GEORGE BERNARD SHAW was born in Dublin in 1856 into a family of Ireland's well-established Protestant Ascendancy. His father's alcoholism and business ineptitude caused the family's fortunes to decline, and Shaw left school at 15 to work as a clerk in a land agent's office. In 1876, he moved to London, where he attended public lectures, joined political and cultural organizations, and, on most days, furthered his learning in the Reading Room of the British Museum. In 1884, he became a member of the newly founded Fabian Society, which was devoted to political reform along socialist principles, and remained one of their leading pamphleteers and campaigners for much of his life. Starting in the mid-1880s, Shaw worked variously as a book, music, art, and theatre reviewer, and this cultural criticism formed the basis of his important studies *The Quintessence of Ibsenism* (1891) and *The Perfect Wagnerite* (1898). He began playwrighting in earnest in the early 1890s, with *Widowers' Houses* (1892), but his early plays were largely unperformed as they did not conform with the commercial theatre's demands for musicals, farces, and melodramas. Shaw finally found success in New York in 1898 with *The Devil's Disciple* (1897). With the windfall from the production, he retired from journalism and married Irish heiress Charlotte Payne-Townshend. In the new century, Shaw embarked on forging a theatre of the future, transforming the problem and discussion play into a theatre of ideas with *Man and Superman* (1903), *John Bull's Other Island*, and *Major Barbara* (1905). The popular writer of *Fanny's First Play* (1911) and *Pygmalion* (1912) became a pariah following his condemnation of jingoistic patriotism at the outset of the First World War. His comeback was slow but he achieved worldwide acclaim as the writer of *Saint Joan* (1923) and was awarded the 1925 Nobel Prize for Literature. He continued to write plays, including *The Apple Cart* (1928) and *Geneva* (1936), but his output dropped off significantly in the 1940s. Shaw died at his home in Ayot St Lawrence in 1950.

JAMES MORAN is Professor of Modern English Literature and Drama at the University of Nottingham, UK. He is a recent recipient of both the Philip Leverhulme Prize and the British Academy mid-career fellowship, and he has presented a monthly book-review feature on BBC Radio Nottingham since 2010. His books include *Staging the Easter Rising* (2006), (as editor) *Four Irish Rebel Plays* (2007), *Irish Birmingham: A History* (2010), *The Theatre of Sean O'Casey* (2013), (as editor with Neal Alexander) *Regional Modernisms* (2013), and *The Theatre of D. H. Lawrence* (2015).

OXFORD WORLD'S CLASSICS

*For over 100 years Oxford World's Classics have brought
readers closer to the world's great literature. Now with over 700
titles—from the 4,000-year-old myths of Mesopotamia to the
twentieth century's greatest novels—the series makes available
lesser-known as well as celebrated writing.*

*The pocket-sized hardbacks of the early years contained
introductions by Virginia Woolf, T. S. Eliot, Graham Greene,
and other literary figures which enriched the experience of reading.
Today the series is recognized for its fine scholarship and
reliability in texts that span world literature, drama and poetry,
religion, philosophy and politics. Each edition includes perceptive
commentary and essential background information to meet the
changing needs of readers.*

OXFORD WORLD'S CLASSICS

GEORGE BERNARD SHAW

Playlets

Edited with an Introduction and Notes by
JAMES MORAN

OXFORD
UNIVERSITY PRESS

OXFORD

UNIVERSITY PRESS

Great Clarendon Street, Oxford, OX2 6DP,
United Kingdom

Oxford University Press is a department of the University of Oxford.
It furthers the University's objective of excellence in research, scholarship,
and education by publishing worldwide. Oxford is a registered trade mark of
Oxford University Press in the UK and in certain other countries

First published as an Oxford World's Classics paperback 2021

Impression: 1

British Library Cataloguing in Publication Data

Data available

ISBN 978-0-19-880498-7

Printed and bound in Great Britain by
Clays Ltd, Elcograf S.p.A.

ACKNOWLEDGEMENTS

I HAVE accrued a number of scholarly debts during the editing of this book. I am particularly thankful for the advice and good sense of Sarah Badcock, Ian Beckett, Mike Carey, Eric Colleary, Stephen Enniss, Keith Gildart, Nicky Grene, David Howell, and Brad Kent. I am grateful to the University of Texas at Austin, for the award of a visiting British Studies Fellowship that allowed me to complete much of my research for this volume. I have also been greatly helped by staff at the Billy Rose Theatre Division of The New York Public Library; the staff at the National Library of Ireland; and those in the Manuscripts Reading Room at the British Library. On a personal level, I am grateful, as always, for the friendship of my close colleagues at the University of Nottingham; and to Maria, Thomas, and Joseph for their forbearance and love.

Macbeth Skit is reproduced by permission of the Society of Authors as agents for the Bernard Shaw Estate. Manuscript material is published with the agreement of the Society of Authors as agents for the Bernard Shaw Estate, the British Library, and the Harry Ransom Center, The University of Texas at Austin.

CONTENTS

INTRODUCTION

GEORGE BERNARD SHAW was one of the leading playwrights and public intellectuals of the nineteenth and twentieth centuries. He helped propel drama towards the unexpected, into a realm where it might shock audiences into new viewpoints and into fresh understandings of society. The British critic Kenneth Tynan declared that 'he attempted, and almost pulled off, two mountainous tasks: he cleared the English stage of humbug, and the English mind of cant'.[1] The Irish playwright Sean O'Casey said that Shaw made 'the Theatre a fit place for man and God to go to, to laugh, and to think out life as life was lived'.[2] Shaw won the Nobel Prize for Literature in 1925; Bertolt Brecht praised him as a figure of 'sagacity and such fearless eloquence'; and Albert Einstein declared that Shaw had 'succeeded in gaining the love and the joyful admiration of mankind'.[3]

The life of Shaw gives the impression of being a lengthy affair in every respect. For one thing, the playwright lived for almost a century, born in 1856 and dying shortly after he toppled from a ladder while trimming a tree in 1950. For another thing, during that lifetime he churned out a simply enormous quantity of written material, producing a substantial body of novels, lectures, letters, political journalism, and cultural criticism. His playwriting alone runs to more than sixty works.

Shaw's plays themselves are often characterized as being, in the words of theatre critic Susannah Clapp, 'torrentially loquacious', or, as the literary scholar Terry Eagleton puts it, 'fatiguingly verbose'.[4] For example, *Back to Methuselah* begins in the Garden of Eden in 4,004 BCE and finishes 'As Far as Thought Can Reach' in 31,920 CE, when the futuristic characters boast that they 'have hundreds of years to live:

---

[1] Tynan, 'Shaw: Demolition Expert', *New York Herald Tribune*, 22 July 1956, sect. 4, p. 1.

[2] O'Casey, 'G. B. Shaw: The Lord of a Century', *New York Times*, 22 July 1956, p. X1.

[3] Brecht, 'Three Cheers for Shaw', in *Brecht on Theatre* (3rd edn), ed. Marc Silberman, Steve Giles, and Tom Kuhn (London: Bloomsbury, 2015), 28–31, at 31; Einstein, quoted in Fred D. Crawford (ed.), 'Toast to Albert Einstein', *SHAW* 15 (1995), 231–44, at 239.

[4] Clapp, 'Man and Superman Review', *The Guardian*, 1 March 2015; <https://www.theguardian.com/stage/2015/mar/01/man-and-superman-lyttelton-observer-review-ralph-fiennes>. Eagleton, 'A Row of Shaws', *London Review of Books*, 21 June 2018, pp. 21–22, at 22.

perhaps thousands'.[5] Productions require spectators to attend a five-part work usually staged over several days, as though watching Wagnerian opera at Bayreuth. Even Brecht reflected that 'Shaw actually manages to give the impression that his mental and physical well-being increase with every sentence he writes', and one of the female players for whom Shaw repeatedly created lead roles, Lillah McCarthy, observed that actors encountering his dramas for the first time tended to find the scripts 'longwinded'.[6] Shaw himself eventually reflected that, with *Methuselah*, 'I was too damned discursive'.[7]

In addition, Shaw's plays often feature lengthy stage directions, appendices, and prefaces. Shaw justified his use of prefaces by explaining that 'When the subject of a play is a large one, there is a great deal about it that cannot be put on the stage though it can be said in an essay.'[8] But, as *The Athenaeum* complained in 1907:

It would almost seem as if Mr. Bernard Shaw distrusted his own dramatic powers, and could not express himself to his entire satisfaction in the language of the theatre, for to every volume of his plays which he commits to the press he attaches long prefaces . . . [which] are at best but journalistic essays—witty, pungent, masterful journalism, yet still the work of a man dealing with issues of the moment, and discussing them with the rhetorical extravagance of a partisan; whereas the dramas, although they are all more or less tracts for and of the times, have considerable artistic pretentions.[9]

With his stage directions, Shaw admitted borrowing from Dickens a mode of description 'so vivid and precise that no actor with the faintest sense of character could mistake the sort of figure he has to present'.[10] Shaw had, after all, cut his literary teeth as a novelist, producing five novels in the 1870s and 1880s that were all initially rejected for book publication. In his subsequent dramas, his character-based stage directions give finer comments about motivation that might help an actor create a role and potentially assist a reader of the text to understand

---

[5] Shaw, *Back to Methuselah: A Metabiological Pentateuch* (London: Constable, 1931), 204.

[6] Brecht, 'Three Cheers for Shaw', 30. Recording of Lillah McCarthy, HRC, Sound recording, Interview with Basil Langton and Lillah McCarthy, January 1960.

[7] Shaw to R. & R. Clark, 21 December 1946, in Shaw, *Bernard Shaw and His Publishers*, ed. Michel W. Pharand (Toronto: University of Toronto Press, 2009), 207.

[8] Shaw, *Complete Prefaces*, ed. Dan H. Laurence and Daniel J. Leary, 3 vols (London: Penguin, 1993), vol. i, p. vii.

[9] 'Drama', *The Athenaeum*, 27 July 1907, pp. 107–8.

[10] Shaw, 'Resurrection Pie', *Saturday Review*, 23 May 1896; repr. in Shaw, *Our Theatres in the Nineties*, 3 vols (London: Constable, 1932), ii. 132–8, at 134–5.

a scene. However, some play-readers undoubtedly found such material overwhelming. Indeed, by the mid-twentieth century, the *Times Literary Supplement* disparaged other scripts with the insult: 'The stage directions are as lengthy as Shaw's'.[11] As modernist writers moved towards compression, they expressed impatience with Shaw. Samuel Beckett, for example, increasingly worked with a spare dramatic palette: when he created his script *Quad* in 1981 he included no spoken words at all, and the printed text is little more than three pages in length.[12] Beckett compared Shaw's work unfavourably with that of W. B. Yeats, J. M. Synge, and Sean O'Casey. When asked to comment on Shaw, Beckett declared, 'I wouldn't suggest that G.B.S. is not a great play-wright, whatever that is when it's at home. What I would do is give the whole unupsettable apple-cart for a sup of the Hawk's Well, or the Saints', or a whiff of Juno, to go no further.'[13] The works that Beckett chose to praise ahead of those of Shaw are comparatively brief. Yeats's *At the Hawk's Well* is roughly 3,000 words; Synge's *The Well of the Saints* is about 16,000 words; and O'Casey's *Juno and the Paycock* is around 14,000 words. By contrast, Shaw's *Back to Methuselah* is over 83,000 words in length. That total extends to 122,000 if the preface is included, making the full-length *Methuselah* more than forty times the size of that Yeats play which Beckett admired. No wonder that the modernist writers who were committed to compression and to 'hard light, clear edges' often expressed antipathy towards Shavian drama.[14] Ezra Pound did, however, discern one reduced-size thing about Shaw: the bearded Irishman apparently 'had a tight foreskin'.[15]

The God of Small Things

This volume presents sixteen of Shaw's briefest theatrical scripts, ranging in length from the 1,000-word puppet play *Shakes Versus Shav*, to the 12,000-word *Press Cuttings*. The average length of script in this volume is just over 6,000 words, and presenting them together reveals

[11] Gomme, Andor, 'Writing the Play', *Times Literary Supplement*, 17 November 1966, p. 1041.

[12] As printed in Beckett, *The Complete Dramatic Works* (London: Faber, 1986), 451–4.

[13] Letter of 1 June 1956, in Beckett, *The Letters of Samuel Beckett*, ed. Martha Dow Fehsenfeld et al., 4 vols (Cambridge: Cambridge University Press, 2009–16), ii. 623.

[14] Letter of 1 August 1914, in Pound, *Selected Letters 1907–1942*, ed. D. D. Paige (New York: New Directions, 1950), 38.

[15] Letter of 8 February 1936, in Pound, *Selected Letters of Ezra Pound and William Carlos Williams*, ed. Hugh Witemeyer (New York: New Directions, 1996), 177.

how a playwright often condemned as too wordy was actually a skilled
dramatic miniaturist.

Of course, Shaw himself could be relatively dismissive about the
more succinct dramas that he wrote. As the prefaces included in this
volume reveal, he felt happy to label a short play of his a 'Playlet',
a 'Tomfoolery', or one of his 'turns' (pp. 121, 307, and 197). He even
subtitled one 'a disgrace to the author', and another 'A piece of utter
nonsense'.[16] He also claimed that one of his short dramas was 'a bad
play' and 'such a flimsy play'; he declared that another was full of 'sav-
ageries'; and labelled a third simply 'no use' and 'quite obsolete'.[17]

Yet, at other times, Shaw evidently did take his short plays seriously.
He declared, for example, that 'They may disgust the admirers of my
more pretentious work; but these highbrows must remember that there is
a demand for little things as well as for big things.'[18] He contended that

tomfoolery is as classic as tragedy. High comedy seldom achieves a whole act
without revealing traces of its origin in the altercations and topical discussions
of the circus clown with the ringmaster: what else indeed are the passages
between Monsieur Jourdain and his philosophers and fencing masters in
Molière's most famous comedy [*Le Bourgeois gentilhomme*]?[19]

As the scholar John A. Bertolini has argued, Shaw considered his
shorter plays 'opportunities for the exhibition of the actor's art . . . his
one-act plays present the opportunity to examine his comic art in its
purest manifestation'.[20]

However, the educator and author Helen Louise Cohen observed in
1921 that Shaw's one-act pieces were 'generally ignored in books on
dramatic workmanship', and her observation was reiterated more than
seven decades later, when the academic Stanley Weintraub declared
that Shaw's short plays continued to attract 'little scholarly attention'.[21]
Indeed, significant commentators have worried that Shaw's playlets are

---

[16] Shaw, *The Fascinating Foundling, a Disgrace to the Author*, in *Translations and
Tomfooleries* (London: Constable, 1932), 205–20, at 205; Shaw, *The Music Cure, a Piece of
Utter Nonsense*, in *Translations and Tomfooleries*, 221–35, at 221.

[17] These plays were, in turn, *Great Catherine, Press Cuttings*, and *The Music Cure*. See
CL ii. 208 and 103, and iv. 754.

[18] Shaw, 'Trifles and Tomfooleries', in *Translations and Tomfooleries*, 81. Comments
also printed as 'Jaunts and Jollities', *Saturday Review*, 6 November 1926, p. 555.

[19] Shaw, 'Trifles and Tomfooleries', 81.

[20] John A. Bertolini, *The Playwrighting Self of Bernard Shaw* (Carbondale: Southern
Illinois University Press, 1991), 145.

[21] Helen Louise Cohen (ed.), *One-Act Plays by Modern Authors* (New York: Harcourt
Brace, 1921), 1; Stanley Weintraub, *Bernard Shaw: A Guide to Research* (University Park:
University of Pennsylvania Press, 1992), 89.

simply too trivial to be ranked alongside his best work. The influential American reviewer Brooks Atkinson, for example, declared in the 1960s that Shaw's short plays proved 'astonishingly silly since they come from the same man who wrote "Saint Joan" and "Caesar and Cleopatra" '.[22] There is, here, a sense that Shaw was slumming it when writing his shorter scripts, scribbling the kind of tuppenny-ha'penny skits that could be churned out by any music-hall sketch-writer.

Nonetheless, such critics have often manifestly enjoyed these works. Brooks Atkinson went on to describe one of Shaw's playlets (*How He Lied to Her Husband*) as 'most entertaining . . . an original curtain rais-er'.[23] Another prominent critic, the Irish writer St John Ervine, declared that Shaw's short scripts 'need not detain us long' before going on to describe some of them as 'very good fun'.[24]

Of course, not all of Shaw's short plays function in the same way. Although they share a comparatively modest length, Shaw wrote these pieces for a variety of purposes and at different times in his career. In order to emphasize some of the shared themes and ideas of Shaw's briefer works, then, this volume divides Shaw's playlets into four subcategories: Farces; War Playlets; Historical Sketches; and Shakespearean Shorts.

Farces

'Nothing in the theatre is staler than the situation of the husband, wife and lover, or the fun of knockabout farce,' wrote Shaw in the preface to *How He Lied to Her Husband*. 'I have taken both, and got an original play out of them' (p. 5). One of the repeated features of his short dramas is this comic focus on marital and extramarital relationships. 'Farce' is a term that has shifted in meaning over the years, but ultimately derives from the Latin *farsa* (stuffed), and tends to signify a light-hearted drama in which scenes are cleverly concocted to deliver a rush of increasingly over-the-top situations. In Shaw's short farces, we see him pushing at the boundaries of the form, and exploring what such comedy involving marriage might be capable of doing.

Shaw's 1904 play *How He Lied to Her Husband* uses the situation of a married couple caught in a love triangle to satirize some of his own earlier writing. Six months later he wrote another farce, *Passion, Poison,*

[22] Brooks Atkinson, 'To G.B.S. the Idea was the Thing', *New York Times*, 6 May 1962, p. 300.

[23] Atkinson, 'To G.B.S. the Idea was the Thing', 300.

[24] John Ervine, 'Books of the Day', *The Observer*, 28 September 1919, p. 3.

and Petrifaction, which again features a love triangle involving a married couple, but this time strives for a far darker, and far more surreal, set of theatrical effects. By 1909 Shaw had created another short comedy involving jealousy and marriage, *Press Cuttings*, in which two army generals have a professional rivalry and both decide to bolster their position by marrying a forthright woman. On this occasion, however, Shaw set his play against a backdrop of suffragette militancy, and so the basic interpersonal comic set-up is deployed in order to comment upon a wider set of changing gender roles and cultural realignments. Subsequently, in 1912, Shaw wrote the farce *Overruled*, which saw him once more return to his theme of 'husband, wife and lover', but which concludes with two married couples accepting that adultery should be a perfectly acceptable part of their life. Hence, by this stage, what looked like the set-up for simple knockabout humour had become, in Shaw's hands, an opportunity for reflection on moral norms and on the boundaries of socially acceptable behaviour.

HOW HE LIED TO HER HUSBAND

The first farce of this sequence was written by Shaw during a rainy Scottish holiday in the summer of 1904. He had been asked for a piece by Arnold Daly, the actor-manager who had enjoyed success with Shaw's *Candida*, a show that had made Shaw's name in the 1890s and which revolved around a love triangle featuring a married woman, her clergyman husband, and her poet-admirer. *Candida* became a box-office smash, but Shaw felt dissatisfied with how the work had been understood, and so now wrote *How He Lied to Her Husband* in order 'to satirize those who took Candida to be a sentimental glorification of eroticism'.[25] Hence, in *How He Lied to Her Husband* he replicated the same dramatic situation that featured in his earlier drama, but altered certain details for comic effect. For example, in *Candida*, the wife's poet-admirer Marchbanks is described as a 'little snivelling cowardly whelp' who tells the husband 'I cant fight you for your wife as a drunken navvy would'.[26] But in *How He Lied to Her Husband*, the poet-admirer is capable of adopting '*the manner of a well taught boxer*' (p. 19) and a slapstick tussle ensues when the poet tells the husband that 'I'll land you one on the chin thatll make your head sing for a week' (p. 19).

[25] Quoted in Michael Holroyd, *Bernard Shaw*, 4 vols (London: Chatto & Windus, 1988–92), iii. 375–6.

[26] Shaw, *Candida*, in *Plays Pleasant and Unpleasant: The Second Volume Containing the Four Pleasant Plays by Bernard Shaw* (London: Constable, 1931), 73–141, at 99.

Arnold Daly premiered *How He Lied to Her Husband* at New York's Berkeley Lyceum in November 1904.[27] Spectators who recognized Daly as the actor who had once played the celebrated role of Marchbanks would have appreciated the references to *Candida* that Shaw included in his new play.[28] Indeed, Shaw specifically included a moment in the original performance script of *How He Lied to Her Husband* that saw Daly's character being addressed in the following way, 'Now that I come to look at you, you <u>are</u> rather like him [the poet from *Candida*]', with Shaw then adding a moment of mugging for the actor: '<u>Applause and laughter, Mr Arnold Daly grins feebly at the audience) Play resumed.</u>'[29]

The piece was sufficiently well received for Daly to revive the work in the United States across the next two decades, despite his falling out of favour with Shaw.[30] Meanwhile, in March 1905, London's Court Theatre staged the piece, with Shaw making revisions to excise the Americanisms that he had included in the first publicly performed version, and to relocate the characters and setting from New York to London. The *Manchester Guardian* heralded Shaw's 'exquisite' one-act play as 'certainly one of the most brilliant things that have been seen on the stage in our time'.[31] *Vogue* magazine lauded *How He Lied to Her Husband* as 'that delicious skit of Shaw at the expense of Shaw'.[32]

Yet who remembers *Candida* today? Very soon after *How He Lied to Her Husband* first appeared onstage, the fact that Shaw had written the script as a response to his own earlier work became obscured. In 1904, Shaw felt that his 'screaming curtain raiser' was 'specialized for a theatre at which Candida has been raging, and for an actor who has played Eugene'.[33] But in 1906, one audience member was heard asking, 'I wonder just what he's making fun of?'[34] By 1911, *The Observer* noted that the 'merry farce' still rouses 'plenty of laughter', but that 'Some of

---

[27] <http://www.irishplayography.com/play.aspx?playid=3272>.

[28] See Bernard F. Dukore, 'Shaw Improves Shaw', *Modern Drama*, 6/1 (1963), 26–31, at 30.

[29] Shaw erased this stage direction before the play was first printed in 1907. He then deleted the spoken line too before the standard edition of the play was published in 1931. *HHL* Carb, fo. 7.

[30] 'Arnold Daly in Vaudeville', *New York Times*, 7 April 1914, p. 9; 'Gossip of the Vaudeville Stage', *New York Times*, 28 September 1924, p. X2. See also Shaw's letter of c.25 May 1911, in *CL* iii. 38–9.

[31] W.A., 'New Comedietta by Mr. Bernard Shaw', *Manchester Guardian*, 3 March 1905, p. 7.

[32] 'What They Read', *Vogue*, 5 September 1907, p. 258.

[33] Letter of 18 August 1904, in Shaw, *Bernard Shaw's Letters to Granville Barker*, ed. C. B. Purdom (London: Phoenix, 1956), 23.

[34] 'G. B. Shaw in Vaudeville', *New York Times*, 30 October 1906, p. 9.

the early part of it is evidently Greek to its new audience, which knows nothing of "Candida" '.[35] On 4 March 1930, Shaw therefore made a second major set of revisions to the play, sending a list of 'important changes' to his publisher, asking for the references to *Candida* to be deleted for the 1931 printing of *How He Lied* (the version reprinted in this edition).[36] For example, in the 1907 version of *How He Lied*, the female lead asks about her own husband, 'do you think for a moment he'd stand it [an adulterous affair], like that half-baked clergyman in the play? He'd just kill you.'[37] In the revised 1931 version, however, that line is shortened to, 'do you think for a moment he'd stand it? He'd just kill you' (p. 10).

Such was Shaw's confidence that *How He Lied to Her Husband* could transcend the circumstances of its composition, and appeal to audience members who knew nothing of *Candida*, that in 1931 he agreed this short play would be the very first of his works to be made into a 'talkie'. Shaw had long felt bewitched by the cinema, and realized the disruptive potential that this technology might have upon the world of theatre. As he put it in 1930, 'I believe that acting and drama can be portrayed far more effectively as well as lucratively from the screen than from the stage.'[38] He decided to supervise the production personally, and at one stage even demonstrated how the actors should behave during the fight scene by rolling around on a studio floor.[39]

Although some critics expressed disappointment with the resulting thirty-three-minute film, Shaw pronounced himself satisfied, claiming that he had 'shown the way' for others to produce 'plays on the screen just as they are produced on the stage'.[40] Certainly, the film of *How He Lied to Her Husband* opened the gates for numerous cinematic renderings

[35] 'How He Lied to Her Husband', *The Observer*, 10 December 1911, p. 11.

[36] *HHL* Hol, fo. 1. For more on the changes see Dukore, 'Shaw Improves Shaw', 26–31.

[37] Shaw, *The Man of Destiny and How He Lied to Her Husband* (New York: Brentanos, 1916), 17.

[38] Holroyd, *Bernard Shaw*, iii. 375.

[39] Ernest Marshall, 'Notes of London Screen', *New York Times*, 24 August 1930, p. X4; 'Shaw Helps Direct Talkie', *New York Times*, 28 October 1930, p. 12. Shaw appears to have rather enjoyed rolling on the floor in this way and 1930 was not the first time he did it: Margaret Halstan, who played Aurora Bompas in the 1911 revival of *How He Lied to Her Husband* at the Palace theatre, recalled that, on that occasion, 'Shaw directed, playing every part to show us exactly what he wanted. He thoroughly enjoyed himself doing it, especially the scene between the husband and the lover where they both fall down on the floor' (Recording of Margaret Halstan, HRC, Sound recording, Interview with Basil Langton and Margaret Halstan, 29 October 1960).

[40] 'Shaw Says U.S. Does Fine When Britain Shows How', *Washington Post*, 2 March 1931, p. 5.

of Shaw's plays, which soon included versions of *Pygmalion* in 1938, *Major Barbara* in 1941, and *Caesar and Cleopatra* in 1945.

Furthermore, the 1931 film was not the end of the formal adaptation of *How He Lied to Her Husband*. Once the BBC had started broadcasting a regular high-definition public television service from Alexandra Palace in November 1936, the first Shaw play to be broadcast from there was *How He Lied* in 1937, which, according to L. W. Conolly, left the 'happy' BBC management pressing 'to get more Shaw plays on television'.[41] A different production of the play would later appear upon the small screen in the United States, where the influential theatre critic Walter Kerr hosted a 1965 series about drama that opened with a version of Shaw's playlet.[42] Farce may trace its roots back to Aristophanes, but *How He Lied to Her Husband* showed that this theatrical form could be retooled for experiments with the most modern of dramatic technologies.

PASSION, POISON, AND PETRIFACTION; OR THE FATAL GAZOGENE

In June 1905, the year after he had written *How He Lied to Her Husband*, Shaw completed another short play about a love triangle involving a married couple: *Passion, Poison, and Petrifaction*. This time, however, Shaw experimented with a darker kind of comedy. An upper-class wife is at risk of being murdered by her husband, with her admirer ultimately ending up poisoned. Shaw based his play, which he labelled 'a new Startling, Original, Pathetic, Bloodcurdling and Entrancing Tragedy, in One Act and Ten Mechanical Effects', on a story he had written some years earlier for the children of his friend William Archer, about a cat which became petrified after lapping up some liquid plaster of Paris.[43] Hence the humour of the stage play takes a decidedly surreal turn. A clock strikes sixteen; the husband insists that his dagger is a fish slice; and, ultimately, the potential adulterer turns into a limestone statue. The wild comic leaps of logic in this well-heeled British setting make the piece feel something like a precursor to *Monty Python*.

---

[41] L. W. Conolly, *Bernard Shaw and the BBC* (Toronto: University of Toronto Press, 2009), 92–3.

[42] Jack Gould, 'TV: Experimental Repertory Dramas', *New York Times*, 18 February 1965, p. 67.

[43] Raymond Mander and Joe Michenson, 'The Stage History of the Plays', in programme for 'Trifles and Tomfooleries' at the Mermaid Theatre in 1967, in HRC, Shaw Collection, Vertical Files, box 697, #G30.

Shaw penned this piece 'mostly in Great Northern Express trains' in response to a request from the actor-manager Cyril Maude, who was president of a charity that helped the orphans and illegitimate children of actors.[44] Maude asked Shaw to draft a fundraising piece, and Shaw agreed, beginning the work in May 1905 and completing it in time for performance on 14 July 1905. The premiere occurred in a 'sweltering marquee' at Regent's Park, where the surreal aspects of Shaw's comic script were set within an equally bizarre context.[45] Just outside, as the actors sweated away inside the tent, a 9-year-old composer conducted a group of musicians; an elephant from the Italian circus rambled around; and the younger brother of the Antarctic explorer Captain Robert Scott impersonated Henry VIII's wife, Catherine Parr.[46]

At the end of that afternoon, Shaw auctioned off his manuscript, then forgot that he had given it away and, two years later, wrote an irate letter to a New York book-collector who had taken possession of the papers (Shaw subsequently remembered what had been done and apologized to the American).[47] But the play was nonetheless soon staged in the United States, with the Young Men's Hebrew Association of Philadelphia giving an amateur performance in March 1915, and the Stage Society of the same city presenting a professional version in March 1916.[48]

Just as with *How He Lied to Her Husband*, Shaw wanted *Passion, Poison, and Petrifaction* to reach an audience outside the playhouse, and he authorized the BBC to broadcast a radio version of the latter work, which was duly transmitted on 13 January 1926. Although some critics felt underwhelmed by this broadcast—*The Times*'s theatre reviewer A. B. Walkley declared the production 'dismal fooling'—others have pointed out that again the piece reveals Shaw to have been distinctly ahead of his time.[49] As the critics Paul Silverstein and Irving Wardle

[44] *PPP* Hol, fos. 1–2.

[45] 'Our London Correspondence', *Manchester Guardian*, 15 July 1905, p. 8.

[46] 'The Actors' Orphanage Fund', *The Times*, 15 July 1905, p. 8.

[47] 'The Play Shaw Forgot and Philadelphia Saved', *Evening Ledger—Philadelphia*, n.d., HRC, Shaw Collection, Vertical Files, box 699, #G120.

[48] 'Entertainments', *Evening Ledger—Philadelphia*, 19 March 1915, p. 9; 'Theatrical Baedekker', *Evening Ledger—Philadelphia*, 25 March 1916, Amusement Section. Later London productions included a revival at the Chanticleer Theatre Club in Kensington in July 1945, a staging as part of a season of Shaw one-act plays at the Arts Theatre Club in April 1951, and a production at the Mermaid Theatre in February 1967.

[49] A.B.W., 'Wirelessed Shaw', *The Times*, 20 January 1926, p. 10.

observe, this script moves towards theatrical absurdism and shows a particular affinity with Ionesco's playhouse classic *The Bald Soprano*.[50]

PRESS CUTTINGS

Less than four years after the premiere of *Passion, Poison, and Petrifaction*, Shaw penned another short comedy, in response to prompting from the painter Bertha Newcombe, an old flame from before he met his wife in 1896.[51] Again, with this script, Shaw intended to confound audience expectations, presenting ideas about gender identity that anticipate the later thinking of figures such as the theorist Judith Butler and playwright Caryl Churchill.

The kernel of the idea for this play came from 1906, when a group from the Women's Social and Political Union had been arrested at Westminster for agitating in favour of votes for women. Shaw petitioned the Home Secretary in protest, and wrote a satirical response in *The Times*, pointing out that previous threats to the British government, including that offered by Guy Fawkes or by the Spanish Armada, had come only from men. The twentieth-century threat, by contrast, came from 'Ten women—ten petticoated, long-stockinged, corseted females [who] have hurled themselves on the British Houses of Parliament', prompting Shaw to highlight (with his tongue firmly in his cheek) 'woman's terrible strength and man's miserable weakness'.[52]

He then wrote *Press Cuttings* in 1909 as a gift for the Women's Suffrage Society. The play features an army leader, General Mitchener, facing professional competition from his rival General Sandstone, but Sandstone is kept offstage throughout the piece and instead two women arrive onstage who manifest traditional masculine qualities of decisiveness and forcefulness. One of those female characters is capable of throwing a man through a glass door, and declares that all the really strong 'men' of history, including Napoleon, have actually been women. By contrast, General Mitchener is accused of being 'hysterical' and criticized for his 'tears and entreaties—a man's last resource' (p. 65). In this way, Shaw's work anticipates a discussion about gender performance, stereotyped behaviours, and non-binary identities that would come to the fore a century after he wrote the play.

---

[50] Paul Silverstein, 'Barns, Booths, and Shaw', *Shaw Review*, 12/3 (1969), 111–16, at 111; Wardle quoted in Holroyd, *Bernard Shaw*, ii. 102.

[51] See Peter Gahan, *Bernard Shaw and Beatrice Webb on Poverty and Equality in the Modern World 1905–1914* (Cham: Palgrave Macmillan, 2017), 42.

[52] Shaw, 'Woman Suffrage', *The Times*, 31 October 1906, p. 8.

Shaw's satirical drama, set on April Fool's Day, also involves mockery of the real-life prime minister, Herbert Henry Asquith, and the real-life military leader, General Herbert Kitchener. The characters of 'Balsquith' and 'Mitchener' feature prominently in the text. But the play's incorporation of such living figures meant that the censor refused to sanction it for the stage, writing to the Court Theatre on 24 June 1909 to declare 'I am returning the copy in order to give you the opportunity of eliminating all personalities expressed or understood'.[53] Shaw in turn protested that Balsquith and Mitchener were 'grotesquely imaginary', but, with the censor forbidding a public production of the work, the premiere in July had to be given as two private rather than public performances at the Court Theatre, under the auspices of a newly formed 'Civic and Dramatic Guild' and with Shaw directing.[54] Shaw fumed about 'all the trouble, expense, and loss that the withholding of a licence entails. The money paid for seats had to be returned; a proposal from one of the most popular actor-managers in London for the inclusion of the play in his programme fell through.'[55] *The Athenaeum* nonetheless pronounced the private production of the playlet 'undeniably amusing'.[56]

Shaw then edited the names in the script for public performance, shifting the name of Mitchener to 'Bones' and Balsquith to 'Johnson' (the revised names were taken from blackface minstrelsy theatre, which was considered perfectly acceptable).[57] The revised script appeared onstage in September 1909 at the Manchester Gaiety, where the *Manchester Guardian* observed that a 'fine large house . . . was laughing from the moment the curtain rose. The farce looks like giving the Gaiety one of its greatest popular successes.'[58] In June 1919 another production directed by Shaw was given at the Kingsway Theatre, organized by the Actresses' Franchise League, although the city then had to wait until May 1951 to see the play again, when it appeared at the

---

[53] HRC Lic.

[54] 'Shaw Tilts With Censor', *New York Times*, 27 June 1909, p. C2; Mander and Michenson, 'The Stage History of the Plays', in HRC, Shaw Collection, Vertical Files, box 697, #G30.

[55] Shaw, 'Bernard Shaw's Play and the Censor', *The Times*, 14 July 1909, p. 10.

[56] 'Drama: The Week', *The Athenaeum*, 17 July 1909, p. 79.

[57] See Benjamin Brühwiler, 'Blackface in America and Africa: Popular Arts and Diaspora Consciousness in Cape Town and the Gold Coast', in Toyin Falola and Tyler Flemi (eds), *Music, Performance and African Identities* (London: Routledge, 2012), 125–43, at 127.

[58] 'Gaiety Theatre', *Manchester Guardian*, 28 September 1909, p. 7.

Arts Theatre Club.[59] Shaw had originally aimed his mockery squarely at British society and institutions of the early twentieth century: he had, after all, begun writing the script at roughly the same time that he signed a petition in support of women's suffrage that appeared in *The Times* on 23 March 1909. The scarcity of revivals after 1919 perhaps revealed how dependent the play was upon that original cultural moment, although at times the text has demonstrated some wider appeal. *Press Cuttings* appeared in the United States in 1914; Brooks Atkinson declared an off-Broadway revival in 1957 to be 'witty' and 'hilarious'; and in 1980 the BBC transmitted a radio version featuring the British television comedy star Arthur Lowe to mark the thirtieth anniversary of Shaw's death.[60]

OVERRULED

In January 1895, Shaw visited the Garrick Theatre to watch a new play, *Slaves of the Ring*, by Sydney Grundy, and reviewed the performance for the *Saturday Review*. Grundy had been trying to demonstrate the outmoded nature of the marriage laws, and although Shaw hated the old-fashioned form of that script, he admired Grundy for describing an issue of great contemporary resonance: the 'cruel social evil' of making marriage indissoluble.[61]

By the summer of 1912, Shaw had decided to write his own punchy playlet that revisited the ideas set out in *Slaves of the Ring*, partly inspired by the fact that Shaw (aged 56, and married) had just fallen wildly in love with the actress Mrs Patrick Campbell.[62] Shaw spent three weeks working on his drama, entitled *Overruled*, which he described as 'a clinical study of how polygamy actually occurs among quite ordinary people, innocent of all unconventional views concerning it' (p. 81). In fact, in today's parlance, we might well choose the term 'wife swapping' rather than 'polygamy' to describe the play's subject matter. After all, Shaw's play revolves around a man and a woman who are having a sexual relationship despite both being married already to other people, and who discover that their own spouses are in turn

[59] Mander and Michenson, 'The Stage History of the Plays', in HRC, Shaw Collection, Vertical Files, box 697, #G30.

[60] Brooks Atkinson, 'Theatre: Two by Shaw: "O'Flaherty, V.C." and "Press Cuttings"', *New York Times*, 19 February 1957, p. 35; 'Plays', *The Listener*, 1 May 1980, p. 574 (the Lowe version had first been broadcast in 1971).

[61] Shaw, 'Slaves of the Ring', *Saturday Review*, 5 January 1895; repr. in Shaw, *Our Theatres in the Nineties*, i. 1–5.

[62] Gahan, *Bernard Shaw and Beatrice Webb on Poverty and Equality*, 94.

enjoying an affair with one another. Both couples then have a discussion about the situation, before eventually deciding to carry on regardless. In writing this way, Shaw seems to have deliberately been playing up to those who suspected him of immorality: after all, *The Academy* had declared in 1909, 'There is a natural decency about marriage, and Shaw and his gang are, of course, irked by it. For the last five years at any rate they have been labouring and shrieking hard to get rid of it. What they want is free love.'[63]

When the play came before the British censor, two official readers differed in their view about what Shaw had written: the first felt that the piece was 'happily quite innocuous', but the second suspected that parts of the dialogue were not 'quite innocent'.[64] Indeed, Shaw *had* written a script that foregrounded the idea of adulterous sex, although he obviously refrained from directly representing the physical act on the stage. So the censor granted a licence for *Overruled* to appear in October 1912 at London's Duke of York Theatre, where, unfortunately, Shaw's audience remained bemused: 'It is not quite clear what it is intended to demonstrate', declared one critic.[65] Shaw himself attended the first performance, and described it as 'the most appalling failure on record: the only regular right down failure I ever had'.[66]

Nonetheless, as the academic Fred D. Crawford observes, Noël Coward's hit play of 1930, *Private Lives*, owes 'a considerable debt' to Shaw's playlet. As Crawford points out, there is a pronounced similarity in plotting between the two works, and 'Coward's dialogue in *Private Lives* echoes many of Shaw's themes in *Overruled*'.[67]

War Playlets

A second major subgroup of Shaw's short plays is found in his 'war playlets'. During the years of the First World War, Shaw felt disinclined to write full-length plays. As he explained in the preface to *Heartbreak House*, he felt that theatrical culture had profoundly changed during the conflict: 'The cultivated soldier, who in time of peace would look at

---

[63] 'Life and Letters', *The Academy*, 29 May 1909, pp. 147–8, at 148. Retained by Shaw and now held in HRC, Shaw Collection, Vertical Files, box 700, #144.

[64] British Library, Add. MS 65987F, *Overruled*, comments by Ernest A. Bendall of 27 September 1912, and D.D. of 30 September 1912.

[65] 'Shaw, Barrie, Pinero: A Triple Bill at the Duke of York's Theatre', *Manchester Guardian*, 15 October 1912, p. 16.

[66] Quoted by Holroyd, *Bernard Shaw*, ii. 275.

[67] Fred D. Crawford, 'Shaw's British Inheritors', *SHAW* 13 (1993), 103–11, at 104–5.

nothing except the most advanced post-Ibsen plays in the most artistic settings, found himself, to his own astonishment, thirsting for silly jokes, dances, and brainlessly sensuous exhibitions of pretty girls.'[68] Shaw's status as pariah during the conflict may also have diminished his enthusiasm for writing at length for the public stage. The London theatres provided little room for him between 1914 and 1920.[69] During the fighting, he was often considered a German sympathizer, largely because of his 1914 pamphlet 'Common Sense About the War', which rejected popular jingoism, described the conflict in terms of class, and stated that 'I shall retain my Irish capacity for criticizing England with something of the detachment of a foreigner, and perhaps with a certain slightly malicious taste for taking the conceit out of her'.[70] Shaw's secretary later recalled that, after publication, 'he got two hundred letters, abusive letters I think, from people saying he ought to be hung, drawn and quartered'.[71] His attitude even repelled friends such as H. G. Wells and Henry James; newspapers printed pictures of Shaw wearing an Iron Cross; and the former American president Theodore Roosevelt called him a 'blue-rumped ape'.[72]

Yet, despite this, Shaw did continue to write playlets during the war years, with the shorter form allowing him to rattle off work relatively quickly, and to continue refining his idea of theatrical dialogue. The author wrote each of these pieces during the First World War at the instigation of four female theatre-makers he knew (Gertrude Kingston, Lalla Vandervelde, Lillah McCarthy, and Augusta Gregory), and he then put the scripts together under the title 'playlets of the war' for publication in a volume of 1919.

These war playlets show that, despite his reputation, Shaw was scarcely pro-German. Indeed, one of the scripts, *The Inca of Perusalem*, revolves around a scathing depiction of the Kaiser. But in these texts,

[68] Shaw, *Heartbreak House* (London: Constable, 1931), 30–1.

[69] Thomas Postlewait, 'Introduction', in *Selected Correspondence of Bernard Shaw: Bernard Shaw and William Archer*, ed. Thomas Postlewait (Toronto: University of Toronto Press, 2017), pp. x–lxxi, at p. xlviii.

[70] Shaw, 'Common Sense About the War', *New York Times*, 15 November 1914, p. SM1. During the same month, this piece was reprinted as a special supplement in the *New Statesman*, and was later reproduced as part of the volume *What I Really Wrote About the War* (London: Constable, 1931), 22–110.

[71] Recording of Ann Jackson, HRC, Sound recording, Interview with Basil Langton and Ann Jackson, 12 July 1962.

[72] Gareth Griffith, *Socialism and Superior Brains: The Political Thought of George Bernard Shaw* (London: Routledge, 1993), 220. Roosevelt quoted by Edmund Fuller and David E. Green, *God in the White House* (New York: Crown, 1968), 166.

Shaw shows his willingness to mock all sides in the conflict: *Augustus Does His Bit* satirizes the upper-crust English commanders of the war effort; *O'Flaherty V.C.* mocks Ireland as a place that would drive men willingly to the trenches; and *Annajanksa, The Bolshevik Empress* burlesques the disorder of revolutionary Russia. Shaw enjoyed casting his insults widely: if British and Irish claims to virtue had been exaggerated, then German militarism and Russian chaos were scarcely any more attractive.

The war playlets show the dramatist's delight in social reversals, in absurdly titled characters, and in philosophical thinking. As his biographer Michael Holroyd puts it: 'Shaw made the plots of these playlets more ludicrous and their action more knock-about than any bedroom farce—then having appealed to the national nonsensical mood (what he called a "national disaffection to intellect"), he tried to introduce a few moments of serious reflection.'[73] After all, Shaw was fascinated and repelled by the war, and although he came to support a British victory, he was alert to the absurdity of the situation. He may have been lambasted, but today his wartime views appear remarkably prescient: he criticized the militarism of the major European powers for the conflict, and pointed to the likelihood that imposing eye-watering reparations on Germany would likely lead to future conflagration.

THE INCA OF PERUSALEM

Shaw created the first of his war playlets in August 1915, when he wrote a script for the actress Gertrude Kingston to perform in the United States.[74] Kingston had, that January, corresponded with Shaw after being arrested in Boston for suffrage activities while preparing to perform in three of his playlets on a single bill.[75] Shaw's new drama, *The Inca of Perusalem*, revolved around a ruler who 'has made war on everybody' and who sports a 'moustache . . . so watched and studied that it has made his face the political barometer of the whole continent' (p. 136). Although the ruler was called the 'Inca', the depiction was an obvious satire on the Kaiser, a figure in the play so recognizable that the British censor worried:

It is, in effect, an elaborate presentment, partly satirical & comical, partly (at least in intention) profound, of the German Emperor. In its course it glances at his family & other royalties, & the propriety of all this may be a delicate

---

[73] Holroyd, *Bernard Shaw*, ii. 377.   [74] Holroyd, *Bernard Shaw*, ii. 377.
[75] Kingston had been preparing *Great Catherine*, *Overruled*, and *The Dark Lady of the Sonnets*. See letter of 25 January 1915, in *CL* iii. 289.

question. . . . I think that since it is agreed that he need no longer be treated with respect this more intimate & searching picture can be allowed—but it needs consideration.[76]

The censor demanded of the company premiering the play: 'see that the make up of the Inca does not too closely resemble the German Emperor'.[77] When Shaw reviewed the proofs of his 1915 publication of the play he noted that the text was 'Cut to comply with Licence' (Shaw deleted the stage direction that described the Inca as wearing '*a German military uniform*' and erased the description of the Inca being a figure who '*strongly resembles the Kaiser, and copies his moustache*').[78] Indeed, in order to protect Shaw's reputation in Germany, the play appeared onstage during the war years as an anonymous piece written by 'A Member of the Royal Society of Literature'.[79]

Still, *The Inca* did appear while the war continued, featuring onstage in Birmingham in 1916, then in Dublin and New York, before an outing in late 1917 at the Criterion Theatre in London. When the Abbey Theatre's actors performed the piece in Ireland during March 1917, there was little doubt about which real-life character was being burlesqued. The Dublin *Evening Herald* noted that the Inca

is dressed in a German military uniform, very stiff, very solemn, walks with an imposing stage gait, clicks his heels. He strongly resembles the Kaiser, and fondles the famous Imperial moustache. . . . The little play gave Mr. Fred O'Donovan an opportunity of dressing up as the Kaiser in the manner acceptable to cartoonists and readers of picture papers. He was the All Highest from the point of his kultured moustache to the heel of his high-legged boots . . . [and] the audience laughed and cheered by turns.[80]

Yet Shaw worried about the text becoming obsolete as events of the war drifted into memory, and in his later preface he reminded readers that the playlet was written 'when its principal character, far from being a fallen

[76] Letter by G. S. Street of 11 November 1915, in British Library, LCP Corr 1915-3885 *The Inca of Perusalem*.

[77] Letter by Trundell of 15 November 1915, in British Library, LCP Corr 1915-3885 *The Inca of Perusalem*.

[78] *Inc* Proof, fo. 12.

[79] See Samuel A. Weiss's annotation to Shaw's letter of 9 November 1915, in Shaw, *Bernard Shaw's Letters to Siegfried Trebitsch*, ed. Samuel A. Weiss (Stanford, CA: Stanford University Press, 1986), 195. In the press, nonetheless, Shaw's workmanship was 'generally assumed', see 'The Inca of Jerusalem' [*sic*], *Manchester Guardian*, 18 December 1917, p. 4.

[80] Jacques, 'GBS Explains a Tongue and Moustache Play at the Abbey', *Evening Herald*, 13 March 1917, in HRC, Shaw Collection, Vertical Files, box 708, folder 281.

foe and virtually a prisoner in our victorious hands, was still the Caesar whose legions we were resisting with our hearts in our mouths' (p. 121).

The script's broader thesis is that responsibility for war is not just the Kaiser's, but is shared by all those who devour and deploy belligerent rhetoric, a lesson that could be applied to almost any age. In 1955, the script was broadcast on American television, with the *New York Times* commenting that this piece, with its 'wit and intelligence', remained a 'delight'.[81]

O'FLAHERTY V.C.

A month after writing *The Inca of Perusalem*, Shaw wrote another short play about the war, with the script developing from a line he had included in *The Inca of Perusalem* in 1915 (but entirely deleted by 1918) in which the Kaiser-figure describes how sending men 'to sacrifice their lives in a quarrel that not one in a thousand of them understands' potentially rescues them 'from unworthy drudgeries, shrewish wives, squalling children, and all the horrors of home'.[82] Shaw planned the latter script, *O'Flaherty V.C.*, when staying at the home of his friend Lady Gregory, the Irish playwright and theatre manager. Here, at Coole Park in County Galway, he specified the stage properties required as 'a garden seat and an iron chair (as at Coole)', and designed the work to assist the Abbey Theatre, which Gregory had co-founded in Dublin.[83] The play might, Shaw hoped, revive his theatrical career from its wartime slump, and provide a much-needed boost to the coffers of the Abbey Theatre by appealing to a music-hall crowd.[84]

Shaw's play was also written, in part, as a response to the wartime recruitment drive in Ireland, which—as he explains in his preface—Shaw felt was being 'badly bungled' by a British government that was trying to drum up patriotic feelings based on 'devotion to England and England's king' (p. 148). One prominent wallposter of the time, headed 'An Irish Hero', pictured the real-life Irish winner of the Victoria Cross, Sergeant Michael O'Leary, along with the line, '1 Irishman defeats 10 Germans'.[85] O'Leary was the first Irishman to win the Victoria

---

[81] J. P. Shanley, 'TV: Saved by Shaw', *New York Times*, 5 July 1955, p. 59.

[82] Holroyd, *Bernard Shaw*, ii. 379. *Inc* Proof, fol. 24.

[83] Terry Phillips, 'Shaw, Ireland, and World War I: *O'Flaherty V.C.*, an Unlikely Recruiting Play', *SHAW* 30 (2010), 133–46, at 134. Letter of 14 September 1915, in *CL* iii. 309.

[84] See Nelson O'Ceallaigh Ritschel, *Bernard Shaw, W. T. Stead, and the New Journalism* (Cham: Palgrave Macmillan, 2017), 197.

[85] Phillips, 'Shaw, Ireland, and World War I', p. 135.

Cross, and so achieved widespread celebrity, particularly in Dublin.[86] Shaw declared that O'Leary's 'famous exploit created the situation which I dramatized', with Shaw now creating a fictional character, in O'Flaherty, with a similar name and the same decoration, but who is driven to join the war effort by unhappy domestic circumstances.[87] The playwright described how, in *O'Flaherty V.C.*, an Irish soldier 'sees Ireland as it is, his mother as she is, his sweetheart as she is; and he goes back to the trenches joyfully for the sake of peace and quietness'.[88] That message would scarcely endear Shaw to anti-war Irish patriots who professed to love their country. Equally, of course, Shaw's depiction was likely to rile those supporting the war effort: O'Flaherty declares 'No war is right' (p. 155) and 'Youll never have a quiet world til you knock the patriotism out of the human race' (p. 158). With this play, Shaw thumbed his nose at all sides of Irish public opinion.

The Abbey manager St John Ervine remembered how 'the moment public announcement of the production was made a large crowd of persons began to besiege the box office'.[89] But the British government in Ireland objected to the proposed production, slated to appear on 23 November 1915, and so the playhouse's directors withdrew the work. The premiere occurred instead on 3 February 1917 on the Western Front in Treizennes, directed by the actor Robert Loraine (who had starred in Shaw's plays before the war) with an amateur cast drawn from the Royal Flying Corps. One of those performing in the play was Lady Gregory's son Robert, who was then in 40 Squadron and who wrote to his mother to tell her that he was taking on the role of Teresa.[90] In this way, Robert Gregory, who would die the following year, found himself performing at a makeshift 250-seat theatre constructed from an abandoned Red Cross building, in the same play that had been inspired by his family homestead back at Coole.[91]

---

[86] See Lauren Arrington, 'The Censorship of *O'Flaherty V.C.*', *SHAW* 28 (2008), 85–106, at 90.

[87] Letter of 18 April 1921, in *CL* iii. 717.

[88] Letter from Shaw to Gregory, 14 September 1915, in *CL* iii. 309.

[89] St. John Ervine, 'At the Play: The Secret History of "O'Flaherty, V.C"', *The Observer*, 12 December 1920, p. 11.

[90] David Gunby, 'The First Night of *O'Flaherty, V.C.*', *SHAW* 19 (1999), 85–97, at 89.

[91] Later in 1917, after the premiere performance at the Western Front, Shaw performed the script to 250 laughing and cheering soldiers near his own Hertfordshire home of Ayot St Lawrence (although he noted 'the best bits were when they sat very tight and said nothing'). He then had the play published in *Hearst's Magazine* in New York during that year, before versions appeared onstage in New York and London in 1920, with a 'rapturously received' production then given by London's Stage Society in 1921. *O'Flaherty*

On 20 November 1924, Shaw made his first ever radio broadcast to an estimated audience of 4 million people, and selected *O'Flaherty V.C.* as the piece for transmission.[92] Shaw suggested this script to the BBC because the piece 'never fails when I read it; and I should like to make my first experiment with it'.[93] He then performed the work by speaking all of the different roles, and singing part of the wartime song 'Tipperary', before concluding with the declaration: 'The play is over. I hope I have not bored you.'[94] The *Manchester Guardian* responded by hailing his virtuosity in performing so many different voices, and labelling him 'The Perfect Broadcaster'.[95]

AUGUSTUS DOES HIS BIT

Shaw's war playlet, *Augustus Does His Bit*, is a whimsical comedy about spying and was written in August 1916 for the actress Lalla Vandervelde. She was married to a Belgian Socialist minister, lived in London during the wartime occupation of her homeland, and would perform in the piece (as the glamorous female protagonist) at its first production. This premiere was given by the Stage Society for two performances at the Court Theatre in January 1917, and was subtitled *An Unofficial Dramatic Tract on War Saving and Cognate Topics by the Author of the Inca of Perusalem.*[96]

The script revolves around the aristocratic Augustus Highcastle, a British army colonel who has been sent home from the front after displaying a zealous incompetence in battle (captured by the Germans, who then realized he would do more damage if they released him). Highcastle now makes recruiting speeches in which he urges listeners to die 'for Little Pifflington', and he remains oblivious when a potential female spy arrives in his office. Today, this male figure looks very much like the forerunner of characters such as Field Marshal Haig in Theatre Workshop's *Oh What a Lovely War* and General Melchett in the BBC's

---

V.C. did not reach the Abbey Theatre until 1920, when it appeared on the bill as work of historical rather than contemporary concern: 'A Reminiscence of 1915'. Letter of 27 November 1917, in *CL* iii. 517. David Clare, *Bernard Shaw's Irish Outlook* (Houndmills: Palgrave Macmillan, 2016), 101. 'Stage Society: "O'Flaherty, V.C."', *The Observer*, 2 January 1921, p. 17. Holroyd, *Bernard Shaw*, ii. 381.

[92] 'Shaw Makes Debut on Radio to 4,000,000', *New York Times*, 21 November 1924, p. 2.
[93] Letter of 24 June 1924, in *CL* iii. 882.
[94] 'Shaw Makes Debut on Radio to 4,000,000', *New York Times*, 21 November 1924, p. 2.
[95] '"G.B.S." The Perfect Broadcaster', *Manchester Guardian*, 21 November 1924, p. 9.
[96] Stanley Weintraub, 'Shaw's Musician: Edward Elgar', *SHAW* 22 (2002), 1–18, at 3. Original programme for *Augustus Does His Bit*, in HRC, Shaw Collection, Vertical Files, box 697, #G30.

Blackadder Goes Forth. But the first staging of *Augustus Does His Bit* followed the previous year's slaughter on the Somme, and some of those in Shaw's audience felt unready for such fare. *The Observer* reported hissing from some spectators, and condemned the show because, despite Shaw's 'genius for writing witty dialogue', the playlet dwells 'on an idea which is almost an obsession with him—the ineptitude and stupidity of the well-born Englishman brought up at a public school'.[97] Shaw's friend William Archer, whose son had enlisted in 1914 and would die on the Western Front, wrote that 'After the war, those of us who are still above ground will no doubt relish our Shaw again; but in the thick of its storm and stress he somehow seems an incongruity . . . Anything less helpful than *Augustus Does His Bit* it would be hard to imagine.'[98]

The play constituted part of Shaw's ongoing attempt to highlight the absurdity of the British ruling classes, although some felt that the midst of wartime was scarcely the time for such mockery, and after the premiere, the play disappeared from the London stage for seven years.[99] Nonetheless, Shaw felt that some of the men who were actually fighting the war recognized and appreciated his portrayal of official incompetence. He recorded that, following the first London production in 1917, he received an invitation to travel to the Western Front, where he could see the devastation for himself, and could dine with Douglas Haig. After meeting the real-life commander, Shaw wrote: 'He seemed to me a first rate specimen of the British gentleman and conscientiously studious soldier, trained socially and professionally to behave and work in a groove from which nothing could move him.'[100]

ANNAJANSKA, THE BOLSHEVIK EMPRESS

After attacking the wartime folly of British military leaders, in December 1917 Shaw turned his attention to Russian politics, setting a play in the fictional post-revolutionary Republic of Beotia, where rival factions vie for power. As one of Shaw's characters asks, 'How can I obey six different

[97] 'The Stage Society: Augustus Does His Bit', *The Observer*, 28 January 1917, p. 5.

[98] Archer, 'The Nation', 26 April 1917, quoted in *Selected Correspondence of Bernard Shaw: Bernard Shaw and William Archer*, ed. Postlewait, p. xlix.

[99] After the play's 1917 premiere, London did not see another production of the work until Norman Macdermott revived it at Hampstead's Everyman Theatre in June 1924, although the piece did play in the United States where it was given by an amateur company (the Drama League Players at Polio's Theatre) in Washington DC on 16 December 1917, and by a professional group (John D. Williams's company at the Comedy Theatre) in New York on 12 March 1919. Mander and Michenson, 'The Stage History of the Plays', in HRC, Shaw Collection, Vertical Files, box 697, #G30.

[100] Shaw, *What I Really Wrote About the War* (London: Constable, 1931), 244.

dictators, and not one gentleman among the lot of them?' (p. 207). In real-life Russia, of course, the February Revolution of that year had overthrown the Tsar, and installed a provisional government. Then, one month before Shaw wrote his script, the October Revolution had abolished the provisional government, handing power to the Bolsheviks.[101]

Shaw's script responds to this febrile situation. 'Annajanska' herself is the daughter of the former imperial ruler, and has escaped from the royal palace—where her family is now imprisoned—in order to join the revolt. She urges the revolutionaries against allowing the restoration of their old rulers (her own family), and, with some irony, demands that the men take their orders from her to avoid reinstating the former regime. At the end of 1917, the British censor fretted that 'whether it is just now desirable to get entertainment of such a fable is perhaps open to doubt', concluding that he would recommend a licence for public performance 'only with hesitation'.[102]

If Shaw had written *The Inca of Perusalem* for Gertrude Kingston, and *Augustus Does His Bit* for Lalla Vandervelde, the new playlet—with its scene-stealing role of Annajanska—was written for another female actress, Lillah McCarthy. Shaw had known McCarthy's work since 1895, and she had thereafter incarnated many of his characters, with Shaw observing that 'with that young lady I achieved performances of my plays which will probably never be surpassed'.[103] But by 1917 McCarthy had suffered from a significant personal and professional blow when her husband, the actor and manager Granville Barker, abandoned their marriage. Her career now trundled to a standstill from which it would never really recover, and Shaw tried to help by creating *Annajanska* for her. The dominant character of Annajanska spends her time firing '*shot after shot*' (p. 206) with her gun, commanding those around her with threats of violence, and creating a memorable finale when she reveals her military uniform. If he sought to bring Lillah McCarthy back to the fore, though, Shaw himself attempted to disappear from view: just as with *The Inca of Perusalem*, in *Annajanska* he presented a work about contemporary politics under a disguised name. *Annajanska* was advertised as being 'from the Russian of Gregory

[101] The revolution took place on 24–5 October on the Julian calendar. However, after the revolution, Russia adopted the Gregorian calendar, according to which the date of the revolution became 6–7 November.

[102] Ernest A. Bendall, letter of 29 December 1917, British Library, Add. MS 66183.

[103] Dennis Kennedy, 'McCarthy, Lila Emma', *ODNB*, <http://www.oxforddnb.com/view/article/34682>.

Biessipoff', although newspapers noted that 'Mr Bernard Shaw may know who the author really is'.[104]

When the piece premiered on 21 January 1918 at London's Coliseum, critics tended to see only 'horseplay' or 'a music-hall "sketch" '.[105] But Shaw's script asks a more profound question: if the public could not be relied upon to act in its own best interests, what might be the role of the political strong man (or woman)? As Annajanska puts it, 'if the people cannot govern themselves, they must be governed by somebody. If they will not do their duty without being half forced and half humbugged, somebody must force them and humbug them' (p. 211).

When the BBC later broadcast the work on television, on 2 May 1939, the script revealed what the Shaw expert L. W. Conolly calls a 'timely political relevance'.[106] After all, Annajanska promises to defend the revolution and declares that 'a great common danger and a great common duty can unite us' (p. 211). The day before that BBC broadcast, Hitler had spoken to a crowd of 132,000 in Berlin, promising to defend his revolution and declaring, 'Let the rest of the world threaten and bluster. They will come to grief where they have always come to grief—on German unity.'[107]

Historical Sketches

Shaw's war playlets had been written during the First World War, and were set in places designed to resemble Europe at the time of the conflict. But outside those wartime years, Shaw also created a group of short plays that tackle a broader range of historical subjects. In these historical sketches, he describes a range of more distant settings, which nonetheless reveal a great deal about Shaw's reactions to the political and artistic world of the first half of the twentieth century. If Victorian historians such as Carlyle and Macaulay had written about the past in order to draw lessons for their own age, a similar approach characterizes Shaw's short historical works.[108] For example, his 1909 play, *The Shewing-up of Blanco Posnet*, may have been set in nineteenth-century America, but Shaw intended the script to reveal more about the system of theatrical censorship in twentieth-century Britain than anything

---

[104] 'The Theatres', *The Times*, 21 January 1918, p. 9.
[105] 'Annajanska, the Wild Duchess', *The Observer*, 27 January 1918, p. 5; 'A Revolutionary Playlet', *The Times*, 22 January 1918, p. 9.
[106] Conolly, *Bernard Shaw and the BBC*, p. 96.
[107] 'The German May Day', *The Times*, 2 May 1939, p. 14.
[108] See J. L. Wisenthal, *Shaw's Sense of History* (Oxford: Clarendon Press, 1988), 2.

historically accurate about the United States. Meanwhile, his 1913 drama *Great Catherine* is set in eighteenth-century Russia, yet also revels in the kind of international misunderstandings between the English, Russians, and Germans that would become central to the entire fate of Europe in the year after the piece was written. Shaw's 1934 piece *The Six of Calais* derived from his response to the historical chronicles of Jean Froissart and the sculpture of Auguste Rodin, but, as his 'Prefatory' to the piece explains, the playlet also set out to teach an audience in the age of George V that a king might not necessarily be 'a pleasant and highly respectable gentleman in a bowler hat' but might be a 'soldier monarch publicly raging and cursing' (p. 351). Meanwhile, the piece that Shaw published in 1944, *The British Party System*, which is set amongst the politicians of late seventeenth- and early eighteenth-century London, was also Shaw's response to feeling, in an age of 'Adolf Hitler, Pilsudski, Benito Mussolini, Stalin', that 'government by Parliaments modelled on the British Party System, far from being a guarantee of liberty and enlightened progress, must be ruthlessly discarded'.[109]

THE SHEWING-UP OF BLANCO POSNET

Between February and March 1909 Shaw wrote what he subtitled *A Sermon in Crude Melodrama*, set vaguely at some point during the nineteenth century '*in a territory of the United States of America*' (p. 274). Shaw had written the piece to raise money for a children's charity, and intended to cast the prominent actor Herbert Beerbohm Tree in the main part. But one of Shaw's characters describes God as 'a sly one. He's a mean one. He lies low for you. He plays cat and mouse with you' (p. 282), and the same character describes one woman in the drama as having 'immoral relations with every man in this town' (p. 291). The British censor found these lines unacceptable, and demanded them cut from public performance.[110]

The message of *Blanco Posnet* was actually a broadly Christian one about a redeemed sinner. Blanco, a horse thief, ends up admitting that he gave away the horse he had stolen in order to help a sick child. In fact, the playwright Sean O'Casey declared that the playlet told a religious story that could be bracketed alongside the writings of St Paul.[111] With such material, Shaw was therefore setting a trap for the censor.

[109] Shaw, *Everybody's Political What's What* (London: Constable, 1944), 29.

[110] British Library, Add. MS 65866E, *The Shewing Up of Blanco Posnet*, and HRC Lic.

[111] Letter of 17 March 1942, in O'Casey, *The Letters of Sean O'Casey*, ed. David Krause, 4 vols (London: Macmillan; Washington: Catholic University Press, 1975–92), ii. 30.

Shaw wrote: 'I have taken advantage of the Blanco Posnet affair to write a tremendous series of letters to The Times; and the result has been that the Prime Minister has promised to appoint a select committee of both Houses of Parliament to enquire into the whole question of Censorship.'[112]

Shaw sensed an opportunity to highlight the absurdity of British censorship by producing *Blanco Posnet* at the Abbey Theatre in Dublin, where the writ of the British censor did not apply (the Irish capital had a long-standing method of licensing the premises rather than the play).[113] 'I think we could do it well,' Lady Gregory told Shaw, 'and I don't think anything could show up the hypocrisy of the British Censor more than a performance in Dublin where the audience is known to be so sensitive.'[114] Despite threats from the British government in Ireland, the Abbey managers remained defiant, issuing a public statement to emphasize that 'the decisions of the English Censor are being brought into Ireland', and the playhouse thus drew the support of Irish nationalists.[115] The theatre historian Christopher Morash writes that

In the end, the Castle [the centre of British government in Ireland] blinked, hoping for objections from the churches once the play was staged; none were forthcoming, and *Blanco Posnet* played to large (and well-heeled) audiences, most of whom enjoyed it, but left a bit mystified as to the source of the controversy. In the end, it was an almost perfect public relations victory for the Abbey.[116]

One regular Dublin playgoer observed that 'an event of a lifetime was taking place', whilst Lady Gregory declared, 'The shouts are still in our ears! Never was such a victory. From first line to last of the play sustained and intense attention, and applause.'[117] *The Times* reported that 'Everybody to-day is enjoying the story of Mr. Shaw's cleverness and the Censor's folly.'[118] When the Stage Society produced the play in London as a private performance in December 1909, the audience

[112] Letter of June 1909, in Shaw, *Bernard Shaw's Letters to Siegfried Trebitsch*, 144.

[113] Joan FitzPatrick Dean, *Riot and Great Anger: Stage Censorship in Twentieth-Century Ireland* (Madison: University of Wisconsin Press, 2004), 18.

[114] Quoted by Holroyd, *Bernard Shaw*, ii. 228.

[115] Yeats and Gregory, '*The Arrow*: 25 August 1909—*The Shewing-up of Blanco Posnet*: Statement by the Directors', in Yeats, *The Irish Dramatic Movement*, ed. Mary FitzGerald and Richard J. Finneran (New York: Scribner, 2003), 207–8, at 208.

[116] Christopher Morash, *A History of Irish Theatre, 1601–2000* (Cambridge: Cambridge University Press, 2002), 144.

[117] Joseph Holloway and Lady Gregory, both quoted by A. M. Gibbs, *Bernard Shaw: A Life* (Gainesville: University Press of Florida, 2005), 262.

[118] 'Ireland', *The Times*, 27 August 1909, p. 8.

again wondered at a piece that had 'no hint in it all of anything more immoral than bad taste'.[119] Kenneth Tynan later commented that this 'immensely lively' play pointed forward to the Wild West films of John Ford, although he claimed Shaw's 'plot is tighter'.[120]

Some rival writers felt irritated by Shaw's success here. James Joyce reviewed the Dublin production for *Il Piccolo della sera* and noted that Shaw's 'loquacious and lively spirit cannot suffer the imposition of the noble, spare style that befits a modern playwright'.[121] Meanwhile W. B. Yeats and Ezra Pound went to watch the Stage Society production, and Yeats was left feeling so 'cantankerous' that afterwards he spent time antagonizing the polyglot Pound by arguing that acquiring foreign languages provided absolutely no indication of intellectual ability.[122] Still, today *Blanco Posnet* is one of the best known of Shaw's short dramas, remembered as a piece that provoked the first major agitation about theatre censorship in twentieth-century Ireland, as well as being a work that enabled Shaw to take a prominent stand against the British system of dramatic licensing, which eventually crumbled away in 1968.[123]

GREAT CATHERINE (WHOM GLORY STILL ADORES)

Between 29 July and 13 August 1913, Shaw wrote another short play with a historical setting, this time taking his cue from the longest-serving female monarch of Russia, Catherine the Great. The real-life Catherine had been a complex, powerful, and rather intellectual figure, yet when Byron came to write cantos 6–10 of his poem *Don Juan*, he condemned her in sexualized terms. Hence, in Byron's poem, Catherine becomes 'the greatest of all sovereigns and w[hore]s'. In turn, Shaw's 'Author's Apology' for the play declares that 'what Byron said was all there really is to say that is worth saying' (p. 308). Shaw therefore created the role of Catherine for the actress Gertrude Kingston, who had

---

[119] 'The Shewing-Up of Blanco Posnet', *The Observer*, 12 December 1909, p. 8.

[120] Tynan, 'Shaw's Adult Western', undated newspaper column, in HRC, Shaw Theatre Biography, box 762, envelope labelled Gassner 'Shaw, George Bernard Short Plays'.

[121] Joyce, 'The Battle Between Bernard Shaw and the Censor: "The Shewing-up of Blanco Posnet"', in James Joyce, *Occasional, Critical, and Political Writing*, ed. Kevin Barry (Oxford: Oxford University Press, 2000), 152–4, at 154.

[122] Grace Lovat Fraser, *In the Days of My Youth* (London: Cassell, 1970), 130.

[123] W. N. Osborough, *The Irish Stage: A Legal History* (Dublin: Four Courts Press, 2015), 234–5.

come to fame in the 1890s, and was known for portraying what William Archer called 'saccharine maliciousness'.[124]

The British censor felt wary of a script that was 'all incredibly silly as well as vulgar'.[125] Douglas Dawson, the comptroller of the Lord Chamberlain's Office, even contacted the Russian Embassy for an opinion about the play, pointing out that Shaw 'turns everything into ridicule'.[126] The embassy responded, 'the Empress Catherine, whatever her morals may have been, is still considered by the whole country as the greatest Sovereign Russia has ever had with Peter the Great'.[127] Still, the play did eventually appear in November 1913 at the Vaudeville Theatre for a run of thirty performances. Unfortunately for Shaw, there was a danger of Shavian fatigue at this time: the play marked the third new Shaw script to appear onstage in as many months, and was tightly sandwiched between two of his greatest hits, *Fanny's First Play* (1911) and *Pygmalion* (1913).[128] Critical reaction to *Great Catherine* was, therefore, somewhat muted. 'Perhaps one expected a little more', sighed *The Times*, the 'joke has run a little thin'.[129]

Still, the script subsequently won some significant admirers. By 1919 the piece had been seen in Frankfurt am Main, where the press reported that 'the applause was on the whole hearty'.[130] When it appeared at New York's Neighborhood Theatre three years after the London premiere, the *New York Times* judged the drama 'vastly entertaining', and in 1926, the play appeared in Monaco's Théâtre de Monte-Carlo, followed by a production at the Théâtre des Arts in Paris in 1927.[131] There followed an operatic version, several television adaptations in the 1940s and 1950s, and a film version starring Peter

---

[124] 'Obituary: Miss Gertrude Kingston', *Manchester Guardian*, 9 November 1937, p. 5.

[125] British Library, Add. MS 66042 A: 1913, Lord Chamberlain's Plays: 'Great Catherine' by George Bernard Shaw, 1913, Typewritten, together with MS and typewritten report and recommendation for licence by E. A. Bendall. Holroyd, *Bernard Shaw*, ii. 322.

[126] Quoted by Brad Kent, 'Bernard Shaw, the British Censorship of Plays, and Modern Celebrity', *English Literature in Transition, 1880–1923*, 57/2 (2014), 231–49, at 246.

[127] Quoted by Kent, 'Bernard Shaw, the British Censorship of Plays', 246.

[128] 'Mr Shaw's New Play', *The Observer*, 16 November 1913, p. 13.

[129] 'Mr Shaw's New Play', *The Times*, 19 November 1913, p. 11.

[130] 'Shaw und Wied im Schausspielhaus', newspaper clipping in HRC, Shaw Collection, Vertical Files, box 698, #G88.

[131] 'Shaw and Dunsany in Grand Street', *New York Times*, 15 November 1916, p. 9; letter of 2 February 1927, in *CL* iv. 38.

O'Toole.[132] The film flopped, but O'Toole felt enthused by Shaw's script, remembering that he had acted in the playlet when at drama school: 'I've never heard such laughter in a theatre in my life,' O'Toole remembered. 'Never taken so many curtain calls either.'[133]

THE SIX OF CALAIS

By the 1930s, Shaw had become a pre-eminent figure in world literature and a Nobel Laureate. Shaw now penned another historical sketch, when he set down *The Six of Calais* during the middle of May 1934, taking just four days to complete the writing, although he had been contemplating the subject for far longer. Indeed, he had originally formed the idea for the script seventeen years earlier, when travelling through the Lorraine region of France. Shaw had become fascinated by the six leading denizens of Calais who had been under siege by the English troops of Edward III, and who volunteered to surrender themselves seemingly to execution in order to save their city.[134]

Jean Froissart penned his account of this siege during the fourteenth century, and in the late 1880s, August Rodin completed a famous sculpture of *The Burghers of Calais*, one cast of which stands in Westminster near the Houses of Parliament to this day.[135] Shaw had a long-standing interest in Rodin's work, with Rodin modelling a bust of Shaw in 1906.[136] Then in 1920, following the First World War, Shaw found

---

[132] The Dutch composer Ignace Lilien created an operatic version that appeared in German at the Staatstheater, Wiesbaden, on 8 May 1932; letter of 19 May 1932, in *CL* iv. 297. The television adaptations included one broadcast by NBC in the United States in 1948; a second by the BBC in Britain in 1953; and a third by CBC in Canada in 1958. ('Radio: Program Preview', *Time*, 3 May 1938, <http://content.time.com/time/magazine/article/0,9171,798550,00.html>; 'Great Catherine', <http://www.bfi.org.uk/films-tv-people/4ce2b7213f8b4>; Robert E. Wood and Anthony Wynn, *Valiant for Truth: Barry Morse and His Lifelong Association with Bernard Shaw* (Portland, OR: Planet, 2012), 53–4.)

[133] Stephen Watts, 'A Funny Thing is Happening to GBS', *New York Times*, 12 March 1967, p. 125.

[134] Michel W. Pharand, *Bernard Shaw and the French* (Gainesville: University Press of Florida, 2000), 235.

[135] Jean Froissart, *Chronicles*, trans. and ed. Geoffrey Brereton (Harmondsworth: Penguin, 1978); Albert E. Elsen, with Rosalyn Frankel Jamison, *Rodin's Art: The Rodin Collection of Iris & B. Gerald Cantor Center for Visual Arts Stanford University*, ed. Bernard Barryte (Oxford: Oxford University Press, 2003), 65.

[136] Shaw later commented that Rodin had 'won immortality for me, as the biographical dictionaries 1000 years hence would all contain an item—<u>Shaw, George Bernard, sujet d'un buste par Rodin: d'ailleurs inconnu</u> [subject of a bust by Rodin: otherwise unknown]'. Note for Catalogue of the August Rodin Exhibition, July–August 1931, in HRC, Shaw Collection, Vertical Files, box 696, folder G11.

a parallel between the way the victorious Allies were treating Germany and the historical subject of Rodin's work, writing:

573 years ago, King Edward III, the Attila of his day, captured Calais after a siege lasting a year. Instead of admiring the men of Calais for holding out against him so long, and yielding only to famine, he, in mere doglike vengeance, demanded that they should send him six of their leading citizens that he might murder them in cold blood. . . . At the present moment the honor of England is at stake in exactly the same way.[137]

In 1934, Shaw scripted his own version of the tale, subtitling his text 'A Medieval War Story told by Froissart, Auguste Rodin and Bernard Shaw'.[138] Indeed, when *The Six of Calais* first appeared onstage, at the Open Air Theatre in Regent's Park during July that year (the same park where *Passion, Poison, and Petrifaction* had premiered nearly three decades before), there were loud calls for the author to appear, and when Shaw strode on to the stage he declared: 'Ladies and gentlemen, be reasonable. You can see for yourselves that the author isn't in the house.'[139]

In *The Observer*, reviewer Ivor Brown responded to the playlet by praising Shaw's mastery of the short form, commenting:

Shaw, in performing the same tail-treading office for Froissart, and giving eloquence to Rodin's burgher, has also done something that is less native to his habit. He has known when to stop. He has cut his joke short, a shrewd method of improving its appearance; it can do with the improvement.[140]

In his 'Prefatory' to the play, Shaw claimed that he had improved the story and made the plot suitable for acting. He claimed that his work was meant 'to provide an exhibition of the art of acting', that it was 'an acting piece and nothing else', and that he felt he needed to improve upon 'the story as told by that absurd old snob Froissart' (p. 352). Shaw could be very protective of his own texts and wanted them performed as he had written them, at times checking on whether actors performed the words as well as the stage directions that he had set down.[141] Still, Shaw's treatment of Froissart offered a premonition of the more modern directorial approach, evinced today in the work of figures such as

---

[137] *Six* Pref, fos. 1–4.

[138] Shaw vacillated over the subtitle of this play, also calling it 'a medieval war story told by Froissart and now retold with Certain Necessary Improvements by a Fellow of the Royal Society of Literature' (*Six* Proof 2, title page).

[139] 'Shaw's New Play on London Stage', *New York Times*, 18 July 1934, p. 20.

[140] Ivor Brown, 'The Week's Theatres', *The Observer*, 22 July 1934, p. 13.

[141] See Bernard F. Dukore, *Crimes and Punishments and Bernard Shaw* (Cham: Springer, 2017), 89.

Thomas Ostermeier, who see the original text as ripe for adaptation and only the starting point of any new theatrical exploration.

THE BRITISH PARTY SYSTEM

The final historical piece included in this volume, *The British Party System*, was written by Shaw during the Second World War, but he had been dwelling on the subject of this sketch since long before the outbreak of hostilities. Indeed, the idea of rulers, the ruling class, and how they governed was one of his most abiding preoccupations. In a book review of 1917, Shaw described the late seventeenth-century 'establishment of the party system in Parliament', and lamented that, although people did not now know much about the system, it meant a politician did not 'vote on the merits of the measure before him' but 'on the question whether his party will remain in power or not'.[142] Shaw despised the figure generally recognized as Britain's first prime minister, Robert Walpole. At one point Shaw characterized Walpole as 'unable to govern without corruption'.[143] Thus, in Shaw's 1917 book review, he described how the arrival of the party system 'under the pressure of a European conflict prototypical of the present war' had not only 'made Walpole possible' but 'made any other sort of man than Walpole impossible'.[144]

Shaw returned to this theme in his 1928 volume *The Intelligent Woman's Guide to Socialism and Capitalism*, where he wrote of the deficiencies of the twentieth-century political system, and traced those flaws back to William III's interaction with Robert Spencer, a 'clever statesman' who told the king 'that if he chose his ministers always from the strongest party in the House of Commons, which happened just then to be the Whig party, that party would have to back him'.[145]

During the Second World War, the theme appeared more urgent: how had universal franchise again led to universal slaughter? Shaw felt sure that he had identified a fundamental problem that plagues democracies to this day, namely that, in any party system, politicians debate any question not on its merits, but according to the party line. Shaw now put this same idea into 'the form of a little historical drama' (p. 369),

---

[142] Shaw, 'Something Like a History of England at Last' (review of 4 November 1917), in Shaw, *Bernard Shaw's Book Reviews*, ed. Brian Tyson, 2 vols (University Park: Pennsylvania State University Press, 1991 and 1996), ii. 366–72, at 368–9.

[143] Shaw, 'Preface: Mainly About Myself', in *Plays Pleasant and Unpleasant: The First Volume Containing Three Unpleasant Plays by Bernard Shaw* (London: Constable, 1931), pp. v–xxiii, at p. xii.

[144] Shaw, 'Something Like a History of England at Last', 369–70.

[145] Shaw, *The Intelligent Woman's Guide to Socialism and Capitalism* (London: Constable, 1928), 350.

The British Party System, bringing together the historical figures of Walpole, Spencer, and William III. Clearly Shaw wrote this piece to inform his own contemporaries, feeling that 'PRACTICALLY nobody in these islands understands the Party System. Britons do not know its history' (p. 369). He himself realized that the problems of the twentieth-century British party system had been present since its inception, and wanted to communicate these flaws to a wider public.

Yet, unlike all of the other playlets in this volume, Shaw did not intend *The British Party System* to be seen onstage. Although the sketch is written in theatrical dialogue, Shaw included it in chapter 3 of his book *Everybody's Political What's What?*, which was, as he told the *Daily Telegraph*, intended as 'an elementary text-book' about politics.[146] He filled this ragbag volume, which appeared in September 1944 when the author was 89, with the kind of truths he felt should be known by every democratically active citizen. The book itself received a mixed critical reception, with historian A. L. Rowse writing in the *Sunday Times* that 'the bright little skit about Sunderland, William III and the party system, which is the best thing in the book, makes one regret that he did not say what he has to say in a series of dialogues'.[147] Only after the author's death was his playlet separated from the rest of the volume and included in the Dodd-Mead edition of Shaw's *Complete Plays with Prefaces*, serving perhaps to endorse T. S. Eliot's contention that there exists the 'unmistakable personal rhythm' of prose style in Shaw's stage plays.[148] After all, in Shaw's prose writings, as in his dramatic works, his argument is frequently advanced through a disputatious array of voices and a demonstration of clashing ideas.

Shakespearean Shorts

In 1896, Shaw famously declared: 'With the single exception of Homer, there is no eminent writer, not even Sir Walter Scott, whom I can despise so entirely as I despise Shakespeare when I measure my mind against his.'[149] Yet paradoxically, in that same essay, Shaw added, 'I pity the man who cannot enjoy Shakespeare. He has outlasted thousands of

---

[146] Holroyd, *Bernard Shaw*, iii. 441.

[147] A. L. Rowse, 'Sense and Nonsense About Politics', *Sunday Times*, 17 September 1944, in HRC, Shaw Collection, Vertical Files, box 701, #G167.

[148] See Shaw, *Complete Plays with Prefaces*, 6 vols (New York: Dodd, Mead, 1962), vol. v; T. S. Eliot, *Poetry and Drama* (London: Faber, 1951), 12.

[149] Shaw, 'Blaming the Bard', review of *Cymbeline*, *Saturday Review*, 26 September 1896; repr. in Shaw, *Our Theatres in the Nineties*, ii. 195–202, at 195.

abler thinkers, and will outlast a thousand more.'[150] During his lifetime,
Shaw became well known for denouncing Shakespeare, often in comic
terms, and yet Shaw obviously had a deep familiarity with, and admiration for, Shakespeare's work. Indeed, when Shaw wrote the manuscript of *Passion, Poison, and Petrifaction* in 1905 he described it as
being written 'by The Chelsea Shakespeare' and pictured the setting as
being, in an echo of Ben Jonson's description of Shakespeare, 'not for
an age but for all time'.[151] Lillah McCarthy noted how Shaw peppered
his conversations with Shakespearean quotations; the actor Cedric
Hardwicke paired Shaw and Shakespeare as 'the two most important
playwrights of all time'; whilst the critic Sonya Freeman Loftis has
recently asserted that 'a key element in the complex performance of
G.B.S. is the act of destroying Shakespeare and replacing him with
Shaw'.[152]

Shaw saw Shakespeare as a long-term rival, but Shaw's target was
not simply the writer himself. As Shaw explained in *Three Plays for the
Puritans*, he hated the 'Bardolatry' of those who blindly worshipped
Shakespeare and whose efforts led to 'spurious and silly representations of his plays'.[153]

This volume's final subgroup of short plays, then, dramatizes the
figure of Shakespeare, and serves to knock him down from the lofty
pedestal on which Romantic critics had placed him. In *The Dark Lady
of the Sonnets* and *Shakes Versus Shav*, Shaw instead reduces the bard to
human—or smaller-than-human—scale. Although Shaw expressed
critical opinions about Henry Irving in part because of how that
actor-manager trimmed Shakespeare's works, Shaw also sought to
show the Bard's writing need not be treated like Holy Writ. Instead,
scripts such as *Macbeth* and *Cymbeline* were apt for reworking by
someone who could see the deficiencies and absurdities of those texts.
At times, in his longer plays, Shaw adapted Shakespeare: for instance,
Shaw's three-act play *Heartbreak House* (1919) provides a rewriting of
King Lear, and his five-act play *Caesar and Cleopatra* (1898) revises
Antony and Cleopatra. Likewise, Shaw found that in his short playlets,
Shakespeare's life and work could be revisited, reconsidered, and
revamped.

---

[150] Shaw, 'Blaming the Bard', 196.   [151] *PPP* Hol, fol. 1.
[152] McCarthy and Hardwicke, quoted in 'Biography in Sound: They Knew Bernard
Shaw' (radio broadcast), NBC, 27 March 1955. Loftis, *Shakespeare's Surrogates:
Rewriting Renaissance Drama* (Houndmills: Palgrave Macmillan, 2013), 3.
[153] Shaw, *Three Plays for Puritans* (London: Grant Richards, 1931), p. xxxi.

THE DARK LADY OF THE SONNETS

In June 1910, Shaw spent three days writing 'An Interlude' called *The Dark Lady of the Sonnets*. He was inspired to do this by Edith Lyttleton, one of the driving forces behind the campaign to establish a National Theatre in Britain and who had recently secured a donation of £70,000 to further that cause.[154]

Lyttleton now turned to Shaw for help, and he responded by writing this short work in which Shakespeare meets Queen Elizabeth I and asks her to establish 'a National Theatre, for the better instruction' (p. 413) of her subjects. The script also features Shakespeare overhearing lines that he would later recycle in his own dramatic works, such as the following moment that Shaw cut from his script at a late stage:

ELIZABETH. Go [*the Dark Lady tries to kiss her hand*]. Go. No more. The rest is silence. [*The Dark Lady goes*].

SHAKESPEAR. Good. Good.

ELIZABETH. What mean you by good?

SHAKESPEAR. 'The rest is silence'. I shall kill somebody with that—in a play.[155]

The premiere performance, in November 1910, occurred at London's Haymarket Theatre, as a charity matinee aimed at raising money for a modern National Theatre, and starring an actress Shaw admired, Mona Limerick, as the Dark Lady.[156] But Shaw's versions of Shakespeare and Elizabeth proved sufficiently fascinating to captivate audiences in places unconnected to the National Theatre campaign and without Mona Limerick in the title role. For example, the playlet appeared as part of a music-hall bill at the London Coliseum in October 1923, and at Cabaret ABC in Vienna in 1935. Newspapers deemed the Coliseum performance a demonstration of 'intelligent "variety"', whilst the 'cheerful, funny' Vienna production won praise as 'the highlight of the programme'.[157] The professional American premiere occurred as

[154] Daniel Rosenthal, *The National Theatre Story* (London: Oberon, 2013), 16.
[155] British Library, Add. MS 50626, *The Dark Lady of the Sonnets*, 11. Shaw deleted this passage from the rough proofs of the 1910 Constable edition of the play.
[156] 'The Shakespeare Memorial National Theatre', *The Times*, 25 November 1910, p. 13. Mona Limerick's daughter later recounted 'Shaw insisted that mummy should play the Dark Lady. He gave the plays to my father Iden Payne, primarily because of her. At least that is mummy's story' (Recording of Mona Limerick, HRC, Sound recording, Interview with Basil Langton and Mona Limerick, 5 July 1962).
[157] 'Dramatis Personae: G.B.S. at the Coliseum', *The Observer*, 28 October 1923, p. 11. NYPL, Billy Rose Theatre Division, Uta Hagen/Herbert Berghof Papers, 1889–2004

part of a charity revue in 1950 at the Ziegfeld Theatre on Broadway, and starred Rex Harrison, the actor who would later appear in the Shaw-inspired musical *My Fair Lady*.[158]

Still, on 22 April 1938, the BBC emphasized *The Dark Lady*'s connections with Britain's National Theatre by broadcasting a radio version of the play to coincide with another milestone in the battle to establish that playhouse. The broadcast marked the transfer of deeds for the National Theatre's proposed site, and Shaw himself drafted and delivered a new prologue for the occasion. In that prologue, Shaw explained that the text was really a plea for a national theatre, and that he himself had been battling against government ministers who 'had never heard of Shakespeare'.[159] In *The Listener*, Grace Wyndham Goldie wrote that this work 'seized and held the attention as few radio plays do', and that the two main actors delivered Shaw's 'brilliant prose' with 'super-excellence'.[160] When, in November 1969, construction finally began on the site that is today's National Theatre, *The Guardian* announced the news by pointing back to Shaw's 'campaign for an English national theatre', and quoting from Queen Elizabeth I's words in *The Dark Lady of the Sonnets*.[161]

MACBETH SKIT

In addition to his work on the campaign for a National Theatre, Shaw liaised closely with individual Shakespearean actors. He knew Lillah McCarthy from the 1890s, when he saw her playing Lady Macbeth, and subsequently created a number of prominent roles for her, including—as we have seen—the lead role in *Annajanska*. In January 1916, Shaw completed another piece for her, a 'Macbeth Skit', consisting of two scenes from the first act of Shakespeare's play.

and undated, *T-Mss 2007-001, Box 51, fo. 3, Productions, 1932–1937 and undated, *The Dark Lady of the Sonnets*, 1935 and undated. Unnamed newspaper review. Esme Percy gave a performance of *The Dark Lady of the Sonnets* in Manchester in 1911 to mark 'Shakespeare's Birth and Death-day'; the piece appeared alongside Shaw's *Candida* at the second Malvern festival in 1930; and by 1945 it was being staged at the Bedford Park Club in London in aid of the Red Cross and Prisoners of War Fund. Programmes from productions of *The Dark Lady of the Sonnets*, in HRC, Shaw Collection, Vertical Files, box 698, #G66. Clipping about the Bedford Park production in HRC, Shaw Collection, Vertical Files, box 698, #G67.

[158] First professional US performance of *The Dark Lady of the Sonnets* given at ANTA (American National Theatre and Academy) Album, 29 January 1950. See HRC, Theatre Biography collection, box 763.

[159] 'The National Theatre: Many Seats Endowed After the Site Ceremony', *Manchester Guardian*, 23 April 1938, p. 12.

[160] *The Listener*, 4 May 1938, quoted by Conolly, *Bernard Shaw and the BBC*, p. 83.

[161] 'The National Theatre at Last?', *The Guardian*, 4 November 1969, p. 8.

In 'Macbeth Skit', Lady Macbeth's words are largely rendered as in the original text of 1623, but those lines are undercut by a very modern-sounding Macbeth:

LADY M . . . .

Like the poor cat i' the adage?

MACBETH. Like what?

LADY M. (*Louder*) Like the cat.

MACBETH. Oh, the cat. In the *what*, did you say?

LADY M. In the adage.

MACBETH. Never heard of it. (p. 421)

At the end of Shaw's script, Lillah McCarthy was to break role and declare to her co-star, the West End actor Gerald du Maurier, 'Gerald: come off it. I shall never make a Shakespearian actor of you', before '*She leads him ignominiously from the stage*' (p. 423). But Gerald du Maurier—who was on course to be knighted in 1922—could not quite bear to be treated in this way, and so refused to take part. Du Maurier was, after all, criticized for 'always being himself' in performance: the prominent reviewer James Agate even referred to the 'theatrical presentation of *Geraldism*'.[162] Shaw's skit therefore cut too close to the bone. Shaw wrote in the margin of his script, 'Gerald would not burlesque himself. Probably he considered himself an ideal Macbeth.'[163] In any event, Lillah McCarthy may have had similar reservations: she reflected shortly before her death that instead of playing roles like 'Lady Macbeth, all the big parts' she had ended up with 'all the silly things of Shaw', and that 'I was supposed to be . . . a tragedienne; not be playing skittles'.[164] So although *Macbeth Skit* anticipates something of the playfulness and clashing registers of recent Shakespearean productions by theatrical innovators such as Emma Rice or The Wooster Group, Shaw's skit remained unperformed and unpublished until printed in an academic journal in 1967.

CYMBELINE REFINISHED

Macbeth, however, was scarcely the only Shakespeare play that Shaw wished to rewrite. In 1896, the actress Ellen Terry had taken on the role

---

[162] Quoted by James Harding, 'Du Maurier, Sir Gerald Hubert Edward Busson', *ODNB*, <http://www.oxforddnb.com/view/article/32928?docPos=3>.

[163] *MacS* Type, fo. 1.

[164] Recording of Lillah McCarthy, HRC, Sound recording, Interview with Basil Langton and Lillah McCarthy, January 1960.

of Imogen in Henry Irving's production of Shakespeare's _Cymbeline_, which ran for eighty-eight performances. She asked Shaw's advice about the character, and he responded by telling her that parts of Imogen's role were 'idiotic', and advised her to edit the script: 'do it with a bold hand', he told her. 'Oh what a DAMNED fool Shakespear was!'[165] When Shaw reviewed the resultant production, he wrote that Shakespeare's play was 'vulgar, foolish, offensive, indecent and exasperating beyond all tolerance'.[166]

Shaw repeatedly returned to _Cymbeline_ in later years. He complained about it in the preface to his 1901 play, _The Admirable Bashville_, and in the early 1930s he wrote 'Cymbeline be blowed!' to the director of the Old Vic, adding, 'Probably Shakespeare had a bet that he could write a worse last act than that of the _Two Gentlemen of Verona_. If so, he won it.'[167] In the 1930s, the governors of the Shakespeare Memorial Theatre at Stratford-upon-Avon discussed the idea of producing _Cymbeline_. Shaw, still feeling troubled by the play, offered to rewrite the concluding act for them, and, as he put it, 'to my surprise they jumped at it. Curiosity, no doubt; but it stuck in my mind like a mosquito until I actually perpetuated the outrage.'[168]

By December 1936, Shaw had completed _Cymbeline Refinished_, but the Shakespeare Memorial Theatre's management now felt wary of alienating Stratford's theatre-goers and so opted to retain the traditional fifth act. Meanwhile, Ronald Adam, who ran the Embassy Theatre in London, heard about what Shaw had drafted, and sought permission to try the piece there instead.[169] Shaw agreed that _Cymbeline Refinished_ could be staged at the Embassy, where it appeared for three weeks from 16 November 1937, with the programme announcing a production of 'Cymbeline: by William Shakespeare and Bernard Shaw'.[170] Joyce Bland, the actress playing Imogen in the Stratford production, took the same role in Shaw's revised script. The _Manchester Guardian_ commented that Shaw's new setting 'certainly removes a great deal of tedium' and that Shaw should be employed on 'cutting of the redundancies in the

[165] Shaw, to Ellen Terry on 6 September 1896, in _CL_ i. 647.

[166] Shaw, 'Blaming the Bard' (review originally published in the _Saturday Review_, 26 September 1896), in Shaw, _Our Theatres in the Nineties_, ii. 195–202, at 195.

[167] Shaw quoted in E. Harcourt Williams, _Four Years at the Old Vic, 1929–1933_ (London: Putnam, 1935), 188.

[168] Letter of 11 January 1937, in _CL_ iv. 459.

[169] Holroyd, _Bernard Shaw_, iii. 395.

[170] Cymbeline programme from Embassy, in HRC, Shaw Collection, Vertical Files, box 698, #G164.

rest of the text'.[171] In fact, when the play premiered, audiences gasped with shock at Shaw's allusions to the recent abdication of the British monarch.[172] Shaw sent a copy of *Cymbeline Refinished* to the actor and author Hesketh Pearson, asking him to read it aloud to another acquaintance 'and see whether he can spot the two authors, and if so, which he prefers'.[173] The *New York Post* commented 'it appears, after all these years, that Shaw and Shakespeare are collaborators at last. And don't forget, Shaw's name always goes first.'[174]

SHAKES VERSUS SHAV

During what Shaw claimed was 'two days' of writing in January 1949, he wrote the concluding play that would be performed during his lifetime, a work that once again deals with Shakespeare and which Shaw named *Shakes Versus Shav*.[175] 'This', wrote Shaw, 'in all actuarial probability is my last play and the climax of my eminence' (p. 447).

Of course, *Shakes Versus Shav* does have one major difference from his other works: it is written not for human actors, but for puppets. Shaw claimed to have found marionettes thrilling during his childhood, and at one point had written to Clumm Lewis, a Kent showman who performed puppet shows at Canterbury fair, to declare that with mannequins:

the dramatic effect is sometimes actually greater than that produced by living performers. Nobody who has not seen marionette shows can be persuaded to believe this but it is so. . . . I could name actors, among them one no less eminent than Henry Irving, delayed for years in their career because they never learned from a puppet show how much must be done by suggestion and illusion, and how fatal to this is a too industrious effort to imitate and simulate every action or symptom of emotion instead of merely setting the audience to work to imagine it.[176]

---

[171] A.D., 'The New "Cymbeline"', *Manchester Guardian*, 17 November 1937, p. 12.

[172] 'Shaw Puts Abdication Lines in Shakespeare', *Daily Express*, 17 November 1937, in HRC, Shaw Collection, Vertical Files, box 706, folder G241.

[173] HRC, *Cymbeline Refinished*, private pamphlet, 20pp, 1937, Shaw Collection, box 6, folder 10, inscription to Hesketh Pearson.

[174] Wilella Waldorf, ' "Cymbeline" by G.B. Shaw and William Shakespeare', *New York Post*, 16 November 1937, p. 12.

[175] *SvS* Type, fo. 1.

[176] Undated letter to Lewis, in the possession of Waldo Lanchester and read aloud on HRC, Sound recordings, Waldo Lanchester interview with Basil Langton, interview of 7 July 1962 at 39 Henley Street, Stratford-on-Avon, R2566.

In the early 1930s, the puppeteer (and brother of film star Elsa Lanchester) Waldo Lanchester had set up a marquee for puppet shows in Malvern, where he and his wife Muriel gave three shows a day. One afternoon, Shaw wandered into the tent for the teatime production. He was the only audience member in the venue, so the startled Lanchesters begged a few friends to fill out the marquee, and performed a show for Shaw that involved a pianist, dancing grasshoppers, and a circus. Shaw felt sufficiently impressed to give a speech when Waldo Lanchester opened a more formal, fifty-seat marionette theatre in Malvern in 1936. Thereafter, when the Lanchesters bumped into Shaw at Malvern, according to Waldo, Shaw would always 'ask after the family, meaning the puppets'.[177] Waldo Lanchester then decided to take advantage of Shaw's approval, and wrote to the playwright on 1 January 1949:

Without beating about the bush I will come straight to the point. We have been making a marionette of yourself and of William Shakespeare. We hope that you will consent to write a dialogue, something to last five or six minutes. We enclose a photo or two of your illustrious self. William is still in the making. I was thinking of you standing on one side of the marionette stage with the background of gates of Shaw's corner and William on the other.[178]

Shaw responded:

I will send you a dialogue presently; but it may not be suitable, as I do not know how much acrobatics puppets are capable of. Do not elaborate the scenery: it distracts the attention of the audience from the actors. . . . For Shakespear must begin with a speech addressed directly to the audience, as Richard III does, explaining who he is.[179]

Shaw then wrote the piece, and added four more characters.[180] Lanchester arranged to have the extra puppets made, and a group of actors recorded the voices at the Abbey Road Studios as soon as Shaw had approved the cast list (Shaw objected to his character being voiced by an actor with an Irish accent, even though Shaw retained that accent in real life: he therefore stipulated that the English actor Ernest Thesiger had to play

---

[177] HRC, Sound recordings, Waldo Lanchester interview with Basil Langton, R2566.
[178] Waldo Lanchester letter to Shaw of 1 January 1949, in the possession of Waldo Lanchester and read aloud on HRC, Sound recordings, Waldo Lanchester interview with Basil Langton, R2566.
[179] Letter of 20 January 1949, in *CL* iv. 839.
[180] The puppets were carved from limewood by Jack Whitehead, a Devon lifeguard. Waldo Lanchester and his wife then painted and clothed them. 'He Had G.B.S. on a Piece of String', *Hertfordshire Pictorial*, 19 October 1949, in HRC, Shaw Collection, Vertical Files, box 700, #G140, press clippings on *Shakes versus Shav*.

the part).[181] Lanchester then staged the premiere of this puppet drama in August 1949 as part of a newly revived Malvern Festival, an event founded two decades before and initially dedicated to the work of Shaw, but which had been mothballed since 1939.[182]

In 1949, only 100 people could fit inside the old school hall where *Shakes Versus Shav* appeared, but critics proved generally appreciative: one claimed 'there is more merit in its ten minutes of Shavian nonsense than in the whole two hours' of a main-stage Malvern Festival show being given around the corner.[183] Waldo Lanchester then toured *Shakes Versus Shav* extensively around England and Scotland. A German production of the script soon appeared at Hilmar Binter's marionette theatre in Munich.[184] Indeed, after Shaw's death the famous poster that Al Hirschfeld designed for the 1956 Broadway production of *My Fair Lady* echoed something of Shaw's marionette show, with the poster depicting Shaw (from heaven) pulling the strings of his characters.

However, not everyone who attended the 1949 Malvern Festival appreciated Shaw's puppet play. At one of the festival's events, the novelist and dramatist John Beverley Nichols declared that linking Shaw with Shakespeare was 'infantile', like 'comparing Walt Disney with Michelangelo'. That statement in turn prompted the writer Compton Mackenzie to condemn Nichols as 'vilely totalitarian' and to praise Shaw as the writer of 'the most lucid prose since Swift'.[185]

A similar battle was waged on the stage itself. In *Shakes Versus Shav*, an angry puppet Shakespeare feels annoyed that his words are being stolen by an 'infamous imposter' (p. 449) called Shaw, and, when the puppet Shaw appears, the duo start to fight *à la* Punch and Judy. A pair of Shakespeare and Shaw surrogates, Macbeth and Rob Roy, also battle, with Rob Roy cutting off Macbeth's head. The real-life Shaw admits in his preface that, when writing *Shakes Versus Shav*, he had felt

---

[181] According to Waldo Lanchester, Lewis Casson 'was trying to get a well-known Irish actor, you see—and Bernard Shaw said "oh oh no, anyone, I won't be depicted with anyone with an Irish accent because immediately people will think of the Dublin porter. No, Ernest Thesiger's got to do my voice"'. HRC, Sound recordings, Waldo Lanchester interview with Basil Langton, R2566. For more on Shaw's own Irish accent see Clare, *Bernard Shaw's Irish Outlook*, 24.

[182] 'Malvern Festival Revived: Mr. Shaw's Latest', *Manchester Guardian*, 8 August 1949, p. 3.

[183] 'Shakes' Battle with Shav', *Birmingham Mail*, 10 August 1949, in HRC, Shaw Collection, Vertical Files, box 700, #G140, press clippings on *Shakes versus Shav*.

[184] '"Shakes v Shav" in Munich', *Malvern Gazette*, 22 September 1950, in HRC, Shaw Collection, Vertical Files, box 700, #G140, press clippings on *Shakes versus Shav*.

[185] 'Shakespeare–Shaw Comparison: A Critic Criticised', *Manchester Guardian*, 27 August 1949, p. 4.

pleased to write for puppets that 'can survive treatment that would kill live actors' (p. 447), and if Shaw had been tussling mentally with Shakespeare for much of his career, here was the opportunity to physicalize that battle. At the end of each performance, Waldo Lanchester put the two main puppets of the show back into separate white bags, one labelled 'Bard I' and the other 'Bard II' ('strictly chronological order' claimed Lanchester).[186] Yet as the theatre scholar Richard G. Scharine has emphasized, although Shaw's presumed antipathy towards Shakespeare may look like 'egotistical self-aggrandizement', in reality Shaw's perceived attacks actually contained 'calls for the kind of theatre Peter Hall would establish with the Royal Shakespeare Company a decade after Shaw's death: a classical theatre embracing a modern social viewpoint and utilizing the staging methods employed by the Elizabethans three hundred years earlier'.[187]

Indeed, some of Shaw's major fights—including those against censorship, in support of establishing a British National Theatre, and in favour of votes for women—were advanced via his short plays. These texts allowed him to promote culturally significant ideas; involved some of his key theatrical collaborators; and encouraged Shaw to distribute his work through experimental technologies. Thus, although each of the playlets is small in size, they have proved capable of doing some intellectual heavy lifting, and of providing a great deal of entertainment. After all, as Michael Frayn quipped after publishing his own collection of miniature dramatic scripts in 2014: 'Wittgenstein's Tractatus Logico-Philosophicus is very short—if he can give a complete account of the logic of the universe in 20,000 words why does anyone need more for anything?'[188]

---

[186] Lanchester quoted in 'Knickerbocker Glory', *News Chronicle*, 9 August 1949, in HRC, Shaw Collection, Vertical Files, box 700, #G140, press clippings on *Shakes versus Shav*.

[187] Scharine, 'Blaming the Bard: Shaw's Fifty Years of Refinishing *Cymbeline*', *Journal of the Wooden O Symposium*, 2 (2002), 150–60, at 151–2. Hall himself directed a number of Shaw plays in his later years and his daughter Rebecca made her West End debut as Vivie Warren in his production of *Mrs Warren's Profession*.

[188] Dominic Cavendish, 'Michael Frayn: "I was in a very lucky generation"', *Daily Telegraph*, 3 May 2015, <http://www.telegraph.co.uk/culture/theatre/theatre-features/11578286/Michael-Frayn-I-was-in-a-very-lucky-generation.html>.

NOTE ON THE TEXT

IN this volume, the text of the plays is taken from the Constable edition of Shaw's works, published in 1931–2, which, in most cases, is the latest text under Shaw's guidance. There are, however, five exceptions to that general rule. Three of the plays had not been written by this point in Shaw's career, and hence *The Six of Calais* is taken from Shaw, *The Simpleton, The Six, and the Millionairess: Being Three More Plays* (London: Constable and Company, 1936), 89–101; *Cymbeline Refinished* is taken from Shaw, *Geneva, Cymbeline Refinished, & Good King Charles* (London: Constable and Company, 1946), 139–50; and *Shakes Versus Shav* is taken from Shaw, *Buoyant Billions, Farfetched Fables, & Shakes Versus Shav* (London: Constable and Company, 1950), 139–43. Furthermore, *The British Party System* was originally published not as a dramatic work but as part of a prose volume, and so the text here is an excerpt from Shaw's *Everybody's Political What's What?* (London: Constable and Company, 1944), 23–8. Finally, *Macbeth Skit* remained unpublished in Shaw's lifetime (first printed by Bernard F. Dukore, as 'Macbeth Skit', in *Educational Theatre Journal*, 19/3 (1967), 343–8) so the text here is taken from Harry Ransom Center (HRC), *Macbeth Skit*, typescript with emendations and notes, and printed Shakespearean sections pasted in, 1916, 7 pp., Shaw collection, box 20 folder 1.

In this volume, there are a number of Shavian peculiarities of which readers should be aware. Shaw uses archaic spellings in some cases (for example 'shew' for 'show'); in some circumstances he prefers American spelling ('favorite', although he keeps words such as 'centre'); he spells other words in his own idiosyncratic way (notably 'Shakespear'); and he avoids 'unsightly' apostrophes (spelling 'wont' and 'doesnt'; but using them where confusion might reign, as in 'she'll' and 'he'll', though oddly not for 'cant'). In print he also suggests emphases in words longer than 'I' either in capitals or by spacing, although this volume (in accordance with the editorial rules of the Oxford University Press series) represents such emphasis in italics to make the script clearer for the reader. In keeping with Shaw's own practice, no list of dramatis personae is printed with the plays, and sometimes characters are introduced by disguised names until the text makes clear who they are (for example, in *The Dark Lady of the Sonnets*, William Shakespeare's lines are initially designation as the lines of 'the man' until the character reveals his identity).

Of necessity, this World's Classics edition does not attempt a comprehensive inclusion of all Shaw's shorter theatrical ideas and fragments of dialogue, but instead offers a selection of Shaw's playlets in four dramatic modes where he repeatedly focused his attention (farces, war playlets, historical sketches, and Shakespearean shorts). These groupings are, in part, designed to assist actors and theatre producers who may wish to stage the works. Individually, the pieces may not fill an entire evening in the playhouse, so directors may wish to present two or more thematically related playlets together. Half the playlets in this volume require a cast of only between two and four actors, and so these scripts may provide an opportunity to stage Shavian drama in venues where the cost of employing performers for one of Shaw's longer dramas might be prohibitive.

SELECT BIBLIOGRAPHY

Editions

Shaw, Bernard, *Bernard Shaw: Theatrics*, ed. Dan H. Laurence (Toronto: University of Toronto Press, 1995).

Shaw, Bernard, *Our Theatre in the Nineties*, 3 vols (London: Constable, 1932).

Shaw, G. B., *Collected Letters*, ed. Dan H. Laurence, 4 vols (London: Max Reinhardt: 1965–88).

Biography

Gibbs, A. M., *Bernard Shaw: A Life* (Gainesville: University Press of Florida, 2005).

Holroyd, Michael, *Bernard Shaw*, 4 vols (London: Chatto & Windus, 1988–92).

General Studies

Clare, David, *Bernard Shaw's Irish Outlook* (Houndmills: Palgrave Macmillan, 2016).

Evans, T. F. (ed.), *Shaw: The Critical Heritage* (London: Routledge & Kegan Paul, 1976).

Ganz, Arthur, *George Bernard Shaw* (London: Macmillan, 1983).

Grene, Nicholas, *Bernard Shaw: A Critical View* (London: Macmillan, 1984).

Hadfield, D. A., and Reynolds, Jean (eds), *Shaw and Feminisms: On Stage and Off* (Gainesville: University Press of Florida, 2013).

Innes, Christopher (ed.), *The Cambridge Companion to George Bernard Shaw* (Cambridge: Cambridge University Press, 1998).

Kent, Brad, 'George Bernard Shaw', Oxford Bibliographies, <http://www.oxfordbibliographies.com/view/document/obo-9780199846719/obo-9780199846719-0045.xml> (New York: Oxford University Press, 2016).

Kent, Brad (ed.), *George Bernard Shaw in Context* (Cambridge: Cambridge University Press, 2015).

Laurence, Dan H., *Bernard Shaw: A Bibliography*, 2 vols (Oxford: Clarendon, 1983).

Morgan, Margery (ed.), *File on Shaw* (London: Methuen, 1989).

O'Toole, Fintan, *Judging Shaw* (Dublin: RIA, 2017).

Phillips, Jill, *Bernard Shaw: A Review of the Literature* (New York: Gordon Press, 1976).

Weintraub, Stanley, *Bernard Shaw: Guide to Research* (University Park: Pennsylvania State University Press, 1992).

Weintraub, Stanley, *Who's Afraid of Bernard Shaw?: Some Personalities in Shaw's Plays* (Gainesville: University Press of Florida, 2011).

Wisenthal, J. L., *Shaw's Sense of History* (Oxford: Clarendon Press, 1988).

Yde, Matthew, *Bernard Shaw and Totalitarianism: Longing for Utopia* (Houndmills: Palgrave Macmillan, 2013).

Criticism on Farces

Conolly, L. W., *Bernard Shaw and the BBC* (Toronto: University of Toronto Press, 2009), 7–8, 75, 91–3 [on *How He Lied to Her Husband*].

Dukore, Bernard F., 'Shaw Improves Shaw', *Modern Drama*, 6/1 (1963), 26–31 [on *How He Lied to Her Husband*].

Gahan, Peter, *Shaw Shadows: Rereading the Texts of Bernard Shaw* (Gainesville: University Press of Florida, 2004), 147–51 [on *How He Lied to Her Husband*].

Gibbs, A. M., 'Bernard Shaw's Other Island', in Oliver MacDonagh, W. F. Mandle, and Pauric Travers (eds), *Irish Culture and Nationalism, 1750–1950* (Houndmills: Macmillan, 1983), 122–36 [on *Press Cuttings*].

Hark, Ina Rae, 'Tomfooling with Melodrama in *Passion, Poison, and Petrifaction*', *SHAW*, 7 (1987), 137–50 [on *Passion, Poison, and Petrifaction*].

Rosset, B. C., *Shaw of Dublin: The Formative Years* (University Park: Pennsylvania State University Press, 1964), 21–2 [on *Press Cuttings*].

Silverstein, Paul, 'Barns, Booths, and Shaw', *Shaw Review*, 12/3 (1969), 111–16 [on *Passion, Poison, and Petrifaction*].

Turco, Alfred Jr, 'Shaw 40 Years Later: Eric Bentley Speaks His Mind on Eleven Neglected Plays: *Getting Married, Overruled, On the Rocks*, and Others', *SHAW* 7 (1987), 7–29 [on *Passion, Poison, and Petrifaction* and *Overruled*].

Valency, Maurice, *The Cart and the Trumpet: The Plays of George Bernard Shaw* (New York: Oxford University Press, 1973), 300–2 [on *Overruled*].

Weimer, Michael, '*Press Cuttings*: G.B.S. and Women's Suffrage', in Rodelle Weintraub (ed.), *Fabian Feminist: Bernard Shaw and Women* (University Park: Pennsylvania State University Press, 1977), 84–9.

Criticism on War Playlets

Arrington, Lauren, 'The Censorship of *O'Flaherty V.C.*', *SHAW* 28 (2008), 85–106.

Bertolini, John A., *The Playwrighting Self of Bernard Shaw* (Carbondale: Southern Illinois UP, 1991), 155–66 [on *The Inca of Perusalem* and *Annajanska, The Bolshevik Empress*].

Biggs, Murray, 'Shaw's Recruiting Pamphlet', *SHAW* 28 (2008), 107–11.

Clare, David, 'Landlord–Tenant (Non)Relations in the Work of Bernard Shaw', *SHAW* 36/1 (2016), 124–41 [on *O'Flaherty V.C.*].

Gunby, David, 'The First Night of *O'Flaherty, V.C.*', *Shaw: The Journal of Bernard Shaw Studies*, 19 (1999), 85–97 [on *O'Flaherty V.C.* and also *The Inca of Perusalem*].

Innes, Christopher, 'Defining Irishness: Bernard Shaw and the Irish Connection on the English Stage', in Julia M. Wright (ed.), *A Companion to Irish Literature*, 2 vols (Oxford: Wiley-Blackwell, 2010), ii. 35–49 [on *O'Flaherty V.C.*].

McDiarmid, Lucy, *The Irish Art of Controversy* (Dublin: Lilliput, 2005), 118–19. [on *O'Flaherty V.C.*].

Murray, Stephen, 'Shaw, the Kaiser and the Victoria Cross', *Shavian: The Journal of the Shaw Society*, 7/5 (Winter 1993–4), 12–14 [on *The Inca of Perusalem* and *O'Flaherty V.C.*].

Phillips, Terry, 'Shaw, Ireland, and World War I: *O'Flaherty V.C.*, an Unlikely Recruiting Play', *SHAW* 30 (2010), 133–46.

Regan, Arthur E., 'The Fantastic Reality of Bernard Shaw: A Look at "Augustus" and "Too True"', *Shaw Review*, 11/1 (1968), 2–10 [on *Augustus Does His Bit*].

Weintraub, Stanley, 'Bernard Shaw's Other Irelands: 1915–1919', *English Language in Transition, 1880–1920*, 42/4 (1999), 433–42 [on *O'Flaherty V.C.*].

Criticism on Historical Sketches

Abbott, A., *Shaw and Christianity* (New York: Seabury Press, 1965), 108–18 [on *The Shewing-Up of Blanco Posnet*].

Bertolini, John A., *The Playwrighting Self of Bernard Shaw* (Carbondale: Southern Illinois University Press, 1991), 151–5, 163–5 [on *Great Catherine* and *The Six of Calais*].

Étienne, Anne, ' "England's Trouble is Ireland's Opportunity": *Blanco Posnet* à l'Abbey Théâtre, *Études irlandaises*, 33/1 (2008), 83–98.

Foster, R. F., *W. B. Yeats: A Life*, i. *The Apprentice Mage* (Oxford: Oxford University Press, 1998), 409–11 [on *The Shewing-Up of Blanco Posnet*].

Kent, Brad, 'Censorship and Immorality: Bernard Shaw's *The Devil's Disciple*, *Modern Drama*, 54/4 (2011), 511–33 [on *The Shewing-Up of Blanco Posnet*].

McDiarmid, Lucy, 'The Shewing-up of Dublin Castle: Lady Gregory, Shaw, and *Blanco Posnet*, August 1909', in McDiarmid, *The Irish Art of Controversy* (Dublin: Lilliput Press, 2005), 87–122.

McKenna, Bernard, 'Yeats, The Arrow, and the Aesthetics of a "National, Moral Culture", the Blanco Posnet Affair', *Journal of Modern Literature*, 38/2 (2015 Winter), 16–28.

Matual, David, '*The Shewing-Up of Blanco Posnet* and Tolstoy's *The Power of Darkness*: Dramatic Kingship and Theological Opposition', *SHAW* 1 (1981), 129–39.

Morash, Christopher, *A History of Irish Theatre 1601–2000* (Cambridge: Cambridge University Press, 2002), 143–4 [on *The Shewing-Up of Blanco Posnet*].

Osborough, W. N., *The Irish Stage: A Legal History* (Dublin: Four Courts Press, 2015), 234–6 [on *The Shewing-Up of Blanco Posnet* and *O'Flaherty V.C.*].

Weintraub, S., 'Exploiting Art', in *The Unexpected Shaw: Biographical Approaches to G.B.S. and His Work* (New York: Ungar, 1982), 89–90 [on *The Six of Calais*].

Criticism on Shakespearean Shorts

Barret, J. K., 'The Crowd in Imogen's Bedroom: Allusion and Ethics in Cymbeline', *Shakespeare Quarterly*, 66/4 (2015), 440–62 [on *Cymbeline Refinished*].

Bates, Robin E., 'Cymbeline and Cymbeline Refinished: G. B. Shaw and the Unresolved Empire', in Willy Maley and Rory Loughnane (eds), *Celtic Shakespeare: The Bard and the Borderers* (London: Routledge, 2013), 231–44.

DiPietro, Cary, *Shakespeare and Modernism* (Cambridge: Cambridge University Press, 2006), 43–84 [on *The Dark Lady of the Sonnets*].

Dukore, Bernard F., 'Macbeth Skit', *Educational Theatre Journal*, 19 (1967), 343–8.

Larson, Gale K., and Bernard Shaw, '"The Dark Lady": G.B.S. Replies to Frank Harris', *SHAW* 19 (1999), 79–83.

Loftis, Sonya Freeman, '"Blaming the Bard": Shaw, Shakespeare, Shotover', in *Shakespeare's Surrogates: Rewriting Renaissance Drama* (New York: Palgrave Macmillan, 2013), 1–31 [on *Cymbeline Refinished* and *Shakes Versus Shav*].

Peters, Sally, 'Shaw's Double Dethroned: *The Dark Lady of the Sonnets, Cymbeline Refinished*, and *Shakes versus Shav*', *SHAW* 7 (1987), 301–16.

Pierce, Robert B., 'Bernard Shaw as Shakespeare Critic', *SHAW* 31 (2011), 118–32 [on *Cymbeline Refinished*].

Scharine, Richard G., 'Blaming the Bard: Shaw's Fifty Years of Refinishing *Cymbeline*', *Journal of the Wooden O Symposium*, 2 (2002), 150–60.

West, E. J., 'Shaw, Shakespeare, and *Cymbeline*', *Theatre Annual*, 8 (1950), 7–24.

Wixon, Christopher, 'Authorship and Shaw's *Shakes Versus Shav*', *SHAW* 33 (2013), 79–94.

Further Reading in Oxford World's Classics

Shaw, George Bernard, *Arms and the Man, The Devil's Disciple, and Caesar and Cleopatra*, ed. Lawrence Switzky.

Shaw, George Bernard, *The Apple Cart, Too True to Be Good, On the Rocks, and The Millionairess*, ed. Matthew Yde.

Shaw, George Bernard, *Major Cultural Essays*, ed. David Kornhaber.

Shaw, George Bernard, *Man and Superman, John Bull's Other Island, and Major Barbara*, ed. Brad Kent.

Shaw, George Bernard, *Mrs Warren's Profession, Candida, and You Never Can Tell*, ed. Sos Eltis.

Shaw, George Bernard, *Political Writings*, ed. Elizabeth Miller.

Shaw, George Bernard, *Pygmalion, Heartbreak House, and Saint Joan*, ed. Brad Kent.

A CHRONOLOGY OF
GEORGE BERNARD SHAW

Plays and novels are listed according to the dates on which their composition was completed. The parenthetical information provides the date and place of the play's first performance, not including specially arranged copyright performances, as well as the subtitle in some instances; in the case of novels, the date on which each was first published as a book—as opposed to serialized in a journal—is indicated. Other major writings are listed according to their date of publication.

1856   Born in Dublin on 26 July.

1871   Leaves school for good in October; begins work as an office boy for a Dublin land agent in November.

1873   Promoted to cashier in February.

1876   Leaves job with Dublin land agent in March; moves to London on 1 April.

1878   *Passion Play* (unfinished).

1879   *Immaturity* (1930).

1880   *The Irrational Knot* (1905).

1882   *Love Among the Artists* (1900).

1883   *Cashel Byron's Profession* (1886); *An Unsocial Socialist* (1887).

1884   The Fabian Society is founded on 4 January; GBS attends his first meeting on 16 May and formally joins on 5 September; publishes his first pamphlet for them, 'A Manifesto', in October.

1886   Begins as art critic for *The World*, a position he will keep until January 1890.

1889   Begins as music critic for *The Star* under the pseudonym 'Corno di Bassetto' in February; *Fabian Essays in Socialism*.

1890   Resigns as music critic for *The Star* and begins as music critic for *The World* in May under the name G.B.S.

1891   *The Quintessence of Ibsenism*.

1892   *Widowers' Houses* (9 December 1892, Royalty Theatre, London).

1893   *The Philanderer: A Topical Comedy* (20 February 1905, Cripplegate Institute, London); *Mrs Warren's Profession* (5 January 1902, New Lyric Club, London).

1894 *Arms and the Man: An Anti-Romantic Comedy* (21 April 1894, Avenue
      Theatre, London); *Candida: A Mystery* (30 July 1897, Her Majesty's
      Theatre, Aberdeen); writes last article for *The World* in August.

1895 Begins as theatre critic at the *Saturday Review* in January; *The Man
      of Destiny: A Fictitious Paragraph of History* (1 July 1897, Grand
      Theatre, Croydon).

1896 *You Never Can Tell: A Comedy* (26 November 1899, Royalty Theatre,
      London).

1897 *The Devil's Disciple: A Melodrama* (1 October 1897, Harmanus
      Bleecker Hall, Albany, NY); elected as a member of the Vestry of the
      Parish of St Pancras, 18 May 1897.

1898 Resigns as theatre critic at the *Saturday Review* in May; marries
      Charlotte Frances Payne-Townshend at the Registry Office, Henrietta
      Street, Covent Garden, on 1 June; *The Perfect Wagnerite*; *Caesar and
      Cleopatra: A History* (1 May 1901, Anna Morgan Studios for Art and
      Expression at the Fine Arts Building, Chicago).

1899 *Captain Brassbound's Conversion: An Adventure* (16 December 1900,
      Strand Theatre, London).

1900 Re-elected for a second (and final) three-year term as a member of
      the St Pancras Borough Council (reconfigured since the prior
      election of 1897); *Fabianism and the Empire*.

1901 *The Admirable Bashville: or, Constancy Unrewarded* (14 December
      1902, Pharos Club, London).

1903 *Man and Superman: A Comedy and a Philosophy* (21 May 1905,
      Court Theatre, London, though without Act III; *Don Juan in Hell* is
      first performed on 4 June 1907, Court Theatre, London; the entire
      play is first performed on 11 June 1915, Lyceum Theatre, Edinburgh).

1904 *How He Lied to Her Husband* (26 September 1904, Berkeley Lyceum,
      New York); *John Bull's Other Island* (1 November 1904, Court
      Theatre, London).

1905 *Passion, Poison, and Petrifaction: or the Fatal Gazogene* (A Brief
      Tragedy for Barns and Booths) (14 July 1905, Theatrical Garden
      Party, Regent's Park, London); *Major Barbara* (A Discussion) (28
      November 1905, Court Theatre, London).

1906 *The Doctor's Dilemma: A Tragedy* (20 November 1906, Court Theatre,
      London).

1908 *The Sanity of Art* (First published as 'A Degenerate's View of
      Nordau', in *Liberty* (New York), 27 July 1895); *Getting Married:
      A Disquisitory Play* (12 May 1908, Haymarket Theatre, London).

1909 *The Shewing-up of Blanco Posnet: A Sermon in Crude Melodrama* (25 August 1909, Abbey Theatre, Dublin); *Press Cuttings* (A Topical Sketch Compiled from the Editorial and Correspondence Columns of the Daily Papers during the Women's War in 1909) (9 July 1909, Court Theatre, London); *The Fascinating Foundling* (A Disgrace to the Author) (28 January 1928, Arts Theatre Club, London); *Misalliance* (A Debate in One Sitting) (23 February 1910, Duke of York's Theatre, London).

1910 *The Dark Lady of the Sonnets: An Interlude* (24 November 1910, Haymarket Theatre, London); *The Glimpse of Reality: A Tragedietta* (8 October 1927, Fellowship Hall, Glasgow).

1911 *Fanny's First Play: An Easy Play for a Little Theatre* (19 April 1911, Little Theatre, London).

1912 *Androcles and the Lion: A Fable Play* (1 September 1913, St James's Theatre, London); *Pygmalion* (A Romance) (16 October 1913, Hofburg Theater, Vienna); *Overruled: A Demonstration* (14 October 1912, Duke of York's Theatre, London).

1913 *Great Catherine (Whom Glory Still Adores)* (A Thumbnail Sketch of Russian Court Life in the XVIII Century) (18 November 1913, Vaudeville Theatre, London).

1914 *The Music-Cure: A Piece of Utter Nonsense* (28 January 1914, Little Theatre, London); outbreak of the First World War on 28 July—Britain enters on 4 August; *Common Sense About the War* (supplement to *The New Statesman*, 14 November).

1915 *The Inca of Perusalem: An Almost Historical Comedietta* (7 October 1916, Repertory Theatre, Birmingham); *O'Flaherty V.C.: A Recruiting Pamphlet* (17 February 1917, Western Front, Treizennes, Belgium).

1916 *Augustus Does His Bit: A True-to-Life Farce* (An Unofficial Dramatic Tract on War Saving and Cognate Topics) (21 January 1917, Court Theatre, London).

1917 *Annajanska, The Bolshevik Empress: A Revolutionary Romancelet* (21 January 1918, Coliseum Theatre, London); *Heartbreak House: A Fantasia in the Russian Manner on English Themes* (10 November 1920, Garrick Theatre, New York).

1918 First World War ends, 11 November.

1920 *Back to Methuselah: A Metabiological Pentateuch* (A Play Cycle) (Parts I and II, 27 February 1922; Parts III and IV, 6 March 1922; Part V, 13 March 1922, Garrick Theatre, New York).

1921 *Jitta's Atonement*, by Siegfried Trebitsch, translated by Shaw (8 January 1923, Shubert-Garrick Theatre, Washington, DC).

1923 *Saint Joan: A Chronicle Play in Six Scenes and an Epilogue* (28 December 1923, Garrick Theatre, New York).

1926 *Translations and Tomfooleries*; the Swedish Academy announces that Shaw has won the 1925 Nobel Prize for Literature, 12 November.

1927 Accepts the Nobel Prize in February.

1928 *The Intelligent Woman's Guide to Socialism and Capitalism*; *The Apple Cart: A Political Extravaganza* (14 June 1929, Teatr Polski, Warsaw).

1931 *Music in London 1890–94: Criticisms contributed Week by Week to the World*; *Our Theatres in the Nineties*; *Too True To Be Good: A Political Extravaganza* (29 February 1932, Colonial Theatre, Boston, MA).

1932 *The Adventures of the Black Girl in Her Search for God.*

1933 *Village Wooing: A Comedietta for Two Voices* (16 April 1934, Little Theatre, Dallas, TX); *On the Rocks: A Political Comedy* (25 November 1933, Winter Garden Theatre, London).

1934 *The Simpleton of the Unexpected Isles: A Vision of Judgment* (18 February 1935, Guild Theatre, New York); *The Six of Calais: A Medieval War Story* (17 July 1934, Open Air Theatre, Regent's Park, London).

1935 *The Millionairess* (A Jonsonian Comedy) (4 January 1936, Akademie Theater, Vienna).

1936 *Geneva: Another Political Extravaganza* (25 July 1938, Teatr Polski, Warsaw).

1937 *Cymbeline Refinished: A Variation on Shakespear's Ending* (16 November 1937, Embassy Theatre, London).

1939 Wins the Academy Award for the best screenplay for the cinematic adaptation of *Pygmalion*; *'In Good King Charles's Golden Days': A True History that Never Happened* (12 August 1939, Festival Theatre, Malvern); outbreak of the Second World War: Britain and France declare war on Germany on 3 September.

1944 *Everybody's Political What's What.*

1945 Second World War ends.

1947 *Buoyant Billions: A Comedy of No Manners* (21 October 1948, Schauspielhaus, Zurich, Switzerland).

1949 *Sixteen Self Sketches*; *Shakes Versus Shav: A Puppet Play* (9 August 1949, Lyttelton Hall, Malvern).

1950 *Farfetched Fables* (6 September 1950, Watergate Theatre, London). Dies in Ayot St Lawrence on 2 November.

ABBREVIATIONS

Anna Proof Harry Ransom Center, Shaw Collection, Box 2 Folder 1: *Annajanska, the Bolshevik Empress*, rough proof with corrections and emendations, n.d., 17 pp.

Aug Play Harry Ransom Center, Shaw Collection, Box 4 Folder 7: *Augustus Does His Bit*, playscript, n.d., 26 pp.

CL *Bernard Shaw: Collected Letters*, ed. Dan H. Laurence, 4 vols: vol. i. *1874–1897* (London: Max Reinhardt; New York: Dodd, Mead, 1965); vol. ii. *1898–1910* (London: Max Reinhardt; New York: Dodd, Mead, 1972); vol. iii. *1911–1925* (London and New York: Penguin Viking Group, 1985); vol. iv. *1926–1950* (London and New York: Penguin Viking Group, 1988)

CR Pamp Harry Ransom Center, Shaw Collection, Box 6, Folder 10: *Cymbeline Refinished*, private pamphlet, 1937, 20 pp.

CR Var Harry Ransom Center, Shaw Collection, Box 6, Folder 10: *Cymbeline Refinished*, a variation, proof, December 1945

DLS Carb Harry Ransom Center, Shaw Collection, Box 7, Folder 1: *The Dark Lady of the Sonnets*, preface carbon copy with revisions

DLS Type Harry Ransom Center, Shaw Collection, Box 7, Folder 1: *The Dark Lady of the Sonnets*, typescript with extensive revisions 1910, 20 pp.; bound with this, revised conclusion of the play, n.d., 2 pp., and new ending holograph draft with revisions, 1910, 2 pp.

GC Type Harry Ransom Center, Shaw Collection, Box 15, Folder 6: *Great Catherine*, earliest typescript draft with revisions, 1913, 59 pp.

HHL Carb Harry Ransom Center, Shaw Collection, Box 16, Folder 3: *How He Lied to Her Husband*, carbon copy typescript with revisions and additions and insert

HHL Hol Harry Ransom Center, Shaw Collection, Box 16, Folder 3: *How He Lied to Her Husband*, holograph 1930, 1 p.

HRC Harry Ransom Center

HRC Lic	Harry Ransom Center, Shaw Collection, Box 63, Folder 6: Licenses and notices from the Lord Chamberlain's Office, Great Britain, 1897–1916
Inc Proof	Harry Ransom Center, Shaw Collection, Box 17, Folder 6: *The Inca of Perusalem*, Rough proof with emendations and notes 1915, with corrections and emendations 1918
Inc Type	Harry Ransom Center, Shaw Collection, Box 17, Folder 4: *The Inca of Perusalem*, typescript with revisions and additions
MacS Draft	Harry Ransom Center, Shaw Collection, Box 20, Folder 1: *Macbeth Skit*, holograph/shorthand draft, 1916, 2 pp.
MacS Type	Harry Ransom Center, Shaw Collection, Box 20, Folder 1: *Macbeth Skit*, typescript with emendations and notes, and printed Shakespearean sections pasted in, 1916, 7 pp.
NYPL	New York Public Library
ODNB	*Oxford Dictionary of National Biography*
OVC Type	Harry Ransom Center, Shaw Collection, Box 22, Folder 1: *O'Flaherty V.C.*, typescript with revisions and title page, 1915, 36 pp.
Over Type	Harry Ransom Center, Shaw Collection, Box 20, Folder 1: *Overruled*, TMS with revisions, *c.*1912, 41 pp.
PC Type	Harry Ransom Center, Shaw Collection, Box 24, Folder 3: *Press Cuttings*, typescript with revisions, n.d., 49 pp.
PPP Hol	Harry Ransom Center, Shaw Collection, Box 22, Folder 8: *Passion, Poison, and Petrifaction*, holograph draft with revisions and note, 1905, 41 pp.
PPP Type	Harry Ransom Center, Shaw Collection, Box 22, Folder 8: *Passion, Poison, and Petrifaction*, typescript production copy, n.d.
SHAW	*SHAW: The Annual of Bernard Shaw Studies* (1981 to 2014); *SHAW: The Journal of Bernard Shaw Studies* (2015–)
Six MS	Harry Ransom Center, Shaw Collection, Box 29, Folder 2: *The Six of Calais*, shorthand MS, 1934, 8 pp.
Six Pref	Harry Ransom Center, Shaw Collection, Box 29, Folder 2: *The Six of Calais*, preface, typescript with emendations, n.d., and typescript 1934, 4 pp. each
Six Proof 1	Harry Ransom Center, Shaw Collection, Box 29, Folder 2: *The Six of Calais*, first proof with corrections, revisions, and note, 1934, 16 pp.

Six Proof 2	Harry Ransom Center, Shaw Collection, Box 29, Folder 2: *The Six of Calais*, second rough proof, 1934, 16 pp.
Six Syd	Harry Ransom Center, Shaw Collection, Box 29, Folder 2: *The Six of Calais*, first rough proof sent to Sydney Carroll, 1934
SUBP Rev	Harry Ransom Center, Shaw Collection, Box 28, Folder 7: *The Shewing-up of Blanco Posnet*, typescript with revisions, notes, title page, and initial stage setting, n.d., 65 pp.
SUBP Type	Harry Ransom Center, Shaw Collection, Box 28, Folder 6: *The Shewing-up of Blanco Posnet*, typescript with corrections, emendations, and notes, 1909, 39 pp.
SvS Type	Harry Ransom Center, Shaw Collection, Box 28, Folder 3: *Shakes Versus Shav*, typescript with revisions, n.d., 5 pp.

FARCES

HOW HE LIED TO HER HUSBAND

PREFACE

LIKE many other works of mine, this playlet is a *pièce d'occasion*.* In 1905 it happened that the late Arnold Daly,* who was then playing the part of Napoleon in The Man of Destiny* in New York, found that whilst the play was too long to take a secondary place in the evening's performance, it was too short to suffice by itself. I therefore took advantage of four days continuous rain during a holiday in the north of Scotland to write How He Lied To Her Husband for Daly. In his hands, it served its turn very effectively.

Trifling as it is, I print it as a sample of what can be done with even the most hackneyed stage framework by filling it in with an observed touch of actual humanity instead of with doctrinaire romanticism. Nothing in the theatre is staler than the situation of husband, wife, and lover, or the fun of knockabout farce. I have taken both, and got an original play out of them, as anybody else can if only he will look about him for his material instead of plagiarizing Othello* and the thousand plays that have proceeded on Othello's romantic assumptions and false point of honor.*

HOW HE LIED TO HER HUSBAND

It is eight o'clock in the evening. The curtains are drawn and the lamps lighted in the drawing room of Her flat in Cromwell Road.* Her lover, a beautiful youth of eighteen, in evening dress and cape, with a bunch of flowers and an opera hat in his hands, comes in alone. The door is near the corner; and as he appears in the doorway, he has the fireplace on the nearest wall to his right, and the grand piano along the opposite wall to his left. Near the fireplace a small ornamental table has on it a hand mirror, a fan, a pair of long white gloves, and a little white woollen cloud to wrap a woman's head in. On the other side of the room, near the piano, is a broad, square, softly upholstered stool. The room is furnished in the most approved South Kensington fashion:* that is, it is as like a shop window as possible, and is intended to demonstrate the social position and spending powers of its owners, and not in the least to make them comfortable.

He is, be it repeated, a very beautiful youth, moving as in a dream, walking as on air. He puts his flowers down carefully on the table beside the fan; takes off his cape, and, as there is no room on the table for it, takes it to the piano; puts his hat on the cape; crosses to the hearth;* looks at his watch; puts it up again; notices the things on the table; lights up as if he saw heaven opening before him; goes to the table and takes the cloud in both hands, nestling his nose into its softness and kissing it; kisses the gloves one after another; kisses the fan; gasps a long shuddering sigh of ecstasy; sits down on the stool and presses his hands to his eyes to shut out reality and dream a little; takes his hands down and shakes his head with a little smile of rebuke for his folly; catches sight of a speck of dust on his shoes and hastily and carefully brushes it off with his handkerchief; rises and takes the hand mirror from the table to make sure of his tie with the gravest anxiety; and is looking at his watch again when She comes in, much flustered. As she is dressed for the theatre;* has spoilt, petted ways; and wears many diamonds, she has an air of being a young and beautiful woman; but as a matter of hard fact, she is, dress and pretensions apart, a very ordinary South Kensington female* of about 37, hopelessly inferior in physical and spiritual distinction to the beautiful youth, who hastily puts down the mirror as she enters.

HE [*kissing her hand*] At last!

SHE. Henry: something dreadful has happened.

HE. Whats the matter?

SHE. I have lost your poems.

HE. They were unworthy of you. I will write you some more.

SHE. No, thank you. Never any more poems for me. Oh, how could I have been so mad! so rash! so imprudent!

HE. Thank Heaven for your madness, your rashness, your imprudence!

SHE [*impatiently*] Oh, be sensible, Henry. Cant you see what a terrible thing this is for me? Suppose anybody finds these poems! what will they think?

HE. They will think that a man once loved a woman more devotedly than ever man loved woman before. But they will not know what man it was.

SHE. What good is that to me if everybody will know what woman it was?

HE. But how will they know?

SHE. How will they know! Why, my name is all over them: my silly, unhappy name. Oh, if I had only been christened Mary Jane, or Gladys Muriel, or Beatrice, or Francesca, or Guinevere, or something quite common! But Aurora! Aurora! I'm the only Aurora in London;* and everybody knows it. I believe I'm the only Aurora in the world. And it's so horribly easy to rhyme to it! Oh, Henry, why didnt you try to restrain your feelings a little in common consideration for me? Why didnt you write with some little reserve?

HE. Write poems to you with reserve! You ask me that!

SHE [*with perfunctory tenderness*] Yes, dear, of course it was very nice of you; and I know it was my own fault as much as yours. I ought to have noticed that your verses ought never to have been addressed to a married woman.

HE. Ah, how I wish they had been addressed to an *un*married woman! *how* I wish they had!

SHE. Indeed you have no right to wish anything of the sort. They are quite unfit for anybody but a married woman. Thats just the difficulty. What will my sisters-in-law think of them?

HE [*painfully jarred*] Have *you* got sisters-in-law?

SHE. Yes, of course I have. Do you suppose I am an angel?

HE [*biting his lips*] I do. Heaven help me, I do—or I did—or [*he almost chokes a sob*].

SHE [*softening and putting her hand caressingly on his shoulder*] Listen to me, dear. It's very nice of you to live with me in a dream, and to love me, and so on; but I cant help my husband having disagreeable relatives, can I?

HE [*brightening up*] Ah, of course they are your husband's relatives: I forgot that. Forgive me, Aurora. [*He takes her hand from his shoulder and kisses it. She sits down on the stool. He remains near the table, with his back to it, smiling fatuously down at her*].

SHE. The fact is, Teddy's got nothing but relatives. He has eight sisters and six half-sisters, and ever so many brothers—but I dont mind his brothers. Now if you only knew the least little thing about the world, Henry, youd know that in a large family, though the sisters quarrel with one another like mad all the time, yet let one of the brothers marry, and they all turn on their unfortunate sister-in-law and devote the rest of their lives with perfect unanimity to persuading him that his wife is unworthy of him. They can do it to her very face without her knowing it, because they always have a lot of stupid low family jokes that nobody understands but themselves. Half the time you cant tell what theyre talking about: it just drives you wild. There ought to be a law against a man's sister ever entering his house after he's married. I'm as certain as that I'm sitting here that Georgina stole those poems out of my workbox.*

HE. She will not understand them, I think.

SHE. Oh, wont she! She'll understand them only too well. She'll understand more harm than ever was in them: nasty vulgar-minded cat!

HE [*going to her*] Oh dont, dont think of people in that way. Dont think of her at all. [*He takes her hand and sits down on the carpet at her feet*]. Aurora: do you remember the evening when I sat here at your feet and read you those poems for the first time?

SHE. I shouldnt have let you: I see that now. When I think of Georgina sitting there at Teddy's feet and reading them to *him* for the first time, I feel I shall just go distracted.

HE. Yes, you are right. It will be a profanation.

SHE. Oh, I dont care about the profanation; but what will Teddy think? what will he do? [*Suddenly throwing his head away from her knee*] You dont seem to think a bit about Teddy. [*She jumps up, more and more agitated*].

HE [*supine on the floor; for she has thrown him off his balance*] To me Teddy is nothing, and Georgina less than nothing.

SHE. Youll soon find out how much less than nothing she is. If you think a woman cant do any harm because she's only a scandalmongering dowdy ragbag, youre greatly mistaken. [*She flounces about the room. He gets up slowly and dusts his hands. Suddenly she runs to him and throws herself into his arms*]. Henry: help me. Find a way out of this for me; and I'll bless you as long as you live. Oh, how wretched I am! [*She sobs on his breast*].

HE. And oh! how happy I am!

SHE [*whisking herself abruptly away*] Dont be selfish.

HE [*humbly*] Yes: I deserve that. I think if I were going to the stake with you, I should still be so happy with you that I should forget your danger as utterly as my own.

SHE [*relenting and patting his hand fondly*] Oh, you are a dear darling boy, Henry; but [*throwing his hand away fretfully*] youre no *use*. I want somebody to tell me what to do.

HE [*with quiet conviction*] Your heart will tell you at the right time. I have thought deeply over this; and I know what we two *must* do, sooner or later.

SHE. No, Henry. I will do nothing improper, nothing dishonorable. [*She sits down plump on the stool and looks inflexible*].

HE. If you did, you would no longer be Aurora. Our course is perfectly simple, perfectly straightforward, perfectly stainless and true. We love one another. I am not ashamed of that: I am ready to go out and proclaim it to all London* as simply as I will declare it to your husband when you see—as you soon will see—that this is the only way honorable enough for your feet to tread. Let us go out together to our own house, this evening, without concealment and without shame. Remember! we owe something to your husband. We are his guests here: he is an honorable man: he has been kind to us: he has perhaps loved you as well as his prosaic nature and his sordid commercial environment permitted. We owe it to him in all honor not to let him learn the truth from the lips of a scandalmonger. Let us go to him now quietly, hand in hand; bid him farewell; and walk out of the house without concealment or subterfuge, freely and honestly, in full honor and self-respect.

SHE [*staring at him*] And where shall we go to?

HE. We shall not depart by a hair's breadth from the ordinary natural current of our lives. We were going to the theatre when the loss of the poems compelled us to take action at once. We shall go to the theatre still; but we shall leave your diamonds here; for we cannot afford diamonds, and do not need them.

SHE [*fretfully*] I have told you already that I hate diamonds; only Teddy insists on hanging me all over with them. You need not preach simplicity to me.

HE. I never thought of doing so, dearest: I know that these trivialities are nothing to you. What was I saying?—oh yes. Instead of coming back here from the theatre, you will come with me to my home—now and henceforth *our* home—and in due course of time, when you are divorced, we shall go through whatever idle legal ceremony you may desire. *I* attach no importance to the law: my love was not created in me by the law, nor can it be bound or loosed by it. That is simple enough, and sweet enough, is it not? [*He takes the flowers from the table*]. Here are flowers for you: I have the tickets: we will ask your husband to lend us the carriage to shew that there is no malice, no grudge, between us. Come!*

SHE. Do you mean to say that you propose that we should walk right bang up to Teddy and tell him we're going away together?

HE. Yes. What can be simpler?

SHE. And do you think for a moment he'd stand it?* He'd just kill you.

HE [*coming to a sudden stop and speaking with considerable confidence*] You dont understand these things, my darling: how could you? I have followed the Greek ideal* and not neglected the culture of my body. Like all poets I have a passion for pugilism.* Your husband would make a tolerable second-rate heavy weight if he were in training and ten years younger. As it is, he could, if strung up to a great effort by a burst of passion, give a good account of himself for perhaps fifteen seconds. But I am active enough to keep out of his reach for fifteen seconds; and after that I should be simply all over him.

SHE [*rising and coming to him in consternation*] What do you mean by all over him?

HE [*gently*] Dont ask me, dearest. At all events, I swear to you that you need not be anxious about *me*.

SHE. And what about Teddy? Do you mean to tell me that you are going to beat Teddy before my face like a brutal prizefighter?

HE. All this alarm is needless, dearest. Believe me, nothing will happen. Your husband knows that I am capable of defending myself. Under such circumstances nothing ever does happen. And of course *I* shall do nothing. The man who once loved you is sacred to me.

SHE [*suspiciously*] Doesnt he love me still? Has he told you anything?

HE. No, no. [*He takes her tenderly in his arms*]. Dearest, dearest: how agitated you are! how unlike yourself! All these worries belong to the lower plane. Come up with me to the higher one. The heights, the solitudes, the soul world!

SHE [*avoiding his gaze*] No: stop: it's no use, Mr Apjohn.

HE [*recoiling*] Mr Apjohn!!!

SHE. Excuse me: I meant Henry, of course.

HE. How could you even think of me as Mr Apjohn? I never think of you as Mrs Bompas: it is always Aurora, Aurora, Auro—

SHE. Yes, yes: thats all very well, Mr Apjohn [*he is about to interrupt again: but she wont have it*]: no: it's no use: Ive suddenly begun to think of you as Mr Apjohn; and it's ridiculous to go on calling you Henry. I thought you were only a boy, a child, a dreamer. I thought you would be too much afraid to do anything. And now you want to beat Teddy and to break up my home and disgrace me and make a horrible scandal in the papers. It's cruel, unmanly, cowardly.

HE [*with grave wonder*] Are you afraid?

SHE. Oh, of course I'm afraid. So would you be if you had any common sense. [*She goes to the hearth, turning her back to him, and puts one tapping foot on the fender*].*

HE [*watching her with great gravity*] Perfect love casteth out fear.* That is why I am not afraid. Mrs Bompas: you do not love me.

SHE [*turning to him with a gasp of relief*] Oh, thank you, thank you! You really can be very nice, Henry.

HE. Why do you thank me?

SHE [*coming prettily to him from the fireplace*] For calling me Mrs Bompas again. I feel now that you are going to be reasonable and behave like a gentleman. [*He drops on the stool; covers his face with his hands; and groans*]. Whats the matter?

HE. Once or twice in my life I have dreamed that I was exquisitely happy and blessed. But oh! the misgiving at the first stir of consciousness! the stab of reality! the prison walls of the bedroom! the bitter, bitter disappointment of waking! And this time! oh, this time I thought I was awake.

SHE. Listen to me, Henry: we really havnt time for all that sort of flapdoodle* now [*He starts to his feet as if she had pulled a trigger and straightened him by the release of a powerful spring, and goes past her with set teeth to the little table*]. Oh, take care: you nearly hit me in the chin with the top of your head.

HE [*with fierce politeness*] I beg your pardon. What is it you want me to do? I am at your service. I am ready to behave like a gentleman if you will be kind enough to explain exactly how.

SHE [*a little frightened*] Thank you, Henry: I was sure you would. Youre not angry with me, are you?

HE. Go on. Go on quickly. Give me something to think about, or I will—I will—[*he suddenly snatches up her fan and is about to break it in his clenched fists*].

SHE [*running forward and catching at the fan, with loud lamentation*] Dont break my fan—no, dont. [*He slowly relaxes his grip of it as she draws it anxiously out of his hands*] No, really, thats a stupid trick: I dont like that. Youve no right to do that [*She opens the fan, and finds that the sticks are disconnected*]. Oh, how could you be so inconsiderate?

HE. I beg your pardon. I will buy you a new one.

SHE [*querulously*] You will never be able to match it. And it was a particular favorite of mine.

HE [*shortly*] Then you will have to do without it: thats all.

SHE. Thats not a very nice thing to say after breaking my pet fan, I think.

HE. If you knew how near I was to breaking Teddy's pet wife and presenting him with the pieces, you would be thankful that you are alive instead of—of—of howling about fiveshillingsworth* of ivory. Damn your fan!

SHE. Oh! Dont you dare swear in my presence. One would think you were my husband.

HE [*again collapsing on the stool*] This is some horrible dream. What has become of you? *You* are not my Aurora.

SHE. Oh, well, if you come to that, what has become of *you*? Do you think I would ever have encouraged you if I had known you were such a little devil?

HE. Dont drag me down—dont—dont. Help me to find the way back to the heights.

SHE [*kneeling beside him and pleading*] If you would only be reasonable, Henry. If you would only remember that I am on the brink of ruin, and not go on calmly saying it's all quite simple.

HE. It seems so to me.

SHE [*jumping up distractedly*] If you say that again I shall do something I'll be sorry for. Here we are, standing on the edge of a frightful precipice. No doubt it's quite simple to go over and have done with it. But cant you suggest anything more agreeable?

HE. I can suggest nothing now. A chill black darkness has fallen: I can see nothing but the ruins of our dream. [*He rises with a deep sigh*].

SHE. Cant you? Well, I can. I can see Georgina rubbing those poems into Teddy. [*Facing him determinedly*] And I tell you, Henry Apjohn, that *you* got me into this mess; and *you* must get me out of it again.

HE [*polite and hopeless*] All I can say is that I am entirely at your service. What do you wish me to do?

SHE. Do you know anybody else named Aurora?

HE. No.

SHE. Theres no use in saying No in that frozen pigheaded way. You *must* know some Aurora or other somewhere.

HE. You said you were the only Aurora in the world. And [*lifting his clasped fists with a sudden return of his emotion*] oh God! you were the only Aurora in the world for me. [*He turns away from her, hiding his face*].

SHE [*petting him*] Yes, yes, dear: of course. It's very nice of you; and I appreciate it: indeed I do; but it's not seasonable just at present. Now just listen to me. I suppose you know all those poems by heart.

HE. Yes, by *heart*. [*Raising his head and looking at her with a sudden suspicion*] Dont you?

SHE. Well, I never can remember verses; and besides, Ive been so busy that Ive not had time to read them all; though I intend to the very first moment I can get: I promise you that most faithfully, Henry. But now try and remember very particularly. Does the name of Bompas occur in any of the poems?

HE [*indignantly*] No.

SHE. Youre quite sure?

HE. Of course I am quite sure. How could I use such a name in a poem?

SHE. Well, I dont see why not. It rhymes to rumpus, which seems appropriate enough at present, goodness knows! However, youre a poet, and you ought to know.

HE. What does it matter—now?

SHE. It matters a lot, I can tell you. If theres nothing about Bompas in the poems, we can say that they were written to some other Aurora, and that you shewed them to me because my name was Aurora too. So youve got to invent another Aurora for the occasion.

HE [*very coldly*] Oh, if you wish me to tell a lie—

SHE. Surely, as a man of honor—as a gentleman, you wouldnt tell the truth: would you?

HE. Very well. You have broken my spirit and desecrated my dreams. I will lie and protest and stand on my honor: oh, I will play the gentleman, never fear.

SHE. Yes, put it all on me, of course. Dont be mean, Henry.

HE [*rousing himself with an effort*] You are quite right, Mrs Bompas: I beg your pardon. You must excuse my temper. I am having growing pains, I think.

SHE. Growing pains!

HE. The process of growing from romantic boyhood into cynical maturity usually takes fifteen years. When it is compressed into fifteen minutes, the pace is too fast; and growing pains are the result.

SHE. Oh, is this a time for cleverness? It's settled, isnt it, that youre going to be nice and good, and that youll brazen it out to Teddy that you have some other Aurora?

HE. Yes: I'm capable of anything now. I should not have told him the truth by halves; and now I will not lie by halves. I'll wallow in the honor of a gentleman.

SHE. Dearest boy, I knew you would. I—Sh! [*She rushes to the door, and holds it ajar, listening breathlessly*].

HE. What is it?

SHE [*white with apprehension*] It's Teddy: I hear him tapping the new barometer. He cant have anything serious on his mind or he wouldnt do that. Perhaps Georgina hasnt said anything.* [*She steals back to the hearth*]. Try and look as if there was nothing the matter. Give me my gloves, quick. [*He hands them to her. She pulls on one hastily and begins buttoning it with ostentatious unconcern*]. Go further away from me, quick. [*He walks doggedly away from her until the piano prevents his going farther*]. If I button my glove, and you were to hum a tune, dont you think that—

HE. The tableau would be complete in its guiltiness. For Heaven's sake, Mrs Bompas, let that glove alone: you look like a pickpocket.

Her husband comes in: a robust, thicknecked, well groomed city man, *with a strong chin but a blithering eye and credulous mouth. He has a momentous air, but shews no sign of displeasure: rather the contrary.*

HER HUSBAND. Hallo! I thought you two were at the theatre.

SHE. I felt anxious about you, Teddy. Why didnt you come home to dinner?

HER HUSBAND. I got a message from Georgina. She wanted me to go to her.

SHE. Poor dear Georgina! I'm sorry I havnt been able to call on her this last week. I hope theres nothing the matter with her.

HER HUSBAND. Nothing, except anxiety for my welfare—and yours. [*She steals a terrified look at Henry*]. By the way, Apjohn, I should like a word with you this evening, if Aurora can spare you for a moment.

HE [*formally*] I am at your service.

HER HUSBAND. No hurry. After the theatre will do.

HE. We have decided not to go.

HER HUSBAND. Indeed! Well, then, shall we adjourn to my snuggery?*

SHE. You neednt move. I shall go and lock up my diamonds since I'm not going to the theatre. Give me my things.

HER HUSBAND [*as he hands her the cloud and the mirror*] Well, we shall have more room here.

HE [*looking about him and shaking his shoulders loose*] I think I should prefer plenty of room.

HER HUSBAND. So, if it's not disturbing you, Rory—?

SHE. Not at all. [*She goes out*].

When the two men are alone together, Bompas deliberately takes the poems from his breast pocket; looks at them reflectively; then looks at Henry, mutely inviting his attention. Henry refuses to understand, doing his best to look unconcerned.

HER HUSBAND. Do these manuscripts seem at all familiar to you, may I ask?

HE. Manuscripts?

HER HUSBAND. Yes. Would you like to look at them a little closer? [*He proffers them under Henry's nose*].

HE [*as with a sudden illumination of glad surprise*] Why, these are my poems!

HER HUSBAND. So I gather.

HE. What a shame! Mrs Bompas has shewn them to you! You must think me an utter ass. I wrote them years ago after reading Swinburne's Songs Before Sunrise.* Nothing would do me then but I must reel off a set of Songs to the Sunrise. Aurora, you know: the rosy fingered Aurora.* Theyre all about Aurora. When Mrs Bompas told me her name was Aurora, I couldnt resist the temptation to lend them to her to read. But I didnt bargain for your unsympathetic eyes.

HER HUSBAND [*grinning*] Apjohn: thats really very ready of you. You are cut out for literature; and the day will come when Rory and I will be proud to have you about the house.* I have heard far thinner stories from much older men.

HE [*with an air of great surprise*] Do you mean to imply that you dont believe me?

HER HUSBAND. Do you expect me to believe you?

HE. Why not? I dont understand.

HER HUSBAND. Come! Dont underrate your own cleverness, Apjohn. I think you understand pretty well.

HE. I assure you I am quite at a loss. Can you not be a little more explicit?

HER HUSBAND. Dont overdo it, old chap.* However, I will just be so far explicit as to say that if you think these poems read as if they were addressed, not to a live woman, but to a shivering cold time of day at which you were never out of bed in your life, you hardly do justice to your own literary powers—which I admire and appreciate, mind you, as much as any man. Come! own up. You wrote those poems to my wife. [*An internal struggle prevents Henry from answering*]. Of course you did. [*He throws the poems on the table; and goes to the hearthrug, where he plants himself solidly, chuckling a little and waiting for the next move*].

HE [*formally and carefully*] Mr Bompas: I pledge you my word you are mistaken. I need not tell you that Mrs Bompas is a lady of stainless honor, who has never cast an unworthy thought on me. The fact that she has shewn you my poems—

HER HUSBAND. Thats not a fact. I came by them without her knowledge. She didnt shew them to me.

HE. Does not that prove their perfect innocence? She would have shewn them to you at once if she had taken your quite unfounded view of them.

HER HUSBAND [*shaken*] Apjohn: play fair. Dont abuse your intellectual gifts. Do you really mean that I am making a fool of myself?*

HE [*earnestly*] Believe me, you are. I assure you, on my honor as a gentleman, that I have never had the slightest feeling for Mrs Bompas beyond the ordinary esteem and regard of a pleasant acquaintance.

HER HUSBAND [*shortly, shewing ill humor for the first time*] Oh! Indeed! [*He leaves his hearth and begins to approach Henry slowly, looking him up and down with growing resentment*].

HE [*hastening to improve the impression made by his mendacity*] I should never have dreamt of writing poems to her. The thing is absurd.

HER HUSBAND [*reddening ominously*] Why is it absurd?

HE [*shrugging his shoulders*] Well, it happens that I do not admire Mrs Bompas—in that way.

HER HUSBAND [*breaking out in Henry's face*] Let me tell you that Mrs Bompas has been admired by better men than you, you soapy headed little puppy, you.

HE [*much taken aback*] There is no need to insult me like this. I assure you, on my honor as a—

HER HUSBAND [*too angry to tolerate a reply, and boring Henry more and more towards the piano*] *You* dont admire Mrs Bompas! *You* would never dream of writing poems to Mrs Bompas! My wife's not good enough for you, isnt she? [*Fiercely*] Who are you, pray, that you should be so jolly superior?

HE. Mr Bompas: I can make allowances for your jealousy—

HER HUSBAND. Jealousy! do you suppose I'm jealous of *you*? No, nor of ten like you. But if you think I'll stand here and let you insult my wife in her own house, youre mistaken.

HE [*very uncomfortable with his back against the piano and Teddy standing over him threateningly*] How can I convince you? Be reasonable. I tell you my relations with Mrs Bompas are relations of perfect coldness— of indifference—

HER HUSBAND [*scornfully*] Say it again: say it again. Youre proud of it, arnt you? Yah! youre not worth kicking.

Henry suddenly executes the feat known to pugilists as slipping, and changes sides with Teddy, who is now between Henry and the piano.*

HE. Look here: I'm not going to stand this.

HER HUSBAND. Oh, you *have* some blood in your body after all! Good job!

HE. This is ridiculous. I assure you Mrs Bompas is quite—

HER HUSBAND. What is Mrs Bompas to you, I'd like to know. I'll tell you what Mrs Bompas is. She's the smartest woman in the smartest set in South Kensington, and the handsomest, and the cleverest, and the most fetching to experienced men who know a good thing when they see it, whatever she may be to conceited penny-a-lining puppies* who think nothing good enough for them. It's admitted by the best people; and not to know it argues yourself unknown. Three of our first actor-managers* have offered her a hundred a week if she'll go on the stage when they start a repertory theatre;* and I think they know what theyre about as well as you. The only member of the present Cabinet that you might call a handsome man has neglected the business of the country to dance with her, though he dont belong to our set as a regular thing. One of the first professional poets in Bedford Park* wrote a sonnet to her, worth all your amateur trash. At Ascot* last season the eldest son of a duke excused himself from calling on me on the ground that his feelings for Mrs Bompas were not consistent with his duty to me as host; and it did him honor and me too. But [*with gathering fury*] she isnt good enough for *you*, it seems. You regard her with coldness, with indifference; and you have the cool cheek to tell me so to my face. For two pins I'd flatten your nose in to teach you manners. Introducing a fine woman to you is casting pearls before swine [*yelling at him*] before SWINE! d'ye hear?*

HE [*with a deplorable lack of polish*] You call me a swine again and I'll land you one on the chin thatll make your head sing for a week.

HER HUSBAND [*exploding*] What!

He charges at Henry with bull-like fury. Henry places himself on guard in the manner of a well taught boxer, and gets away smartly, but unfortunately forgets the stool which is just behind him. He falls backwards over it, unintentionally pushing it against the shins of Bompas, who falls forward over it. Mrs Bompas, with a scream, rushes into the room between the sprawling champions, and sits down on the floor in order to get her right arm round her husband's neck.

SHE. You shant, Teddy: you shant. You will be killed: he is a prizefighter.

HER HUSBAND [*vengefully*] I'll prizefight him. [*He struggles vainly to free himself from her embrace*].

SHE. Henry: dont let him fight you. Promise me that you wont.

HE [*ruefully*] I have got a most frightful bump on the back of my head. [*He tries to rise*].

SHE [*reaching out her left hand to seize his coat tail, and pulling him down again, whilst keeping fast hold of Teddy with the other hand*] Not until you have promised: not until you both have promised. [*Teddy tries to rise: she pulls him back again*]. Teddy: you promise, dont you? Yes, yes. Be good: you promise.

HER HUSBAND. I wont, unless he takes it back.

SHE. He will: he does. You take it back, Henry?—yes.

HE [*savagely*] Yes. I take it back. [*She lets go his coat. He gets up. So does Teddy*]. I take it all back, all, without reserve.

SHE [*on the carpet*] Is nobody going to help me up? [*They each take a hand and pull her up*]. Now wont you shake hands and be good?

HE [*recklessly*] I shall do nothing of the sort. I have steeped myself in lies for your sake; and the only reward I get is a lump on the back of my head the size of an apple. Now I will go back to the straight path.

SHE. Henry: for Heaven's sake—

HE. It's no use. Your husband is a fool and a brute—

HER HUSBAND. Whats that you say?

HE. I say you are a fool and a brute; and if youll step outside with me I'll say it again. [*Teddy begins to take off his coat for combat*]. Those poems *were* written to your wife, every word of them, and to nobody else. [*The scowl clears away from Bompas's countenance. Radiant, he replaces his coat*]. I wrote them because I loved her. I thought her the most beautiful woman in the world, and I told her so over and over again. I adored her: do you hear? I told her that you were a sordid commercial chump, utterly unworthy of her; and so you are.

HER HUSBAND [*so gratified, he can hardly believe his ears*] You dont mean it!*

HE. Yes, I do mean it, and a lot more too. I asked Mrs Bompas to walk out of the house with me—to leave you—to get divorced from you and marry me. I begged and implored her to do it this very night. It was her refusal that ended everything between us. [*Looking very disparagingly at him*] What she can see in you, goodness only knows!

HER HUSBAND [*beaming with remorse*] My dear chap, why didnt you say so before?* I apologize. Come! dont bear malice: shake hands. Make him shake hands, Rory.

SHE. For my sake, Henry. After all, he's my husband. Forgive him. Take his hand.* [*Henry, dazed, lets her take his hand and place it in Teddy's*].

HER HUSBAND [*shaking it heartily*] Youve got to own that none of your literary heroines can touch my Rory. [*He turns to her and claps her with fond pride on the shoulder*]. Eh, Rory? They cant resist you: none of em. Never knew a man yet that could hold out three days.

SHE. Dont be foolish, Teddy. I hope you were not really hurt, Henry [*She feels the back of his head. He flinches*]. Oh, poor boy, what a bump! I must get some vinegar and brown paper.* [*She goes to the bell and rings*].

HER HUSBAND. Will you do me a great favor, Apjohn. I hardly like to ask; but it would be a real kindness to us both.*

HE. What can I do?

HER HUSBAND [*taking up the poems*] Well, may I get these printed? It shall be done in the best style. The finest paper, sumptuous binding, everything first class. Theyre beautiful poems. I should like to shew them about a bit.

SHE [*running back from the bell, delighted with the idea, and coming between them*] Oh Henry, if you wouldnt mind?

HE. Oh, *I* dont mind. I am past minding anything.*

HER HUSBAND. What shall we call the volume? To Aurora, or something like that, eh?

HE. I should call it *How He Lied to Her Husband*.*

PASSION, POISON, AND PETRIFACTION*
OR
THE FATAL GAZOGENE*
A BRIEF TRAGEDY FOR BARNS AND BOOTHS*

PREFACE

THIS tragedy was written at the request of Mr Cyril Maude,* under whose direction it was performed repeatedly, with colossal success, in a booth in Regent's Park, for the benefit of The Actors' Orphanage,* on the 14th July 1905, by Miss Irene Vanbrugh, Miss Nancy Price, Mr G. P. Huntley, Mr Cyril Maude, Mr Eric Lewis, Mr Arthur Williams, and Mr Lennox Pawle.*

As it is extremely difficult to find an actor capable of eating a real ceiling, it will be found convenient in performance to substitute the tops of old wedding cakes for bits of plaster. There is but little difference in material between the two substances; but the taste of the wedding cake is considered more agreeable by many people.

The orchestra should consist of at least a harp, a drum, and a pair of cymbals, these instruments being the most useful in enhancing the stage effect.

The landlord may with equal propriety be a landlady, if that arrangement be better suited to the resources of the company.

As the Bill Bailey* song has not proved immortal, any equally appropriate ditty of the moment may be substituted.

PASSION, POISON, AND PETRIFACTION

In a bed-sitting room* in a fashionable quarter of London* a lady sits at her dressing-table, with her maid combing her hair. It is late; and the electric lamps are glowing. Apparently the room is bedless; but there stands against the opposite wall to that at which the dressing-table is placed a piece of furniture that suggests a bookcase without carrying conviction. On the same side is a chest of drawers of that disastrous kind which, recalcitrant to the opener until she is provoked to violence, then suddenly come wholly out and defy all her efforts to fit them in again. Opposite this chest of drawers, on the lady's side of the room, is a cupboard. The presence of a row of gentleman's boots beside the chest of drawers proclaims that the lady is married. Her own boots are beside the cupboard. The third wall is pierced midway by the door, above which is a cuckoo clock. Near the door a pedestal bears a portrait bust of the lady in plaster. There is a fan on the dressing-table, a hatbox and rug strap on the chest of drawers, an umbrella and a bootjack* against the wall near the bed. The general impression is one of brightness, beauty, and social ambition, damped by somewhat inadequate means. A certain air of theatricality is produced by the fact that though the room is rectangular it has only three walls. Not a sound is heard except the overture and the crackling of the lady's hair as the maid's brush draws electric sparks from it in the dry air of the London midsummer. The cuckoo clock strikes sixteen.

THE LADY. How much did the clock strike, Phyllis?

PHYLLIS. Sixteen, my lady.

THE LADY. That means eleven o'clock, does it not?

PHYLLIS. Eleven at night, my lady. In the morning it means half-past two; so if you hear it strike sixteen during your slumbers, do not rise.

THE LADY. I will not, Phyllis. Phyllis: I am weary. I will go to bed. Prepare my couch.

Phyllis crosses the room to the bookcase and touches a button. The front of the bookcase falls out with a crash and becomes a bed. A roll of distant thunder echoes the crash.

PHYLLIS [*shuddering*] It is a terrible night. Heaven help all poor mariners at sea! My master is late. I trust nothing has happened to him. Your bed is ready, my lady.

THE LADY. Thank you, Phyllis. [*She rises and approaches the bed*]. Goodnight.

PHYLLIS. Will your ladyship not undress?

THE LADY. Not tonight, Phyllis. [*Glancing through where the fourth wall is missing*] Not under the circumstances.

PHYLLIS [*impulsively throwing herself on her knees by her mistress's side, and clasping her round the waist*] Oh, my beloved mistress, I know not why or how; but I feel that I shall never see you alive again. There is murder in the air. [*Thunder*]. Hark!

THE LADY. Strange! As I sat there methought I heard angels singing, Oh, wont you come home, Bill Bailey? Why should angels call me Bill Bailey? My name is Magnesia* Fitztollemache.

PHYLLIS [*emphasizing the title*] *Lady* Magnesia Fitztollemache.

LADY MAGNESIA. In case we should never again meet in this world, let us take a last farewell.

PHYLLIS [*embracing her* with tears] My poor murdered angel mistress!

LADY MAGNESIA. In case we *should* meet again, call me at half-past eleven.

PHYLLIS. I will, I will.

Phyllis withdraws, overcome by emotion. Lady Magnesia switches off the electric light, and immediately hears the angels quite distinctly. They sing Bill Bailey so sweetly that she can attend to nothing else, and forgets to remove even her boots as she draws the coverlet over herself and sinks to sleep, lulled by celestial harmony. A white radiance plays on her pillow, and lights up her beautiful face. But the thunder growls again; and a lurid red glow concentrates itself on the door, which is presently flung open, revealing a saturnine figure in evening dress, partially concealed by a crimson cloak. As he steals towards the bed the unnatural glare in his eyes and the broad-bladed dagger nervously gripped in his right hand bode ill for the sleeping lady. Providentially she sneezes on the very brink of eternity; and the tension of the murderer's nerves is such that he bolts precipitately under the bed at the sudden and startling Atscha! A dull, heavy, rhythmic thumping—the beating of his heart—betrays his whereabouts. Soon he emerges cautiously and raises his head above the bed coverlet level.*

THE MURDERER. I can no longer cower here listening to the agonized thumpings of my own heart. She but snooze in her sleep. I'll do't.* [*He again raises the dagger. The angels sing again. He cowers*] What is this? Has that tune reached Heaven?*

LADY MAGNESIA [*waking and sitting up*] My husband! [*All the colors of the rainbow chase one another up his face with ghastly brilliancy*]. Why do you change color? And what on earth are you doing with that dagger?

FITZ [*affecting unconcern, but unhinged*] It is a present for you: a present from mother. Pretty, isnt it? [*he displays it fatuously*].

LADY MAGNESIA. But she promised me a fish slice.

FITZ. This is a combination fish slice and dagger. One day you have salmon for dinner. The next you have a murder to commit. See?

LADY MAGNESIA. My sweet mother-in-law! [*Someone knocks at the door*]. That is Adolphus's knock. [*Fitz's face turns a dazzling green*]. What has happened to your complexion? You have turned green. Now I think of it, you always do when Adolphus is mentioned. Arnt you going to let him in?

FITZ. Certainly not. [*He goes to the door*] Adolphus: you cannot enter. My wife is undressed and in bed.

LADY MAGNESIA [*rising*] I am not. Come in, Adolphus [*she switches on the electric light*].

ADOLPHUS [*without*] Something most important has happened. I must come in for a moment.

FITZ [*calling to Adolphus*] Something important happened? What is it?

ADOLPHUS [*without*] My new clothes have come home.

FITZ. He says his new clothes have come home.

LADY MAGNESIA [*running to the door and opening it*] Oh, come in, come in. Let me see.

Adolphus Bastable enters. He is in evening dress, made in the latest fashion, with the right half of the coat and the left half of the trousers yellow and the other halves black. His silver-spangled waistcoat has a crimson handkerchief stuck between it and his shirt front.

ADOLPHUS. What do you think of it?

LADY MAGNESIA. It is a dream! a creation! [*she turns him about to admire him*].

ADOLPHUS [*proudly*] I shall never be mistaken for a waiter again.

FITZ. A drink, Adolphus?

ADOLPHUS. Thanks.

Fitztollemache goes to the cupboard and takes out a tray with tumblers and a bottle of whisky. He puts them on the dressing-table.

FITZ. Is the gazogene full?

LADY MAGNESIA. Yes: you put in the powders* yourself today.

FITZ [*sardonically*] So I did. The special powders! Ha! ha! ha! ha! ha! [*his face is again strangely variegated*].

LADY MAGNESIA. Your complexion is really going to pieces. Why do you laugh in that silly way at nothing?

FITZ. Nothing! Ha, ha! Nothing! Ha, ha, ha!

ADOLPHUS. I hope, Mr Fitztollemache, you are not laughing at my clothes. I warn you that I am an Englishman. You may laugh at my manners, at my brains, at my national institutions; but if you laugh at my clothes, one of us must die.

Thunder.

FITZ. I laughed but at the irony of Fate [*he takes a gazogene from the cupboard*].

ADOLPHUS [*satisfied*] Oh, *that*! Oh, yes, of course!*

FITZ. Let us drown all unkindness in a loving cup.* [*He puts the gazogene on the floor in the middle of the room*]. Pardon the absence of a table: we found it in the way and pawned it. [*He takes the whisky bottle from the dressing-table*].

LADY MAGNESIA. We picnic at home now. It is delightful.

She takes three tumblers from the dressing-table and sits on the floor, presiding over the gazogene, with Fitz and Adolphus squatting on her left and right respectively. Fitz pours whisky into the tumblers.

FITZ [*as Magnesia is about to squirt soda into his tumbler*] Stay! No soda for me. Let Adolphus have it all—*all*. I will take mine neat.

LADY MAGNESIA [*proffering tumbler to Adolphus*] Pledge me,*Adolphus.*

FITZ. Kiss the cup, Magnesia. Pledge her, man. Drink deep.

ADOLPHUS. To Magnesia!

FITZ. To Magnesia! [*The two men drink*] It is done. [*Scrambling to his feet*] Adolphus: you have but ten minutes to live—if so long.

ADOLPHUS. What mean you?

MAGNESIA [*rising*] My mind misgives me. I have a strange feeling here [*touching her heart*].

ADOLPHUS. So have I, but lower down [*touching his stomach*]. That gazogene is disagreeing with me.

FITZ. It was poisoned!

*Sensation.**

ADOLPHUS [*rising*] Help! Police!

FITZ. Dastard! you would appeal to the law! Can you not die like a gentleman?

ADOLPHUS. But so young! when I have only worn my new clothes once.

MAGNESIA. It is too horrible. [*To Fitz*] Fiend! what drove you to this wicked deed?

FITZ. Jealousy. You admired his clothes: you did not admire mine.

ADOLPHUS. My clothes [*his face lights up with heavenly radiance*]! Have I indeed been found worthy to be the first clothes-martyr? Welcome, death! Hark! angels call me. [*The celestial choir again raises its favorite chant. He listens with a rapt expression. Suddenly the angels sing out of tune; and the radiance on the poisoned man's face turns a sickly green*] Yah—ah! Oh—ahoo! The gazogene is disagreeing extremely. Oh! [*he throws himself on the bed, writhing*].

MAGNESIA [*to Fitz*] Monster: what have you done? [*She points to the distorted figure on the bed*]. That was once a Man, beautiful and glorious. What have you made of it? A writhing, agonized, miserable, moribund worm.

ADOLPHUS [*in a tone of the strongest remonstrance*] Oh, I say! Oh, come! No: look here, Magnesia! Really!

MAGNESIA. Oh, is this a time for petty vanity? Think of your misspent life—

ADOLPHUS [*much injured*] *Whose* misspent life?

MAGNESIA [*continuing relentlessly*] Look into your conscience: look into your stomach. [*Adolphus collapses in hideous spasms. She turns to Fitz*] And this is *your* handiwork!

FITZ. Mine is a passionate nature, Magnesia. I must have your undivided love. I must have your love: do you hear? LOVE! LOVE!! LOVE!!! LOVE!!!! LOVE!!!!!

He raves, accompanied by a fresh paroxysm from the victim on the bed.

MAGNESIA [*with sudden resolution*] You *shall* have it.

FITZ [*enraptured*] Magnesia! I have recovered your love! Oh, how slight appears the sacrifice of this man compared to so glorious a reward! I would poison ten men without a thought of self to gain one smile from you.

ADOLPHUS [*in a broken voice*] Farewell, Magnesia: my last hour is at hand. Farewell, farewell, farewell!

MAGNESIA. At this supreme moment, George Fitztollemache, I solemnly dedicate to you all that I formerly dedicated to poor Adolphus.

ADOLPHUS. Oh, please not poor Adolphus yet. I still live, you know.

MAGNESIA. The vital spark but flashes before it vanishes. [*Adolphus groans*]. And now, Adolphus, take this last comfort from the unhappy Magnesia Fitztollemache. As I have dedicated to George all that I gave to you, so I will bury in your grave—or in your urn if you are cremated—all that I gave to him.

FITZ. I hardly follow this.

MAGNESIA. I will explain. George: hitherto I have given Adolphus all the romance of my nature—all my love—all my dreams—all my caresses. Henceforth they are yours!

FITZ. Angel!

MAGNESIA. Adolphus: forgive me if this pains you.

ADOLPHUS. Dont mention it. I hardly feel it. The gazogene is so much worse. [*Taken bad again*] Oh!

MAGNESIA. Peace, poor sufferer: there is still some balm. You are about to hear what I am going to dedicate to *you*.

ADOLPHUS. All I ask is a peppermint lozenge,* for mercy's sake.

MAGNESIA. I have something far better than any lozenge: the devotion of a lifetime. Formerly it was George's. I kept his house, or rather, his lodgings. I mended his clothes. I darned his socks. I bought his food. I interviewed his creditors. I stood between him and the servants. I administered his domestic finances. When his hair needed cutting or his countenance was imperfectly washed, I pointed it out to him. The trouble that all this gave me made him prosaic in my eyes. Familiarity bred contempt. Now all that shall end. My husband shall be my hero, my lover, my perfect knight. He shall shield me from all care and trouble. He shall ask nothing in return but love—boundless, priceless, rapturous, soul-enthralling love, LOVE! LOVE!! LOVE!!! [*she raves and flings her arms about Fitz*]. And the duties I formerly discharged shall be replaced by the one supreme duty of duties: the duty of weeping at Adolphus's tomb.

FITZ [*reflectively*] My ownest, this sacrifice makes me feel that I have perhaps been a little selfish. I cannot help feeling that there is much to be said for the old arrangement. Why should Adolphus die for my sake?

ADOLPHUS. I am not dying for your sake, Fitz. I am dying because you poisoned me.

MAGNESIA. You do not *fear* to die, Adolphus, do you?

ADOLPHUS. N-n-no, I dont exactly fear to die. Still—

FITZ. Still, if an antidote—

ADOLPHUS [*bounding from the bed*] Antidote!

MAGNESIA [*with wild hope*] Antidote!

FITZ. If an antidote would not be too much of an anti-climax.

ADOLPHUS. Anti-climax be blowed! Do you think I am going to die to please the critics? Out with your antidote. Quick!

FITZ. The best antidote to the poison I have given you is lime, plenty of lime.

ADOLPHUS. Lime! You mock me! Do you think I carry lime about in my pockets?

FITZ. There is the plaster ceiling.*

MAGNESIA. Yes, the ceiling. Saved, saved, saved!

All three frantically shy boots at the ceiling. Flakes of plaster rain down which Adolphus devours, at first ravenously, then with a marked falling off in relish.*

MAGNESIA [*picking up a huge slice*] Take this, Adolphus: it is the largest [*she crams it into his mouth*].

FITZ. Ha! a lump off the cornice! Try this.

ADOLPHUS [*desperately*] Stop! stop!

MAGNESIA. Do not stop. You will die. [*She tries to stuff him again*].

ADOLPHUS [*resolutely*] I prefer death.

MAGNESIA and FITZ [*throwing themselves on their knees on either side of him*] For our sakes, Adolphus, persevere.

ADOLPHUS. No: unless you can supply lime in liquid form, I must perish. Finish that ceiling I cannot and will not.

MAGNESIA. I have a thought—an inspiration. My bust. [*She snatches it from its pedestal and brings it to him*].

ADOLPHUS [*gazing fondly at it*] Can I resist it?

FITZ. Try the bun.

ADOLPHUS [*gnawing the knot of hair at the back of the bust's head: it makes him ill*]. Yah, I cannot. I cannot. Not even *your* bust, Magnesia. Do not ask me. Let me die.

FITZ [*pressing the bust on him*] Force yourself to take a mouthful. Down with it, Adolphus!

ADOLPHUS. Useless. It would not stay down. Water! Some fluid! Ring for something to drink [*he chokes*].

MAGNESIA. I will save you [*she rushes to the bell and rings*].

Phyllis, in her night-gown, with her hair prettily made up into a chevaux de fries* of crocuses with pink and yellow curl papers,* rushes in straight to Magnesia.

PHYLLIS [*hysterically*] My beloved mistress, once more we meet. [*She sees Fitztollemache and screams*] Ah! ah! ah! A man! [*She sees Adolphus*] Men!! [*She flies; but Fitztollemache seizes her by the night-gown just as she is escaping*]. Unhand me, villain!

FITZ. This is no time for prudery, girl. Mr Bastable is dying.

PHYLLIS [*with concern*] Indeed, sir? I hope he will not think it unfeeling of me to appear at his deathbed in curl papers.

MAGNESIA. We know you have a good heart, Phyllis. Take this [*giving her the bust*]; dissolve it in a jug of hot water; and bring it back instantly. Mr Bastable's life depends on your haste.

PHYLLIS [*hesitating*] It do seem a pity, dont it, my lady, to spoil your lovely bust?

ADOLPHUS. Tush! This craze for fine art is beyond all bounds. Off with you [*he pushes her out*]. Drink, drink, drink! My entrails are parched. Drink! [*he rushes deliriously to the gazogene*].

FITZ [*rushing after him*] Madman, you forget! It is poisoned!

ADOLPHUS. I dont care. Drink, drink! [*They wrestle madly for the gazogene. In the struggle they squirt all its contents away, mostly into one another's face. Adolphus at last flings Fitztollemache to the floor, and puts the spout into his mouth*]. Empty! empty! [*with a shriek of despair he collapses on the bed, clasping the gazogene like a baby, and weeping over it*].

FITZ [*aside to Magnesia*] Magnesia: I have always pretended not to notice it; but you keep a siphon for your private use in my hat-box.

MAGNESIA. I use it for washing old lace; but no matter: he shall have it [*she produces a siphon from the hat-box, and offers a tumbler of soda-water to Adolphus*].

ADOLPHUS. Thanks, thanks, oh, thanks! [*he drinks. A terrific fizzing is heard. He starts up screaming*] Help! help! The ceiling is effervescing! I am BURSTING! [*He wallows convulsively on the bed*].

FITZ. Quick! the rug strap! [*They pack him with blankets and strap him*]. Is that tight enough?

MAGNESIA [*anxiously*] Will you hold, do you think?

ADOLPHUS. The peril is past. The soda-water has gone flat.

MAGNESIA and FITZ. Thank heaven!

Phyllis returns with a washstand ewer,* in which she has dissolved the bust.

MAGNESIA [*snatching it*] At last!

FITZ. You are saved. Drain it to the dregs.

Fitztollemache* holds the lip of the ewer to Adolphus's mouth and gradually raises it until it stands upside down. Adolphus's efforts to swallow it are *fearful, Phyllis thumping his back when he chokes, and Magnesia loosening the straps when he moans. At last, with a sigh of relief, he sinks back in the women's arms. Fitz shakes the empty ewer upside down like a potman shaking the froth out of a flagon.**

ADOLPHUS. How inexpressibly soothing to the chest! A delicious numbness steals through all my members. I would sleep.

MAGNESIA ⎫

FITZ   ⎬ *[whispering]* Let him sleep.

PHYLLIS ⎭

He sleeps. Celestial harps are heard; but their chords cease* on the abrupt entrance of the landlord, a vulgar person in pyjamas.

THE LANDLORD. Eah! Eah! Wots this? Wots all this noise? Ah kin ennybody sleep through it? *[Looking at the floor and ceiling]* Ellow! wot you bin doin te maw ceilin?

FITZ. Silence, or leave the room. If you wake that man he dies.

THE LANDLORD. If e kin sleep through the noise you three mikes e kin sleep through ennythink.

MAGNESIA. Detestable vulgarian: your pronunciation jars on the finest chords of my nature. Begone!

THE LANDLORD *[looking at Adolphus]* Aw downt blieve eze esleep. Aw blieve eze dead. *[Calling]* Pleece! Pleece! Merder! *[A blue halo plays mysteriously on the door, which opens and reveals a policeman. Thunder]*. Eah, pleecmin: these three's bin an merdered this gent between em, an naw tore moy ahse dahn.**

THE POLICEMAN *[offended]* Policeman, indeed! Wheres your manners?

FITZ. Officer—

THE POLICEMAN *[with distinguished consideration]* Sir?

FITZ. As between gentlemen—

THE POLICEMAN *[bowing]* Sir: to you.

FITZ *[bowing]* I may inform you that my friend had an acute attack of indigestion. No carbonate of soda being available, he swallowed a portion of this man's ceiling. *[Pointing to Adolphus]* Behold the result!

THE POLICEMAN. The ceiling was poisoned! Well, of all the artful— [*he collars the landlord*]. I arrest you for wilful murder.

THE LANDLORD [*appealing to the heavens*] Ow, is this jestice! Ah could aw tell e wiz gowin te eat moy ceilin?

THE POLICEMAN [*releasing him*] True. The case is more complicated than I thought. [*He tries to lift Adolphus's arm but cannot*]. Stiff already.

THE LANDLORD [*trying to lift Adolphus's leg*] An' precious evvy. [*Feeling the calf*] Woy, eze gorn ez awd ez niles.*

FITZ [*rushing to the bed*] What is this?

MAGNESIA. Oh, say not he is dead. Phyllis: fetch a doctor. [*Phyllis runs out. They all try to lift Adolphus; but he is perfectly stiff, and as heavy as lead*]. Rouse him. Shake him.

THE POLICEMAN [*exhausted*] Whew!* Is he a man or a statue? [*Magnesia utters a piercing scream*]. Whats wrong, Miss?

MAGNESIA [*to Fitz*] Do you not see what has happened?

FITZ [*striking his forehead*] Horror on horror's head!

THE LANDLORD. Wotjemean?

MAGNESIA. The plaster has set inside him. The officer was right: he is indeed a living statue.

Magnesia flings herself on the stony breast of Adolphus. Fitztollemache buries his head in his hands; and his chest heaves convulsively. The policeman takes a small volume from his pocket and consults it.

THE POLICEMAN. This case is not provided for in my book of instructions. It dont seem no use trying artificial respiration, do it? [*To the landlord*] Here! lend a hand, you. We'd best take him and set him up in Trafalgar Square.*

THE LANDLORD. Aushd pat im in the cestern an worsh it aht of im.*

Phyllis comes back with a Doctor.

PHYLLIS. The medical man, my lady.

THE POLICEMAN. A poison case, sir.

THE DOCTOR. Do you mean to say that an unqualified person! a layman! has dared to administer poison in my district?

THE POLICEMAN [*raising Magnesia tenderly*] It looks like it. Hold up, my lady.

THE DOCTOR. Not a moment must be lost. The patient must be kept awake at all costs. Constant and violent motion is necessary.

He snatches Magnesia from the policeman, and rushes her about the room.

FITZ. Stop! That is not the poisoned person!

THE DOCTOR. It is you, then. Why did you not say so before?

He seizes Fitztollemache and rushes him about.

THE LANDLORD. Naow, naow, thet ynt im.

THE DOCTOR. What, you!

He pounces on the landlord and rushes him round.

THE LANDLORD. Eah! chack it.* [*He trips the doctor up. Both fall*]. Jest owld this leoonatic, will you, Mister Horficer?*

THE POLICEMAN [*dragging both of them to their feet*] Come out of it, will you. You must all come with me to the station.

Thunder.

MAGNESIA. What! In this frightful storm!

The hail patters noisily on the window.

PHYLLIS. I think it's raining.

The wind howls.

THE LANDLORD. It's thanderin and lawtnin.

FITZ. It's dangerous.

THE POLICEMAN [*drawing his baton and whistle*] If you wont come quietly, then—

He whistles. A fearful flash is followed by an appalling explosion of heaven's artillery. A thunderbolt enters the room, and strikes the helmet of the devoted constable, whence it is attracted to the waistcoat of the doctor by the lancet* in his pocket. Finally it leaps with fearful force on the landlord, who, being of a gross and spongy nature, absorbs the electric fluid at the cost of his life. The others look on horror-stricken as the three victims, after reeling, jostling, cannoning through a ghastly quadrille,* at last sink inanimate on the carpet.

MAGNESIA [*listening at the doctor's chest*] Dead!

FITZ [*kneeling by the landlord, and raising his hand, which drops with a thud*] Dead!

PHYLLIS [*seizing the looking-glass and holding it to the Policeman's lips*] Dead!

FITZ [*solemnly rising*] The copper* attracted the lightning.

MAGNESIA [*rising*] After life's fitful fever they sleep well.* Phyllis: sweep them up.

Phyllis replaces the looking-glass on the dressing-table; takes up the fan; and fans the policeman, who rolls away like a leaf before the wind to the wall. She disposes similarly of the landlord and doctor.

PHYLLIS. Will they be in your way if I leave them there until morning, my lady? Or shall I bring up the ashpan* and take them away?

MAGNESIA. They will not disturb us. Goodnight, Phyllis.

PHYLLIS. Goodnight, my lady. Goodnight, sir.

She retires.

MAGNESIA. And now, husband, let us perform our last sad duty to our friend. He has become his own monument. Let us erect him. He is heavy; but love can do much.

FITZ. A little leverage will get him on his feet. Give me my umbrella.

MAGNESIA. True.

She hands him the umbrella, and takes up the bootjack. They get them under Adolphus's back, and prize him up on his feet.

FITZ. Thats done it! Whew!

MAGNESIA [*kneeling at the left hand of the statue*] For ever and for ever, Adolphus.

FITZ [*kneeling at the right hand of the statue*] The rest is silence.*

*The Angels sing Bill Bailey. The statue raises its hands in an attitude of blessing, and turns its limelit face to heaven as the curtain falls. National Anthem.**

ATTENDANTS [*in front*] All out for the next performance. Pass along, please, ladies and gentlemen: pass along.

PRESS CUTTINGS*

A TOPICAL SKETCH COMPILED FROM THE EDITORIAL
AND CORRESPONDENCE COLUMNS OF THE DAILY
PAPERS DURING THE WOMEN'S WAR IN 1909

PREFACE

By direction of the Lord Chamberlain* the General and the Prime Minister in this play must in all public performances of it be addressed and described as General Bones and Mr Johnson,* and by no means as General Mitchener and Mr Balsquith. The allusions to commoner persons are allowed to stand as they are.

General Mitchener, by the way, is not the late Lord Kitchener,* but an earlier and more highly connected commander. Balsquith (Balfour-Asquith*) is obviously neither of these statesmen, and cannot in the course of nature be both.

PRESS CUTTINGS

The forenoon of the first of April,* three years hence.*

General Mitchener is at his writing-table in the War Office,* opening letters. On his left is the fireplace, with a fire burning. On his right, against the opposite wall, is a standing desk with an office stool. The door is in the wall behind him, half way between the table and the desk. The table is not quite in the middle of the room: it is nearer to the hearthrug than to the desk. There is a chair at each end of it for persons having business with the General. There is a telephone on the table.

Long silence.

A VOICE FROM THE STREET. Votes for Women!*

The General starts convulsively; snatches a revolver from a drawer; and listens in an agony of apprehension. Nothing happens. He puts the revolver back, ashamed; wipes his brow; and resumes his work. He is startled afresh by the entry of an Orderly.* This Orderly is an unsoldierly, slovenly, discontented young man.

MITCHENER. Oh, it's only you. Well?

THE ORDERLY. Another one, sir. She's chained herself.

MITCHENER. Chained herself? How? To what? Weve taken away the railings and everything that a chain can be passed through.

THE ORDERLY. We forgot the door-scraper,* sir. She lay down on the flags* and got the chain through before she started hollerin. She's lyin there now; and she downfaces* us that youve got the key of the padlock in a letter in a buff envelope, and that youll see her when you open it.

MITCHENER. She's mad. Have the scraper dug up and let her go home with it hanging round her neck.

THE ORDERLY. There *is* a buff envelope there, sir.

MITCHENER. Youre all afraid of these women.* [*He picks the letter up*] It does seem to have a key in it. [*He opens the letter; takes out a key and a note; and reads*] 'Dear Mitch'—Well, I'm dashed!*

THE ORDERLY. Yes, sir.

MITCHENER. What do you mean by Yes, sir?

THE ORDERLY. Well, you said you was dashed, sir; and you did look—if youll excuse my saying it, sir—well, you looked it.

MITCHENER [*who has been reading the letter, and is too astonished to attend to the Orderly's reply*] This is a letter from the Prime Minister asking me to release the woman with this key if she padlocks herself, and to have her shewn up and see her at once.

THE ORDERLY [*tremulously*] Dont do it, governor.

MITCHENER [*angrily*] How often have I ordered you not to address me as governor? Remember that you are a soldier and not a vulgar civilian. Remember also that when a man enters the army he leaves fear behind him. Heres the key. Unlock her and shew her up.

THE ORDERLY. *Me* unlock her! I dursent.* Lord knows what she'd do to me.

MITCHENER [*pepperily,* rising*] Obey your orders instantly, sir; and dont presume to argue. Even if she kills you, it is your duty to die for your country. Right about face.* March.

The Orderly goes out, trembling.

THE VOICE OUTSIDE. Votes for Women! Votes for Women! Votes for Women!

MITCHENER [*mimicking her*] Votes for Women! Votes for Women! Votes for Women! [*In his natural voice*] Votes for children! Votes for babies! Votes for monkeys!* [*He posts himself on the hearthrug and awaits the enemy*].

THE ORDERLY [*outside*] In you go. [*He pushes a panting Suffraget* into the room*] The person, sir. [*He withdraws*].

The Suffraget takes off her tailor-made skirt and reveals a pair of fashionable trousers.

MITCHENER [*horrified*] Stop, madam. What are you doing? you must not undress in my presence. I protest. Not even your letter from the Prime Minister—

THE SUFFRAGET. My dear Mitchener: I *am* the Prime Minister. [*He takes off his hat and cloak; throws them on the desk; and confronts the General in the ordinary costume of a Cabinet Minister*].

MITCHENER. Good heavens! Balsquith!*

BALSQUITH [*throwing himself into Mitchener's chair*] Yes: it is indeed Balsquith. It has come to this: that the only way the Prime Minister of England can get from Downing Street to the War Office is by assuming this disguise; shrieking 'VOTES FOR WOMEN'; and chaining himself to your doorscraper. They were at the corner in force. They cheered me. Bellachristina* herself was there. She shook my hand and told me to say I was a vegetarian, as the diet was better in Holloway* for vegetarians.

MITCHENER. Why didnt you telephone?

BALSQUITH. They tap the telephone. Every switchboard in London is in their hands, or in those of their young men.

MITCHENER. Where on earth did you get the dress? I hope it's not a French dress!

BALSQUITH. Great heavens, no. We're not allowed even to put on our gloves with French chalk.* Everything's labelled 'Made in Camberwell.'*

MITCHENER. As a Tariff Reformer,* I must say Quite right. [*Balsquith has a strong controversial impulse and is evidently going to dispute this profession of faith*]. No matter. Dont argue. What have you come for?

BALSQUITH. Sandstone* has resigned.

MITCHENER [*amazed*] Old Red resigned!

BALSQUITH. Resigned.

MITCHENER. But how? Why? Oh, impossible! the proclamation of martial law last Tuesday made Sandstone virtually Dictator in the metropolis; and to resign now is flat desertion.

BALSQUITH. Yes, yes, my dear Mitchener: I know all that as well as you do: I argued with him until I was black in the face, and he so red about the neck that if I had gone on he would have burst. He is furious because we have abandoned his plan.

MITCHENER. But you accepted it unconditionally.

BALSQUITH. Yes, before we knew what it was. It was unworkable, you know.

MITCHENER. I *dont* know. Why is it unworkable?

BALSQUITH. I mean the part about drawing a cordon round Westminster* at a distance of two miles, and turning all women out of it.

MITCHENER. A masterpiece of strategy. Let me explain. The Suffragets are a very small body; but they are numerous enough to be troublesome—even dangerous—when they are all concentrated in one place—say in Parliament Square.* But by making a two-mile radius and pushing them beyond it, you scatter their attack over a circular line twelve miles long. Just what Wellington* would have done.

BALSQUITH. But the women wont go.

MITCHENER. Nonsense: they must go.

BALSQUITH. They wont.

MITCHENER. What does Sandstone say?

BALSQUITH. He says: Shoot them down.

MITCHENER. Of course.

BALSQUITH. Youre not serious?

MITCHENER. I'm perfectly serious.

BALSQUITH. But you cant shoot them down! Women, you know!

MITCHENER [*straddling confidently*] Yes you can. Strange as it may seem to you as a civilian, Balsquith, if you point a rifle at a woman and fire it, she will drop exactly as a man drops.

BALSQUITH. But suppose your own daughters—Helen and Georgina*—

MITCHENER. My daughters would not dream of disobeying the proclamation. [*As an afterthought*] At least Helen wouldnt.

BALSQUITH. But Georgina?

MITCHENER. Georgina would if she knew she'd be shot if she didnt. Thats how the thing would work. Military methods are really the most merciful in the end. You keep sending these misguided women to Holloway and killing them slowly and inhumanly by ruining their health; and it does no good: they go on worse than ever. Shoot a few, promptly and humanely; and there will be an end at once of all resistance and of all the suffering that resistance entails.

BALSQUITH. But public opinion would never stand it.

MITCHENER [*walking about and laying down the law*] Theres no such thing as public opinion.

BALSQUITH. No such thing as public opinion!!

MITCHENER. Absolutely no such thing. There are certain persons who entertain certain opinions. Well, shoot them down. When you have shot them down, there are no longer any persons entertaining those opinions alive; consequently there is no longer any more of the public opinion you are so much afraid of. Grasp that fact, my dear Balsquith; and you have grasped the secret of government. Public opinion is mind. Mind is inseparable from matter. Shoot down the matter and you kill the mind.

BALSQUITH. But hang it all—

MITCHENER [*intolerantly*] No I wont hang it all. It's no use coming to me and talking about public opinion. You have put yourself into the hands of the army; and you are committed to military methods. And the basis of all military methods is that when people wont do what theyre told to do, you shoot them down.

BALSQUITH. Oh yes; it's all jolly fine for you and Old Red. You dont depend on votes for your places. What do you suppose would happen at the next election?

MITCHENER. Have no next election. Bring in a Bill* at once repealing all the Reform Acts* and vesting the Government in a properly trained magistracy responsible only to a Council of War.* It answers perfectly in India.* If anyone objects, shoot him down.

BALSQUITH. But none of the members of my party would be on the Council of War. Neither should I. Do you expect us to vote for making ourselves nobodies?

MITCHENER. Youll have to, sooner or later, or the Socialists will make nobodies of the lot of you by collaring every penny you possess. Do you suppose this damned democracy can be allowed to go on now that the mob is beginning to take it seriously and using its power to lay hands on property? Parliament must abolish itself. The Irish parliament voted for its own extinction.* The English parliament will do the same if the same means are taken to persuade it.

BALSQUITH. That would cost a lot of money.

MITCHENER. Not money necessarily. Bribe them with titles.

BALSQUITH. Do you think we dare?

MITCHENER [*scornfully*] Dare! Dare! What is life but daring, man? 'To dare, to dare, and again to dare—'*

FEMALE VOICE IN THE STREET. Votes for Women! [*Mitchener, revolver in hand, rushes to the door and locks it. Balsquith hides under the table*]. Votes for Women!

A shot is heard.

BALSQUITH [*emerging in the greatest alarm*] Good heavens, you havent given orders to fire on them: have you?

MITCHENER. No: but it's a sentinel's duty to fire on anyone who persists in attempting to pass without giving the word.

BALSQUITH [*wiping his brow*] This military business is really awful.

MITCHENER. Be calm, Balsquith. These things must happen: they save bloodshed in the long run, believe me. Ive seen plenty of it; and I know.

BALSQUITH. I havnt; and I dont know. I wish those guns didnt make such a devil of a noise. We must adopt Maxim's Silencer* for the army rifles if we're going to shoot women. I really couldnt stand hearing it. [*Someone outside tries to open the door and then knocks*]. Whats that?

MITCHENER. Who's there?

THE ORDERLY. It's only me, governor. It's all right.

MITCHENER [*unlocking the door and admitting the Orderly, who comes between them*] What was it?

THE ORDERLY. Suffraget, sir.

BALSQUITH. Did the sentry shoot her?

THE ORDERLY. No, sir: she shot the sentry.

BALSQUITH [*relieved*] Oh: is that all?

MITCHENER [*most indignantly*] All! A civilian shoots down one of His Majesty's soldiers on duty; and the Prime Minister of England asks, Is that all?!!! Have you no regard for the sanctity of human life?*

BALSQUITH [*much relieved*] Well, getting shot is what a soldier is for.* Besides, he doesnt vote.

MITCHENER. Neither do the Suffragets.

BALSQUITH. Their husbands do. [*To the Orderly*] Did she kill him?

THE ORDERLY. No, sir. He got a stinger on his trousers, sir; but it didnt penetrate. He lost his temper a bit and put down his gun and clouted her head for her. So she said he was no gentleman; and we let her go, thinking she'd had enough, sir.

MITCHENER [*groaning*] Clouted her head! These women are making the army as lawless as themselves. Clouted her head indeed! A purely civil procedure.

THE ORDERLY. Any orders, sir?

MITCHENER. No. Yes. No. Yes: send everybody who took part in this disgraceful scene to the guard-room. No. I'll address the men on the subject after lunch. Parade them for that purpose: full kit. Dont grin at me, sir. Right about face. March.

The Orderly obeys and goes out.

BALSQUITH [*taking Mitchener affectionately by the arm and walking him persuasively to and fro*] And now, Mitchener, will you come to the rescue of the Government and take the command that Old Red has thrown up?

MITCHENER. How can I? You know that the people are devoted heart and soul to Sandstone. He is only bringing you 'on the knee,' as we say in the army. Could any other living man have persuaded the British nation to accept universal compulsory military service* as he did last year? Why, even the Church refused exemption. He is supreme—omnipotent.

BALSQUITH. He *was*, a year ago. But ever since your book of reminiscences went into two more editions than his, and the rush for it led to the wrecking of the Times Book Club,* you have become to all intents and purposes his senior. He lost ground by saying that the wrecking was got up by the booksellers. It shewed jealousy; and the public felt it.

MITCHENER. But I cracked him up in my book—you see I could do no less after the handsome way he cracked me up in his—and I cant go back on it now. [*Breaking loose from Balsquith*] No: it's no use, Balsquith: he can dictate his terms to you.

BALSQUITH. Not a bit of it. That affair of the curate—*

MITCHENER [*impatiently*] Oh, damn that curate. Ive heard of nothing but that wretched mutineer for a fortnight past. He's not a curate: whilst he's serving in the army he's a private soldier and nothing else. I really havnt time to discuss him further. I'm busy. Good morning. [*He sits down at his table and takes up his letters*].

BALSQUITH [*near the door*] I'm sorry you take that tone, Mitchener. Since you *do* take it, let me tell you frankly that I think Lieutenant Chubbs-Jenkinson* shewed a great want of consideration for the Government in giving an unreasonable and unpopular order, and bringing compulsory military service into disrepute.

MITCHENER. No order is unreasonable; and all orders are unpopular.

BALSQUITH. When the leader of the Labor Party* appealed to me and to the House* last year not to throw away all the liberties of Englishmen by accepting compulsory military service without full civil rights for the soldier—

MITCHENER. Rot.

BALSQUITH. —I said that no British officer would be capable of abusing the authority with which it was absolutely necessary to invest him.

MITCHENER. Quite right.

BALSQUITH. That carried the House;—

MITCHENER. Naturally.

BALSQUITH. —and the feeling was that the Labor Party were soulless cads.

MITCHENER. So they are.

BALSQUITH. And now comes this unmannerly young whelp Chubbs-Jenkinson, the only son of what they call a soda king,* and orders a curate to lick his boots. And when the curate punches his head, you first sentence him to be shot; and then make a great show of clemency by commuting it to a flogging. What did you expect the curate to do?

MITCHENER [*throwing down his pen and his letters and jumping up to confront Balsquith*] His duty was perfectly simple. He should have obeyed the order; and then laid his complaint against the officer in proper form. He would have received the fullest satisfaction.

BALSQUITH. What satisfaction?

MITCHENER. Chubbs-Jenkinson would have been reprimanded. In fact, he *was* reprimanded. Besides, the man was thoroughly insubordinate. You cant deny that the very first thing he did when they took him down after flogging him was to walk up to Chubbs-Jenkinson and break his jaw. That shewed there was no use flogging him; so now he will get two years' hard labor; and serve him right!

BALSQUITH. I bet you a guinea he wont get even a week. I bet you another that Chubbs-Jenkinson apologizes abjectly. You evidently havnt heard the news.

MITCHENER. What news?

BALSQUITH. It turns out that the curate is well connected. [*Mitchener staggers at the shock. He reels into his chair and buries his face in his hands over the blotter*]. He has three aunts in the peerage; Lady Richmond's one of them [*Mitchener punctuates these announcements with heartrending groans*]; and they all adore him. The invitations for six garden parties and fourteen dances have been cancelled for all the subalterns* in Chubbs's regiment. [*Mitchener attempts to shoot himself*].

BALSQUITH [*seizing the pistol*] No: your country needs you, Mitchener.

MITCHENER [*putting down the pistol*] For my country's sake. [*Balsquith, reassured, sits down*]. But what an infernal young fool Chubbs-Jenkinson is, not to know the standing of his man better! Why didnt he know? It was his business to know. He ought to be flogged.

BALSQUITH. Probably he will be, by the other subalterns.

MITCHENER. I hope so. Anyhow, out he goes. Out of the army. He or I.

BALSQUITH. Steady, steady. His father has subscribed a million to the party funds. *We* owe him a peerage.*

MITCHENER. I dont care.

BALSQUITH. I do. How do you think parties are kept up? Not by the subscriptions of the local associations, I hope. They dont pay for the gas at the meetings.

MITCHENER. Man: can you not be serious? Here are we, face to face with Lady Richmond's grave displeasure; and you talk to me about gas and subscriptions. Her own nephew!!!!!

BALSQUITH [*gloomily*] It's unfortunate. He was at Oxford with Bobby Bessborough.*

MITCHENER. Worse and worse. What shall we do?

A VOICE IN THE STREET. Votes for Women! Votes for Women!

A terrific explosion shakes the building. They take no notice.

MITCHENER [*breaking down*] You dont know what this means to me, Balsquith. I love the army. I love my country.

BALSQUITH. It certainly is rather awkward.

The Orderly comes in.

MITCHENER [*angrily*] What is it? How dare you interrupt us like this?

THE ORDERLY. Didnt you hear the explosion, sir?

MITCHENER. Explosion. What explosion? No: I heard no explosion: I have something more serious to attend to than explosions. Great Heavens! Lady Richmond's nephew has been treated like any common laborer; and while England is reeling under the shock, a private walks in and asks me if I heard an explosion.

BALSQUITH. By the way, what was the explosion?

THE ORDERLY. Only a sort of bombshell, sir.

BALSQUITH. Bombshell!

THE ORDERLY. A pasteboard one,* sir. Full of papers with Votes for Women in red letters. Fired into the yard from the roof of the Alliance Office.*

MITCHENER. Pooh! Go away. GO away.

The Orderly, bewildered, goes out.

BALSQUITH. Mitchener: you can save the country yet. Put on your full dress uniform and your medals and orders and so forth. Get a guard of honor—something showy—horse guards or something of that sort; and call on the old girl—

MITCHENER. The old girl?

BALSQUITH. Well, Lady Richmond. Apologize to her. Ask her leave to accept the command. Tell her that youve made the curate your adjutant or your aide-de-camp* or whatever is the proper thing. By the way, what *can* you make him?

MITCHENER. I might make him my chaplain. I dont see why I shouldnt have a chaplain on my staff. He shewed a very proper spirit in punching that young cub's head. I should have done the same myself.

BALSQUITH. Then Ive your promise to take command if Lady Richmond consents?

MITCHENER. On condition that I have a free hand. No nonsense about public opinion or democracy.

BALSQUITH. As far as possible, I think I may say yes.

MITCHENER [*rising intolerantly and going to the hearthrug*] That wont do for me. Dont be weak-kneed, Balsquith. You know perfectly well that the real government of this country is and always must be the government of the masses by the classes. You know that democracy is damned nonsense, and that no class stands less of it than the working class. You know that we are already discussing the steps that will have to be taken if the country should ever be face to face with the possibility of a Labor majority in Parliament. You know that in that case we should disfranchise the mob, and if they made a fuss, shoot them down. You know that if we need public opinion to support us, we can get any quantity of it manufactured in our papers by poor devils of journalists who will sell their souls for five shillings. You know——

BALSQUITH. Stop. Stop, I say. I dont know. That is the difference between your job and mine, Mitchener. After twenty years in the army a man thinks he knows everything. After twenty months in the Cabinet he knows that he knows nothing.

MITCHENER. We learn from history——

BALSQUITH. We learn from history that men never learn anything from history. That's not my own: it's Hegel.*

MITCHENER. Who's Hegel?

BALSQUITH. Dead. A German philosopher. [*He half rises, but recollects something and sits down again*]. Oh, confound it: that reminds me. The Germans have laid down four more Dreadnoughts.*

MITCHENER. Then you must lay down twelve.

BALSQUITH. Oh yes: it's easy to say that; but think of what theyll cost.

MITCHENER. Think of what it would cost to be invaded by Germany and forced to pay an indemnity of five hundred millions.

BALSQUITH. But you said that if you got compulsory military service there would be an end of the danger of invasion.

MITCHENER. On the contrary, my dear fellow, it increases the danger tenfold, because it increases German jealousy of our military supremacy.

BALSQUITH. After all, why should the Germans invade us?

MITCHENER. Why shouldnt they? What else has their army to do? What else are they building a navy for?

BALSQUITH. Well, we never think of invading Germany.

MITCHENER. Yes, we do. I have thought of nothing else for the last ten years. Say what you will, Balsquith, the Germans have never recognized, and until they get a stern lesson they never *will* recognize, the plain fact that the interests of the British Empire are paramount, and that the command of the sea belongs by nature to England.

BALSQUITH. But if they wont recognize it, what can I do?

MITCHENER. Shoot them down.

BALSQUITH. I *cant* shoot them down.

MITCHENER. Yes you can. You dont realize it; but if you fire a rifle into a German he drops just as surely as a rabbit does.

BALSQUITH. But dash it all, man, a rabbit hasnt got a rifle and a German has. Suppose he shoots you down.

MITCHENER. Excuse me, Balsquith; but that consideration is what we call cowardice in the army. A soldier always assumes that he is going to shoot, not to be shot.

BALSQUITH [*jumping up and walking about sulkily*] Oh come! I like to hear you military people talking of cowardice. Why, you spend your lives in an ecstasy of terror of imaginary invasions. I dont believe you ever go to bed without looking under it for a burglar.

MITCHENER [*calmly*] A very sensible precaution, Balsquith. I always take it; and, in consequence, Ive never been burgled.

BALSQUITH. Neither have I. Anyhow, dont you taunt me with cowardice. [*He posts himself on the hearthrug beside Mitchener, on his left*]. I never look under my bed for a burglar. I'm not always looking under the nation's bed for an invader. And if it comes to fighting, I'm quite willing to fight without being three to one.

MITCHENER. These are the romantic ravings of a Jingo civilian,* Balsquith. At least youll not deny that the absolute command of the sea is essential to our security.

BALSQUITH. The absolute command of the sea is essential to the security of the principality of Monaco. But Monaco isnt going to get it.

MITCHENER. And consequently Monaco enjoys no security.* What a frightful thing! How do the inhabitants sleep with the possibility of invasion, of bombardment, continually present to their minds? Would you have our English slumbers broken in the same way? Are we also to live without security?

BALSQUITH [*dogmatically*] Yes. Theres no such thing as security in the world; and there never can be as long as men are mortal. England will be secure when England is dead, just as the streets of London will be safe when theres no longer a man in her streets to be run over or a vehicle to run over him. When you military chaps ask for security you are crying for the moon.

MITCHENER [*very seriously*] Let me tell you, Balsquith, that in these days of aeroplanes and Zeppelin airships* the question of the moon is becoming one of the greatest importance. It will be reached at no very distant date. Can you, as an Englishman, tamely contemplate the possibility of having to live under a German moon? The British flag must be planted there at all hazards.

BALSQUITH. My dear Mitchener, the moon is outside practical politics. I'd swop it for a coaling-station* tomorrow with Germany or any other Power sufficiently military in its way of thinking to attach any importance to it.

MITCHENER [*losing his temper*] You are the friend of every country but your own.

BALSQUITH. Say nobody's enemy but my own. It sounds nicer. You really neednt be so horribly afraid of the other countries. Theyre all in the same fix as we are. I'm much more interested in the death-rate in Lambeth* than in the German fleet.

MITCHENER. You darent say that in Lambeth.

BALSQUITH. I'll say it the day after you publish your scheme for invading Germany and repealing all the Reform Acts.

The Orderly comes in.

MITCHENER. What do you want?

THE ORDERLY. I dont want anything, governor, thank you. The secretary and president of the Anti-Suffraget League says they had an appointment with the Prime Minister, and that theyve been sent on here from Downing Street.

BALSQUITH [*going to the table*] Quite right. I forgot them. [*To Mitchener*] Would you mind my seeing them here? I feel extraordinarily grateful to these women for standing by us and facing the Suffragets, especially as they are naturally the gentler and timider sort of women. [*The Orderly moans*]. Did you say anything?

THE ORDERLY. No, sir.

BALSQUITH. Did you catch their names?

THE ORDERLY. Yes, sir. The president is Lady Corinthia Fanshawe;* and the secretary is Mrs Banger.

MITCHENER [*abruptly*] Mrs what?

THE ORDERLY. Mrs Banger.

BALSQUITH. Curious that quiet people always seem to have violent names.

THE ORDERLY. Not much quiet about *her*, sir.

MITCHENER [*outraged*] Attention! Speak when youre spoken to. Hold your tongue when youre not. Right about face. March. [*The Orderly obeys*]. Thats the way to keep these chaps up to the mark. [*The Orderly returns*]. Back again! What do you mean by this mutiny?

THE ORDERLY. What am I to say to the ladies, sir?

BALSQUITH. You dont mind my seeing them somewhere, do you?

MITCHENER. Not at all. Bring them in to see me when youve done with them. I understand that Lady Corinthia is a very fascinating woman. Who is she, by the way?

BALSQUITH. Daughter of Lord Broadstairs,* the automatic turbine man.* Gave quarter of a million to the party funds. She's musical and romantic and all that—dont hunt: hates politics: stops in town all the year round: one never sees her except at the opera and at musical at-homes and so forth.

MITCHENER. What a life! [*To the Orderly*] Where are the ladies?

THE ORDERLY. In No. 17, sir.

MITCHENER. Shew Mr Balsquith there; and send Mrs Farrell here.

THE ORDERLY [*calling into the corridor*] Mrs Farrell! [*To Balsquith*] This way, sir. [*He goes out with Balsquith*].

Mrs Farrell, a lean, highly respectable Irish charwoman of about fifty, comes in.*

MITCHENER. Mrs Farrell: Ive a very important visit to pay: I shall want my full dress uniform and all my medals and orders and my presentation sword. There was a time when the British Army contained men capable of discharging these duties for their commanding officer. Those days are over. The compulsorily enlisted soldier runs to a woman for everything. I'm therefore reluctantly obliged to trouble you.

MRS FARRELL. Your meddles n ordhers n the crooked sword widh the ivory handle n your full dress uniform is in the wax-works in the Chamber o Military Glory* over in the place they used to call the Banquetin Hall. I told you youd be sorry for sendin them away; and you told me to mind me own business. Youre wiser now.

MITCHENER. I am. I had not at that time discovered that you were the only person in the whole military establishment of this capital who could be trusted to remember where anything was, or to understand an order and obey it.

MRS FARRELL. It's no good flattherin me. I'm too old.

MITCHENER. Not at all, Mrs Farrell. How is your daughter?

MRS FARRELL. Which daughter?

MITCHENER. The one who has made such a gratifying success in the Music Halls.*

MRS FARRELL. Theres no Music Halls nowadays: theyre Variety Theatres.* She's got an offer of marriage from a young jook.*

MITCHENER. Is it possible? What did you do?

MRS FARRELL. I told his mother on him.

MITCHENER. Oh! What did she say?

MRS FARRELL. She was as pleased as Punch.* Thank Heaven, she says, he's got somebody thatll be able to keep him when the supertax is put up to twenty shillings in the pound.*

MITCHENER. But your daughter herself? What did she say?

MRS FARRELL. Accepted him, of course. What else would a young fool like her do? He inthrojooced her to the Poet Laureate* thinkin she'd inspire him.

MITCHENER. Did she?

MRS FARRELL. Faith, I dunna. All I know is she walked up to him as bold as brass n said, 'Write me a sketch, dear.' Afther all the throuble Ive took with that child's manners she's no more notion how to behave herself than a pig. Youll have to wear General Sandstone's uniform: it's the only one in the place, because he wont lend it to the shows.

MITCHENER. But Sandstone's clothes wont fit me.

MRS FARRELL [*unmoved*] Then youll have to fit *them*. Why shouldnt they fitchya as well as they fitted General Blake at the Mansion House?*

MITCHENER. They didnt fit him. He looked a frightful guy.

MRS FARRELL. Well, you must do the best you can with them. You cant exhibit your clothes and wear them too.

MITCHENER. And the public thinks the lot of a commanding officer a happy one! Oh, if they could only see the seamy* side of it. [*He returns to his table to resume work*].

MRS FARRELL. If they could only see the seamy side o General Sandstone's uniform, where his flask rubs agen the buckle of his braces, theyd tell him he ought to get a new one. Let alone the way he swears at me.

MITCHENER. When a man has risked his life on eight battlefields, Mrs Farrell, he has given sufficient proof of his self-control to be excused a little strong language.

MRS FARRELL. Would you put up with bad language from me because Ive risked me life eight times in childbed?

MITCHENER. My dear Mrs Farrell, you surely would not compare a risk of that harmless domestic kind to the fearful risks of the battlefield.

MRS FARRELL. I wouldnt compare risks run to bear livin people into the world to risks run to blow dhem out of it. A mother's risk is jooty: a soldier's is nothin but divilmint.*

MITCHENER [*nettled*] Let me tell you, Mrs Farrell, that if the men did not fight, the women would have to fight themselves. We spare you that at all events.

MRS FARRELL. You cant help yourselves. If three-quarters of you was killed we could replace you with the help of the other quarter. If three-quarters of us was killed how many people would there be in England in another generation? If it wasnt for that, the men'd put the fightin on us just as they put all the other dhrudgery. What would *you* do if we was all kilt? Would you go to bed and have twins?

MITCHENER. Really, Mrs Farrell, you must discuss these questions with a medical man. You make me blush, positively.

MRS FARRELL [*grumbling to herself*] A good job too. If I could have made Farrell blush I wouldnt have had to risk me life so often. You n your risks n your bravery n your self-conthrol indeed. 'Why dont you conthrol yourself?' I sez to Farrell. 'It's agen me religion,' he sez.

MITCHENER [*plaintively*] Mrs Farrell: youre a woman of very powerful mind. I'm not qualified to argue these delicate matters with you. I ask you to spare me, and to be good enough to take these clothes to Mr Balsquith when the ladies leave.

The Orderly comes in.

THE ORDERLY. Lady Corinthia Fanshawe and Mrs Banger want to see you, sir. Mr Balsquith told me to tell you.

MRS FARRELL. Theyve come about the vote. I dont know whether it's dhem dhat want it or dhem dhat doesnt want it: anyhow, theyre all alike when they get into a state about it. [*She goes out, having gathered Balsquith's Suffraget disguise from the desk*].

MITCHENER. Is Mr Balsquith not with them.

THE ORDERLY. No, sir. Couldnt stand Mrs Banger, I expect. Fair
caution* she is. [*Chuckling*] Couldnt help larfin when I sor im op it.*

MITCHENER [*highly incensed*] How dare you indulge in this unseemly
mirth in the presence of your commanding officer? Have you no
sense of a soldier's duty?

THE ORDERLY [*sadly*] I'm afraid I shant ever get the ang of it, sir. You
see, my father has a tidy little barber's business down off Shoreditch;*
and I was brought up to be chatty and easy-like with everybody. I tell
you, when I drew the number in the conscription it gev my old
mother the needle and it gev me the ump.* I should take it very kind,
sir, if youd let me off the drill* and let me shave you instead. Youd
appreciate my qualities then: you would indeed, sir. I shant never do
myself jastice at soljerin, sir. I cant bring myself to think of it as
proper work for a man with an active mind, as you might say, sir. Arf
of it's only ousemaidin; and tother arf is dress-up and make-believe.

MITCHENER. Stuff, sir. It's the easiest life in the world. Once you learn
your drill, all you have to do is to hold your tongue and obey your orders.

THE ORDERLY. But I do assure you, sir, arf the time theyre the wrong
orders; and I get into trouble when I obey them. The sergeant's*
orders is all right; but the officers dont know what theyre talkin about.
Why, the orses knows better sometimes. 'Fours,'* says Lieutenant*
Trevor at the gate of Bucknam Palace only this mornin when we was
on dooty for a State visit to the Coal Trust.* I was fourth man like in
the first file; and when I started the orse eld back; and the sergeant
was on to me straight. Threes,* you bally* fool, e whispers. An e was
on to me again about it when we come back, and called me a fathead,
e did. What am I to do, I says: the lieutenant's orders was fours,
I says. I'll shew you who's lieutenant here, e says. In future you
attend to my orders and not to iz, e says: what does e know about it?
e says. You didnt give me any orders, I says. Couldnt you see for
yourself there wasnt room for fours, e says: why cant you *think*?
General Mitchener tells me I'm not to think, but to obey orders,
I says. Is Mitchener your sergeant or am I? e says in his bullyin way.
You are, I says. Well, e says, you got to do what your sergeant tells
you: thats discipline, e says. And what am I to do for the General?
I says. Youre to let him talk, e says: thats what e's for.

MITCHENER [*groaning*] It is impossible for the human mind to conceive
anything more dreadful than this. Youre a disgrace to the service.

THE ORDERLY [*deeply wounded*] The service is a disgrace to me. When my mother's people pass me in the street with this uniform on, I ardly know which way to look. There never was a soldier in my family before.

MITCHENER. There never was anything else in mine, sir.

THE ORDERLY. My mother's second cousin was one of the Parkinsons o Stepney.* [*Almost in tears*] What do *you* know of the feelings of a respectable family in the middle station of life? I cant bear to be looked down on as a common soldier. Why cant my father be let buy my discharge? Youve done away with the soldier's right to ave his discharge bought for him by his relations.* The country didnt know you were going to do that or it'd never ave stood it. Is an Englishman to be made a mockery like this?

MITCHENER. Silence. Attention. Right about face. March.

THE ORDERLY [*retiring to the standing desk and bedewing it with passionate tears*] Oh that I should have lived to be spoke to as if I was the lowest of the low! Me! that has shaved a City o London alderman* wiv me own and.

MITCHENER. Poltroon.* Crybaby. Well, better disgrace yourself here than disgrace your country on the field of battle.

THE ORDERLY [*angrily coming to the table*] Who's going to disgrace his country on the field of battle? It's not fightin I object to: it's soljerin. Shew me a German and I'll ave a go at him as fast as you or any man. But to ave me time wasted like this, an be stuck in a sentry-box* at a street corner for an ornament to be stared at; and to be told 'right about face: march,' if I speak as one man to another: that aint pluck: that aint fightin: that aint patriotism: it's bein made a bloomin sheep of.

MITCHENER. A sheep has many valuable military qualities. Emulate them, dont disparage them.

THE ORDERLY. Oh, wots the good of talkin to you? If I wasnt a poor soldier I could punch your ed for forty shillins or a month. But because youre my commandin officer you deprive me of my right to a magistrate, and make a compliment of giving me two years ard* stead o shootin me. Why cant you take your chance the same as any civilian does?

MITCHENER [*rising majestically*] I search the pages of history in vain for a parallel to such a speech made by a private to a General. But for the coherence of your remarks I should conclude that you were drunk. As it is, you must be mad. You shall be placed under restraint at once. Call the guard.

THE ORDERLY. Call your grandmother. If you take one man off the doors the place'll be full of Suffragets before you can wink.

MITCHENER. Then arrest yourself; and off with you to the guard-room.

THE ORDERLY. What am I to arrest myself for?

MITCHENER. Thats nothing to you. You have your orders: obey them. Do you hear? Right about face. March.*

THE ORDERLY. How would *you* feel if you was told to right-about-face and march as if you was a door-mat?

MITCHENER. I should feel as if my country had spoken through the voice of my officer. I should feel proud and honored to be able to serve my country by obeying its commands. No thought of self, no vulgar preoccupation with my own petty vanity, could touch my mind at such a moment. To me my officer would not be a mere man: he would be for the moment—whatever his personal frailties—the incarnation of our national destiny.

THE ORDERLY. What I'm saying to you is the voice of old England a jolly sight more than all this rot that you get out of books. I'd rather be spoke to by a sergeant than by you. He tells me to go to hell when I challenges him to argue it out like a man. It aint polite; but it's English. What you say aint anything at all. You dont act on it yourself. You dont believe in it. Youd punch my head if I tried it on you; and serve me right. And look here. Heres another point for you to argue—

MITCHENER [*with a shriek of protest*] No—

Mrs Banger comes in followed by Lady Corinthia Fanshawe. Mrs Banger is a masculine woman of forty with a powerful voice and great physical strength. Lady Corinthia, who is also over thirty, is beautiful and romantic.

MRS BANGER [*throwing the door open decisively and marching straight to Mitchener*] Pray how much longer is the Anti-Suffraget League to be kept waiting? [*She passes him contemptuously and sits down with impressive confidence in the chair next the fireplace. Lady Corinthia takes the chair on the opposite side of the table with equal aplomb*].

MITCHENER. I'm extremely sorry. You really do not know what I have to put up with. This imbecile, incompetent, unsoldierly disgrace to the uniform he should never have been allowed to put on, ought to have shewn you in fifteen minutes ago.

THE ORDERLY. All I said was——

MITCHENER. Not another word. Attention. Right about face. March. [*The Orderly sits down doggedly*]. Get out of the room this instant, you fool; or I'll kick you out.

THE ORDERLY [*civilly*] I dont mind that, sir. It's human. It's English. Why couldn't you have said it before? [*He goes out*].

MITCHENER. Take no notice, I beg: these scenes are of daily occurrence now that we have compulsory service* under the command of the halfpenny papers.* Pray sit down.

LADY CORINTHIA
AND MRS BANGER } [*rising*] { Thank you. [*They sit down again*].

MITCHENER [*sitting down with a slight chuckle of satisfaction*] And now, ladies, to what am I indebted——

MRS BANGER. Let me introduce us. I am Rosa Carmina Banger: Mrs Banger, organizing secretary of the Anti-Suffraget League. This is Lady Corinthia Fanshawe, the president of the League, known in musical circles—*I* am not musical—as the Richmond Park nightingale.* A soprano. I am myself said to be almost a baritone; but I do not profess to understand these distinctions.

MITCHENER [*murmuring politely*] Most happy, I'm sure.

MRS BANGER. We have come to tell you plainly that the Anti-Suffragets are going to fight.

MITCHENER [*gallantly*] Oh, pray leave that to the men, Mrs Banger.

LADY CORINTHIA. We can no longer trust the men.

MRS BANGER. They have shewn neither the strength, the courage, nor the determination which are needed to combat women like the Suffragets.

LADY CORINTHIA. Nature is too strong for the combatants.

MRS BANGER. Physical struggles between persons of opposite sexes are unseemly.

LADY CORINTHIA. Demoralizing.

MRS BANGER. Insincere.

LADY CORINTHIA. They are merely embraces in disguise.

MRS BANGER. No such suspicion can attach to combats in which the antagonists are of the same sex.

LADY CORINTHIA. The Anti-Suffragets have resolved to take the field.

MRS BANGER. They will enforce the order of General Sandstone for the removal of all women from the two-mile radius—that is, all women except themselves.

MITCHENER. I am sorry to have to inform you, madam, that the Government has given up that project, and that General Sandstone has resigned in consequence.

MRS BANGER. That does not concern us in the least. We approve of the project and will see that it is carried out. We have spent a good deal of money arming ourselves; and we are not going to have that money thrown away through the pusillanimity* of a Cabinet of males.

MITCHENER. Arming yourselves! But, my dear ladies, under the latest proclamation women are strictly forbidden to carry chains, padlocks, tracts on the franchise, or weapons of any description.

LADY CORINTHIA [*producing an ivory-handled revolver and pointing it at his nose*] You little know your countrywomen, General Mitchener.

MITCHENER [*without flinching*] Madam: it is my duty to take possession of that weapon in accordance with the proclamation. Be good enough to put it down.

MRS BANGER [*producing an XVIII century horse pistol*]* Is it your duty to take possession of this also?

MITCHENER. That, madam, is not a weapon: it is a curiosity. If you would be kind enough to place it in some museum instead of pointing it at my head, I should be obliged to you.

MRS BANGER. This pistol, sir, was carried at Waterloo* by my grandmother.

MITCHENER. I presume you mean your grandfather.

MRS BANGER. You presume unwarrantably.

LADY CORINTHIA. Mrs Banger's grandmother commanded a canteen at that celebrated battle.

MRS BANGER. Who my grandfather was is a point that has never been quite clearly settled. I put my trust, not in my ancestors, but in my good sword, which is at my lodgings.

MITCHENER. Your sword!

MRS BANGER. The sword with which I slew five Egyptians with my own hand at Kassassin,* where I served as a trooper.

MITCHENER. Lord bless me! But was your sex never discovered?

MRS BANGER. It was never even suspected. I had a comrade—a gentleman ranker—whom they called Fanny. They never called *me* Fanny.

LADY CORINTHIA. The Suffragets have turned the whole woman movement on to the wrong track. They ask for a vote.

MRS BANGER. What use is a vote? Men have the vote.

LADY CORINTHIA. And men are slaves.

MRS BANGER. What women need is the right to military service. Give me a well-mounted regiment of women with sabres, opposed to a regiment of men with votes. We shall see which will go down before the other. No: we have had enough of these gentle pretty creatures who merely talk and cross-examine ministers in police courts,* and go to prison like sheep, and suffer and sacrifice themselves. This question must be solved by blood and iron, as was well said by Bismarck,* whom I have reason to believe was a woman in disguise.

MITCHENER. Bismarck a woman!

MRS BANGER. All the really strong men of history have been disguised women.

MITCHENER. [*remonstrating*] My dear lady!

MRS BANGER. How can you tell? You never knew that the hero of the charge at Kassassin was a woman: yet she was: it was I, Rosa Carmina Banger. Would Napoleon* have been so brutal to women, think you, had he been a man?

MITCHENER. Oh, come, come! Really! Surely female rulers have often shewn all the feminine weaknesses. Queen Elizabeth,* for instance. Her vanity, her levity—

MRS BANGER. Nobody who has studied the history of Queen Elizabeth can doubt for a moment that she was a disguised man.

LADY CORINTHIA [*admiring Mrs Banger*] Isnt she splendid!

MRS BANGER [*rising with a large gesture*] This very afternoon I shall cast off this hampering skirt for ever; mount my charger; and with my good sabre lead the Anti-Suffragets to victory. [*She strides to the other side of the room, snorting*].

MITCHENER. But I cant allow anything of the sort, madam. I shall stand no such ridiculous nonsense. I'm perfectly determined to put my foot down—

LADY CORINTHIA. Dont be hysterical, General.

MITCHENER. Hysterical!

MRS BANGER. Do you think we are to be stopped by these childish exhibitions of temper? They are useless; and your tears and entreaties—a man's last resource—will avail you just as little. I sweep them away, just as I sweep your plans of campaign 'made in Germany'—*

MITCHENER [*flying into a transport of rage*] How dare you repeat that infamous slander! [*He rings the bell violently*]. If this is the alternative to votes for women, I shall advocate giving every woman in the country six votes. [*The Orderly comes in*]. Remove that woman. See that she leaves the building at once.

The Orderly forlornly contemplates the iron front presented by Mrs Banger.

THE ORDERLY [*propitiatorily*] Would you ave the feelin art to step out, madam?

MRS BANGER. You are a soldier. Obey your orders. Put me out. If I got such an order I should not hesitate.

THE ORDERLY [*to Mitchener*] Would you mind lendin me a and, Guvner?

LADY CORINTHIA [*raising her revolver*]* I shall be obliged to shoot you if you stir, General.

MRS BANGER [*to the Orderly*] When you are ordered to put a person out you should do it like this. [*She hurls him from the room. He is heard falling headlong downstairs and crashing through a glass door*]. I shall now wait on General Sandstone. If he shews any sign of weakness, he shall share that poor wretch's fate. [*She goes out*].

LADY CORINTHIA. Isnt she magnificent?

MITCHENER. Thank heaven she's gone. And now, my dear lady, is it necessary to keep that loaded pistol to my nose all through our conversation?

LADY CORINTHIA. It's not loaded. It's heavy enough, goodness knows, without putting bullets in it.

MITCHENER [*triumphantly snatching his revolver from the drawer*] Then I am master of the situation. This *is* loaded. Ha, ha!

LADY CORINTHIA. But since we are not really going to shoot one another, what difference can it possibly make?

MITCHENER [*putting his pistol down on the table*] True. Quite true. I recognize there the practical good sense that has prevented you from falling into the snares of the Suffragets.

LADY CORINTHIA. The Suffragets, General, are the dupes of dowdies. A really attractive and clever woman—

MITCHENER [*gallantly*] Yourself, for instance.

LADY CORINTHIA [*snatching up his revolver*] Another step and you are a dead man.

MITCHENER [*amazed*] My dear lady!

LADY CORINTHIA. I am not your dear lady. You are not the first man who has concluded that because I am devoted to music and can reach F in alt* with the greatest facility—Patti* never got above E flat*— I am marked out as the prey of every libertine. You think I am like the thousands of weak women whom you have ruined—

MITCHENER. I solemnly protest—

LADY CORINTHIA. Oh, I know what you officers are. To you a woman's honor is nothing, and the idle pleasure of the moment is everything.

MITCHENER. This is perfectly ridiculous. I never ruined anyone in my life.

LADY CORINTHIA. Never! Are you in earnest?

MITCHENER. Certainly I am in earnest. Most indignantly in earnest.

LADY CORINTHIA [*throwing down the pistol contemptuously*] Then you have no temperament: you are not an artist. You have no soul for music.

MITCHENER. Ive subscribed to the regimental band all my life. I bought two sarrusophones* for it out of my own pocket. When I sang Tosti's Goodbye for Ever* at Knightsbridge* in 1880 the whole regiment wept. You are too young to remember that.

LADY CORINTHIA. Your advances are useless. I—

MITCHENER. Confound it, madam, can you not receive an innocent compliment without suspecting me of dishonorable intentions?

LADY CORINTHIA. Love—real love—makes *all* intentions honorable. But *you* could never understand that.

MITCHENER. I'll not submit to the vulgar penny-novelette notion that an officer is less honorable than a civilian in his relations with women. While I live I'll raise my voice—

LADY CORINTHIA. Tush!*

MITCHENER. What do you mean by tush?

LADY CORINTHIA. You cant raise your voice above its natural compass. What sort of voice have you?

MITCHENER. A tenor.* What sort had you?

LADY CORINTHIA. Had! I have it still. I tell you I am the highest living soprano. [*Scornfully*] What was *your* highest note, pray?

MITCHENER. B flat—once—in 1879. I was drunk at the time.

LADY CORINTHIA [*gazing at him almost tenderly*] Though you may not believe me, I find you are more interesting when you talk about music than when you are endeavoring to betray a woman who has trusted you by remaining alone with you in your apartment.

MITCHENER [*springing up and fuming away to the fireplace*] Those repeated insults to a man of blameless life are as disgraceful to you as they are undeserved by me, Lady Corinthia. Such suspicions invite the conduct they impute. [*She raises the pistol*]. You need not be alarmed: I am only going to leave the room.

LADY CORINTHIA. Fish.

MITCHENER. Fish! This is worse than tush. Why fish?

LADY CORINTHIA. Yes, fish: cold-blooded fish.

MITCHENER. Dash it all, madam, do you *want* me to make advances to you?

LADY CORINTHIA. I have not the slightest intention of yielding to them; but to make them would be a tribute to romance. What is life without romance?

MITCHENER [*making a movement towards her*] I tell you—

LADY CORINTHIA. Stop. No nearer. No vulgar sensuousness. If you must adore, adore at a distance.

MITCHENER. This is worse than Mrs Banger. I shall ask that estimable woman to come back.

LADY CORINTHIA. Poor Mrs Banger! Do not for a moment suppose, General Mitchener, that Mrs Banger represents my views on the suffrage question. Mrs Banger is a man in petticoats. I am every inch a woman; but I find it convenient to work with her.

MITCHENER. Do you find the combination comfortable?

LADY CORINTHIA. I do not wear combinations,* General: [*with dignity*] they are unwomanly.

MITCHENER [*throwing himself despairingly into the chair next the hearthrug*] I shall go mad. I never for a moment dreamt of alluding to anything of the sort.

LADY CORINTHIA. There is no need to blush and become self-conscious at the mention of underclothing. You are extremely vulgar, General.

MITCHENER. Lady Corinthia: you have my pistol. Will you have the goodness to blow my brains out? I should prefer it to any other effort to follow the gyrations of the weathercock you no doubt call your mind. If you refuse, then I warn you that youll not get another word out of me—not if we sit here until doomsday.

LADY CORINTHIA. I dont want you to talk. I want you to listen. You do not understand my views on the question of the suffrage. [*She rises to make a speech*]. I must preface my remarks by reminding you that the Suffraget movement is essentially a dowdy movement. The Suffragets are not all dowdies; but they are mainly supported by dowdies. Now I am not a dowdy. Oh, no compliments—

MITCHENER. I did not utter a sound.

LADY CORINTHIA [*smiling*] It is easy to read your thoughts. I am one of those women who are accustomed to rule the world through men. Man is ruled by beauty, by charm. The men who are not have no influence. The Salic Law,* which forbade women to occupy a throne, is founded on the fact that when a woman is on the throne the country is ruled by men, and therefore ruled badly; whereas when a man is on the throne the country is ruled by women, and therefore ruled well. The Suffragets would degrade women from being rulers to being voters, mere politicians, the drudges of the caucus and the polling booth. We should lose our influence completely under such a state of affairs. The New Zealand women have the vote.* What is the result? No poet ever makes a New Zealand woman his heroine. One might as well be romantic about New Zealand mutton. Look at the Suffragets themselves. The only ones who are popular are the pretty ones, who flirt with mobs as ordinary women flirt with officers.

MITCHENER. Then I understand you to hold that the country should be governed by the women after all.

LADY CORINTHIA. Not by all the women. By certain women. I had almost said by one woman. By the women who have charm—who have artistic talent—who wield a legitimate, a refining influence over the men. [*She sits down gracefully, smiling, and arranging her draperies with conscious elegance*].

MITCHENER. In short, madam, you think that if you give the vote to the man, you give the power to the woman who can get round the man.

LADY CORINTHIA. That is not a very delicate way of putting it; but I suppose that is how *you* would express what I mean.

MITCHENER. Perhaps youve never had any experience of garrison life. If you had, youd have noticed that the sort of woman who's clever at getting round men is sometimes rather a bad lot.

LADY CORINTHIA. What do you mean by a bad lot?

MITCHENER. I mean a woman who would play the very devil if the other women didnt keep her in pretty strict order. I dont approve of democracy, because it's rot; and I'm against giving the vote to women, because I'm not accustomed to it, and therefore am able to see with an unprejudiced eye what infernal nonsense it is. But I tell you plainly, Lady Corinthia, that there is one game that I dislike more than either democracy or votes for women; and that is the game of Antony and Cleopatra.* If I must be ruled by women, let me have decent women, and not——well, not the other sort.

LADY CORINTHIA. You have a coarse mind, General Mitchener.

MITCHENER. So has Mrs Banger. And, by George! I prefer Mrs Banger to you!

LADY CORINTHIA [*bounding to her feet*] You prefer Mrs Banger to me!!!

MITCHENER. I do. You said yourself she was splendid.

LADY CORINTHIA. You are no true man. You are one of those unsexed creatures who have no joy in life, no sense of beauty, no high notes.

MITCHENER. No doubt I am, madam. As a matter of fact, I am not clever at discussing public questions, because, as an English gentleman, I was not brought up to use my brains. But occasionally, after a number of remarks which are perhaps sometimes rather idiotic, I get certain convictions. Thanks to you, I have now got a conviction that this woman question is not a question of lovely and accomplished females, but of dowdies. The average Englishwoman is a dowdy and never has half a chance of becoming anything else. She hasnt any charm; and she has no high notes, except when she's giving her husband a piece of her mind, or calling down the street for one of the children.

LADY CORINTHIA. How disgusting!

MITCHENER. Somebody must do the dowdy work! If we had to choose between pitching all the dowdies into the Thames and pitching all the lovely and accomplished women, the lovely ones would have to go.

LADY CORINTHIA. And if you had to do without Wagner's music* or do without your breakfast, you would do without Wagner. Pray does that make eggs and bacon more precious than music, or the butcher and baker better than the poet and philosopher? The scullery may be more necessary to our bare existence than the cathedral. Even humbler apartments might make the same claim. But which is the more essential to the higher life?

MITCHENER. Your arguments are so devilishly ingenious that I feel convinced you got them out of some confounded book. Mine—such as they are—are my own. I imagine it's something like this. There is an old saying that if you take care of the pence, the pounds will take care of themselves.* Well, perhaps if we take care of the dowdies and the butchers and the bakers, the beauties and the bigwigs will take care of themselves. [*Rising and facing her determinedly*] Anyhow, I dont want to have things arranged for me by Wagner. I'm not Wagner. How does he know where the shoe pinches *me*? How do *you* know where the shoe pinches your washerwoman? you and your high F in alt! How are you to know when you havnt made her comfortable unless she has a vote? Do you want her to come and break your windows?

LADY CORINTHIA. Am I to understand that General Mitchener is a Democrat and a Suffraget?

MITCHENER. Yes: you have converted me—you and Mrs Banger.

LADY CORINTHIA. Farewell, creature. [*Balsquith enters hurriedly*]. Mr Balsquith: I am going to wait on General Sandstone. He, at least, is an officer and a gentleman. [*She sails out*].

BALSQUITH. Mitchener: the game is up.

MITCHENER. What do you mean?

BALSQUITH. The strain is too much for the Cabinet. The old Liberal and Unionist Free Traders* declare that if they are defeated on their resolution to invite tenders from private contractors for carrying on the Army and Navy, they will go solid for votes for women as the only means of restoring the liberties of the country which we have destroyed by compulsory military service.

MITCHENER. Infernal impudence!

BALSQUITH. The Labor Party is taking the same line. They say the men got the Factory Acts* by hiding behind the women's petticoats, and that they will get votes for the army in the same way.

MITCHENER. Balsquith: we must not yield to clamor. I have just told that woman that I am at last convinced—

BALSQUITH [*joyfully*]—that the Suffragets must be supported?

MITCHENER. No: that the Anti-Suffragets must be put down at all hazards.

BALSQUITH. Same thing.

MITCHENER. No. For you now tell me that the Labor Party demands votes for women. That makes it impossible to give them, because it would be yielding to clamor. The one condition on which we can consent to grant anything in this country is that nobody shall presume to ask for it.

BALSQUITH [*earnestly*] Mitchener: it's no use. You cant have the conveniences of Democracy without its occasional inconveniences.

MITCHENER. What are its conveniences, I should like to know?

BALSQUITH. Well, when you tell people that they are the real rulers and they can do what they like, nine times out of ten they say 'All right: tell us what to do.' But it happens sometimes that they get an idea of their own; and then of course youre landed.

MITCHENER. Sh—

BALSQUITH [*desperately shouting him down*] No: it's no use telling me to shoot them down: I'm not going to do it. After all, I dont suppose votes for women will make much difference. It hasnt in the other countries in which it has been tried.*

MITCHENER. I never supposed it would make *any* difference. What I cant stand is giving in to that Pankhurst lot.* Hang it all, Balsquith, it seems only yesterday that we put them in quad* for a month. I said at the time that it ought to have been ten years. If my advice had been taken this wouldnt have happened. It's a consolation to me that events are proving how thoroughly right I was.

The Orderly rushes in.

THE ORDERLY. Look 'ere, sir: Mrs Banger's locked the door of General Sandstone's room on the inside; an' she's sittin on his ed til he signs a proclamation for women to serve in the army.

MITCHENER. Put your shoulder to the door and burst it open.

THE ORDERLY. It's only in story books that doors burst open as easy as that. Besides, I'm only too thankful to av a locked door between me and Mrs B.; and so is all the rest of us.

MITCHENER. Cowards. Balsquith: to the rescue! [*He dashes out*].

BALSQUITH [*ambling calmly to the hearth*] This is the business of the Sergeant-at-Arms* rather than of the leader of the House.* Theres no use in my tackling Mrs Banger: she would only sit on my head too.

THE ORDERLY. You take my tip, Mr Balsquith. Give the women the vote and give the army civil rights; and av done with it.

Mitchener returns and comes between them.

MITCHENER. Balsquith: prepare to hear the worst.

BALSQUITH. Sandstone is no more?

MITCHENER. On the contrary, he is particularly lively. He has softened Mrs Banger by a proposal of marriage in which he appears to be perfectly in earnest. He says he has met his ideal at last, a really soldierly woman. She will sit on his head for the rest of his life; and the British Army is now to all intents and purposes commanded by Mrs Banger. When I remonstrated with Sandstone she positively shouted 'Right about face. March' at me in the most offensive tone. If she hadnt been a woman I should have punched her head. I precious nearly punched Sandstone's. The horrors of martial law administered by Mrs Banger are too terrible to be faced. I demand civil rights for the army.

THE ORDERLY [*chuckling*] Wot oh, General! Wot oh!

MITCHENER. Hold your tongue. [*He goes to the door and calls*] Mrs Farrell! [*He returns, and again addresses the Orderly*]. Civil rights dont mean the right to be uncivil. [*Pleased with his own wit*] Almost a pun. Ha ha!

MRS FARRELL [*entering*] Whats the matther now? [*She comes to the table*].

MITCHENER [*to the Orderly*] I have private business with Mrs Farrell. Outside, you infernal blackguard.

THE ORDERLY [*arguing, as usual*] Well, I didnt ask to—[*Mitchener seizes him by the nape; marches him out; slams the door; and comes* solemnly to Mrs Farrell*].

MITCHENER. Excuse the abruptness of this communication, Mrs Farrell; but I know only one woman in the country whose practical ability and force of character can maintain her husband in competition with the husband of Mrs Banger. I have the honor to propose for your hand.

MRS FARRELL. D'ye mean you want to marry me?

MITCHENER. I do.

MRS FARRELL. No thank you. I'd have to work for you just the same; only I shouldnt get any wages for it.

BALSQUITH. That will be remedied when women get the vote. Ive had to promise that.

MITCHENER [*winningly*] Mrs Farrell: you have been charwoman here now ever since I took up my duties. Have you really never, in your more romantic moments, cast a favorable eye on my person?

MRS FARRELL. Ive been too busy casting an unfavorable eye on your cloze an on the litther you make with your papers.

MITCHENER [*wounded*] Am I to understand that you refuse me?

MRS FARRELL. Just wait a bit. [*She takes Mitchener's chair and rings up the telephone*] Double three oh seven Elephant.*

MITCHENER. I trust youre not ringing for the police, Mrs Farrell. I assure you I'm perfectly sane.

MRS FARRELL [*into the telephone*] Is that you, Eliza? [*She listens for the answer*]. Not out o bed yet! Go and pull her out be the heels, the lazy sthreel;* an tell her her mother wants to speak to her very particularly about General Mitchener. [*To Mitchener*] Dont you be afeard: I know youre sane enough when youre not talkin about the Germans. [*Into the telephone*] Is that you, Eliza? [*She listens for the answer*]. D'ye remember me givin you a clout on the side of the head for tellin me that if I only knew how to play me cards I could marry any General on the staff instead o disgracin you be bein a charwoman? [*She listens for the answer*]. Well, I can have General Mitchener without playin any cards at all. What d'ye think I ought to say? [*She listens*]. Well, I'm no chicken* meself. [*To Mitchener*] How old are you?

MITCHENER [*with an effort*] Fifty-two.

MRS FARRELL [*into the telephone*] He says he's fifty-two. [*She listens; then, to Mitchener*] She says youre down in Who's Who* as sixty-one.

MITCHENER. Damn Who's Who!

MRS FARRELL [*into the telephone*] Anyhow I wouldnt let that stand in the way. [*She listens*]. If I really *what*? [*She listens*]. I cant hear you. If I really *what*? [*She listens*]. *Who* druv him? I never said a word to—Eh? [*She listens*]. Oh, *love* him. Arra,* dont be a fool, child. [*To Mitchener*] She wants to know do I really love you. [*Into the telephone*] It's likely indeed I'd frighten the man off with any such nonsense at my age. What? [*She listens*]. Well, thats just what I was thinkin.

MITCHENER. May I ask what you were thinking, Mrs Farrell? This suspense is awful.

MRS FARRELL. I was thinkin that praps the Duchess might like her daughther-in-law's mother to be a General's lady bether than to be a charwoman. [*Into the telephone*] Waitle youre married yourself, me fine lady: youll find out that every woman's a charwoman from the day she's married. [*She listens*]. Then you think I might take him? [*She listens*]. G'lang,* you young scald:* if I had you here I'd teach you manners. [*She listens*]. Thats enough now. Back wid you to bed; and be thankful I'm not there to put me slipper across you. [*She rings off*]. The impudence! [*To Mitchener*] Bless you, me childher, may you be happy, she says. [*To Balsquith, going to his side of the room*] Give dear old Mitch me love, she says.

The Orderly opens the door, ushering in Lady Corinthia.

THE ORDERLY. Lady Corinthia Fanshawe to speak to you, sir.

LADY CORINTHIA. General Mitchener: your designs on Mrs Banger are defeated. She is engaged to General Sandstone. Do you still prefer her to me?

MRS FARRELL. He's out o the hunt. He's engaged to me.

The Orderly, overcome by this news, reels from the door to the standing desk and clutches the stool to save himself from collapsing.

MITCHENER. And extremely proud of it, Lady Corinthia.

LADY CORINTHIA [*contemptuously*] She suits you exactly. [*Coming to Balsquith*] Mr Balsquith: you, at least, are not a Philistine.

BALSQUITH. No, Lady Corinthia; but I'm a confirmed bachelor. I dont want a wife; but I want an Egeria.*

MRS FARRELL. More shame for you!

LADY CORINTHIA. Silence, woman. The position and functions of a wife may suit your gross nature. An Egeria is exactly what I desire to be. [*To Balsquith*] Can you play accompaniments?

BALSQUITH. Melodies only, I regret to say. With one finger. But my brother, who is a very obliging fellow, and not unlike me personally, is acquainted with three chords, with which he manages to accompany most of the comic songs of the day.

LADY CORINTHIA. I do not sing comic songs. Neither will you when I am your Egeria. You must come to my musical at-home this afternoon. I will allow you to sit at my feet.

BALSQUITH [*doing so*] That is my ideal of romantic happiness. It commits me exactly as far as I desire to venture. Thank you.

THE ORDERLY. Wot price me, General? Wont you celebrate your engagement by doin somethin for me? Maynt I be promoted to be a sergeant?

MITCHENER. Youre too utterly incompetent to discharge the duties of a sergeant. You are only fit to be a lieutenant.* I shall recommend you for a commission.

THE ORDERLY. Hooray! The Parkinsons o Stepney'll be proud to have me call on em now. I'll go and tell the sergeant what I think of him. Hooray! [*He rushes out*].

MRS FARRELL [*going to the door and calling after him*] You might have the manners to shut the door afther you. [*She shuts it and comes between Mitchener and Lady Corinthia*].

MITCHENER. Poor wretch! the day after civil rights are conceded to the army he and Chubbs-Jenkinson will be found incapable of maintaining discipline. They will be sacked and replaced by really capable men. Mrs Farrell: as we are engaged, and I am anxious to do the correct thing in every way, I am quite willing to kiss you if you wish it.

MRS FARRELL. Youd only feel like a fool; and so would I.

MITCHENER. You are really the most sensible woman. Ive made an extremely wise choice. [*He kisses her hand*].

LADY CORINTHIA [*to Balsquith*] You may kiss my hand, if you wish.

BALSQUITH [*cautiously*] I think we had better not commit ourselves too far. Let us change a subject which threatens to become embarrassing. [*To Mitchener*] The moral of the occasion for you, Mitchener, appears to be that youve got to give up treating soldiers as if they were schoolboys.

MITCHENER. The moral for you, Balsquith, is that youve got to give up treating women as if they were angels. Ha ha!

MRS FARRELL. It's a mercy youve found one another out at last. Thats enough now.

OVERRULED

PREFACE

The Alleviations of Monogamy

THIS piece is not an argument for or against polygamy. It is a clinical study of how the thing actually occurs among quite ordinary people, innocent of all unconventional views concerning it. The enormous majority of cases in real life are those of people in that position. Those who deliberately and conscientiously profess what are oddly called advanced views by those others who believe them to be retrograde, are often, and indeed mostly, the last people in the world to engage in unconventional adventures of any kind, not only because they have neither time nor disposition for them, but because the friction set up between the individual and the community by the expression of unusual views of any sort is quite enough hindrance to the heretic without being complicated by personal scandals. Thus the theoretic libertine is usually a person of blameless family life, whilst the practical libertine is mercilessly severe on all other libertines, and excessively conventional in professions of social principle.

What is more, these professions are not hypocritical: they are for the most part quite sincere. The common libertine, like the drunkard, succumbs to a temptation which he does not defend, and against which he warns others with an earnestness proportionate to the intensity of his own remorse. He (or she) may be a liar and a humbug, pretending to be better than the detected libertines, and clamoring for their condign* punishment; but this is mere self-defence. No reasonable person expects the burglar to confess his pursuits, or to refrain from joining in the cry of Stop Thief when the police get on the track of another burglar. If society chooses to penalize candor, it has itself to thank if its attack is countered by falsehood. The clamorous virtue of the libertine is therefore no more hypocritical than the plea of Not Guilty which is allowed to every criminal. But one result is that the theorists who write most sincerely and favorably about polygamy know least about it; and the practitioners who know most about it keep their knowledge very jealously to themselves. Which is hardly fair to the practice.

Inaccessibility of the Facts

Also, it is impossible to estimate its prevalence. A practice to which nobody confesses may be both universal and unsuspected, just as a virtue which everybody is expected, under heavy penalties, to claim, may have no existence. It is often assumed—indeed it is the official assumption of the Churches and the divorce courts—that a gentleman and a lady cannot be alone together innocently. And that is manifest blazing nonsense, though many women have been stoned to death in the east, and divorced in the west, on the strength of it. On the other hand, the innocent and conventional people who regard gallant adventures as crimes of so horrible a nature that only the most depraved and desperate characters engage in them or would listen to advances in that direction without raising an alarm with the noisiest indignation, are clearly examples of the fact that most sections of society do not know how the other sections live. Industry is the most effective check on gallantry. Women may, as Napoleon said, be the occupation of the idle man just as men are the preoccupation of the idle woman;* but the mass of mankind is too busy and too poor for the long and expensive sieges which the professed libertine lays to virtue. Still, wherever there is idleness or even a reasonable supply of elegant leisure there is a good deal of coquetry and philandering. It is so much pleasanter to dance on the edge of a precipice than to go over it that leisured society is full of people who spend a great part of their lives in flirtation, and conceal nothing but the humiliating secret that they have never gone any further. For there is no pleasing people in the matter of reputation in this department: every insult is a flattery: every testimonial is a disparagement: Joseph* is despised and promoted, Potiphar's wife* admired and condemned: in short, you are never on solid ground until you get away from the subject altogether. There is a continual and irreconcilable conflict between the natural and conventional sides of the case, between spontaneous human relations between independent men and women on the one hand and the property relation between husband and wife on the other, not to mention the confusion under the common name of love of a generous natural attraction and interest with the murderous jealousy that fastens on and clings to its mate (especially a hated mate) as a tiger fastens on a carcase. And the confusion is natural; for these extremes are extremes of the same passion; and most cases lie somewhere on the scale between them, and are so complicated by ordinary likes and dislikes, by incidental wounds to vanity or gratifications of it, and by class feeling, that A will be jealous of B and not of C, and will tolerate infidelities on the part of D whilst being furiously angry when they are committed by E.

The Convention of Jealousy

That jealousy is independent of sex is shewn by its intensity in children, and by the fact that very jealous people are jealous of everybody without regard to relationship or sex, and cannot bear to hear the person they 'love' speak favorably of anyone under any circumstances (many women, for instance, are much more jealous of their husbands' mothers and sisters than of unrelated women whom they suspect him of fancying); but it is seldom possible to disentangle the two passions in practice. Besides, jealousy is an inculcated passion, forced by society on people in whom it would not occur spontaneously. In Brieux's Bourgeois aux Champs,* the benevolent hero finds himself detested by the neighboring peasants and farmers, not because he preserves game, and sets mantraps for poachers, and defends his legal rights over his land to the extremest point of unsocial savagery, but because, being an amiable and public-spirited person, he refuses to do all this, and thereby offends and disparages the sense of property in his neighbors. The same thing is true of matrimonial jealousy: the man who does not at least pretend to feel it, and behave as badly as if he really felt it, is despised and insulted; and many a man has shot or stabbed a friend or been shot or stabbed by him in a duel, or disgraced himself and ruined his own wife in a divorce scandal, against his conscience, against his instinct, and to the destruction of his home, solely because Society conspired to drive him to keep its own lower morality in countenance in this miserable and undignified manner.

Morality is confused in such matters. In an elegant plutocracy, a jealous husband is regarded as a boor. Among the tradesmen who supply that plutocracy with its meals, a husband who is not jealous, and refrains from assailing his rival with his fists, is regarded as a ridiculous, contemptible, and cowardly cuckold. And the laboring class is divided into the respectable section which takes the tradesman's view, and the disreputable section which enjoys the license of the plutocracy without its money: creeping below the law as its exemplars prance above it; cutting down all expenses of respectability and even decency; and frankly accepting squalor and disrepute as the price of anarchic self-indulgence. The conflict between Malvolio and Sir Toby,* between the marquis and the bourgeois, the cavalier and the puritan, the ascetic and the voluptuary,* goes on continually, and goes on not only between class and class and individual and individual, but in the selfsame breast in a series of reactions and revulsions in which the irresistible becomes the unbearable, and the unbearable the irresistible, until none of us can say what our characters really are in this respect.

The Missing Data of a Scientific
Natural History of Marriage

Of one thing I am persuaded: we shall never attain to a reasonably
healthy public opinion on sex questions until we offer, as the data for
that opinion, our actual conduct and our real thoughts instead of
a moral fiction which we agree to call virtuous conduct, and which we
then—and here comes in the mischief—pretend is our conduct and
our thoughts. If the result were that we all believed one another to be
better than we really are, there would be something to be said for it; but
the actual result appears to be a monstrous exaggeration of the power
and continuity of sexual passion. The whole world shares the fate of
Lucrezia Borgia, who, though she seems on investigation to have been
quite a suitable wife for a modern British Bishop, has been invested
by the popular historical imagination with all the extravagances of
a Messalina or a Cenci.* Writers of belles lettres who are rash enough
to admit that their whole life is not one constant preoccupation with
adored members of the opposite sex, and who even countenance La
Rochefoucauld's* remark that very few people would ever imagine
themselves in love if they had never read anything about it, are gravely
declared to be abnormal or physically defective by critics of crushing
unadventurousness and domestication. French authors of saintly temperament are forced to include in their retinue countesses of ardent
complexion with whom they are supposed to live in sin. Sentimental
controversies on the subject are endless; but they are useless, because
nobody tells the truth. Rousseau* did it by an extraordinary effort,
aided by a superhuman faculty for human natural history; but the
result was curiously disconcerting because, though the facts were so
conventionally shocking that people felt that they ought to matter
a great deal, they actually mattered very little. And even at that everybody pretends not to believe him.

Artificial Retribution

The worst of this is that busybodies with perhaps rather more than
a normal taste for mischief are continually trying to make negligible
things matter as much in fact as they do in convention by deliberately
inflicting injuries—sometimes atrocious injuries—on the parties concerned. Few people have any knowledge of the savage punishments that
are legally inflicted for aberrations and absurdities to which no sanely
instructed community would call any attention. We create an artificial

morality, and consequently an artificial conscience, by manufacturing disastrous consequences for events which, left to themselves, would do very little harm (sometimes not any) and be forgotten in a few days.

But the artificial morality is not therefore to be condemned offhand. In many cases it may save mischief instead of making it: for example, though the hanging of a murderer is the duplication of a murder, yet it may be less murderous than leaving the matter to be settled by blood feud or vendetta. As long as human nature insists on revenge, the official organization and satisfaction of revenge by the State may be also its minimization. The mischief begins when the official revenge persists after the passion it satisfies has died out of the race. Stoning a woman to death in the east because she has ventured to marry again after being deserted by her husband may be more merciful than allowing her to be mobbed to death; but the official stoning or burning of an adulteress in the west would be an atrocity, because few of us hate an adulteress to the extent of desiring such a penalty, or of being prepared to take the law into our own hands if it were withheld. Now what applies to this extreme case applies also in due degree to the other cases. Offences in which sex is concerned are often needlessly magnified by penalties, ranging from various forms of social ostracism to long sentences of penal servitude, which would be seen to be monstrously disproportionate to the real feeling against them if the removal of both the penalties and the taboo on their discussion made it possible for us to ascertain their real prevalence and estimation. Fortunately there is one outlet for the truth. We are permitted to discuss in jest what we may not discuss in earnest. A serious comedy about sex is taboo: a farcical comedy is privileged.

The Favorite Subject of Farcical Comedy*

The little piece which follows this preface accordingly takes the form of a farcical comedy, because it is a contribution to the very extensive dramatic literature which takes as its special department the gallantries of married people. The stage has been preoccupied by such affairs for centuries, not only in the jesting vein of Restoration Comedy* and Palais Royal farce,* but in the more tragically turned adulteries of the Parisian school* which dominated the stage until Ibsen* put them out of countenance* and relegated them to their proper place as articles of commerce. Their continued vogue in that department maintains the tradition that adultery is the dramatic subject *par excellence*, and indeed that a play that is not about adultery is not a play at all. I was considered a heresiarch* of the most extravagant kind when I expressed my opinion, at the outset of my career as a playwright, that adultery is the dullest of themes on the stage, and that from Francesca and Paolo* down to the latest guilty couple of the school of Dumas *fils*, the romantic adulterers have all been intolerable bores.

The Pseudo Sex Play

Later on, I had occasion to point out to the defenders of sex as the proper theme of drama, that though they were right in ranking sex as an intensely interesting subject, they were wrong in assuming that sex is an indispensable motive in popular plays.* The plays of Molière* are, like the novels of the Victorian epoch or Don Quixote,* as nearly sexless as anything not absolutely inhuman can be; and some of Shakespear's plays are sexually on a par with the census: they contain women as well as men, and that is all. This had to be admitted; but it was still assumed that the plays of the nineteenth century Paris school are, in contrast with the sexless masterpieces, saturated with sex; and this I strenuously denied. A play about the convention that a man should fight a duel or come to fisticuffs with his wife's lover if she has one, or the convention that he should strangle her like Othello,* or turn her out of the house and never see her or allow her to see her children again, or the convention that she should never be spoken to again by any decent person and should finally drown herself, or the convention that persons involved in scenes of recrimination or confession by these conventions should call each other certain abusive names and describe their conduct as guilty and frail and so on: all these may provide material for very effective plays; but such plays are not dramatic studies of sex: one might as well say that Romeo and Juliet* is a dramatic study of pharmacy because the catastrophe is brought about through an apothecary. Duels are not sex; divorce cases are not sex; the Trade Unionism of married women is not sex. Only the most insignificant fraction of the gallantries of married people produce any of the conventional results; and plays occupied wholly with the conventional results are therefore utterly unsatisfying as sex plays, however interesting they may be as plays of intrigue and plot puzzles.

The world is finding this out rapidly. The Sunday papers, which in the days when they appealed almost exclusively to the lower middle class were crammed with police intelligence, and more especially with divorce and murder cases, now lay no stress on them; and police papers which confined themselves entirely to such matters, and were once eagerly read, have perished through the essential dulness of their topics. And yet the interest in sex is stronger than ever: in fact, the literature that has driven out the journalism of the divorce courts is a literature occupied with sex to an extent and with an intimacy and frankness that would have seemed utterly impossible to Thackeray* or Dickens* if they had been told that the change would complete itself within fifty years of their own time.

Art and Morality

It is ridiculous to say, as inconsiderate amateurs of the arts do, that art has nothing to do with morality. What is true is that the artist's business is not that of the policeman; and that such factitious consequences and put-up jobs as divorces and executions and the detective operations that lead up to them are no essential part of life, though, like poisons and buttered slides and red-hot pokers, they provide material for plenty of thrilling or amusing stories suited to people who are incapable of any interest in psychology. But the fine artist must keep the policeman out of his studies of sex and studies of crime. It is by clinging nervously to the policeman that most of the pseudo sex plays convince me that the writers have either never had any serious personal experience of their ostensible subject, or else have never conceived it possible that the stage dare present the phenomena of sex as they appear in nature.

The Limits of Stage Presentation

But the stage presents much more shocking phenomena than those of sex. There is, of course, a sense in which you cannot present sex on the stage, just as you cannot present murder. Macbeth must no more really kill Duncan than he must himself be really slain by Macduff.* But the feelings of a murderer can be expressed in a certain artistic convention; and a carefully prearranged sword exercise can be gone through with sufficient pretence of earnestness to be accepted by the willing imaginations of the younger spectators as a desperate combat.

The tragedy of love has been presented on the stage in the same way. In Tristan and Isolde,* the curtain does not, as in Romeo and Juliet, rise with the lark: the whole night of love is played before the spectators. The lovers do not discuss marriage in an elegantly sentimental way: they utter the visions and feelings that come to lovers at the supreme moments of their love, totally forgetting that there are such things in the world as husbands and lawyers and duelling codes and theories of

sin and notions of propriety and all the other irrelevancies which
provide hackneyed and bloodless material for our so-called plays of
passion.

Pruderies of the French Stage

To all stage presentations there are limits. If Macduff were to stab
Macbeth, the spectacle would be intolerable; and even the pretence
which we allow on our stage is ridiculously destructive to the illusion of
the scene. Yet pugilists and gladiators will actually fight and kill in public without shame, even as a spectacle for money. But no sober couple
of lovers of any delicacy could endure to be watched. We in England,
accustomed to consider the French stage much more licentious than
the British, are always surprised and puzzled when we learn, as we may
do any day if we come within reach of such information, that French
actors are often scandalized by what they consider the indecency of the
English stage, and that French actresses who desire a greater license in
appealing to the sexual instincts than the French stage allows them,
learn English and establish themselves on the English stage. The
German and Russian stages are in the same relation to the French and,
perhaps more or less, all the Latin stages. The reason is that, partly
from a want of respect for the theatre, partly from a sort of respect for
art in general which moves them to accord moral privileges to artists,
partly from the very objectionable tradition that the realm of art is
Alsatia* and the contemplation of works of art a holiday from the burden of virtue, partly because French prudery does not attach itself to
the same points of behavior as British prudery, and has a different code
of the mentionable and the unmentionable, and for many other reasons,
the French tolerate plays which are never performed in England until
they have been spoiled by a process of bowdlerization; yet French taste
is more fastidious than ours as to the exhibition and treatment on the
stage of the physical incidents of sex. On the French stage a kiss is as
obvious a convention as the thrust under the arm by which Macduff
runs Macbeth through. It is even a purposely unconvincing convention: the actors rather insisting that it shall be impossible for any spectator to mistake a stage kiss for a real one. In England, on the contrary,
realism is carried to the point at which nobody except the two performers can perceive that the caress is not genuine. And here the English
stage is certainly in the right; for whatever question there arises as to
what incidents are proper for representation on the stage or not, my
experience as a playgoer leaves me in no doubt that once it is decided to

represent an incident, it will be offensive, no matter whether it be a prayer or a kiss, unless it is presented with a convincing appearance of sincerity.

Our Disillusive* Scenery

For example, the main objection to the use of illusive scenery (in most modern plays scenery is not illusive: everything visible is as real as in your drawing room at home) is that it is unconvincing; whilst the imaginary scenery with which the audience transfigures a platform or tribune like the Elizabethan stage or the Greek stage used by Sophocles,* is quite convincing. In fact, the more scenery you have the less illusion you produce. The wise playwright, when he cannot get absolute reality of presentation, goes to the other extreme, and aims at atmosphere and suggestion of mood rather than at direct simulative illusion. The theatre, as I first knew it, was a place of wings and flats which destroyed both atmosphere and illusion. This was tolerated, and even intensely enjoyed, but not in the least because nothing better was possible; for all the devices employed in the productions of Mr Granville Barker or Max Reinhardt or the Moscow Art Theatre* were equally available for Colley Cibber and Garrick, except the intensity of our artificial light. When Garrick played Richard III* in slashed trunk hose and plumes,* it was not because he believed that the Plantagenets* dressed like that, or because the costumiers could not have made him a XV century dress as easily as a nondescript combination of the state robes of George III* with such scraps of older fashions as seemed to playgoers for some reason to be romantic. The charm of the theatre in those days was its makebelieve. It has that charm still, not only for the amateurs, who are happiest when they are most unnatural and impossible and absurd, but for audiences as well. I have seen performances of my own plays which were to me far wilder burlesques than Sheridan's Critic or Buckingham's Rehearsal;* yet they have produced sincere laughter and tears such as the most finished metropolitan productions have failed to elicit. Fielding* was entirely right when he represented Partridge as enjoying intensely the performance of the king in Hamlet because anybody could see that the king was an actor, and resenting Garrick's Hamlet* because it might have been a real man. Yet we have only to look at the portraits of Garrick to see that his performances would nowadays seem almost as extravagantly stagey as his costumes. In our day Calvé's intensely real Carmen* never pleased the mob as much as the obvious fancy ball masquerading of suburban young ladies in the same character.

Holding the Mirror up to Nature

Theatrical art begins as the holding up to Nature of a distorting mirror. In this phase it pleases people who are childish enough to believe that they can see what they look like and what they are when they look at a true mirror. Naturally they think that a true mirror can teach them nothing. Only by giving them back some monstrous image can the mirror amuse them or terrify them. It is not until they grow up to the point at which they learn that they know very little about themselves, and that they do not see themselves in a true mirror as other people see them, that they become consumed with curiosity as to what they really are like, and begin to demand that the stage shall be a mirror of such accuracy and intensity of illumination that they shall be able to get glimpses of their real selves in it, and also learn a little how they appear to other people.

For audiences of this highly developed class, sex can no longer be ignored or conventionalized or distorted by the playwright who makes the mirror. The old sentimental extravagances and the old grossnesses are of no further use to him. Don Giovanni and Zerlina* are not gross: Tristan and Isolde are not extravagant or sentimental. They say and do nothing that you cannot bear to hear and see; and yet they give you, the one pair briefly and slightly, and the other fully and deeply, what passes in the minds of lovers. The love depicted may be that of a philosophic adventurer tempting an ignorant country girl, or of a tragically serious poet entangled with a woman of noble capacity in a passion which has become for them the reality of the whole universe. No matter: the thing is dramatized and dramatized directly, not talked about as something that happened before the curtain rose, or that will happen after it falls.

Farcical Comedy Shrinking its Subject

Now if all this can be done in the key of tragedy and philosophic comedy, it can, I have always contended, be done in the key of farcical comedy; and Overruled is a trifling experiment in that manner. Conventional farcical comedies are always finally tedious because the heart of them, the inevitable conjugal infidelity, is always evaded. Even its consequences are evaded. Mr Granville Barker has pointed out rightly that if the third acts of our farcical comedies dared to describe the consequences that would follow from the first and second in real life, they would end as squalid tragedies; and in my opinion they would be greatly improved thereby even as entertainments; for I have never seen

a three-act farcical comedy without being bored and tired by the third
act, and observing that the rest of the audience were in the same condition, though they were not vigilantly introspective enough to find that
out, and were apt to blame one another, especially the husbands and
wives, for their crossness. But it is happily by no means true that conjugal infidelities always produce tragic consequences, or that they need
produce even the unhappiness which they often do produce. Besides,
the more momentous the consequences, the more interesting become
the impulses and imaginations and reasonings, if any, of the people who
disregard them. If I had an opportunity of conversing with the ghost of
an executed murderer, I have no doubt he would begin to tell me eagerly
about his trial, with the names of the distinguished ladies and gentlemen who honored him with their presence on that occasion, and then
about his execution. All of which would bore me exceedingly. I should
say, 'My dear sir: such manufactured ceremonies do not interest me in
the least. I know how a man is tried, and how he is hanged. I should
have had you killed in a much less disgusting, hypocritical, and
unfriendly manner if the matter had been in my hands. What I want to
know about is the murder. How did you feel when you committed it?
Why did you do it? What did you say to yourself about it? If, like most
murderers, you had not been hanged, would you have committed other
murders? Did you really dislike the victim, or did you want his money,
or did you murder a person whom you did not dislike, and from whose
death you had nothing to gain, merely for the sake of murdering? If so,
can you describe the charm to me? Does it come upon you periodically;
or is it chronic? Has curiosity anything to do with it?' I would ply him
with all manner of questions to find out what murder is really like; and
I should not be satisfied until I had realized that I, too, might commit
a murder, or else that there is some specific quality present in a murderer and lacking in me. And, if so, what that quality is.

In just the same way, I want the unfaithful husband or the unfaithful
wife in a farcical comedy not to bother me with their divorce cases or
the stratagems they employ to avoid a divorce case, but to tell me how
and why married couples are unfaithful. I dont want to hear the lies
they tell one another to conceal what they have done, but the truths
they tell one another when they have to face what they have done without concealment or excuse. No doubt prudent and considerate people
conceal such adventures, when they can, from those who are most likely
to be wounded by them; but it is not to be presumed that, when found
out, they necessarily disgrace themselves by irritating lies and trans-
parent subterfuges.

My playlet, which I offer as a model to all future writers of farcical comedy, may now, I hope, be read without shock. I may just add that Mr Sibthorpe Juno's* view that morality demands, not that we should behave morally (an impossibility to our sinful nature) but that we shall not attempt to defend our immoralities, is a standard view in England, and was advanced in all seriousness by an earnest and distinguished British moralist* shortly after the first performance of Overruled. My objection to that aspect of the doctrine of original sin* is that no necessary and inevitable operation of human nature can reasonably be regarded as sinful at all, and that a morality which assumes the contrary is an absurd morality, and can be kept in countenance only by hypocrisy. When people were ashamed of sanitary problems, and refused to face them, leaving them to solve themselves clandestinely in dirt and secrecy, the solution arrived at was the Black Death.* A similar policy as to sex problems has solved itself by an even worse plague than the Black Death; and the remedy for that is not salvarsan,* but sound moral hygiene, the first foundation of which is the discontinuance of our habit of telling not only the comparatively harmless lies that we know we ought not to tell, but the ruinous lies that we foolishly think we ought to tell.

OVERRULED

A lady and gentleman are sitting together on a chesterfield* in a retired corner of the lounge of a seaside hotel.* It is a summer night: the French window behind them stands open. The terrace without overlooks a moonlit harbor. The lounge is dark. The chesterfield, upholstered in silver grey, and the two figures on it in evening dress, catch the light from an arc lamp somewhere; but the walls, covered with a dark green paper, are in gloom. There are two stray chairs, one on each side. On the gentleman's right, behind him up near the window, is an unused fireplace. Opposite it on the lady's left is a door. The gentleman is on the lady's right.

The lady is very attractive, with a musical voice and soft appealing manners. She is young: that is, one feels sure that she is under thirty-five and over twenty-four. The gentleman does not look much older. He is rather handsome, and has ventured as far in the direction of poetic dandyism* in the arrangement of his hair as any man who is not a professional artist can afford to in England. He is obviously very much in love with the lady, and is, in fact, yielding to an irresistible impulse to throw his arms round her.

THE LADY. Dont—oh dont be horrid. Please, Mr Lunn [*she rises from the lounge and retreats behind it*]! Promise me you wont be horrid.

GREGORY LUNN. I'm not being horrid, Mrs Juno.* I'm not going to be horrid. I love you: thats all. I'm extraordinarily happy.

MRS JUNO. You will really be good?

GREGORY. I'll be whatever you wish me to be. I tell you I love you. I love loving you. I dont want to be tired and sorry, as I should be if I were to be horrid. I dont want you to be tired and sorry.* Do come and sit down again.

MRS JUNO [*coming back to her seat*] Youre sure you dont want anything you oughtnt to?

GREGORY. Quite sure. I only want you [*she recoils*]. Dont be alarmed: I *like* wanting you. As long as I have a want, I have a reason for living. Satisfaction is death.

MRS JUNO. Yes; but the impulse to commit suicide is sometimes irresistible.

GREGORY. Not with you.

MRS JUNO. What!

GREGORY. Oh, it sounds uncomplimentary; but it isnt really. Do you know why half the couples who find themselves situated as we are now behave horridly?

MRS JUNO. Because they cant help it if they let things go too far.

GREGORY. Not a bit of it. It's because they have nothing else to do, and no other way of entertaining each other. You dont know what it is to be alone with a woman who has little beauty and less conversation. What is a man to do? She cant talk interestingly; and if he talks that way himself she doesnt understand him. He cant look at her: if he does, he only finds out that she isnt beautiful. Before the end of five minutes they are both hideously bored. Theres only one thing that can save the situation; and thats what you call being horrid. With a beautiful, witty, kind woman, theres no time for such follies. It's so delightful to look at her, to listen to her voice, to hear all she has to say, that nothing else happens. That is why the woman who is supposed to have a thousand lovers seldom has one; whilst the stupid, graceless animals of women have dozens.

MRS JUNO. I wonder! It's quite true that when one feels in danger one talks like mad to stave it off, even when one doesnt quite want to stave it off.

GREGORY. One never does quite want to stave it off. Danger is delicious. But death isnt. We court the danger; but the real delight is in escaping, after all.

MRS JUNO. I dont think we'll talk about it any more. Danger is all very well when you *do* escape; but sometimes one doesnt. I tell you frankly I dont feel as safe as you do—if you really do.

GREGORY. But surely you can do as you please without injuring anyone, Mrs Juno. That is the whole secret of your extraordinary charm for me.

MRS JUNO. I dont understand.

GREGORY. Well, I hardly know how to begin to explain. But the root of the matter is that I am what people call a good man.

MRS JUNO. I thought so until you began making love to me.*

GREGORY. But you knew I loved you all along.

MRS JUNO. Yes, of course; but I depended on you not to tell me so; because I thought you were good. Your blurting it out spoilt it. And it was wicked besides.

GREGORY. Not at all. You see, it's a great many years since Ive been able to allow myself to fall in love. I know lots of charming women; but the worst of it is, theyre all married. Women dont become charming, to my taste, until theyre fully developed; and by that time, if theyre really nice, theyre snapped up and married. And then, because I am a good man, I have to place a limit to my regard for them. I may be fortunate enough to gain friendship and even very warm affection from them; but my loyalty to their husbands and their hearths and their happiness obliges me to draw a line and not overstep it. Of course I value such affectionate regard very highly indeed. I am surrounded with women who are most dear to me. But every one of them has a post sticking up, if I may put it that way, with the inscription: Trespassers Will Be Prosecuted. How we all loathe that notice! In every lovely garden, in every dell full of primroses, on every fair hillside, we meet that confounded board; and there is always a game-keeper round the corner. But what is that to the horror of meeting it on every beautiful woman, and knowing that there is a husband round the corner? I have had this accursed board standing between me and every dear and desirable woman until I thought I had lost the power of letting myself fall really and whole-heartedly in love.

MRS JUNO. Wasnt there a widow?

GREGORY. No. Widows are extraordinarily scarce in modern society. Husbands live longer than they used to; and even when they do die, their widows have a string of names down for their next.

MRS JUNO. Well, what about the young girls?

GREGORY. Oh, who cares for young girls? Theyre unsympathetic. Theyre beginners. They dont attract me. I'm afraid of them.

MRS JUNO. Thats the correct thing to say to a woman of my age. But it doesnt explain why you seem to have put your scruples in your pocket when you met me.

GREGORY. Surely thats quite clear. I—

MRS JUNO. No: please dont explain. I dont want to know. I take your word for it. Besides, it doesnt matter now. Our voyage is over; and tomorrow I start for the north to my poor father's place.

GREGORY [*surprised*] Your poor father! I thought he was alive.

MRS JUNO. So he is. What made you think he wasnt?

GREGORY. You said your *poor* father.

MRS JUNO. Oh, thats a trick of mine. Rather a silly trick, I suppose; but theres something pathetic to me about men: I find myself calling them poor So-and-So when theres nothing whatever the matter with them.*

GREGORY [*who has listened in growing alarm*] But—I—is?—wa—? Oh Lord!

MRS JUNO. Whats the matter?

GREGORY. Nothing.

MRS JUNO. Nothing! [*Rising anxiously*] Nonsense: youre ill.

GREGORY. No. It was something about your late husband—

MRS JUNO. My *late* husband! What do you mean? [*Clutching him, horror-stricken*] Dont tell me he's dead.

GREGORY [*rising, equally appalled*] Dont tell *me* he's alive.

MRS JUNO. Oh, dont frighten me like this. Of course he's alive—unless youve heard anything.

GREGORY. The first day we met—on the boat—you spoke to me of your poor dear husband.

MRS JUNO [*releasing him, quite reassured*] Is that all?

GREGORY. Well, afterwards you called him poor Tops. Always poor Tops, or poor dear Tops. What could I think?

MRS JUNO [*sitting down again*] I wish you hadnt given me such a shock about him; for I havnt been treating him at all well. Neither have you.

GREGORY [*relapsing into his seat, overwhelmed*] And you mean to tell me youre not a widow!

MRS JUNO. Gracious, no! I'm not in black.

GREGORY. Then I have been behaving like a blackguard! I have broken my promise to my mother. I shall never have an easy conscience again.

MRS JUNO. I'm sorry. I thought you knew.

GREGORY. You thought I was a libertine?*

MRS JUNO. No: of course I shouldnt have spoken to you if I had thought that. I thought you liked me, but that you knew, and would be good.

GREGORY [*stretching his hand towards her breast*] I thought the burden of being good had fallen from my soul at last. I saw nothing there but a bosom to rest on: the bosom of a lovely woman of whom I could dream without guilt. What do I see now?

MRS JUNO. Just what you saw before.

GREGORY [*despairingly*] No, no.

MRS JUNO. What else?

GREGORY. Trespassers Will Be Prosecuted: Trespassers Will Be Prosecuted.

MRS JUNO. They wont if they hold their tongues. Dont be such a coward. My husband wont eat you.

GREGORY. I'm not afraid of your husband. I'm afraid of my conscience.

MRS JUNO [*losing patience*] Well! I dont consider myself at all a badly behaved woman; for nothing has passed between us that was not perfectly nice and friendly; but really! to hear a grown-up man talking about promises to his mother!——

GREGORY [*interrupting her*] Yes, yes: I know all about that. It's not romantic: it's not Don Juan:* it's not advanced; but we feel it all the same. It's far deeper in our blood and bones than all the romantic stuff. My father got into a scandal once: that was why my mother made me promise never to make love to a married woman. And now Ive done it I cant feel honest. Dont pretend to despise me or laugh at me. You feel it too. You said just now that your own conscience was uneasy when you thought of your husband. What must it be when you think of my wife?

MRS JUNO [*rising aghast*] Your wife!!! You dont dare sit* there and tell me coolly that youre a married man!

GREGORY. I never led you to believe I was unmarried.

MRS JUNO. Oh! You never gave me the faintest hint that you had a wife.

GREGORY. I did indeed. I discussed things with you that only married people really understand.

MRS JUNO. Oh!!

GREGORY. I thought it the most delicate way of letting you know.

MRS JUNO. Well, you *are* a daisy, I must say. I suppose thats vulgar; but really! really!! You and your goodness! However, now weve found one another out theres only one thing to be done. Will you please go?

GREGORY [*rising slowly*] I *ought* to go.

MRS JUNO. Well, go.

GREGORY. Yes. Er—[*he tries to go*] I—I somehow cant. [*He sits down again helplessly*] My conscience is active: my will is paralyzed. This is really dreadful. Would you mind ringing the bell and asking them to throw me out? You ought to, you know.

MRS JUNO. What! make a scandal in the face of the whole hotel! Certainly not. Dont be a fool.

GREGORY. Yes; but I cant go.

MRS JUNO. Then I can. Goodbye.

GREGORY [*clinging to her hand*] Can you really?

MRS JUNO. Of course I—[*she wavers*] Oh dear! [*They contemplate one another helplessly*]. I cant. [*She sinks on the lounge, hand in hand with him*].

GREGORY. For heaven's sake pull yourself together. It's a question of self-control.

MRS JUNO [*dragging her hand away and retreating to the end of the chesterfield*] No: it's a question of distance. Self-control is all very well two or three yards off, or on a ship, with everybody looking on. Dont come any nearer.

GREGORY. This is a ghastly business. I want to go away; and I cant.

MRS JUNO. I think you ought to go [*he makes an effort; and she adds quickly*] but if you try to I shall grab you round the neck and disgrace myself. I implore you to sit still and be nice.

GREGORY. I implore you to run away. I believe I can trust myself to let you go for your own sake. But it will break my heart.

MRS JUNO. I dont want to break your heart. I cant bear to think of your sitting here alone. I cant bear to think of sitting alone myself somewhere else. It's so senseless—so ridiculous—when we might be so happy. I dont want to be wicked, or coarse. But I like you very much; and I *do* want to be affectionate and human.

GREGORY. I ought to draw a line.

MRS JUNO. So you shall, dear. Tell me: do you really like me? I dont mean *love* me: you might love the housemaid—

GREGORY [*vehemently*] No!

MRS JUNO. Oh yes you might; and what does that matter, anyhow? Are you really fond of me? Are we friends—comrades? Would you be sorry if I died?

GREGORY [*shrinking*] Oh dont.

MRS JUNO. Or was it the usual aimless man's lark: a mere shipboard flirtation?

GREGORY. Oh no, no: nothing half so bad, so vulgar, so wrong. I assure you I only meant to be agreeable. It grew on me before I noticed it.

MRS JUNO. And you were glad to let it grow?

GREGORY. I let it grow because the board was not up.

MRS JUNO. Bother the board! I am just as fond of Sibthorpe as—

GREGORY. Sibthorpe!

MRS JUNO. Sibthorpe is my husband's Christian name. I oughtnt to call him Tops to you now.

GREGORY [*chuckling*] It sounded like something to drink.* But I have no right to laugh at him. *My* Christian name is Gregory, which sounds like a powder.*

MRS JUNO [*chilled*] That is so like a man! I offer you my heart's warmest friendliest feeling; and you think of nothing but a silly joke. A quip like that makes you forget me.

GREGORY. Forget you! Oh, if only I could!

MRS JUNO. If you could, would you?

GREGORY [*burying his shamed face in his hands*] No: I'd die first. Oh, I hate myself.

MRS JUNO. I glory in myself. It's so jolly to be reckless. *Can* a man be reckless, I wonder?

GREGORY [*straightening himself desperately*] No. I'm not reckless. I know what I'm doing: my conscience is awake. Oh, where is the intoxication of love? the delirium? the madness that makes a man think the world well lost for the woman he adores? I dont think anything of the sort: I see that it's not worth it: I know that it's wrong: I have never in my life been cooler, more businesslike.

MRS JUNO [*opening her arms to him*] But you cant resist me.

GREGORY. I must. I ought. [*Throwing himself into her arms*] Oh my darling, my treasure, we shall be sorry for this.

MRS JUNO. We can forgive ourselves. Could we forgive ourselves if we let this moment slip?

GREGORY. I protest to the last. I'm against this. I have been pushed over a precipice. I'm innocent. This wild joy, this exquisite tenderness, this ascent into heaven can thrill me to the uttermost fibre of my heart [*with a gesture of ecstasy she hides her face on his shoulder*]; but it cant subdue my mind or corrupt my conscience, which still shouts to the skies that I'm not a willing party to this outrageous conduct. I repudiate the bliss with which you are filling me.

MRS JUNO. Never mind your conscience. Tell me how happy you are.

GREGORY. No: I recall you to your duty. But oh, I will give you my life with both hands if you can tell me that you feel for me one millionth part of what I feel for you now.

MRS JUNO. Oh yes, yes. Be satisfied with that. Ask for no more. Let me go.

GREGORY. I cant. I have no will. Something stronger than either of us is in command here. Nothing on earth or in heaven can part us now. You know that, dont you?

MRS JUNO. Oh, dont make me say it. Of course I know. Nothing—not life nor death nor shame nor *anything* can part us.

A MATTER-OF-FACT MALE VOICE IN THE CORRIDOR. All right. This must be it.

The two recover with a violent start; release one another; and spring back to opposite sides of the lounge.

GREGORY. That did it.

MRS JUNO [*in a thrilling whisper*] Sh-sh-sh! That was my husband's voice.

GREGORY. Impossible: it's only our guilty fancy.

A WOMAN'S VOICE. This is the way to the lounge. I know it.

GREGORY. Great Heaven! we're both mad. Thats my wife's voice.

MRS JUNO. Ridiculous! Oh, we're dreaming it all. We—[*the door opens; and Sibthorpe Juno appears in the roseate glow of the corridor (which happens to be papered in pink) with Mrs Lunn, like Tannhäuser in the hill of Venus.* He is a fussily energetic little man, who gives himself an air of gallantry by greasing the points of his moustaches and dressing very carefully. She is a tall, imposing, handsome, languid woman, with flashing dark eyes and long lashes. They make for the chesterfield, not noticing the two palpitating figures blotted against the walls in the gloom on either side. The figures flit away noiselessly through the window and disappear*].

JUNO [*officiously*] Ah: here we are. [*He leads the way to the sofa*]. Sit down: I'm sure youre tired. [*She sits*]. Thats right. [*He sits beside her on her left*]. Hullo! [*he rises*] this sofa's quite warm.

MRS LUNN [*bored*] Is it? I dont notice it. I expect the sun's been on it.

JUNO. I felt it quite distinctly: I'm more thinly clad than you. [*He sits down again, and proceeds, with a sigh of satisfaction*] What a relief to get off the ship and have a private room! Thats the worst of a ship. Youre under observation all the time.

MRS LUNN. But why not?

JUNO. Well, of course theres no reason: at least I suppose not. But, you know, part of the romance of a journey is that a man keeps imagining that something might happen; and he cant do that if there are a lot of people about and it simply cant happen.

MRS LUNN. Mr Juno: romance is all very well on board ship; but when your foot touches the soil of England theres an end of it.

JUNO. No: believe me, thats a foreigner's mistake: we are the most romantic people in the world, we English. Why, my very presence here is a romance.

MRS LUNN [*faintly ironical*] Indeed?

JUNO. Yes. Youve guessed, of course, that I'm a married man.

MRS LUNN. Oh, thats all right. I'm a married woman.

JUNO. Thank Heaven for that! To my English mind, passion is not real passion without guilt. I am a red-blooded man, Mrs Lunn: I cant help it. The tragedy of my life is that I married, when quite young, a woman whom I couldnt help being very fond of. I longed for a guilty passion—for the real thing—the wicked thing; and yet I couldnt care twopence for any other woman when my wife was about. Year after year went by: I felt my youth slipping away without ever having had a romance in my life; for marriage is all very well; but it isnt romance. Theres nothing wrong in it, you see.

MRS LUNN. Poor man! How you must have suffered!

JUNO. No: that was what was so tame about it. I *wanted* to suffer. You get so sick of being happily married. It's always the happy marriages that break up. At last my wife and I agreed that we ought to take a holiday.

MRS LUNN. Hadnt you holidays every year?

JUNO. Oh, the seaside and so on! Thats not what we meant. We meant a holiday from one another.

MRS LUNN. How very odd!

JUNO. She said it was an excellent idea; that domestic felicity was making us perfectly idiotic; that she wanted a holiday too. So we agreed to go round the world in opposite directions. I started for Suez* on the day she sailed for New York.

MRS LUNN [*suddenly becoming attentive*] Thats precisely what Gregory and I did. Now I wonder did he want a holiday from me! What he said was that he wanted the delight of meeting me after a long absence.

JUNO. Could anything be more romantic than that? Would anyone else than an Englishman have thought of it? I daresay my temperament seems tame to your boiling southern blood—

MRS LUNN. My what!

JUNO. Your southern blood. Dont you remember how you told me, that night in the saloon when I sang 'Farewell and adieu to you dear

Spanish ladies,'* that you were by birth a lady of Spain? Your splendid Andalusian beauty speaks for itself.

MRS LUNN. Stuff! I was born in Gibraltar.* My father was Captain Jenkins. In the artillery.

JUNO [*ardently*] It is climate and not race that determines the temperament. The fiery sun of Spain blazed on your cradle; and it rocked to the roar of British cannon.

MRS LUNN. What eloquence!* It reminds me of my husband when he was in love—before we were married. Are you in love?

JUNO. Yes; and with the same woman.

MRS LUNN. Well, of course, I didnt suppose you were in love with two women.

JUNO. I dont think you quite understand. I meant that I am in love with you.

MRS LUNN [*relapsing into deepest boredom*] Oh, that! Men do fall in love with me. They all seem to think me a creature with volcanic passions: I'm sure I dont know why; for all the volcanic women I know are plain little creatures with sandy hair. I dont consider human volcanoes respectable. And I'm so tired of the subject! Our house is always full of women who are in love with my husband and men who are in love with me. We encourage it because it's pleasant to have company.

JUNO. And is your husband as insensible as yourself?

MRS LUNN. Oh, Gregory's not insensible: very far from it; but I am the only woman in the world for him.*

JUNO. But you? Are you really as insensible as you say you are?

MRS LUNN. I never said anything of the kind. I'm not at all insensible by nature; but (I dont know whether youve noticed it) I am what people call rather a fine figure of a woman.

JUNO [*passionately*] Noticed it! Oh, Mrs Lunn! Have I been able to notice anything else since we met?

MRS LUNN. There you go, like all the rest of them! I ask you, how do you expect a woman to keep up what you call her sensibility when this sort of thing has happened to her about three times a week ever since she was seventeen? It used to upset me and terrify me at first. Then I got rather a taste for it. It came to a climax with Gregory: that was why I married him. Then it became a mild lark, hardly worth the trouble. After that I found it valuable once or twice as a spinal tonic* when I was run down; but now it's an unmitigated bore. I dont mind your declaration: I daresay it gives you a certain pleasure to make it. I quite understand that you adore me; but (if you dont mind) I'd rather you didnt keep on saying so.

JUNO. Is there then no hope for me?

MRS LUNN. Oh, yes. Gregory has an idea that married women keep lists of the men theyll marry if they become widows. I'll put your name down, if that will satisfy you.

JUNO. Is the list a long one?

MRS LUNN. Do you mean the real list? Not the one I shew to Gregory: there are hundreds of names on that; but the little private list that he'd better not see?

JUNO. Oh, will you really put me on that? Say you will.

MRS LUNN. Well, perhaps I will. [*He kisses her hand*]. Now dont begin abusing the privilege.

JUNO. May I call you by your Christian name?

MRS LUNN. No: it's too long. You cant go about calling a woman Seraphita.*

JUNO [*ecstatically*] Seraphita!

MRS LUNN. I used to be called Sally at home; but when I married a man named Lunn, of course that became ridiculous. Thats my one little pet joke.* Call me Mrs Lunn for short. And change the subject, or I shall go to sleep.

JUNO. I cant change the subject. For me there is no other subject. Why else have you put me on your list?

MRS LUNN. Because youre a solicitor. Gregory's a solicitor. I'm accustomed to my husband being a solicitor and telling me things he oughtnt to tell anybody.

JUNO [*ruefully*] Is that all? Oh, I cant believe that the voice of love has ever thoroughly awakened you.

MRS LUNN. No: it sends me to sleep. [*Juno appeals against this by an amorous demonstration*]. It's no use, Mr Juno: I'm hopelessly respectable: the Jenkinses always were. Dont you realize that unless most women were like that, the world couldnt go on as it does?

JUNO [*darkly*] You think it goes on respectably; but I can tell you as a solicitor—

MRS LUNN. Stuff! of course all the disreputable people who get into trouble go to you, just as all the sick people go to the doctors; but most people never go to a solicitor.

JUNO [*rising, with a growing sense of injury*] Look here, Mrs Lunn: do you think a man's heart is a potato? or a turnip? or a ball of knitting wool? that you can throw it away like this?

MRS LUNN. I dont throw away balls of knitting wool. A man's heart seems to me much like a sponge: it sops up dirty water as well as clean.

JUNO. I have never been treated like this in my life. Here am I, a married man, with a most attractive wife: a wife I adore, and who adores me, and has never as much as looked at any other man since we were married. I come and throw all this at your feet. I! I, a solicitor! braving the risk of your husband putting me into the divorce court and making me a beggar and an outcast! I do this for your sake. And you go on as if I were making no sacrifice: as if I had told you it's a fine evening, or asked you to have a cup of tea. It's not human. It's not right. Love has its rights as well as respectability [*he sits down again, aloof and sulky*].

MRS LUNN. Nonsense! Here! heres a flower [*she gives him one*]. Go and dream over it until you feel hungry. Nothing brings people to their senses like hunger.

JUNO [*contemplating the flower without rapture*] What good's this?

MRS LUNN [*snatching it from him*] Oh! you dont love me a bit.

JUNO. Yes I do. Or at least I did. But I'm an Englishman; and I think you ought to respect the conventions of English life.

MRS LUNN. But I *am* respecting them; and youre not.

JUNO. Pardon me. I may be doing wrong; but I'm doing it in a proper and customary manner. You may be doing right; but youre doing it in an unusual and questionable manner. I am not prepared to put up with that. I can stand being badly treated: I'm no baby, and can take care of myself with anybody. And of course I can stand being well treated. But the one thing I cant stand is being unexpectedly treated. It's outside my scheme of life. So come now! youve got to behave naturally and straightforwardly with me. You can leave husband and child, home, friends, and country, for my sake, and come with me to some southern isle—or say South America—where we can be all in all to one another. Or you can tell your husband and let him jolly well punch my head if he can. But I'm damned if I'm going to stand any eccentricity. It's not respectable.

GREGORY [*coming in from the terrace and advancing with dignity to his wife's end of the chesterfield*] Will you have the goodness, sir, in addressing this lady, to keep your temper and refrain from using profane language?

MRS LUNN [*rising, delighted*] Gregory! Darling [*she enfolds him in a copious embrace*]!

JUNO [*rising*] You make love to another man to my face!

MRS LUNN. Why, he's my husband.

JUNO. That takes away the last rag of excuse for such conduct. A nice world it would be if married people were to carry on their endearments before everybody!

GREGORY. This is ridiculous. What the devil business is it of yours what passes between my wife and myself? Youre not her husband, are you?

JUNO. Not at present; but I'm on the list. I'm her prospective husband: youre only her actual one. I'm the anticipation: youre the disappointment.

MRS LUNN. Oh, my Gregory is not a disappointment. [*Fondly*] Are you, dear?

GREGORY. You just wait, my pet. I'll settle this chap for you. [*He disengages himself from her embrace, and faces Juno. She sits down placidly*]. You call me a disappointment, do you? Well, I suppose every husband's a disappointment. What about yourself? Dont try to look like an unmarried man. I happen to know the lady *you* disappointed. I travelled in the same ship with her; and—

JUNO. And you fell in love with her.

GREGORY [*taken aback*] Who told you that?

JUNO. Aha! you confess it. Well, if you want to know, nobody told me. Everybody falls in love with my wife.

GREGORY. And do you fall in love with everybody's wife?

JUNO. Certainly not. Only with yours.

MRS LUNN. But whats the good of saying that, Mr Juno? I'm married to him; and theres an end of it.

JUNO. Not at all. You can get a divorce.

MRS LUNN. What for?

JUNO. For his misconduct with my wife.

GREGORY [*deeply indignant*] How dare you, sir, asperse the character of that sweet lady? a lady whom I have taken under my protection.

JUNO. Protection!

MRS JUNO [*returning hastily*] Really you must be more careful what you say about me, Mr Lunn.*

JUNO. My precious! [*He embraces her*]. Pardon this betrayal of feeling; but Ive not seen my wife for several weeks; and she is very dear to me.

GREGORY. I call this cheek. Who is making love to his own wife before people now, pray?

MRS LUNN. Wont you introduce me to your wife, Mr Juno?

MRS JUNO. How do you do? [*They shake hands; and Mrs Juno sits down beside Mrs Lunn, on her left*].

MRS LUNN. I'm so glad to find you do credit to Gregory's taste. I'm naturally rather particular about the women he falls in love with.

JUNO [*sternly*] This is no way to take your husband's unfaithfulness. [*To Lunn*] You ought to teach your wife better. Wheres her feelings? It's scandalous.

GREGORY. What about your own conduct, pray?

JUNO. I dont defend it; and theres an end of the matter.

GREGORY. Well, upon my soul! What difference does your not defending it make?

JUNO. A fundamental difference. To serious people I may appear wicked. I dont defend myself: I *am* wicked, though not bad at heart.

To thoughtless people I may even appear comic. Well, laugh at me: I have given myself away. But Mrs Lunn seems to have no opinion at all about me. She doesnt seem to know whether I'm wicked or comic. She doesnt seem to care. She has no moral sense. I say it's not right. I repeat, I have sinned; and I'm prepared to suffer.

MRS JUNO. Have you really sinned, Tops?

MRS LUNN [*blandly*] I dont remember your sinning. I have a shocking bad memory for trifles; but I think I should remember that—if you mean me.

JUNO [*raging*] Trifles! I have fallen in love with a monster.

GREGORY. Dont you dare call my wife a monster.

MRS JUNO [*rising quickly and coming between them*] Please dont lose your temper, Mr Lunn: I wont have my Tops bullied.

GREGORY. Well, then, let him not brag about sinning with my wife. [*He turns impulsively to his wife; makes her rise; and takes her proudly on his arm*]. What pretension has he to any such honor?

JUNO. I sinned in intention. [*Mrs Juno abandons him and resumes her seat, chilled*]. I'm as guilty as if I had actually sinned. And I insist on being treated as a sinner, and not walked over as if I'd done nothing, by your wife or any other man.

MRS LUNN. Tush! [*She sits down again contemptuously*].

JUNO [*furious*] I wont be belittled.

MRS LUNN [*to Mrs Juno*] I hope youll come and stay with us now that you and Gregory are such friends, Mrs Juno.

JUNO. This insane magnanimity—

MRS LUNN. Dont you think youve said enough, Mr Juno? This is a matter for two women to settle. Wont you take a stroll on the beach with my Gregory while we talk it over. Gregory is a splendid listener.

JUNO. I dont think any good can come of a conversation between Mr Lunn and myself. We can hardly be expected to improve one another's morals. [*He passes behind the chesterfield to Mrs Lunn's end; seizes a chair; deliberately pushes it between Gregory and Mrs Lunn; and sits down with folded arms, resolved not to budge*].

GREGORY. Oh! Indeed! Oh, all right. If you come to that—[*he crosses to Mrs Juno; plants a chair by her side; and sits down with equal determination*].

JUNO. Now we are both equally guilty.

GREGORY. Pardon me. I'm not guilty.

JUNO. In intention. Dont quibble. You were guilty in intention, as I was.

GREGORY. No. I should rather describe myself as being guilty in fact, but not in intention.

JUNO		What!
MRS JUNO	[*rising and exclaiming simultaneously*]	No, really—
MRS LUNN		Gregory!

GREGORY. Yes: I maintain that I am responsible for my intentions only, and not for reflex actions over which I have no control. [*Mrs Juno sits down, ashamed*]. I promised my mother that I would never tell a lie, and that I would never make love to a married woman. I never *have* told a lie—

MRS LUNN [*remonstrating*] Gregory! [*She sits down again*].

GREGORY. I say never. On many occasions I have resorted to prevarication; but on great occasions I have always told the truth. I regard this as a great occasion; and I wont be intimidated into breaking my promise. I solemnly declare that I did not know until this evening that Mrs Juno was married. She will bear me out when I say that from that moment my intentions were strictly and resolutely honorable; though my conduct, which I could not control and am therefore not responsible for, was disgraceful—or would have been had this gentleman not walked in and begun making love to my wife under my very nose.

JUNO [*flinging himself back into his chair*] Well, I like this!

MRS LUNN. Really, darling, theres no use in the pot calling the kettle black.

GREGORY. When you say darling, may I ask which of us you are addressing?

MRS LUNN. I really dont know. I'm getting hopelessly confused.

JUNO. Why dont you let my wife say something? I dont think she ought to be thrust into the background like this.

MRS LUNN. I'm sorry, I'm sure. Please excuse me, dear.

MRS JUNO [*thoughtfully*] I dont know what to say. I must think over it. I have always been rather severe on this sort of thing; but when it came to the point I didnt behave as I thought I should behave. I didnt intend to be wicked; but somehow or other, Nature, or whatever you choose to call it, didnt take much notice of my intentions. [*Gregory instinctively seeks her hand and presses it*]. And I really did think, Tops, that I was the only woman in the world for you.

JUNO [*cheerfully*] Oh, thats all right, my precious. Mrs Lunn thought she was the only woman in the world for him.

GREGORY [*reflectively*] So she is, in a sort of way.

JUNO [*flaring up*] And so is my wife. Dont you set up to be a better husband than I am; for youre not. Ive owned I'm wrong. You havnt.

MRS LUNN. Are you sorry, Gregory?

GREGORY [*perplexed*] Sorry?

MRS LUNN. Yes, sorry. I think it's time for you to say youre sorry, and to make friends with Mr Juno before we all dine together.

GREGORY. Seraphita: I promised my mother—

MRS JUNO [*involuntarily*] Oh, bother your mother! [*Recovering herself*] I beg your pardon.

GREGORY. A promise is a promise. I cant tell a deliberate lie. I know I ought to be sorry; but the flat fact is that I'm not sorry. I find that in this business, somehow or other, there is a disastrous separation between my moral principles and my conduct.

JUNO. Theres nothing disastrous about it. It doesnt matter about your conduct if your principles are all right.

GREGORY. Bosh! It doesnt matter about your principles if your conduct is all right.

JUNO. But your conduct isnt all right; and my principles are.

GREGORY. Whats the good of your principles being right if they wont work?

JUNO. They *will* work, sir, if you exercise self-sacrifice.

GREGORY. Oh yes: if, if, if. You know jolly well that self-sacrifice doesnt work either when you really want a thing. How much have you sacrificed yourself, pray?

MRS LUNN. Oh, a great deal, Gregory. Dont be rude. Mr Juno is a very nice man: he has been most attentive to me on the voyage.

GREGORY. And Mrs Juno's a very nice woman. She oughtnt to be; but she is.

JUNO. Why oughtnt she to be a nice woman, pray?

GREGORY. I mean she oughtnt to be nice to me. And you oughtnt to be nice to my wife. And your wife oughtnt to like me. And my wife oughtnt to like you. And if they do, they oughtnt to go on liking us. And I oughtnt to like your wife; and you oughtnt to like mine; and if we do, we oughtnt to go on liking them. But we do, all of us. We oughtnt; but we do.

JUNO. But, my dear boy, if we admit we are in the wrong wheres the harm of it? We're not perfect; but as long as we keep the ideal before us——

GREGORY. How?

JUNO. By admitting we're wrong.

MRS LUNN [*springing up, out of patience, and pacing round the lounge intolerantly*] Well, really, I must have my dinner. These two men, with their morality, and their promises to their mothers, and their admissions that they were wrong, and their sinning and suffering, and their going on at one another as if it meant anything, or as if it mattered, are getting on my nerves. [*Stooping over the back of the chesterfield to address Mrs Juno*] If you will be so very good, my dear, as to take my sentimental husband off my hands occasionally, I shall be more than obliged to you: I'm sure you can stand more male sentimentality than I can. [*Sweeping away to the fireplace*] I, on my part, will do my best to amuse your excellent husband when you find him tiresome.

JUNO. I call this polyandry.*

MRS LUNN. I wish you wouldnt call innocent things by offensive names, Mr Juno. What do you call your own conduct?

JUNO [*rising*] I tell you I have admitted—

GREGORY		Whats the good of keeping on at that?
MRS JUNO	[*together*]	Oh, not that again, please.
MRS LUNN		Tops: I'll scream if you say that again.

JUNO. Oh, well, if you wont listen to me—! [*He sits down again*].

MRS JUNO. What is the position now exactly? [*Mrs Lunn shrugs her shoulders and gives up the conundrum. Gregory looks at Juno. Juno turns away his head huffily*]. I mean, what are we going to do?

MRS LUNN. What would you advise, Mr Juno?

JUNO. I should advise you to divorce your husband.

MRS LUNN. You want me to drag your wife into court and disgrace her?

JUNO. No: I forgot that. Excuse me; but for the moment I thought I was married to you.

GREGORY. I think we had better let bygones be bygones. [*To Mrs Juno, very tenderly*] You will forgive me, wont you? Why should you let a moment's forgetfulness embitter all our future life?

MRS JUNO. But it's Mrs Lunn who has to forgive you.

GREGORY. Oh, dash it, I forgot. This is getting ridiculous.

MRS LUNN. I'm getting hungry.

MRS JUNO. Do you really mind, Mrs Lunn?

MRS LUNN. My dear Mrs Juno, Gregory is one of those terribly uxorious* men who ought to have ten wives. If any really nice woman will take him off my hands for a day or two occasionally, I shall be greatly obliged to her.

GREGORY. Seraphita: you cut me to the soul [*he weeps*].

MRS LUNN. Serve you right! Youd think it quite proper if it cut me to the soul.

MRS JUNO. Am I to take Sibthorpe off your hands too, Mrs Lunn?

JUNO [*rising*] Do you suppose I'll allow this?

MRS JUNO. Youve admitted that youve done wrong, Tops. Whats the use of your allowing or not allowing after that?

JUNO. I do not admit that I have done wrong. I admit that what I did was wrong.

GREGORY. Can you explain the distinction?

JUNO. It's quite plain to anyone but an imbecile. If you tell me Ive done something wrong you insult me. But if you say that something that I did is wrong you simply raise a question of morals. I tell you flatly if you say I did anything wrong you will have to fight me. In fact I think we ought to fight anyhow. I dont particularly want to; but I feel that England expects us to.

GREGORY. I wont fight. If you beat me my wife would share my humiliation. If I beat you, she would sympathize with you and loathe me for my brutality.

MRS LUNN. Not to mention that as we are human beings and not reindeer or barndoor fowl, if two men presumed to fight for us we couldnt decently ever speak to either of them again.

GREGORY. Besides, neither of us could beat the other, as we neither of us know how to fight. We should only blacken each other's eyes and make fools of ourselves.

JUNO. I dont admit that. Every Englishman can use his fists.

GREGORY. Youre an Englishman. Can you use yours?

JUNO. I presume so: I never tried.

MRS JUNO. You never told me you couldnt fight, Tops. I thought you were an accomplished boxer.

JUNO. My precious: I never gave you any ground for such a belief.

MRS JUNO. You always talked as if it were a matter of course. You spoke with the greatest contempt of men who didnt kick other men downstairs.

JUNO. Well, I cant kick Mr Lunn downstairs. We're on the ground floor.

MRS JUNO. You could throw him into the harbor.

GREGORY. Do you want me to be thrown into the harbor?

MRS JUNO. No: I only want to shew Tops that he's making a ghastly fool of himself.

GREGORY [*rising and prowling disgustedly between the chesterfield and the windows*] We're all making fools of ourselves.

JUNO [*following him*] Well, if we're not to fight, I must insist at least on your never speaking to my wife again.

GREGORY. Does my speaking to your wife do you any harm?

JUNO. No. But it's the proper course to take. [*Emphatically*] We *must* behave with some sort of decency.

MRS LUNN. And are you never going to speak to me again, Mr Juno?

JUNO. I'm prepared to promise never to do so. I think your husband has a right to demand that. Then if I speak to you after, it will not be his fault. It will be a breach of my promise; and I shall not attempt to defend my conduct.

GREGORY [*facing him*] I shall talk to your wife as often as she'll let me.

MRS JUNO. I have no objection to your speaking to me, Mr Lunn.

JUNO. Then I shall take steps.

GREGORY. What steps?

JUNO. Steps. Measures. Proceedings. Such steps as may seem advisable.

MRS LUNN [*to Mrs Juno*] Can *your* husband afford a scandal, Mrs Juno?

MRS JUNO. No.

MRS LUNN. Neither can mine.

GREGORY. Mrs Juno: I'm very sorry I let you in for all this. I dont know how it is that we contrive to make feelings like ours, which seem to me to be beautiful and sacred feelings, and which lead to such interesting and exciting adventures, end in vulgar squabbles and degrading scenes.

JUNO. I decline to admit that my conduct has been vulgar or degrading.

GREGORY. I promised—

JUNO. Look here, old chap: I dont say a word against your mother; and I'm sorry she's dead; but really, you know, most women are mothers; and they all die some time or other; yet that doesnt make them infallible authorities on morals, does it?

GREGORY. I was about to say so myself. Let me add that if you do things merely because you think some other fool expects you to do them, and he expects you to do them because he thinks you expect him to expect you to expect him to expect you to do them, it will end in everybody doing what nobody wants to do, which is in my opinion a silly state of things.

JUNO. Lunn: I love your wife; and thats all about it.

GREGORY. Juno: I love yours. What then?

JUNO. Clearly she must never see you again.

MRS JUNO. Why not?

JUNO. Why not! My love: I'm surprised at you.

MRS JUNO. Am I to speak only to men who dislike me?

JUNO. Yes: I think that is, properly speaking, a married woman's duty.

MRS JUNO. Then I wont do it: thats flat. I like to be liked. I like to be loved. I want everyone round me to love me. I dont want to meet or speak to anyone who doesnt like me.

JUNO. But, my precious, this is the most horrible immorality.

MRS LUNN. I dont intend to give up meeting you, Mr Juno. You amuse me very much. I dont like being loved: it bores me. But I do like to be amused.

JUNO. I hope we shall meet very often. But I hope also we shall not defend our conduct.

MRS JUNO. [*rising*] This is unendurable. Weve all been flirting. Need we go on footling* about it?

JUNO. [*huffily*] I dont know what you call footling—

MRS JUNO. [*cutting him short*] You do. *Youre* footling. Mr Lunn is footling. Cant we admit that we're human and have done with it?

JUNO. I have admitted it all along. I—

MRS JUNO. [*almost screaming*] Then stop footling.

The dinner gong sounds.

MRS LUNN. [*rising*] Thank heaven! Lets go into dinner. Gregory: take in Mrs Juno.

GREGORY. But surely I ought to take in our guest, and not my own wife.

MRS LUNN. Well, Mrs Juno is not your wife, is she?

GREGORY. Oh, of course: I beg your pardon. I'm hopelessly confused. [*He offers his arm to Mrs Juno, rather apprehensively*].

MRS JUNO. You seem quite afraid of me [*she takes his arm*].

GREGORY. I am. I simply adore you. [*They go out together; and as they pass through the door he turns and says in a ringing voice to the other couple*] I have said to Mrs Juno that I simply adore her. [*He takes her out defiantly*].

MRS LUNN [*calling after him*] Yes, dear. She's a darling. [*To Juno*] Now, Sibthorpe.

JUNO [*giving her his arm gallantly*] You have called me Sibthorpe! Thank you. I think Lunn's conduct fully justifies me in allowing you to do it.

MRS LUNN. Yes: I think you may let yourself go now.

JUNO. Seraphita: I worship you beyond expression.

MRS LUNN. Sibthorpe: you amuse me beyond description. Come. [*They go in to dinner together*].

WAR PLAYLETS

THE INCA OF PERUSALEM

AN ALMOST HISTORICAL COMEDIETTA

PREFACE

I MUST remind the reader that this playlet was written when its principal character, far from being a fallen foe and virtually a prisoner in our victorious hands, was still the Caesar* whose legions we were resisting with our hearts in our mouths. Many were so horribly afraid of him that they could not forgive me for not being afraid of him: I seemed to be trifling heartlessly with a deadly peril. I knew better; and I have represented Caesar as knowing better himself.* But it was one of the quaintnesses of popular feeling during the war that anyone who breathed the slightest doubt of the absolute perfection of German organization, the Machiavellian depth of German diplomacy, the omniscience of German science, the equipment of every German with a complete philosophy of history, and the consequent hopelessness of overcoming so magnificently accomplished an enemy except by the sacrifice of every recreative activity to incessant and vehement war work, including a heartbreaking mass of fussing and cadging and bluffing that did nothing but waste our energies and tire our resolution, was called a pro-German.

Now that this is all over, and the upshot of the fighting has shewn that we could quite well have afforded to laugh at the doomed Inca, I am in another difficulty. I may be supposed to be hitting Caesar when he is down. That is why I preface the play with this reminder that when it was written he was not down. To make quite sure, I have gone through the proof sheets very carefully, and deleted everything that could possibly be mistaken for a foul blow.* I have of course maintained the ancient privilege of comedy to chasten Caesar's foibles by laughing at them, whilst introducing enough obvious and outrageous fiction to relieve both myself and my model from the obligations and responsibilities of sober history and biography. But I should certainly put the play in the fire instead of publishing it if it contained a word against our defeated enemy that I would not have written in 1913.

THE INCA OF PERUSALEM

PROLOGUE

The tableau curtains are closed. An English archdeacon* comes through them in a condition of extreme irritation. He speaks through the curtains to someone behind them.

THE ARCHDEACON. Once for all, Ermyntrude, I cannot afford to maintain you in your present extravagance. [*He goes to a flight of steps leading to the stalls and sits down disconsolately on the top step. A fashionably dressed lady comes through the curtains and contemplates him with patient obstinacy. He continues, grumbling*] An English clergyman's daughter should be able to live quite respectably and comfortably on an allowance of £150 a year, wrung with great difficulty from the domestic budget.

ERMYNTRUDE. You are not a common clergyman: you are an archdeacon.

THE ARCHDEACON [*angrily*] That does not affect my emoluments* to the extent of enabling me to support a daughter whose extravagance would disgrace a royal personage. [*Scrambling to his feet and scolding at her*] What do you mean by it, Miss?

ERMYNTRUDE. Oh really, father! Miss! Is that the way to talk to a widow.

THE ARCHDEACON. Is that the way to talk to a father? Your marriage was a most disastrous imprudence. It gave you habits that are absolutely beyond your means—I mean beyond *my* means: you have no means. Why did you not marry Matthews: the best curate I ever had?

ERMYNTRUDE. I wanted to; and you wouldnt let me. You insisted on my marrying Roosenhonkers-Pipstein.*

THE ARCHDEACON. I had to do the best for you, my child. Roosenhonkers-Pipstein was a millionaire.

ERMYNTRUDE. How do you know he was a millionaire?

THE ARCHDEACON. He came from America. Of course he was

a millionaire. Besides, he proved to my solicitors that he had fifteen million dollars* when you married him.

ERMYNTRUDE. His solicitors proved to me that he had sixteen millions when he died. He was a millionaire to the last.

THE ARCHDEACON. O Mammon, Mammon!* I am punished now for bowing the knee to him. Is there nothing left of your settlement? Fifty thousand dollars a year it secured to you, as we all thought. Only half the securities* could be called speculative. The other half were gilt-edged. What has become of it all?

ERMYNTRUDE. The speculative ones were not paid up; and the gilt-edged ones just paid the calls on them until the whole show burst up.*

THE ARCHDEACON. Ermyntrude: what expressions!

ERMYNTRUDE. Oh bother! If you had lost ten thousand a year what expressions would you use, do you think? The long and the short of it is that I cant live in the squalid way you are accustomed to.

THE ARCHDEACON. Squalid!

ERMYNTRUDE. I have formed habits of comfort.

THE ARCHDEACON. Comfort!!

ERMYNTRUDE. Well, elegance if you like. Luxury, if you insist. Call it what you please. A house that costs less than a hundred thousand dollars* a year to run is intolerable to me.

THE ARCHDEACON. Then, my dear, you had better become lady's maid to a princess until you can find another millionaire to marry you.

ERMYNTRUDE. Thats an idea. I will [*She vanishes through the curtains*].

THE ARCHDEACON. What!* Come back, Miss. Come back this instant. [*The lights are lowered*]. Oh, very well: I have nothing more to say. [*He descends the steps into the auditorium and makes for the door, grumbling all the time*]. Insane, senseless extravagance! [*Barking*] Worthlessness!! [*Muttering*] I will not bear it any longer. Dresses, hats, furs, gloves, motor rides: one bill after another: money going like water. No restraint, no self-control, no decency. [*Shrieking*] I say, no decency! [*Muttering again*] Nice state of things we are coming to! A pretty world! But I simply will not bear it. She can do as she likes. I wash my hands of her: I am not going to die in the workhouse* for any good-for-nothing, undutiful, spendthrift daughter; and the sooner that is understood by everybody the better for all par—[*He is by this time out of hearing in the corridor*].

THE PLAY

A hotel sitting room. A table in the centre. On it a telephone. Two chairs at it, opposite one another. Behind it, the door. The fireplace has a mirror in the mantelpiece.

A spinster Princess, hatted and gloved, is ushered in by the Hotel Manager, spruce and artificially bland by professional habit, but treating his customer with a condescending affability which sails very close to the east wind of insolence.

THE MANAGER. I am sorry I am unable to accommodate Your Highness on the first floor.

THE PRINCESS [*very shy and nervous*] Oh please dont mention it. This is quite nice. Very nice. Thank you very much.

THE MANAGER. We could prepare a room in the annexe—

THE PRINCESS. Oh no. This will do very well.

She takes off her gloves and hat; puts them on the table; and sits down.

THE MANAGER. The rooms are quite as good up here. There is less noise; and there is the lift. If Your Highness desires anything, there is the telephone—

THE PRINCESS. Oh, thank you, I dont want anything. The telephone is so difficult: I am not accustomed to it.

THE MANAGER. Can I take any order? Some tea?

THE PRINCESS. Oh, thank you. Yes: I should like some tea, if I might— if it would not be too much trouble.

He goes out. The telephone rings. The Princess starts out of her chair, terrified, and recoils as far as possible from the instrument.

THE PRINCESS. Oh dear! [*It rings again. She looks scared. It rings again. She approaches it timidly. It rings again. She retreats hastily. It rings repeatedly. She runs to it in desperation and puts the receiver to her ear*]. Who is there? What do I do? I am not used to the telephone: I dont know how— What! Oh, I can hear you speaking quite distinctly. [*She sits down, delighted, and settles herself for a conversation*]. How wonderful! What! A lady? Oh! a person. Oh yes: I know. Yes, please, send her up. Have my servants finished their lunch yet? Oh no: please dont disturb them: I'd rather not. It doesnt matter. Thank you. What? Oh yes, it's quite easy. I had no idea—am I to hang it up just as it was? Thank you. [*She hangs it up*].

Ermyntrude enters, presenting a plain and staid appearance in a long straight waterproof with a hood over her head gear. She comes to the end of the table opposite to that at which the Princess is seated.

THE PRINCESS. Excuse me. I have been talking through the telephone; and I heard quite well, though I have never ventured before. Wont you sit down?

ERMYNTRUDE. No, thank you, Your Highness. I am only a lady's maid. I understood you wanted one.

THE PRINCESS. Oh no: you mustnt think I want one. It's so unpatriotic to want anything now, on account of the war,* you know. I sent my maid away as a public duty; and now she has married a soldier and is expecting a war baby. But I dont know how to do without her. Ive tried my very best; but somehow it doesnt answer: everybody cheats me; and in the end it isnt any saving. So Ive made up my mind to sell my piano and have a maid. That will be a real saving, because I really dont care a bit for music, though of course one has to pretend to. Dont you think so?

ERMYNTRUDE. Certainly I do, Your Highness. Nothing could be more correct. Saving and self-denial both at once; and an act of kindness to me, as I am out of place.

THE PRINCESS. I'm so glad you see it in that way. Er—you wont mind my asking, will you?—how did you lose your place?

ERMYNTRUDE. The war, Your Highness, the war.

THE PRINCESS. Oh yes, of course. But how—

ERMYNTRUDE [*taking out her handkerchief and shewing signs of grief*] My poor mistress—

THE PRINCESS. Oh *please* say no more. Dont think about it. So tactless of me to mention it.

ERMYNTRUDE [*mastering her emotion and smiling through her tears*] Your Highness is too good.

THE PRINCESS. Do you think you could be happy with me? I attach such importance to that.

ERMYNTRUDE [*gushing*] Oh, I *know* I shall.

THE PRINCESS. You must not expect too much. There is my uncle. He is very severe and hasty; and he is my guardian. I once had a maid I liked very much; but he sent her away the very first time.

ERMYNTRUDE. The first time of what, Your Highness?

THE PRINCESS. Oh, something she did. I am sure she had never done it before; and I *know* she would never have done it again, she was so truly contrite and nice about it.

ERMYNTRUDE. About what, Your Highness?

THE PRINCESS. Well, she wore my jewels and one of my dresses at a rather improper ball with her young man; and my uncle saw her.

ERMYNTRUDE. Then he was at the ball too, Your Highness?

THE PRINCESS [*struck by the inference*] I suppose he must have been. I wonder! You know, it's very sharp of you to find that out. I hope you are not too sharp.

ERMYNTRUDE. A lady's maid has to be, Your Highness. [*She produces some letters*]. Your Highness wishes to see my testimonials, no doubt. I have one from an Archdeacon. [*She proffers the letters*].

THE PRINCESS [*taking them*] Do archdeacons have maids? How curious!

ERMYNTRUDE. No, Your Highness. They have daughters. I have first-rate testimonials from the Archdeacon and from his daughter.

THE PRINCESS [*reading them*] The daughter says you are in every respect a treasure. The Archdeacon says he would have kept you if he could possibly have afforded it. Most satisfactory, I'm sure.

ERMYNTRUDE. May I regard myself as engaged then, Your Highness?

THE PRINCESS [*alarmed*] Oh, I'm sure I dont know. If you like, of course; but do you think I ought to?

ERMYNTRUDE. Naturally I think Your Highness ought to, most decidedly.

THE PRINCESS. Oh well, if you think that, I daresay youre quite right. Youll excuse my mentioning it, I hope; but what wages—er—?

ERMYNTRUDE. The same as the maid who went to the ball. Your Highness need not make any change.

THE PRINCESS. M'yes. Of course she began with less. But she had such a number of relatives to keep! It was quite heartbreaking: I had to raise her wages again and again.

ERMYNTRUDE. I shall be quite content with what she began on; and I have no relatives dependent on me. And I am willing to wear my own dresses at balls.

THE PRINCESS. I am sure nothing could be fairer than that. My uncle cant object to that: can he?

ERMYNTRUDE. If he does, Your Highness, ask him to speak to me about it. I shall regard it as part of my duties to speak to your uncle about matters of business.

THE PRINCESS. Would you? You must be frightfully courageous.

ERMYNTRUDE. May I regard myself as engaged, Your Highness? I should like to set about my duties immediately.

THE PRINCESS. Oh yes, I think so. Oh certainly. I—

A waiter comes in with the tea. He places the tray on the table.

THE PRINCESS. Oh, thank you.

ERMYNTRUDE [*raising the cover from the tea cake and looking at it*] How long has that been standing at the top of the stairs?

THE PRINCESS [*terrified*] Oh please! It doesnt matter.

THE WAITER. It has not been waiting. Straight from the kitchen, madam, believe me.

ERMYNTRUDE. Send the manager here.

THE WAITER. The manager! What do you want with the manager?

ERMYNTRUDE. He will tell you when I have done with him. How dare you treat Her Highness in this disgraceful manner? What sort of pothouse* is this? Where did you learn to speak to persons of quality? Take away your cold tea and cold cake instantly. Give them to the chambermaid you were flirting with whilst Her Highness was waiting. Order some fresh tea at once; and do not presume to bring it yourself: have it brought by a civil waiter who is accustomed to wait on ladies, and not, like you, on commercial travellers.

THE WAITER. Alas, madam, I am not accustomed to wait on anybody. Two years ago I was an eminent medical man.* My waiting-room was crowded with the flower of the aristocracy and the higher bourgeoisie from nine to six every day. But the war came; and my patients were ordered to give up their luxuries. They gave up their doctors, but kept their week-end hotels, closing every career to me except the career of a waiter. [*He puts his fingers on the teapot to test its temperature, and automatically takes out his watch with the other hand as if to count the teapot's pulse*]. You are right: the tea is cold: it was made by the wife of a once fashionable architect. The cake is only half toasted: what can you expect from a ruined west-end tailor whose attempt to establish a second-hand business failed last Tuesday week? Have you the heart to complain to the manager? Have we not suffered enough? Are our miseries nev—[*the manager enters*] Oh Lord! here he is. [*The waiter withdraws abjectly, taking the tea tray with him*].

THE MANAGER. Pardon, Your Highness; but I have received an urgent inquiry for rooms from an English family of importance; and I venture to ask you to let me know how long you intend to honor us with your presence.

THE PRINCESS [*rising anxiously*] Oh! am I in the way?

ERMYNTRUDE [*sternly*] Sit down, madam [*The Princess sits down forlornly. Ermyntrude turns imperiously to the Manager*]. Her Highness will require this room for twenty minutes.

THE MANAGER. Twenty minutes!

ERMYNTRUDE. Yes: it will take fully that time to find a proper apartment in a respectable hotel.

THE MANAGER. I do not understand.

ERMYNTRUDE. You understand perfectly. How dare you offer Her Highness a room on the second floor?

THE MANAGER. But I have explained. The first floor is occupied. At least—

ERMYNTRUDE. Well? At least?

THE MANAGER. It is occupied.

ERMYNTRUDE. Dont you dare tell Her Highness a falsehood. It is not occupied. You are saving it up for the arrival of the five fifteen express, from which you hope to pick up some fat armaments contractor* who will drink all the bad champagne in your cellar at 25 francs a bottle, and pay twice over for everything because he is in the same hotel with Her Highness, and can boast of having turned her out of the best rooms.

THE MANAGER. But Her Highness was so gracious. I did not know that her Highness was at all particular.

ERMYNTRUDE. And you take advantage of Her Highness's graciousness. You impose on her with your stories. You give her a room not fit for a dog. You send cold tea to her by a decayed professional person disguised as a waiter.* But dont think you can trifle with me. I am a lady's maid; and I know the ladies' maids and valets of all the aristocracies of Europe and all the millionaires of America. When I expose your hotel as the second-rate little hole it is, not a soul above the rank of a curate with a large family will be seen entering it. I shake its dust off my feet.* Order the luggage to be taken down at once.

THE MANAGER [*appealing to the Princess*] Can Your Highness believe this of me? Have I had the misfortune to offend Your Highness?

THE PRINCESS. Oh no. I am quite satisfied. Please—

ERMYNTRUDE. Is Your Highness dissatisfied with *me*?

THE PRINCESS [*intimidated*] Oh no: please dont think that. I only meant—

ERMYNTRUDE [*to the Manager*] You hear. Perhaps you think Her Highness is going to do the work of teaching you your place herself, instead of leaving it to her maid.

THE MANAGER. Oh please, mademoiselle. Believe me: our only wish is to make you perfectly comfortable. But in consequence of the war, all royal personages now practise a rigid economy, and desire us to treat them like their poorest subjects.

THE PRINCESS. Oh yes. You are quite right—

ERMYNTRUDE [*interrupting*] There! Her Highness forgives you; but dont do it again. Now go downstairs, my good man, and get that suite on the first floor ready for us. And send some proper tea. And turn on the heating apparatus until the temperature in the rooms is comfortably warm. And have hot water put in all the bedrooms—

THE MANAGER. There are basins with hot and cold taps.

ERMYNTRUDE [*scornfully*] Yes: there *would* be. I suppose we must put up with that: sinks in our rooms, and pipes that rattle and bang and guggle all over the house whenever anyone washes his hands. *I* know.

THE MANAGER [*gallant*] You are hard to please, mademoiselle.

ERMYNTRUDE. No harder than other people. But when I'm not pleased I'm not too ladylike to say so. Thats all the difference. There is nothing more, thank you.

The Manager shrugs his shoulders resignedly; makes a deep bow to the Princess; goes to the door; wafts a kiss surreptitiously to Ermyntrude; and goes out.

THE PRINCESS. It's wonderful! How have you the courage?

ERMYNTRUDE. In Your Highness's service I know no fear. Your Highness can leave all unpleasant people to me.

THE PRINCESS. How I wish I could! The most dreadful thing of all I have to go through myself.

ERMYNTRUDE. Dare I ask what it is, Your Highness?

THE PRINCESS. I'm going to be married. I'm to be met here and married to a man I never saw. A boy! A boy who never saw *me*! One of the sons of the Inca of Perusalem.

ERMYNTRUDE. Indeed? Which son?

THE PRINCESS. I dont know. They havnt settled which. It's a dreadful thing to be a princess: they just marry you to anyone they like. The Inca is to come and look at me, and pick out whichever of his sons he thinks will suit. And then I shall be an alien enemy everywhere except in Perusalem, because the Inca has made war on everybody. And I shall have to pretend that everybody has made war on him. It's too bad.

ERMYNTRUDE. Still, a husband is a husband. I wish I had one.

THE PRINCESS. Oh, how can you say that! I'm afraid youre not a nice woman.

ERMYNTRUDE. Your Highness is provided for. I'm not.

THE PRINCESS. Even if you could bear to let a man touch you, you shouldnt say so.

ERMYNTRUDE. I shall not say so again, Your Highness, except perhaps to the man.

THE PRINCESS. It's too dreadful to think of. I wonder you can be so coarse. I really dont think youll suit. I feel sure now that you know more about men than you should.

ERMYNTRUDE. I am a widow, Your Highness.

THE PRINCESS [*overwhelmed*] Oh, I BEG your pardon. Of course I ought to have known you would not have spoken like that if you were not married. That makes it all right, doesnt it? I'm so sorry.

The Manager returns, white, scared, hardly able to speak.

THE MANAGER. Your Highness: an officer asks to see you on behalf of the Inca of Perusalem.

THE PRINCESS [*rising distractedly*] Oh, I cant, really. Oh, what shall I do?

THE MANAGER. On important business, he says, Your Highness. Captain Duval.

ERMYNTRUDE. Duval! Nonsense! The usual thing. It is the Inca himself, incognito.

THE PRINCESS. Oh, send him away. Oh, I'm so afraid of the Inca. I'm not properly dressed to receive him; and he is so particular: he would order me to stay in my room for a week. Tell him to call tomorrow: say I'm ill in bed. I cant: I wont: I darent: you must get rid of him somehow.

ERMYNTRUDE. Leave him to me, Your Highness.

THE PRINCESS. Youd never dare!

ERMYNTRUDE. I am an Englishwoman, Your Highness, and perfectly capable of tackling ten Incas if necessary. I will arrange the matter. [*To the Manager*] Shew Her Highness to her bedroom; and then shew Captain Duval in here.

THE PRINCESS. Oh, thank you so much. [*She goes to the door. Ermyntrude, noticing that she has left her hat and gloves on the table, runs after her with them*]. Oh, *thank* you. And oh, please, if I must have one of his sons, I should like a fair one that doesnt shave, with soft hair and a beard. I couldnt bear being kissed by a bristly person. [*She runs out, the Manager bowing as she passes. He follows her*].

Ermyntrude whips off her waterproof; hides it; and gets herself swiftly into perfect trim at the mirror, before the Manager, with a large jewel case in his hand, returns, ushering in the Inca.

THE MANAGER. Captain Duval.

*The Inca, in military uniform, advances with a marked and imposing stage walk; stops; orders the trembling Manager by a gesture to place the jewel case on the table; dismisses him with a frown; touches his helmet graciously to Ermyntrude; and takes off his cloak.**

THE INCA. I beg you, madam, to be quite at your ease, and to speak to me without ceremony.

ERMYNTRUDE [*moving haughtily and carelessly to the table*] I hadnt the slightest intention of treating you with ceremony. [*She sits down: a liberty which gives him a perceptible shock*]. I am quite at a loss to imagine why I should treat a perfect stranger named Duval: a captain! almost a subaltern! with the smallest ceremony.

THE INCA. That is true. I had for the moment forgotten my position.

ERMYNTRUDE. It doesnt matter. You may sit down.

THE INCA [*frowning*] What!

ERMYNTRUDE. I said, you...may...sit...down.

THE INCA. Oh [*His moustache droops. He sits down*].

ERMYNTRUDE. What is your business?

THE INCA. I come on behalf of the Inca of Perusalem.

ERMYNTRUDE. The Allerhöchst?*

THE INCA. Precisely.

ERMYNTRUDE. I wonder does he feel ridiculous when people call him the Allerhöchst.

THE INCA [*surprised*] Why should he? He is the Allerhöchst.

ERMYNTRUDE. Is he nice looking?

THE INCA. I—er. Er—I. I—er. I am not a good judge.

ERMYNTRUDE. They say he takes himself very seriously.

THE INCA. Why should he not, madam? Providence* has entrusted to his family the care of a mighty empire. He is in a position of half divine, half paternal responsibility towards sixty millions of people, whose duty it is to die for him at the word of command. To take himself otherwise than seriously would be blasphemous. It is a punishable offence—severely punishable—in Perusalem. It is called Incadisparagement.

ERMYNTRUDE. How cheerful! Can he laugh?

THE INCA. Certainly, madam. [*He laughs, harshly and mirthlessly*]. Ha ha! Ha ha ha!

ERMYNTRUDE [*frigidly*] I asked could the Inca laugh. I did not ask could *you* laugh.

THE INCA. That is true, madam. [*Chuckling*] Devilish amusing, that! [*He laughs, genially and sincerely, and becomes a much more agreeable person*]. Pardon me: I am now laughing because I cannot help it. I am amused. The other was merely an imitation: a failure, I admit.

ERMYNTRUDE. You intimated that you had some business?

THE INCA [*producing a very large jewel case, and relapsing into solemnity*] I am instructed by the Allerhöchst to take a careful note of your features and figure, and, if I consider them satisfactory, to present you with this trifling token of His Imperial Majesty's regard, I do consider them satisfactory. Allow me [*he opens the jewel case and presents it*]!

ERMYNTRUDE [*staring at the contents*] What awful taste he must have! I cant wear that.

THE INCA [*reddening*] Take care, madam! This brooch was designed by the Inca himself. Allow me to explain the design. In the centre, the shield of Arminius.* The ten surrounding medallions represent the ten castles of His Majesty. The rim is a piece of the telephone cable laid by His Majesty across the Shipskeel canal.* The pin is a model in miniature of the sword of Henry the Birdcatcher.*

ERMYNTRUDE. Miniature! It must be bigger than the original. My good man, you dont expect me to wear this round my neck: it's as big as a turtle. [*He shuts the case with an angry snap*]. How much did it cost?

THE INCA. For materials and manufacture alone, half a million Perusalem dollars,* madam. The Inca's design constitutes it a work of art. As such, it is now worth probably ten million dollars.

ERMYNTRUDE. Give it to me [*she snatches it*]. I'll pawn it and buy something nice with the money.

THE INCA. Impossible, madam. A design by the Inca must not be exhibited for sale in the shop window of a pawnbroker. [*He flings himself into his chair, fuming*].

ERMYNTRUDE. So much the better. The Inca will have to redeem it to save himself from that disgrace; and the poor pawnbroker will get his money back. Nobody would buy it, you know.

THE INCA. May I ask why?

ERMYNTRUDE. Well, look at it! Just look at it! I ask you!*

THE INCA [*his moustache drooping ominously*] I am sorry to have to report to the Inca that you have no soul for fine art. [*He rises sulkily*]. The position of daughter-in-law* to the Inca is not compatible with the tastes of a pig. [*He attempts to take back the brooch*].

ERMYNTRUDE [*rising and retreating behind her chair with the brooch*] Here! you let that brooch alone. You presented it to me on behalf of the Inca. It is mine. You said my appearance was satisfactory.

THE INCA. Your appearance is *not* satisfactory. The Inca would not allow his son to marry you if the boy were on a desert island and you were the only other human being on it* [*he strides up the room*].

ERMYNTRUDE [*calmly sitting down and replacing the case on the table*] How could he? There would be no clergyman to marry us. It would have to be quite morganatic.*

THE INCA [*returning*] Such an expression is out of place in the mouth of a princess aspiring to the highest destiny on earth. You have the morals of a dragoon.* [*She receives this with a shriek of laughter. He struggles with his sense of humor*]. At the same time [*he sits down*] there is a certain coarse fun in the idea which compels me to smile [*he turns up his moustache and smiles*].

ERMYNTRUDE. When I marry the Inca's son, Captain, I shall make the Inca order you to cut off that moustache.* It is too irresistible. Doesnt it fascinate everyone in Perusalem?

THE INCA [*leaning forward to her energetically*] By all the thunders of Thor,* madam, it fascinates the whole world.

ERMYNTRUDE. What I like about you, Captain Duval, is your modesty.

THE INCA [*straightening up suddenly*] Woman: do not be a fool.

ERMYNTRUDE [*indignant*] Well!

THE INCA. You must look facts in the face. This moustache is an exact copy of the Inca's moustache. Well, does the world occupy itself with the Inca's moustache or does it not? Does it ever occupy itself with anything else? If that is the truth, does its recognition constitute the Inca a coxcomb? Other potentates have moustaches: even beards and moustaches. Does the world occupy itself with those beards and moustaches? Do the hawkers in the streets of every capital on the civilized globe sell ingenious cardboard representations of *their* faces on which, at the pulling of a simple string, the moustaches turn up and down, so—[*he makes his moustache turn up and down several times*]? No! I say No.* The Inca's moustache is so watched and studied that it has made his face the political barometer of the whole continent. When that moustache goes up, culture rises with it. Not what *you* call culture; but Kultur,* a word so much more significant that I hardly understand it myself except when I am in specially good form. When it goes down, millions of men perish.

ERMYNTRUDE. You know, if I had a moustache like that, it would turn my head. I should go mad. Are you quite sure the Inca isnt mad?

THE INCA. How can he be mad, madam? What is sanity? The condition of the Inca's mind. What is madness? The condition of the people who disagree with the Inca.

ERMYNTRUDE. Then I am a lunatic because I dont like that ridiculous brooch.

THE INCA. No, madam: you are only an idiot.

ERMYNTRUDE. Thank you.

THE INCA. Mark you: it is not to be expected that you should see eye to eye with the Inca. That would be presumption. It is for you to accept without question or demur the assurance of your Inca that the brooch is a masterpiece.

ERMYNTRUDE. My Inca! Oh, come! I like that. He is not my Inca yet.

THE INCA. He is everybody's Inca, madam. His realm will yet extend to the confines of the habitable earth. It is his divine right; and let those who dispute it look to themselves. Properly speaking, all those who are now trying to shake his world predominance are not at war with him, but in rebellion against him.

ERMYNTRUDE. Well, he started it, you know.*

THE INCA. Madam, be just. When the hunters surround the lion, the lion will spring. The Inca had kept the peace for years. Those who attacked him were steeped in blood, black blood, white blood, brown blood, yellow blood, blue blood. The Inca had never shed a drop.

ERMYNTRUDE. He had only talked.

THE INCA. Only *talked*! *Only* talked! What is more glorious than talk? Can anyone in the world talk like him? Madam: when he signed the declaration of war, he said to his foolish generals and admirals, 'Gentlemen: you will all be sorry for this.' And they are. They know now that they had better have relied on the sword of the spirit: in other words, on their Inca's talk, than on their murderous cannons. The world will one day do justice to the Inca as the man who kept the peace with nothing but his tongue and his moustache. While he talked: talked just as I am talking now to you, simply, quietly, sensibly, but GREATLY, there was peace; there was prosperity; Perusalem went from success to success. He has been silenced for a year by the roar of trinitrotoluene* and the bluster of fools; and the world is in ruins. What a tragedy! [*He is convulsed with grief*].*

ERMYNTRUDE. Captain Duval: I dont want to be unsympathetic; but suppose we get back to business.

THE INCA. Business! What business?

ERMYNTRUDE. Well, *my* business. You want me to marry one of the Inca's sons: I forget which.

THE INCA. As far as I can recollect the name, it is His Imperial Highness Prince Eitel William Frederick George Franz Josef Alexander Nicholas Victor Emmanuel Albert Theodore Wilson—*

ERMYNTRUDE [*interrupting*] Oh, please, *please*, maynt I have one with a shorter name? What is he called at home?

THE INCA. He is usually called Sonny, madam. [*With great charm of manner*] But you will please understand that the Inca had no desire to pin you to any particular son. There is Chips and Spots and Lulu and Pongo and the Corsair and the Piffler and Jack Johnson the

Second,* all unmarried. At least not seriously married: nothing, in short, that cannot be arranged. They are all at your service.

ERMYNTRUDE. Are they all as clever and charming as their father?

THE INCA [*lifts his eyebrows pityingly; shrugs his shoulders; then, with indulgent paternal contempt*] Excellent lads, madam. Very honest affectionate creatures. I have nothing against them. Pongo imitates farmyard sounds—cock-crowing and that sort of thing—extremely well. Lulu plays Strauss's Sinfonia Domestica* on the mouth organ* really screamingly. Chips keeps owls and rabbits. Spots motor bicycles. The Corsair commands canal barges and steers them himself. The Piffler writes plays, and paints most abominably. Jack Johnson trims ladies' hats, and boxes with professionals hired for that purpose. He is invariably victorious. Yes: they all have their different little talents. And also, of course, their family resemblances. For example, they all smoke; they all quarrel with one another; and they none of them appreciate their father, who, by the way, is no mean painter, though the Piffler pretends to ridicule his efforts.

ERMYNTRUDE. Quite a large choice, eh?

THE INCA. But very little to choose, believe me. I should not recommend Pongo, because he snores so frightfully that it has been necessary to build him a sound-proof bedroom: otherwise the royal family would get no sleep. But any of the others would suit equally well—if you are really bent on marrying one of them.

ERMYNTRUDE. If! What is this! I never wanted to marry one of them. I thought you wanted me to.

THE INCA. I did, madam; but [*confidentially, flattering her*] you are not quite the sort of person I expected you to be; and I doubt whether any of these young degenerates* would make you happy. I trust I am not shewing any want of natural feeling when I say that from the point of view of a lively, accomplished, and beautiful woman [*Ermyntrude bows*] they might pall after a time. I suggest that you might prefer the Inca himself.

ERMYNTRUDE. Oh, Captain, how could a humble person like myself be of any interest to a prince who is surrounded with the ablest and most far-reaching intellects in the world?

THE INCA [*explosively*] What on earth are you talking about, madam? Can you name a single man in the entourage of the Inca who is not a born fool?

ERMYNTRUDE. Oh, how can you say that! There is Admiral von Cockpits—*

THE INCA [*rising intolerantly and striding about the room*] Von Cockpits! Madam: if Von Cockpits ever goes to heaven, before three weeks are over, the Angel Gabriel* will be at war with the man in the moon.

ERMYNTRUDE. But General Von Schinkenburg—*

THE INCA. Schinkenburg!* I grant you, Schinkenburg has a genius for defending market gardens. Among market gardens he is invincible. But what is the good of that? The world does not consist of market gardens. Turn him loose in pasture and he is lost. The Inca has defeated all these generals again and again at manœuvres; and yet he has to give place to them in the field because he would be blamed for every disaster—accused of sacrificing the country to his vanity. Vanity! Why do they call him vain? Just because he is one of the few men who are not afraid to live. Why do they call themselves brave? Because they have not sense enough to be afraid to die. Within the last year the world has produced millions of heroes. Has it produced more than one Inca? [*He resumes his seat*].

ERMYNTRUDE. Fortunately not, Captain. I'd rather marry Chips.

THE INCA [*making a wry face*] Chips! Oh no: I wouldnt marry Chips.

ERMYNTRUDE. Why?

THE INCA [*whispering the secret*] Chips talks too much about himself.

ERMYNTRUDE. Well, what about Snooks?

THE INCA. Snooks? Who is he? Have I a son named Snooks? There are so many—[*wearily*] so many—that I often forget. [*Casually*] But I wouldnt marry him, anyhow, if I were you.

ERMYNTRUDE. But hasnt any of them inherited the family genius? Surely, if Providence has entrusted them with the care of Perusalem— if they are all descended from Bedrock the Great—*

THE INCA [*interrupting her impatiently*] Madam: if you ask me, I consider Bedrock a grossly overrated monarch.

ERMYNTRUDE [*shocked*] Oh, Captain! Take care! Incadisparagement.

THE INCA. I repeat, grossly overrated. Strictly between ourselves, I do not believe all this about Providence entrusting the care of sixty million human beings to the abilities of Chips and the Piffler and Jack Johnson. I believe in individual genius. That is the Inca's secret. It must be. Why, hang it all, madam, if it were a mere family matter, the Inca's uncle* would have been as great a man as the Inca. And—well, everybody knows what the Inca's uncle was.

ERMYNTRUDE. My experience is that the relatives of men of genius are always the greatest duffers* imaginable.

THE INCA. Precisely. That is what proves that the Inca is a man of genius. His relatives *are* duffers.

ERMYNTRUDE. But bless my soul, Captain, if all the Inca's generals are incapables, and all his relatives duffers, Perusalem will be beaten in the war; and then it will become a republic, like France after 1871,* and the Inca will be sent to St Helena.*

THE INCA [*triumphantly*] That is just what the Inca is playing for, madam. It is why he consented to the war.

ERMYNTRUDE. What!

THE INCA. Aha! The fools talk of crushing the Inca; but they little know their man. Tell me this. Why did St Helena extinguish Napoleon?

ERMYNTRUDE. I give it up.

THE INCA. Because, madam, with certain rather remarkable qualities, which I should be the last to deny, Napoleon lacked versatility. After all, any fool can be a soldier: we know that only too well in Perusalem, where every fool *is* a soldier. But the Inca has a thousand other resources. He is an architect. Well, St Helena presents an unlimited field to the architect. He is a painter: need I remind you that St Helena is still without a National Gallery? He is a composer: Napoleon left no symphonies in St Helena. Send the Inca to St Helena, madam, and the world will crowd thither to see his works as they crowd now to Athens to see the Acropolis,* to Madrid to see the pictures of Velasquez,* to Bayreuth* to see the music dramas of that egotistical old rebel Richard Wagner, who ought to have been shot before he was forty, as indeed he very nearly was.* Take this from me: hereditary monarchs are played out: the age for men of genius has come: the career is open to the talents: before ten years have elapsed every civilized country from the Carpathians to the Rocky Mountains* will be a Republic.

ERMYNTRUDE. Then goodbye to the Inca.

THE INCA. On the contrary, madam, the Inca will then have his first real chance. He will be unanimously invited by those Republics to return from his exile and act as Super-president of all the republics.

ERMYNTRUDE. But wont that be a come down for him? Think of it! after being Inca, to be a mere President!

THE INCA. Well, why not! An Inca can do nothing. He is tied hand and foot. A constitutional monarch is openly called an india-rubber stamp.* An emperor is a puppet. The Inca is not allowed to make a speech: he is compelled to take up a screed of flatulent twaddle written by some noodle of a minister and read it aloud. But look at the American President!* He is the Allerhöchst, if you like. No, madam, believe me, there is nothing like Democracy, American Democracy. Give the people voting papers: good long voting papers, American fashion;* and while the people are reading the voting papers the Government does what it likes.

ERMYNTRUDE. What! You too worship before the statue of Liberty, like the Americans?

THE INCA. Not at all, madam. The Americans do not worship the statue of Liberty. They have erected it in the proper place for a statue of Liberty: on its tomb* [*he turns down his moustaches*].

ERMYNTRUDE [*laughing*] Oh! Youd better not let them hear you say that, Captain.

THE INCA. Quite safe, madam: they would take it as a joke. [*He rises*]. And now, prepare yourself for a surprise. [*She rises*]. A shock. Brace yourself. Steel yourself. And do not be afraid.

ERMYNTRUDE. Whatever on earth can you be going to tell me, Captain?

THE INCA. Madam: I am no captain. I—

ERMYNTRUDE. You are the Inca in disguise.

THE INCA. Good heavens! how do you know that? Who has betrayed me?

ERMYNTRUDE. How could I help divining it, Sir? Who is there in the world like you? Your magnetism—

THE INCA. True: I had forgotten my magnetism. But you know now that beneath the trappings of Imperial Majesty there is a Man: simple,

frank, modest, unaffected, colloquial: a sincere friend, a natural human
being, a genial comrade, one eminently calculated to make a woman
happy. You, on the other hand, are the most charming woman I have
ever met. Your conversation is wonderful. I have sat here almost in
silence, listening to your shrewd and penetrating account of my
character, my motives, if I may say so, my talents. Never has such
justice been done me: never have I experienced such perfect sympathy.
Will you—I hardly know how to put this—will you be mine?

ERMYNTRUDE. Oh, Sir, you are married.

THE INCA. I am prepared to embrace the Mahometan faith,* which
allows a man four wives, if you will consent. It will please the Turks. But
I had rather you did not mention it to the Inca-ess, if you dont mind.

ERMYNTRUDE. This is really charming of you. But the time has come
for me to make a revelation. It is your Imperial Majesty's turn now to
brace yourself. To steel yourself. I am not the princess. I am—

THE INCA. The daughter of my old friend Archdeacon Daffodil
Donkin, whose sermons are read to me every evening after dinner.
I never forget a face.

ERMYNTRUDE. You knew all along!

THE INCA [*bitterly, throwing himself into his chair*] And you supposed
that I, who have been condemned to the society of princesses all my
wretched life, believed for a moment that any princess that ever
walked could have your intelligence!

ERMYNTRUDE. How clever of you, Sir! But you cannot afford to marry
me.

THE INCA [*springing up*] Why not?

ERMYNTRUDE. You are too poor. You have to eat war bread.* Kings
nowadays belong to the poorer classes. The King of England does
not even allow himself wine at dinner.*

THE INCA [*delighted*] Haw! Ha ha! Haw! haw! [*he is convulsed with laughter,
and finally has to relieve his feelings by waltzing half round the room*].

ERMYNTRUDE. You may laugh, Sir; but I really could not live in that
style.* I am the widow of a millionaire, ruined by your little war.

THE INCA. A millionaire! What are millionaires now, with the world
crumbling?

ERMYNTRUDE. Excuse me: mine was a hyphenated millionaire.*

THE INCA. A highfalutin millionaire, you mean. [*Chuckling*] Haw! ha ha! really very nearly a pun, that. [*He sits down in her chair*].

ERMYNTRUDE [*revolted, sinking into his chair*] I think it quite the worst pun I ever heard.

THE INCA. The best puns have all been made years ago: nothing remained but to achieve the worst. However, madam [*he rises majestically; and she is about to rise also*] No: I prefer a seated audience [*she falls back into her seat at the imperious wave of his hand*] So [*he clicks his heels*]. Madam: I recognize my presumption in having sought the honor of your hand. As you say, I cannot afford it. Victorious as I am, I am hopelessly bankrupt; and the worst of it is, I am intelligent enough to know it. And I shall be beaten in consequence, because my most implacable enemy,* though only a few months further away from bankruptcy than myself, has not a ray of intelligence, and will go on fighting until civilization is destroyed, unless I, out of sheer pity for the world, condescend to capitulate.

ERMYNTRUDE. The sooner the better, Sir. Many fine young men are dying while you wait.*

THE INCA [*flinching painfully*] Why? Why do they do it?

ERMYNTRUDE. Because you make them.

THE INCA. Stuff! How can I? I am only one man; and they are millions. Do you suppose they would really kill each other if they didnt want to, merely for the sake of my beautiful eyes? Do not be deceived by newspaper claptrap, madam. I was swept away by a passion not my own, which imposed itself on me. By myself I am nothing. I dare not walk down the principal street of my own capital in a coat two years old, though the sweeper of that street can wear one ten years old. You talk of death as an unpopular thing. You are wrong: for years I gave them art, literature, science, prosperity, that they might live more abundantly; and they hated me, ridiculed me, caricatured me. Now that I give them death in its frightfullest forms, they are devoted to me. If you doubt me, ask those who for years have begged our taxpayers in vain for a few paltry thousands to spend on Life: on the bodies and minds of the nation's children, on the beauty and healthfulness of its cities, on the honor and comfort of its wornout workers. They refused; and because they refused, death is let loose on them. They grudged a few hundreds a year for their salvation: they now pay millions a day for their own destruction and damnation. And this they call *my* doing! Let them say it, if they dare, before the judgment-seat at which they and I shall answer at last for what we have left undone no less than for what we have done. [*Pulling himself together suddenly*] Madam: I have the honor to be your most obedient [*he clicks his heels and bows*].

ERMYNTRUDE. Sir! [*she curtsies*].

THE INCA [*turning at the door*] Oh, by the way, there is a princess, isnt there, somewhere on the premises?

ERMYNTRUDE. There is. Shall I fetch her?

THE INCA [*dubious*] Pretty awful, I suppose, eh?

ERMYNTRUDE. About the usual thing.

THE INCA [*sighing*] Ah well! What can one expect? I dont think I need trouble her personally. Will you explain to her about the boys?

ERMYNTRUDE. I am afraid the explanation will fall rather flat without your magnetism.

THE INCA [*returning to her and speaking very humanly*] You are making fun of me. Why does everybody make fun of me? Is it fair?

ERMYNTRUDE [*seriously*] Yes: it is fair. What other defence have we poor common people against your shining armor, your mailed fist, your pomp and parade, your terrible power over us? Are these things fair?

THE INCA. Ah, well, perhaps, perhaps. [*He looks at his watch*]. By the way, there is time for a drive round the town and a cup of tea at the Zoo. Quite a bearable band there: it does not play any patriotic airs. I am sorry you will not listen to any more permanent arrangement; but if you would care to come—

ERMYNTRUDE [*eagerly*] Ratherrrrr. I shall be delighted.

THE INCA [*cautiously*] In the strictest honor, you understand.

ERMYNTRUDE. Dont be afraid. I promise to refuse any incorrect proposals.

THE INCA [*enchanted*] Oh! Charming woman: how well you understand men!

He offers her his arm: they go out together.

O'FLAHERTY V.C.

A RECRUITING PAMPHLET

PREFACE

IT may surprise some people to learn that in 1915 this little play was a recruiting poster in disguise. The British officer seldom likes Irish soldiers; but he always tries to have a certain proportion of them in his battalion, because, partly from a want of common sense which leads them to value their lives less than Englishmen do (lives are really less worth living in a poor country), and partly because even the most cowardly Irishman feels obliged to outdo an Englishman in bravery if possible, and at least to set a perilous pace for him, Irish soldiers give impetus to those military operations which require for their spirited execution more devilment than prudence.

Unfortunately, Irish recruiting was badly bungled in 1915. The Irish were for the most part Roman Catholics and loyal Irishmen, which means that from the English point of view they were heretics and rebels. But they were willing enough to go soldiering on the side of France and see the world outside Ireland, which is a dull place to live in. It was quite easy to enlist them by approaching them from their own point of view. But the War Office insisted on approaching them from the point of view of Dublin Castle.* They were discouraged and repulsed by refusals to give commissions to Roman Catholic officers, or to allow distinct Irish units to be formed. To attract them, the walls were covered with placards headed REMEMBER BELGIUM.* The folly of asking an Irishman to remember anything when you want him to fight for England was apparent to everyone outside the Castle: FORGET AND FORGIVE* would have been more to the point. Remembering Belgium and its broken treaty* led Irishmen to remember Limerick and its broken treaty;* and the recruiting ended in a rebellion,* in suppressing which the British artillery quite unnecessarily reduced the centre of Dublin to ruins, and the British commanders killed their leading prisoners of war in cold blood morning after morning with an effect of long drawn out ferocity.* Really it was only the usual childish petulance in which John Bull* does things in a week that disgrace him for a century, though he soon recovers his good humor, and cannot understand why the survivors of his wrath do not feel as jolly with him as he does with them. On the smouldering ruins of Dublin* the appeals to remember Louvain* were presently supplemented by a fresh appeal. IRISHMEN: DO YOU WISH TO HAVE THE HORRORS OF WAR BROUGHT TO YOUR OWN HEARTHS AND HOMES? Dublin laughed sourly.

As for me, I addressed myself quite simply to the business of obtaining recruits. I knew by personal experience and observation what anyone might have inferred from the records of Irish emigration, that all an Irishman's hopes and ambitions turn on his opportunities of getting out of Ireland. Stimulate his loyalty, and he will stay in Ireland and die for her; for, incomprehensible as it seems to an Englishman, Irish patriotism does not take the form of devotion to England and England's king. Appeal to his discontent, his deadly boredom, his thwarted curiosity and desire for change and adventure, and, to escape from Ireland, he will go abroad to risk his life for France, for the Papal States, for secession in America,* and even, if no better may be, for England. Knowing that the ignorance and insularity of the Irishman is a danger to himself and to his neighbors, I had no scruple in making that appeal when there was something for him to fight which the whole world had to fight unless it meant to come under the jack boot of the German version of Dublin Castle.

There was another consideration, unmentionable by the recruiting sergeants and war orators, which must nevertheless have helped them powerfully in procuring soldiers by voluntary enlistment. The happy home of the idealist may become common under millennial conditions. It is not common at present. No one will ever know how many men joined the army in 1914 and 1915 to escape from tyrants and taskmasters, termagants* and shrews, none of whom are any the less irksome when they happen by ill-luck to be also our fathers, our mothers, our wives and our children. Even at their amiablest, a holiday from them may be a tempting change for all parties. That is why I did not endow O'Flaherty V.C. with an ideal Irish colleen* for his sweetheart, and gave him for his mother a Volumnia* of the potato patch rather than an affectionate parent from whom he could not so easily have torn himself away.

I need hardly say that a play thus carefully adapted to its purpose was voted utterly inadmissible; and in due course the British Government, frightened out of its wits for the moment by the rout of the Fifth Army,* ordained Irish Conscription,* and then did not dare to go through with it. I still think my own line was the more businesslike. But during the war everyone except the soldiers at the front imagined that nothing but an extreme assertion of our most passionate prejudices, without the smallest regard to their effect on others, could win the war. Finally the British blockade* won the war; but the wonder is that the British blockhead did not lose it. I suppose the enemy was no wiser. War is not a sharpener of wits; and I am afraid I gave great offence by keeping my head in this matter of Irish recruiting. What can I do but apologize, and publish the play now that it can no longer do any good?

O'FLAHERTY V.C.

At the door of an Irish country house in a park. Fine summer weather: the summer of 1915. The porch, painted white, projects into the drive; but the door is at the side and the front has a window. The porch faces east; and the door is in the north side of it. On the south side is a tree in which a thrush is singing. Under the window is a garden seat with an iron chair at each end of it.

The last four bars of God Save the King* *are heard in the distance, followed by three cheers. Then the band strikes up* It's a Long Way to Tipperary* *and recedes until it is out of hearing.*

Private O'Flaherty *V.C. comes wearily southward along the drive, and falls exhausted into the garden seat. The thrush utters a note of alarm and flies away. The tramp of a horse is heard.*

A GENTLEMAN'S VOICE. Tim! Hi! Tim! [*He is heard dismounting*].

A LABORER'S VOICE. Yes, your honor.

THE GENTLEMAN'S VOICE. Take this horse to the stables, will you?

A LABORER'S VOICE. Right, your honor. Yup there. Gwan now. Gwan. [*The horse is led away*].

General Sir Pearce Madigan, an elderly baronet *in* khaki, beaming with enthusiasm, arrives. O'Flaherty rises and stands at attention.*

SIR PEARCE. No, no, O'Flaherty: none of that now. Youre off duty. Remember that though I am a general of forty years service, that little Cross of yours gives you a higher rank in the roll of glory than I can pretend to.

O'FLAHERTY [*relaxing*] I'm thankful to you, Sir Pearce; but I wouldnt have anyone think that the baronet of my native place would let a common soldier like me sit down in his presence without leave.

SIR PEARCE. Well, youre not a common soldier, O'Flaherty: youre a very uncommon one; and I'm proud to have you for my guest here today.

O'FLAHERTY. Sure I know, sir. You have to put up with a lot from the like of me for the sake of the recruiting.* All the quality* shakes hands with me and says theyre proud to know me, just the way the king said when he pinned the Cross on me. And it's as true as I'm standing here, sir, the queen* said to me 'I hear you were born on the estate of General Madigan,' she says; 'and the General himself tells me you were always a fine young fellow.' 'Bedad,* Mam,' I says to her, 'if the General knew all the rabbits I snared on him, and all the salmon I snatched on him, and all the cows I milked on him, he'd think me the finest ornament for the county jail he ever sent there for poaching.'

SIR PEARCE [*laughing*] Youre welcome to them all, my lad. Come [*he makes him sit down again on the garden seat*]! sit down and enjoy your holiday [*he sits down on one of the iron chairs: the one at the doorless side of the porch*].

O'FLAHERTY. Holiday, is it? I'd give five shillings to be back in the trenches for the sake of a little rest and quiet. I never knew what hard work was til I took to recruiting. What with the standing on my legs all day, and the shaking hands, and the making speeches, and—whats worse—the listening to them, and the calling for cheers for king and country, and the saluting the flag til I'm stiff with it, and the listening to them playing God Save the King and Tipperary, and the trying to make my eyes look moist like a man in a picture book, I'm that bet* that I hardly get a wink of sleep. I give you my word, Sir Pearce, that I never heard the tune of Tipperary in my life til I came back from Flanders;* and already it's drove me to that pitch of tiredness of it that when a poor little innocent slip of a boy in the street the other night drew himself up and saluted and began whistling it at me, I clouted his head for him, God forgive me.

SIR PEARCE [*soothingly*] Yes, yes: I know. *I* know. One does get fed up with it: Ive been dog tired myself on parade many a time. But still, you know, theres a gratifying side to it, too. After all, he is our king; and it's our own country, isnt it?*

O'FLAHERTY. Well, sir, to you that have an estate in it, it would feel like your country. But the divil a perch of it ever I owned.* And as to the king, God help him, my mother would have taken the skin off my back if I'd ever let on to have any other king than Parnell.*

SIR PEARCE [*rising, painfully shocked*] Your mother! What are you dreaming about, O'Flaherty? A most loyal woman. Always *most* loyal. Whenever there is an illness in the Royal Family, she asks me every time we meet about the health of the patient as anxiously as if it were yourself, her only son.

O'FLAHERTY. Well, she's my mother; and I wont utter a word agen her. But I'm not saying a word of lie when I tell you that that old woman is the biggest kanatt* from here to the cross of Monasterboice.* Sure she's the wildest Fenian* and rebel, and always has been, that ever taught a poor innocent lad like myself to pray night and morning to St Patrick* to clear the English out of Ireland the same as he cleared the snakes. Youll be surprised at my telling you that now, maybe, Sir Pearce?

SIR PEARCE [*unable to keep still, walking away from O'Flaherty*] Surprised! I'm more than surprised, O'Flaherty. I'm overwhelmed. [*Turning and facing him*] Are you—are you joking?

O'FLAHERTY. If youd been brought up by my mother, sir, youd know better than to joke about her. What I'm telling you is the truth; and I wouldnt tell it to you if I could see my way to get out of the fix I'll be in when my mother comes here this day to see her boy in his glory, and she after thinking all the time it was against the English I was fighting.

SIR PEARCE. Do you mean to say you told her such a monstrous falsehood as that you were fighting in the German army?

O'FLAHERTY. I never told her one word that wasnt the truth and nothing but the truth. I told her I was going to fight for the French and for the Russians; and sure who ever heard of the French or the Russians doing anything to the English but fighting them? That was how it was, sir. And sure the poor woman kissed me and went about the house singing in her old cracky voice that the French was on the sea, and theyd be here without delay, and the Orange will decay, says the Shan Van Vocht.*

SIR PEARCE [*sitting down again, exhausted by his feelings*] Well, I never could have believed this. Never. What do you suppose will happen when she finds out?

O'FLAHERTY. She mustnt find out. It's not that she'd half kill me, as big as I am and as brave as I am. It's that I'm fond of her, and cant bring myself to break the heart in her. You may think it queer that a man should be fond of his mother, sir, and she having bet him from the time he could feel to the time she was too slow to ketch him; but I'm fond of her; and I'm not ashamed of it. Besides, didnt she win the Cross for me?

SIR PEARCE. Your mother! How?

O'FLAHERTY. By bringing me up to be more afraid of running away than of fighting. I was timid by nature; and when the other boys hurted me, I'd want to run away and cry. But she whaled me for disgracing the blood of the O'Flahertys until I'd have fought the divil himself sooner than face her after funking* a fight. That was how I got to know that fighting was easier than it looked, and that the others was as much afeard of me as I was of them, and that if I only held out long enough theyd lose heart and give up. Thats the way I came to be so courageous. I tell you, Sir Pearce, if the German army had been brought up by my mother, the Kaiser* would be dining in the banqueting hall at Buckingham Palace this day, and King George polishing his jack boots for him in the scullery.

SIR PEARCE. But I dont like this, O'Flaherty. You cant go on deceiving your mother, you know. It's not right.

O'FLAHERTY. Cant go on deceiving her, cant I? It's little you know what a son's love can do, sir. Did you ever notice what a ready liar I am?

SIR PEARCE. Well, in recruiting a man gets carried away. I stretch it a bit occasionally myself. After all, it's for king and country. But if you wont mind my saying it, O'Flaherty, I think that story about your fighting the Kaiser and the twelve giants of the Prussian guard* singlehanded would be the better for a little toning down. I dont ask you to drop it, you know; for it's popular, undoubtedly; but still, the truth is the truth. Dont you think it would fetch in almost as many recruits if you reduced the number of guardsmen to six?

O'FLAHERTY. Youre not used to telling lies like I am, sir. I got great practice at home with my mother. What with saving my skin when I was young and thoughtless, and sparing her feelings when I was old enough to understand them, Ive hardly told my mother the truth twice a year since I was born; and would you have me turn round on her and tell it now, when she's looking to have some peace and quiet in her old age?

SIR PEARCE [*troubled in his conscience*] Well, it's not my affair, of course, O'Flaherty. But hadnt you better talk to Father Quinlan about it?

O'FLAHERTY. Talk to Father Quinlan, is it! Do you know what Father Quinlan says to me this very morning?

SIR PEARCE. Oh, youve seen him already, have you? What did he say?

O'FLAHERTY. He says 'You know, dont you' he says 'that it's your duty, as a Christian and a good son of the Holy Church, to love your enemies?' he says. 'I know it's my juty as a soldier to kill them' I says. 'That right, Dinny,' he says: 'quite right. But' says he 'you can kill them and do them a good turn afterwards to shew your love for them' he says; 'and it's your duty to have a mass said* for the souls of the hundreds of Germans you say you killed' says he; 'for many and many of them were Bavarians* and good Catholics' he says. 'Is it me that must pay for masses for the souls of the Boshes?'* I says. 'Let the King of England pay for them' I says; 'for it was his quarrel and not mine.'

SIR PEARCE [*warmly*] It is the quarrel of every honest man and true patriot, O'Flaherty. Your mother must see that as clearly as I do. After all, she is a reasonable, well disposed woman, quite capable of understanding the right and the wrong of the war. Why cant you explain to her what the war is about?

O'FLAHERTY. Arra, sir, how the divil do I know what the war is about?

SIR PEARCE [*rising again and standing over him*] What! O'Flaherty: do you know what you are saying? You sit there wearing the Victoria Cross for having killed God knows how many Germans; and you tell me you dont know why you did it!

O'FLAHERTY. Asking your pardon, Sir Pearce, I tell you no such thing. I know quite well why I kilt them. I kilt them because I was afeard that, if I didnt, theyd kill me.

SIR PEARCE [*giving it up, and sitting down again*] Yes, yes, of course; but have you no knowledge of the causes of the war? of the interests at stake? of the importance—I may almost say—in fact I *will* say—the sacred rights for which we are fighting? Dont you read the papers?

O'FLAHERTY. I do when I can get them. Theres not many newsboys crying the evening paper in the trenches. They do say, Sir Pearce, that we shall never beat the Boshes* until we make Horatio Bottomley* Lord Leftnant of England. Do you think thats true, sir?

SIR PEARCE. Rubbish, man! theres no Lord Lieutenant* in England: the king is Lord Lieutenant. It's a simple question of patriotism. Does patriotism mean nothing to you?

O'FLAHERTY. It means different to me than what it would to you, sir. It means England and England's king to you. To me and the like of me, it means talking about the English just the way the English papers talk about the Boshes.* And what good has it ever done here in Ireland? It's kept me ignorant because it filled up my mother's mind, and she thought it ought to fill up mine too. It's kept Ireland poor, because instead of trying to better ourselves we thought we was the fine fellows of patriots when we were speaking evil of Englishmen that was as poor as ourselves and maybe as good as ourselves.* The Boshes I kilt was more knowledgable men than me: and what better am I now that Ive kilt them? What better is anybody?

SIR PEARCE [*huffed, turning a cold shoulder to him*] I am sorry the terrible experience of this war—the greatest war ever fought—has taught you no better, O'Flaherty.

O'FLAHERTY [*preserving his dignity*] I dont know about its being a great war, sir. It's a big war; but thats not the same thing. Father Quinlan's new church is a big church: you might take the little old chapel out of the middle of it and not miss it. But my mother says there was more true religion in the old chapel. And the war has taught me that may be she was right.

SIR PEARCE [*grunts sulkily*]!!

O'FLAHERTY [*respectfully but doggedly*] And theres another thing it's taught me too, sir, that concerns you and me, if I may make bold to tell it to you.

SIR PEARCE [*still sulkily*] I hope it's nothing you oughtnt to say to me, O'Flaherty.

O'FLAHERTY. It's this, sir: that I'm able to sit here now and talk to you without humbugging you; and thats what not one of your tenants or your tenants' childer ever did to you before in all your long life. It's a true respect I'm shewing you at last, sir. Maybe youd rather have me humbug you and tell you lies as I used, just as the boys here, God help them, would rather have me tell them how I fought the Kaiser, that all the world knows I never saw in my life, than tell them the truth. But I cant take advantage of you the way I used, not even if I seem to be wanting in respect to you and cocked up by winning the Cross.

SIR PEARCE [*touched*] Not at all, O'Flaherty. Not at all.

O'FLAHERTY. Sure whats the Cross to me, barring the little pension* it carries? Do you think I dont know that theres hundreds of men as brave as me that never had the luck to get anything for their bravery but a curse from the sergeant, and the blame for the faults of them that ought to have been their betters? Ive learnt more than youd think, sir; for how would a gentleman like you know what a poor ignorant conceited creature I was when I went from here into the wide world as a soldier? What use is all the lying, and pretending, and humbugging, and letting on, when the day comes to you that your comrade is killed in the trench beside you, and you dont as much as look round at him until you trip over his poor body, and then all you say is to ask why the hell the stretcher-bearers dont take it out of the way. Why should I read the papers to be humbugged and lied to by them that had the cunning to stay at home and send me to fight for them? Dont talk to me or to any soldier of the war being right. No war is right; and all the holy water* that Father Quinlan ever blessed couldnt make one right. There, sir! Now you know what O'Flaherty V.C. thinks; and youre wiser so than the others that only knows what he done.

SIR PEARCE [*making the best of it, and turning good-humoredly to him again*] Well, what you did was brave and manly, anyhow.

O'FLAHERTY. God knows whether it was or not, better than you nor me, General. I hope He wont be too hard on me for it, anyhow.

SIR PEARCE [*sympathetically*] Oh yes: we all have to think seriously sometimes, especially when we're a little run down. I'm afraid weve been overworking you a bit over these recruiting meetings. However, we can knock off for the rest of the day; and tomorrow's Sunday. Ive had about as much as I can stand myself. [*He looks at his watch*]. It's teatime. I wonder whats keeping your mother.

O'FLAHERTY. It's nicely cocked up the old woman will be, having tea at the same table as you, sir, instead of in the kitchen. She'll be after dressing in the heighth of grandeur; and stop she will at every house on the way to shew herself off and tell them where she's going, and fill the whole parish with spite and envy. But sure, she shouldnt keep you waiting, sir.

SIR PEARCE. Oh, thats all right: she must be indulged on an occasion like this. I'm sorry my wife is in London: she'd have been glad to welcome your mother.

O'FLAHERTY. Sure, I know she would, sir. She was always a kind friend to the poor. Little her ladyship knew, God help her, the depth of divilment that was in us: we were like a play to her. You see, sir, she was English: that was how it was. We was to her what the Pathans* and Senegalese was to me when I first seen them: I couldnt think, somehow, that they were liars, and thieves, and backbiters, and drunkards, just like ourselves or any other Christians. Oh, her ladyship never knew all that was going on behind her back: how would she? When I was a weeshy* child, she gave me the first penny I ever had in my hand; and I wanted to pray for her conversion* that night the same as my mother made me pray for yours; and—

SIR PEARCE [*scandalized*] Do you mean to say that your mother made you pray for *my* conversion?

O'FLAHERTY. Sure and she wouldnt want to see a gentleman like you going to hell after she nursing your own son and bringing up my sister Annie on the bottle.* That was how it was, sir. She'd rob you; and she'd lie to you; and she'd call down all the blessings of God on your head when she was selling you your own three geese that you thought had been ate by the fox the day after youd finished fattening them, sir; and all the time you were like a bit of her own flesh and blood to her. Often has she said she'd live to see you a good Catholic yet, leading victorious armies against the English and wearing the collar of gold that Malachi won from the proud invader.* Oh, she's the romantic woman is my mother, and no mistake.

SIR PEARCE [*in great perturbation*] I really cant believe this, O'Flaherty. I could have sworn your mother was as honest a woman as ever breathed.

O'FLAHERTY. And so she is, sir. She's as honest as the day.

SIR PEARCE. Do you call it honest to steal my geese?

O'FLAHERTY. She didnt steal them, sir. It was me that stole them.

SIR PEARCE. Oh! And why the devil *did* you steal them?

O'FLAHERTY. Sure we needed them, sir. Often and often we had to sell our own geese to pay you the rent to satisfy your needs; and why shouldnt we sell your geese to satisfy ours?

SIR PEARCE. Well, damn me!

O'FLAHERTY [*sweetly*] Sure you had to get what you could out of us; and we had to get what we could out of you. God forgive us both!

SIR PEARCE. Really, O'Flaherty, the war seems to have upset you a little.

O'FLAHERTY. It's set me thinking, sir; and I'm not used to it. It's like the patriotism of the English. They never thought of being patriotic until the war broke out; and now the patriotism has took them so sudden and come so strange to them that they run about like frightened chickens, uttering all manner of nonsense. But please God theyll forget all about it when the war's over. Theyre getting tired of it already.

SIR PEARCE. No, no: it has uplifted us all in a wonderful way. The world will never be the same again, O'Flaherty. Not after a war like this.

O'FLAHERTY. So they all say, sir. I see no great differ myself. It's all the fright and the excitement; and when that quiets down theyll go back to their natural divilment and be the same as ever. It's like the vermin: itll wash off after a while.

SIR PEARCE [*rising and planting himself firmly behind the garden seat*] Well, the long and the short of it is, O'Flaherty, I must decline to be a party to any attempt to deceive your mother. I thoroughly disapprove of this feeling against the English, especially at a moment like the present. Even if your mother's political sympathies are really what you represent them to be, I should think that her gratitude to Gladstone* ought to cure her of such disloyal prejudices.

O'FLAHERTY [*over his shoulder*] She says Gladstone was an Irishman, sir. What call would he have to meddle with Ireland as he did if he wasnt?

SIR PEARCE. What nonsense! Does she suppose Mr Asquith* is an Irishman?

O'FLAHERTY. She wont give him any credit for Home Rule,* sir. She says Redmond* made him do it. She says you told her so.

SIR PEARCE [*convicted out of his own mouth*] Well, I never meant her to take it up in that ridiculous way. [*He moves to the end of the garden seat on O'Flaherty's left*] I'll give her a good talking to when she comes. I'm not going to stand any of her nonsense.

O'FLAHERTY. It's not a bit of use, sir. She says all the English generals is Irish. She says all the English poets and great men was Irish. She says the English never knew how to read their own books until we taught them. She says we're the lost tribes of the house of Israel* and the chosen people of God. She says that the goddess Venus,* that was born out of the foam of the sea, came up out of the water in Killiney Bay off Bray Head.* She says that Moses built the seven churches,* and that Lazarus was buried in Glasnevin.*

SIR PEARCE. Bosh! How does she know he was? Did you ever ask her?

O'FLAHERTY. I did, sir, often.

SIR PEARCE. And what did she say?

O'FLAHERTY. She asked me how did I know he wasnt, and fetched me a clout on the side of my head.

SIR PEARCE. But have you never mentioned any famous Englishman to her, and asked her what she had to say about him?

O'FLAHERTY. The only one I could think of was Shakespear, sir; and she says he was born in Cork.*

SIR PEARCE [*exhausted*] Well, I give it up [*he throws himself into the nearest chair*]. The woman is— Oh, well! No matter.

O'FLAHERTY [*sympathetically*] Yes, sir: she's pigheaded and obstinate: theres no doubt about it. She's like the English: they think theres no one like themselves. It's the same with the Germans, though theyre educated and ought to know better. Youll never have a quiet world til you knock the patriotism out of the human race.

SIR PEARCE. Still, we—

O'FLAHERTY. Whisht,* sir, for God's sake: here she is.

The General jumps up. Mrs O'Flaherty arrives, and comes between the two men. She is very clean, and carefully dressed in the old fashioned peasant costume: black silk sunbonnet with a tiara of trimmings, and black cloak.

O'FLAHERTY [*rising shyly*] Good evening, mother.

MRS O'FLAHERTY [*severely*] You hold your whisht,* and learn behavior while I pay my juty to his honor. [*To Sir Pearce, heartily*] And how is your honor's good self? And how is her ladyship and all the young ladies? Oh, it's right glad we are to see your honor back again and looking the picture of health.

SIR PEARCE [*forcing a note of extreme geniality*] Thank you, Mrs O'Flaherty. Well, you see weve brought you back your son safe and sound. I hope youre proud of him.

MRS O'FLAHERTY. And indeed and I am, your honor. It's the brave boy he is; and why wouldnt he be, brought up on your honor's estate and with you before his eyes for a pattern of the finest soldier in Ireland? Come and kiss your old mother, Dinny darlint.* [*O'Flaherty does so sheepishly*]. Thats my own darling boy. And look at your fine new uniform stained already with the eggs youve been eating and the porter youve been drinking. [*She takes out her handkerchief; spits on it; and scrubs his lapel with it*]. Oh, it's the untidy slovenly one you always were. There! It wont be seen on the khaki: it's not like the old red coat* that would shew up everything that dribbled down on it. [*To Sir Pearce*] And they tell me down at the lodge that her ladyship is staying in London, and that Miss Agnes is to be married to a fine young nobleman. Oh, it's your honor that is the lucky and happy father! It will be bad news for many of the young gentlemen of the quality round here, sir. Theres lots thought she was going to marry young Master Lawless—

SIR PEARCE. What! That—that—that bosthoon!*

MRS O'FLAHERTY [*hilariously*] Let your honor alone for finding the right word! A big bosthoon he is indeed, your honor. Oh, to think of the times and times I have said that Miss Agnes would be my lady as her mother was before her! Didnt I, Dinny?

SIR PEARCE. And now, Mrs O'Flaherty, I daresay you have a great deal to say to Dennis that doesnt concern me. I'll just go in and order tea.

MRS O'FLAHERTY. Oh, why would your honor disturb yourself? Sure I can take the boy into the yard.

SIR PEARCE. Not at all. It wont disturb me in the least. And he's too big a boy to be taken into the yard now. He has made a front seat for himself. Eh? [*He goes into the house*].

MRS O'FLAHERTY. Sure he has that, your honor. God bless your honor! [*The General being now out of hearing, she turns threateningly to her son with one of those sudden Irish changes of manner which amaze and scandalize less flexible nations, and exclaims*] And what do you mean, you lying young scald, by telling me you were going to fight agen the English? Did you take me for a fool that couldnt find out, and the papers all full of you shaking hands with the English king at Buckingham Palace?

O'FLAHERTY. I didnt shake hands with him: he shook hands with me. Could I turn on the man in his own house, before his own wife, with his money in my pocket and in yours, and throw his civility back in his face?

MRS O'FLAHERTY. You would take the hand of a tyrant red with the blood of Ireland—

O'FLAHERTY. Arra hold your nonsense, mother: he's not half the tyrant you are, God help him. His hand was cleaner than mine that had the blood of his own relations on it, may be.

MRS O'FLAHERTY [*threateningly*] Is that a way to speak to your mother, you young spalpeen?*

O'FLAHERTY [*stoutly*] It is so, if you wont talk sense to me. It's a nice thing for a poor boy to be made much of by kings and queens, and shook hands with by the heighth of his country's nobility in the capital cities of the world, and then to come home and be scolded and insulted by his own mother. I'll fight for who I like; and I'll shake hands with what kings I like; and if your own son is not good enough for you, you can go and look for another. Do you mind me now?

MRS O'FLAHERTY. And was it the Belgians learned you such brazen impudence?

O'FLAHERTY. The Belgians is good men; and the French ought to be more civil to them, let alone their being half murdered by the Boshes.*

MRS O'FLAHERTY. Good men is it! Good men! to come over here when they were wounded because it was a Catholic country, and then to go to the Protestant Church because it didnt cost them anything, and some of them to never go near a church at all. Thats what you call good men!

O'FLAHERTY. Oh, youre the mighty fine politician, arnt you? Much you know about Belgians or foreign parts or the world youre living in, God help you!

MRS O'FLAHERTY. Why wouldnt I know better than you? Amment I your mother?

O'FLAHERTY. And if you are itself, how can you know what you never seen as well as me that was dug into the continent of Europe for six months, and was buried in the earth of it three times with the shells bursting on the top of me? I tell you I know what I'm about. I have my own reasons for taking part in this great conflict. I'd be ashamed to stay at home and not fight when everybody else is fighting.

MRS. O'FLAHERTY. If you wanted to fight, why couldnt you fight in the German army?

O'FLAHERTY. Because they only get a penny a day.

MRS O'FLAHERTY. Well, and if they do itself, isnt there the French army?

O'FLAHERTY. They only get a hapenny a day.

MRS O'FLAHERTY [*much dashed*] Oh murder! They must be a mean lot, Dinny.

O'FLAHERTY [*sarcastic*] Maybe youd have me join the Turkish army, and worship the heathen Mahomet that put a corn in his ear and pretended it was a message from the heavens when the pigeon come to pick it out and eat it.* I went where I could get the biggest allowance for you; and little thanks I get for it!

MRS O'FLAHERTY. Allowance, is it! Do you know what the thieving blackguards did on me? They came to me and they says, 'Was your son a big eater?' they says. 'Oh, he was that' says I: 'ten shillings a week wouldnt keep him.' Sure I thought the more I said the more theyd give me. 'Then' says they, 'thats ten shillings a week off your allowance' they says, 'because you save that by the king feeding him.' 'Indeed!' says I: 'I suppose if I'd six sons, youd stop three pound a week from me, and make out that I ought to pay you money instead of you paying me.' 'Theres a fallacy in your argument' they says.

O'FLAHERTY. A what?

MRS O'FLAHERTY. A fallacy: thats the word he said. I says to him, 'It's a Pharisee* I'm thinking you mean, sir; but you can keep your dirty money that your king grudges a poor old widow; and please God the English will be bet yet for the deadly sin of oppressing the poor'; and with that I shut the door in his face.

O'FLAHERTY [*furious*] Do you tell me they knocked ten shillings off you for my keep?

MRS O'FLAHERTY [*soothing him*] No, darlint: they only knocked off half a crown. I put up with it because Ive got the old age pension; and they know very well I'm only sixty-two;* so Ive the better of them by half a crown a week anyhow.

O'FLAHERTY. It's a queer way of doing business. If theyd tell you straight out what they was going to give you, you wouldnt mind; but if there was twenty ways of telling the truth and only one way of telling a lie, the Government would find it out. It's in the nature of governments to tell lies.

Teresa Driscoll, a parlor maid, comes from the house.

TERESA. Youre to come up to the drawing room to have your tea, Mrs O'Flaherty.

MRS O'FLAHERTY. Mind you have a sup of good black tea for me in the kitchen afterwards, acushla.* That washy drawing room tea will give me the wind if I leave it on my stomach. [*She goes into the house, leaving the two young people alone together*].

O'FLAHERTY. Is that yourself, Tessie?* And how are you?

TERESA. Nicely, thank you. And hows yourself?

O'FLAHERTY. Finely, thank God. [*He produces a gold chain*]. Look what Ive brought you, Tessie.

TERESA [*shrinking*] Sure I dont like to touch it, Denny. Did you take it off a dead man?

O'FLAHERTY. No: I took it off a live one; and thankful he was to me to be alive and kept a prisoner in ease and comfort, and me left fighting in peril of my life.

TERESA [*taking it*] Do you think it's real gold, Denny?

O'FLAHERTY. It's real German gold, anyhow.

TERESA. But German silver* isnt real, Denny.

O'FLAHERTY [*his face darkening*] Well, it's the best the Bosh* could do for me, anyhow.

TERESA. Do you think I might take it to the jeweller next market day and ask him?

O'FLAHERTY [*sulkily*] You may take it to the divil if you like.

TERESA. You neednt lose your temper about it. I only thought I'd like to know. The nice fool I'd look if I went about shewing off a chain that turned out to be only brass!

O'FLAHERTY. I think you might say Thank you.

TERESA. Do you? I think you might have said something more to me than 'Is that yourself?' You couldnt say less to the postman.

O'FLAHERTY [*his brow clearing*] Oh, is that whats the matter? Here! come and take the taste of the brass out of my mouth. [*He seizes her and kisses her*].

Teresa, without losing her Irish dignity, takes the kiss as appreciatively as a connoisseur might take a glass of wine, and sits down with him on the garden seat.

TERESA [*as he squeezes her waist*] Thank God the priest cant see us here!

O'FLAHERTY. It's little they care for priests in France, alanna.*

TERESA. And what had the queen on her, Denny, when she spoke to you in the palace?

O'FLAHERTY. She had a bonnet on without any strings to it. And she had a plakeen* of embroidery down her bosom. And she had her waist where it used to be, and not where the other ladies had it.* And she had little brooches in her ears, though she hadnt half the jewelry of Mrs Sullivan that keeps the popshop in Drumpogue.* And she dresses her hair down over her forehead, in a fringe like. And she has an Irish look about her eyebrows. And she didnt know what to say to me,* poor woman! and I didnt know what to say to her, God help me!

TERESA. Youll have a pension now with the Cross, wont you, Denny?

O'FLAHERTY. Sixpence three farthings a day.*

TERESA. That isnt much.

O'FLAHERTY. I take out the rest in glory.

TERESA. And if youre wounded, youll have a wound pension, wont you?

O'FLAHERTY. I will, please God.

TERESA. Youre going out again, arnt you, Denny?

O'FLAHERTY. I cant help myself. I'd be shot for a deserter if I didnt go; and may be I'll be shot by the Boshes if I do go; so between the two of them I'm nicely fixed up.

MRS O'FLAHERTY [*calling from within the house*] Tessie! Tessie darlint!

TERESA [*disengaging herself from his arm and rising*] I'm wanted for the tea table. Youll have a pension anyhow, Denny, wont you, whether youre wounded or not?

MRS O'FLAHERTY. Come, child, come.

TERESA [*impatiently*] Oh, sure I'm coming. [*She tries to smile at Denny, not very convincingly, and hurries into the house*].

O'FLAHERTY [*alone*] And if I do get a pension itself, the divil a penny* of it youll ever have the spending of.

MRS O'FLAHERTY [*as she comes from the porch*] Oh, it's a shame for you to keep the girl from her juties, Dinny. You might get her into trouble.

O'FLAHERTY. Much I care whether she gets into trouble or not! I pity the man that gets *her* into trouble.* He'll get himself into worse.

MRS O'FLAHERTY. Whats that you tell me? Have you been falling out with her, and she a girl with a fortune of ten pounds?

O'FLAHERTY. Let her keep her fortune. I wouldnt touch her with the tongs if she had thousands and millions.

MRS O'FLAHERTY. Oh fie for shame, Dinny! why would you say the like of that of a decent honest girl, and one of the Driscolls too?

O'FLAHERTY. Why wouldnt I say it? She's thinking of nothing but to get me out there again to be wounded so that she may spend my pension, bad scran* to her!

MRS O'FLAHERTY. Why, whats come over you, child, at all at all?

O'FLAHERTY. Knowledge and wisdom has come over me with pain and fear and trouble. Ive been made a fool of and imposed upon all my life. I thought that covetious sthreal in there was a walking angel; and now if ever I marry at all I'll marry a Frenchwoman.

MRS O'FLAHERTY [*fiercely*] Youll not, so; and dont you dar repeat such a thing to me.

O'FLAHERTY. Wont I, faith! Ive been as good as married to a couple of them already.

MRS O'FLAHERTY. The Lord be praised, what wickedness have you been up to, you young blackguard?

O'FLAHERTY. One of them Frenchwomen would cook you a meal twice in the day and all days and every day that Sir Pearce himself might go begging through Ireland for, and never see the like of. I'll have a French wife, I tell you; and when I settle down to be a farmer I'll have a French farm, with a field as big as the continent of Europe that ten of your dirty little fields here wouldnt so much as fill the ditch of.

MRS O'FLAHERTY [*furious*] Then it's a French mother you may go look for; for I'm done with you.

O'FLAHERTY. And it's no great loss youd be if it wasnt for my natural feelings for you; for it's only a silly ignorant old countrywoman you are with all your fine talk about Ireland: you that never stepped beyond the few acres of it you were born on!

MRS O'FLAHERTY [*tottering to the garden seat and shewing signs of breaking down*] Dinny darlint, why are you like this to me? Whats happened to you?

O'FLAHERTY [*gloomily*] Whats happened to everybody? thats what I want to know. Whats happened to you that I thought all the world of and was afeared of? Whats happened to Sir Pearce, that I thought was a great general, and that I now see to be no more fit to command an army than an old hen? Whats happened to Tessie,* that I was mad to marry a year ago, and that I wouldnt take now with all Ireland for her fortune? I tell you the world's creation is crumbling in ruins about me; and then you come and ask whats happened to *me*?

MRS O'FLAHERTY [*giving way to wild grief*] Ochone!* ochone! my son's turned agen me. Oh, whatll I do at all at all? Oh! oh! oh! oh!

SIR PEARCE [*running out of the house*] Whats this infernal noise? What on earth is the matter?

O'FLAHERTY. Arra hold your whisht, mother. Dont you see his honor?

MRS O'FLAHERTY. Oh, sir, I'm ruined and destroyed. Oh, wont you speak to Dinny, sir: I'm heart scalded* with him. He wants to marry a Frenchwoman on me, and to go away and be a foreigner and desert his mother and betray his country. It's mad he is with the roaring of the cannons and he killing the Germans and the Germans killing him, bad cess* to them? My boy is taken from me and turned agen me? and who is to take care of me in my old age after all Ive done for him, ochone! ochone!

O'FLAHERTY. Hold your noise, I tell you. Who's going to leave you? I'm going to take you with me. There now: does that satisfy you?

MRS O'FLAHERTY. Is it take me into a strange land among heathens and pagans and savages, and me not knowing a word of their language nor them of mine?

O'FLAHERTY. A good job they dont: may be theyll think youre talking sense.

MRS O'FLAHERTY. Ask me to die out of Ireland, is it? and the angels not to find me when they come for me!

O'FLAHERTY. And would you ask me to live in Ireland where Ive been imposed on and kept in ignorance, and to die where the divil himself wouldnt take me as a gift, let alone the blessed angels? You can come or stay. You can take your old way or take my young way. But stick in this place I will not among a lot of good-for-nothing divils thatll not do a hand's turn but watch the grass growing and build up the stone wall where the cow walked through it. And Sir Horace Plunkett* breaking his heart all the time telling them how they might put the land into decent tillage like the French and Belgians.

SIR PEARCE. Yes: he's quite right, you know, Mrs O'Flaherty: quite right there.

MRS O'FLAHERTY. Well, sir, please God the war will last a long time yet: and may be I'll die before it's over and the separation allowance* stops.

O'FLAHERTY. Thats all you care about. It's nothing but milch cows we men are for the women, with their separation allowances, ever since the war began, bad luck to them that made it!

TERESA [*coming from the porch between the General and Mrs O'Flaherty*] Hannah sent me out for to tell you, sir, that the tea will be black and the cake not fit to eat with the cold if yous all dont come at wanst.

MRS O'FLAHERTY [*breaking out again*] Oh, Tessie darlint, what have you been saying to Dinny at all at all? Oh! oh—

SIR PEARCE [*out of patience*] You cant discuss that here. We shall have Tessie beginning now.

O'FLAHERTY. Thats right, sir: drive them in.

TERESA. I havnt said a word to him. He—

SIR PEARCE. Hold your tongue; and go in and attend to your business at the tea table.

TERESA. But amment I telling your honor that I never said a word to him? He gave me a beautiful gold chain. Here it is to shew your honour thats it's no lie I'm telling you.

SIR PEARCE. Whats this, O'Flaherty? Youve been looting some unfortunate officer.

O'FLAHERTY. No sir: I stole it from him of his own accord.

MRS O'FLAHERTY. Wouldnt your honor tell him that his mother has the first call on it? What would a slip of a girl like that be doing with a gold chain round her neck?

TERESA [*venomously*] Anyhow, I have a neck to put it round and not a hank of wrinkles.

At this unfortunate remark, Mrs O'Flaherty bounds from her seat; and an appalling tempest of wordy wrath breaks out. The remonstrances and commands of the General, and the protests and menaces of O'Flaherty, only increase the hubbub. They are soon all speaking at once at the top of their voices.

MRS O'FLAHERTY [*solo*] You impudent young heifer, how dar you say such a thing to me? [*Teresa retorts furiously; the men interfere; and the solo becomes a quartet, fortissimo*]. Ive a good mind to clout your ears for you to teach you manners. Be ashamed of yourself, do; and learn to know who youre speaking to. That I maytnt sin! but I dont know what the good God was thinking about when he made the like of you. Let me not see you casting sheeps' eyes* at my son again. There never was an O'Flaherty yet that would demean himself by keeping company with a dirty Driscoll; and if I see you next or nigh my house I'll put you in the ditch with a flea in your ear: * mind that now.

TERESA. Is it me you offer such a name to, you foul-mouthed, dirty minded, lying, sloothering* old sow, you? I wouldnt soil my tongue by calling you in your right name and telling Sir Pearce whats the common talk of the town about you. You and your O'Flahertys! setting yourself up agen the Driscolls that would never lower themselves to be seen in conversation with you at the fair. You can keep your ugly stingy lump of a son; for what is he but a common soldier? and God help the girl that gets him, say I! So the back of my hand to you, Mrs O'Flaherty; and that the cat may tear your ugly old face!

SIR PEARCE. Silence. Tessie: did you hear me ordering you to go into the house? Mrs O'Flaherty! [*Louder*] Mrs O'Flaherty!! Will you just listen to me one moment? Please. [*Furiously*] Do you hear me speaking to you, woman? Are you human beings or are you wild beasts? Stop that noise immediately: do you hear? [*Yelling*] Are you going to do what I order you, or are you not? Scandalous! Disgraceful! This comes of being too familiar with you, O'Flaherty: shove them into the house. Out with the whole damned pack of you.

O'FLAHERTY [*to the women*] Here now: none of that, none of that. Go easy, I tell you. Hold your whisht, mother, will you, or youll be sorry for it after. [*To Teresa*] Is that the way for a decent young girl to speak? [*Despairingly*] Oh, for the Lord's sake, shut up, will yous? Have yous no respect for yourselves or your betters? [*Peremptorily*] Let me have no more of it, I tell you. Och! the divil's in the whole crew of you. In with you into the house this very minute and tear one another's eyes out in the kitchen if you like. In with you.

The two men seize the two women, and push them, still violently abusing one another, into the house. Sir Pearce slams the door upon them savagely. Immediately a heavenly silence falls on the summer afternoon. The two sit down out of breath; and for a long time nothing is said. Sir Pearce sits on an iron chair. O'Flaherty sits on the garden seat. The thrush begins to sing melodiously. O'Flaherty cocks his ears, and looks up at it. A smile spreads over his troubled features. Sir Pearce, with a long sigh, takes out his pipe, and begins to fill it.

O'FLAHERTY [*idyllically*] What a discontented sort of an animal a man is, sir! Only a month ago, I was in the quiet of the country out at the front, with not a sound except the birds and the bellow of a cow in the distance as it might be, and the shrapnel making little clouds in the heavens, and the shells whistling, and may be a yell or two when one of us was hit; and would you believe it, sir, I complained of the noise and wanted to have a peaceful hour at home. Well: them two has taught me a lesson. This morning, sir, when I was telling the boys here how I was longing to be back taking my part for king and country with the others, I was lying, as you well knew, sir. Now I can go and say it with a clear conscience. Some likes war's alarums; and some likes home life. Ive tried both, sir; and I'm all for war's alarums now. I always was a quiet lad by natural disposition.

SIR PEARCE. Strictly between ourselves, O'Flaherty, and as one soldier to another [*O'Flaherty salutes, but without stiffening*], do you think we should have got an army without conscription if domestic life had been as happy as people say it is?

O'FLAHERTY. Well, between you and me and the wall, Sir Pearce, I think the less we say about that until the war's over, the better.

He winks at the General. The General strikes a match. The thrush sings. A jay laughs. The conversation drops.

AUGUSTUS DOES HIS BIT

A TRUE-TO-LIFE FARCE

PREFACE

I WISH to express my gratitude for certain good offices which Augustus secured for me in January 1917. I had been invited to visit the theatre of war in Flanders by the Commander-in-Chief:* an invitation which was, under the circumstances, a summons to duty. Thus I had occasion to spend some days in procuring the necessary passports and other official facilities for my journey. It happened just then that the Stage Society* gave a performance of this little play. It opened the heart of every official to me. I have always been treated with distinguished consideration in my contacts with bureaucracy during the war; but on this occasion I found myself *persona grata** in the highest degree. There was only one word when the formalities were disposed of; and that was 'We are up against Augustus all day.' The shewing-up of Augustus scandalized one or two innocent and patriotic critics who regarded the prowess of the British army as inextricably bound up with Highcastle prestige. But our Government departments knew better: their problem was how to win the war with Augustus on their backs, well-meaning, brave, patriotic, but obstructively fussy, self-important, imbecile, and disastrous.

Save for the satisfaction of being able to laugh at Augustus in the theatre, nothing, as far as I know, came of my dramatic reduction of him to absurdity. Generals, admirals, Prime Ministers and Controllers, not to mention Emperors, Kaisers and Tsars, were scrapped remorselessly at home and abroad, for their sins or services, as the case might be. But Augustus stood like the Eddystone* in a storm, and stands so to this day. He gave us his word that he was indispensable; and we took it.

AUGUSTUS DOES HIS BIT

The Mayor's parlor in the Town Hall of Little Pifflington. Lord Augustus Highcastle, a distinguished member of the governing class, in the uniform of a colonel, and very well preserved at 45, is comfortably seated at a writing table with his heels on it, reading The Morning Post.* The door faces him, a little to his left, at the other side of the room. The window is behind him. In the fireplace, a gas stove. On the table a bell button and a telephone. Portraits of past Mayors, in robes and gold chains, adorn the walls. An elderly clerk with a short white beard and whiskers, and a very red nose, shuffles in.

AUGUSTUS [*hastily putting aside his paper and replacing his feet on the floor*] Hullo! Who are you?

THE CLERK. The staff [*a slight impediment in his speech adds to the impression of incompetence produced by his age and appearance*].

AUGUSTUS. You the staff! What do you mean, man?

THE CLERK. What I say. There aint anybody else.

AUGUSTUS. Tush! Where are the others?

THE CLERK. At the front.

AUGUSTUS. Quite right. Most proper. Why arnt *you* at the front?

THE CLERK. Over age. Fiftyseven.

AUGUSTUS. But you can still do your bit. Many an older man is in the G.R.'s,* or volunteering for home defence.

THE CLERK. I have volunteered.

AUGUSTUS. Then why are you not in uniform?

THE CLERK. They said they wouldnt have me if I was given away with a pound of tea. Told me to go home and not be an old silly. [*A sense of unbearable wrong, til now only smouldering in him, bursts into flame*]. Young Bill Knight, that I took with me, got two and sevenpence. I got nothing. Is it justice? This country is going to the dogs, if you ask me.

AUGUSTUS [*rising indignantly*] I do not ask you, sir; and I will not allow you to say such things in my presence. Our statesmen are the greatest known to history. Our generals are invincible. Our army is the admiration of the world. [*Furiously*] How dare you tell me that the country is going to the dogs!

THE CLERK. Why did they give young Bill Knight two and sevenpence, and not give me even my tram fare? Do you call that being great statesmen? As good as robbing me, I call it.

AUGUSTUS. Thats enough. Leave the room. [*He sits down and takes up his pen, settling himself to work. The clerk shuffles to the door. Augustus adds, with cold politeness*] Send me the Secretary.

THE CLERK. I'm the Secretary. I cant leave the room and send myself to you at the same time, can I?

AUGUSTUS. Dont be insolent. Where is the gentleman I have been corresponding with: Mr Horatio Floyd Beamish?

THE CLERK [*returning and bowing*] Here. Me.

AUGUSTUS. You! Ridiculous. What right have you to call yourself by a pretentious name of that sort?

THE CLERK. You may drop the Horatio Floyd. Beamish is good enough for me.

AUGUSTUS. Is there nobody else to take my instructions?

THE CLERK. It's me or nobody. And for two pins I'd chuck it. Dont you drive me too far. Old uns like me is up in the world now.

AUGUSTUS. If we were not at war, I should discharge you on the spot for disrespectful behavior. But England is in danger; and I cannot think of my personal dignity at such a moment. [*Shouting at him*] Dont you think of yours, either, worm that you are; or I'll have you arrested under the Defence of the Realm Act,* double quick.

THE CLERK. What do I care about the realm? They done me out of two and seven—

AUGUSTUS. Oh, damn your two and seven! Did you receive my letters?

THE CLERK. Yes.

AUGUSTUS. I addressed a meeting here last night—went straight to the platform from the train. I wrote to you that I should expect you to be present and report yourself. Why did you not do so?

THE CLERK. The police wouldnt let me on the platform.

AUGUSTUS. Did you tell them who you were?

THE CLERK. They knew who I was. Thats why they wouldnt let me up.

AUGUSTUS. This is too silly for anything. This town wants waking up.
I made the best recruiting speech I ever made in my life; and not
a man joined.

THE CLERK. What did you expect? You told them our gallant fellows is
falling at the rate of a thousand a day in the big push. Dying for
Little Pifflington, you says. Come and take their places, you says.
That aint the way to recruit.

AUGUSTUS. But I expressly told them their widows would have
pensions.

THE CLERK. I heard you. Would have been all right if it had been the
widows you wanted to get round.

AUGUSTUS [*rising angrily*] This town is inhabited by dastards. I say it
with a full sense of responsibility, *dastards*! They call themselves
Englishmen; and they are afraid to fight.

THE CLERK. Afraid to fight! You should see them on a Saturday night.

AUGUSTUS. Yes: they fight one another; but they wont fight the
Germans.

THE CLERK. They got grudges again one another: how can they have
grudges again the Huns* that they never saw? Theyve no imagination:
thats what it is. Bring the Huns here; and theyll quarrel with them
fast enough.

AUGUSTUS [*returning to his seat with a grunt of disgust*] Mf! Theyll
have them here if theyre not careful. [*Seated*] Have you carried out
my orders about the war saving?*

THE CLERK. Yes.

AUGUSTUS. The allowance of petrol has been reduced by three quarters?

THE CLERK. It has.

AUGUSTUS. And you have told the motor-car people to come here and
arrange to start munition work now that their motor business is
stopped?

THE CLERK. It aint stopped. Theyre busier than ever.

AUGUSTUS. Busy at what?

THE CLERK. Making small cars.

AUGUSTUS. *New* cars!

THE CLERK. The old cars only do twelve miles to the gallon. Everybody has to have a car that will do thirtyfive now.

AUGUSTUS. Cant they take the train?

THE CLERK. There aint no trains now. Theyve tore up the rails and sent them to the front.

AUGUSTUS. Psha!

THE CLERK. Well, we have to get about somehow.

AUGUSTUS. This is perfectly monstrous. Not in the least what I intended.

THE CLERK. Hell—

AUGUSTUS. Sir!

THE CLERK [*explaining*] Hell, they says, is paved with good intentions.

AUGUSTUS [*springing to his feet*] Do you mean to insinuate that hell is paved with *my* good intentions—with the good intentions of His Majesty's Government?

THE CLERK. I dont mean to insinuate anything until the Defence of the Realm Act is repealed. It aint safe.

AUGUSTUS. They told me that this town had set an example to all England in the matter of economy. I came down here to promise the Mayor a knighthood for his exertions.

THE CLERK. The Mayor! Where do *I* come in?

AUGUSTUS. You dont come in. You go out. This is a fool of a place. I'm greatly disappointed. Deeply disappointed. [*Flinging himself back into his chair*] Disgusted.

THE CLERK. What more can we do? Weve shut up everything. The picture gallery is shut. The museum is shut. The theatres and picture shows is shut: I havnt seen a movy picture for six months.

AUGUSTUS. Man, man: do you *want* to see picture shows when the Hun is at the gate?

THE CLERK [*mournfully*] I dont now, though it drove me melancholy mad at first. I was on the point of taking a pennorth* of rat poison—

AUGUSTUS. Why didnt you?

THE CLERK. Because a friend advised me to take to drink instead. That saved my life, though it makes me very poor company in the mornings, as [*hiccuping*] perhaps youve noticed.

AUGUSTUS. Well, upon my soul! You are not ashamed to stand there and confess yourself a disgusting drunkard.

THE CLERK. Well, what of it? We're at war now; and everything's changed. Besides, I should lose my job here if I stood drinking at the bar. I'm a respectable man and must buy my drink and take it home with me. And they wont serve me with less than a quart.* If youd told me before the war that I could get through a quart of whisky in a day, I shouldnt have believed you. Thats the good of war: it brings out powers in a man that he never suspected himself capable of. You said so yourself in your speech last night.

AUGUSTUS. I did not know that I was talking to an imbecile. You ought to be ashamed of yourself. There must be an end of this drunken' slacking. I'm going to establish a new order of things here. I shall come down every morning before breakfast until things are properly in train. Have a cup of coffee and two rolls for me here every morning at half-past ten.

THE CLERK. You cant have no rolls. The only baker that baked rolls was a Hun; and he's been interned.

AUGUSTUS. Quite right, too. And was there no Englishman to take his place?

THE CLERK. There was. But he was caught spying; and they took him up to London and shot him.

AUGUSTUS. Shot an Englishman!

THE CLERK. Well, it stands to reason if the Germans wanted a spy they wouldnt employ a German that everybody would suspect, dont it?

AUGUSTUS [*rising again*] Do you mean to say, you scoundrel, that an Englishman is capable of selling his country to the enemy for gold?

THE CLERK. Not as a general thing I wouldnt say it; but theres men here would sell their own mothers for two coppers if they got the chance.

AUGUSTUS. Beamish: it's an ill bird that fouls its own nest.

THE CLERK. It wasnt me that let Little Pifflington get foul. *I* dont belong to the governing classes. I only tell you why you cant have no rolls.

AUGUSTUS [*intensely irritated*] Can you tell me where I can find an intelligent being to take my orders?

THE CLERK. One of the street sweepers used to teach in the school until it was shut up for the sake of economy. Will he do?

AUGUSTUS. What! You mean to tell me that when the lives of the gallant fellows in our trenches, and the fate of the British Empire, depend on our keeping up the supply of shells, you are wasting money on sweeping the streets?

THE CLERK. We have to. We dropped it for a while; but the infant death rate went up something frightful.

AUGUSTUS. What matters the death rate of Little Pifflington in a moment like this? Think of our gallant soldiers, not of your squalling infants.

THE CLERK. If you want soldiers you must have children. You cant buy em in boxes, like toy soldiers.

AUGUSTUS. Beamish: the long and the short of it is, you are no patriot. Go downstairs to your office; and have that gas stove taken away and replaced by an ordinary grate. The Board of Trade* has urged on me the necessity for economizing gas.

THE CLERK. Our orders from the Minister of Munitions* is to use gas instead of coal, because it saves material. Which is it to be?

AUGUSTUS [*bawling furiously at him*] Both! Dont criticize your orders: obey them. Yours not to reason why: yours but to do and die.* Thats war. [*Cooling down*] Have you anything else to say?

THE CLERK. Yes: I want a rise.

AUGUSTUS [*reeling against the table in his horror*] A rise! Horatio Floyd Beamish: do you know that we are at war?

THE CLERK [*feebly ironical*] I *have* noticed something about it in the papers. Heard *you* mention it once or twice, now I come to think of it.

AUGUSTUS. Our gallant fellows are dying in the trenches; and you want a rise!

THE CLERK. What are they dying for? To keep me alive, aint it? Well, whats the good of that if I'm dead of hunger by the time they come back?

AUGUSTUS. Everybody else is making sacrifices without a thought of self; and you—

THE CLERK. Not half, they aint. Wheres the baker's sacrifice? Wheres the coal merchant's? Wheres the butcher's? Charging me double: thats how they sacrifice themselves. Well, I want to sacrifice myself that way too. Just double next Saturday: double and not a penny less; or no secretary for you [*he stiffens himself shakily, and makes resolutely for the door*].

AUGUSTUS [*looking after him contemptuously*] Go: miserable pro–German.

THE CLERK [*rushing back and facing him*] Who are you calling a pro–German?

AUGUSTUS. Another word, and I charge you under the Act with discouraging me. Go.

The clerk blenches and goes out, cowed.
The telephone rings.

AUGUSTUS [*taking up the telephone receiver*] Hallo...Yes: who are you?...oh, Blueloo, is it?...Yes: theres nobody in the room: fire away...What?...A spy!...A woman!...Yes: I brought it down with me. Do you suppose I'm such a fool as to let it out of my hands? Why, it gives a list of all our anti-aircraft emplacements from Ramsgate to Skegness. The Germans would give a million for it—what?...But how could she possibly know about it? I havnt mentioned it to a soul, except, of course, dear Lucy....Oh, Toto and Lady Popham and that lot: they dont count: theyre all right. I mean that I havnt mentioned it to any Germans....Pooh! Dont you be nervous, old chap. I know you think me a fool: but I'm not such a fool as all that. If she tries to get it out of me I'll have her in the Tower* before you ring up again. [*The clerk returns*]. Sh-sh! Somebody's just come in: ring off. Goodbye. [*He hangs up the receiver*].

THE CLERK. Are you engaged? [*His manner is strangely softened*].

AUGUSTUS. What business is that of yours? However, if you will take the trouble to read the society papers for this week, you will see that I am engaged to the Honorable Lucy Popham, youngest daughter of—

THE CLERK. That aint what I mean. Can you see a female?

AUGUSTUS. Of course I can see a female as easily as a male. Do you suppose I'm blind?

THE CLERK. You dont seem to follow me, somehow. Theres a female downstairs: what you might call a lady. She wants to know can you see her if I let her up.

AUGUSTUS. Oh, you mean am I *dis*engaged. Tell the lady I have just received news of the greatest importance which will occupy my entire attention for the rest of the day, and that she must write for an appointment.

THE CLERK. I'll ask her to explain her business to me. *I* aint above talking to a handsome young female when I get the chance [*going*].

AUGUSTUS. Stop. Does she seem to be a person of consequence?

THE CLERK. A regular marchioness,* if you ask me.

AUGUSTUS. Hm! Beautiful, did you say?

THE CLERK. A human chrysanthemum, sir, believe me.

AUGUSTUS. It will be extremely inconvenient for me to see her; but the country is in danger; and we must not consider our own comfort. Think how our gallant fellows are suffering in the trenches! Shew her up. [*The clerk makes for the door, whistling the latest popular love ballad*]. Stop whistling instantly, sir. This is not a casino.

THE CLERK. Aint it? You just wait til you see her. [*He goes out*].

*Augustus produces a mirror, a comb, and a pot of moustache pomade from the drawer of the writing-table, and sits down before the mirror to put some touches to his toilet.**

The clerk returns, devotedly ushering a very attractive lady, brilliantly dressed, She has a dainty wallet hanging from her wrist. Augustus hastily covers up his toilet apparatus with The Morning Post, and rises in an attitude of pompous condescension.

THE CLERK [*to Augustus*] Here she is. [*To the lady*] May I offer you a chair, lady? [*He places a chair at the writing-table opposite Augustus, and steals out on tiptoe*].

AUGUSTUS. Be seated, madam.

THE LADY [*sitting down*] Are you Lord Augustus Highcastle?

AUGUSTUS [*sitting also*] Madam: I am.

THE LADY [*with awe*] The great Lord Augustus?

AUGUSTUS. I should not dream of describing myself so, madam; but no doubt I have impressed my countrymen—and [*bowing gallantly*] may I say my countrywomen—as having some exceptional claims to their consideration.

THE LADY [*emotionally*] What a beautiful voice you have!

AUGUSTUS. What you hear, madam, is the voice of my country, which now takes a sweet and noble tone even in the harsh mouth of high officialism.

THE LADY. Please go on. You express yourself so wonderfully.

AUGUSTUS. It would be strange indeed if, after sitting on thirty-seven Royal Commissions,* mostly as chairman, I had not mastered the art of public expression. Even the Radical papers* have paid me the high compliment of declaring that I am never more impressive than when I have nothing to say.

THE LADY. I never read the Radical papers. All I can tell you is that what we women admire in you is not the politician, but the man of action, the heroic warrior, the *beau sabreur*.*

AUGUSTUS [*gloomily*] Madam, I beg! Please! My military exploits are not a pleasant subject, unhappily.

THE LADY. Oh, I know, I know. How shamefully you have been treated! What ingratitude! But the country is with you. The women are with you. Oh, do you think all our hearts did not throb and all our nerves thrill when we heard how, when you were ordered to occupy that terrible quarry in Hulluch,* and you swept into it at the head of your men like a sea-god riding on a tidal wave, you suddenly sprang over the top shouting 'To Berlin! Forward!'; dashed at the German army single-handed; and were cut off and made prisoner by the Huns?

AUGUSTUS. Yes, madam; and what was my reward? They said I had disobeyed orders, and sent me home. Have they forgotten Nelson in the Baltic?* Has any British battle ever been won except by a bold individual initiative? I say nothing of professional jealousy: it exists in the army as elsewhere; but it is a bitter thought to me that the recognition denied me by my own country—or rather by the Radical cabal in the Cabinet which pursues my family with rancorous class hatred—that this recognition, I say, came to me at the hands of an enemy—of a rank Prussian.

THE LADY. You dont say so!

AUGUSTUS. How else should I be here instead of starving to death in Ruhleben?* Yes, madam: the Colonel of the Pomeranian* regiment which captured me, after learning what I had done, and conversing for an hour with me on European politics and military strategy, declared that nothing would induce him to deprive my country of my services, and set me free. I offered, of course, to procure the release in exchange of a German officer of equal quality; but he would not hear of it. He was kind enough to say he could not believe that a German officer answering to that description existed. [*With emotion*] I had my first taste of the ingratitude of my own country as I made my way back to our lines. A shot from our front trench struck me in the head. I still carry the flattened projectile as a trophy [*he throws it on the table: the noise it makes testifies to its weight*]. Had it penetrated to the brain I might never have sat on another Royal Commission. Fortunately we have strong heads, we Highcastles. Nothing has ever penetrated to our brains.

THE LADY. How thrilling! How simple! And how tragic! But you will forgive England? Remember: *England*! Forgive her.

AUGUSTUS [*with gloomy magnanimity*] It will make no difference whatever to my services to my country. Though she slay me, yet will I, if not exactly trust in her, at least take my part in her government. I am ever at my country's call. Whether it be the embassy in a leading European capital, a governor-generalship in the tropics, or my humble mission here to make Little Pifflington do its bit, I am always ready for the sacrifice. Whilst England remains England, wherever there is a public job to be done you will find a Highcastle sticking to it. And now, madam, enough of my tragic personal history. You have called on business. What can I do for you?

THE LADY. You have relatives at the Foreign Office,* have you not?

AUGUSTUS [*haughtily*] Madam: the Foreign Office is staffed by my relatives exclusively.

THE LADY. Has the Foreign Office warned you that you are being pursued by a female spy who is determined to obtain possession of a certain list of gun emplacements—

AUGUSTUS [*interrupting her somewhat loftily*] All that is perfectly well known to this department, madam.

THE LADY [*surprised and rather indignant*] Is it? Who told you? Was it one of your German brothers-in-law?

AUGUSTUS [*injured, remonstrating*] I have only three German brothers-in-law, madam. Really, from your tone, one would suppose that I had several. Pardon my sensitiveness on that subject; but reports are continually being circulated that I have been shot as a traitor in the courtyard of the Ritz Hotel* simply because I have German brothers-in-law. [*With feeling*] If you had a German brother-in-law, madam, you would know that nothing else in the world produces so strong an anti-German feeling. Life affords no keener pleasure than finding a brother-in-law's name in the German casualty list.

THE LADY. Nobody knows that better than I. Wait until you hear what I have come to tell you: you will understand me as no one else could. Listen. This spy, this woman—

AUGUSTUS [*all attention*] Yes?

THE LADY. She is a German. A Hun.

AUGUSTUS. Yes, yes. She would be. Continue.

THE LADY. She is my sister-in-law.

AUGUSTUS [*deferentially*] I see you are well connected, madam. Proceed.

THE LADY. Need I add that she is my bitterest enemy?

AUGUSTUS. May I—[*he proffers his hand. They shake, fervently. From this moment onward Augustus becomes more and more confidential, gallant, and charming*].

THE LADY. Quite so. Well, she is an intimate friend of your brother at the War Office,* Hungerford Highcastle: Blueloo as you call him: I dont know why.

AUGUSTUS [*explaining*] He was originally called The Singing Oyster, because he sang drawing-room ballads with such an extraordinary absence of expression. He was then called the Blue Point for a season or two. Finally he became Blueloo.

THE LADY. Oh, indeed: I didnt know. Well, Blueloo is simply infatuated with my sister-in-law; and he has rashly let out to her that this list is in your possession. He forgot himself because he was in a towering rage at its being entrusted to you: his language was terrible. He ordered all the guns to be shifted at once.

AUGUSTUS. What on earth did he do that for?

THE LADY. I cant imagine. But this I know. She made a bet with him that she would come down here and obtain possession of that list and get clean away into the street with it. He took the bet on condition that she brought it straight back to him at the War Office.

AUGUSTUS. Good heavens! And you mean to tell me that Blueloo was such a dolt as to believe that she could succeed? Does he take me for a fool?

THE LADY. Oh, impossible! He is jealous of your intellect. The bet is an insult to you: dont you feel that? After what you have done for our country—

AUGUSTUS. Oh, never mind that. It is the idiocy of the thing I look at. He'll lose his bet; and serve him right!

THE LADY. You feel sure you will be able to resist the siren? I warn you, she is very fascinating.

AUGUSTUS. You need have no fear, madam. I hope she will come and try it on. Fascination is a game that two can play at. For centuries the younger sons of the Highcastles have had nothing to do but fascinate attractive females when they were not sitting on Royal Commissions or on duty at Knightsbridge barracks.* By Gad, madam, if the siren comes here she will meet her match.

THE LADY. I feel that. But if she fails to seduce you—

AUGUSTUS [*blushing*] Madam!

THE LADY [*continuing*]—from your allegiance—

AUGUSTUS. Oh, that!

THE LADY. —she will resort to fraud, to force, to anything. She will burgle your office: she will have you attacked and garotted at night in the street.

AUGUSTUS. Pooh! I'm not afraid.

THE LADY. Oh, your courage will only tempt you into danger. She may get the list after all. It is true that the guns are moved. But she would win her bet.

AUGUSTUS [*cautiously*] You did not say that the guns were moved. You said that Blueloo had ordered them to be moved.

THE LADY. Well, that is the same thing, isnt it?

AUGUSTUS. Not quite—at the War Office. No doubt those guns *will* be moved: possibly even before the end of the war.

THE LADY. Then you think they are there still! But if the German War Office gets the list—and she will copy it before she gives it back to Blueloo, you may depend on it—all is lost.

AUGUSTUS [*lazily*] Well, I should not go as far as that. [*Lowering his voice*] Will you swear to me not to repeat what I am going to say to you; for if the British public knew that I had said it, I should be at once hounded down as a pro-German.

THE LADY. I will be silent as the grave. I swear it.

AUGUSTUS [*again taking it easily*] Well, our people have for some reason made up their minds that the German War Office is everything that our War Office is not—that it carries promptitude, efficiency, and organization to a pitch of completeness and perfection that must be, in my opinion, destructive to the happiness of the staff. My own view—which you are pledged, remember, not to betray—is that the German War Office is no better than any other War Office. I found that opinion on my observation of the characters of my brothers-in-law: one of whom, by the way, is on the German general staff. I am not at all sure that this list of gun emplacements would receive the smallest attention. You see, there are always so many more important things to be attended to. Family matters, and so on, you understand.

THE LADY. Still, if a question were asked in the House of Commons—

AUGUSTUS. The great advantage of being at war, madam, is that nobody takes the slightest notice of the House of Commons. No

doubt it is sometimes necessary for a Minister to soothe the more
seditious members of that assembly by giving a pledge or two; but
the War Office takes no notice of such things.

THE LADY [*staring at him*] Then you think this list of gun emplacements
doesnt matter!!

AUGUSTUS. By no means, madam. It matters very much indeed. If this
spy were to obtain possession of the list, Blueloo would tell the story
at every dinner-table in London; and—

THE LADY. And you might lose your post. Of course.

AUGUSTUS [*amazed and indignant*] *I* lose my post! What are you
dreaming about, madam? How could I possibly be spared? There are
hardly Highcastles enough at present to fill half the posts created by
this war. No: Blueloo would not go that far. He is at least a gentleman.
But I should be chaffed; and, frankly, I dont like being chaffed.

THE LADY. Of course not. Who does? It would never do. Oh never,
never.

AUGUSTUS. I'm glad you see it in that light. And now, as a measure of
security, I shall put that list in my pocket. [*He begins searching vainly
from drawer to drawer in the writing-table*]. Where on earth—? What
the dickens did I—? Thats very odd: I—Where the deuce—? I thought
I had put it in the— Oh, here it is! No: this is Lucy's last letter.

THE LADY [*elegiacally*] Lucy's Last Letter! What a title for a picture
play!

AUGUSTUS [*delighted*] Yes: it is, isnt it? Lucy appeals to the imagination
like no other woman. By the way [*handing over the letter*] I wonder
could you read it for me? Lucy is a darling girl; but I really cant read
her writing. In London I get the office typist to decipher it and make
me a typed copy; but here there is nobody.

THE LADY [*puzzling over it*] It is really almost illegible. I think the
beginning is meant for 'Dearest Gus'.

AUGUSTUS [*eagerly*] Yes: that is what she usually calls me. Please go on.

THE LADY [*trying to decipher it*] 'What a'—'what a'—oh yes: 'what
a forgetful old'—something—'you are!' I cant make out the word.

AUGUSTUS [*greatly interested*] Is it blighter? That is a favorite
expression of hers.

THE LADY. I think so. At all events it begins with a B. [*Reading*] 'What a forgetful old'—[*she is interrupted by a knock at the door*].

AUGUSTUS [*impatiently*] Come in. [*The clerk enters, clean shaven and in khaki, with an official paper and an envelope in his hand*]. What is this ridiculous mummery, sir?

THE CLERK [*coming to the table and exhibiting his uniform to both*] Theyve passed me. The recruiting officer come for me. Ive had my two and seven.

AUGUSTUS [*rising wrathfully*] I shall not permit it. What do they mean by taking my office staff? Good God! they will be taking our hunt servants next. [*Confronting the clerk*] What did the man mean? What did he say?

THE CLERK. He said that now you was on the job we'd want another million men, and he was going to take the old-age pensioners or anyone he could get.

AUGUSTUS. And did you dare to knock at my door and interrupt my business with this lady to repeat this man's ineptitudes?

THE CLERK. No. I come because the waiter from the hotel brought this paper. You left it on the coffee-room breakfast-table this morning.

THE LADY [*intercepting it*] It is the list. Good heavens!

THE CLERK [*proffering the envelope*] He says he thinks this is the envelope belonging to it.

THE LADY [*snatching the envelope also*] Yes! Addressed to you. Lord Augustus! [*Augustus comes back to the table to look at it*] Oh, how imprudent! Everybody would guess its importance with your name on it. Fortunately I have some letters of my own here [*opening her wallet*]. Why not hide it in one of my envelopes? then no one will dream that the enclosure is of any political value. [*Taking out a letter, she crosses the room towards the window, whispering to Augustus as she passes him*] Get rid of that man.

AUGUSTUS [*haughtily approaching the clerk, who humorously makes a paralytic attempt to stand at attention*]* Have you any further business here, pray?

THE CLERK. Am I to give the waiter anything; or will you do it yourself?

AUGUSTUS. Which waiter is it? The English one?

THE CLERK. No: the one that calls hisself a Swiss. Shouldnt wonder if he'd made a copy of that paper.

AUGUSTUS. Keep your impertinent surmises to yourself, sir. Remember that you are in the army now; and let me have no more of your civilian insubordination. Attention! Left turn! Quick march!

THE CLERK [*stolidly*] I dunno what you mean.

AUGUSTUS. Go to the guard-room and report yourself for disobeying orders. Now do you know what I mean?

THE CLERK. Now look here. I aint going to argue with you—

AUGUSTUS. Nor I with you. Out with you.

He seizes the clerk, and rushes him through the door. The moment the lady is left alone, she snatches a sheet of official paper from the stationery rack; folds it so that it resembles the list; compares the two to see that they look exactly alike; whips the list into her wallet; and substitutes the facsimile for it. Then she listens for the return of Augustus. A crash is heard, as of the clerk falling downstairs.

Augustus returns and is about to close the door when the voice of the clerk is heard from below:

THE CLERK. I'll have the law of you for this, I will.

AUGUSTUS [*shouting down to him*] Theres no more law for you, you scoundrel. Youre a soldier now. [*He shuts the door and comes to the lady*]. Thank heaven, the war has given us the upper hand of these fellows at last. Excuse my violence; but discipline is absolutely necessary in dealing with the lower middle classes.

THE LADY. Serve the insolent creature right! Look! I have found you a beautiful envelope for the list, an unmistakeable lady's envelope. [*She puts the sham list into her envelope and hands it to him*].

AUGUSTUS. Excellent. Really very clever of you. [*Slyly*] Come: would you like to have a peep at the list [*beginning to take the blank paper from the envelope*]?

THE LADY [*on the brink of detection*] No no. Oh, *please*, no.

AUGUSTUS. Why? It wont bite you [*drawing it out further*].

THE LADY [*snatching at his hand*] Stop. Remember: if there should be an inquiry, you must be able to swear that you never shewed that list to a mortal soul.

AUGUSTUS. Oh, that is a mere form. If you are really curious—

THE LADY. I am not. I couldnt bear to look at it. One of my dearest friends was blown to pieces by an aircraft gun; and since then I have never been able to think of one without horror.

AUGUSTUS. You mean it was a real gun, and actually went off. How sad! how sad! [*He pushes the sham list back into the envelope, and pockets it*].

THE LADY. Ah! [*great sigh of relief*]. And now, Lord Augustus, I have taken up too much of your valuable time. Goodbye.

AUGUSTUS. What! Must you go?

THE LADY. You are so busy.

AUGUSTUS. Yes; but not before lunch, you know. I never can do much before lunch. And I'm no good at all in the afternoon. From five to six is my real working time. Must you really go?

THE LADY. I must, really. I have done my business very satisfactorily. Thank you ever so much [*she proffers her hand*].

AUGUSTUS [*shaking it affectionately as he leads her to the door, but first pressing the bell button with his left hand*] Goodbye. Goodbye. So sorry to lose you. Kind of you to come; but there was no real danger. You see, my dear little lady, all this talk about war saving, and secrecy, and keeping the blinds down at night, and so forth, is all very well; but unless it's carried out with intelligence, believe me, you may waste a pound to save a penny; you may let out all sorts of secrets to the enemy; you may guide the Zeppelins right on to your own chimneys. Thats where the ability of the governing class comes in. Shall the fellow call a taxi for you?

THE LADY. No, thanks: I prefer walking. Goodbye. Again, many, *many* thanks.

She goes out. Augustus returns to the writing-table smiling, and takes another look at himself in the mirror. The clerk returns with his head bandaged, carrying a poker.

THE CLERK. What did you ring for? [*Augustus hastily drops the mirror*]. Dont you come nigh me or I'll split your head with this poker, thick as it is.

AUGUSTUS. It does not seem to me an exceptionally thick poker. I rang for you to shew the lady out.

THE CLERK. She's gone. She run out like a rabbit. I ask myself, why was she in such a hurry?

THE LADY'S VOICE [*from the street*] Lord Augustus. Lord Augustus.

THE CLERK. She's calling you.

AUGUSTUS [*running to the window and throwing it up*] What is it? Wont you come up?

THE LADY. Is the clerk there?

AUGUSTUS. Yes. Do you want him?

THE LADY. Yes.

AUGUSTUS. The lady wants you at the window.

THE CLERK [*rushing to the window and putting down the poker*] Yes, maam? Here I am, maam. What is it, maam?

THE LADY. I want you to witness that I got clean away into the street. I am coming up now.

The two men stare at one another.

THE CLERK. Wants me to witness that she got clean away into the street!

AUGUSTUS. What on earth does she mean?

The lady returns.

THE LADY. May I use your telephone?

AUGUSTUS. Certainly. Certainly. [*Taking the receiver down*] What number shall I get you?

THE LADY. The War Office, please.

AUGUSTUS. The War Office!?

THE LADY. If you will be so good.

AUGUSTUS. But— Oh, very well. [*Into the receiver*] Hallo. This is the Town Hall Recruiting Office. Give me Colonel Bogey,* sharp.

A pause.

THE CLERK [*breaking the painful silence*] I dont think I'm awake. This is a dream of a movy picture, this is.

AUGUSTUS [*his ear at the receiver*] Shut up, will you? [*Into the telephone*] What?...[*To the lady*] Whom do you want to get on to?

THE LADY. Blueloo.

AUGUSTUS [*into the telephone*] Put me through to Lord Hungerford Highcastle....I'm his brother, idiot....That you, Blueloo? Lady here at Little Pifflington wants to speak to you. Hold the line. [*To the lady*] Now, madam [*he hands her the receiver*].

THE LADY [*sitting down in Augustus's chair to speak into the telephone*] Is that Blueloo?...Do you recognize my voice?...Ive won our bet....

AUGUSTUS. *Your* bet!

THE LADY [*into the telephone*] Yes: I have the list in my wallet....

AUGUSTUS. Nothing of the kind, madam. I have it here in my pocket. [*He takes the envelope from his pocket; draws out the paper; and unfolds it*].

THE LADY [*continuing*] Yes: I got clean into the street with it. I have a witness. I could have got to London with it. Augustus wont deny it....

AUGUSTUS [*contemplating the blank paper*] Theres nothing written on this. Where is the list of guns?

THE LADY [*continuing*] Oh, it was quite easy. I said I was my sister-in-law and that I was a Hun. He lapped it up like a kitten....

AUGUSTUS. You dont mean to say that—

THE LADY [*continuing*] I got hold of the list for a moment and changed it for a piece of paper out of his stationery rack: it was quite easy [*she laughs; and it is clear that Blueloo is laughing too*].

AUGUSTUS. What!

THE CLERK [*laughing slowly and laboriously, with intense enjoyment*] Ha ha! Ha ha ha! Ha! [*Augustus rushes at him: he snatches up the poker and stands on guard*]. No you dont.

THE LADY [*still at the telephone, waving her disengaged hand behind her impatiently at them to stop making a noise*] Sh-sh-sh-sh-sh!!! [*Augustus, with a shrug, goes up the middle of the room. The lady resumes her conversation with the telephone*] What?...Oh yes: I'm coming up by the 12.35: why not have tea with me at Rumpelmeister's?...

Rum-pel-meister's. You know: they call it Robinson's now.... Right. Ta ta. [*She hangs up the receiver, and is passing round the table on her way towards the door when she is confronted by Augustus*].

AUGUSTUS. Madam: I consider your conduct most unpatriotic. You make bets and abuse the confidence of the hardworked officials who are doing their bit for their country whilst our gallant fellows are perishing in the trenches—

THE LADY. Oh, the gallant fellows are not all in the trenches, Augustus. Some of them have come home for a few days hard-earned leave; and I am sure you wont grudge them a little fun at your expense.

THE CLERK. Hear! Hear!

AUGUSTUS [*amiably*] Ah, well! For my country's sake—!

ANNAJANSKA, THE BOLSHEVIK EMPRESS

A REVOLUTIONARY ROMANCELET

PREFACE

ANNAJANSKA is frankly a bravura* piece. The modern variety theatre demands for its 'turns' little plays called sketches, to last twenty minutes or so, and to enable some favorite performer to make a brief but dazzling appearance on some barely passable dramatic pretext. Miss Lillah McCarthy and I, as author and actress, have helped to make one another famous on many serious occasions, from Man and Superman to Androcles;* and Mr Charles Ricketts* has not disdained to snatch moments from his painting and sculpture to design some wonderful dresses for us. We three unbent as Mrs Siddons, Sir Joshua Reynolds, and Dr Johnson* might have unbent, to devise a 'turn' for the Coliseum variety theatre.* Not that we would set down the art of the variety theatre as something to be condescended to, or our own art as elephantine. We should rather crave indulgence as three novices fresh from the awful legitimacy of the highbrow theatre.

Well, Miss McCarthy and Mr Ricketts justified themselves easily in the glamor of the footlights, to the strains of Tchaikovsky's 1812.* I fear I did not. I have received only one compliment on my share; and that was from a friend who said 'it is the only one of your works that is not too long.' So I have made it a page or two longer, according to my own precept: EMBRACE YOUR REPROACHES: THEY ARE OFTEN GLORIES IN DISGUISE.

ANNAJANSKA, THE BOLSHEVIK EMPRESS

The General's office in a military station on the east front in Beotia.* An office table with a telephone, writing materials, official papers, etc., is set across the room. At the end of the table, a comfortable chair for the General. Behind the chair, a window. Facing it at the other end of the table, a plain wooden bench. At the side of the table, with its back to the door, a common chair, with a typewriter before it. Beside the door, which is opposite the end of the bench, a rack for caps and coats. There is nobody in the room.

General Strammfest enters, followed by Lieutenant Schneidekind. They hang up their cloaks and caps. Schneidekind takes a little longer than Strammfest, who comes to the table.

STRAMMFEST. Schneidekind.

SCHNEIDEKIND. Yes, sir.

STRAMMFEST. Have you sent my report yet to the government [*he sits down*].

SCHNEIDEKIND [*coming to the table*] Not yet, sir. Which government do you wish it sent to? [*He sits down*].

STRAMMFEST. That depends. Whats the latest? Which of them do you think is most likely to be in power tomorrow morning?

SCHNEIDEKIND. Well, the provisional government* was going strong yesterday. But today they say that the prime minister has shot himself,* and that the extreme left fellow* has shot all the others.

STRAMMFEST. Yes: thats all very well; but these fellows always shoot themselves with blank cartridge.

SCHNEIDEKIND. Still, even the blank cartridge means backing down. I should send the report to the Maximilianists.*

STRAMMFEST. Theyre no stronger than the Oppidoshavians;* and in my own opinion the Moderate Red Revolutionaries* are as likely to come out on top as either of them.

SCHNEIDEKIND. I can easily put a few carbon sheets* in the typewriter and send a copy each to the lot.

STRAMMFEST. Waste of paper. You might as well send reports to an infant school. [*He throws his head on the table with a groan*].

SCHNEIDEKIND. Tired out, sir?

STRAMMFEST. O Schneidekind, Schneidekind, how can you bear to live?

SCHNEIDEKIND. At my age, sir, I ask myself how can I bear to die?

STRAMMFEST. You are young, young and heartless. You are excited by the revolution: * you are attached to abstract things like liberty. But my family has served the Panjandrums of Beotia* faithfully for seven centuries. The Panjandrums have kept our place for us at their courts, honored us, promoted us, shed their glory on us, made us what we are. When I hear you young men declaring that you are fighting for civilization, for democracy, for the overthrow of militarism, I ask myself how can a man shed his blood for empty words used by vulgar tradesmen and common laborers: mere wind and stink. [*He rises, exalted by his theme*]. A king is a splendid reality, a man raised above us like a god. You can see him; you can kiss his hand; you can be cheered by his smile and terrified by his frown. I would have died for my Panjandrum as my father died for his father. Your toiling millions were only too honored to receive the toes of our boots in the proper spot for them when they displeased their betters. And now what is left in life for me? [*He relapses into his chair discouraged*] My Panjandrum is deposed* and transported to herd with convicts. The army, his pride and glory, is paraded to hear seditious speeches from penniless rebels, with the colonel actually forced to take the chair and introduce the speaker. I myself am made Commander-in-Chief by my own solicitor: a Jew, Schneidekind! a Hebrew Jew!* It seems only yesterday that these things would have been the ravings of a madman: today they are the commonplaces of the gutter press.* I live now for three objects only: to defeat the enemy, to restore the Panjandrum, and to hang my solicitor.

SCHNEIDEKIND. Be careful, sir: these are dangerous views to utter nowadays. What if I were to betray you?

STRAMMFEST. What!

SCHNEIDEKIND. I wont, of course: my own father goes on just like that; but suppose I did?

STRAMMFEST [*chuckling*] I should accuse you of treason to the Revolution, my lad; and they would immediately shoot you, unless you cried and asked to see your mother before you died, when they would probably change their minds and make you a brigadier. Enough. [*He rises and expands his chest*]. I feel the better for letting myself go. To business. [*He takes up a telegram; opens it; and is thunderstruck by its contents*]. Great heaven! [*He collapses into his chair*]. This is the worst blow of all.

SCHNEIDEKIND. What has happened? Are we beaten?

STRAMMFEST. Man: do you think that a mere defeat could strike me down as this news does: I, who have been defeated thirteen times since the war began? O, my master, my master, my Panjandrum! [*he is convulsed with sobs*].

SCHNEIDEKIND. They have killed him?

STRAMMFEST. A dagger has been struck through his heart—

SCHNEIDEKIND. Good God!

STRAMMFEST. —and through mine, through mine.

SCHNEIDEKIND [*relieved*] Oh: a metaphorical dagger. I thought you meant a real one. What has happened?

STRAMMFEST. His daughter, the Grand Duchess Annajanska, she whom the Panjandrina loved beyond all her other children, has—has—[*he cannot finish*].

SCHNEIDEKIND. Committed suicide?

STRAMMFEST. No. Better if she had. Oh, far far better.

SCHNEIDEKIND [*in hushed tones*] Left the Church?

STRAMMFEST [*shocked*] Certainly not. Do not blaspheme, young man.

SCHNEIDEKIND. Asked for the vote?*

STRAMMFEST. I would have given it to her with both hands* to save her from this.

SCHNEIDEKIND. Save her from what? Dash it, sir, out with it.

STRAMMFEST. She has joined the Revolution.

SCHNEIDEKIND. But so have you, sir. Weve all joined the Revolution. She doesnt mean it any more than we do.

STRAMMFEST. Heaven grant you may be right! But that is not the worst. She has eloped with a young officer. Eloped, Schneidekind, eloped!

SCHNEIDEKIND [*not particularly impressed*] Yes, sir.

STRAMMFEST. Annajanska, the beautiful, the innocent, my master's daughter! [*He buries his face in his hands*].

The telephone rings.

SCHNEIDEKIND [*taking the receiver*] Yes: G.H.Q.* Yes.... Dont bawl: I'm not a general. Who is it speaking?... Why didnt you say so? dont you know your duty? Next time you will lose your stripe.... Oh, theyve made you a colonel, have they? Well, theyve made me a field-marshal: now what have you to say?... Look here: what did you ring up for? I cant spend the day here listening to your cheek.... What! the Grand Duchess! [*Strammfest starts*]. Where did you catch her?

STRAMMFEST [*snatching the telephone and listening for the answer*] Speak louder, will you: I am a General.... I know that, you dolt. Have you captured the officer that was with her?... Damnation! You shall answer for this: you let him go: he bribed you.... You *must* have seen him: the fellow is in the full dress court uniform of the Panderobajensky Hussars.* I give you twelve hours to catch him or... whats that you say about the devil? Are you swearing at me, you... Thousand thunders! [*To Schneidekind*] The swine says that the Grand Duchess is a devil incarnate. [*Into the telephone*] Filthy traitor: is that the way you dare speak of the daughter of our anointed Panjandrum? I'll—

SCHNEIDEKIND [*pulling the telephone from his lips*] Take care, sir.

STRAMMFEST. I wont take care: I'll have him shot. Let go that telephone.

SCHNEIDEKIND. But for her own sake, sir—

STRAMMFEST. Eh?

SCHNEIDEKIND. For her own sake they had better send her here. She will be safe in your hands.

STRAMMFEST [*yielding the receiver*] You are right. Be civil to him. I should choke [*he sits down*].

SCHNEIDEKIND [*into the telephone*] Hullo. Never mind all that: it's only a fellow here who has been fooling with the telephone. I had to leave the room for a moment. Wash out; and send the girl along. We'll jolly soon teach her to behave herself here.... Oh, youve sent her already. Then why the devil didnt you say so, you—[*he hangs up *the telephone angrily*]. Just fancy: they started her off this morning: and all this is because the fellow likes to get on the telephone and hear himself talk now that he is a colonel. [*The telephone rings again. He snatches the receiver furiously*] Whats the matter now?...[*To the General*] It's our own people downstairs. [*Into the receiver*] Here! do you suppose Ive nothing else to do than to hang on to the telephone all day?...Whats that? Not men enough to hold her! What do you mean? [*To the General*] She is there, sir.

STRAMMFEST. Tell them to send her up. I shall have to receive her without even rising, without kissing her hand, to keep up appearances before the escort. It will break my heart.

SCHNEIDEKIND [*into the receiver*] Send her up....Tcha! [*He hangs up the receiver*]. He says she is half way up already: they couldnt hold her.

The Grand Duchess bursts into the room, dragging with her two exhausted soldiers hanging on desperately to her arms. She is enveloped from head to foot by a fur-lined cloak, and wears a fur cap.

SCHNEIDEKIND [*pointing to the bench*] At the word Go, place your prisoner on the bench in a sitting posture; and take your seats right and left of her. Go.

The two soldiers make a supreme effort to force her to sit down. She flings them back so that they are forced to sit on the bench to save themselves from falling backwards over it, and is herself dragged into sitting between them. The second soldier, holding on tight to the Grand Duchess with one hand, produces papers with the other, and waves them towards Schneidekind, who takes them from him and passes them on to the General. He opens them and reads them with a grave expression.

SCHNEIDEKIND. Be good enough to wait, prisoner, until the General has read the papers on your case.

THE GRAND DUCHESS [*to the soldiers*] Let go. [*To Strammfest*] Tell them to let go, or I'll upset the bench backwards and bash our three heads on the floor.

FIRST SOLDIER. No, little mother. Have mercy on the poor.

STRAMMFEST [*growling over the edge of the paper he is reading*] Hold your tongue.

THE GRAND DUCHESS [*blazing*] Me, or the soldier?

STRAMMFEST [*horrified*] The soldier, madam.

THE GRAND DUCHESS. Tell him to let go.

STRAMMFEST. Release the lady.

The soldiers take their hands off her. One of them wipes his fevered brow. The other sucks his wrist.

SCHNEIDEKIND [*fiercely*] 'ttention!

The two soldiers sit up stiffly.

THE GRAND DUCHESS. Oh, let the poor man suck his wrist. It may be poisoned. I bit it.

STRAMMFEST [*shocked*] You bit a common soldier!

THE GRAND DUCHESS. Well, I offered to cauterize it with the poker in the office stove. But he was afraid. What more could I do?

SCHNEIDEKIND. Why did you bite him, prisoner?

THE GRAND DUCHESS. He would not let go.

STRAMMFEST. Did he let go when you bit him?

THE GRAND DUCHESS. No. [*Patting the soldier on the back*] You should give the man a cross* for his devotion. I could not go on eating him; so I brought him along with me.

STRAMMFEST. Prisoner—

THE GRAND DUCHESS. Dont call me prisoner, General Strammfest. My grandmother dandled you on her knee.

STRAMMFEST [*bursting into tears*] O God, yes. Believe me, my heart is what it was then.

THE GRAND DUCHESS. Your brain also is what it was then. I will not be addressed by you as prisoner.

STRAMMFEST. I may not, for your own sake, call you by your rightful and most sacred titles. What am I to call you?

THE GRAND DUCHESS. The Revolution has made us comrades. Call me comrade.*

STRAMMFEST. I had rather die.

THE GRAND DUCHESS. Then call me Annajanska; and I will call you Peter Piper,* as grandmamma did.

STRAMMFEST [*painfully agitated*] Schneidekind: you must speak to her: I cannot—[*he breaks down*].

SCHNEIDEKIND [*officially*] The Republic of Beotia has been compelled to confine the Panjandrum and his family, for their own safety, within certain bounds. You have broken those bounds.

STRAMMFEST [*taking the word from him*] You are—I must say it—a prisoner. What am I to do with you?

THE GRAND DUCHESS. You should have thought of that before you arrested me.

STRAMMFEST. Come, come, prisoner! do you know what will happen to you if you compel me to take a sterner tone with you?

THE GRAND DUCHESS. No. But I know what will happen to you.

STRAMMFEST. Pray what, prisoner?

THE GRAND DUCHESS. Clergyman's sore throat.*

Schneidekind splutters: drops a paper; and conceals his laughter under the table.

STRAMMFEST [*thunderously*] Lieutenant Schneidekind.

SCHNEIDEKIND [*in a stifled voice*] Yes, sir. [*The table vibrates visibly*].

STRAMMFEST. Come out of it, you fool: youre upsetting the ink.

Schneidekind emerges, red in the face with suppressed mirth.

STRAMMFEST. Why dont you laugh? Dont you appreciate Her Imperial Highness's joke?

SCHNEIDEKIND [*suddenly becoming solemn*] I dont want to, sir.

STRAMMFEST. Laugh at once, sir. I order you to laugh.

SCHNEIDEKIND [*with a touch of temper*] I really cant, sir. [*He sits down decisively*].

STRAMMFEST [*growling at him*] Yah! [*He turns impressively to the Grand Duchess*] Your Imperial Highness desires me to address you as comrade?

THE GRAND DUCHESS [*rising and waving a red handkerchief*] Long live the Revolution, comrade!

STRAMMFEST [*rising and saluting*] Proletarians of all lands, unite.* Lieutenant Schneidekind: you will rise and sing the Marseillaise.*

SCHNEIDEKIND [*rising*] But I cannot, sir. I have no voice, no ear.

STRAMMFEST. Then sit down; and bury your shame in your typewriter [*Schneidekind sits down*]. Comrade Annajanska: you have eloped with a young officer.

THE GRAND DUCHESS [*astounded*] General Strammfest: you lie.

STRAMMFEST. Denial, comrade, is useless. It is through that officer that your movements have been traced. [*The Grand Duchess is suddenly enlightened, and seems amused. Strammfest continues in a forensic manner*] He joined you at the Golden Anchor in Hakonsburg. You gave us the slip there; but the officer was traced to Potterdam, where you rejoined him and went alone to Premsylople.* What have you done with that unhappy young man? Where is he?

THE GRAND DUCHESS [*pretending to whisper an important secret*] Where he has always been.

STRAMMFEST [*eagerly*] Where is that?

THE GRAND DUCHESS [*impetuously*] In your imagination. I came alone. I *am* alone. Hundreds of officers travel every day from Hakonsburg to Potterdam. What do I know about them?

STRAMMFEST. They travel in khaki. They do not travel in full dress court uniform as this man did.

SCHNEIDEKIND. Only officers who are eloping with grand duchesses wear court uniform: otherwise the grand duchesses could not be seen with them.

STRAMMFEST. Hold your tongue [*Schneidekind, in high dudgeon, folds his arms and retires from the conversation. The General returns to his paper and to his examination of the Grand Duchess*] This officer travelled with your passport. What have you to say to that?

THE GRAND DUCHESS. Bosh! How could a man travel with a woman's passport?

STRAMMFEST. It is quite simple, as you very well know. A dozen travellers arrive at the boundary. The official collects their passports.

He counts twelve persons; then counts the passports. If there are twelve, he is satisfied.

THE GRAND DUCHESS. Then how do you know that one of the passports was mine?

STRAMMFEST. A waiter at the Potterdam Hotel looked at the officer's passport when he was in his bath. It was your passport.

THE GRAND DUCHESS. Stuff! Why did he not have me arrested?

STRAMMFEST. When the waiter returned to the hotel with the police the officer had vanished; and you were there with your own passport. They knouted* him.

THE GRAND DUCHESS. Oh! Strammfest: send these men away. I must speak to you alone.

STRAMMFEST [*rising in horror*] No: this is the last straw: I cannot consent. It is impossible, utterly, eternally impossible, that a daughter of the Imperial House should speak to anyone alone, were it even her own husband.

THE GRAND DUCHESS. You forget that there is an exception. She may speak to a child alone. [*She rises*] Strammfest: you have been dandled on my grandmother's knee. By that gracious action the dowager* Panjandrina made you a child forever. So did Nature, by the way. I order you to speak to me alone. Do you hear? I *order* you. For seven hundred years no member of your family has ever disobeyed an order from a member of mine. Will you disobey me?

STRAMMFEST. There is an alternative to obedience. The dead cannot disobey. [*He takes out his pistol and places the muzzle against his temple*].

SCHNEIDEKIND [*snatching the pistol from him*] For God's sake, General—

STRAMMFEST [*attacking him furiously to recover the weapon*] Dog of a subaltern, restore that pistol, and my honor.

SCHNEIDEKIND [*reaching out with the pistol to the Grand Duchess*] Take it: quick: he is as strong as a bull.

THE GRAND DUCHESS [*snatching it*] Aha! Leave the room, all of you except the General. At the double! lightning! electricity! [*she fires shot after shot, spattering bullets about the ankles of the soldiers. They fly precipitately. She turns to Schneidekind, who has by this time been flung on the floor by the General*] You too. [*He scrambles up*]. March [*He flies to the door*].

SCHNEIDEKIND [*turning at the door*] For your own sake, comrade—

THE GRAND DUCHESS [*indignantly*] Comrade! You!!! Go. [*She fires two more shots. He vanishes*].

STRAMMFEST [*making an impulsive movement towards her*] My Imperial Mistress—

THE GRAND DUCHESS. Stop. I have one bullet left, if you attempt to take this from me [*putting the pistol to her temple*].

STRAMMFEST [*recoiling, and covering his eyes with his hands*] No no: put it down: put it down. I promise everything: I swear anything; put it down, I implore you.

THE GRAND DUCHESS [*throwing it on the table*] There!

STRAMMFEST [*uncovering his eyes*] Thank God!

THE GRAND DUCHESS [*gently*] Strammfest: I am your comrade. Am I nothing more to you?

STRAMMFEST [*falling on his knee*] You are, God help me, all that is left to me of the only power I recognize on earth [*he kisses her hand*].

THE GRAND DUCHESS [*indulgently*] Idolater! When will you learn that our strength has never been in ourselves, but in your illusions about us? [*She shakes off her kindliness, and sits down in his chair*] Now tell me, what are your orders? And do you mean to obey them?

STRAMMFEST [*starting like a goaded ox, and blundering fretfully about the room*] How can I obey six different dictators, and not one gentleman among the lot of them? One of them orders me to make peace with the foreign enemy. Another orders me to offer all the neutral countries 48 hours to choose between adopting his views on the single tax* and being instantly invaded and annihilated. A third orders me to go to a damned Socialist Conference and explain that Beotia will allow no annexations and no indemnities,* and merely wishes to establish the Kingdom of Heaven on Earth throughout the universe. [*He finishes behind Schneidekind's chair*].

THE GRAND DUCHESS. Damn their trifling!

STRAMMFEST. I thank Your Imperial Highness from the bottom of my heart for that expression. Europe thanks you.

THE GRAND DUCHESS. M'yes; but—[*rising*] Strammfest: you know that your cause—the cause of the dynasty—is lost.

STRAMMFEST. You must not say so. It is treason, even from you. [*He sinks, discouraged, into the chair, and covers his face with his hand*].

THE GRAND DUCHESS. Do not deceive yourself, General: never again will a Panjandrum reign in Beotia. [*She walks slowly across the room, brooding bitterly, and thinking aloud*]. We are so decayed, so out of date, so feeble, so wicked in our own despite, that we have come at last to will our own destruction.*

STRAMMFEST. You are uttering blasphemy.

THE GRAND DUCHESS. All great truths begin as blasphemies. All the king's horses and all the king's men* cannot set up my father's throne again. If they could, you would have done it, would you not?

STRAMMFEST. God knows I would!*

THE GRAND DUCHESS. You really mean that? You would keep the people in their hopeless squalid misery? you would fill those infamous prisons again with the noblest spirits in the land? you would thrust the rising sun of liberty back into the sea of blood from which it has risen? And all because there was in the middle of the dirt and ugliness and horror a little patch of court splendor in which you could stand with a few orders on your uniform, and yawn day after day and night after night in unspeakable boredom until your grave yawned wider still, and you fell into it because you had nothing better to do. How can you be so stupid, so heartless?

STRAMMFEST. You must be mad to think of royalty in such a way. I never yawned at court. The dogs yawned; but that was because they were dogs: they had no imagination, no ideals, no sense of honor and dignity to sustain them.

THE GRAND DUCHESS. My poor Strammfest: you were not often enough at court to tire of it. You were mostly soldiering; and when you came home to have a new order* pinned on your breast, your happiness came through looking at my father and mother and at me, and adoring us. Was that not so?

STRAMMFEST. Do *you* reproach me with it? I am not ashamed of it.

THE GRAND DUCHESS. Oh, it was all very well for you, Strammfest. But think of me, of me! standing there for you to gape at, and knowing that I was no goddess, but only a girl like any other girl! It was cruelty to animals: you could have stuck up a wax doll or a golden calf to worship;* it would not have been bored.

STRAMMFEST. Stop; or I shall renounce my allegiance to you. I have had women flogged for such seditious chatter as this.

THE GRAND DUCHESS. Do not provoke me to send a bullet through your head for reminding me of it.

STRAMMFEST. You always had low tastes. You are no true daughter of the Panjandrums: you are a changeling,* thrust into the Panjandrina's bed by some profligate nurse. I have heard stories of your childhood: of how—

THE GRAND DUCHESS. Ha, ha! Yes: they took me to the circus when I was a child. It was my first moment of happiness, my first glimpse of heaven. I ran away and joined the troupe. They caught me and dragged me back to my gilded cage; but I had tasted freedom; and they never could make me forget it.

STRAMMFEST. Freedom! To be the slave of an acrobat! to be exhibited to the public! to—

THE GRAND DUCHESS. Oh, I was trained to that. I had learnt that part of the business at court.

STRAMMFEST. You had not been taught to strip yourself half naked and turn head over heels—

THE GRAND DUCHESS. Man: I *wanted* to get rid of my swaddling clothes and turn head over heels. I wanted to, I wanted to, I wanted to. I can do it still. Shall I do it now?

STRAMMFEST. If you do, I swear I will throw myself from the window so that I may meet your parents in heaven without having my medals torn from my breast by them.

THE GRAND DUCHESS. Oh, you are incorrigible. You are mad, infatuated. You will not believe that we royal divinities are mere common flesh and blood even when we step down from our pedestals and tell you ourselves what a fool you are. I will argue no more with you: I will use my power. At a word from me your men will turn against you: already half of them do not salute you; and you dare not punish them: you have to pretend not to notice it.

STRAMMFEST. It is not for you to taunt me with that if it is so.

THE GRAND DUCHESS [*haughtily*] Taunt! *I* condescend to taunt! To taunt a common General! You forget yourself, sir.

STRAMMFEST [*dropping on his knee submissively*] Now at last you speak like your royal self.

THE GRAND DUCHESS. Oh, Strammfest, Strammfest, they have driven your slavery into your very bones. Why did you not spit in my face?

STRAMMFEST [*rising with a shudder*] God forbid!

THE GRAND DUCHESS. Well, since you will be my slave, take your orders from me. I have not come here to save our wretched family and our bloodstained crown. I am come to save the Revolution.

STRAMMFEST. Stupid as I am, I have come to think that I had better save that than save nothing. But what will the Revolution do for the people? Do not be deceived by the fine speeches of the revolutionary leaders and the pamphlets of the revolutionary writers. How much liberty is there where *they* have gained the upper hand? Are they not hanging, shooting, imprisoning as much as ever we did? Do they ever tell the people the truth? No: if the truth does not suit them they spread lies instead, and make it a crime to tell the truth.

THE GRAND DUCHESS. Of course they do. Why should they not?

STRAMMFEST [*hardly able to believe his ears*] Why should they not!

THE GRAND DUCHESS. Yes: why should they not? We did it. You did it, whip in hand: you flogged women for teaching children to read.

STRAMMFEST. To read sedition. To read Karl Marx.*

THE GRAND DUCHESS. Pshaw! How could they learn to read the Bible without learning to read Karl Marx? Why do you not stand to your guns and justify what you did, instead of making silly excuses. Do you suppose *I* think flogging a woman worse than flogging a man? I, who am a woman myself!

STRAMMFEST. I am at a loss to understand your Imperial Highness. You seem to me to contradict yourself.

THE GRAND DUCHESS. Nonsense! I say that if the people cannot govern themselves, they must be governed by somebody. If they will not do their duty without being half forced and half humbugged, somebody must force them and humbug them. Some energetic and capable minority must always be in power. Well, I am on the side of the energetic minority whose principles I agree with. The Revolution is as cruel as we were; but its aims are my aims. Therefore I stand for the Revolution.

STRAMMFEST. You do not know what you are saying. This is pure Bolshevism.* Are you, the daughter of a Panjandrum, a Bolshevist?

THE GRAND DUCHESS. I am anything that will make the world less like a prison and more like a circus.

STRAMMFEST. Ah! You still want to be a circus star.

THE GRAND DUCHESS. Yes, and be billed as the Bolshevik Empress. Nothing shall stop me. You have your orders, General Strammfest: save the Revolution.

STRAMMFEST. What Revolution? Which Revolution? No two of your rabble of revolutionists mean the same thing by the Revolution. What can save a mob in which every man is rushing in a different direction?

THE GRAND DUCHESS. I will tell you. The war can save it.

STRAMMFEST. The war?

THE GRAND DUCHESS. Yes, the war. Only a great common danger and a great common duty can unite us and weld these wrangling factions into a solid commonwealth.

STRAMMFEST. Bravo! War sets everything right: I have always said so. But what is a united people without a united army? And what can *I* do? I am only a soldier. I cannot make speeches: I have won no victories: they will not rally to *my* call [*again he sinks into his chair with his former gesture of discouragement*].

THE GRAND DUCHESS. Are you sure they will not rally to mine?

STRAMMFEST. Oh, if only you were a man and a soldier!

THE GRAND DUCHESS. Suppose I find you a man and a soldier?

STRAMMFEST [*rising in a fury*] Ah! the scoundrel you eloped with! You think you will shove this fellow into an army command, over my head. Never.

THE GRAND DUCHESS. You promised everything. You swore anything. [*She marches as if in front of a regiment*]. I know that this man alone can rouse the army to enthusiasm.

STRAMMFEST. Delusion! Folly! He is some circus acrobat; and you are in love with him.

THE GRAND DUCHESS. I swear I am not in love with him. I swear I will never marry him.

STRAMMFEST. Then who is he?

THE GRAND DUCHESS. Anybody in the world but you would have guessed long ago. He is under your very eyes.

STRAMMFEST [*staring past her right and left*] Where?

THE GRAND DUCHESS. Look out of the window.

He rushes to the window, looking for the officer. The Grand Duchess takes off her cloak and appears in the uniform of the Panderobajensky Hussars.

STRAMMFEST [*peering through the window*] Where is he? I can see no one.

THE GRAND DUCHESS. Here, silly.

STRAMMFEST [*turning*] You! Great Heavens! The Bolshevik Empress!

HISTORICAL SKETCHES

THE SHEWING-UP OF BLANCO POSNET

A SERMON IN CRUDE MELODRAMA

PREFACE

The Censorship

THIS little play is really a religious tract in dramatic form. If our silly censorship would permit its performance, it might possibly help to set right-side-up the perverted conscience and re-invigorate the starved self-respect of our considerable class of loose-lived playgoers whose point of honor is to deride all official and conventional sermons. As it is, it only gives me an opportunity of telling the story of the Select Committee of both Houses of Parliament* which sat last year to inquire into the working of the censorship, against which it was alleged by myself and others that as its imbecility and mischievousness could not be fully illustrated within the limits of decorum imposed on the press, it could only be dealt with by a parliamentary body subject to no such limits.

A Readable Bluebook*

Few books of the year 1909 can have been cheaper and more entertaining than the report of this Committee. Its full title is REPORT FROM THE JOINT SELECT COMMITTEE OF THE HOUSE OF LORDS AND THE HOUSE OF COMMONS ON THE STAGE PLAYS (CENSORSHIP) TOGETHER WITH THE PROCEEDINGS OF THE COMMITTEE, MINUTES OF EVIDENCE, AND APPENDICES. What the phrase 'the Stage Plays' means in this title I do not know; nor does anyone else. The number of the Bluebook is 214. How interesting it is may be judged from the fact that it contains verbatim reports of long and animated interviews between the Committee and such witnesses as Mr William Archer, Mr Granville Barker, Mr J. M. Barrie, Mr Forbes Robertson, Mr Cecil Raleigh, Mr John Galsworthy, Mr Laurence Housman, Sir Herbert Beerbohm Tree, Mr W. L. Courtney, Sir William Gilbert, Mr A. B. Walkley, Miss Lena Ashwell, Professor Gilbert Murray, Mr George Alexander, Mr George Edwardes, Mr Comyns Carr,* the Speaker of the House of Commons,* the Bishop of Southwark,* Mr Hall Caine, Mr Israel Zangwill, Sir Squire Bancroft, Sir Arthur Pinero, and Mr Gilbert Chesterton,* not to mention myself and a number of gentlemen less well known to the general public, but important in the world of the theatre. The publication of a book by so many famous contributors would be beyond the means of any commercial publishing firm. His Majesty's Stationery Office* sells it to all comers by weight at the very reasonable price of three-and-threepence a copy.

How Not To Do It

It was pointed out by Charles Dickens in Little Dorrit,* which remains the most accurate and penetrating study of the genteel littleness of our class governments in the English language, that whenever an abuse becomes oppressive enough to persuade our party parliamentarians that something must be done, they immediately set to work to face the situation and discover How Not To Do It. Since Dickens's day the exposures effected by the Socialists have so shattered the self-satisfaction of modern commercial civilization that it is no longer difficult to convince our governments that something must be done, even to the extent of attempts at a reconstruction of civilization on a thoroughly uncommercial basis. Consequently, the first part of the process described by Dickens: that in which the reformers were snubbed by front bench demonstrations that the administrative departments were consuming miles of red tape in the correctest forms of activity, and that everything was for the best in the best of all possible worlds,* is out of fashion; and we are in that other phase, familiarized by the history of the French Revolution,* in which the primary assumption is that the country is in danger, and that the first duty of all parties, politicians, and governments is to save it. But as the effect of this is to give governments a great many more things to do, it also gives a powerful stimulus to the art of How Not To Do Them: that is to say, the art of contriving methods of reform which will leave matters exactly as they are.

The report of the Joint Select Committee is a capital illustration of this tendency. The case against the censorship was overwhelming; and the defence was more damaging to it than no defence at all could have been. Even had this not been so, the mere caprice of opinion had turned against the institution; and a reform was expected, evidence or no evidence. Therefore the Committee was unanimous as to the necessity of reforming the censorship; only, unfortunately, the majority attached to this unanimity the usual condition that nothing should be done to disturb the existing state of things. How this was effected may be gathered from the recommendations finally agreed on, which are as follows.

1. The drama is to be set entirely free by the abolition of the existing obligation to procure a licence from the Censor before performing a play; but every theatre lease is in future to be construed as if it contained a clause giving the landlord power to break it and evict the lessee

if he produces a play without first obtaining the usual licence from the Lord Chamberlain.*

2. Some of the plays licensed by the Lord Chamberlain are so vicious that their present practical immunity from prosecution must be put an end to; but no manager who procures the Lord Chamberlain's licence for a play can be punished in any way for producing it, though a special tribunal may order him to discontinue the performance; and even this order must not be recorded to his disadvantage on the licence of his theatre, nor may it be given as a judicial reason for cancelling that licence.

3. Authors and managers producing plays without first obtaining the usual licence from the Lord Chamberlain shall be perfectly free to do so, and shall be at no disadvantage compared to those who follow the existing practice, except that they may be punished, have the licences of their theatres endorsed and cancelled, and have the performance stopped pending the proceedings without compensation in the event of the proceedings ending in their acquittal.

4. Authors are to be rescued from their present subjection to an irresponsible secret tribunal which can condemn their plays without giving reasons, by the substitution for that tribunal of a Committee of the Privy Council,* which is to be the final authority on the fitness of a play for representation; and this Committee is to sit *in camera** if and when it pleases.

5. The power to impose a veto on the production of plays is to be abolished because it may hinder the growth of a great national drama; but the Office of Examiner of Plays* shall be continued; and the Lord Chamberlain shall retain his present powers to license plays, but shall be made responsible to Parliament to the extent of making it possible to ask questions there concerning his proceedings, especially now that members have discovered a method of doing this indirectly.

And so on, and so forth. The thing is to be done; and it is not to be done. Everything is to be changed and nothing is to be changed. The problem is to be faced and the solution to be shirked. And the word of Dickens is to be justified.

The Story of the Joint Select Committee

Let me now tell the story of the Committee in greater detail, partly as a contribution to history; partly because, like most true stories, it is more amusing than the official story.

All commissions of public enquiry are more or less intimidated both by the interests on which they have to sit in judgment and, when their members are party politicians, by the votes at the back of those interests; but this unfortunate Committee sat under a quite exceptional cross fire. First, there was the king.* The Censor is a member of his household retinue; and as a king's retinue has to be jealously guarded to avoid curtailment of the royal state no matter what may be the function of the particular retainer threatened, nothing but an express royal intimation to the contrary, which is a constitutional impossibility, could have relieved the Committee from the fear of displeasing the king by any proposal to abolish the censorship of the Lord Chamberlain. Now all the lords on the Committee and some of the commoners could have been wiped out of society (in their sense of the word) by the slightest intimation that the king would prefer not to meet them; and this was a heavy risk to run on the chance of 'a great and serious national drama' ensuing on the removal of the Lord Chamberlain's veto on Mrs Warren's Profession.* Second, there was the Nonconformist conscience,* holding the Liberal Government* responsible for the Committee it had appointed, and holding also, to the extent of votes enough to turn the scale in some constituencies, that the theatre is the gate of hell, to be tolerated, as vice is tolerated, only because the power to suppress it could not be given to any public body without too serious an interference with certain Liberal traditions of liberty which are still useful to Nonconformists in other directions. Third, there was the commercial interest of the theatrical managers and their syndicates of backers in the City,* to whom, as I shall shew later on, the censorship affords a cheap insurance of enormous value. Fourth, there was the powerful interest of the trade in intoxicating liquors, fiercely determined to resist any extension of the authority of teetotaller-led local governing bodies over theatres. Fifth, there were the playwrights, without political power, but with a very close natural monopoly of a talent not only for playwriting but for satirical polemics. And since every interest has its opposition, all these influences had created hostile bodies by the operation of the mere impulse to contradict them, always strong in English human nature.

Why the Managers Love the Censorship

The only one of these influences which seems to be generally misunderstood is that of the managers. It has been assumed repeatedly that managers and authors are affected in the same way by the censorship. When a prominent author protests against the censorship, his opinion is supposed to be balanced by that of some prominent manager who

declares that the censorship is the mainstay of the theatre, and his relations with the Lord Chamberlain and the Examiner of Plays a cherished privilege and an inexhaustible joy. This error was not removed by
the evidence given before the Joint Select Committee. The managers
did not make their case clear there, partly because they did not understand it, and partly because their most eminent witnesses were not personally affected by it, and would not condescend to plead it, feeling
themselves, on the contrary, compelled by their self-respect to admit
and even emphasize the fact that the Lord Chamberlain in the exercise
of his duties as licenser had done those things which he ought not to
have done, and left undone those things which he ought to have done.
Mr Forbes Robertson and Sir Herbert Tree, for instance, had never felt
the real disadvantage of which managers have to complain. This disadvantage was not put directly to the Committee; and though the managers are against me on the question of the censorship, I will now put
their case for them as they should have put it themselves, and as it can
be read between the lines of their evidence when once the reader has
the clue.

The manager of a theatre is a man of business. He is not an expert in
politics, religion, art, literature, philosophy, or law. He calls in a playwright just as he calls in a doctor, or consults a lawyer, or engages an
architect, depending on the playwright's reputation and past achievements for a satisfactory result. A play by an unknown man may attract
him sufficiently to induce him to give that unknown man a trial; but this
does not occur often enough to be taken into account: his normal course
is to resort to a well-known author and take (mostly with misgiving) what
he gets from him. Now this does not cause any anxiety to Mr Forbes
Robertson and Sir Herbert Tree, because they are only incidentally
managers and men of business: primarily they are highly cultivated artists, quite capable of judging for themselves anything that the most
abstruse playwright is likely to put before them. But the plain-sailing
tradesman who must be taken as the typical manager (for the west end
of London* is not the whole theatrical world) is by no means equally
qualified to judge whether a play is safe from prosecution or not. He
may not understand it, may not like it, may not know what the author
is driving at, may have no knowledge of the ethical, political, and sectarian controversies which may form the intellectual fabric of the play,
and may honestly see nothing but an ordinary 'character part' in
a stage figure which may be a libellous and unmistakeable caricature of
some eminent living person of whom he has never heard. Yet if he
produces the play he is legally responsible just as if he had written it

himself. Without protection he may find himself in the dock answering a charge of blasphemous libel, seditious libel, obscene libel, or all three together, not to mention the possibility of a private action for defamatory libel. His sole refuge is the opinion of the Examiner of Plays, his sole protection the licence of the Lord Chamberlain. A refusal to license does not hurt him, because he can produce another play: it is the author who suffers. The granting of the licence practically places him above the law; for though it may be legally possible to prosecute a licensed play, nobody ever dreams of doing it. The really responsible person, the Lord Chamberlain, could not be put into the dock; and the manager could not decently be convicted when he could produce in his defence a certificate from the chief officer of the King's Household that the play was a proper one.

A Two Guinea Insurance Policy

The censorship, then, provides the manager, at the negligible premium of two guineas* per play, with an effective insurance against the author getting him into trouble, and a complete relief from all conscientious responsibility for the character of the entertainment at his theatre. Under such circumstances, managers would be more than human if they did not regard the censorship as their most valuable privilege. This is the simple explanation of the rally of the managers and their Associations to the defence of the censorship, of their reiterated resolutions of confidence in the Lord Chamberlain, of their presentations of plate, and, generally, of their enthusiastic contentment with the present system, all in such startling contrast to the denunciations of the censorship by the authors. It also explains why the managerial witnesses who had least to fear from the Censor were the most reluctant in his defence, whilst those whose practice it is to strain his indulgence to the utmost were almost rapturous in his praise. There would be absolute unanimity among the managers in favor of the censorship if they were all simply tradesmen. Even those actor-managers who made no secret before the Committee of their contempt for the present operation of the censorship, and their indignation at being handed over to a domestic official as casual servants of a specially disorderly kind, demanded, not the abolition of the institution, but such a reform as might make it consistent with their dignity and unobstructive to their higher artistic aims. Feeling no personal need for protection against the author, they perhaps forgot the plight of many a manager to whom the modern advanced drama is so much Greek;* but they did feel very strongly the need of being protected against Vigilance Societies and Municipalities* and common informers in a country where a large section of the community still believes that art of all kinds is inherently sinful.

Why the Government Interfered

It may now be asked how a Liberal government had been persuaded to meddle at all with a question in which so many conflicting interests were involved, and which had probably no electoral value whatever. Many simple souls believed that it was because certain severely virtuous plays by Ibsen, by M. Brieux, by Mr Granville Barker, and by me,* were suppressed by the censorship, whilst plays of a scandalous character were licensed without demur. No doubt this influenced public opinion; but those who imagine that it could influence British governments little know how remote from public opinion and how full of their own little family and party affairs British governments, both Liberal and Unionist,* still are. The censorship scandal had existed for years without any parliamentary action being taken in the matter, and might have existed for as many more had it not happened in 1906 that Mr Robert Vernon Harcourt entered parliament as a member of the Liberal Party, of which his father had been one of the leaders during the Gladstone era.* Mr Harcourt was thus a young man marked out for office both by his parentage and his unquestionable social position as one of the governing class. Also, and this was much less usual, he was brilliantly clever, and was the author of a couple of plays* of remarkable promise. Mr Harcourt informed his leaders that he was going to take up the subject of the censorship. The leaders, recognizing his hereditary right to a parliamentary canter of some sort as a prelude to his public career, and finding that all the clever people seemed to be agreed that the censorship was an anti-Liberal institution and an abominable nuisance to boot, indulged him by appointing a Select Committee of both Houses to investigate the subject. The then Chancellor of the Duchy of Lancaster,* Mr Herbert Samuel (now Postmaster-General),* who had made his way into the Cabinet twenty years ahead of the usual age, was made Chairman. Mr Robert Harcourt himself was of course a member. With him, representing the Commons, were Mr Alfred Mason,* a man of letters who had won a seat in parliament as offhandedly as he has since discarded it, or as he once appeared on the stage to help me out of a difficulty in casting Arms and the Man* when that piece was the newest thing in the advanced drama. There was Mr Hugh Law, an Irish member, son of an Irish Chancellor,* presenting a keen and joyous front to English intellectual sloth. Above all, there was Colonel Lockwood* to represent at one stroke the Opposition and the average popular man. This he did by standing up gallantly for the Censor, to whose support the Opposition was in no way committed, and by visibly defying the most cherished conventions of the average man with a bunch of carnations in his buttonhole as large as a dinner-plate, which would have made a Bunthorne blench,* and which very nearly did make Mr Granville Barker (who has an antipathy to the scent of carnations) faint.

The Peers on the Joint Select Committee

The House of Lords then proceeded to its selection. As fashionable drama in Paris and London concerns itself almost exclusively with adultery, the first choice fell on Lord Gorell,* who had for many years presided over the Divorce Court. Lord Plymouth,* who had been Chairman to the Shakespear Memorial project* (now merged in the Shakespear Memorial National Theatre),* was obviously marked out for selection; and it was generally expected that the Lords Lytton and Esher,* who had taken a prominent part in the same movement, would have been added. This expectation was not fulfilled. Instead, Lord Willoughby de Broke, who had distinguished himself as an amateur actor,* was selected along with Lord Newton,* whose special qualifications for the Committee, if he had any, were unknown to the public. Finally Lord Ribblesdale, the argute* son of a Scotch mother, was thrown in to make up for any shortcoming in intellectual subtlety that might arise in the case of his younger colleagues; and this completed the two teams.

The Committee's Attitude towards the Theatre

In England, thanks chiefly to the censorship, the theatre is not respected. It is indulged and despised as a department of what is politely called gaiety. It is therefore not surprising that the majority of the Committee began by taking its work uppishly and carelessly. When it discovered that the contemporary drama, licensed by the Lord Chamberlain, included plays which could be described only behind closed doors, and in the discomfort which attends discussions of very nasty subjects between men of widely different ages, it calmly put its own convenience before its public duty by ruling that there should be no discussion of particular plays, much as if a committee on temperance were to rule that drunkenness was not a proper subject of conversation among gentlemen.

A Bad Beginning

This was a bad beginning. Everybody knew that in England the censorship would not be crushed by the weight of the constitutional argument against it, heavy as that was, unless it were also brought home to the Committee and to the public that it had sanctioned and protected the very worst practicable examples of the kind of play it professed to extirpate. For it must be remembered that the other half of the practical side of the case, dealing with the merits of the plays it had suppressed, could never secure a unanimous assent. If the Censor had suppressed Hamlet,* as he most certainly would have done had it been submitted to him as a new play, he would have been supported by a large body of people to whom incest is a tabooed subject which must not be mentioned on the stage or anywhere else outside a criminal court. Hamlet, Oedipus, and The Cenci, Mrs Warren's Profession, Brieux's Maternité, and Les Avariés, Maeterlinck's Monna Vanna* and Mr Granville Barker's Waste may or may not be great poems, or edifying sermons, or important documents, or charming romances: our tribal citizens know nothing about that and do not want to know anything: all that they do know is that incest, prostitution, abortion, contagious diseases, and nudity are improper, and that all conversations, or books, or plays in which they are discussed are improper conversations, improper books, improper plays, and should not be allowed. The Censor may prohibit all such plays with complete certainty that there will be a chorus of 'Quite right too' sufficient to drown the protests of the few who know better. The Achilles heel of the censorship is therefore not the fine plays it has suppressed, but the abominable plays it has licensed: plays which the Committee itself had to turn the public out of the room and close the doors before it could discuss, and which I myself have found it impossible to expose in the press because no editor of a paper or magazine intended for general family reading could admit into his columns the baldest narration of the stories which the Censor has not only tolerated but expressly certified as fitting for presentation on the stage. When the Committee ruled out this part of the case it shook the confidence of the authors in its impartiality and its seriousness. Of course it was not able to enforce its ruling thoroughly. Plays which were merely lightminded and irresponsible in their viciousness were repeatedly mentioned by Mr Harcourt and others. But the really detestable plays, which would have damned the censorship beyond all apology or salvation, were never referred to; and the moment Mr Harcourt or anyone else made the Committee uncomfortable by a move in their direction, the ruling was appealed to at once, and the censorship saved.

A Comic Interlude

It was part of this nervous dislike of the unpleasant part of its business that led to the comic incident of the Committee's sudden discovery that I had insulted it, and its suspension of its investigation for the purpose of elaborately insulting me back again. Comic to the lookers-on, that is; for the majority of the Committee made no attempt to conceal the fact that they were wildly angry with me; and I, though my public experience and skill in acting enabled me to maintain an appearance of imperturbable good-humor, was equally furious. The friction began as follows.

The precedents for the conduct of the Committee were to be found in the proceedings of the Committee of 1892.* That Committee, no doubt recognizing the absurdity of calling on distinguished artists to give their views before it, and then refusing to allow them to state their views except in nervous replies to such questions as it might suit members to put to them, allowed Sir Henry Irving* and Sir John Hare to prepare and read written statements, and formally invited them to read them to the Committee before being questioned. I accordingly prepared such a statement. For the greater convenience of the Committee, I offered to have this statement printed at my own expense, and to supply the members with copies. The offer was accepted; and the copies supplied. I also offered to provide the Committee with copies of those plays of mine which had been refused a licence by the Lord Chamberlain. That offer also was accepted; and the books duly supplied.

An Anti-Shavian Panic

As far as I can guess, the next thing that happened was that some timid or unawakened member of the Committee read my statement and was frightened or scandalized out of his wits by it. At all events it is certain that the majority of the Committee allowed themselves to be persuaded to refuse to allow any statement to be read; but to avoid the appearance of pointing this expressly at me, the form adopted was a resolution to adhere strictly to precedent, the Committee being then unaware that the precedents were on my side. Accordingly, when I appeared before the Committee, and proposed to read my statement 'according to precedent,' the Committee was visibly taken aback. The Chairman was bound by the letter of the decision arrived at to allow me to read my statement, since that course was according to precedent; but as this was exactly what the decision was meant to prevent, the majority of the Committee would have regarded this hoisting of them with their own petard* as a breach of faith on the part of the Chairman, who, I infer, was not in agreement with the suppressive majority. There was nothing for it, after a somewhat awkward pause, but to clear me and the public out of the room and reconsider the situation *in camera*. When the doors were opened again I was informed simply that the Committee would not hear my statement. But as the Committee could not very decently refuse my evidence altogether, the Chairman, with a printed copy of my statement in his hand as 'proof,' was able to come to the rescue to some extent by putting to me a series of questions to which no doubt I might have replied by taking another copy out of my pocket, and quoting my statement paragraph by paragraph, as some of the later witnesses did. But as in offering the Committee my statement for burial in their bluebook I had made a considerable sacrifice, being able to secure greater publicity for it by independent publication on my own account; and as, further, the circumstances of the refusal made it offensive enough to take all heart out of the scrupulous consideration with which I had so far treated the Committee, I was not disposed to give its majority a second chance, or to lose the opportunity offered me by the questions to fire an additional broadside into the censorship. I pocketed my statement, and answered the questions *viva voce*.* At the conclusion of this, my examination-in-chief, the Committee adjourned, asking me to present myself again for (virtually) cross-examination. But this cross-examination never came off, as the sequel will shew.

A Rare and Curious First Edition

The refusal of the Committee to admit my statement had not unnaturally created the impression that it must be a scandalous document; and a lively demand for copies at once set in. And among the very first applicants were members of the majority which had carried the decision to exclude the document. They had given so little attention to the business that they did not know, or had forgotten, that they had already been supplied with copies at their own request. At all events, they came to me publicly and cleaned me out of the handful of copies I had provided for distribution to the press. And after the sitting it was intimated to me that yet more copies were desired for the use of the Committee: a demand, under the circumstances, of breath-bereaving coolness. At the same time, a brisk demand arose outside the Committee, not only among people who were anxious to read what I had to say on the subject, but among victims of the craze for collecting first editions, copies of privately circulated pamphlets, and other real or imaginary rarities. Such maniacs will cheerfully pay five guineas for any piece of discarded old rubbish of mine when they will not pay as many shillings for a clean new copy of it, because everyone else can get it for the same price too.*

The Times to the Rescue

The day after the refusal of the Committee to face my statement, I transferred the scene of action to the columns of The Times, which did yeoman's service* to the public on this, as on many other occasions, by treating the question as a public one without the least regard to the supposed susceptibilities of the Court on the one side, or the avowed prejudices of the Free Churches* or the interests of the managers or theatrical speculators on the other. The Times published* the summarized conclusions of my statement, and gave me an opportunity of saying as much as it was then advisable to say of what had occurred. For it must be remembered that, however impatient and contemptuous I might feel of the intellectual cowardice shewn by the majority of the Committee face to face with myself, it was none the less necessary to keep up its prestige in every possible way, not only for the sake of the dignity and importance of the matter with which it had to deal, and in the hope that the treatment of subsequent witnesses and the final report might make amends for a feeble beginning, but also out of respect and consideration for the minority. For it is fair to say that the majority was never more than a bare majority, and that the worst thing the Committee did—the exclusion of references to particular plays—was perpetrated in the absence of the Chairman.

I, therefore, had to treat the Committee in The Times very much better than its majority deserved, an injustice for which I now apologize. I did not, however, resist the temptation to hint, quite good-humoredly, that my politeness to the Committee had cost me quite enough already, and that I was not prepared to supply the members of the Committee, or anyone else, with extra copies merely as collectors' curiosities.

The Council of Ten

Then the fat was in the fire. The majority, chaffed for its eagerness to obtain copies of scarce pamphlets retailable at five guineas, went dancing mad. When I presented myself, as requested, for cross-examination, I found the doors of the Committee room shut, and the corridors of the House of Lords filled by a wondering crowd, to whom it had somehow leaked out that something terrible was happening inside. It could not be another licensed play too scandalous to be discussed in public, because the Committee had decided to discuss no more of these examples of the Censor's notions of purifying the stage; and what else the Committee might have to discuss that might not be heard by all the world was not easily guessable.

Without suggesting that the confidence of the Committee was in any way violated by any of its members further than was absolutely necessary to clear them from suspicion of complicity in the scene which followed, I think I may venture to conjecture what was happening. It was felt by the majority, first, that it must be cleared at all costs of the imputation of having procured more than one copy each of my statement, and that one not from any interest in an undesirable document by an irreverent author, but in the reluctant discharge of its solemn public duty; second, that a terrible example must be made of me by the most crushing public snub in the power of the Committee to administer. To throw my wretched little pamphlet at my head and to kick me out of the room was the passionate impulse which prevailed in spite of all the remonstrances of the Commoners, seasoned to the give-and-take of public life, and of the single peer who kept his head. The others, for the moment, had no heads to keep. And the fashion in which they proposed to wreak their vengeance was as follows.

The Sentence

I was to be admitted, as a lamb to the slaughter, and allowed to take my place as if for further examination. The Chairman was then to inform me coldly that the Committee did not desire to have anything more to say to me. The members were thereupon solemnly to hand me back the copies of my statement as so much waste paper, and I was to be suffered to slink away with what countenance I could maintain in such disgrace.

But this plan required the active co-operation of every member of the Committee; and whilst the majority regarded it as an august and impressive vindication of the majesty of parliament, the minority regarded it with equal conviction as a puerile tomfoolery, and declined altogether to act their allotted parts in it. Besides, they did not all want to part with the books. For instance, Mr Hugh Law, being an Irishman, with an Irishman's sense of how to behave like a gallant gentleman on occasion, was determined to be able to assure me that nothing should induce him to give up my statement or prevent him from obtaining and cherishing as many copies as possible. (I quote this as an example to the House of Lords of the right thing to say in such emergencies.) So the program had to be modified. The minority could not prevent the enraged majority from refusing to examine me further; nor could the Chairman refuse to communicate that decision to me. Neither could the minority object to the secretary handing me back such copies as he could collect from the majority. And at that the matter was left. The doors were opened; the audience trooped in; I was called to my place in the dock (so to speak); and all was ready for the sacrifice.

The Execution

Alas! the majority reckoned without Colonel Lockwood. That hardy and undaunted veteran refused to shirk his share in the scene merely because the minority was recalcitrant and the majority perhaps subject to stage fright. When Mr Samuel had informed me that the Committee had no further questions to ask me with an urbanity which gave the public no clue as to the temper of the majority; when I had jumped up with the proper air of relief and gratitude; when the secretary had handed me his little packet of books with an affability which effectually concealed his dramatic function as executioner; when the audience was simply disappointed at being baulked of the entertainment of hearing Mr Robert Harcourt cross-examine me; in short, when the situation was all but saved by the tact of the Chairman and secretary, Colonel Lockwood rose, with all his carnations blazing, and gave away the whole case by handing me, with impressive simplicity and courtesy, his *two* copies of the precious statement. And I believe that if he had succeeded in securing ten, he would have handed them all back to me with the most sincere conviction that every one of the ten must prove a crushing addition to the weight of my discomfiture. I still cherish that second copy, a little blue-bound pamphlet, methodically autographed 'Lockwood B' among my most valued literary trophies.

An innocent lady told me afterwards that she never knew that I could smile so beautifully, and that she thought it shewed very good taste on my part. I was not conscious of smiling; but I should have embraced the Colonel had I dared. As it was, I turned expectantly to his colleagues, mutely inviting them to follow his example. But there was only one Colonel Lockwood on that Committee. No eye met mine except minority eyes, dancing with mischief. There was nothing more to be said. I went home to my morning's work, and returned in the afternoon to receive the apologies of the minority for the conduct of the majority, and to see Mr Granville Barker, overwhelmed by the conscience-stricken politeness of the now almost abject Committee, and by a powerful smell of carnations, heading the long list of playwrights who came there to testify against the censorship, and whose treatment, I am happy to say, was everything they could have desired.

After all, ridiculous as the scene was, Colonel Lockwood's simplicity and courage were much more serviceable to his colleagues than their own inept *coup de théâtre* would have been if he had not spoiled it. It was plain to everyone that he had acted in entire good faith, without a thought as to these apparently insignificant little books being of any importance or having caused me or anybody else any trouble, and that he was wounded in his most sensitive spot by the construction my Times letter had put on his action. And in Colonel Lockwood's case one saw the case of his party on the Committee. They had simply been thoughtless in the matter.

I hope nobody will suppose that this in any way exonerates them. When people accept public service for one of the most vital duties that can arise in our society, they have no right to be thoughtless. In spite of the fun of the scene on the surface, my public sense was, and still is, very deeply offended by it. It made an end for me of the claim of the majority to be taken seriously. When the Government comes to deal with the question, as it presumably will before long, I invite it to be guided by the Chairman, the minority, and by the witnesses according to their weight, and to pay no attention whatever to those recommendations which were obviously inserted solely to conciliate the majority and get the report through and the Committee done with.

My evidence will be found in the Bluebook, pp. 46–53.* And here is the terrible statement which the Committee went through so much to suppress.

THE REJECTED STATEMENT — PART I

The Witness's Qualifications

I AM by profession a playwright. I have been in practice since 1892.*
I am a member of the Managing Committee of the Society of Authors*
and of the Dramatic Sub-Committee of that body. I have written nineteen plays, some of which have been translated and performed in all
European countries except Turkey, Greece, and Portugal. They have
been performed extensively in America. Three of them have been
refused licences* by the Lord Chamberlain. In one case a licence has
since been granted.* The other two are still unlicensed. I have suffered
both in pocket and reputation by the action of the Lord Chamberlain.
In other countries I have not come into conflict with the censorship
except in Austria, where the production of a comedy of mine* was
postponed for a year because it alluded to the part taken by Austria
in the Servo-Bulgarian war. This comedy was not one of the plays
suppressed in England by the Lord Chamberlain. One of the plays so
suppressed* was prosecuted in America by the police in consequence
of an immense crowd of disorderly persons having been attracted to
the first performance by the Lord Chamberlain's condemnation of it;
but on appeal to a higher court it was decided that the representation
was lawful and the intention innocent, since when it has been repeatedly performed.

I am not an ordinary playwright in general practice. I am a specialist
in immoral and heretical plays. My reputation has been gained by
my persistent struggle to force the public to reconsider its morals. In
particular, I regard much current morality as to economic and sexual
relations as disastrously wrong; and I regard certain doctrines of the
Christian religion as understood in England today with abhorrence.
I write plays with the deliberate object of converting the nation to
my opinions in these matters. I have no other effectual incentive to
write plays, as I am not dependent on the theatre for my livelihood. If
I were prevented from producing immoral and heretical plays, I should
cease to write for the theatre, and propagate my views from the platform and through books. I mention these facts to shew that I have
a special interest in the achievement by my profession of those rights
of liberty of speech and conscience which are matters of course in
other professions. I object to censorship not merely because the existing form of it grievously injures and hinders me individually, but on
public grounds.

The Definition of Immorality

In dealing with the question of the censorship, everything depends on the correct use of the word immorality, and a careful discrimination between the powers of a magistrate or judge to administer a code, and those of a censor to please himself.

Whatever is contrary to established manners and customs is immoral. An immoral act or doctrine is not necessarily a sinful one: on the contrary, every advance in thought and conduct is by definition immoral until it has converted the majority. For this reason it is of the most enormous importance that immorality should be protected jealously against the attacks of those who have no standard except the standard of custom, and who regard any attack on custom—that is, on morals— as an attack on society, on religion, and on virtue.

A censor is never intentionally a protector of immorality. He always aims at the protection of morality. Now morality is extremely valuable to society. It imposes conventional conduct on the great mass of persons who are incapable of original ethical judgment, and who would be quite lost if they were not in leading-strings* devised by lawgivers, philosophers, prophets, and poets for their guidance. But morality is not dependent on censorship for protection. It is already powerfully fortified by the magistracy and the whole body of law. Blasphemy, indecency, libel, treason, sedition, obscenity, profanity, and all the other evils which a censorship is supposed to avert, are punishable by the civil magistrate with all the severity of vehement prejudice. Morality has not only every engine that lawgivers can devise in full operation for its protection, but also that enormous weight of public opinion enforced by social ostracism which is stronger than all the statutes. A censor pretending to protect morality is like a child pushing the cushions of a railway carriage to give itself the sensation of making the train travel at sixty miles an hour. It is immorality, not morality, that needs protection: it is morality, not immorality, that needs restraint; for morality, with all the dead weight of human inertia and superstition to hang on the back of the pioneer, and all the malice of vulgarity and prejudice to threaten him, is responsible for many persecutions and many martyrdoms.

Persecutions and martyrdoms, however, are trifles compared to the mischief done by censorships in delaying the general march of enlightenment. This can be brought home to us by imagining what would have been the effect of applying to all literature the censorship we still apply to the stage. The works of Linnaeus* and the evolutionists of 1790–1830, of Darwin, Wallace, Huxley, Helmholtz, Tyndall, Spencer, Carlyle,

Ruskin, and Samuel Butler,* would not have been published, as they were all immoral and heretical in the very highest degree, and gave pain to many worthy and pious people. They are at present condemned by the Greek and Roman Catholic censorships* as unfit for general reading. A censorship of conduct would have been equally disastrous. The disloyalty of Hampden and of Washington; the revolting immorality of Luther in not only marrying when he was a priest, but actually marrying a nun; the heterodoxy of Galileo;* the shocking blasphemies and sacrileges of Mahomet against the idols whom he dethroned to make way for his conception of one god; the still more startling blasphemy of Jesus when He declared God to be the son of man and Himself to be the son of God, are all examples of shocking immoralities (every immorality shocks somebody), the suppression and extinction of which would have been more disastrous than the utmost mischief that can be conceived as ensuing from the toleration of vice.

These facts, glaring as they are, are disguised by the promotion of immoralities into moralities which is constantly going on. Christianity and Mahometanism,* once thought of and dealt with exactly as Anarchism is thought of and dealt with today,* have become established religions; and fresh immoralities are persecuted in their name. The truth is that the vast majority of persons professing these religions have never been anything but simple moralists. The respectable Englishman who is a Christian because he was born in Clapham* would be a Mahometan for the cognate reason if he had been born in Constantinople.* He has never willingly tolerated immorality. He did not adopt any innovation until it had become moral; and then he adopted it, not on its merits, but solely because it had become moral. In doing so he never realized that it had ever been immoral: consequently its early struggles taught him no lesson; and he has opposed the next step in human progress as indignantly as if neither manners, customs, nor thought had ever changed since the beginning of the world. Toleration must be imposed on him as a mystic and painful duty by his spiritual and political leaders, or he will condemn the world to stagnation, which is the penalty of an inflexible morality.

What Toleration Means

This must be done all the more arbitrarily because it is not possible to make the ordinary moral man understand what toleration and liberty really mean. He will accept them verbally with alacrity, even with enthusiasm, because the word toleration has been moralized by eminent

Whigs;* but what he means by toleration is toleration of doctrines that he considers enlightened, and, by liberty, liberty to do what he considers right: that is, he does not mean toleration or liberty at all; for there is no need to tolerate what appears enlightened or to claim liberty to do what most people consider right. Toleration and liberty have no sense or use except as toleration of opinions that are considered damnable, and liberty to do what seems wrong. Setting Englishmen free to marry their deceased wife's sisters is not tolerated by the people who approve of it, but by the people who regard it as incestuous. Catholic Emancipation and the admission of Jews to parliament* needed no toleration from Catholics and Jews: the toleration they needed was that of the people who regarded the one measure as a facilitation of idolatry, and the other as a condonation of the crucifixion. Clearly such toleration is not clamored for by the multitude or by the press which reflects its prejudices. It is essentially one of those abnegations of passion and prejudice which the common man submits to because uncommon men whom he respects as wiser than himself assure him that it must be so, or the higher affairs of human destiny will suffer.

Such submission is the more difficult because the arguments against tolerating immorality are the same as the arguments against tolerating murder and theft; and this is why the Censor seems to the inconsiderate as obviously desirable a functionary as the police magistrate. But there is this simple and tremendous difference between the cases: that whereas no evil can conceivably result from the total suppression of murder and theft, and all communities prosper in direct proportion to such suppression, the total suppression of immorality, especially in matters of religion and sex, would stop enlightenment, and produce what used to be called a Chinese civilization until the Chinese lately took to immoral courses by permitting railway contractors to desecrate the graves of their ancestors, and their soldiers to wear clothes which indecently revealed the fact that they had legs and waists and even posteriors. At about the same moment a few bold Englishwomen ventured on the immorality of riding astride their horses, a practice that has since established itself so successfully that before another generation has passed away there may not be a new side-saddle in England, or a woman who could use it if there was.

The Case for Toleration

Accordingly, there has risen among wise and far-sighted men a perception of the need for setting certain departments of human activity

entirely free from legal interference. This has nothing to do with any
sympathy these liberators may themselves have with immoral views.
A man with the strongest conviction of the Divine ordering of the universe and of the superiority of monarchy to all forms of government
may nevertheless quite consistently and conscientiously be ready to lay
down his life for the right of every man to advocate Atheism or
Republicanism if he believes in them. An attack on morals may turn out
to be the salvation of the race. A hundred years ago nobody foresaw that
Tom Paine's centenary* would be the subject of a laudatory special
article in The Times; and only a few understood that the persecution of
his works and the transportation of men for the felony of reading them
was a mischievous mistake. Even less, perhaps, could they have guessed
that Proudhon,* who became notorious by his essay entitled 'What is
Property? It is Theft,' would have received, on the like occasion and
in the same paper, a respectful consideration which nobody would
now dream of according to Lord Liverpool or Lord Brougham.*
Nevertheless there was a mass of evidence to shew that such a development was not only possible but fairly probable, and that the risks of
suppressing liberty of propaganda were far graver than the risk of
Paine's or Proudhon's writings wrecking civilization. Now there was no
such evidence in favor of tolerating the cutting of throats and the robbing of tills. No case whatever can be made out for the statement that
a nation cannot do without common thieves and homicidal ruffians.
But an overwhelming case can be made out for the statement that
no nation can prosper or even continue to exist without heretics and
advocates of shockingly immoral doctrines. The Inquisition and the
Star Chamber,* which were nothing but censorships, made ruthless
war on impiety and immorality. The result was once familiar to
Englishmen, though of late years it seems to have been forgotten. It
cost England a revolution to get rid of the Star Chamber.* Spain did
not get rid of the Inquisition,* and paid for that omission by becoming
a barely third-rate power politically, and intellectually no power at
all, in the Europe she had once dominated as the mightiest of the
Christian empires.

The Limits to Toleration

But the large toleration these considerations dictate has limits. For
example, though we tolerate, and rightly tolerate, the propaganda of
Anarchism as a political theory which embraces all that is valuable in
the doctrine of Laisser-Faire* and the method of Free Trade as well as

all that is shocking in the views of Bakounine,* we clearly cannot, or at all events will not, tolerate assassination of rulers on the ground that it is 'propaganda by deed' or sociological experiment. A play inciting to such an assassination cannot claim the privileges of heresy or immorality, because no case can be made out in support of assassination as an indispensable instrument of progress. Now it happens that we have in the Julius Cæsar* of Shakespear a play which the Tsar of Russia* or the Governor-General of India* would hardly care to see performed in their capitals just now. It is an artistic treasure; but it glorifies a murder which Goethe* described as the silliest crime ever committed. It may quite possibly have helped the regicides of 1649* to see themselves, as it certainly helped generations of Whig statesmen to see them, in a heroic light; and it unquestionably vindicates and ennobles a conspirator who assassinated the head of the Roman State not because he abused his position but solely because he occupied it, thus affirming the extreme republican principle that all kings, good or bad, should be killed because kingship and freedom cannot live together. Under certain circumstances this vindication and ennoblement might act as an incitement to an actual assassination as well as to Plutarchian republicanism;* for it is one thing to advocate republicanism or royalism: it is quite another to make a hero of Brutus or Ravaillac, or a heroine of Charlotte Corday.* Assassination is the extreme form of censorship; and it seems hard to justify an incitement to it on anti-censorial principles. The very people who would have scouted* the notion of prohibiting the performances of Julius Cæsar at His Majesty's Theatre in London* last year, might now entertain very seriously a proposal to exclude Indians from them, and to suppress the play completely in Calcutta and Dublin;* for if the assassin of Cæsar was a hero, why not the assassins of Lord Frederick Cavendish, Presidents Lincoln and McKinley, and Sir Curzon Wyllie?* Here is a strong case for some constitutional means of preventing the performance of a play. True, it is an equally strong case for preventing the circulation of the Bible, which was always in the hands of our regicides; but as the Roman Catholic Church does not hesitate to accept that consequence of the censorial principle, it does not invalidate the argument.

Take another actual case. A modern comedy, Arms and The Man, though not a comedy of politics, is nevertheless so far historical that it reveals the unacknowledged fact that as the Servo-Bulgarian War of 1885 was much more than a struggle between the Servians and Bulgarians, the troops engaged were officered by two European Powers of the first magnitude.* In consequence, the performance of the play was for some time forbidden in Vienna, and more recently it gave offence in Rome* at a moment when popular feeling was excited as to the relations of Austria with the Balkan States. Now if a comedy so remote from political passion as Arms and The Man can, merely because it refers to political facts, become so inconvenient and inopportune that Foreign Offices take the trouble to have its production postponed, what may not be the effect of what is called a patriotic drama produced at a moment when the balance is quivering between peace and war? Is there not something to be said for a political censorship, if not for a moral one? May not those continental governments who leave the stage practically free in every other respect, but muzzle it politically, be justified by the practical exigencies of the situation?

The Difference between Law and Censorship

The answer is that a pamphlet, a newspaper article, or a resolution moved at a political meeting can do all the mischief that a play can, and often more; yet we do not set up a permanent censorship of the press or of political meetings. Any journalist may publish an article, any demagogue may deliver a speech without giving notice to the government or obtaining its licence. The risk of such freedom is great; but as it is the price of our political liberty, we think it worth paying. We may abrogate it in emergencies by a Coercion Act, a suspension of the Habeas Corpus Act, or a proclamation of martial law,* just as we stop the traffic in a street during a fire, or shoot thieves at sight if they loot after an earthquake. But when the emergency is past, liberty is restored everywhere except in the theatre. The Act of 1843* is a permanent Coercion Act for the theatre, a permanent suspension of the Habeas Corpus Act as far as plays are concerned, a permanent proclamation of martial law with a single official substituted for a court martial. It is, in fact, assumed that actors, playwrights, and theatre managers are dangerous and dissolute characters whose existence creates a chronic state of emergency, and who must be treated as earthquake looters are treated. It is not necessary now to discredit this assumption. It was broken down by the late Sir Henry Irving when he finally shamed the Government into extending to his profession the official recognition enjoyed by the other branches of fine art.* Today we have on the roll of knighthood actors, authors, and managers. The rogue and vagabond theory of the depravity of the theatre is as dead officially as it is in general society; and with it has perished the sole excuse for the Act of 1843 and for the denial to the theatre of the liberties secured, at far greater social risk, to the press and the platform.

There is no question here of giving the theatre any larger liberties than the press and the platform, or of claiming larger powers for Shakespear to eulogize Brutus than Lord Rosebery has to eulogize Cromwell.* The abolition of the censorship does not involve the abolition of the magistrate and of the whole civil and criminal code. On the contrary, it would make the theatre more effectually subject to them than it is at present; for once a play now runs the gauntlet of the censorship, it is practically placed above the law. It is almost humiliating to have to demonstrate the essential difference between a censor and a magistrate or a sanitary inspector; but it is impossible to ignore the carelessness with which even distinguished critics of the theatre assume that all the arguments proper to the support of a magistracy and body of jurisprudence apply equally to a censorship.

A magistrate has laws to administer: a censor has nothing but his own opinion. A judge leaves the question of guilt to the jury: the Censor is jury and judge as well as lawgiver. A magistrate may be strongly prejudiced against an atheist or an anti-vaccinator, just as a sanitary inspector may have formed a careful opinion that drains are less healthy than cesspools; but the magistrate must allow the atheist to affirm instead of to swear, and must grant the anti-vaccinator an exemption certificate, when their demands are lawfully made; and in cities the inspector must compel the builder to make drains and must prosecute him if he makes cesspools. The law may be only the intolerance of the community; but it is a defined and limited intolerance. The limitation is sometimes carried so far that a judge cannot inflict the penalty for housebreaking on a burglar who can prove that he found the door open and therefore made only an unlawful entry. On the other hand, it is sometimes so vague, as for example in the case of the American law against obscenity, that it makes the magistrate virtually a censor.* But in the main a citizen can ascertain what he may do and what he may not do; and, though no one knows better than a magistrate that a single ill-conducted family may demoralize a whole street, no magistrate can imprison or otherwise restrain its members on the ground that their immorality may corrupt their neighbors. He can prevent any citizen from carrying certain specified weapons, but not from handling pokers, table-knives, bricks or bottles of corrosive fluid, on the ground that he might use them to commit murder or inflict malicious injury. He has no general power to prevent citizens from selling unhealthy or poisonous substances, or judging for themselves what substances are unhealthy and what wholesome, what poisonous and what innocuous: what he *can* do is to prevent anybody who has not a specific qualification from selling certain specified poisons of which a schedule is kept. Nobody is forbidden to sell minerals without a licence; but everybody is forbidden to sell silver without a licence. When the law has forgotten some atrocious sin—for instance, contracting marriage whilst suffering from contagious disease—the magistrate cannot arrest or punish the wrong-doer, however he may abhor his wickedness. In short, no man is lawfully at the mercy of the magistrate's personal caprice, prejudice, ignorance, superstition, temper, stupidity, resentment, timidity, ambition, or private conviction. But a playwright's livelihood, his reputation, and his inspiration and mission are at the personal mercy of the Censor. The two do not stand, as the criminal and the judge stand, in the presence of a law that binds them both equally, and was made by neither of them, but by the deliberate collective wisdom of the community. The only law that affects them is the Act of 1843, which empowers one of them to do absolutely and finally what he likes with the other's work. And when it is remembered that the slave in this case is the man whose profession is that of Eschylus and Euripides,* of Shakespear and Goethe, of Tolstoy and Ibsen, and the master the holder of a party appointment which by the nature of its duties practically excludes the possibility of its acceptance by a serious statesman or great lawyer, it will be seen that the playwrights are justified in reproaching the framers of that Act for having failed not only to appreciate the immense importance of the theatre as a most powerful instrument for teaching the nation how and what to think and feel, but even to conceive that those who make their living by the theatre are normal human beings with the common rights of English citizens. In this extremity of inconsiderateness it is not surprising that they also did not trouble themselves to study the difference between a censor and a magistrate. And it will be found that almost all the people who disinterestedly defend the censorship today are defending him on the assumption that there is no constitutional difference between him and any other functionary whose duty it is to restrain crime and disorder.

One further difference remains to be noted. As a magistrate grows old his mind may change or decay; but the law remains the same. The censorship of the theatre fluctuates with every change in the views and character of the man who exercises it. And what this implies can only be appreciated by those who can imagine what the effect on the mind must be of the duty of reading through every play that is produced in the kingdom year in, year out.

Why the Lord Chamberlain?

What may be called the high political case against censorship as a principle is now complete. The pleadings are those which have already
freed books and pulpits and political platforms in England from censorship, if not from occasional legal persecution. The stage alone
remains under a censorship of a grotesquely unsuitable kind. No play
can be performed if the Lord Chamberlain happens to disapprove of it.
And the Lord Chamberlain's functions have no sort of relationship to
dramatic literature. A great judge of literature, a far-seeing statesman,
a born champion of liberty of conscience and intellectual integrity—
say a Milton, a Chesterfield, a Bentham*—would be a very bad Lord
Chamberlain: so bad, in fact, that his exclusion from such a post may
be regarded as decreed by natural law. On the other hand, a good Lord
Chamberlain would be a stickler for morals in the narrowest sense,
a busy-body, a man to whom a matter of two inches in the length of
a gentleman's sword or the absence of a feather from a lady's head-
dress would be a graver matter than the Habeas Corpus Act. The Lord
Chamberlain, as Censor of the theatre, is a direct descendant of the
King's Master of the Revels, appointed in 1544 by Henry VIII to keep
order among the players and musicians of that day when they performed at Court. This first appearance of the theatrical censor in politics as the whipper-in* of the player, with its conception of the player as
a rich man's servant hired to amuse him, and, outside his professional
duties, as a gay, disorderly, anarchic spoilt child, half privileged, half
outlawed, probably as much vagabond as actor, is the real foundation of
the subjection of the whole profession, actors, managers, authors and
all, to the despotic authority of an officer whose business it is to pre-
serve decorum among menials. It must be remembered that it was not
until a hundred years later, in the reaction against the Puritans, that
a woman could appear on the English stage without being pelted off as
the Italian actresses were. The theatrical profession was regarded as
a shameless one; and it is only of late years that actresses have at last
succeeded in living down the assumption that actress and prostitute are
synonymous terms, and made good their position in respectable society. This makes the survival of the old ostracism in the Act of 1843
intolerably galling; and though it explains the apparently unaccountable absurdity of choosing as Censor of dramatic literature an official
whose functions and qualifications have nothing whatever to do with
literature, it also explains why the present arrangement is not only
criticized as an institution, but resented as an insult.

The Diplomatic Objection to the Lord Chamberlain

There is another reason, quite unconnected with the susceptibilities of authors, which makes it undesirable that a member of the King's Household should be responsible for the character and tendency of plays. The drama, dealing with all departments of human life, is necessarily political. Recent events have shewn—what indeed needed no demonstration—that it is impossible to prevent inferences being made, both at home and abroad, from the action of the Lord Chamberlain. The most talked-about play of the present year (1909), An Englishman's Home,* has for its main interest an invasion of England by a fictitious power which is understood, as it is meant to be understood, to represent Germany. The lesson taught by the play is the danger of invasion and the need for every English citizen to be a soldier. The Lord Chamberlain licensed this play, but refused to license a parody of it.* Shortly afterwards he refused to license another play* in which the fear of a German invasion was ridiculed. The German press drew the inevitable inference that the Lord Chamberlain was an anti-German alarmist, and that his opinions were a reflection of those prevailing in St James's Palace.* Immediately after this, the Lord Chamberlain licensed the play. Whether the inference, as far as the Lord Chamberlain was concerned, was justified, is of no consequence. What is important is that it was sure to be made, justly or unjustly, and extended from the Lord Chamberlain to the Throne.

The Objection of Court Etiquet

There is another objection to the Lord Chamberlain's censorship which affects the author's choice of subject. Formerly very little heed was given in England to the susceptibilities of foreign courts. For instance, the notion that the Mikado* of Japan should be as sacred to the English playwright as he is to the Japanese Lord Chamberlain would have seemed grotesque a generation ago. Now that the maintenance of *entente cordiale** between nations is one of the most prominent and most useful functions of the crown, the freedom of authors to deal with political subjects, even historically, is seriously threatened by the way in which the censorship makes the King responsible for the contents of every play. One author—the writer of these lines, in fact—has long desired to dramatize the life of Mahomet. But the possibility of a protest from the Turkish Ambassador—or the fear of it—causing the Lord Chamberlain to refuse to license such a play has prevented the play from being written. Now, if the censorship were abolished, nobody but the author could be held responsible for the play. The Turkish Ambassador does not now protest against the publication of Carlyle's essay on the prophet,* or of the English translations of the Koran in the prefaces to which Mahomet is criticized as an impostor,* or of the older books in which he is reviled as Mahound* and classed with the devil himself. But if these publications had to be licensed by the Lord Chamberlain it would be impossible for the King to allow the licence to be issued, as he would thereby be made responsible for the opinions expressed. This restriction of the historical drama is an unmixed evil. Great religious leaders are more interesting and more important subjects for the dramatist than great conquerors. It is a misfortune that public opinion would not tolerate a dramatization of Mahomet in Constantinople. But to prohibit it here, where public opinion would tolerate it, is an absurdity which, if applied in all directions, would make it impossible for the Queen to receive a Turkish ambassador without veiling herself, or the Dean and Chapter of St Paul's* to display a cross on the summit of their Cathedral in a city occupied largely and influentially by Jews. Court etiquet is no doubt an excellent thing for court ceremonies; but to attempt to impose it on the drama is about as sensible as an attempt to make everybody in London wear court dress.

Why not an Enlightened Censorship?

In the above cases the general question of censorship is separable from the question of the present form of it. Everyone who condemns the principle of censorship must also condemn the Lord Chamberlain's control of the drama; but those who approve of the principle do not necessarily approve of the Lord Chamberlain being the Censor *ex officio*.* They may, however, be entirely opposed to popular liberties, and may conclude from what has been said, not that the stage should be made as free as the church, press, or platform, but that these institutions should be censored as strictly as the stage. It will seem obvious to them that nothing is needed to remove all objections to a censorship except the placing of its powers in better hands.

Now though the transfer of the censorship to, say, the Lord Chancellor, or the Primate,* or a Cabinet Minister, would be much less humiliating to the persons immediately concerned, the inherent vices of the institution would not be appreciably less disastrous. They would even be aggravated, for reasons which do not appear on the surface, and therefore need to be followed with some attention.

It is often said that the public is the real censor. That this is to some extent true is proved by the fact that plays which are licensed and produced in London have to be expurgated for the provinces. This does not mean that the provinces are more strait-laced, but simply that in many provincial towns there is only one theatre for all classes and all tastes, whereas in London there are separate theatres for separate sections of playgoers: so that, for example, Sir Herbert Beerbohm Tree can conduct His Majesty's Theatre without the slightest regard to the tastes of the frequenters of the Gaiety Theatre;* and Mr George Edwardes can conduct the Gaiety Theatre without catering in any way for lovers of Shakespear. Thus the farcical comedy which has scandalized the critics in London by the libertinage of its jests is played to the respectable dress circle of Northampton* with these same jests slurred over so as to be imperceptible by even the most prurient spectator. The public, in short, takes care that nobody shall outrage it.

But the public also takes care that nobody shall starve it, or regulate its dramatic diet as a schoolmistress regulates the reading of her pupils. Even when it wishes to be debauched, no censor can—or at least no censor does—stand out against it. If a play is irresistibly amusing, it gets licensed no matter what its moral aspect may be. A brilliant instance is the Divorçons of the late Victorien Sardou,* which may not have been the naughtiest play of the 19th century, but was certainly the very naughtiest that any English manager in his senses would have ventured to produce. Nevertheless, being a very amusing play, it passed the licenser with the exception of a reference to impotence as a ground for divorce which no English actress would have ventured on in any case. Within the last few months a very amusing comedy* with a strongly polygamous moral was found irresistible by the Lord Chamberlain. Plenty of fun and a happy ending will get anything licensed, because the public will have it so, and the Examiner of Plays, as the holder of the office testified before the Commission of 1892 (Report, page 330),* feels with the public, and knows that his office could not survive a widespread unpopularity. In short, the support of the mob—that is, of the unreasoning, unorganized, uninstructed mass of popular sentiment—is indispensable to the censorship as it exists today in England. This is the explanation of the toleration by the Lord Chamberlain of coarse and vicious plays. It is not long since a judge before whom a licensed play came in the course of a lawsuit expressed his scandalized astonishment at the licensing of such a work. Eminent churchmen have made similar protests. In some plays the simulation of criminal assaults on the stage has been carried to a point at which a step further would have involved the interference of the police. Provided the treatment of the theme is gaily or hypocritically popular, and the ending happy, the indulgence of the Lord Chamberlain can be counted on. On the other hand, anything unpleasing and unpopular is rigorously censored. Adultery and prostitution are tolerated and even encouraged to such an extent that plays which do not deal with them are commonly said not to be plays at all. But if any of the unpleasing consequences of adultery and prostitution—for instance, an *unsuccessful* illegal operation* (successful ones are tolerated) or venereal disease—are mentioned, the play is prohibited. This principle of shielding the playgoer from unpleasant reflections is carried so far that when a play was submitted for licence in which the relations of a prostitute with all the male characters in the piece was described as 'immoral,' the Examiner of Plays objected to that passage, though he made no objection to the relations themselves. The Lord Chamberlain dare not, in short, attempt to exclude from the stage the tragedies of murder and lust, or the farces of mendacity, adultery, and dissolute gaiety in which vulgar people delight. But when these same vulgar people are threatened with an unpopular play in which dissoluteness is shewn to be no laughing matter, it is prohibited at once amid the vulgar applause, the net result being that vice is made delightful and virtue banned by the very institution which is supported on the understanding that it produces exactly the opposite result.

The Weakness of the Lord Chamberlain's Department

Now comes the question, Why is our censorship, armed as it is with apparently autocratic powers, so scandalously timid in the face of the mob? Why is it not as autocratic in dealing with playwrights below the average as with those above it? The answer is that its position is really a very weak one. It has no direct coercive forces, no funds to institute prosecutions and recover the legal penalties of defying it, no powers of arrest or imprisonment, in short, none of the guarantees of autocracy. What it can do is to refuse to renew the licence of a theatre at which its orders are disobeyed. When it happens that a theatre is about to be demolished, as was the case recently with the Imperial Theatre* after it had passed into the hands of the Wesleyan Methodists, unlicensed plays can be performed, technically in private, but really in full publicity, without risk. The prohibited plays of Brieux and Ibsen have been performed in London in this way with complete impunity. But the impunity is not confined to condemned theatres. Not long ago a West End manager* allowed a prohibited play to be performed at his theatre, taking his chance of losing his licence in consequence. The event proved that the manager was justified in regarding the risk as negligible; for the Lord Chamberlain's remedy—the closing of a popular and well-conducted theatre—was far too extreme to be practicable. Unless the play had so outraged public opinion as to make the manager odious and provoke a clamor for his exemplary punishment, the Lord Chamberlain could only have had his revenge at the risk of having his powers abolished as unsupportably tyrannical.

The Lord Chamberlain then has his powers so adjusted that he is tyrannical just where it is important that he should be tolerant, and tolerant just where he could screw up the standard a little by being tyrannical. His plea that there are unmentionable depths to which managers and authors would descend if he did not prevent them is disproved by the plain fact that his indulgence goes as far as the police, and sometimes further than the public, will let it. If our judges had so little power there would be no law in England. If our churches had so much, there would be no theatre, no literature, no science, no art, possibly no England. The institution is at once absurdly despotic and abjectly weak.

An Enlightened Censorship still worse than the Lord Chamberlain's

Clearly a censorship of judges, bishops, or statesmen would not be in this abject condition. It would no doubt make short work of the coarse and vicious pieces which now enjoy the protection of the Lord Chamberlain, or at least of those of them in which the vulgarity and vice are discoverable by merely reading the prompt copy.* But it would certainly disappoint the main hope of its advocates: the hope that it would protect and foster the higher drama. It would do nothing of the sort. On the contrary, it would inevitably suppress it more completely than the Lord Chamberlain does, because it would understand it better. The one play of Ibsen's which is prohibited on the English stage, Ghosts, is far less subversive than A Doll's House.* But the Lord Chamberlain does not meddle with such far-reaching matters as the tendency of a play. He refuses to license Ghosts exactly as he would refuse to license Hamlet if it were submitted to him as a new play. He would license even Hamlet if certain alterations were made in it. He would disallow the incestuous relationship between the King and Queen. He would probably insist on the substitution of some fictitious country for Denmark in deference to the near relations of our reigning house with that realm. He would certainly make it an absolute condition that the closet scene, in which a son, in an agony of shame and revulsion, reproaches his mother for her relations with his uncle, should be struck out as unbearably horrifying and improper. But compliance with these conditions would satisfy him. He would raise no speculative objections to the tendency of the play.

This indifference to the larger issues of a theatrical performance could not be safely predicated of an enlightened censorship. Such a censorship might be more liberal in its toleration of matters which are only objected to on the ground that they are not usually discussed in general social conversation or in the presence of children; but it would presumably have a far deeper insight to and concern for the real ethical tendency of the play. For instance, had it been in existence during the last quarter of a century, it would have perceived that those plays of Ibsen's which have been licensed without question are fundamentally immoral to an altogether extraordinary degree. Every one of them is a deliberate act of war on society as at present constituted. Religion, marriage, ordinary respectability, are subjected to a destructive exposure and criticism which seems to mere moralists—that is, to persons of no more than average depth of mind—to be diabolical. It is no exaggeration to say that Ibsen gained his overwhelming reputation by undertaking a task of no less magnitude than changing the mind of Europe with the view of changing its morals. Now you cannot license work of that sort without making yourself responsible for it. The Lord Chamberlain accepted the responsibility because he did not understand it or concern himself about it. But what really enlightened and conscientious official dare take such a responsibility? The strength of character and range of vision which made Ibsen capable of it are not to be expected from any official, however eminent. It is true that an enlightened censor might, whilst shrinking even with horror from Ibsen's views, perceive that any nation which suppressed Ibsen would presently find itself falling behind the nations which tolerated him just as Spain fell behind England; but the proper action to take on such a conviction is the abdication of censorship, not the practice of it. As long as a censor is a censor, he cannot endorse by his licence opinions which seem to him dangerously heretical.

We may, therefore, conclude that the more enlightened a censorship is, the worse it would serve us. The Lord Chamberlain, an obviously unenlightened Censor, prohibits Ghosts and licenses all the rest of Ibsen's plays. An enlightened censorship would possibly license Ghosts; but it would certainly suppress many of the other plays. It would suppress subversiveness as well as what is called bad taste. The Lord Chamberlain prohibits one play by Sophocles* because, like Hamlet, it mentions the subject of incest; but an enlightened censorship might suppress all the plays of Euripides because Euripides, like Ibsen, was a revolutionary Freethinker.* Under the Lord Chamberlain, we can smuggle a good deal of immoral drama and almost as much coarsely vulgar and furtively lascivious drama as we like. Under a college of cardinals, or bishops, or judges, or any other conceivable form of experts in morals, philosophy, religion, or politics, we should get little except stagnant mediocrity.

The Practical Impossibilities of Censorship

There is, besides, a crushing material difficulty in the way of an enlightened censorship. It is not too much to say that the work involved would drive a man of any intellectual rank mad. Consider, for example, the Christmas pantomimes. Imagine a judge of the High Court, or an archbishop, or a Cabinet Minister, or an eminent man of letters, earning his living by reading through the mass of trivial doggerel represented by all the pantomimes which are put into rehearsal simultaneously at the end of every year. The proposal to put such mind-destroying drudgery upon an official of the class implied by the demand for an enlightened censorship falls through the moment we realize what it implies in practice.

Another material difficulty is that no play can be judged by merely reading the dialogue. To be fully effective a censor should witness the performance. The *mise-en-scène** of a play is as much a part of it as the words spoken on the stage. No censor could possibly object to such a speech as 'Might I speak to you for a moment, miss?' yet that apparently innocent phrase has often been made offensively improper on the stage by popular low comedians, with the effect of changing the whole character and meaning of the play as understood by the official Examiner. In one of the plays* of the present season, the dialogue was that of a crude melodrama dealing in the most conventionally correct manner with the fortunes of a good-hearted and virtuous girl. Its morality was that of the Sunday school. But the principal actress, between two speeches which contained no reference to her action, changed her underclothing on the stage! It is true that in this case the actress was so much better than her part that she succeeded in turning what was meant as an impropriety into an inoffensive stroke of realism; yet it is none the less clear that stage business of this character, on which there can be no check except the actual presence of a censor in the theatre, might convert any dialogue, however innocent, into just the sort of entertainment against which the Censor is supposed to protect the public.

It was this practical impossibility that prevented the London County Council* from attempting to apply a censorship of the Lord

Chamberlain's pattern to the London music halls. A proposal to examine all entertainments before permitting their performance was actually made; and it was abandoned, not in the least as contrary to the liberty of the stage, but because the executive problem of how to do it at once reduced the proposal to absurdity. Even if the Council devoted all its time to witnessing rehearsals of variety performances, and putting each item to the vote, possibly after a prolonged discussion followed by a division, the work would still fall into arrear. No committee could be induced to undertake such a task. The attachment of an inspector of morals to each music hall would have meant an appreciable addition to the ratepayers' burden. In the face of such difficulties the proposal melted away. Had it been pushed through, and the inspectors appointed, each of them would have become a censor, and the whole body of inspectors would have become a *police des mœurs*.* Those who know the history of such police forces on the Continent will understand how impossible it would be to procure inspectors whose characters would stand the strain of their opportunities of corruption, both pecuniary and personal, at such salaries as a local authority could be persuaded to offer.

It has been suggested that the present censorship should be supplemented by a board of experts, who should deal, not with the whole mass of plays sent up for licence, but only those which the Examiner of Plays refuses to pass. As the number of plays which the Examiner refuses to pass is never great enough to occupy a Board in permanent session with regular salaries, and as casual employment is not compatible with public responsibility, this proposal would work out in practice as an addition to the duties of some existing functionary. A Secretary of State* would be objectionable as likely to be biased politically. An ecclesiastical referee* might be biased against the theatre altogether. A judge in chambers would be the proper authority. This plan would combine the inevitable intolerance of an enlightened censorship with the popular laxity of the Lord Chamberlain. The judge would suppress the pioneers, whilst the Examiner of Plays issued two guinea certificates for the vulgar and vicious plays. For this reason the plan would no doubt be popular; but it would be very much as a relaxation of the administration of the Public Health Acts* accompanied by the cheapening of gin would be popular.

The Arbitration Proposal

On the occasion of a recent deputation* of playwrights to the Prime Minister it was suggested that if a censorship be inevitable, provision should be made for an appeal from the Lord Chamberlain in cases of refusal of licence. The authors of this suggestion propose that the Lord Chamberlain shall choose one umpire and the author another. The two umpires shall then elect a referee, whose decision shall be final.

This proposal is not likely to be entertained by constitutional lawyers. It is a naïve offer to accept the method of arbitration in what is essentially a matter, not between one private individual or body and another, but between a public offender and the State. It will presumably be ruled out as a proposal to refer a case of manslaughter to arbitration would be ruled out. But even if it were constitutionally sound, it bears all the marks of that practical inexperience which leads men to believe that arbitration either costs nothing or is at least cheaper than law. Who is to pay for the time of the three arbitrators, presumably men of high professional standing? The author may not be able: the manager may not be willing: neither of them should be called upon to pay for a public service otherwise than by their contributions to the revenue. Clearly the State should pay. But even so, the difficulties are only beginning. A licence is seldom refused except on grounds which are controversial. The two arbitrators selected by the opposed parties to the controversy are to agree to leave the decision to a third party unanimously chosen by themselves. That is very far from being a simple solution. An attempt to shorten and simplify the passing of the Finance Bill* by referring it to an arbitrator chosen unanimously by Mr Asquith and Mr Balfour might not improbably cost more and last longer than a civil war. And why should the chosen referee—if he ever succeeded in getting chosen— be assumed to be a safer authority than the Examiner of Plays? He would certainly be a less responsible one: in fact, being (however eminent) a casual person called in to settle a single case, he would be virtually irresponsible. Worse still, he would take all responsibility away from the Lord Chamberlain, who is at least an official of the King's Household and a nominee of the Government. The Lord Chamberlain, with all his shortcomings, thinks twice before he refuses a licence, knowing that his refusal is final and may promptly be made public. But if he could transfer his responsibility to an arbitrator, he would naturally do so whenever he felt the slightest misgiving, or whenever, for diplomatic reasons, the licence would come more gracefully from an authority unconnected with the court. These considerations, added to the general objection to the principle of censorship, seem sufficient to put the arbitration expedient quite out of the question.

END OF THE FIRST PART OF THE REJECTED STATEMENT

THE REJECTED STATEMENT — PART II

The Licensing of Theatres

The Distinction between Licensing and Censorship

IT must not be concluded that the uncompromising abolition of all censorship involves the abandonment of all control and regulation of theatres. Factories are regulated in the public interest; but there is no censorship of factories. For example, many persons are sincerely convinced that cotton clothing is unhealthy; that alcoholic drinks are demoralizing; and that playing-cards are the devil's picture-books. But though the factories in which cotton, whiskey, and cards are manufactured are stringently regulated under the factory code* and the Public Health and Building Acts,* the inspectors appointed to carry out these Acts never go to a manufacturer and inform him that unless he manufactures woollens instead of cottons, ginger-beer instead of whiskey, Bibles instead of playing-cards, he will be forbidden to place his products on the market. In the case of premises licensed for the sale of spirits the authorities go a step further. A public-house differs from a factory in the essential particular that whereas disorder in a factory is promptly and voluntarily suppressed, because every moment of its duration involves a measurable pecuniary loss to the proprietor, disorder in a public-house may be a source of profit to the proprietor by its attraction for disorderly customers. Consequently a publican is compelled to obtain a licence to pursue his trade; and this licence lasts only a year, and need not be renewed if his house has been conducted in a disorderly manner in the meantime.

Prostitution and Drink in Theatres

The theatre presents the same problem as the public-house in respect to disorder. To begin with, a theatre is actually a place licensed for the sale of spirits. The bars at a London theatre can be let without difficulty for £30 a week and upwards. And though it is clear that nobody will pay from a shilling to half a guinea for access to a theatre bar when he can obtain access to an ordinary public-house for nothing, there is no law to prevent the theatre proprietor from issuing free passes broadcast and recouping himself by the profit on the sale of drink. Besides, there may be some other attraction than the sale of drink. When this attraction is that of the play no objection need be made. But it happens that the auditorium of a theatre, with its brilliant lighting and luxurious decorations, makes a very effective shelter and background for the display of fine dresses and pretty faces. Consequently theatres have been used for centuries in England as markets by prostitutes. From the Restoration to the days of Macready* all theatres were made use of in this way as a matter of course; and to this, far more than to any prejudice against dramatic art, we owe the Puritan formula that the theatre door is the gate of hell. Macready had a hard struggle to drive the prostitutes from his theatre;* and since his time the London theatres controlled by the Lord Chamberlain have become respectable and even socially pretentious. But some of the variety theatres still derive a revenue by selling admissions to women who do not look at the performance, and men who go to purchase or admire the women. And in the provinces this state of things is by no means confined to the variety theatres. The real attraction is sometimes not the performance at all. The theatre is not really a theatre: it is a drink shop and a prostitution market; and the last shred of its disguise is stripped by the virtually indiscriminate issue of free tickets to the men. Access to the stage is also easily obtained; and the plays preferred by the management are those in which the stage is filled with young women who are not in any serious technical sense of the word actresses at all. Considering that all this is now possible at any theatre, and actually occurs at some theatres, the fact that our best theatres are as respectable as they are is much to their credit; but it is still an intolerable evil that respectable managers should have to fight against the free tickets and disorderly housekeeping of unscrupulous competitors. The dramatic author is equally injured. He finds that unless he writes plays which make suitable side-shows for drinking-bars and brothels, he may be excluded from towns where there is not room for two theatres, and where the one existing theatre is exploiting drunkenness and prostitution instead of carrying on a legitimate dramatic business. Indeed everybody connected with the theatrical profession suffers in reputation from the detestable tradition of such places, against which the censorship has proved quite useless.

Here we have a strong case for applying either the licensing system or whatever better means may be devized for securing the orderly conduct of houses of public entertainment, dramatic or other. Liberty must, no doubt, be respected in so far that no manager should have the right to refuse admission to decently dressed, sober, and well-conducted persons, whether they are prostitutes, soldiers in uniform, gentlemen not in evening dress, Indians, or what not; but when disorder is stopped, disorderly persons will either cease to come or else reform their manners. It is, however, quite arguable that the indiscriminate issue of free admissions, though an apparently innocent and good-natured, and certainly a highly popular proceeding, should expose the proprietor of the theatre to the risk of a refusal to renew his licence.

Why the Managers dread Local Control

All this points to the transfer of the control of theatres from the Lord Chamberlain to the municipality. And this step is opposed by the long-run managers,* partly because they take it for granted that municipal control must involve municipal censorship of plays, so that plays might be licensed in one town and prohibited in the next, and partly because, as they have no desire to produce plays which are in advance of public opinion, and as the Lord Chamberlain in every other respect gives more scandal by his laxity than trouble by his severity, they find in the present system a cheap and easy means of procuring a certificate which relieves them of all social responsibility, and provides them with so strong a weapon of defence in case of a prosecution that it acts in practice as a bar to any such proceedings. Above all, they know that the Examiner of Plays is free from the pressure of that large body of English public opinion already alluded to, which regards the theatre as the Prohibitionist Teetotaller* regards the public-house: that is, as an abomination to be stamped out unconditionally. The managers rightly dread this pressure more than anything else; and they believe that it is so strong in local governments as to be a characteristic bias of municipal authority. In this they are no doubt mistaken. There is not a municipal authority of any importance in the country in which a proposal to stamp out the theatre, or even to treat it illiberally, would have a chance of adoption. Municipal control of the variety theatres (formerly called music halls) has been very far from illiberal, except in the one particular in which the Lord Chamberlain is equally illiberal. That particular is the assumption that a draped figure is decent and an undraped one indecent. It is useless to point to actual experience, which proves abundantly that naked or apparently naked figures, whether exhibited as living pictures, animated statuary, or in a dance, are at their best not only innocent, but refining in their effect, whereas those actresses and skirt dancers who have brought the peculiar aphrodisiac effect which is objected to to the highest pitch of efficiency wear twice as many petticoats as an ordinary lady does, and seldom exhibit more than their ankles. Unfortunately, municipal councillors persist in confusing decency with drapery; and both in London and the provinces certain

positively edifying performances have been forbidden or withdrawn
under pressure, and replaced by coarse and vicious ones. There is not
the slightest reason to suppose that the Lord Chamberlain would have
been any more tolerant; but this does not alter the fact that the municipal licensing authorities have actually used their powers to set up a censorship which is open to all the objections to censorship in general, and
which, in addition, sets up the objection from which central control is
free: namely, the impossibility of planning theatrical tours without the
serious commercial risk of having the performance forbidden in some
of the towns booked. How can this be prevented?

Desirable Limitations of Local Control

The problem is not a difficult one. The municipality can be limited just
as the monarchy is limited. The Act transferring theatres to local control can be a charter of the liberties of the stage as well as an Act to
reform administration. The power to refuse to grant or renew a licence
to a theatre need not be an arbitrary one. The municipality may be
required to state the ground of refusal; and certain grounds can be
expressly declared as unlawful; so that it shall be possible for the manager to resort to the courts for a mandamus* to compel the authority to
grant a licence. It can be declared unlawful for a licensing authority to
demand from the manager any disclosure of the nature of any entertainment he proposes to give, or to prevent its performance, or to refuse
to renew his licence on the ground that the tendency of his entertainments is contrary to religion and morals, or that the theatre is an
undesirable institution, or that there are already as many theatres as are
needed, or that the theatre draws people away from the churches, chap-
els, mission halls, and the like in its neighborhood. The assumption
should be that every citizen has a right to open and conduct a theatre,
and therefore has a right to a licence unless he has forfeited that right
by allowing his theatre to become a disorderly house, or failing to provide a building which complies with the regulations concerning sanitation and egress in case of fire, or being convicted of an offence against
public decency. Also, the licensing powers of the authority should not
be delegated to any official or committee; and the manager or lessee of
the theatre should have a right to appear in person or by counsel to
plead against any motion to refuse to grant or renew his licence. With
these safeguards the licensing power could not be stretched to censorship. The manager would enjoy liberty of conscience as far as the local
authority is concerned; but on the least attempt on his part to keep

a disorderly house under cover of opening a theatre he would risk his licence.

But the managers will not and should not be satisfied with these limits to the municipal power. If they are deprived of the protection of the Lord Chamberlain's licence, and at the same time efficiently protected against every attempt at censorship by the licensing authority, the enemies of the theatre will resort to the ordinary law, and try to get from the prejudices of a jury what they are debarred from getting from the prejudices of a County Council or City Corporation.* Moral Reform Societies, 'Purity' Societies, Vigilance Societies, exist in England and America for the purpose of enforcing the existing laws against obscenity, blasphemy, Sabbath-breaking,* the debauchery of children, prostitution, and so forth. The paid officials of these societies, in their anxiety to produce plenty of evidence of their activity in the annual reports which go out to the subscribers, do not always discriminate between an obscene postcard and an artistic one, or to put it more exactly, between a naked figure and an indecent one. They often combine a narrow but terribly sincere sectarian bigotry with a complete ignorance of art and history. Even when they have some culture, their livelihood is at the mercy of subscribers and committee men who have none. If these officials had any power of distinguishing between art and blackguardism, between morality and virtue, between immorality and vice, between conscientious heresy and mere baseness of mind and foulness of mouth, they might be trusted by theatrical managers not to abuse the powers of the common informer. As it is, it has been found necessary, in order to enable good music to be performed on Sunday, to take away these powers in that particular, and vest them solely in the Attorney-General.* This disqualification of the common informer should be extended to the initiation of all proceedings of a censorial character against theatres. Few people are aware of the monstrous laws against blasphemy* which still disgrace our statute book. If any serious attempt were made to carry them out, prison accommodation would have to be provided for almost every educated person in the country, beginning with the Archbishop of Canterbury.* Until some government with courage and character enough to repeal them comes into power, it is not too much to ask that such infamous powers of oppression should be kept in responsible hands and not left at the disposal of every bigot ignorant enough to be unaware of the social dangers of persecution. Besides, the common informer is not always a sincere bigot who believes he is performing an action of signal merit in silencing and ruining a heretic. He is unfortunately just as often a blackmailer, who has studied his powers as a common informer in order that he may extort money for refraining from exercising them. If the manager is to be responsible he should be made responsible to a responsible functionary. To be responsible to every fanatical ignoramus who chooses to prosecute him for exhibiting a cast of the Hermes of Praxiteles* in his vestibule, or giving a performance of Measure for Measure,* is mere slavery. It is made bearable at present by the protection of the Lord Chamberlain's certificate. But when that is no longer available, the common informer must be disarmed if the manager is to enjoy security.

SUMMARY

THE general case against censorship as a principle, and the particular case against the existing English censorship and against its replacement by a more enlightened one, is now complete. The following is a recapitulation of the propositions and conclusions contended for.

1. The question of censorship or no censorship is a question of high political principle and not of petty policy.

2. The toleration of heresy and shocks to morality on the stage, and even their protection against the prejudices and superstitions which necessarily enter largely into morality and public opinion, are essential to the welfare of the nation.

3. The existing censorship of the Lord Chamberlain does not only intentionally suppress heresy and challenges to morality in their serious and avowed forms, but unintentionally gives the special protection of its official licence to the most extreme impropriety that the lowest section of London playgoers will tolerate in theatres especially devoted to their entertainment, licensing everything that is popular and forbidding any attempt to change public opinion or morals.

4. The Lord Chamberlain's censorship is open to the special objection that its application to political plays is taken to indicate the attitude of the Crown on questions of domestic and foreign policy, and that it imposes the limits of etiquet on the historical drama.

5. A censorship of a more enlightened and independent kind, exercised by the most eminent available authorities, would prove in practice more disastrous than the censorship of the Lord Chamberlain, because the more eminent its members were the less possible would it be for them to accept the responsibility for heresy or immorality by licensing them, and because the many heretical and immoral plays which now

pass the Lord Chamberlain because he does not understand them, would be understood and suppressed by a more highly enlightened censorship.

6. A reconstructed and enlightened censorship would be armed with summary and effective powers which would stop the evasions by which heretical and immoral plays are now performed in spite of the Lord Chamberlain; and such powers would constitute a tyranny which would ruin the theatre spiritually by driving all independent thinkers from the drama into the uncensored forms of art.

7. The work of critically examining all stage plays in their written form, and of witnessing their performance in order to see that the sense is not altered by the stage business, would, even if it were divided among so many officials as to be physically possible, be mentally impossible to persons of taste and enlightenment.

8. Regulation of theatres is an entirely different matter from censorship, inasmuch as a theatre, being not only a stage, but a place licensed for the sale of spirits, and a public resort capable of being put to disorderly use, and needing special provision for the safety of audiences in cases of fire, etc., cannot be abandoned wholly to private control, and may therefore reasonably be made subject to an annual licence like those now required before allowing premises to be used publicly for music and dancing.

9. In order to prevent the powers of the licensing authority being abused so as to constitute a virtual censorship, any Act transferring the theatres to the control of a licensing authority should be made also a charter of the rights of dramatic authors and managers by the following provisions:

A. The public prosecutor (the Attorney-General) alone should have the right to set the law in operation against the manager of a theatre or the author of a play in respect of the character of the play or entertainment.

B. No disclosure of the particulars of a theatrical entertainment shall be required before performance.

C. Licences shall not be withheld on the ground that the existence of theatres is dangerous to religion and morals, or on the ground that any entertainment given or contemplated is heretical or immoral.

D. The licensing area shall be no less than that of a County Council or City Corporation, which shall not delegate its licensing powers to any minor local authority or to any official or committee; it shall decide all questions affecting the existence of a theatrical licence by vote of the entire body; managers, lessees, and proprietors of theatres shall have the right to plead, in person or by counsel, against a proposal to withhold a licence; and the licence shall not be withheld except for stated reasons, the validity of which shall be subject to the judgment of the high courts.

E. The annual licence, once granted, shall not be cancelled or suspended unless the manager has been convicted by public prosecution of an offence against the ordinary laws against disorderly housekeeping, indecency, blasphemy, etc., except in cases where some structural or sanitary defect in the building necessitates immediate action for the protection of the public against physical injury.

F. No licence shall be refused on the ground that the proximity of the theatre to a church, mission hall, school, or other place of worship, edification, instruction, or entertainment (including another theatre) would draw the public away from such places into its own doors.

PREFACE RESUMED

Mr George Alexander's Protest

On the facts mentioned in the foregoing statement, and in my evidence before the Joint Select Committee, no controversy arose except on one point. Mr George Alexander protested vigorously and indignantly against my admission that theatres, like public-houses, need special control on the ground that they can profit by disorder, and are sometimes conducted with that end in view. Now, Mr Alexander is a famous actor-manager; and it is very difficult to persuade the public that the more famous an actor-manager is the less he is likely to know about any theatre except his own. When the Committee of 1892 reported, I was considered guilty of a perverse paradox when I said that the witness who knew least about the theatre was Henry Irving. Yet a moment's consideration would have shewn that the paradox was a platitude. For about quarter of a century Irving was confined night after night to his own theatre and his own dressing-room, never seeing a play even there because he was himself part of the play; producing the works of long departed authors; and, to the extent to which his talent was extraordinary, necessarily making his theatre unlike any other theatre. When he went to the provinces or to America, the theatres to which he went were swept and garnished for him, and their staffs replaced—as far as he came in contact with them—by his own lieutenants. In the end, there was hardly a first-nighter* in his gallery who did not know more about the London theatres and the progress of dramatic art than he; and as to the provinces, if any chief constable had told him the real history and character of many provincial theatres, he would have denounced that chief constable as an ignorant libeller of a noble profession. But the constable would have been right for all that. Now if this was true of Sir Henry Irving, who did not become a London manager until he had roughed it for years in the provinces, how much more true must it be of, say, Mr George Alexander, whose successful march* through his profession has passed as far from the purlieus* of our theatrical world as the king's naval career from the Isle of Dogs?* The moment we come to that necessary part of the censorship question which deals with the control of theatres from the point of view of those who know how much money can be made out of them by managers who seek to make the auditorium attractive rather than the stage, you find the managers divided into two sections. The first section consists of honorable and successful managers like Mr Alexander, who know nothing of such abuses, and deny, with perfect sincerity and indignant vehemence, that they exist except, perhaps, in certain notorious variety theatres. The other is the silent section which knows better, but is very well content to be publicly defended and privately amused by Mr Alexander's innocence. To accept a West End manager as an expert in theatres because he is an actor is much as if we were to accept the organist of St Paul's Cathedral as an expert on music halls because he is a musician. The real experts are all in the conspiracy to keep the police out of the theatre. And they are so successful that even the police do not know as much as they should.

The police should have been examined by the Committee, and the whole question of the extent to which theatres are disorderly houses in disguise sifted to the bottom. For it is on this point that we discover behind the phantoms of the corrupt dramatists who are restrained by the censorship from debauching the stage, the reality of the corrupt managers and theatre proprietors who actually do debauch it without let or hindrance from the censorship. The whole case for giving control over theatres to local authorities rests on this reality.

Eliza and Her Bath

The persistent notion that a theatre is an Alsatia where the king's writ does not run, and where any wickedness is possible in the absence of a special tribunal and a special police, was brought out by an innocent remark made by Sir William Gilbert, who, when giving evidence before the Committee, was asked by Colonel Lockwood whether a law sufficient to restrain impropriety in books would also restrain impropriety in plays. Sir William replied: 'I should say there is a very wide distinction between what is read and what is seen. In a novel one may read that "Eliza stripped off her dressing-gown and stepped into her bath" without any harm; but I think if that were presented on the stage it would be shocking.' All the stupid and inconsiderate people seized eagerly on this illustration as if it were a successful attempt to prove that without a censorship we should be unable to prevent actresses from appearing naked on the stage. As a matter of fact, if an actress could be persuaded to do such a thing (and it would be about as easy to persuade a bishop's wife to appear in church in the same condition) the police would simply arrest her on a charge of indecent exposure. The extent to which this obvious safeguard was overlooked may be taken as a measure of the thoughtlessness and frivolity of the excuses made for the censorship.

It should be added that the artistic representation of a bath, with every suggestion of nakedness that the law as to decency allows, is one of the most familiar subjects of scenic art. From the Rhine maidens* in Wagner's Trilogy, and the bathers in the second act of Les Huguenots,* to the ballets of water nymphs in our Christmas pantomimes and at our variety theatres, the sound hygienic propaganda of the bath, and the charm of the undraped human figure, are exploited without offence on the stage to an extent never dreamt of by any novelist.

A King's Proctor

Another hare was started by Professor Gilbert Murray and Mr Laurence Housman, who, in pure kindness to the managers, asked whether it would not be possible to establish for their assistance a sort of King's Proctor* to whom plays might be referred for an official legal opinion as to their compliance with the law before production. There are several objections to this proposal; and they may as well be stated in case the proposal should be revived. In the first place, no lawyer with the most elementary knowledge of the law of libel in its various applications to sedition, obscenity, and blasphemy, could answer for the consequences of producing any play whatsoever as to which the smallest question could arise in the mind of any sane person. I have been a critic and an author in active service for thirty years; and though nothing I have written has ever been prosecuted in England or made the subject of legal proceedings, yet I have never published in my life an article, a play, or a book, as to which, if I had taken legal advice, an expert could have assured me that I was proof against prosecution or against an action for damages by the persons criticized. No doubt a sensible solicitor might have advised me that the risk was no greater than all men have to take in dangerous trades; but such an opinion, though it may encourage a client, does not protect him. For example, if a publisher asks his solicitor whether he may venture on an edition of Sterne's Sentimental Journey,* or a manager whether he may produce King Lear* without risk of prosecution, the solicitor will advise him to go ahead. But if the solicitor or counsel consulted by him were asked for a guarantee that neither of these works was a libel, he would have to reply that he could give no such guarantee; that, on the contrary, it was his duty to warn his client that both of them are obscene libels; that King Lear, containing as it does perhaps the most appalling blasphemy* that despair ever uttered, is a blasphemous libel, and that it is doubtful whether it could not be construed as a seditious libel as well. As to

Ibsen's Brand* (the play which made him popular with the most earnestly religious people) no sane solicitor would advise his client even to
chance it except in a broadly cultivated and tolerant (or indifferent)
modern city. The lighter plays would be no better off. What lawyer could
accept any responsibility for the production of Sardou's Divorçons
or Clyde Fitch's The Woman in the Case?* Put the proposed King's
Proctor in operation tomorrow; and what will be the result? The managers will find that instead of insuring them as the Lord Chamberlain
does, he will warn them that every play they submit to him is vulnerable
to the law, and that they must produce it not only on the ordinary risk
of acting on their own responsibility, but at the very grave additional
risk of doing so in the teeth of an official warning. Under such circumstances, what manager would resort a second time to the Proctor; and
how would the Proctor live without fees, unless indeed the Government
gave him a salary for doing nothing? The institution would not last
a year, except as a job for somebody.

Counsel's Opinion

The proposal is still less plausible when it is considered that at present,
without any new legislation at all, any manager who is doubtful about
a play can obtain the advice of his solicitor, or Counsel's opinion, if he
thinks it will be of any service to him. The verdict of the proposed
King's Proctor would be nothing but Counsel's opinion without the
liberty of choice of Counsel, possibly cheapened, but sure to be adverse;
for an official cannot give practical advice as a friend and a man of the
world; he must stick to the letter of the law and take no chances. And as
far as the law is concerned, journalism, literature, and the drama exist
only by custom or sufferance.

Wanted: A New Magna Charta*

This leads us to a very vital question. Is it not possible to amend the law
so as to make it possible for a lawyer to advise his client that he may
publish the works of Blake, Zola, and Swinburne,* or produce the plays
of Ibsen and Mr Granville Barker, or print an ordinary criticism in his
newspaper, without the possibility of finding himself in prison, or
mulcted* in damages and costs in consequence? No doubt it is; but
only by a declaration of constitutional right to blaspheme, rebel, and
deal with tabooed subjects. Such a declaration is not just now within
the scope of practical politics, although we are compelled to act to

a great extent as if it was actually part of the constitution. All that can be done is to take my advice and limit the necessary public control of the theatres in such a manner as to prevent its being abused as a censorship. We have ready to our hand the machinery of licensing as applied to public-houses. A licensed victualler* can now be assured confidently by his lawyer that a magistrate cannot refuse to renew his licence on the ground that he (the magistrate) is a teetotaller and has seen too much of the evil of drink to sanction its sale. The magistrate must give a judicial reason for his refusal, meaning really a constitutional reason; and his teetotalism is not such a reason. In the same way you can protect a theatrical manager by ruling out certain reasons as unconstitutional, as suggested in my statement. Combine this with the abolition of the common informer's power to initiate proceedings; and you will have gone as far as seems possible at present. You will have local control of the theatres for police purposes and sanitary purposes without censorship; and I do not see what more is possible until we get a formal Magna Charta declaring all the categories of libel and the blasphemy laws contrary to public liberty, and repealing and defining accordingly.

Proposed: A New Star Chamber

Yet we cannot mention Magna Charta without recalling how useless such documents are to a nation which has no more political comprehension nor political virtue than King John. When Henry VII* calmly proceeded to tear up Magna Charta by establishing the Star Chamber (a criminal court consisting of a committee of the Privy Council without a jury) nobody objected until, about a century and a half later, the Star Chamber began cutting off the ears of eminent Nonconformist divines* and standing them in the pillory; and then the Nonconformists, and nobody else, abolished the Star Chamber. And if anyone doubts that we are quite ready to establish the Star Chamber again, let him read the Report of the Joint Select Committee, on which I now venture to offer a few criticisms.

The report of the Committee, which will be found in the bluebook, should be read with attention and respect as far as page x, up to which point it is an able and well-written statement of the case. From page x onward, when it goes on from diagnosing the disease to prescribing the treatment, it should be read with even greater attention but with no respect whatever, as the main object of the treatment is to conciliate the How Not To Do It majority. It contains, however, one very notable proposal, the same being nothing more nor less than to revive the Star

Chamber for the purpose of dealing with heretical or seditious plays and their authors, and indeed with all charges against theatrical entertainments except common police cases of indecency. The reason given is that for which the Star Chamber was created by Henry VII: that is, the inadequacy of the ordinary law. 'We consider,' says the report, 'that the law which prevents or punishes indecency, blasphemy and libel in printed publications [it does not, by the way, except in the crudest police cases]* would not be adequate for the control of the drama.' Therefor a committee of the Privy Council is to be empowered to suppress plays and punish managers and authors at its pleasure, on the motion of the Attorney-General, without a jury. The members of the Committee will, of course, be men of high standing and character: otherwise they would not be on the Privy Council. That is to say, they will have all the qualifications of Archbishop Laud.*

Now I have no guarantee that any member of the majority of the Joint Select Committee ever heard of the Star Chamber or of Archbishop Laud. One of them did not know that politics meant anything more than party electioneering. Nothing is more alarming than the ignorance of our public men of the commonplaces of our history, and their consequent readiness to repeat experiments which have in the past produced national catastrophes. At all events, whether they knew what they were doing or not, there can be no question as to what they did. They proposed virtually that the Act of the Long Parliament in 1641* shall be repealed, and the Star Chamber re-established, in order that playwrights and managers may be punished for unspecified offences unknown to the law. When I say unspecified, I should say specified as follows (see page xi of the report) in the case of a play:—

(*a*) To be indecent.

(*b*) To contain offensive personalities.

(*c*) To represent on the stage in an invidious manner a living person, or any person recently dead.

(*d*) To do violence to the sentiment of religious reverence.

(*e*) To be calculated to conduce to vice or crime.

(*f*) To be calculated to impair friendly relations with any foreign power.

(*g*) To be calculated to cause a breach of the peace.

Now it is clear that there is no play yet written, or possible to be written, in this world, that might not be condemned under one or other of these heads. How any sane man, not being a professed enemy of public liberty, could put his hand to so monstrous a catalogue passes my understanding. Had a comparatively definite and innocent clause been added forbidding the affirmation or denial of the doctrine of Transubstantiation,* the country would have been up in arms at once. Lord Ribblesdale made an effort to reduce the seven categories to the old formula 'not to be fitting for the preservation of good manners, decorum, or the public peace'; but this proposal was not carried; whilst on Lord Gorell's motion a final widening of the net was achieved by adding the phrase 'to be calculated to'; so that even if a play does not produce any of the results feared, the author can still be punished on the ground that his play is 'calculated' to produce them. I have no hesitation in saying that a committee capable of such an outrageous display of thoughtlessness and historical ignorance as this paragraph of its report implies deserves to be haled before the tribunal it has itself proposed, and dealt with under a general clause levelled at conduct 'calculated to' overthrow the liberties of England.

Possibilities of the Proposal

Still, though I am certainly not willing to give Lord Gorell the chance of seeing me in the pillory with my ears cut off if I can help it, I daresay many authors would rather take their chance with a Star Chamber than with a jury, just as some soldiers would rather take their chance with a court-martial than at Quarter Sessions.* For that matter, some of them would rather take their chance with the Lord Chamberlain than with either. And though this is no reason for depriving the whole body of authors of the benefit of Magna Charta, still, if the right of the proprietor of a play to refuse the good offices of the Privy Council and to perform the play until his accusers had indicted him at law, and obtained the verdict of a jury against him, were sufficiently guarded, the proposed Committee might be set up and used for certain purposes. For instance, it might be made a condition of the intervention of the Attorney-General or the Director of Public Prosecutions* that he should refer an accused play to the Committee, and obtain their sanction before taking action, offering the proprietor of the play, if the Committee thought fit, an opportunity of voluntarily accepting trial by the Committee as an alternative to prosecution in the ordinary course of law. But the Committee should have no powers of punishment beyond the power (formidable enough) of suspending performances of the play. If it thought that additional punishment was called for, it could order a prosecution without allowing the proprietor or author of the play the alternative of a trial by itself. The author of the play should be made a party to all proceedings of the Committee, and have the right to defend himself in person or by counsel. This would provide a check on the Attorney-General (who might be as bigoted as any of the municipal aldermen* who are so much dreaded by the actor-managers) without enabling the Committee to abuse its powers for party, class, or sectarian ends beyond that irreducible minimum of abuse which a popular jury would endorse, for which minimum there is no remedy.

But when everything is said for the Star Chamber that can be said, and every precaution taken to secure to those whom it pursues the alternative of trial by jury, the expedient still remains a very questionable one, to be endured for the sake of its protective rather than its repressive powers. It should abolish the present quaint toleration of rioting in theatres. For example, if it is to be an offence to perform a play which the proposed new Committee shall condemn, it should also be made an offence to disturb a performance which the Committee has not condemned. 'Brawling' at a theatre should be dealt with as severely as brawling in church if the censorship is to be taken out of the hands of the public. At present Jenny Geddes* may throw her stool at the head of a playwright who preaches unpalatable doctrine to her, or rather, since her stool is a fixture, she may hiss and hoot and make it impossible to proceed with the performance, even although nobody has compelled her to come to the theatre or suspended her liberty to stay away, and although she has no claim on an unendowed theatre for her spiritual necessities, as she has on her parish church. If mob censorship cannot be trusted to keep naughty playwrights in order, still less can it be trusted to keep the pioneers of thought in countenance; and I submit that anyone hissing a play permitted by the new censorship should be guilty of contempt of court.

Star Chamber Sentimentality

But what is most to be dreaded in a Star Chamber is not its sternness but its sentimentality. There is no worse censorship than one which considers only the feelings of the spectators, except perhaps one which considers the feelings of people who do not even witness the performance. Take the case of the Passion Play at Oberammergau.* The offence given by a representation of the Crucifixion on the stage is not bounded by frontiers: further, it is an offence of which the voluntary spectators are guilty no less than the actors. If it is to be tolerated at all: if we are not to make war on the German Empire for permitting it, nor punish the English people who go to Bavaria to see it and thereby endow it with

English money, we may as well tolerate it in London, where nobody need go to see it except those who are not offended by it. When Wagner's Parsifal* becomes available for representation in London, many people will be sincerely horrified when the miracle of the Mass* is simulated on the stage of Covent Garden,* and the Holy Ghost* descends in the form of a dove. But if the Committee of the Privy Council, or the Lord Chamberlain, or anyone else, were to attempt to keep Parsifal from us to spare the feelings of these people, it would not be long before even the most thoughtless champions of the censorship would see that the principle of doing nothing that could shock anybody had reduced itself to absurdity. No quarter whatever should be given to the bigotry of people so unfit for social life as to insist not only that their own prejudices and superstitions should have the fullest toleration but that everybody else should be compelled to think and act as they do. Every service in St Paul's Cathedral is an outrage to the opinions of the congregation of the Roman Catholic Cathedral of Westminster. Every Liberal meeting is a defiance and a challenge to the most cherished opinions of the Unionists. A law to compel the Roman Catholics to attend service at St Paul's, or the Liberals to attend the meetings of the Primrose League* would be resented as an insufferable tyranny. But a law to shut up both St Paul's and the Westminster Cathedral, and to put down political meetings and associations because of the offence given by them to many worthy and excellent people, would be a far worse tyranny, because it would kill the religious and political life of the country outright, whereas to compel people to attend the services and meetings of their opponents would greatly enlarge their minds, and would actually be a good thing if it were enforced all round. I should not object to a law to compel everybody to read two newspapers, each violently opposed to the other in politics; but to forbid us to read newspapers at all would be to maim us mentally and cashier our country in the ranks of civilization. I deny that anybody has the right to demand more from me, over and above lawful conduct in a general sense, than liberty to stay away from the theatre in which my plays are represented. If he is unfortunate enough to have a religion so petty that it can be insulted (any man is as welcome to insult my religion, if he can, as he is to insult the universe) I claim the right to insult it to my heart's content, if I choose, provided I do not compel him to come and hear me. If I think this country ought to make war on any other country, then, so long as war remains lawful, I claim full liberty to write and perform a play inciting the country to that war without interference from the ambassadors of the menaced country. I may 'give pain to many worthy people, and pleasure to none,' as the Censor's pet phrase puts it: I may even make Europe a cockpit and Asia a shambles: no matter: if preachers and politicians, statesmen and soldiers, may do these things—if it is right that such things should be done, then I claim my share in the right to do them. If the proposed Committee is meant to prevent me from doing these things whilst men of other professions are permitted to do them, then I protest with all my might against the formation of such a Committee. If it is to protect me, on the contrary, against the attacks that bigots and corrupt pornographers may make on me by appealing to the ignorance and prejudices of common jurors, then I welcome it; but is that really the object of its proposers? And if it is, what guarantee have I that the new tribunal will not presently resolve into a mere committee to avoid unpleasantness and keep the stage 'in good taste'? It is no more possible for me to do my work honestly as a playwright without giving pain than it is for a dentist. The nation's morals are like its teeth: the more decayed they are the more it hurts to touch them. Prevent dentists and dramatists from giving pain, and not only will our morals become as carious as our teeth, but toothache and the plagues that follow neglected morality will presently cause more agony than all the dentists and dramatists at their worst have caused since the world began.

Anything for a Quiet Life

Another doubt: would a Committee of the Privy Council really face the risks that must be taken by all communities as the price of our freedom to evolve? Would it not rather take the popular English view that freedom and virtue generally are sweet and desirable only when they cost nothing? Nothing worth having is to be had without risk. A mother risks her child's life every time she lets it ramble through the countryside, or cross the street, or clamber over the rocks on the shore by itself. A father risks his son's morals when he gives him a latchkey. The members of the Joint Select Committee risked my producing a revolver and shooting them when they admitted me to the room without having me handcuffed. And these risks are no unreal ones. Every day some child is maimed or drowned and some young man infected with disease; and political assassinations have been appallingly frequent of late years. Railway travelling has its risks; motoring has its risks; aeroplaning has its risks; every advance we make costs us a risk of some sort. And though these are only risks to the individual, to the community they are certainties. It is not certain that I will be killed this year in a railway accident; but it is certain that somebody will. The invention of printing and the freedom of the press have brought upon us, not merely risks of their abuse, but the establishment as part of our social routine of some of the worst evils a community can suffer from. People who realize these evils shriek for the suppression of motor cars, the virtual imprisonment and enslavement of the young, the passing of Press Laws (especially in Egypt, India, and Ireland),* exactly as they shriek for a censorship of the stage. The freedom of the stage will be abused just as certainly as the complaisance and innocence of the censorship is abused at present. It will also be used by writers like myself for raising very difficult and disturbing questions, social, political, and religious, at moments which may be extremely inconvenient to the government. Is it certain that a Committee of the Privy Council would stand up to all this as the price of liberty? I doubt it. If I am to be at the mercy of a nice amiable Committee of elderly gentlemen (I know all about elderly gentlemen, being one myself) whose motto is the highly popular one, 'Anything for a quiet life,' and who will make the inevitable abuses of freedom by our blackguards an excuse for interfering with any disquieting use of it by myself, then I shall be worse off than I am with the Lord Chamberlain, whose mind is not broad enough to obstruct the whole range of thought. If it were, he would be given a more difficult post.

Shall the Examiner of Plays Starve?

And here I may be reminded that if I prefer the Lord Chamberlain I can go to the Lord Chamberlain, who is to retain all his present functions for the benefit of those who prefer to be judged by him. But I am not so sure that the Lord Chamberlain will be able to exercise those functions for long if resort to him is to be optional. Let me be kinder to him than he has been to me, and uncover for him the pitfalls which the Joint Select Committee have dug (and concealed) in his path. Consider how the voluntary system must inevitably work. The Joint Select Committee expressly urges that the Lord Chamberlain's licence must not be a bar to a prosecution. Granted that in spite of this reservation the licence would prove in future as powerful a defence as it has been in the past, yet the voluntary clause nevertheless places the manager at the mercy of any author who makes it a condition of his contract that his play shall not be submitted for licence. I should probably take that course without opposition from the manager. For the manager, knowing that three of my plays have been refused a licence, and that it would be far safer to produce a play for which no licence had been asked than one for which it had been asked and refused, would agree that it was more prudent, in my case, to avail himself of the power of dispensing with the Lord Chamberlain's licence. But now mark the consequences. The manager, having thus discovered that his best policy was to dispense with the licence in the few doubtful cases, would presently ask himself why he should spend two guineas each on licences for the many plays as to which no question could conceivably arise. What risk does any manager run in producing such works as Sweet Lavender, Peter Pan, The Silver King,* or any of the 99 per cent of plays that are equally neutral on controversial questions. Does anyone seriously believe that the managers would continue to pay the Lord Chamberlain two guineas a play out of mere love and loyalty, only to create an additional risk in the case of controversial plays, and to guard against risks that do not exist in the case of the great bulk of other productions? Only those would remain faithful to him who produce such plays as the Select Committee began by discussing *in camera*, and ended by refusing to discuss at all because they were too nasty. These people would still try to get a licence, and would still no doubt succeed as they do today. But could the King's Reader of Plays live on his fees from these plays alone; and if he could how long would his post survive the discredit of licensing only pornographic plays? It is clear to me that the Examiner would be starved out of existence, and the censorship perish of desuetude.* Perhaps that is exactly what the Select Committee contemplated. If so, I have nothing more to say, except that I think sudden death would be more merciful.

Lord Gorell's Awakening

In the meantime, conceive the situation which would arise if a licensed play were prosecuted. To make it clearer, let us imagine any other offender—say a company promoter with a fraudulent prospectus—pleading in Court that he had induced the Lord Chamberlain to issue a certificate that the prospectus contained nothing objectionable, and that on the strength of that certificate he issued it; also, that by law the Court could do nothing to him except order him to wind up his company. Some such vision as this must have come to Lord Gorell when he at last grappled seriously with the problem. Mr Harcourt seized the opportunity to make a last rally. He seconded Lord Gorell's proposal that the Committee should admit that its scheme of an optional censorship was an elaborate absurdity, and report that all censorship before production was out of the question. But it was too late: the *volte face* was too sudden and complete. It was Lord Gorell whose vote had turned the close division which took place on the question of receiving my statement. It was Lord Gorell without whose countenance and authority the farce of the books could never have been performed. Yet here was Lord Gorell, after assenting to all the provisions for the optional censorship paragraph by paragraph, suddenly informing his colleagues that they had been wrong all through and that I had been right all through, and inviting them to scrap half their work and adopt my conclusion. No wonder Lord Gorell got only one vote: that of Mr Harcourt. But the incident is not the less significant. Lord Gorell carried more weight than any other member of the Committee on the legal and constitutional aspect of the question. Had he begun where he left off—had he at the outset put down his foot on the notion that an optional penal law could ever be anything but a gross contradiction in terms, that part of the Committee's proposals would never have come into existence.

Judges: Their Professional Limitations

I do not, however, appeal to Lord Gorell's judgment on all points. It is inevitable that a judge should be deeply impressed by his professional experience with a sense of the impotence of judges and laws and courts to deal satisfactorily with evils which are so Protean and elusive as to defy definition, and which yet seem to present quite simple problems to the common sense of men of the world. You have only to imagine the Privy Council as consisting of men of the world highly endowed with common sense, to persuade yourself that the supplementing of the law by the common sense of the Privy Council would settle the whole difficulty. But no man knows what he means by common sense, though every man can tell you that it is very uncommon, even in Privy Councils. And since every ploughman is a man of the world, it is evident that even the phrase itself does not mean what it says. As a matter of fact, it means in ordinary use simply a man who will not make himself disagreeable for the sake of a principle: just the sort of man who should never be allowed to meddle with political rights. Now to a judge a political right, that is, a dogma which is above our laws and conditions our laws, instead of being subject to them, is anarchic and abhorrent. That is why I trust Lord Gorell when he is defending the integrity of the law against the proposal to make it in any sense optional, whilst I very strongly mistrust him, as I mistrust all professional judges, when political rights are in danger.

Conclusion

I must conclude by recommending the Government to take my advice wherever it conflicts with that of the Joint Select Committee. It is, I think, obviously more deeply considered and better informed, though I say it that should not. At all events, I have given my reasons; and at that I must leave it. As the tradition which makes Malvolio not only Master of the Revels* but Master of the Mind of England, and which has come down to us from Henry VIII,* is manifestly doomed to the dustbin, the sooner it goes there the better; for the democratic control which naturally succeeds it can easily be limited so as to prevent it becoming either a censorship or a tyranny. The Examiner of Plays should receive a generous pension, and be set free to practise privately as an expert adviser of theatrical managers. There is no reason why they should be deprived of the counsel they so highly value.

It only remains to say that public performances of The Shewing-Up of Blanco Posnet are still prohibited in Great Britain by the Lord Chamberlain. An attempt was made to prevent even its performance in Ireland by some indiscreet Castle officials in the absence of the Lord Lieutenant. This attempt gave extraordinary publicity to the production of the play; and every possible effort was made to persuade the Irish public that the performance would be an outrage to their religion, and to provoke a repetition of the rioting that attended the first performances of Synge's Playboy of the Western World* before the most sensitive and, on provocation, the most turbulent audience in the kingdom. The directors of the Irish National Theatre,* Lady Gregory and Mr William Butler Yeats,* rose to the occasion with inspiriting courage. I am a conciliatory person, and was willing, as I always am, to make every concession in return for having my own way. But Lady Gregory and Mr Yeats not only would not yield an inch, but insisted, within the due limits of gallant warfare, on taking the field with every circumstance of defiance, and winning the battle with every trophy of victory. Their triumph was as complete as they could have desired. The performance exhausted the possibilities of success, and provoked no murmur, though it inspired several approving sermons. Later on, Lady Gregory and Mr Yeats brought the play to London* and performed it under the Lord Chamberlain's nose, through the instrumentality of the Stage Society.

After this, the play was again submitted to the Lord Chamberlain. But, though beaten, he, too, understands the art of How Not To Do It. He licensed the play, but endorsed on his licence the condition that all the passages which implicated God in the history of Blanco Posnet must be omitted in representation. All the coarseness, the profligacy, the prostitution, the violence, the drinking-bar humor into which the light shines in the play are licensed, but the light itself is extinguished. I need hardly say that I have not availed myself of this licence, and do not intend to. There is enough licensed darkness in our theatres today without my adding to it.

AYOT ST LAWRENCE,
14th July 1910.

POSTSCRIPT.—Since the above was written the Lord Chamberlain has made an attempt to evade his responsibility and perhaps to postpone his doom by appointing an advisory committee, unknown to the law, on which he will presumably throw any odium that may attach to refusals of licences in the future. This strange and lawless body will hardly reassure our moralists, who object much more to the plays he licenses than to those he suppresses, and are therefore unmoved by his plea that his refusals are few and far between. It consists of two eminent actors (one retired),* an Oxford professor of literature,* and two eminent barristers.* As their assembly is neither created by statute nor sanctioned by custom, it is difficult to know what to call it until it advises the Lord Chamberlain to deprive some author of his means of livelihood, when it will, I presume, become a conspiracy, and be indictable accordingly; unless, indeed, it can persuade the Courts to recognize it as a new Estate of the Realm,* created by the Lord Chamberlain. This constitutional position is so questionable that I strongly advise the members to resign promptly before the Lord Chamberlain gets them into trouble.

THE SHEWING UP OF BLANCO POSNET

A number of women are sitting together in a big room not unlike an old English tithe barn* in its timbered construction, but with windows high up next the roof. It is furnished as a courthouse, with the floor raised next the walls, and on this raised flooring a seat for the Sheriff,* a rough jury box on his right, and a bar to put prisoners to on his left. In the well in the middle is a table with benches round it. A few other benches are in disorder round the room. The autumn sun is shining warmly through the windows and the open door. The women, whose dress and speech are those of pioneers of civilization* in a territory of the United States of America, are seated round the table and on the benches, shucking nuts.* The conversation is at its height.

BABSY [*a bumptious young slattern,* with some good looks*] I say that a man that would steal a horse would do anything.

LOTTIE [*a sentimental girl, neat and clean*] Well, I never should look at it in that way. I do think killing a man is worse any day than stealing a horse.

HANNAH [*elderly and wise*] I dont say it's right to kill a man. In a place like this, where every man has to have a revolver, and where theres so much to try people's tempers, the men get to be a deal too free with one another in the way of shooting. God knows it's hard enough to have to bring a boy into the world and nurse him up to be a man only to have him brought home to you on a shutter, perhaps for nothing, or only just to shew that the man that killed him wasnt afraid of him. But men are like children when they get a gun in their hands: theyre not content til theyve used it on somebody.*

JESSIE [*a good-natured but sharp-tongued, hoity-toity young woman; Babsy's rival in good looks and her superior in tidiness*] They shoot for the love of it. Look at them at a lynching. Theyre not content to hang the man; but directly the poor creature is swung up they all shoot him full of holes, wasting their cartridges that cost solid money, and pretending they do it in horror of his wickedness, though half of them would have a rope round their own necks if all they did was known. Let alone the mess it makes.

LOTTIE. I wish we could get more civilized. I dont like all this lynching and shooting. I dont believe any of us like it, if the truth were known.

BABSY. Our Sheriff is a real strong man. You want a strong man for a rough lot like our people here. He aint afraid to shoot and he aint afraid to hang. Lucky for us quiet ones, too.

JESSIE. Oh, dont talk to me. I know what men are. Of course he aint afraid to shoot and he aint afraid to hang. Wheres the risk in that with the law on his side and the whole crowd at his back longing for the lynching as if it was a spree?* Would one of them own to it or let him own to it if they lynched the wrong man? Not them. What they call justice in this place is nothing but a breaking out of the devil thats in all of us. What I want to see is a Sheriff that aint afraid not to shoot and not to hang.

EMMA [*a sneak who sides with Babsy or Jessie, according to the fortune of war*] Well, I must say it does sicken me to see Sheriff Kemp putting down his foot, as he calls it. Why dont he put it down on his wife? She wants it worse than half the men he lynches. He and his Vigilance Committee,* indeed!

BABSY [*incensed*] Oh, well! if people are going to take the part of horse-thieves against the Sheriff—?

JESSIE. Who's taking the part of horse-thieves against the Sheriff?

BABSY. *You* are. Waitle your own horse is stolen, and youll know better. I had an uncle that died of thirst in the sage brush because a negro stole his horse. But they caught him and burned him; and serve him right, too.

EMMA. I have known a child that was born crooked because its mother had to do a horse's work that was stolen.*

BABSY. There! You hear that? I say stealing a horse is ten times worse than killing a man. And if the Vigilance Committee ever gets hold of you, youd better have killed twenty men than as much as stole a saddle or bridle, much less a horse.

Elder Daniels comes in.

ELDER DANIELS. Sorry to disturb you, ladies; but the Vigilance Committee has taken a prisoner, and they want the room to try him in.

JESSIE. But they cant try him til Sheriff Kemp comes back from the wharf.

ELDER DANIELS. Yes; but we have to keep the prisoner here til he comes.

BABSY. What do you want to put him here for? Cant you tie him up in the Sheriff's stable?

ELDER DANIELS. He has a soul to be saved, almost like the rest of us. I am bound to try to put some religion into him before he goes into his Maker's presence after the trial.

HANNAH. What has he done, Mr Daniels?

ELDER DANIELS. Stole a horse.

BABSY. And are we to be turned out of the town hall for a horse-thief? Aint a stable good enough for *his* religion?

ELDER DANIELS. It may be good enough for his, Babsy; but, by your leave, it is not good enough for mine. While I am Elder here, I shall umbly endeavor to keep up the dignity of Him I serve to the best of my small ability. So I must ask you to be good enough to clear out. Allow me. [*He takes the sack of husks and puts it out of the way against the panels of the jury box*].

THE WOMEN [*murmuring*] Thats always the way. Just as we'd settled down to work. What harm are we doing? Well, it is tiresome. Let them finish the job themselves. Oh dear, oh dear! We cant have a minute to ourselves. Shoving us out like that!

HANNAH. Whose horse was it, Mr Daniels?

ELDER DANIELS [*returning to move the other sack*] I am sorry to say it was the Sheriff's horse—the one he loaned to young Strapper. Strapper loaned it to me; and the thief stole it, thinking it was mine. If it had been mine, I'd have forgiven him cheerfully. I'm sure I hoped he would get away; for he had two hours start of the Vigilance Committee. But they caught him. [*He disposes of the other sack also*].

JESSIE. It cant have been much of a horse if they caught him with two hours start.

ELDER DANIELS [*coming back to the centre of the group*] The strange thing is that he wasnt on the horse when they took him. He was walking; and of course he denies that he ever had the horse. The Sheriff's brother wanted to tie him up and lash him til he confessed what he'd done with it; but I couldnt allow that: it's not the law.

BABSY. Law! What right has a horse-thief to any law? Law is thrown away on a brute like that.

ELDER DANIELS. Dont say that, Babsy. No man should be made to confess by cruelty until religion has been tried and failed. Please God I'll get the whereabouts of the horse from him if youll be so good as to clear out from this. [*Disturbance*]. They are bringing him in. Now ladies! please, please.

They rise reluctantly. Hannah, Jessie, and Lottie retreat to the Sheriff's bench, shepherded by Daniels; but the other women crowd forward behind Babsy and Emma to see the prisoner.

Blanco Posnet is brought in by Strapper Kemp, the Sheriff's brother, and a cross-eyed man called Squinty. Others follow. Blanco is evidently a blackguard.* It would be necessary to clean him to make a close guess at his age; but he is under forty, and an upturned, red moustache, and the arrangement of his hair in a crest on his brow, proclaim the dandy in spite of his intense disreputableness. He carries his head high, and has a fairly resolute mouth, though the fire of incipient delirium tremens* is in his eye.

His arms are bound with a rope with a long end, which Squinty holds. They release him when he enters; and he stretches himself and lounges across the courthouse in front of the women. Strapper and the men remain between him and the door.

BABSY [*spitting at him as he passes her*] Horse-thief! horse-thief!

OTHERS. You will hang for it; do you hear? And serve you right. Serve you right. That will teach you. I wouldnt wait to try you. Lynch him straight off, the varmint.* Yes, yes. Tell the boys. Lynch him.

BLANCO [*mocking*] 'Angels ever bright and fair—'

BABSY. You call me an angel, and I'll smack your dirty face for you.

BLANCO. 'Take, oh take me to your care.'*

EMMA. There wont be any angels where youre going to.

OTHERS. Aha! Devils, more likely. And too good company for a horse-thief.

ALL. Horse-thief! Horse-thief! Horse-thief!

BLANCO. Do women make the law here, or men? Drive these heifers out.

THE WOMEN. Oh! [*They rush at him, vituperating, screaming passionately, tearing at him. Lottie puts her fingers in her ears and runs out. Hannah follows, shaking her head. Blanco is thrown down*]. Oh, did you hear what he called us? You foul-mouthed brute! You liar! How dare you

put such a name to a decent woman? Let me get at him. You coward!
Oh, he struck me: did you see that? Lynch him! Pete, will you stand
by and hear me called names by a skunk like that? Burn him: burn
him! Thats what I'd do with him. Aye, burn him!

THE MEN [*pulling the women away from Blanco, and getting them out
partly by violence and partly by coaxing*] Here! come out of this. Let
him alone. Clear the courthouse. Come on now. Out with you. Now,
Sally: out you go. Let go my hair, or I'll twist your arm out. Ah,
would you? Now, then: get along. You know you must go. Whats the
use of scratching like that? Now, ladies, ladies, ladies. How would you
like it if you were going to be hanged?

*At last the women are pushed out, leaving Elder Daniels, the Sheriff's
brother Strapper Kemp, and a few others with Blanco. Strapper is a lad
just turning into a man: strong, selfish, sulky, and determined.*

BLANCO [*sitting up and tidying himself*]—

> Oh woman, in our hours of ease,
> Uncertain, coy, and hard to please—*

Is my face scratched? I can feel their damned claws all over me still. Am
I bleeding? [*He sits on the nearest bench*].

ELDER DANIELS. Nothing to hurt. Theyve drawn a drop or two under
your left eye.

STRAPPER. Lucky for you to have an eye left in your head.

BLANCO [*wiping the blood off*]—

> When pain and anguish wring the brow,
> A ministering angel thou.*

Go out to them, Strapper Kemp; and tell them about your big
brother's little horse that some wicked man stole. Go and cry in your
mammy's lap.

STRAPPER [*furious*] You jounce me any more about that horse, Blanco
Posnet; and I'll—I'll—

BLANCO. Youll scratch my face, wont you? Yah! Your brother's the
Sheriff, aint he?

STRAPPER. Yes, he is. He hangs horse-thieves.

BLANCO [*with calm conviction*] He's a rotten Sheriff. Oh, a rotten
Sheriff. If he did his first duty he'd hang himself. This is a rotten

town. Your fathers came here on a false alarm of gold-digging; and when the gold didnt pan out, they lived by licking their young into habits of honest industry.

STRAPPER. If I hadnt promised Elder Daniels here to give him a chance to keep you out of Hell, I'd take the job of twisting your neck off the hands of the Vigilance Committee.

BLANCO [*with infinite scorn*] You and your rotten Elder, and your rotten Vigilance Committee!

STRAPPER. Theyre sound enough to hang a horse-thief, anyhow.

BLANCO. Any fool can hang the wisest man in the country. Nothing he likes better. But you cant hang me.

STRAPPER. Cant we?

BLANCO. No, you cant. I left the town this morning before sunrise, because it's a rotten town, and I couldnt bear to see it in the light. Your brother's horse did the same, as any sensible horse would. Instead of going to look for the horse, you went looking for me. That was a rotten thing to do, because the horse belonged to your brother—or to the man he stole it from—and I dont belong to him. Well, you found me; but you didnt find the horse. If I had took the horse, I'd have been on the horse. Would I have taken all that time to get to where I did if I'd a horse to carry me?

STRAPPER. I dont believe you started not for two hours after you say you did.

BLANCO. Who cares what you believe or dont believe? Is a man worth six of you to be hanged because youve lost your big brother's horse, and youll want to kill somebody to relieve your rotten feelings when he licks you for it? Not likely. Til you can find a witness that saw me with that horse you cant touch me; and you know it.

STRAPPER. Is that the law, Elder?

ELDER DANIELS. The Sheriff knows the law. I wouldnt say for sure; but I think it would be more seemly to have a witness. Go and round one up, Strapper; and leave me here alone to wrestle with his poor blinded soul.*

STRAPPER. I'll get a witness all right enough. I know the road he took; and I'll ask at every house within sight of it for a mile out. Come, boys.

Strapper goes out with the others, leaving Blanco and Elder Daniels together. Blanco rises and strolls over to the Elder, surveying him with extreme disparagement.

BLANCO. Well, brother? Well, Boozy Posnet, alias Elder Daniels? Well, thief? Well, drunkard?

ELDER DANIELS. It's no good, Blanco. Theyll never believe we're brothers.

BLANCO. Never fear. Do you suppose I want to claim you? Do you suppose I'm proud of you? Youre a rotten brother, Boozy Posnet. All you ever did when I owned you was to borrow money from me to get drunk with. Now you lend money and sell drink to other people. I was ashamed of you before; and I'm worse ashamed of you now. I wont have you for a brother. Heaven gave you to me; but I return the blessing without thanks. So be easy: I shant blab. [*He turns his back on him and sits down*].

ELDER DANIELS. I tell you they wouldnt believe you; so what does it matter to me whether you blab or not? Talk sense, Blanco: theres no time for your foolery now; for youll be a dead man an hour after the Sheriff comes back. What possessed you to steal that horse?

BLANCO. I didnt steal it. I distrained on it for what you owed me.* I thought it was yours. I was a fool to think that you owned anything but other people's property. You laid your hands on everything father and mother had when they died. I never asked you for a fair share. I never asked you for all the money I'd lent you from time to time. I asked you for mother's old necklace with the hair locket in it. You wouldnt give me that: you wouldnt give me anything. So as you refused me my due I took it, just to give you a lesson.

ELDER DANIELS. Why didnt you take the necklace if you must steal something? They wouldnt have hanged you for that.

BLANCO. Perhaps I'd rather be hanged for stealing a horse than let off for a damned piece of sentimentality.

ELDER DANIELS. Oh, Blanco, Blanco: spiritual pride has been your ruin. If youd only done like me, youd be a free and respectable man this day instead of laying there with a rope round your neck.

BLANCO [*turning on him*] Done like you! What do you mean? Drink like you, eh? Well, Ive done some of that lately. I see things.

ELDER DANIELS. Too late, Blanco: too late. [*Convulsively*] Oh, why didnt you drink as I used to? Why didnt you drink as I was led to by the Lord for my good, until the time came for me to give it up? It was drink that saved my character when I was a young man; and it was the want of it that spoiled yours. Tell me this. Did I ever get drunk when I was working?

BLANCO. No; but then you never worked when you had money enough to get drunk.

ELDER DANIELS. That just shews the wisdom of Providence and the Lord's mercy. God fulfils Himself in many ways:* ways we little think of when we try to set up our own shortsighted laws against His Word. When does the Devil catch hold of a man? Not when he's working and not when he's drunk; but when he's idle and sober. Our own natures tell us to drink when we have nothing else to do. Look at you and me! When we'd both earned a pocketful of money, what did we do? Went on the spree,* naturally. But I was humble minded. I did as the rest did. I gave my money in at the drink-shop; and I said, 'Fire me out when I have drunk it all up.' Did you ever see me sober while it lasted?

BLANCO. No; and you looked so disgusting that I wonder it didnt set me against drink for the rest of my life.

ELDER DANIELS. That was your spiritual pride, Blanco. You never reflected that when I was drunk I was in a state of innocence. Temptations and bad company and evil thoughts passed by me like the summer wind as you might say: I was too drunk to notice them. When the money was gone, and they fired me out, I was fired out like gold out of the furnace, with my character unspoiled and unspotted; and when I went back to work, the work kept me steady. Can you say as much, Blanco? Did *your* holidays leave *your* character unspoiled? Oh, no, no. It was theatres: it was gambling: it was evil company: it was reading vain romances: it was women, Blanco, women: it was wrong thoughts and gnawing discontent. It ended in your becoming a rambler and a gambler: it is going to end this evening on the gallows tree. Oh, what a lesson against spiritual pride! Oh, what a—[*Blanco throws his hat at him*].

BLANCO. Stow it, Boozy. Sling it. Cut it. Cheese it.* Shut up. 'Shake not the dying sinner's sand.'*

ELDER DANIELS. Aye: there you go, with your scraps of lustful poetry. But you cant deny what I tell you. Why, do you think I would put my soul in peril by selling drink if I thought it did no good, as them silly temperance reformers* make out, flying in the face of the natural tastes implanted in us all for a good purpose? Not if I was to starve for it tomorrow. But I know better. I tell you, Blanco, what keeps America today the purest of the nations is that when she's not working she's too drunk to hear the voice of the tempter.*

BLANCO. Dont deceive yourself, Boozy. You sell drink because you make a bigger profit out of it than you can by selling tea. And you gave up drink yourself because when you got that fit at Edwardstown the doctor told you youd die the next time; and that frightened you off it.*

ELDER DANIELS [*fervently*] Oh thank God selling drink pays me! And thank God He sent me that fit as a warning that my drinking time was past and gone, and that He needed me for another service!

BLANCO. Take care, Boozy. He hasnt finished with you yet. He always has a trick up His sleeve—

ELDER DANIELS. Oh, is that the way to speak of the ruler of the universe—the great and almighty God?

BLANCO. He's a sly one. He's a mean one. He lies low for you. He plays cat and mouse with you. He lets you run loose until you think youre shut of Him; and then, when you least expect it, He's got you.

ELDER DANIELS. Speak more respectful, Blanco—more reverent.

BLANCO [*springing up and coming at him*] Reverent! Who taught you your reverent cant? Not your Bible. It says He cometh like a thief in the night*—aye, like a thief—a horse-thief—

ELDER DANIELS [*shocked*] Oh!

BLANCO [*overbearing him*] And it's true. Thats how He caught me and put my neck into the halter. To spite me because I had no use for Him—because I lived my own life in my own way, and would have no truck with His 'Dont do this,' and 'You mustnt do that,' and 'Youll go to Hell if you do the other.' I gave Him the go-bye and did without Him all these years. But He caught me out at last. The laugh is with Him as far as hanging me goes.* [*He thrusts his hands into his pockets and lounges moodily away from Daniels, to the table, where he sits facing the jury box*].

ELDER DANIELS. Dont dare to put your theft on Him, man. It was the Devil tempted you to steal the horse.

BLANCO. Not a bit of it. Neither God nor Devil tempted me to take the horse: I took it on my own. He had a cleverer trick than that ready for me. [*He takes his hands out of his pockets and clenches his fists*]. Gosh! When I think that I might have been safe and fifty miles away by now with that horse; and here I am waiting to be hung up and filled with lead! What came to me? What made me such a fool? Thats what I want to know. Thats the great secret.

ELDER DANIELS [*at the opposite side of the table*] Blanco: the great secret now is, what did you do with the horse?

BLANCO [*striking the table with his fist*] May my lips be blighted like my soul if ever I tell that to you or any mortal man! They may roast me alive or cut me to ribbons; but Strapper Kemp shall never have the laugh on me over that job. Let them hang me. Let them shoot. So long as they are shooting a man and not a snivelling skunk and softy, I can stand up to them and take all they can give me—game.

ELDER DANIELS. Dont be headstrong, Blanco. Whats the use? [*Slyly*] They might let up on you if you put Strapper in the way of getting his brother's horse back.

BLANCO. Not they. Hanging's too big a treat for them to give up a fair chance. Ive done it myself. Ive yelled with the dirtiest of them when a man no worse than myself was swung up. Ive emptied my revolver into him, and persuaded myself that he deserved it and that I was doing justice with strong stern men. Well, my turn's come now. Let the men I yelled at and shot at look up out of Hell and see the boys yelling and shooting at me as *I* swing up.

ELDER DANIELS. Well, even if you want to be hanged, is that any reason why Strapper shouldnt have his horse? I tell you I'm responsible to him for it. [*Bending over the table and coaxing him*]. Act like a brother, Blanco: tell me what you done with it.

BLANCO [*shortly, getting up, and leaving the table*] Never you mind what I done with it. I was done out of it: let that be enough for you.

ELDER DANIELS [*following him*] Then why dont you put us on to the man that done you out of it?

BLANCO. Because he'd be too clever for you, just as he was too clever for me.

ELDER DANIELS. Make your mind easy about that, Blanco. He wont be too clever for the boys and Sheriff Kemp if you put them on his trail.

BLANCO. Yes, he will. It wasnt a man.

ELDER DANIELS. Then what was it?

BLANCO [*pointing upward*] Him.

ELDER DANIELS. Oh what a way to utter His holy name!

BLANCO. He done me out of it. He meant to pay off old scores by bringing me here. He means to win the deal and you cant stop Him. Well, He's made a fool of me; but He cant frighten me. I'm not going to beg off. I'll fight off if I get a chance. I'll lie off if they cant get a witness against me. But back down I never will, not if all the hosts of heaven come to snivel at me in white surplices* and offer me my life in exchange for an umble and a contrite heart.

ELDER DANIELS. Youre not in your right mind, Blanco. I'll tell em youre mad. I believe theyll let you off on that. [*He makes for the door*].

BLANCO [*seizing him, with horror in his eyes*] Dont go: dont leave me alone: do you hear?

ELDER DANIELS. Has your conscience brought you to this that youre afraid to be left alone in broad daylight, like a child in the dark.

BLANCO. I'm afraid of Him and His tricks. When I have you to raise the devil in me—when I have people to shew off before and keep me game, I'm all right; but Ive lost my nerve for being alone since this morning. It's when youre alone that He takes His advantage. He might turn my head again. He might send people to me—not real people perhaps. [*Shivering*] By God, I dont believe that woman and the child were real. I dont. I never noticed them til they were at my elbow.

ELDER DANIELS. What woman and what child? What are you talking about? Have you been drinking too hard?

BLANCO. Never you mind. Youve got to stay with me: thats all; or else send someone else—someone rottener than yourself to keep the devil in me. Strapper Kemp will do. Or a few of those scratching devils of women.

Strapper Kemp comes back.

ELDER DANIELS [*to Strapper*] He's gone off his head.

STRAPPER. Foxing,* more likely. [*Going past Daniels and talking to Blanco nose to nose*]. It's no good: we hang madmen here; and a good job too!

BLANCO. I feel safe with you, Strapper. Youre one of the rottenest.*

STRAPPER. You know youre done, and that you may as well be hanged for a sheep as a lamb.* So talk away. Ive got my witness; and I'll trouble you not to make a move towards her when she comes in to identify you.

BLANCO [*retreating in terror*] A woman? She aint real: neither is the child.

ELDER DANIELS. He's raving about a woman and a child. I tell you he's gone off his chump.

STRAPPER [*calling to those without*] Shew the lady in there.

Feemy Evans comes in. She is a young woman of 23 or 24, with impudent manners, battered good looks, and dirty-fine dress.

ELDER DANIELS. Morning, Feemy.

FEEMY. Morning, Elder. [*She passes on and slips her arm familiarly through Strapper's*].

STRAPPER. Ever see him before, Feemy?

FEEMY. Thats the little lot that was on your horse this morning, Strapper. Not a doubt of it.

BLANCO [*implacably contemptuous*] Go home and wash yourself, you slut.

FEEMY [*reddening, and disengaging her arm from Strapper's*] I'm clean enough to hang you, anyway. [*Going over to him threateningly*]. Youre no true American man, to insult a woman like that.

BLANCO. A woman! Oh Lord!* You saw me on a horse, did you?

FEEMY. Yes, I did.

BLANCO. Got up early on purpose to do it, didnt you?

FEEMY. No I didnt: I stayed up late on a spree.*

BLANCO. I was on a horse, was I?

FEEMY. Yes you were; and if you deny it youre a liar.

BLANCO [*to Strapper*] She saw a man on a horse when she was too drunk to tell which was the man and which was the horse—

FEEMY [*breaking in*] You lie. I wasnt drunk—at least not as drunk as that.

BLANCO [*ignoring the interruption*]—and you found a man without a horse. Is a man on a horse the same as a man on foot? Yah! Take your witness away. Who's going to believe her? Throw her out on the dump. Youve got to find that horse before you get a rope round my neck. [*He turns away from her contemptuously, and sits at the table with his back to the jury box*].

FEEMY [*following him*] I'll hang you, you dirty horse-thief; or not a man in this camp will ever get a word or a look from me again. Youre just trash: thats what you are. White trash.

BLANCO. And what are you, darling? What are you? Youre a worse danger to a town like this than ten horse-thieves.

FEEMY. Mr Kemp: will you stand by and hear me insulted in that low way? [*To Blanco, spitefully*] I'll see you swung up and I'll see you cut down: I'll see you high and I'll see you low, as dangerous as I am. [*He laughs*]. Oh you neednt try to brazen it out. Youll look white enough before the boys are done with you.

BLANCO. You do me good, Feemy. Stay by me to the end, wont you? Hold my hand to the last; and I'll die game.* [*He puts out his hand: she strikes savagely at it; but he withdraws it in time and laughs at her discomfiture*].

FEEMY. You—

ELDER DANIELS. Never mind him, Feemy: he's not right in his head today. [*She receives the assurance with contemptuous incredulity, and sits down on the step of the Sheriff's dais*].

Sheriff Kemp comes in: a stout man, with large flat ears, and a neck thicker than his head.

ELDER DANIELS. Morning, Sheriff.

THE SHERIFF. Morning, Elder. [*Passing on*]. Morning, Strapper. [*Passing on*]. Morning, Miss Evans. [*Stopping between Strapper and Blanco*]. Is this the prisoner?

BLANCO [*rising*] Thats so. Morning, Sheriff.

THE SHERIFF. Morning. You know, I suppose, that if youve stole a horse and the jury find against you, you wont have any time to settle your affairs. Consequently, if you feel guilty, youd better settle em now.

BLANCO. Affairs be damned! Ive got none.

THE SHERIFF. Well, are you in a proper state of mind? Has the Elder talked to you?

BLANCO. He has. And I say it's against the law. It's torture: thats what it is.

ELDER DANIELS. He's not accountable. He's out of his mind, Sheriff. He's not fit to go into the presence of his Maker.

THE SHERIFF. You are a merciful man, Elder; but you wont take the boys with you there. [*To Blanco*] If it comes to hanging you, youd better for your own sake be hanged in a proper state of mind than in an improper one. But it wont make any difference to us: make no mistake about that.

BLANCO. Lord keep me wicked til I die! Now Ive said my little prayer. I'm ready. Not that I'm guilty, mind you; but this is a rotten town, dead certain to do the wrong thing.

THE SHERIFF. You wont be asked to live long in it, I guess. [*To Strapper*] Got the witness all right, Strapper?

STRAPPER. Yes, got everything.

BLANCO. Except the horse.

THE SHERIFF. Whats that? Aint you got the horse?

STRAPPER. No. He traded it before we overtook him, I guess. But Feemy saw him on it.

FEEMY. She did.

STRAPPER. Shall I call in the boys?

BLANCO. Just a moment, Sheriff. A good appearance is everything in a low-class place like this. [*He takes out a pocket comb and mirror, and retires towards the dais to arrange his hair*].

ELDER DANIELS. Oh, think of your immortal soul, man, not of your foolish face.

BLANCO. I cant change my soul, Elder: it changes me—sometimes. Feemy: I'm too pale. Let me rub my cheek against yours, darling.

FEEMY. You lie: my color's my own, such as it is. And a pretty color youll be when youre hung white and shot red.

BLANCO. Aint she spiteful, Sheriff?

THE SHERIFF. Time's wasted on you. [*To Strapper*] Go and see if the boys are ready. Some of them were short of cartridges, and went down to the store to buy them. They may as well have their fun; and itll be shorter for him.

STRAPPER. Young Jack has brought a boxful up. Theyre all ready.

THE SHERIFF [*going to the dais and addressing Blanco*] Your place is at the bar there. Take it. [*Blanco bows ironically and goes to the bar*]. Miss Evans: youd best sit at the table. [*She does so, at the corner nearest the bar. The Elder takes the opposite corner. The Sheriff takes his chair*]. All ready, Strapper.

STRAPPER [*at the door*] All in to begin.

The crowd comes in and fills the court. Babsy, Jessie, and Emma come to the Sheriff's right; Hannah and Lottie to his left.

THE SHERIFF. Silence there. The jury will take their places as usual. [*They do so*].

BLANCO. I challenge this jury, Sheriff.

THE FOREMAN. Do you, by Gosh?

THE SHERIFF. On what ground?

BLANCO. On the general ground that it's a rotten jury. [*Laughter*].

THE SHERIFF. Thats not a lawful ground of challenge.

THE FOREMAN. It's a lawful ground for me to shoot yonder skunk at sight, first time I meet him, if he survives this trial.

BLANCO. I challenge the Foreman because he's prejudiced.

THE FOREMAN. I say you lie. We mean to hang you, Blanco Posnet; but you will be hanged fair.

THE JURY. Hear, hear!

STRAPPER [*to the Sheriff*] George: this is rot. How can you get an unprejudiced jury if the prisoner starts by telling them theyre all rotten? If theres any prejudice against him he has himself to thank for it.

THE BOYS. Thats so. Of course he has. Insulting the court! Challenge be jiggered! Gag him.

NESTOR [*a juryman with a long white beard, drunk, the oldest man present*] Besides, Sheriff, I go so far as to say that the man that is not prejudiced against a horse-thief is not fit to sit on a jury in this town.

THE BOYS. Right. Bully for you, Nestor! Thats the straight truth. Of course he aint. Hear, hear!

THE SHERIFF. That is no doubt true, old man. Still, you must get as unprejudiced as you can. The critter has a right to his chance, such as he is. So now go right ahead. If the prisoner dont like this jury, he should have stole a horse in another town; for this is all the jury he'll get here.

THE FOREMAN. Thats so, Blanco Posnet.

THE SHERIFF [*to Blanco*] Dont you be uneasy. You will get justice here. It may be rough justice; but it is justice.

BLANCO. What is justice?

THE SHERIFF. Hanging horse-thieves is justice; so now you know. Now then: weve wasted enough time. Hustle with your witness there, will you?

BLANCO [*indignantly bringing down his fist on the bar*] Swear the jury. A rotten Sheriff you are not to know that the jury's got to be sworn.

THE FOREMAN [*galled*] Be swore for you! Not likely. What do *you* say, old son?

NESTOR [*deliberately and solemnly*] I say: GUILTY!!!

THE BOYS [*tumultuously rushing at Blanco*] Thats it. Guilty, guilty. Take him out and hang him. He's found guilty. Fetch a rope. Up with him. [*They are about to drag him from the bar*].

THE SHERIFF [*rising, pistol in hand*] Hands off that man. Hands off him, I say, Squinty, or I drop you, and would if you were my own son. [*Dead silence*]. I'm Sheriff here; and it's for me to say when he may lawfully be hanged. [*They release him*].

BLANCO. As the actor says in the play, 'a Daniel come to judgment.'* Rotten actor he was, too.

THE SHERIFF. Elder Daniel is come to judgment all right, my lad. Elder: the floor is yours. [*The Elder rises*]. Give your evidence. The truth and the whole truth and nothing but the truth, so help you God.

ELDER DANIELS. Sheriff: let me off this. I didnt ought to swear away this man's life. He and I are, in a manner of speaking, brothers.

THE SHERIFF. It does you credit, Elder: every man here will acknowledge it. But religion is one thing: law is another. In religion we're all brothers. In law we cut our brother off when he steals horses.

THE FOREMAN. Besides, you neednt hang him, you know. Theres plenty of willing hands to take that job off your conscience. So rip ahead, old son.

STRAPPER. Youre accountable to me for the horse until you clear yourself, Elder: remember that.

BLANCO. Out with it, you fool.

ELDER DANIELS. You might own up, Blanco, as far as my evidence goes. Everybody knows I borrowed one of the Sheriff's horses from Strapper because my own's gone lame. Everybody knows you arrived in the town yesterday and put up in my house. Everybody knows that in the morning the horse was gone and you were gone.

BLANCO [*in a forensic manner*] Sheriff: the Elder, though known to you and to all here as no brother of mine and the rottenest liar in this town, is speaking the truth for the first time in his life as far as what he says about me is concerned. As to the horse, I say nothing; except that it was the rottenest horse you ever tried to sell.

THE SHERIFF. How do you know it was a rotten horse if you didnt steal it?

BLANCO. I *dont* know of my own knowledge. I only argue that if the horse had been worth its keep, you wouldnt have lent it to Strapper, and Strapper wouldnt have lent it to this eloquent and venerable ram. [*Suppressed laughter*]. And now I ask him this. [*To the Elder*] Did we or did we not have a quarrel last evening about a certain article that was left by my mother, and that I considered I had a right to more than you?* And did you say one word to me about the horse not belonging to you?

ELDER DANIELS. Why should I? We never said a word about the horse at all. How was I to know what it was in your mind to do?

BLANCO. Bear witness all that I had a right to take a horse from him without stealing to make up for what he denied me. I am no thief. But you havnt proved yet that I took the horse. Strapper Kemp: had I the horse when you took me or had I not?

STRAPPER. No, nor you hadnt a railway train neither. But Feemy Evans saw you pass on the horse at four o'clock twenty-five miles from the spot where I took you at seven on the road to Pony Harbor. Did you walk twenty-five miles in three hours? That so, Feemy? eh?

FEEMY. Thats so. At four I saw him. [*To Blanco*] Thats done for you.

THE SHERIFF. You say you saw him on my horse?

FEEMY. I did.*

BLANCO. And I ate it, I suppose, before Strapper fetched up with me. [*Suddenly and dramatically*] Sheriff: I accuse Feemy of immoral relations with Strapper.

FEEMY. Oh you liar!*

BLANCO. I accuse the fair Euphemia of immoral relations with every man in this town, including yourself, Sheriff. I say this is a conspiracy to kill me between Feemy and Strapper because I wouldnt touch Feemy with a pair of tongs.* I say you darent hang any white man on the word of a woman of bad character. I stand on the honor and virtue of my American manhood. I say that she's not had the oath, and that you darent for the honor of the town give her the oath because her lips would blaspheme the holy Bible if they touched it. I say thats the law; and if you are a proper United States Sheriff and not a low-down lyncher, youll hold up the law and not let it be dragged in the mud by your brother's kept woman.

Great excitement among the women. The men much puzzled.

JESSIE. Thats right. She didnt ought to be let kiss the Book.

EMMA. How could the like of her tell the truth?

BABSY. It would be an insult to every respectable woman here to believe her.

FEEMY. It's easy to be respectable with nobody ever offering you a chance to be anything else.

THE WOMEN [*clamoring all together*] Shut up, you hussy. Youre a disgrace. How dare you open your lips to answer your betters? Hold your tongue and learn your place, miss. You painted slut! Whip her out of the town!

THE SHERIFF. Silence. Do you hear. Silence. [*The clamor ceases*]. Did anyone else see the prisoner with the horse?

FEEMY [*passionately*] Aint I good enough?

BABSY. No. Youre dirt: thats what you are.

FEEMY. And you—

THE SHERIFF. Silence. This trial is a man's job; and if the women forget their sex they can go out or be put out. Strapper and Miss Evans: you cant have it two ways. You can run straight, or you can run gay, so to speak; but you cant run both ways together. There is also a strong feeling among the men of this town that a line should be drawn between those that are straight wives and mothers and those that are, in the words of the Book of Books,* taking the primrose path.* We dont wish to be hard on any woman; and most of us have a personal regard for Miss Evans for the sake of old times; but theres no getting out of the fact that she has private reasons for wishing to oblige Strapper, and that—if she will excuse my saying so—she is not what I might call morally particular as to what she does to oblige him. Therefore I ask the prisoner not to drive us to give Miss Evans the oath. I ask him to tell us fair and square, as a man who has but a few minutes between him and eternity, what he done with my horse.

THE BOYS. Hear, hear! Thats right. Thats fair. That does it. Now, Blanco. Own up.

BLANCO. Sheriff: you touch me home. This is a rotten world; but there is still one thing in it that remains sacred even to the rottenest of us, and that is a horse.

THE BOYS. Good. Well said, Blanco. Thats straight.

BLANCO. You have a right to your horse, Sheriff; and if I could put you in the way of getting it back, I would. But if I had that horse I shouldnt be here. As I hope to be saved, Sheriff—or rather as I hope to be damned; for I have no taste for pious company and no talent for playing the harp—I know no more of that horse's whereabouts than you do yourself.

STRAPPER. Who did you trade him to?

BLANCO. I did not trade him. I got nothing for him or by him. I stand here with a rope round my neck for the want of him. When you took me, did I fight like a thief or run like a thief; and was there any sign of a horse on me or near me?

STRAPPER. You were looking at a rainbow like a damned silly fool instead of keeping your wits about you; and we stole up on you and had you tight before you could draw a bead on us.

THE SHERIFF. That dont sound like good sense. What would he look at a rainbow for?*

BLANCO. I'll tell you, Sheriff. I was looking at it because there was something written on it?

SHERIFF. How do you mean written on it?

BLANCO. The words were, 'Ive got the cinch* on you this time, Blanco Posnet.' Yes, Sheriff, I saw those words in green on the red streak of the rainbow; and as I saw them I felt Strapper's grab on my arm and Squinty's on my pistol.

THE FOREMAN. He's shammin mad:* thats what he is. Aint it about time to give a verdict and have a bit of fun, Sheriff?

THE BOYS. Yes, lets have a verdict. We're wasting the whole afternoon. Cut it short.*

THE SHERIFF [*making up his mind*] Swear Feemy Evans, Elder. She dont need to touch the Book. Let her say the words.

FEEMY. Worse people than me has kissed that Book. What wrong Ive done, most of you went shares in. Ive to live, havnt I? same as the rest of you. However, it makes no odds to me, I guess the truth is the truth and a lie is a lie, on the Book or off it.

BABSY. Do as youre told. Who are you, to be let talk about it?

THE SHERIFF. Silence there, I tell you. Sail ahead, Elder.

ELDER DANIELS. Feemy Evans: do you swear to tell the truth and the whole truth and nothing but the truth, so help you God.

FEEMY. I do, so help me—

SHERIFF. Thats enough. Now, on your oath, did you see the prisoner on my horse this morning on the road to Pony Harbor?

FEEMY. On my oath—[*Disturbance and crowding at the door*].

AT THE DOOR. Now then, now then! Where are you shovin to? Whats up? Order in court. Chuck him out. Silence. You cant come in here. Keep back.

Strapper rushes to the door and forces his way out.

SHERIFF [*savagely*] Whats this noise? Cant you keep quiet there? Is this a Sheriff's court or is it a saloon?

BLANCO. Dont interrupt a lady in the act of hanging a gentleman. Wheres your manners?

FEEMY. I'll hang you, Blanco Posnet. I will. I wouldnt for fifty dollars I hadnt seen you this morning. I'll teach you to be civil to me next time, for all I'm not good enough to kiss the Book.

BLANCO. Lord keep me wicked till I die! I'm game for anything while youre spitting dirt at me, Feemy.

RENEWED TUMULT AT THE DOOR. Here, whats this? Fire them out. Not me. Who are you that I should get out of your way? Oh, stow it. Well, she cant come in. What woman? What horse? Whats the good of shoving like that? Who says? No! you dont say!

THE SHERIFF. Gentlemen of the Vigilance Committee: clear that doorway. Out with them in the name of the law.

STRAPPER [*without*] Hold hard, George. [*At the door*] Theyve got the horse. [*He comes in, followed by Waggoner Jo, an elderly carter, who crosses the court to the jury side. Strapper pushes his way to the Sheriff and speaks privately to him*].

THE BOYS. What! No! Got the horse! Sheriff's horse! Who took it, then? Where? Get out. Yes it is, sure. I tell you it is. It's the horse all right enough. Rot. Go and look. By Gum!*

THE SHERIFF [*to Strapper*] You dont say!

STRAPPER. It's here, I tell you.

WAGGONER JO. It's here all right enough, Sheriff.

STRAPPER. And theyve got the thief too.*

ELDER DANIELS. Then it aint Blanco.

STRAPPER. No: it's a woman. [*Blanco yells and covers his eyes with his hands*].

THE WHOLE CROWD. A woman!

THE SHERIFF. Well, fetch her in. [*Strapper goes out. The Sheriff continues, to Feemy*] And what do *you* mean, you lying jade,* by putting up this story on us about Blanco?

FEEMY. I aint put up no story on you. This is a plant: you see if it isnt.

Strapper returns with a woman. Her expression of intense grief silences them as they crane over one another's heads to see her. Strapper takes her to the corner of the table. The Elder moves up to make room for her.

BLANCO [*terrified*] Sheriff: that woman aint real. You take care. That woman will make you do what you never intended. Thats the rainbow woman. Thats the woman that brought me to this.

THE SHERIFF. Shut your mouth, will you. Youve got the horrors. [*To the woman*] Now you. Who are you? and what are you doing with a horse that doesnt belong to you?

THE WOMAN. I took it to save my child's life. I thought it would get me to a doctor in time. The child was choking with croup.*

BLANCO [*strangling, and trying to laugh*] A little choker: thats the word for him. His choking wasnt real: wait and see mine. [*He feels his neck with a sob*].

THE SHERIFF. Wheres the child?

STRAPPER. On Pug Jackson's bench in his shed. He's makin a coffin for it.

BLANCO [*with a horrible convulsion of the throat—frantically*] Dead! The little Judas* kid! The child I gave my life for! [*He breaks into hideous laughter*].

THE SHERIFF [*jarred beyond endurance by the sound*] Hold your noise, will you. Shove his neckerchief into his mouth if he dont stop. [*To the woman*] Dont you mind him, maam: he's mad with drink and devilment. I suppose theres no fake about this, Strapper. Who found her?

WAGGONER JO. I did, Sheriff. Theres no fake about it. I came on her on the track round by Red Mountain. She was settin on the ground with the dead body on her lap, stupid-like. The horse was grazin on the other side o the road.

THE SHERIFF [*puzzled*] Well, this is blamed queer. [*To the woman*] What call had you to take the horse from Elder Daniels' stable to find a doctor? Theres a doctor in the very next house.

BLANCO [*mopping his dabbled red crest* and trying to be ironically gay*] Story simply wont wash, my angel. You got it from the man that stole the horse. He gave it to you because he was a softy and went to bits when you played off the sick kid on him. Well, I guess that clears me. I'm not that sort. Catch me putting my neck in a noose for anybody's kid!

THE FOREMAN. Dont you go putting her up to what to say. She said she took it.

THE WOMAN. Yes: I took it from a man that met me. I thought God sent him to me. I rode here joyfully thinking so all the time to myself. Then I noticed that the child was like lead in my arms. God would never have been so cruel as to send me the horse to disappoint me like that.

BLANCO. Just what He *would* do.

STRAPPER. We aint got nothin to do with that. This is the man, aint he? [*pointing to Blanco*].

THE WOMAN [*pulling herself together after looking scaredly at Blanco, and then at the Sheriff and at the jury*] No.

THE FOREMAN. You lie.

THE SHERIFF. Youve got to tell us the truth. Thats the law, you know.

THE WOMAN. The man looked a bad man. He cursed me; and he cursed the child: God forgive him! But something came over him. I was desperate. I put the child in his arms; and it got its little fingers down his neck and called him Daddy and tried to kiss him; for it was not right in its head with the fever. He said it was a little Judas kid, and that it was betraying him with a kiss,* and that he'd swing for it. And then he gave me the horse, and went away crying and laughing and singing dreadful dirty wicked words to hymn tunes like as if he had seven devils in him.

STRAPPER. She's lying. Give her the oath, George.

THE SHERIFF. Go easy there. Youre a smart boy, Strapper; but youre not Sheriff yet. This is my job. You just wait. I submit that we're in a difficulty here. If Blanco was the man, the lady cant, as a white woman, give him away. She oughtnt to be put in the position of having either to give him away or commit perjury. On the other hand, we dont want a horse-thief to get off through a lady's delicacy.

THE FOREMAN. No we dont; and we dont intend he shall. Not while I am foreman of this jury.

BLANCO [*with intense expression*] A rotten foreman! Oh, what a rotten foreman!

THE SHERIFF. Shut up, will you. Providence shews us a way out here. Two women saw Blanco with a horse. One has a delicacy about saying so. The other will excuse me saying that delicacy is not her strongest holt.* She can give the necessary witness. Feemy Evans: youve taken the oath. You saw the man that took the horse.

FEEMY. I did. And he was a low-down rotten drunken lying hound that would go further to hurt a woman any day than to help her. And if he ever did a good action it was because he was too drunk to know what he was doing. So it's no harm to hang him. She said he cursed her and went away blaspheming and singing things that were not fit for the child to hear.

BLANCO [*troubled*] I didnt mean them for the child to hear, you venomous devil.

THE SHERIFF. All thats got nothing to do with us. The question you have to answer is, *was* that man Blanco Posnet?

THE WOMAN. No. I say no. I swear it. Sheriff: dont hang that man: oh dont. You may hang me instead if you like: Ive nothing to live for now. You darent take her word against mine. She never had a child: I can see it in her face.

FEEMY [*stung to the quick*] I can hang him in spite of you, anyhow. Much good your child is to you now, lying there on Pug Jackson's bench!

BLANCO [*rushing at her with a shriek*] I'll twist your heart out of you for that. [*They seize him before he can reach her*].

FEEMY [*mocking him as he struggles to get at her*] Ha, ha, Blanco Posnet. You cant touch me; and I can hang you. Ha, ha! Oh, I'll do for you.

I'll twist your heart and I'll twist your neck [*He is dragged back to the bar and leans on it, gasping and exhausted*]. Give me the oath again, Elder. I'll settle him. And do you [*to the woman*] take your sickly face away from in front of me.

STRAPPER. Just turn your back on her there, will you?

THE WOMAN. God knows I dont want to see her commit murder. [*She folds her shawl over her head*].

THE SHERIFF. Now, Miss Evans: cut it short. Was the prisoner the man you saw this morning or was he not? Yes or no?

FEEMY [*a little hysterically*] I'll tell you fast enough. Dont think I'm a softy.

THE SHERIFF [*losing patience*] Here: weve had enough of this. You tell the truth, Feemy Evans; and let us have no more of your lip. Was the prisoner the man or was he not? On your oath?

FEEMY. On my oath and as I'm a living woman—[*flinching*] Oh God! he felt the little child's hands on his neck—I cant [*bursting into a flood of tears and scolding at the other woman*] It's you with your snivelling face that has put me off it. [*Desperately*] No: it wasnt him. I only said it out of spite because he insulted me. May I be struck dead if I ever saw him with the horse!

Everybody draws a long breath. Dead silence.

BLANCO [*whispering at her*] Softy! Cry-baby! Landed like me! Doing what you never intended! [*Taking up his hat and speaking in his ordinary tone*] I presume I may go now, Sheriff.

STRAPPER. Here, hold hard.

THE FOREMAN. Not if we know it, you dont.

THE BOYS [*barring the way to the door*] You stay where you are. Stop a bit, stop a bit. Dont you be in such a hurry. Dont let him go. Not much.

Blanco stands motionless, his eye fixed, thinking hard, and apparently deaf to what is going on.

THE SHERIFF [*rising solemnly*] Silence there. Wait a bit. I take it that if the Sheriff is satisfied and the owner of the horse is satisfied, theres no more to be said. I have had to remark on former occasions that what is wrong with this court is that theres too many Sheriffs in it. Today there is going to be one, and only one; and that one is your humble servant. I call that to the notice of the Foreman of the jury, and also to the notice of young Strapper. I am also the owner of the horse. Does any man say I am not? [*Silence*]. Very well, then. In my opinion, to commandeer a horse for the purpose of getting a dying child to a doctor is not stealing, provided, as in the present case, that the horse is returned safe and sound. I rule that there has been no theft.

NESTOR. That aint the law.

THE SHERIFF. I fine you a dollar for contempt of court, and will collect it myself off you as you leave the building. And as the boys have been disappointed of their natural sport, I shall give them a little fun by standing outside the door and taking up a collection for the bereaved mother of the late kid that shewed up Blanco Posnet.

THE BOYS. A collection. Oh, I say! Calls that sport? Is this a mothers' meeting? Well, I'll be jiggered!* Where does the sport come in?

THE SHERIFF [*continuing*] The sport comes in, my friends, not so much in contributing as in seeing others fork out. Thus each contributes to the general enjoyment; and all contribute to his. Blanco Posnet: you go free under the protection of the Vigilance Committee for just long enough to get you out of this town, which is not a healthy place for you. As you are in a hurry, I'll sell you the horse at a reasonable figure. Now, boys, let nobody go out till I get to the door. The court is adjourned. [*He goes out*].

STRAPPER [*to Feemy, as he goes to the door*] I'm done with you. Do you hear? I'm done with you. [*He goes out sulkily*].

FEEMY [*calling after him*] As if I cared about a stingy brat like you! Go back to the freckled maypole* you left for me: youve been fretting for her long enough.

THE FOREMAN [*To Blanco, on his way out*] A man like you makes me sick. Just sick. [*Blanco makes no sign. The Foreman spits disgustedly, and follows Strapper out. The Jurymen leave the box, except Nestor, who collapses in a drunken sleep*].*

BLANCO [*Suddenly rushing from the bar to the table and jumping up on it*] Boys, I'm going to preach you a sermon on the moral of this day's proceedings.

THE BOYS [*crowding round him*] Yes: lets have a sermon. Go ahead, Blanco. Silence for Elder Blanco. Tune the organ. Let us pray.

NESTOR [*staggering out of his sleep*] Never hold up your head in this town again. I'm done with you.

BLANCO [*pointing inexorably to Nestor*] Drunk in church. Disturbing the preacher. Hand him out.

THE BOYS [*chivying Nestor out*] Now, Nestor, outside. Outside, Nestor. Out you go. Get your subscription ready for the Sheriff. Skiddoo,* Nestor.

NESTOR. Afraid to be hanged! Afraid to be hanged! [*At the door*] Coward! [*He is thrown out*].

BLANCO. Dearly beloved brethren—

A BOY. Same to you, Blanco. [*Laughter*].

BLANCO. And many of them. Boys: this is a rotten world.

ANOTHER BOY. Lord have mercy on us, miserable sinners. [*More laughter*].

BLANCO [*Forcibly*] No: thats where youre wrong. Dont flatter yourselves that youre miserable sinners. Am I a miserable sinner? No: I'm a fraud and a failure.* I started in to be a bad man like the rest of you. You all started in to be bad men or you wouldnt be in this jumped-up, jerked-off, hospital-turned-out camp that calls itself a town. I took the broad path because I thought I was a man and not a snivelling canting turning-the-other-cheek* apprentice angel serving his time in a vale of tears.* They talked Christianity to us on Sundays; but when they really meant business they told us never to take a blow without giving it back, and to get dollars. When they talked the golden rule* to me, I just looked at them as if they werent there, and spat. But when they told me to try to live my life so that I could always look my fellowman straight in the eye and tell him to go to hell, that fetched me.

THE BOYS. Quite right. Good. Bully for you, Blanco, old son. Right good sense too. Aha-a-ah!

BLANCO. Yes; but whats come of it all? Am I a real bad man? a man of game and grit? a man that does what he likes and goes over or through other people to his own gain? or am I a snivelling cry-baby that let

a horse his life depended on be took from him by a woman, and then
sat on the grass looking at the rainbow and let himself be took like
a hare in a trap by Strapper Kemp: a lad whose back I or any grown
man here could break against his knee? I'm a rottener fraud and
failure than the Elder here. And youre all as rotten as me, or youd
have lynched me.

A BOY. Anything to oblige you, Blanco.

ANOTHER. We can do it yet if you feel really bad about it.

BLANCO. No: the devil's gone out of you. We're all frauds. Theres
none of us real good and none of us real bad.

ELDER DANIELS. There is One above, Blanco.

BLANCO. What do you know about Him? you that always talk as if He
never did anything without asking your rotten leave first? Why did
the child die? Tell me that if you can. He cant have wanted to kill the
child. Why did He make me go soft on the child if He was going hard
on it Himself? Why should He go hard on the innocent kid and go
soft on a rotten thing like me? Why did I go soft myself? Why did the
Sheriff go soft? Why did Feemy go soft? Whats this game that upsets
our game? For seems to me theres two games bein played. Our game
is a rotten game that makes me feel I'm dirt and that youre all as
rotten dirt as me. T'other game may be a silly game; but it aint
rotten. When the Sheriff played it he stopped being rotten. When
Feemy played it the paint nearly dropped off her face. When I played
it I cursed myself for a fool; but I lost the rotten feel all the same.

ELDER DANIELS. It was the Lord speaking to your soul, Blanco.

BLANCO. Oh yes: you know all about the Lord, dont you? Youre in
the Lord's confidence. He wouldnt for the world do anything to
shock you, would He, Boozy dear? Yah! What about the croup? It
was early days when He made the croup, I guess. It was the best He
could think of then; but when it turned out wrong on His hands He
made you and me to fight the croup for Him. You bet He didnt
make us for nothing; and He wouldnt have made us at all if He
could have done His work without us. By Gum, that must be
what we're for! He'd never have made us to be rotten drunken
blackguards like me, and good-for-nothing rips* like Feemy. He
made me because He had a job for me. He let me run loose til the
job was ready; and then I had to come along and do it, hanging or

no hanging. And I tell you it didnt feel rotten: it felt *bully*,* just bully. Anyhow, I got the rotten feel off me for a minute of my life; and I'll go through fire to get it off me again.* Look here! which of you will marry Feemy Evans?

THE BOYS [*uproariously*] Who speaks first? Who'll marry Feemy? Come along, Jack. Nows your chance, Peter. Pass along a husband for Feemy. Oh my! Feemy!

FEEMY [*shortly*] Keep your tongue off me, will you?

BLANCO. Feemy was a rose of the broad path, wasnt she? You all thought her the champion bad woman of this district. Well, she's a failure as a bad woman; and I'm a failure as a bad man. So let Brother Daniels marry us to keep all the rottenness in the family. What do you say, Feemy?

FEEMY. Thank you; but when I marry I'll marry a man that could do a decent action without surprising himself out of his senses. Youre like a child with a new toy: you and your bit of human kindness!

THE WOMAN. How many would have done it with their life at stake?

FEEMY. Oh well, if youre so much taken with him, marry him yourself. Youd be what people call a good wife to him, wouldnt you?

THE WOMAN. I was a good wife to the child's father. I dont think any woman wants to be a good wife twice in her life. I want somebody to be a good husband to me now.

BLANCO. Any offer, gentlemen, on that understanding? [*The boys shake their heads*]. Oh, it's a rotten game, our game. Heres a real good woman; and she's had enough of it, finding that it only led to being put upon.

HANNAH. Well, if there was nothing wrong in the world there wouldnt be anything left for us to do, would there?*

ELDER DANIELS. Be of good cheer, brothers. Seek the path.

BLANCO. No. No more paths. No more broad and narrow. No more good and bad. Theres no good and bad;* but by Jiminy, gents, theres a rotten game, and theres a great game. I played the rotten game; but the great game was played on me; and now I'm for the great game every time. Amen. Gentlemen: let us adjourn to the saloon. I stand the drinks. [*He jumps down from the table*].

THE BOYS. Right you are, Blanco. Drinks round. Come along, boys. Blanco's standing. Right along to the Elder's. Hurrah! [*They rush out, dragging the Elder with them*].

BLANCO [*to Feemy, offering his hand*] Shake, Feemy.

FEEMY. Get along, you blackguard.

BLANCO. It's come over me again, same as when the kid touched me, same as when you swore a lie to save my neck.*

FEEMY. Oh well, here. [*They shake hands*].

GREAT CATHERINE

(WHOM GLORY STILL ADORES)

THE AUTHOR'S APOLOGY
FOR GREAT CATHERINE

EXCEPTION has been taken to the title of this seeming tomfoolery on
the ground that the Catherine it represents is not Great Catherine,* but
the Catherine whose gallantries provide some of the lightest pages of
modern history. Great Catherine, it is said, was the Catherine whose
diplomacy, whose campaigns and conquests, whose plans of Liberal
reform, whose correspondence with Grimm and Voltaire* enabled her
to cut such a magnificent figure in the XVIII century. In reply, I can
only confess that Catherine's diplomacy and her conquests do not interest
me. It is clear to me that neither she nor the statesmen with whom she
played this mischievous kind of political chess had any notion of the real
history of their own times, or of the real forces that were moulding Europe.
The French Revolution, which made such short work of Catherine's
Voltairean principles, surprised and scandalized her as much as it surprised and scandalized any provincial governess in the French chateaux.

The main difference between her and our modern Liberal
Governments was that whereas she talked and wrote quite intelligently
about Liberal principles before she was frightened into making such
talking and writing a flogging matter, our Liberal ministers take the
name of Liberalism in vain without knowing or caring enough about its
meaning even to talk and scribble about it, and pass their flogging Bills,
and institute their prosecutions for sedition and blasphemy and so
forth, without the faintest suspicion that such proceedings need any
apology from the Liberal point of view.

It was quite easy for Patiomkin* to humbug* Catherine as to the condition of Russia by conducting her through sham cities run up for the
occasion by scenic artists; but in the little world of European court
intrigue and dynastic diplomacy which was the only world she knew
she was more than a match for him and for all the rest of her contemporaries. In such intrigue and diplomacy, however, there was no
romance, no scientific political interest, nothing that a sane mind can
now retain even if it can be persuaded to waste time in reading it up.
But Catherine as a woman, with plenty of character and (as we should
say) no morals, still fascinates and amuses us as she fascinated and
amused her contemporaries. They were great sentimental comedians,
these Peters, Elizabeths, and Catherines* who played their Tsarships as
eccentric character parts, and produced scene after scene of furious

harlequinade* with the monarch as clown, and of tragic relief in the torture chamber with the monarch as pantomime demon committing real atrocities, not forgetting the indispensable love interest on an enormous and utterly indecorous scale. Catherine kept this vast Guignol Theatre* open for nearly half a century, not as a Russian, but as a highly domesticated German lady whose household routine was not at all so unlike that of Queen Victoria as might be expected from the difference in their notions of propriety in sexual relations.

In short, if Byron* leaves you with an impression that he said very little about Catherine, and that little not what was best worth saying, I beg to correct your impression by assuring you that what Byron said was all there really is to say that is worth saying. His Catherine is my Catherine and everybody's Catherine. The young man who gains her favor is a Spanish nobleman in his version. I have made him an English country gentleman,* who gets out of his rather dangerous scrape by simplicity, sincerity, and the courage of these qualities. By this I have given some offence to the many Britons who see themselves as heroes: what they mean by heroes being theatrical snobs of superhuman pretensions which, though quite groundless, are admitted with awe by the rest of the human race. They say I think an Englishman a fool. When I do, they have themselves to thank.

I must not, however, pretend that historical portraiture was the motive of a play that will leave the reader as ignorant of Russian history as he may be now before he has turned the page. Nor is the sketch of Catherine complete even idiosyncratically, leaving her politics out of the question. For example, she wrote bushels of plays.* I confess I have not yet read any of them. The truth is, this play grew out of the relations which inevitably exist in the theatre between authors and actors. If the actors have sometimes to use their skill as the author's puppets rather than in full self-expression, the author has sometimes to use his skill as the actors' tailor, fitting them with parts written to display the virtuosity of the performer rather than to solve problems of life, character, or history. Feats of this kind may tickle an author's technical vanity; but he is bound on such occasions to admit that the performer for whom he writes is 'the onlie begetter'* of his work, which must be regarded critically as an addition to the debt dramatic literature owes to the art of acting and its exponents. Those who have seen Miss Gertrude Kingston* play the part of Catherine will have no difficulty in believing that it was her talent rather than mine that brought the play into existence. I once recommended Miss Kingston professionally to play queens. Now in the modern drama there were no queens for her to play;

and as to the older literature of our stage, did it not provoke the veteran actress in Sir Arthur Pinero's Trelawny of the Wells* to declare that, as parts, queens are not worth a tinker's oath?* Miss Kingston's comment on my suggestion, though more elegantly worded, was to the same effect; and it ended in my having to make good my advice by writing Great Catherine. History provided no other queen capable of standing up to our joint talents.

In composing such bravura pieces, the author limits himself only by the range of the virtuoso, which by definition far transcends the modesty of nature. If my Russians seem more Muscovite than any Russian, and my English people more insular than any Briton, I will not plead, as I honestly might, that the fiction has yet to be written that can exaggerate the reality of such subjects; that the apparently outrageous Patiomkin is but a timidly bowdlerized ghost of the original; and that Captain Edstaston is no more than a miniature that might hang appropriately on the walls of nineteen out of twenty English country houses to this day. An artistic presentment must not condescend to justify itself by a comparison with crude nature; and I prefer to admit that in this kind my *dramatis personae* are, as they should be, of the stage stagey, challenging the actor to act up to them or beyond them, if he can. The more heroic the overcharging, the better for the performance.

In dragging the reader thus for a moment behind the scenes, I am departing from a rule which I have hitherto imposed on myself so rigidly that I never permit myself, even in a stage direction, to let slip a word that could bludgeon the imagination of the reader by reminding him of the boards and the footlights and the sky borders and the rest of the theatrical scaffolding, for which nevertheless I have to plan as carefully as if I were the head carpenter as well as the author. But even at the risk of talking shop, an honest playwright should take at least one opportunity of acknowledging that his art is not only limited by the art of the actor, but often stimulated and developed by it. No sane and skilled author writes plays that present impossibilities to the actor or to the stage engineer. If, as occasionally happens, he asks them to do things that they have never done before and cannot conceive as presentable or possible (as Wagner and Thomas Hardy have done,* for example), it is always found that the difficulties are not really insuperable, the author having foreseen unsuspected possibilities both in the actor and in the audience, whose will-to-make-believe can perform the quaintest miracles. Thus may authors advance the arts of acting and of staging plays. But the actor also may enlarge the scope of the drama by displaying powers not previously discovered by the author. If the best available actors are only Horatios,* the authors will have to leave Hamlet out, and be content with Horatios for heroes. Some of the difference between Shakespear's Orlandos and Bassanios and Bertrams* and his Hamlets and Macbeths must have been due not only to his development as a dramatic poet, but to the development of Burbage* as an actor. Playwrights do not write for ideal actors when their livelihood is at stake: if they did, they would write parts for heroes with twenty arms like an Indian god.* Indeed the actor often influences the author too much; for I can remember a time (I am not implying that it is yet wholly past) when the art of writing a fashionable play had become very largely the art of writing it 'round' the personalities of a group of fashionable performers of whom Burbage would certainly have said that their parts needed no acting. Everything has its abuse as well as its use.

It is also to be considered that great plays live longer than great actors, though little plays do not live nearly so long as the worst of their exponents. The consequence is that the great actor, instead of putting pressure on contemporary authors to supply him with heroic parts, falls back on the Shakespearean repertory, and takes what he needs from a dead hand. In the nineteenth century, the careers of Kean, Macready, Barry Sullivan,* and Irving, ought to have produced a group of heroic plays comparable in intensity to those of Æschylus, Sophocles, and Euripides; but nothing of the kind happened: these actors played the works of dead authors, or, very occasionally, of live poets who were hardly regular professional playwrights. Sheridan Knowles, Bulwer Lytton, Wills, and Tennyson* produced a few glaringly artificial high horses for the great actors of their time; but the playwrights proper, who really kept the theatre going, and were kept going by the theatre, did not cater for the great actors: they could not afford to compete with a bard who was not of an age but for all time, and who had, moreover, the overwhelming attraction for the actor-managers of not charging author's fees. The result was that the playwrights and the great actors ceased to think of themselves as having any concern with one another: Tom Robertson, Ibsen, Pinero, and Barrie* might as well have belonged to a different solar system as far as Irving was concerned; and the same was true of their respective predecessors.

Thus was established an evil tradition; but I at least can plead that it does not always hold good. If Forbes Robertson had not been there to play Caesar,* I should not have written Caesar and Cleopatra. If Ellen Terry* had never been born, Captain Brassbound's Conversion* would never have been effected. The Devil's Disciple,* with which I won my *cordon bleu** in America as a potboiler,* would have had a different sort of hero if Richard Mansfield* had been a different sort of actor, though the actual commission to write it came from an English actor, William Terriss, who was assassinated* before he recovered from the dismay into which the result of his rash proposal threw him. For it must be said that the actor or actress who inspires or commissions a play as often as not regards it as a Frankenstein's monster,* and will none of it. That does not make him or her any the less parental in the fecundity of the playwright.

To an author who has any feeling of his business there is a keen and whimsical joy in divining and revealing a side of an actor's genius overlooked before, and unsuspected even by the actor himself. When I snatched Mr Louis Calvert* from Shakespear, and made him wear a frock coat and silk hat on the stage for perhaps the first time in his life, I do not think he expected in the least that his performance would enable me to boast of his Tom Broadbent as a genuine stage classic. Mrs Patrick Campbell* was famous before I wrote for her, but not for playing illiterate cockney flowermaidens. And in the case which is provoking me to all these impertinences, I am quite sure that Miss Gertrude Kingston, who first made her reputation as an impersonator of the most delightfully feather-headed and inconsequent ingenues, thought me more than usually mad when I persuaded her to play the Helen of Euripides,* and then launched her on a queenly career as Catherine of Russia.

It is not the whole truth that if we take care of the actors the plays will take care of themselves; nor is it any truer that if we take care of the plays the actors will take care of themselves. There is both give and take in the business. I have seen plays written for actors that made me exclaim, 'How oft the sight of means to do ill deeds makes deeds ill done!'* But Burbage may have flourished the prompt copy of Hamlet under Shakespear's nose at the tenth rehearsal and cried, 'How oft the sight of means to do great deeds makes playwrights great!' I say the tenth because I am convinced that at the first he denounced his part as a rotten one; thought the ghost's speech ridiculously long; and wanted to play the king. Anyhow, whether he had the wit to utter it or not, the boast would have been a valid one. The best conclusion is that every actor should say, 'If I create the hero in myself, God will send an author to write his part.' For in the long run the actors will get the authors, and the authors the actors, they deserve.

GREAT CATHERINE (WHOM GLORY STILL ADORES)

THE FIRST SCENE

1776. *Patiomkin in his bureau in the Winter Palace, St Petersburg.* Huge palatial apartment: style, Russia in the XVIII century imitating the Versailles du Roi Soleil.* Extravagant luxury. Also dirt and disorder.*

Patiomkin, gigantic in stature and build, his face marred by the loss of one eye and a marked squint in the other, sits at the end of a table littered with papers and the remains of three or four successive breakfasts. He has supplies of coffee and brandy at hand sufficient for a party of ten. His coat, encrusted with diamonds, is on the floor. It has fallen off a chair placed near the other end of the table for the convenience of visitors. His court sword, with its attachments, is on the chair. His three-cornered hat, also bejewelled, is on the table. He himself is half dressed in an unfastened shirt and an immense dressing-gown, once gorgeous, now food-splashed and dirty, as it serves him for towel, handkerchief, duster, and every other use to which a textile fabric can be put by a slovenly man. It does not conceal his huge hairy chest, nor his half-buttoned knee breeches, nor his legs. These are partly clad in silk stockings, which he occasionally hitches up to his knees, and presently shakes down to his shins, by his restless movements. His feet are thrust into enormous slippers, worth, with their crust of jewels, several thousand roubles* apiece.

Superficially Patiomkin is a violent, brutal barbarian, an upstart despot of the most intolerable and dangerous type, ugly, lazy, and disgusting in his personal habits. Yet ambassadors report him the ablest man in Russia, and the one who can do most with the still abler Empress Catherine II, who is not a Russian but a German, by no means barbarous or intemperate in her personal habits. She not only disputes with Frederick the Great the reputation of being the cleverest monarch in Europe, but may even put in a very plausible claim to be the cleverest and most attractive individual alive. Now she not only tolerates Patiomkin long after she has got over her first romantic attachment to him, but esteems him highly as a counsellor and a good friend. His love letters are among the best on record. He has a wild sense of humor, which enables him to laugh at himself as well as at everybody else. In the eyes of the English visitor now about to be admitted to his presence he may be an outrageous ruffian. In fact he actually is an outrageous ruffian, in no matter whose eyes; but the visitor will find out, as everyone else sooner or later finds out, that he is a man to be reckoned with even by those who are not intimidated by his temper, bodily strength, and exalted rank.

A pretty young lady, Varinka,* his favorite niece, is lounging on an ottoman between his end of the table and the door, very sulky and dissatisfied, perhaps because he is preoccupied with his papers and his brandy bottle, and she can see nothing of him but his broad back.

There is a screen behind the ottoman.

An old soldier, a Cossack* sergeant, enters.

THE SERGEANT [*softly to the lady, holding the door handle*] Little darling honey: is his Highness the prince very busy?

VARINKA. His Highness the prince is *very* busy. He is singing out of tune; he is biting his nails; he is scratching his head; he is hitching up his untidy stockings; he is making himself disgusting and odious to everybody; and he is pretending to read state papers that he does not understand because he is too lazy and selfish to talk and be companionable.

PATIOMKIN [*growls; then wipes his nose with his dressing-gown*]!!

VARINKA. Pig. Ugh! [*She curls herself up with a shiver of disgust and retires from the conversation*].

THE SERGEANT [*stealing across to the coat, and picking it up to replace it on the back of the chair*] Little Father: the English captain, so highly recommended to you by old Fritz of Prussia,* by the English ambassador, and by Monsieur Voltaire (whom [*crossing himself*] may God in his infinite mercy damn eternally!), is in the antechamber and desires audience.

PATIOMKIN [*deliberately*] To hell with the English captain; and to hell with old Fritz of Prussia; and to hell with the English ambassador; and to hell with Monsieur Voltaire; and to hell with you too!

THE SERGEANT. Have mercy on me, Little Father. Your head is bad this morning. You drink too much French brandy and too little good Russian kvass.*

PATIOMKIN [*with sudden fury*] Why are visitors of consequence announced by a sergeant? [*Springing at him and seizing him by the throat*] What do you mean by this, you hound? Do you want five thousand blows of the stick? Where is General Volkonsky?*

THE SERGEANT [*on his knees*] Little Father: you kicked his Highness downstairs.

PATIOMKIN [*flinging him down and kicking him*] You lie, you dog. You lie.

THE SERGEANT. Little Father: life is hard for the poor. If you say it is a lie, it is a lie. He *fell* downstairs. I picked him up; and he kicked me. They all kick me when you kick them. God knows that is not just, Little Father!

PATIOMKIN [*laughs ogreishly; then returns to his place at the table, chuckling*]!!!

VARINKA. Savage! Boor! It is a disgrace. No wonder the French sneer at us as barbarians.

THE SERGEANT [*who has crept round the table to the screen, and insinuated himself between Patiomkin's back and Varinka*] Do you think the Prince will see the Captain, little darling?

PATIOMKIN. He will not see any captain. Go to the devil!

THE SERGEANT. Be merciful, Little Father. God knows it is your duty to see him! [*To Varinka*] Intercede for him and for me, beautiful little darling. He has given me a rouble.

PATIOMKIN. Oh, send him in, send him in, and stop pestering me. Am I never to have a moment's peace?

The Sergeant salutes joyfully and hurries out, divining that Patiomkin has intended to see the English captain all along, and has played this comedy of fury and exhausted impatience to conceal his interest in the visitor.

VARINKA. Have you no shame? You refuse to see the most exalted persons. You kick princes and generals downstairs. And then you see an English captain merely because he has given a rouble to that common soldier. It is scandalous.

PATIOMKIN. Darling beloved, I am drunk; but I know what I am doing. I wish to stand well with the English.

VARINKA. And you think you will impress an Englishman by receiving him as you are now, half drunk?

PATIOMKIN [*gravely*] It is true: the English despise men who cannot drink. I must make myself *wholly* drunk [*he takes a huge draught of brandy*].

VARINKA. Sot!*

The Sergeant returns ushering a handsome strongly built young English officer in the uniform of a Light Dragoon.* He is evidently on fairly good terms with himself, and very sure of his social position. He crosses the room to the end of the table opposite Patiomkin's, and awaits the civilities of that statesman with confidence. The Sergeant remains prudently at the door.

THE SERGEANT [*paternally*] Little Father: this is the English captain, so well recommended to her sacred Majesty the Empress. God knows, he needs your countenance and protec—[*he vanishes precipitately, seeing that Patiomkin is about to throw a bottle at him. The Captain contemplates these preliminaries with astonishment, and with some displeasure, which is not allayed when Patiomkin, hardly condescending to look at his visitor, of whom he nevertheless takes stock with the corner of his one eye, says gruffly*] Well?

EDSTASTON. My name is Edstaston: * Captain Edstaston of the Light Dragoons. I have the honor to present to your Highness this letter from the British ambassador, which will give you all necessary particulars. [*He hands Patiomkin the letter*].

PATIOMKIN [*tearing it open and glancing at it for about a second*] What do you want?

EDSTASTON. The letter will explain to your Highness who I am.

PATIOMKIN. I dont want to know who you are. What do you want?

EDSTASTON. An audience of the Empress. [*Patiomkin contemptuously throws the letter aside. Edstaston adds hotly*] Also some civility, if you please.

PATIOMKIN [*with derision*] Ho!

VARINKA. My uncle is receiving you with unusual civility, Captain. He has just kicked a general downstairs.

EDSTASTON. A Russian general, madam?

VARINKA. Of course.

EDSTASTON. I must allow myself to say, madam, that your uncle had better not attempt to kick an English officer downstairs.

PATIOMKIN. You want me to kick you upstairs: eh? You want an audience of the Empress.

EDSTASTON. I have said nothing about kicking, sir. If it comes to that, my boots shall speak for me. Her Majesty has signified a desire to have news of the rebellion in America.* I have served against the rebels; and I am instructed to place myself at the disposal of her Majesty, and to describe the events of the war to her, as an eye-witness, in a discreet and agreeable manner.

PATIOMKIN. Psha! I know. You think if she once sets eyes on your face and your uniform your fortune is made. You think that if she could stand a man like me, with only one eye, and a cross eye at that, she must fall down at your feet at first sight, eh?

EDSTASTON [*shocked and indignant*] I think nothing of the sort: and I'll trouble you not to repeat it. If I were a Russian subject and you made such a boast about my queen, I'd strike you across the face with my sword. [*Patiomkin, with a yell of fury, rushes at him*]. Hands off, you swine! [*As Patiomkin, towering over him, attempts to seize him by the throat, Edstaston, who is a bit of a wrestler, adroitly backheels him. He falls, amazed, on his back*].

VARINKA [*rushing out*] Help! Call the guard! The Englishman is murdering my uncle! Help! Help!

The guard and the Sergeant rush in. Edstaston draws a pair of small pistols from his boots, and points one at the Sergeant and the other at Patiomkin, who is sitting on the floor, somewhat sobered. The soldiers stand irresolute.

EDSTASTON. Stand off. [*To Patiomkin*] Order them off, if you dont want a bullet through your silly head.

THE SERGEANT. Little Father: tell us what to do. Our lives are yours; but God knows you are not fit to die.

PATIOMKIN [*absurdly self-possessed*] Get out.

THE SERGEANT. Little Father—

PATIOMKIN [*roaring*] Get out. Get out, all of you. [*They withdraw, much relieved at their escape from the pistol. Patiomkin attempts to rise, and rolls over*]. Here! help me up, will you? Dont you see that I'm drunk and cant get up?

EDSTASTON [*suspiciously*] You want to get hold of me.

PATIOMKIN [*squatting resignedly against the chair on which his clothes hang*] Very well, then: I shall stay where I am, because I'm drunk and youre afraid of me.

EDSTASTON. I'm not afraid of you, damn you!

PATIOMKIN [*ecstatically*] Darling: your lips are the gates of truth. Now listen to me. [*He marks off the items of his statement with ridiculous stiff gestures of his head and arms, imitating a puppet*] You are Captain Whathisname; and your uncle is the Earl of Whatdyecallum; and your father is Bishop of Thingummybob; and you are a young man of the highest spr–promise (I told you I was drunk), educated at Cambridge,* and got your step as captain in the field at the GLORIOUS battle of Bunker's Hill.* Invalided home from America at the request of Aunt Fanny, Lady-in-Waiting to the Queen. All right, eh?

EDSTASTON. How do you know all this?

PATIOMKIN [*crowing fantastically*] In er lerrer, darling, darling, darling, darling. Lerrer you shewed me.

EDSTASTON. But you didnt read it.

PATIOMKIN [*flapping his fingers at him grotesquely*] Only one eye, darling. Cross eye. Sees everything. Read lerrer ince-ince-istastaneously. Kindly give me vinegar borle.* Green borle. On'y to sober me. Too drunk to speak proply. If you would be so kind, darling. Green borle. [*Edstaston, still suspicious, shakes his head and keeps his pistols ready*]. Reach it myself. [*He reaches behind him up to the table, and snatches at the green bottle, from which he takes a copious draught. Its effect is appalling. His wry faces and agonized belchings are so heartrending that they almost upset Edstaston. When the victim at last staggers to his feet, he is a pale fragile nobleman, aged and quite sober, extremely dignified in manner and address, though shaken by his recent convulsions*]. Young man: it is not better to be drunk than sober; but it is happier. Goodness is not happiness. That is an epigram. But I have overdone this. I am too sober to be good company. Let me redress the balance. [*He takes a generous draught of brandy, and recovers his geniality*]. Aha! Thats better. And now listen, darling. You must not come to Court with pistols in your boots.

EDSTASTON. I have found them useful.

PATIOMKIN. Nonsense. I'm your friend. You mistook my intention because I was drunk. Now that I am sober—in moderation—I will prove that I am your friend. Have some diamonds. [*Roaring*] Hullo there! Dogs, pigs: hullo!

The Sergeant comes in.

THE SERGEANT. God be praised, Little Father: you are still spared to us.

PATIOMKIN. Tell them to bring some diamonds. Plenty of diamonds. And rubies. Get out. [*He aims a kick at the Sergeant, who flees*]. Put up your pistols, darling. I'll give you a pair with gold handgrips. I am your friend.

EDSTASTON [*replacing the pistols in his boots rather unwillingly*] Your Highness understands that if I am missing, or if anything happens to me, there will be trouble.

PATIOMKIN [*enthusiastically*] Call me darling.

EDSTASTON. It is not the English custom.

PATIOMKIN. You have no hearts, you English! [*Slapping his right breast*] Heart! Heart!

EDSTASTON. Pardon, your Highness: your heart is on the other side.

PATIOMKIN [*surprised and impressed*] Is it? You are learned! You are a doctor! You English are wonderful! We are barbarians, drunken pigs. Catherine does not know it; but we are. Catherine's a German. But I have given her a Russian heart [*he is about to slap himself again*].

EDSTASTON [*delicately*] The other side, your Highness.

PATIOMKIN [*maudlin*] Darling: a true Russian has a heart on both sides.

The Sergeant enters carrying a goblet filled with precious stones.

PATIOMKIN. Get out. [*He snatches the goblet and kicks the Sergeant out, not maliciously but from habit, indeed not noticing that he does it*]. Darling: have some diamonds. Have a fistful. [*He takes up a handful and lets them slip back through his fingers into the goblet, which he then offers to Edstaston*].

EDSTASTON. Thank you: I dont take presents.

PATIOMKIN [*amazed*] You refuse!

EDSTASTON. I thank your Highness; but it is not the custom for English gentlemen to take presents of that kind.

PATIOMKIN. Are you really an Englishman?

EDSTASTON [*bows*]!

PATIOMKIN. You are the first Englishman I ever saw refuse anything he could get. [*He puts the goblet on the table; then turns again to Edstaston*]. Listen, darling. You are a wrestler: a splendid wrestler. You threw me on my back like magic, though I could lift you with one hand. Darling: you are a giant, a paladin.*

EDSTASTON [*complacently*] We wrestle rather well in my part of England.

PATIOMKIN. I have a Turk who is a wrestler: a prisoner of war. You shall wrestle with him for me. I'll stake a million roubles on you.

EDSTASTON [*incensed*] Damn you! do you take me for a prize-fighter? How dare you make me such a proposal?

PATIOMKIN [*with wounded feeling*] Darling: there is no pleasing you. Dont you like me?

EDSTASTON [*mollified*] Well, in a sort of way I do; though I dont know why I should. But my instructions are that I am to see the Empress; and——

PATIOMKIN. Darling: you *shall* see the Empress. A glorious woman, the greatest woman in the world. But lemme give you piece 'vice—pah! still drunk. They water my vinegar. [*He shakes himself; clears his throat; and resumes soberly*] If Catherine takes a fancy to you, you may ask for roubles, diamonds, palaces, titles, orders, anything! and you may aspire to everything: field-marshal, admiral, minister, what you please—except Tsar.

EDSTASTON. I tell you I dont want to ask for anything. Do you suppose I am an adventurer and a beggar?

PATIOMKIN [*plaintively*] Why not, darling? *I* was an adventurer. *I* was a beggar.

EDSTASTON. Oh, you!

PATIOMKIN. Well: whats wrong with me?

EDSTASTON. You are a Russian. Thats different.

PATIOMKIN [*effusively*] Darling: I am a man; and you are a man; and Catherine is a woman. Woman reduces us all to the common denominator. [*Chuckling*]. Again an epigram! [*Gravely*] You understand it, I hope. Have you had a college education, darling? *I* have.

EDSTASTON. Certainly. I am a Bachelor of Arts.

PATIOMKIN. It is enough that you are a bachelor, darling: Catherine will supply the arts. Aha! Another epigram? I am in the vein today.

EDSTASTON [*embarrassed and a little offended*] I must ask your Highness to change the subject. As a visitor in Russia, I am the guest of the Empress; and I must tell you plainly that I have neither the right nor the disposition to speak lightly of her Majesty.

PATIOMKIN. You have conscientious scruples?

EDSTASTON. I have the scruples of a gentleman.

PATIOMKIN. In Russia a gentleman has no scruples. In Russia we face facts.

EDSTASTON. In England, sir, a gentleman never faces any facts if they are unpleasant facts.

PATIOMKIN. In real life, darling, all facts are unpleasant. [*Greatly pleased with himself*] Another epigram! Where is my accursed chancellor? these gems should be written down and recorded for posterity. [*He rushes to the table; sits down; and snatches up a pen. Then, recollecting himself,*] But I have not asked you to sit down. [*He rises and goes to the other chair*]. I am a savage: a barbarian. [*He throws the shirt and coat over the table on to the floor and puts his sword on the table*]. Be seated, Captain.

EDSTASTON. Thank you.

They bow to one another ceremoniously. Patiomkin's tendency to grotesque exaggeration costs him his balance: he nearly falls over Edstaston, who rescues him and takes the proffered chair.

PATIOMKIN [*resuming his seat*] By the way, what was the piece of advice I was going to give you?

EDSTASTON. As you did not give it, I dont know. Allow me to add that I have not asked for your advice.

PATIOMKIN. I give it to you unasked, delightful Englishman. I remember it now. It was this. Dont try to become Tsar of Russia.

EDSTASTON [*in astonishment*] I havnt the slightest intention—

PATIOMKIN. Not now; but you will have: take my word for it. It will strike you as a splendid idea to have conscientious scruples—to desire the blessing of the Church on your union with Catherine.

EDSTASTON [*rising in utter amazement*] My union with Catherine! Youre mad.

PATIOMKIN [*unmoved*] The day you hint at such a thing will be the day of your downfall. Besides, it is not lucky to be Catherine's husband. You know what happened to Peter?

EDSTASTON [*shortly: sitting down again*] I do not wish to discuss it.

PATIOMKIN. You think she murdered him?

EDSTASTON. I know that people have said so.

PATIOMKIN [*thunderously: springing to his feet*] It is a lie: Orloff murdered him.* [*Subsiding a little*] He also knocked my eye out; but [*sitting down placidly*] I succeeded him for all that. And [*patting Edstaston's hand very affectionately*] I'm sorry to say, darling, that if you become Tsar, *I* shall murder *you*.

EDSTASTON [*ironically returning the caress*] Thank you. The occasion will not arise. [*Rising*] I have the honor to wish your Highness good morning.

PATIOMKIN [*jumping up and stopping him on his way to the door*] Tut tut! I'm going to take you to the Empress *now*, this very instant.

EDSTASTON. In these boots? Impossible! I must change.

PATIOMKIN. Nonsense! You shall come just as you are. You shall shew her your calves later on.

EDSTASTON. But it will take me only half an hour to—

PATIOMKIN. In half an hour it will be too late for the *petit lever*.* Come along. Damn it, man, I must oblige the British ambassador, and the French ambassador, and old Fritz, and Monsieur Voltaire and the rest of them. [*He shouts rudely to the door*] Varinka! [*To Edstaston, with tears in his voice*] Varinka shall persuade you: nobody can refuse Varinka anything. My niece. A treasure, I assure you. Beautiful! devoted! fascinating! [*Shouting again*] Varinka: where the devil are you?

VARINKA [*returning*] I'll not be shouted for. You have the voice of a bear, and the manners of a tinker.

PATIOMKIN. Tsh-sh-sh. Little angel Mother: you must behave yourself before the English captain. [*He takes off his dressing-gown*

*and throws it over the papers and the breakfasts; picks up his coat; and
disappears behind the screen to complete his toilette].**

EDSTASTON. Madam! [*He bows*].

VARINKA [*curtseying*] Monsieur le Capitaine!

EDSTASTON. I must apologize for the disturbance I made, madam.

PATIOMKIN [*behind the screen*] You must not call her madam. You
must call her Little Mother, and beautiful darling.

EDSTASTON. My respect for the lady will not permit it.

VARINKA. Respect! How can you respect the niece of a savage?

EDSTASTON [*deprecating*] Oh, madam!

VARINKA. Heaven is my witness, Little English Father, we need
someone who is not afraid of him. He is so strong! I hope you will
throw him down on the floor many, many, many times.

PATIOMKIN [*behind the screen*] Varinka!

VARINKA. Yes?

PATIOMKIN. Go and look through the keyhole of the Imperial bedchamber; and bring me word whether the Empress is awake yet.

VARINKA. Fi donc!* I do not look through keyholes.

PATIOMKIN [*emerging, having arranged his shirt and put on his diamonded
coat*] You have been badly brought up, little darling. Would any lady
or gentleman walk unannounced into a room without first looking
through the keyhole? [*Taking his sword from the table and putting it
on*] The great thing in life is to be simple; and the perfectly simple
thing is to look through keyholes. Another epigram: the fifth this
morning! Where is my fool of a chancellor? Where is Popof?*

EDSTASTON [*choking with suppressed laughter*]!!!!

PATIOMKIN [*gratified*] Darling: you appreciate my epigram.

EDSTASTON. Excuse me. Pop off! Ha! ha! I cant help laughing. Whats
his real name, by the way, in case I meet him?

VARINKA [*surprized*] His real name? Popof, of course. Why do you
laugh, Little Father?

EDSTASTON. How can anyone with a sense of humor help laughing?
Pop off! [*He is convulsed*].

VARINKA [*looking at her uncle, taps her forehead significantly*]!!

PATIOMKIN [*aside to Varinka*] No: only English. He will amuse Catherine. [*To Edstaston*] Come! you shall tell the joke to the Empress: she is by way of being a humorist [*he takes him by the arm, and leads him towards the door*].

EDSTASTON [*resisting*] No, really. I am not fit—

PATIOMKIN. Persuade him, Little angel Mother.

VARINKA [*taking his other arm*] Yes, yes, yes, Little English Father: God knows it is your duty to be brave and wait on the Empress. Come.

EDSTASTON. No. I had rather—

PATIOMKIN [*hauling him along*] Come.

VARINKA [*pulling him and coaxing him*] Come, little love: you cant refuse me.

EDSTASTON. But how can I?

PATIOMKIN. Why not? She wont eat you.

VARINKA. She will; but you must come.

EDSTASTON. I assure you—it is quite out of the question—my clothes.

VARINKA. You look perfect.

PATIOMKIN. Come along, darling.

EDSTASTON [*struggling*] Impossible—

VARINKA. Come, come, come.

EDSTASTON. No. Believe me—I dont wish—I—

VARINKA. Carry him, uncle.

PATIOMKIN [*lifting him in his arms like a father carrying a little boy*] Yes: I'll carry you.

EDSTASTON. Dash it all, this is ridiculous!

VARINKA [*seizing his ankles and dancing as he is carried out*] You must come. If you kick you will blacken my eyes.

PATIOMKIN. Come, baby, come.

By this time they have made their way through the door and are out of hearing.

THE SECOND SCENE

The Empress's petit lever. The central doors are closed. Those who enter through them find on their left, on a dais of two broad steps, a magnificent curtained bed. Beyond it a door in the panelling leads to the Empress's cabinet. Near the foot of the bed, in the middle of the room, stands a gilt chair, with the Imperial arms carved and the Imperial monogram embroidered.

The Court is in attendance, standing in two melancholy rows down the side of the room opposite to the bed, solemn, bored, waiting for the Empress to awaken. The Princess Dashkoff,* with two ladies, stands a little in front of the line of courtiers, by the Imperial chair. Silence, broken only by the yawns and whispers of the courtiers. Naryshkin, the Chamberlain,* stands by the head of the bed.

A loud yawn is heard from behind the curtains.

NARYSHKIN [*holding up a warning hand*] Ssh!

The courtiers hastily cease whispering; dress up their lines; and stiffen. Dead silence. A bell tinkles within the curtains. Naryshkin and the Princess solemnly draw them and reveal the Empress.
Catherine turns over on her back, and stretches herself.

CATHERINE [*yawning*] Heigho—ah—yah—ah—ow—what o'clock is it? [*Her accent is German*].

NARYSHKIN [*formally*] Her Imperial Majesty is awake. [*The Court falls on its knees*].

ALL. Good morning to your Majesty.

NARYSHKIN. Half-past ten, Little Mother.

CATHERINE [*sitting up abruptly*] Potztausend!* [*Contemplating the kneeling courtiers*] Oh, get up, get up. [*All rise*]. Your etiquette bores me. I am hardly awake in the morning before it begins. [*Yawning again, and relapsing sleepily against her pillows*] Why do they do it, Naryshkin?

NARYSHKIN. God knows it is not for your sake, Little Mother. But you see if you were not a great queen they would all be nobodies.

CATHERINE [*sitting up*] They make me do it to keep up their own little dignities? So?

NARYSHKIN. Exactly. Also because if they didnt you might have them flogged, dear Little Mother.

CATHERINE [*springing energetically out of bed and seating herself on the edge of it*] Flogged! I! A Liberal Empress! A philosopher! You are a barbarian, Naryshkin. [*She rises and turns to the courtiers*] And then, as if I cared! [*She turns again to Naryshkin*] You should know by this time that I am frank and original in character, like an Englishman. [*She walks about restlessly*]. No: what maddens me about all this ceremony is that I am the only person in Russia who gets no fun out of my being Empress. You all glory in me: you bask in my smiles: you get titles and honors and favors from me: you are dazzled by my crown and my robes: you feel splendid when you have been admitted to my presence; and when I say a gracious word to you, you talk about it to everyone you meet for a week afterwards. But what do *I* get out of it? Nothing. [*She throws herself into the chair. Naryshkin deprecates with a gesture: she hurls an emphatic repetition at him*] Nothing!! I wear a crown until my neck aches: I stand looking majestic until I am ready to drop: I have to smile at ugly old ambassadors and frown and turn my back on young and handsome ones. Nobody gives *me* anything. When I was only an Archduchess, the English ambassador used to give me money whenever I wanted it—or rather whenever *he* wanted to get anything out of my sacred predecessor Elizabeth* [*the Court bows to the ground*]; but now that I am Empress he never gives me a kopek.* When I have headaches and colics I envy the scullerymaids. And you are not a bit grateful to me for all my care of you, my work, my thought, my fatigue, my sufferings.

THE PRINCESS DASHKOFF. God knows, Little Mother, we all implore you to give your wonderful brain a rest. That is why you get headaches. Monsieur Voltaire also has headaches. His brain is just like yours.

CATHERINE. Dashkoff: what a liar you are! [*Dashkoff curtsies with impressive dignity*]. And you think you are flattering me! Let me tell you I would not give a rouble to have the brains of all the philosophers in France. What is our business for today?

NARYSHKIN. The new museum, Little Mother. But the model will not be ready until tonight.

CATHERINE [*rising eagerly*] Yes: the museum. An enlightened capital should have a museum. [*She paces the chamber with a deep sense of the importance of the museum*]. It shall be one of the wonders of the world. I must have specimens: specimens, specimens, specimens.

NARYSHKIN. You are in high spirits this morning, Little Mother.

CATHERINE [*with sudden levity*] I am always in high spirits, even when people do not bring me my slippers. [*She runs to the chair and sits down, thrusting her feet out*].

The two ladies rush to her feet, each carrying a slipper. Catherine, about to put her feet into them, is checked by a disturbance in the antechamber.

PATIOMKIN [*carrying Edstaston through the antechamber*] Useless to struggle. Come along, beautiful baby darling. Come to Little Mother. [*He sings*]

> March him baby,
> Baby, baby,
> Lit-tle ba-by bumpkins.*

VARINKA [*joining in to the same doggerel in canon, a third above*]* March him, baby, etc., etc.

EDSTASTON [*trying to make himself heard*] No, no. This is carrying a joke too far. I must insist. Let me down! Hang it, *will* you let me down! Confound it! No, no. Stop playing the fool, will you? We dont understand this sort of thing in England. I shall be disgraced. Let me down.

CATHERINE [*meanwhile*] What a horrible noise! Naryshkin: see what it is.

Naryshkin goes to the door.

CATHERINE [*listening*] That is Prince Patiomkin.

NARYSHKIN [*calling from the door*] Little Mother: a stranger.

Catherine plunges into bed again and covers herself up. Patiomkin, followed by Varinka, carries Edstaston in; dumps him down on the foot of the bed; and staggers past it to the cabinet door. Varinka joins the courtiers at the opposite side of the room. Catherine, blazing with wrath, pushes Edstaston off her bed on to the floor; gets out of bed; and turns on Patiomkin with so terrible an expression that all kneel down hastily except Edstaston, who is sprawling on the carpet in angry confusion.

CATHERINE. Patiomkin: how dare you? [*Looking at Edstaston*] What is this?

PATIOMKIN [*on his knees: tearfully*] I dont know. I am drunk. What is this, Varinka?

EDSTASTON [*scrambling to his feet*] Madam: this drunken ruffian—

PATIOMKIN. Thas true. Drungn ruffian. Took dvantage of my being drunk. Said: take me to Lil angel Mother. Take me to beaufl Empress. Take me to the grea'st woman on earth. Thas whas he said. I took him. I was wrong. I am not sober.

CATHERINE. Men have grown sober in Siberia* for less, Prince.

PATIOMKIN. Serve em right! Sgusting habit. Ask Varinka.

Catherine turns her face from him to the Court. The courtiers see that she is trying not to laugh, and know by experience that she will not succeed. They rise, relieved and grinning.

VARINKA. It is true. He drinks like a pig.

PATIOMKIN [*plaintively*] No: not like pig. Like prince. Lil Mother made poor Patiomkin prince. Whas use being prince if I maynt drink?

CATHERINE [*biting her lips*] Go. I am offended.

PATIOMKIN. Dont scold, Ll Mother.

CATHERINE [*imperiously*] Go.

PATIOMKIN [*rising unsteadily*] Yes: go. Go bye bye. Very sleepy. Berr go bye bye than go Siberia. Go bye bye in Lil Mother's bed [*he pretends to make an attempt to get into the bed*].

CATHERINE [*energetically pulling him back*] No, no! Patiomkin! What are you thinking of? [*He falls like a log on the floor, apparently dead drunk*].

THE PRINCESS DASHKOFF. Scandalous! An insult to your Imperial Majesty!

CATHERINE. Dashkoff: you have no sense of humor. [*She steps down to the floor level and looks indulgently at Patiomkin. He gurgles brutishly. She has an impulse of disgust*]. Hog. [*She kicks him as hard as she can*]. Oh! You have broken my toe. Brute. Beast. Dashkoff is quite right. Do you hear?

PATIOMKIN. If you ask my pi-pinion of Dashkoff, my pipinion is that Dashkoff is drunk. Scanlous. Poor Patiomkin go bye bye. [*He relapses into drunken slumbers*].

Some of the courtiers move to carry him away.

CATHERINE [*stopping them*] Let him lie. Let him sleep it off. If he goes out it will be to a tavern and low company for the rest of the day. [*Indulgently*] There! [*She takes a pillow from the bed and puts it under his head; then turns to Edstaston; surveys him with perfect dignity; and asks, in her queenliest manner*] Varinka: who is this gentleman?

VARINKA. A foreign captain: I cannot pronounce his name. I think he is mad. He came to the Prince and said he must see your Majesty. He can talk of nothing else. We could not prevent him.

EDSTASTON [*overwhelmed by this apparent betrayal*] Oh! Madam: I am perfectly sane: I am actually an Englishman. I should never have dreamt of approaching your Majesty without the fullest credentials. I have letters from the English ambassador, from the Prussian ambassador. [*Naïvely*] But everybody assured me that Prince Patiomkin is all-powerful with your Majesty; so I naturally applied to him.

PATIOMKIN [*interrupts the conversation by an agonized wheezing groan, as of a donkey beginning to bray*]!!!

CATHERINE [*like a fishfag*]* Schweig, du Hund.* [*Resuming her impressive Royal manner*] Have you never been taught, sir, how a gentleman should enter the presence of a sovereign.

EDSTASTON. Yes, Madam; but I did not enter your presence: I was carried.

CATHERINE. But you say you asked the Prince to carry you.

EDSTASTON. Certainly not, Madam. I protested against it with all my might. I appeal to this lady to confirm me.

VARINKA [*pretending to be indignant*] Yes: you protested. But, all the same, you were very very *very* anxious to see her Imperial Majesty. You blushed when the Prince spoke of her. You threatened to strike him across the face with your sword because you thought he did not speak enthusiastically enough of her. [*To Catherine*] Trust me: he has seen your Imperial Majesty before.

CATHERINE [*to Edstaston*] You have seen us before?

EDSTASTON. At the review, Madam.

VARINKA [*triumphantly*] Aha! I knew it. Your Majesty wore the hussar uniform. He saw how radiant! how splendid! your Majesty looked.

Oh! he has dared to admire your Majesty. Such insolence is not to be endured.

EDSTASTON. All Europe is a party to that insolence, Madam.

THE PRINCESS DASHKOFF. All Europe is content to do so at a respectful distance. It is possible to admire her Majesty's policy and her eminence in literature and philosophy without performing acrobatic feats in the Imperial bed.

EDSTASTON. I know nothing about her Majesty's eminence in policy or philosophy: I dont pretend to understand such things. I speak as a practical man. And I never knew that foreigners had any policy: I always thought that policy was Mr Pitt's business.*

CATHERINE [*lifting her eyebrows*] So?

VARINKA. What else did you presume to admire her Majesty for, pray?

EDSTASTON [*addled*] Well, I—I—I—that is, I—[*He stammers himself dumb*].

CATHERINE [*after a pitiless silence*] We are waiting for your answer.

EDSTASTON. But I never said I admired your Majesty. The lady has twisted my words.

VARINKA. You dont admire her, then?

EDSTASTON. Well, I—naturally—of course, I cant deny that the uniform was very becoming—perhaps a little unfeminine—still—

Dead silence. Catherine and the Court watch him stonily. He is wretchedly embarrassed.

CATHERINE [*with cold majesty*] Well, sir: is that all you have to say?

EDSTASTON. Surely there is no harm in noticing that er—that er—[*He stops again*].

CATHERINE. Noticing that er—? [*He gazes at her, speechless, like a fascinated rabbit. She repeats fiercely*] That er—?

EDSTASTON [*startled into speech*] Well, that your Majesty was—was—[*Soothingly*] Well, let me put it this way: that it was rather natural for a man to admire your Majesty without being a philosopher.

CATHERINE [*suddenly smiling and extending her hand to him to be kissed*] Courtier!

EDSTASTON [*kissing it*] Not at all. Your Majesty is very good. I have been very awkward; but I did not intend it. I am rather stupid, I am afraid.

CATHERINE. Stupid! By no means. Courage, Captain: we are pleased. [*He falls on his knee. She takes his cheeks in her hands; turns up his face; and adds*] We are *greatly* pleased. [*She slaps his cheek coquettishly: he bows almost to his knee*]. The *petit lever* is over. [*She turns to go into the cabinet, and stumbles against the supine Patiomkin*]. Ach! [*Edstaston springs to her assistance, seizing Patiomkin's heels and shifting him out of the Empress's path*]. We thank you, Captain.

He bows gallantly, and is rewarded by a very gracious smile. Then Catherine goes into her cabinet, followed by the Princess Dashkoff, who turns at the door to make a deep curtsey to Edstaston.

VARINKA. Happy Little Father! Remember: *I* did this for you. [*She runs out after the Empress*].

Edstaston, somewhat dazed, crosses the room to the courtiers, and is received with marked deference, each courtier making him a profound bow or curtsey before withdrawing through the central doors. He returns each obeisance with a nervous jerk, and turns away from it, only to find another courtier bowing at the other side. The process finally reduces him to distraction, as he bumps into one in the act of bowing to another and then has to bow his apologies. But at last they are all gone except Naryshkin.

EDSTASTON. Ouf!

PATIOMKIN [*jumping up vigorously*] You have done it, darling. Superbly! Beautifully!

EDSTASTON [*astonished*] Do you mean to say you are not drunk?

PATIOMKIN. Not dead drunk, darling. Only diplomatically drunk. As a drunken hog, I have done for you in five minutes what I could not have done in five months as a sober man. Your fortune is made. She likes you.

EDSTASTON. The devil she does!

PATIOMKIN. Why? Arnt you delighted?

EDSTASTON. Delighted! Gracious heavens, man, I am engaged to be married.

PATIOMKIN. What matter? She is in England, isnt she?

EDSTASTON. No. She has just arrived in St Petersburg.

THE PRINCESS DASHKOFF [*returning*] Captain Edstaston: the Empress is robed, and commands your presence.

EDSTASTON. Say I was gone before you arrived with the message. [*He hurries out. The other three, too taken aback to stop him, stare after him in the utmost astonishment*].

NARYSHKIN [*turning from the door*] She will have him knouted. He is a dead man.

THE PRINCESS DASHKOFF. But what am *I* to do? I cannot take such an answer to the Empress.

PATIOMKIN. P-P-P-P-P-P-W-W-W-W-W-rrrrrr [*a long puff, turning into a growl*]! [*He spits*]. I must kick somebody.

NARYSHKIN [*flying precipitately through the central doors*] No, no. Please.

THE PRINCESS DASHKOFF [*throwing herself recklessly in front of Patiomkin as he starts in pursuit of the Chamberlain*] Kick me. Disable me. It will be an excuse for not going back to her. Kick me hard.

PATIOMKIN. Yah! [*He flings her on the bed and dashes after Naryshkin*].

THE THIRD SCENE

In a terrace garden overlooking the Neva.* Claire, a robust young English lady, is leaning on the river wall. She turns expectantly on hearing the garden gate opened and closed. Edstaston hurries in. With a cry of delight she throws her arms round his neck.

CLAIRE. Darling!

EDSTASTON [*making a wry face*] Dont call me darling.

CLAIRE [*amazed and chilled*] Why?

EDSTASTON. I have been called darling all the morning.

CLAIRE [*with a flash of jealousy*] By whom?

EDSTASTON. By everybody. By the most unutterable swine. And if we do not leave this abominable city now: do you hear? *now*: I shall be called darling by the Empress.

CLAIRE [*with magnificent snobbery*] She would not dare. Did you tell her you were engaged to me?

EDSTASTON. Of course not.

CLAIRE. Why?

EDSTASTON. Because I didnt particularly want to have you knouted, and to be hanged or sent to Siberia myself.

CLAIRE. What on earth do you mean?

EDSTASTON. Well, the long and short of it is—dont think me a coxcomb,* Claire: it is too serious to mince matters—I have seen the Empress; and—

CLAIRE. Well: you wanted to see her.

EDSTASTON. Yes; but the Empress has seen *me*.

CLAIRE. She has fallen in love with you.

EDSTASTON. How did you know?

CLAIRE. Dearest: as if anyone could help it.

EDSTASTON. Oh, dont make me feel like a fool. But, though it does sound conceited to say it, I flatter myself I'm better looking than

Patiomkin and the other hogs she is accustomed to. Anyhow, I darent risk staying.

CLAIRE. What a nuisance! Mamma will be furious at having to pack, and at missing the Court ball this evening.

EDSTASTON. I cant help that. We havnt a moment to lose.

CLAIRE. May I tell her she will be knouted if we stay?

EDSTASTON. Do, dearest.

He kisses her and lets her go, expecting her to run into the house.

CLAIRE [*pausing thoughtfully*] Is she—is she good-looking when you see her close?

EDSTASTON. Not a patch on you, dearest.

CLAIRE [*jealous*] Then you *did* see her close?

EDSTASTON. Fairly close.

CLAIRE. Indeed! How close? No: thats silly of me: I will tell mamma. [*She is going out when Naryshkin enters with the Sergeant and a squad of soldiers*]. What do you want here?

The Sergeant goes to Edstaston; plumps down on his knees; and takes out a magnificent pair of pistols with gold grips. He proffers them to Edstaston, holding them by the barrels.

NARYSHKIN. Captain Edstaston: his Highness Prince Patiomkin sends you the pistols he promised you.

THE SERGEANT. Take them, Little Father; and do not forget us poor soldiers who have brought them to you; for God knows we get but little to drink.

EDSTASTON [*irresolutely*] But I cant take these valuable things. By Jiminy, though, theyre beautiful! Look at them, Claire.

As he is taking the pistols the kneeling Sergeant suddenly drops them; flings himself forward; and embraces Edstaston's hips to prevent him from drawing his own pistols from his boots.

THE SERGEANT. Lay hold of him there. Pin his arms. I have his pistols. [*The soldiers seize Edstaston*].

EDSTASTON. Ah, would you, damn you! [*He drives his knee into the Sergeant's epigastrium,* and struggles furiously with his captors*].

THE SERGEANT [*rolling on the ground, gasping and groaning*] Owgh! Murder! Holy Nicholas!* Owwwgh!

CLAIRE. Help! help! They are killing Charles. Help!

NARYSHKIN [*seizing her and clapping his hand over her mouth*] Tie him neck and crop. Ten thousand blows of the stick if you let him go. [*Claire twists herself loose; turns on him; and cuffs him furiously*] Yow—ow! Have mercy, Little Mother.

CLAIRE. You wretch! Help! Help! Police! We are being murdered. Help!

The Sergeant, who has risen, comes to Naryshkin's rescue, and grasps Claire's hands, enabling Naryshkin to gag her again. By this time Edstaston and his captors are all rolling on the ground together. They get Edstaston on his back and fasten his wrists together behind his knees. Next they put a broad strap round his ribs. Finally they pass a pole through this breast strap and through the wrist strap and lift him by it, helplessly trussed up, to carry him off. Meanwhile he is by no means suffering in silence.

EDSTASTON [*gasping*] You shall hear more of this. Damn you, will you untie me? I will complain to the ambassador. I will write to the Gazette.* England will blow your trumpery little fleet out of the water and sweep your tinpot army into Siberia for this. Will you let me go? Damn you! Curse you! What the devil do you mean by it? I'll—I'll—I'll—[*he is carried out of hearing*].

NARYSHKIN [*snatching his hands from Claire's face with a scream, and shaking his finger frantically*] Agh! [*The Sergeant, amazed, lets go her hands*]. She has bitten me, the little vixen.

CLAIRE [*spitting and wiping her mouth disgustedly*] How dare you put your dirty paws on my mouth? Ugh! Psha!

THE SERGEANT. Be merciful, Little angel Mother.

CLAIRE. Do not presume to call me your little angel mother. Where are the police?

NARYSHKIN. We are the police in St Petersburg, little spitfire.

THE SERGEANT. God knows we have no orders to harm you, Little Mother. Our duty is done. You are well and strong; but I shall never be the same man again. He is a mighty and terrible fighter, as stout as a bear. He has broken my sweetbread* with his strong knees. God knows poor folk should not be set upon such dangerous adversaries!

CLAIRE. Serve you right! Where have they taken Captain Edstaston to?

NARYSHKIN [*spitefully*] To the Empress, little beauty. He has insulted the Empress. He will receive a hundred and one blows of the knout. [*He laughs and goes out, nursing his bitten finger*].

THE SERGEANT. He will feel only the first twenty; and he will be mercifully dead long before the end, little darling.

CLAIRE [*sustained by an invincible snobbery*] They dare not touch an English officer. I will go to the Empress myself; she cannot know who Captain Edstaston is—who *we* are.

THE SERGEANT. Do so in the name of the Holy Nicholas, little beauty.

CLAIRE. Dont be impertinent. How can I get admission to the palace?

THE SERGEANT. Everybody goes in and out of the palace, little love.

CLAIRE. But I must get into the Empress's presence. I must speak to her.

THE SERGEANT. You shall, dear Little Mother. You shall give the poor old Sergeant a rouble; and the blessed Nicholas will make your salvation his charge.

CLAIRE [*impetuously*] I will give you [*she is about to say fifty roubles, but checks herself cautiously*]—Well: I dont mind giving you two roubles if I can speak to the Empress.

THE SERGEANT [*joyfully*] I praise Heaven for you, Little Mother. Come. [*He leads the way out*]. It was the temptation of the devil that led your young man to bruise my vitals and deprive me of breath. We must be merciful to one another's faults.

THE FOURTH SCENE

A triangular recess communicating by a heavily curtained arch with the huge ballroom of the palace. The light is subdued by red shades on the candles. In the wall adjoining that pierced by the arch is a door. The only piece of furniture is a very handsome chair on the arch side. In the ballroom they are dancing a polonaise* to the music of a brass band.*

Naryshkin enters through the door, followed by the soldiers carrying Edstaston, still trussed to the pole. Exhausted and dogged, he makes no sound.

NARYSHKIN. Halt. Get that pole clear of the prisoner. [*They dump Edstaston on the floor, and detach the pole. Naryshkin stoops over him and addresses him insultingly*]. Well! are you ready to be tortured? This is the Empress's private torture chamber. Can I do anything to make you quite comfortable? You have only to mention it.

EDSTASTON. Have you any back teeth?

NARYSHKIN [*surprised*] Why?

EDSTASTON. His Majesty King George the Third will send for six of them when the news of this reaches London; so look out, damn your eyes!

NARYSHKIN [*frightened*] Oh, I assure you I am only obeying my orders. Personally I abhor torture, and would save you if I could. But the Empress is proud; and what woman would forgive the slight you put upon her?

EDSTASTON. As I said before: Damn your eyes!

NARYSHKIN [*almost in tears*] Well, it isnt my fault. [*To the soldiers, insolently*] You know your orders? You remember what you have to do when the Empress gives you the word? [*The soldiers salute in assent*].

Naryshkin passes through the curtains, admitting a blare of music and a strip of the brilliant white candle-light from the chandeliers in the ballroom as he does so. The white light vanishes and the music is muffled as the curtains fall together behind him. Presently the band stops abruptly; and Naryshkin comes back through the curtains. He makes a warning gesture to the soldiers, who stand at attention. Then he moves the curtain to allow Catherine to enter. She is in full Imperial regalia, and stops sternly just where she has entered. The soldiers fall on their knees.

CATHERINE. Obey your orders.

The soldiers seize Edstaston, and throw him roughly at the feet of the Empress.

CATHERINE [*looking down coldly on him*] Also [*the German word*]* you have put me to the trouble of sending for you twice. You had better have come the first time.

EDSTASTON [*exsufflicate,* and pettishly angry*] I havnt come either time. Ive been carried. I call it infernal impudence.

CATHERINE. Take care what you say.

EDSTASTON. No use. I daresay you look very majestic and very handsome; but I cant see you; and I am not intimidated. I am an Englishman; and you can kidnap me; but you cant bully me.

NARYSHKIN. Remember to whom you are speaking.

CATHERINE [*violently, furious at his intrusion*] Remember that dogs should be dumb. [*He shrivels*]. And do you, Captain, remember that famous as I am for my clemency, there are limits to the patience even of an Empress.

EDSTASTON. How is a man to remember anything when he is trussed up in this ridiculous fashion? I can hardly breathe. [*He makes a futile struggle to free himself*]. Here: dont be unkind, your Majesty: tell these fellows to unstrap me. You know you really owe me an apology.

CATHERINE. You think you can escape by appealing, like Prince Patiomkin, to my sense of humor?

EDSTASTON. Sense of humor! Ho! Ha, ha! I like that. Would anybody with a sense of humor make a guy of a man like this, and then expect him to take it seriously? I say: *do* tell them to loosen these straps.

CATHERINE [*seating herself*] Why should I, pray?

EDSTASTON. Why! Why!! Why, because theyre hurting me.

CATHERINE. People sometimes learn through suffering. Manners, for instance.

EDSTASTON. Oh, well, of course, if youre an ill-natured woman, hurting me on purpose, I have nothing more to say.

CATHERINE. A monarch, sir, has sometimes to employ a necessary and salutary severity—

EDSTASTON [*interrupting her petulantly*] Quack! quack! quack!

CATHERINE. Donnerwetter!*

EDSTASTON [*continuing recklessly*] This isnt severity: it's tomfoolery.
And if you think it's reforming my character or teaching me anything,
youre mistaken. It may be a satisfaction to you; but if it is, all I can
say is that it's not an amiable satisfaction.

CATHERINE [*turning suddenly and balefully on Naryshkin*] What are
you grinning at?

NARYSHKIN [*falling on his knees in terror*] Be merciful, Little Mother.
My heart is in my mouth.

CATHERINE. Your heart and your mouth will be in two separate parts
of your body if you again forget in whose presence you stand. Go.
And take your men with you. [*Naryshkin crawls to the door. The
soldiers rise*]. Stop. Roll that [*indicating Edstaston*] nearer. [*The
soldiers obey*]. Not so close. Did I ask you for a footstool? [*She pushes
Edstaston away with her foot*].

EDSTASTON [*with a sudden squeal*] Agh!!! I must really ask your Majesty
not to put the point of your Imperial toe between my ribs. I am
ticklesome.

CATHERINE. Indeed? All the more reason for you to treat me with
respect, Captain. [*To the others*] Begone. How many times must
I give an order before it is obeyed?

NARYSHKIN. Little Mother: they have brought some instruments of
torture. Will they be needed?

CATHERINE [*indignantly*] How dare you name such abominations to
a Liberal Empress? You will always be a savage and a fool, Naryshkin.
These relics of barbarism are buried, thank God, in the grave of
Peter the Great.* My methods are more civilized. [*She extends her
toe towards Edstaston's ribs*].

EDSTASTON [*shrieking hysterically*] Yagh! Ah! [*Furiously*] If your
Majesty does that again I will write to the London Gazette.

CATHERINE [*to the soldiers*] Leave us. Quick! do you hear? Five
thousand blows of the stick for the soldier who is in the room when
I speak next. [*The soldiers rush out*]. Naryshkin: are you waiting to
be knouted? [*Naryshkin backs out hastily*].

Catherine and Edstaston are now alone. Catherine has in her hand a sceptre or baton of gold. Wrapped round it is a new pamphlet, in French, entitled L'Homme aux Quarante Écus.* She calmly unrolls this and begins to read it at her ease as if she were quite alone. Several seconds elapse in dead silence. She becomes more and more absorbed in the pamphlet, and more and more amused by it.

CATHERINE [*greatly pleased by a passage, and turning over the leaf*] Ausgezeichnet!*

EDSTASTON. Ahem!

Silence. Catherine reads on.

CATHERINE. Wie komisch!*

EDSTASTON. Ahem! ahem!

Silence.

CATHERINE [*soliloquizing enthusiastically*] What a wonderful author is Monsieur Voltaire! How lucidly he exposes the folly of this crazy plan for raising the entire revenue of the country from a single tax on land! how he withers it with his irony! how he makes you laugh whilst he is convincing you! how sure one feels that the proposal is killed by his wit and economic penetration: killed never to be mentioned again among educated people!

EDSTASTON. For Heaven's sake, Madam, do you intend to leave me tied up like this while you discuss the blasphemies of that abominable infidel? Agh!! [*She has again applied her toe*]. Oh! Oo!

CATHERINE [*calmly*] Do I understand you to say that Monsieur Voltaire is a great philanthropist and a great philosopher as well as the wittiest man in Europe?

EDSTASTON. Certainly not. I say that his books ought to be burnt by the common hangman [*her toe touches his ribs*]. Yagh! Oh dont. I shall faint. I cant bear it.

CATHERINE. Have you changed your opinion of Monsieur Voltaire?

EDSTASTON. But you cant expect me as a member of the Church of England* [*she tickles him*]—Agh! Ow! Oh Lord! he is anything you like. He is a philanthropist, a philosopher, a beauty: he ought to have a statue, damn him! [*she tickles him*] No! bless him! save him victorious, happy and glorious! Oh, let eternal honors crown his name: Voltaire thrice worthy on the rolls of fame! [*Exhausted*]. *Now* will you let me up? And look here! I can see your ankles when you tickle me: it's not ladylike.

CATHERINE [*sticking out her toe and admiring it critically*] Is the spectacle so disagreeable?

EDSTASTON. It's agreeable enough; only [*with intense expression*] for heaven's sake dont touch me in the ribs.

CATHERINE [*putting aside the pamphlet*] Captain Edstaston: why did you refuse to come when I sent for you?

EDSTASTON. Madam: I cannot talk tied up like this.

CATHERINE. Do you still admire me as much as you did this morning?

EDSTASTON. How can I possibly tell when I cant see you? Let me get up and look. I cant see anything now except my toes and yours.

CATHERINE. Do you still intend to write to the London Gazette about me?

EDSTASTON. Not if you will loosen these straps. Quick: loosen me. I'm fainting.

CATHERINE. I dont think you are [*tickling him*].

EDSTASTON. Agh! Cat!

CATHERINE. What [*she tickles him again*]!

EDSTASTON [*with a shriek*] No: angel, angel!

CATHERINE [*tenderly*] Geliebter!*

EDSTASTON. I dont know a word of German; but that sounded kind. [*Becoming hysterical*] Little Mother, beautiful little darling angel mother: dont be cruel: untie me. Oh, I beg and implore you. Dont be unkind. I shall go mad.

CATHERINE. You are expected to go mad with love when an Empress deigns to interest herself in you. When an Empress allows you to see her foot you should kiss it. Captain Edstaston: you are a booby.

EDSTASTON [*indignantly*] I am nothing of the kind. I have been mentioned in dispatches as a highly intelligent officer. And let me warn your Majesty that I am not so helpless as you think. The English Ambassador is in that ballroom. A shout from me will bring him to my side; and then where will your Majesty be?

CATHERINE. I should like to see the English Ambassador or anyone else pass through that curtain against my orders. It might be a stone wall ten feet thick. Shout your loudest. Sob. Curse. Scream. Yell [*she tickles him unmercifully*].

EDSTASTON [*frantically*] Ahowyow!!!! Agh! Ooh! Stop! Oh Lord! Ya-a-a-ah! [*A tumult in the ballroom responds to his cries*].

VOICES FROM THE BALLROOM. Stand back. You cannot pass. Hold her back there. The Empress's orders. It is out of the question. No, little darling, not in there. Nobody is allowed in there. You will be sent to Siberia. Dont let her through there, on your life. Drag her back. You will be knouted. It is hopeless, Mademoiselle: you must obey orders. Guard there! Send some men to hold her.

CLAIRE'S VOICE. Let me go. They are torturing Charles in there. I *will* go. How can you all dance as if nothing was happening? Let me go, I tell you. Let—me—go. [*She dashes through the curtain. No one dares follow her*].

CATHERINE [*rising in wrath*] How dare you?

CLAIRE [*recklessly*] Oh, dare your grandmother! Where is my Charles? What are they doing to him?

EDSTASTON [*shouting*] Claire: loosen these straps, in Heaven's name. Quick.

CLAIRE [*seeing him and throwing herself on her knees at his side*] Oh, how dare they tie you up like that! [*To Catherine*] You wicked wretch! You Russian savage! [*She pounces on the straps, and begins unbuckling them*].

CATHERINE [*conquering herself with a mighty effort*] Now self-control. Self-control, Catherine. Philosophy. Europe is looking on. [*She forces herself to sit down*].

EDSTASTON. Steady, dearest: it is the Empress. Call her your Imperial Majesty. Call her Star of the North, Little Mother, Little Darling: thats what she likes; but get the straps off.

CLAIRE. Keep quiet, dear: I cannot get them off if you move.

CATHERINE [*calmly*] Keep quite still, Captain [*she tickles him*].

EDSTASTON. Ow! Agh! Ahowyow!

CLAIRE [*stopping dead in the act of unbuckling the straps and turning sick with jealousy as she grasps the situation*] Was *that* what I thought was your being tortured?

CATHERINE [*urbanely*] That is the favorite torture of Catherine the Second, Mademoiselle. I think the Captain enjoys it very much.

CLAIRE. Then he can have as much more of it as he wants. I am sorry I intruded. [*She rises to go*].

EDSTASTON [*catching her train in his teeth and holding on like a bull-dog*] Dont go. Dont leave me in this horrible state. Loosen me. [*This is what he is saying; but as he says it with the train in his mouth it is not very intelligible.*]

CLAIRE. Let go. You are undignified and ridiculous enough yourself without making me ridiculous. [*She snatches her train away*].

EDSTASTON. Ow! Youve nearly pulled my teeth out: youre worse than the Star of the North. [*To Catherine*] Darling Little Mother: you have a kind heart, the kindest in Europe. Have pity. Have mercy. I love you. [*Claire bursts into tears*]. Release me.

CATHERINE. Well, just to shew you how much kinder a Russian savage can be than an English one (though I am sorry to say I am a German) here goes! [*She stoops to loosen the straps*].

CLAIRE [*jealously*] You neednt trouble, thank you. [*She pounces on the straps; and the two set Edstaston free between them*]. Now get up, please; and conduct yourself with some dignity if you are not utterly demoralized.

EDSTASTON. Dignity! Ow! I cant. I'm stiff all over. I shall never be able to stand up again. Oh Lord! how it hurts! [*They seize him by the shoulders and drag him up*]. Yah! Agh! Wow! Oh! Mmmmmm! Oh, Little Angel Mother, dont ever do this to a man again. Knout him; kill him; roast him; baste him; head, hang, and quarter him; but dont tie him up like that and tickle him.

CATHERINE. Your young lady still seems to think that you enjoyed it.

CLAIRE. I know what I think. I will never speak to him again. Your Majesty can keep him, as far as I am concerned.

CATHERINE. I would not deprive you of him for worlds; though really I think he's rather a darling [*she pats his cheek*].

CLAIRE [*snorting*] So I see, indeed.

EDSTASTON. Dont be angry, dearest: in this country everybody's a darling. I'll prove it to you. [*To Catherine*] Will your Majesty be good enough to call Prince Patiomkin?

CATHERINE [*surprised into haughtiness*] Why?

EDSTASTON. To oblige me.

Catherine laughs good-humoredly and goes to the curtains and opens them. The band strikes up a Redowa.*

CATHERINE [*calling imperiously*] Patiomkin! [*The music stops suddenly*]. Here! To me! Go on with your music there, you fools. [*The Redowa is resumed*].

The sergeant rushes from the ballroom to relieve the Empress of the curtain. Patiomkin comes in dancing with Varinka.

CATHERINE [*to Patiomkin*] The English captain wants you, little darling.

Catherine resumes her seat as Patiomkin intimates by a grotesque bow that he is at Edstaston's service. Varinka passes behind Edstaston and Claire, and posts herself on Claire's right.

EDSTASTON. Precisely. [*To Claire*] You observe, my love: 'little darling.' Well, if her Majesty calls *him* a darling, is it my fault that she calls me one too?

CLAIRE. I dont care: I dont think you ought to have done it. I am very angry and offended.

EDSTASTON. They tied me up, dear. I couldnt help it. I fought for all I was worth.

THE SERGEANT [*at the curtains*] He fought with the strength of lions and bears. God knows I shall carry a broken sweetbread to my grave.

EDSTASTON. You cant mean to throw me over, Claire. [*Urgently*] Claire. Claire.

VARINKA [*in a transport of sympathetic emotion, pleading with clasped hands to Claire*] Oh, sweet little angel lamb, he loves you: it shines in his darling eyes. Pardon him, pardon him.

PATIOMKIN [*rushing from the Empress's side to Claire and falling on his knees to her*] Pardon him, pardon him, little cherub! little wild duck! little star! little glory! little jewel in the crown of heaven!

CLAIRE. This is perfectly ridiculous.

VARINKA [*kneeling to her*] Pardon him, pardon him, little delight, little sleeper in a rosy cradle.

CLAIRE. I'll do anything if youll only let me alone.

THE SERGEANT [*kneeling to her*] Pardon him, pardon him, lest the mighty man bring his whip to you. God knows we all need pardon!

CLAIRE [*at the top of her voice*] I pardon him! I pardon him!

PATIOMKIN [*springing up joyfully and going behind Claire, whom he raises in his arms*] Embrace her, victor of Bunker's Hill. Kiss her till she swoons.

THE SERGEANT. Receive her in the name of the holy Nicholas.

VARINKA. She begs you for a thousand dear little kisses all over her body.

CLAIRE [*vehemently*] I do not. [*Patiomkin throws her into Edstaston's arms*]. Oh! [*The pair, awkward and shamefaced, recoil from one another, and remain utterly inexpressive*].

CATHERINE [*pushing Edstaston towards Claire*] There is no help for it, Captain. This is Russia, not England.

EDSTASTON [*plucking up some geniality, and kissing Claire ceremoniously on the brow*] I have no objection.

VARINKA [*disgusted*] Only one kiss! and on the forehead! Fish. See how I kiss, though it is only my horribly ugly old uncle [*she throws her arms round Patiomkin's neck and covers his face with kisses*].

THE SERGEANT [*moved to tears*] Sainted Nicholas: bless your lambs!

CATHERINE. Do you wonder now that I love Russia as I love no other place on earth?

NARYSHKIN [*appearing at the door*] Majesty: the model for the new museum has arrived.

CATHERINE [*rising eagerly and making for the curtains*] Let us go. I can think of nothing but my museum. [*In the archway she stops and turns to*

Edstaston, who has hurried to lift the curtain for her]. Captain: I wish you every happiness that your little angel can bring you. [*For his ear alone*] I could have brought you more; but you did not think so. Farewell.

EDSTASTON [*kissing her hand, which, instead of releasing, he holds caressingly and rather patronizingly in his own*] I feel your Majesty's kindness so much that I really cannot leave you without a word of plain wholesome English advice.

CATHERINE [*snatching her hand away and bounding forward as if he had touched her with a spur*] Advice!!!

PATIOMKIN. Madman: take care!

NARYSHKIN. Advise the Empress!!

THE SERGEANT. Sainted Nicholas!

VARINKA. Hoo hoo! [*a stifled splutter of laughter*].

[*exclaiming simultaneously*].

EDSTASTON [*following the Empress and resuming kindly but judicially*] After all, though your Majesty is of course a great queen, yet when all is said, I am a man; and your Majesty is only a woman.

CATHERINE. Only a wo—[*she chokes*].

EDSTASTON [*continuing*] Believe me, this Russian extravagance will not do. I appreciate as much as any man the warmth of heart that prompts it; but it is overdone: it is hardly in the best taste: it is—really I must say it—it is not proper.

CATHERINE [*ironically, in German*] So!*

EDSTASTON. Not that I cannot make allowances. Your Majesty has, I know, been unfortunate in your experience as a married woman—

CATHERINE [*furious*] Alle Wetter!!!*

EDSTASTON [*sentimentally*] Dont say that. Dont think of him in that way. After all, he was your husband; and whatever his faults may have been, it is not for you to think unkindly of him.

CATHERINE [*almost bursting*] I shall forget myself.

EDSTASTON. Come! I am sure he really loved you; and you truly loved him.

CATHERINE [*controlling herself with a supreme effort*] No, Catherine. What would Voltaire say?

EDSTASTON. Oh, never mind that vile scoffer. Set an example to Europe, Madam, by doing what I am going to do. Marry again. Marry some good man who will be a strength and a support to your old age.

CATHERINE. My old—[*she again becomes speechless*].

EDSTASTON. Yes: we must all grow old, even the handsomest of us.

CATHERINE [*sinking into her chair with a gasp*] Thank you.

EDSTASTON. You will thank me more when you see your little ones round your knee, and your man there by the fireside in the winter evenings—by the way, I forgot that you have no firesides here in spite of the coldness of the climate; so shall I say by the stove?

CATHERINE. Certainly, if you wish. The stove, by all means.

EDSTASTON [*impulsively*] Ah, Madam, abolish the stove: believe me, there is nothing like the good old open grate. Home! duty! happiness! they all mean the same thing; and they all flourish best on the drawing room hearthrug. [*Turning to Claire*] And now, my love, we must not detain the Queen: she is anxious to inspect the model of her museum, to which I am sure we wish every success.

CLAIRE [*coldly*] *I* am not detaining her.

EDSTASTON. Well, goodbye [*wringing Patiomkin's hand*], goo-oo-oodbye, Prince: come and see us if ever you visit England. Spire View, Deepdene, Little Mugford, Devon,* will always find me. [*To Varinka, kissing her hand*] Goodbye, Mademoiselle: goodbye, Little Mother, if I may call you that just once. [*Varinka puts up her face to be kissed*]. Eh? No, no, no, no: you dont mean that, you know. Naughty! [*To the Sergeant*] Goodbye, my friend. You will drink our healths with this [*tipping him*].

THE SERGEANT. The blessed Nicholas will multiply your fruits, Little Father.

EDSTASTON. Goodbye, goodbye, goodbye, goodbye, goodbye, goodbye.

He goes out backwards bowing, with Claire curtseying, having been listened to in utter dumbfoundedness by Patiomkin and Naryshkin, in childlike awe by Varinka, and with quite inexpressible feelings by Catherine. When he is out of sight she rises with clenched fists and raises her arm and her closed eyes to Heaven. Patiomkin, rousing himself from his stupor of amazement, springs to her like a tiger, and throws himself at her feet.

PATIOMKIN. What shall I do to him for you? Skin him alive? Cut off his eyelids and stand him in the sun? Tear his tongue out? What shall it be?

CATHERINE [*opening her eyes*] Nothing. But oh, if I could only have had him for my—for my—for my—

PATIOMKIN [*in a growl of jealousy*] For your lover?

CATHERINE [*with an ineffable smile*] No: for my museum.

THE SIX OF CALAIS

PREFATORY TO THE SIX OF CALAIS

THE most amusing thing about the first performance of this little play was the exposure it elicited of the quaint illiteracy of our modern London journalists. Their only notion of a king was a pleasant and highly respectable gentleman in a bowler hat and Victorian beard, shaking hands affably with a blushing football team. To them a queen was a dignified lady, also Victorian as to her coiffure,* graciously receiving bouquets from excessively washed children in beautiful new clothes. Such were their mental pictures of Great Edward's grandson and his queen Philippa.* They were hurt, shocked, scandalized at the spectacle of a medieval soldier-monarch publicly raging and cursing, crying and laughing, asserting his authority with thrasonic* ferocity and the next moment blubbering like a child in his wife's lap or snarling like a savage dog at a dauntless and defiant tradesman: in short, behaving himself like an unrestrained human being in a very trying situation instead of like a modern constitutional monarch on parade keeping up an elaborate fiction of living in a political vacuum and moving only when his ministers pull his strings. Edward Plantagenet the Third* had to pull everybody else's strings and pull them pretty hard, his father having been miserably killed for taking his job too lightly. But the journalist critics knew nothing of this. A King Edward who did not behave like the son of King Edward the Seventh seemed unnatural and indecent to them, and they rent their garments* accordingly.

They were perhaps puzzled by the fact that the play has no moral whatever. Every year or so I hurl at them a long play full of insidious propaganda, with a moral in every line. They never discover what I am driving at: it is always too plainly and domestically stated to be grasped by their subtle and far flung minds; but they feel that I am driving at something: probably something they had better not agree with if they value their livelihoods. A play of mine in which I am not driving at anything more than a playwright's direct business is as inconceivable by them as a medieval king.

Now a playwright's direct business is simply to provide the theatre with a play. When I write one with the additional attraction of providing the twentieth century with an up-to-date religion or the like, that luxury is thrown in gratuitously; and the play, simply as a play, is not necessarily either the better or the worse for it. What, then, is a play simply as a play?

Well, it is a lot of things. Life as we see it is so haphazard that it is only by picking out its key situations and arranging them in their significant order (which is never how they actually occur) that it can be made intelligible. The highbrowed dramatic poet wants to make it intelligible and sublime. The farce writer wants to make it funny. The melodrama merchant wants to make it as exciting as some people find the police news. The pornographer wants to make it salacious. All interpreters of life in action, noble or ignoble, find their instrument in the theatre; and all the academic definitions of a play are variations of this basic function.

Yet there is one function hardly ever alluded to now, though it was made much too much of from Shakespear's time to the middle of the nineteenth century. As I write my plays it is continually in my mind and very much to my taste. This function is to provide an exhibition of the art of acting. A good play with bad parts is not an impossibility; but it is a monstrosity. A bad play with good parts will hold the stage and be kept alive by the actors for centuries after the obsolescence of its mentality would have condemned it to death without them. A great deal of the British Drama, from Shakespear to Bulwer Lytton, is as dead as mutton, and quite unbearable except when heroically acted; yet Othello and Richelieu* can still draw hard money into the pay boxes; and The School For Scandal* revives again and again with unabated vigor. Rosalind can always pull As You Like It* through in spite of the sententious futility of the melancholy Jaques; and Millamant,* impossible as she is, still produces the usual compliments to the wit and style of Congreve, who thought that syphilis and cuckoldry and concupiscent* old women are things to be laughed at.

The Six of Calais is an acting piece and nothing else. As it happened, it was so well acted that in the eighteenth century all the talk would have been about Siddons* as Philippa. But the company got no thanks except from the audience: the critics were prostrated with shock, damn their eyes!

I have had to improve considerably on the story as told by that absurd old snob Froissart,* who believed that 'to rob and pill was a good life' if the robber was at least a baron. He made a very poor job of it in my opinion.

ON THE HIGH SEAS,*
28th May 1935.

THE SIX OF CALAIS

A.D. *4th August 1347. Before the walls of Calais on the last day of the siege.* The pavilion of Edward III,* King of England, is on your left as you face the walls. The pavilion of his consort Philippa of Hainault* is on your right. Between them, near the King's pavilion, is a two-seated chair of state for public audiences. Crowds of tents cover the background; but there is a clear way in the middle through the camp to the great gate of the city with its drawbridge still up and its flag still flying.**

The Black Prince,* aged 17, arrives impetuously past the Queen's tent, a groom running after him.

THE PRINCE. Here is the King's pavilion without a single attendant to announce me. What can the matter be?

A child's scream is heard from the royal pavilion; and John of Gaunt,* aged 7, dashes out and is making for his mother's tent when the Prince seizes him.

THE PRINCE. How now, Johnny? Whats the matter?

JOHN [*struggling*] Let me go. Father is in a frightful wax.*

THE PRINCE. I shall be in a wax myself presently. [*Releasing him*] Off with you to mother. [*The child takes refuge in the Queen's pavilion*].

THE KING'S VOICE. Grrr! Yah! Why was I not told? Gogswoons,* why was I not told? [*Edward III, aged 35,* dashes from his pavilion, foaming*]. Out! [*The groom flies for his life*]. How long have you been here? They never tell me anything. I might be a dog instead of a king.

THE PRINCE [*about to kneel*] Majesty—

THE KING. No no: enough of that. Your news. Anything from Scotland? Anything from Wales?

THE PRINCE. I—

THE KING [*not waiting for the answer*] The state of things here is past words. The wrath of God and all his saints is upon this expedition.

THE PRINCE. I hope not, sir. I—

THE KING [*raging on*] May God wither and blast this accursed town! You would have thought that these dogs would have come out of their kennels and grovelled for mercy at my summons. Am I not their lawful king, ha?

THE PRINCE. Undoubtedly, sir. They—

THE KING. They have held me up for twelve months! A whole year!!
My business ruined! My plans upset! My money exhausted! Death,
disease, mutiny, a dog's life here in the field winter and summer. The
bitch's bastard who is in command of their walls came to demand
terms from me! to demand terms!!! looked me straight in the eyes
with his head up as if I—I, his king! were dirt beneath his feet. By
God, I will have that head: I will kick it to my dogs to eat. I will chop
his insolent herald* into four quarters—

THE PRINCE [*shocked*] Oh no, sir: not a herald: you cannot do that.

THE KING. They have driven me to such extremity that I am capable
of cutting all the heralds in Christendom into their quarterings.
[*He sits down in his chair of state and suddenly becomes ridiculously
sentimental*]. I have not told you the worst. Your mother, the Queen,
my Philippa, is here: here! Edward, in her delicate state of health.
Even that did not move them. They want her to die: they are trying
to murder her and our innocent unborn child.* Think of that, boy:
oh, think of that [*he almost weeps*].

THE PRINCE. Softly, father: that is not their fault: it is yours.

THE KING. Would you make a jest of this? If it is not their fault it shall
be their misfortune; for I will have every man, woman, and child
torn to pieces with red hot pincers for it.

THE PRINCE. Truly, dear Sir, you have great cause to be annoyed; but
in sober earnest how does the matter stand? They must be suffering
the last extremity of famine. Their walls may hold out; but their
stomachs cannot. Cannot you offer them some sort of terms to end
the business? Money is running short. Time is running short. You
only make them more desperate by threatening them. Remember: it
is good policy to build a bridge of silver for a flying foe.

THE KING. Do I not know it? Have I not been kind, magnanimous?
Have I not done all that Christian chivalry could require of me? And
they abuse my kindness: it only encourages them: they despise me
for it.

THE PRINCE. What terms have you offered them?

THE KING. I have not threatened the life of a single knight. I have said
that no man of gentle condition and noble blood shall be denied

quarter and ransom. It was their knightly duty to make a show of arms against me. But [*rising wrathfully*] these base rascals of burgesses:* these huckstering hounds of merchants who have made this port of Calais a nest of pirates: these usurers and tradesmen: these rebel curs who have dared to take up arms against their betters: am I to pardon their presumption? I should be false to our order, to Christendom, if I did not make a signal example.

THE PRINCE. By all means, sir. But what have you demanded?

THE KING. Six of the most purseproud of their burgesses, as they call themselves—by God, they begin to give themselves the airs of barons—six of them are to come in their shirts with halters round their necks for me to hang in the sight of all their people. [*Raising his voice again and storming*] They shall die the dog's death they deserve. They shall—

A court lady comes in.

THE COURT LADY. Sir: the Queen. Sssh!

THE KING [*subsiding to a whisper*] The Queen! Boy: not a word here. Her condition: she must not be upset: she takes these things so amiss: be discreet, for heaven's sake.

Queen Philippa, aged 33, comes from her pavilion, attended.*

THE QUEEN. Dear child: welcome.

THE PRINCE. How do you, lady mother? [*He kisses her hand*].

THE KING [*solicitously*] Madam: are you well wrapped up? Is it wise to come into the cold air here? Had they better not bring a brazier and some cushions, and a hot drink—a posset*—

THE QUEEN [*curtseying*] Sir: beloved: dont fuss. I am very well; and the air does me good. [*To the Prince*] You must cheer up your father, my precious. He will fret about my health when it is his own that needs care. I have borne him eleven children; and St Anne* be my witness they have cost less looking after than this one big soldier, the greatest baby of them all. [*To the King*] Have you put on your flannel belly band, dearest?

THE KING. Yes, yes, yes, my love: do not bother about me. Think of yourself and our child—

THE QUEEN. Oh, leave me to take care of myself and the child. I am no maternal malingreuse* I promise you. And now, sir sonny, tell me all your news. I—

She is interrupted by a shrill trumpet call.

THE KING. What is that? What now?

John of Gaunt, who has been up to the town gates to see the fun, runs in excitedly.

JOHN OF GAUNT [*bending his knee very perfunctorily*] Sire: they have surrendered: the drawbridge is down. The six old men have come out in their shirts with ropes round their necks.

THE KING [*clouting him*] Sssh! Hold your tongue, you young devil.

THE QUEEN. Old men in their shirts in this weather!! They will catch cold.

THE KING. It is nothing, madam my love: only the ceremony of surrender. You must go in: it is not fitting that these half naked men should be in your presence. I will deal with them.

THE QUEEN. Do not keep them too long in the cold, dearest sir.

THE KING [*uxoriously waving her a kiss*] My love!

The Queen goes into her pavilion; and a group of noblemen attendant on the King, including Sir Walter Manny and the Lords Derby, Northampton, and Arundel,* issue from their tents and assemble behind the chair of state, where they are joined by the Black Prince, who stands at the King's right hand and takes charge of John of Gaunt.*

THE KING. Now for these swine, these bloodsuckers. They shall learn—[*shouting*] Fetch me these fellows in here. Drag them in. I'll teach them to hold me up here for twelve months. I'll—

The six burgesses, hustled by men-at-arms, enter in their shirts and halters, each carrying a bunch of massive iron keys. Their leader, Eustache de St Pierre, kneels at the King's feet. Four of his fellow victims, Piers de Wissant, Jacques de Wissant, Jean d'Aire, and Gilles d'Oudebolle,* kneel in pairs behind him, and, following his example, lay their keys on the ground. They are deeply cast down, bearing themselves like condemned men, yet maintaining a melancholy dignity. Not so the sixth, Piers de Rosty (nick-named Hardmouth),* the only one without a grey or white beard. He has an extraordinarily dogged chin with a few bristles on it. He deliberately separates himself from the rest by passing behind the royal chair to the King's* *right and planting himself stiffly erect in an attitude of intense recalcitrance. The King, scowling fiercely at St Pierre and the rest, does not notice this until Peter* flings down his keys with a violence which suggests that he would very willingly have brained Edward with them.*

THE KING. On your knees, hound.

PETER. I am a good dog, but not of your kennel, Neddy.

THE KING. Neddy!!!!

PETER. Order your own curs: I am a free burgess and take commands from nobody.

Before the amazed monarch can retort, Eustache appeals to Peter.

EUSTACHE. Master Peter: if you have no regard for yourself, remember that our people, our wives and children, are at the mercy of this great king.

PETER. You mistake him for his grandfather.* Great! [*He spits*].

EUSTACHE. Is this your promise to be patient?

PETER. Why waste civilities on him, Master Mayor? He can do no worse than hang us; and as to the town, *I* would have burnt it to the last brick, and every man, woman and child along with it, sooner than surrender. I came here to make up the tale of six to be hanged. Well, he can hang me; but he shall not outface me. I am as good a dog as he, any day in the week.

THE PRINCE. Fie,* fellow! is this a way for one of thy degree to speak to an anointed king? Bear thyself as befits one of thy degree in the royal presence, or by Holy Paul—*

PETER. You know how we have borne ourselves in his royal presence these twelve months. We have made some of you skip. Famine and not you, has beaten us. Give me a square meal and a good sword and stake all on a fair single combat with this big bully, or his black whelp here if he is afraid of me; and we shall see which is the better dog of the two.

THE KING. Drag him to his knees. Hamstring him if he resists.

Three men-at-arms dash at Peter and drag him to his knees. They take his halter and tie his ankles and wrists with it. Then they fling him on his side, where he lies helpless.

THE KING. And so, Master Burgess—

PETER. Bow-wow-wow!

THE KING [*furious*] Gag him. Gogswoons, gag him.

> *They tear a piece of linen from the back of his shirt, and bind his mouth*
> *with it. He barks to the last moment. John of Gaunt laughs ecstatically*
> *at this performance, and sets off some of the soldiers.*

THE KING. If a man laughs I will have him flayed alive.

Dead silence.

THE KING. And now, fellows, what have ye to say to excuse your hardy
and stubborn resistance for all these months to me, your king?

EUSTACHE. Sir, we are not fellows. We are free burgesses of this
great city.

THE KING. Free burgesses! Are you still singing that song? Well, I will
bend the necks of your burgesses when the hangman has broken
yours. Am I not your overlord? Am I not your anointed king?

EUSTACHE. That is your claim, sir; and you have made it good by force
of arms. We must submit to you and to God.

THE KING. Leave God out of this! What hast thou or thy like to do
with God?

EUSTACHE. Nothing, sir: we would not so far presume. But with due
respect to your greatness I would humbly submit to your Majesty
that God may have something to do with us, seeing that he created
us all alike and redeemed us by the blood of his beloved son.

THE KING [*to the Prince*] Can you make head or tail of this, boy? Is he
accusing me of impiety? If he is, by God—

EUSTACHE. Sir, is it for me to accuse you of anything? Here we kneel
in the dust before you, naked and with the ropes on our necks with
which you will presently send us into the presence of our maker and
yours. [*His teeth chatter*].

THE KING. Ay: you may well tremble. You have cause.

EUSTACHE. Yes: I tremble; and my teeth chatter: the few I have left.
But you gentlemen that see our miserable plight, I call on your
generosity as noblemen, on your chivalry as good knights, to bear
witness for us that it is the cold of the morning and our naked

condition that shakes us. We kneel to implore your King's mercy for our wretched and starving townsfolk, not for ourselves.

THE KING. Whose fault is it that they are starving? They have themselves to thank. Why did they not open their gates to me? Why did they take arms against their anointed king? Why should I have mercy on them or on you?

EUSTACHE. Sir: one is merciful not for reasons, but for the love of God, at whose hand we must all sue for mercy at the end of our days.

THE KING. You shall not save yourself by preaching. What right have you to preach? It is for churchmen and learned divines to speak of these mysteries, not for tradesmen and usurers. I'll teach you to rebel against your betters, whom God has appointed to keep you in obedience and loyalty. You are traitors; and as traitors you shall die. Thank my mercy that you are spared the torments that traitors and rebels suffer in England. [*Rising*] Away with them to the hangman; and let our trumpeters summon the townspeople to the walls to take warning from their dangling corpses.

The three men-at-arms begin to lift Peter. The others lay hands on his five colleagues.

THE KING. No: let that hound lie. Hanging is too good for him.

The Queen hurries in with her ladies in great concern. The men-at-arms release the burgesses irresolutely. It is evident that the Queen's arrival washes out all the King's orders.

THE QUEEN. Sir, what is this they tell me?

THE KING [*hurrying across to intercept her*] Madam: this is no place for you. I pray you, retire. The business is one in which it becomes you not to meddle.

THE QUEEN [*evading him and passing on to inspect the burgesses*] But these gentlemen. They are almost naked. It is neither seemly nor sufficient. They are old: they are half frozen: they should be in their beds.

THE KING. They soon will be. Leave us, madam. This is business of State. They are suffering no more than they deserve. I beg and pray you—I command you—

THE QUEEN. Dear sir, your wishes are my law and your commands my duty. But these gentlemen are very cold.

THE KING. They will be colder presently; so you need not trouble about that. Will it please you, madam, to withdraw at once?

THE QUEEN. Instantly, my dear lord. [*To Eustache*] Sir: when his Majesty has ended his business with you, will you and your friends partake of some cups of hot wine in my pavilion? You shall be furnished with gowns.

THE KING [*choking with wrath*] Hot w—!

EUSTACHE. Alas, madam, when the King has ended his business with us we shall need nothing but our coffins. I also beg you to withdraw and hasten our despatch to that court where we shall not be held guilty for defending our hearths and homes to the last extremity. The King will not be baulked of* his revenge; and we are shriven* and ready.

THE QUEEN. Oh, you mistake, sir: the King is incapable of revenge: my husband is the flower of chivalry.

EUSTACHE. You little know your husband, madam. We know better what to expect* from Edward Plantagenet.

THE KING [*coming to him threateningly past his consort*] Ha! do you, Master Merchant? You know better than the Queen! You and your like know what to expect from your lords and rulers! Well, this time you shall not be disappointed. You have guessed aright. You shall hang, every man of you, in your shirts, to make mirth for my horseboys and their trulls.*

THE QUEEN. Oh no—

THE KING [*thundering*] Madam: I forbid you to speak. I bade you go: you would not; and now you shall see what I would have spared you had you been obedient. By God, I will be master in my own house and king in my own camp. Take these fellows out and hang them in their white beards.

The King takes his place on his chair of state with his arms folded implacably. The Queen follows him slowly and desolately. She takes her place beside him. The dead silence is very trying.

THE QUEEN [*drooping in tears and covering her face with her hands*] Oh!

THE KING [*flinching*] No no no no no NO. Take her away.

THE QUEEN. Sir: I have been always a great trouble to you. I have asked you for a thousand favors and graces and presents. I am impatient and ungrateful, ever asking, asking, asking. Have you ever refused me even once?

THE KING. Well, is that a reason why I should give and grant, grant and give, for ever? Am I never to have my own way?

THE QUEEN. Oh, dearest sir, when next I ask you for a great thing, refuse me: teach me a lesson. But this is such a little thing. [*Heartbroken*] I cannot bear your refusing me a little thing.

THE KING. A little thing! You call this a little thing!

THE QUEEN. A very very little thing, sir. You are the King: you have at your disposal thousands of lives: all our lives from the noblest to the meanest. All the lives in that city are in your hand to do as you will with in this your hour of victory: it is as if you were God himself. You said once that you would lead ten kings captive to my feet. Much as I have begged from you I have never asked for my ten kings. I ask only for six old merchants, men beneath your royal notice, as my share of the spoils of your conquest. Their ransom will hardly buy me a new girdle; and oh, dear sir, you know that my old one is becoming too strait for me. Will you keep me begging so?

THE KING. I see very well that I shall not be allowed my own way. [*He begins to cry*].

THE QUEEN [*throwing her arms round him*] Oh, dear sir, you know I would die to spare you a moment's distress. There, there, dearest! [*She pets him*].

THE KING [*blubbering*] I am never allowed to do anything I want. I might as well be a dog as a king. You treat me like a baby.

THE QUEEN. Ah no: you are the greatest of kings to me, the noblest of men, my dearest lord and my dearest dearest love. [*Throwing herself on her knees*] Listen: do as you will: I will not say another word: I ask nothing.

THE KING. No: you ask nothing because you know you will get everything. [*He rises, shouting*] Take those men out of my sight.

THE PRINCE. What shall we do with them, sir?

THE KING [*flinging himself back into his seat*] Ask the Queen. Banquet them: feast them: give them my crown, my kingdom. Give them the clothes off my back, the bread out of my mouth, only take them away. Will you go, curses on you.

The five burgesses kneel gratefully to the Queen.

EUSTACHE [*kissing her hand*] Madam: our ransom shall buy you a threefold girdle of gold and a cradle of silver.

THE KING. Aye, well, see that it does: see that it does.

The burgesses retire, bowing to the Queen, who, still on her knees, waves her hand graciously to them.

THE QUEEN. Will you not help me up, dear sir?

THE KING. Oh yes, yes [*raising her*]: you should be more careful: who knows what harm you may have done yourself flopping on your knees like that?

THE QUEEN. I have done myself no harm, dear sir; but you have done me a world of good. I have never been better nor happier in my life. Look at me. Do I not look radiant?

THE KING. And how do I look? Like a fool.

JOHN OF GAUNT. Sir: the men-at-arms want to know what they are to do with this fellow?

THE KING. Aye, I forgot him. Fetch him here.

The three men-at-arms carry Peter to the King, and fling him down. The King is now grinning. His paroxysm of tears has completely discharged his ill temper. It dawns on him that through Peter he may get even with Philippa for his recent domestic defeat.

THE QUEEN. Oh, the poor man has not even a proper shirt to wear. It is all torn: it is hardly decent.

THE KING. Look well at this man, madam. He defied me. He spat at me. There is no insult that he did not heap on me. He looked me in the face and spoke to me as if I were a scullion.* I swear to you by the Holy Rood,* he called me Neddy! Donkeys are called Neddy. What have you to say now? Is he, too, to be spared and petted and fed and have a gown from you?

THE QUEEN [*going to Peter*] But he is blue with cold. I fear he is dying. Untie him. Lift him up. Take that bandage off his mouth. Fie fie! I believe it is the tail of his shirt.

THE KING. It is cleaner than his tongue.

The men-at-arms release Peter from his bonds and his gag. He is too stiff to rise. They pull him to his feet.

PETER [*as they lift him groaning and swearing*] Ah-ooh-oh-ow!

THE KING. Well? Have you learnt your lesson? Are you ready to sue for the Queen's mercy?

PETER. Yah! Henpecked!* Kiss mammy!

THE KING [*chuckles*]!!!

THE QUEEN [*severely*] Are you mad, Master Burgess? Do you not know that your life is in the King's hand? Do you expect me to recommend you to his mercy if you forget yourself in this unseemly fashion?

PETER. Let me tell you, madam, that I came here in no ragged shirt. I have a dozen shirts of as fine a web as ever went on your back. Is it likely that I, a master mercer,* would wear aught but the best of the best to go to my grave in?

THE QUEEN. Mend your manners first, sir; and then mend your linen; or you shall have no countenance* from me.

PETER. I have naught to do with you, madam, though I well see who wears the breeches in this royal household. I am not skilled in dealing with fine handsome ladies. Leave me to settle my business with your henpecked husband.

THE QUEEN. You shall suffer for this insolence. [*To the King*] Will you, my lord, stand by and hear me spoken to in this tone by a haberdasher?*

THE KING [*grinning*] Nay: I am in a merciful mood this morning. The poor man is to be pitied, shivering there in his shirt with his tail torn off.

PETER. Shivering! You lie in your teeth, though you were fifty kings. No man alive shall pity Peter Hardmouth, a dog of lousy Champagne.*

THE KING [*going to him*] Ha! A dog of Champagne! Oh, you must pardon this man, madam; for my grandmother hailed from that lousy province; so I also am a dog of Champagne. We know one another's bark. [*Turning on him with bristling teeth*] Eh?

PETER [*growling in his face like a dog*] Grrrr!!!

THE KING [*returning the growl chin to chin*] Grrrr!!!!!!

They repeat this performance, to the great scandal of the Queen, until it develops into a startling imitation of a dog fight.

THE QUEEN [*tearing the two dogs asunder*] Oh, for shame, sir! And you, fellow: I will have you muzzled and led through the streets on a chain and lodged in a kennel.

THE KING. Be merciful, lady. I have asked you for many favors, and had them granted me too, as the world, please God, will soon have proof. Will you deny me this?

THE QUEEN. Will you mock my condition before this insolent man and before the world? I will not endure it.

THE KING. Faith, no, dearest: no mockery. But you have no skill in dealing with the dogs of lousy Champagne. We must pity this poor trembling fellow.

THE QUEEN [*angrily*] He is *not* trembling.

PETER. No, by all the saints in heaven and devils in hell. Well said, lass.

He nudges her, to her extreme indignation.

THE KING. Hear that, dearest: he calls thee lass. Be kind to him. He is only a poor old cur* who has lost half his teeth. His condition would move a heart of stone.*

PETER. I may be an old cur; but if I had sworn to hang the six of us as he swore, no shrew should scold me out of it, nor any softbosomed beauty wheedle me out of it. Yah, cry baby! Give her your sword and sit in the corner with her distaff.* The grey mare is the better horse here. Do your worst, dame: I like your spunk* better than his snivel.

THE QUEEN [*raging*] Send him away, sir. He is too ugly; and his words are disgusting. Such objects should be kept out of my sight: would you have me bear you a monster? Take him away.

THE KING. Away with him. Hurt him not; but let him not come into the Queen's presence. Quick there. Off with him.

The men-at-arms lay hands on Peter who struggles violently.

PETER. Hands off me, spaniels. Arrr! Grrr! [*As they drag him out overpowered*] Gee-up, Neddy. [*He finishes with a spirited imitation of a donkey's bray*].*

THE KING. That is how they build men in Champagne. By the Holy Rood I care not if a bit of him gets into our baby.

THE QUEEN. Oh, for shame! for shame! Have men no decency?

The King snatches her into his arms, laughing boisterously. The laugh spreads to all the soldiers and courtiers. The whole camp seems in a hilarious uproar.

THE QUEEN. No no: for shame! for shame!

*The King stops her mouth with a kiss. Peter brays melodiously in the distance.**

THE BRITISH PARTY SYSTEM

THE BRITISH PARTY SYSTEM

PRACTICALLY nobody in these islands understands the Party System. Britons do not know its history. They believe that it is founded in human nature and therefore indestructible and eternal. When I point out that it does not exist in our municipalities* they think that I am ignorant or crazy, and assure me that there are Conservative parties and Progressive parties* in the municipal councils and corporations* 'just the same as' in Parliament, and always will be by the immutable law of political human nature.

What are the facts? Let me put them in the form of a little historical drama, as that comes easiest to me and is the most amusing.

Scene: Althorp,* the residence of the Spencers, Earls of Sunderland. Present King William the Third,* aged 45, of glorious pious and immortal memory, and his host Robert Spencer,* the second Earl, ten years older, famous even at the courts of Charles II* and James II for his complete unscrupulousness and political ingenuity. Period 1695.

ROBERT. Your Majesty, has done me a tremendous honor in visiting my humble residence. As I cannot pretend to have deserved it I apprehend that there is some way in which I can be of service to your Majesty.

WILLIAM. There is. I am at my wits' end. I want advice. I am expected to save the Protestant religion in Europe from the Scarlet Woman of Rome.* I am expected to save your country* and my own country from the Bourbons.* I am expected to do everything for everybody. And I am expected to do it all without money and without a standing army. I cannot plan my campaigns for a year ahead because this damnable British Parliament, which is elected to govern England, only wants what all Englishmen want: that is, not to be governed at all. It may leave me at any moment without a penny and without a soldier. France's best general,* who has won all her battles for her, has just died and left King Louis in the hollow of my hand. And this is the moment your parliament chooses to threaten me with a peace. It is intolerable. Damn your parliament! I will go back to Amsterdam:* better be a real Stadtholder* than a sham king. They want liberty, these pigheaded squires and knights of the shire. Well, let them have their liberty: liberty to be broken on the wheel to please the Pope,* liberty to be the vassals of France, liberty to go to the devil their own way and not be interfered with by any king or council. I shall fling the crown in their faces and shake the dust of England off my feet unless you can shew me a way of making Parliament do what I tell it to do.

ROBERT. I cannot do that; but I can shew you a way to prevent Parliament from doing anything at all except vote supplies and stave off the next election as long as it can.

WILLIAM. Can you? The only supplies I care about are supplies of men and money to save the Protestant north from that fat Bourbon bigot.* If I cannot have them your crown is no use to me. You can have James back again. You know where to find him: in Louis' pocket.* I daresay you are in correspondence with him, double-faced schemer that you are.

ROBERT. I am what the times have made me; and I keep in correspondence with everybody: one never knows what will happen next. But I wish I could get your Majesty's mind off the Protestant north and the army for a moment. I wish I could convince you that what you have to fight here is not King Louis, but the British Parliament.

WILLIAM. Well, do I not know it? Am I not telling you so?

ROBERT. Keep to that, your Majesty. Is it agreed, too, that I am a schemer?

WILLIAM. Oh, it is: it is: by God it is!

ROBERT. Would your Majesty condescend so far as to say, a fairly successful schemer?

WILLIAM. A devilishly subtle one, I should say. What then?

ROBERT. I have a scheme for dealing with Parliament, though I have never yet found a king subtle enough to understand it.

WILLIAM. Try me.

ROBERT. You, sir, are the last king on earth to understand it. But I will lay it at your royal feet. Just now you choose your ministers on their merits and capacities without regard to their parties, a Whig here, a Tory* there, each in his department which you call his Cabinet, and the assembly of them forming your council, which may be called *your* Cabinet.

WILLIAM. Just so. What fault have you to find with that?

ROBERT. My advice to your Majesty is that in future you choose all your ministers from the same party, and that this party shall always be the party which has a majority in the House of Commons.

WILLIAM. You are mad. Who ever heard of such a thing?

ROBERT. All things must have a beginning, sir. Think it over.

WILLIAM. I am thinking it over. And I remember what you have forgotten.

ROBERT. What is that, your Majesty?

WILLIAM. That the majority in the House of Commons at present is a Whig majority.

ROBERT. I have not forgotten it, sir. You must at once get rid of all your Tory ministers and replace them by Whigs.

WILLIAM. But, man alive, I am a Tory. Are you out of your senses?

ROBERT. Some day the Tories will have a majority and will defeat the Whig government on some measure. You will then immediately dissolve Parliament; and when the Tories come back from the general election with a majority you will choose Tory ministers only.

WILLIAM. But what is the purpose of this absurdity? You talk as coolly as if you were talking sense. Why are you talking nonsense?

ROBERT. If your Majesty will only deign to do what I advise, I pledge my word—

WILLIAM [*sceptically*]. Hmm!

ROBERT. Pardon: I should have said I pledge my reputation as a schemer. Well, I pledge it that from the moment when your Majesty adopts this plan no member of the House of Commons will ever again vote according to his principles or his convictions or his judgment or his religion or any other of his fancies. The people will think that he is voting on toleration, on peace or war, on whether the crown shall go to the elector of Hanover* if your sister-in-law's children continue to die,* on the enclosure of commons* or billeting* or the window tax* or what not; but the real question on which he will always be voting is whether or no his party shall remain in office or he himself have to spend half his property on another election with the chance of losing his seat* if his opponent has a few thousand pounds more to spend than he.

WILLIAM. Dont be a fool, Robert. I should be the slave of the majority no matter how they voted. And what has all this to do with the army and the money to pay for it?

ROBERT. There would be only one way of voting about the war or about anything; and you could always count on it. No majority, Whig or Tory, dare vote for surrender to our natural enemies the French, or to the Pope.

WILLIAM. The Pope is on my side.

ROBERT. Fortunately only a few of us know that curious fact. Your best card in England is always No Popery.*

WILLIAM. You are laying a trap for me. You want to make the majority in the Commons the real ruler and make the monarch a puppet. And as the majority is always led by the nose by some ambitious schemer with the gift of the gab like yourself, he would be able to dictate to me as if he were the king and I a nobody.

ROBERT. I shall never be a dictator while you live, because you, sir, will never be a nobody. But I give you this further pledge. That if you do as I advise, you will have nothing to fear from the boldest and ablest adventurer, were he Cromwell himself, or Lilburne the Leveller.* He will spend half his life and most of his means in getting into Parliament; and when he at last arrives there he will have no time to think of anything but how to get into your Majesty's Cabinet. When he intrigues his way to the top of that, he will be a master of the Party game and of nothing else. He will feed out of your Majesty's hand. And the people will imagine they are free because they have a parliament. Then you can fight all Europe all the time to your heart's content.

WILLIAM. I dont understand it and dont believe it. But as I cannot go on as at present, not knowing where my next regiment or my next penny is to come from, I will try your plan until I have driven Louis back to his pigstye. And if the plan fails I will have your head off by hook or crook.

ROBERT. You shall, sir. It has been on my weary shoulders too long.

Twentyfive years elapse. William and Sunderland, having died in the same year, have been eighteen years in their coffins. Queen Anne is dead; and*

George the First is King. Sunderland's son Charles,* aged 45, is a member of the Whig Government. Robert Walpole,* aged 44, though a notable Whig Parliamentarian, leads the Opposition to the Peerage Bill.* As it happens, they meet one morning in St James's Park,* where they are taking the air. Walpole is inclined to pass on with a wave of the hand; but Sunderland is determined to engage him in conversation and will not be shaken off. After the usual commonplaces he comes to his point.

SUNDERLAND. I wish I could have your support for this Peerage Bill of mine. Frankly, I fear you will defeat me if you oppose it. Why not come to my aid? It is not a Party question: we are all Whigs, and all equally interested in it.

WALPOLE. How do you make that out?

SUNDERLAND. Well, is it not as plain as a pikestaff?* We Whigs are above all Parliament men: to us British liberty means the supremacy of Parliament. Parliament has two rival powers to fear: the king and the voting mob. My sainted father, a grain or two of whose political genius I may claim to have inherited, rescued us from the tyranny of the mob by the Party System. He made you what you are: the greatest Party leader in the world: you owe your eminence to his invention.

WALPOLE. It costs a lot of money. Every man has his price.

SUNDERLAND. All the more reason for making sure of the cash for us, and not for the mob. But what about Parliament's other rival, the King?

WALPOLE. The king question was settled seventyone years ago.

SUNDERLAND. Nay, my dear Walpole, you cannot kill kingship with a single chop of the axe in Whitehall.* The Restoration* brought back the House of Lords, and the King's power to pack it by making as many new peers as he pleased at any moment. The sole purpose of the Peerage Bill is to destroy that power. It will make it impossible for the king ever to make a single peer in excess of the present number. Surely you agree.

WALPOLE. Do I? I think not. Your sainted father persuaded King William that the Party System would give him the control of Parliament. But it really gave the parliamentary majority the control of the king. That ought to suit you very well, because you have the control of the majority until I get it back again, as I shall do when I defeat your Bill.

SUNDERLAND. But why defeat us on this Bill, which is as much in your interest as in mine? You can choose some other issue.

WALPOLE. It is not as much in my interest as in yours. You are a peer: I am a commoner.* You want to make the Lords supreme by breaking the king's power over them. I want the king to keep his power over the Lords, and the Commons to keep its power over the King. I can see through and through your game. I have English brains, not Dutch ones.

SUNDERLAND. You are too clever for me, I see. But consider. You are a Commoner; but you will not always be a Commoner. You will soon be one of us. You know there is an earldom waiting for you to stretch out your hand and take it.

WALPOLE. Yes, provided the King keeps his power to make me an earl. Your Bill might deprive him of that power.

SUNDERLAND. Pooh! There is always a vacancy.

WALPOLE. Even so, an earldom would be the end of me. I do not look forward to being kicked upstairs. The House of Lords is the springboard from which you plunged into politics at 21.* For me it is the shelf on which I shall be laid by at three score and ten.*

SUNDERLAND. That may be so in your personal case. But take the larger view. Consider the interests of the country. The Upper House, with all its faults, stands between England and the mob of rich commercial upstarts who want to make money out of her: money, money and still more money. You are not an upstart: you are a country gentleman.

WALPOLE. Yes; and you are up to the neck in this commercial South Sea madness.* It will be your ruin. I warn you: it will be the end of you politically* within a year from now.

SUNDERLAND. You are impossible. [*Brusquely*] Good morning. [*He walks quickly away, leaving Walpole to finish his walk alone*].

SHAKESPEAREAN SHORTS

THE DARK LADY OF THE SONNETS

PREFACE

How the Play came to be Written

I HAD better explain why, in this little *pièce d'occasion*,* written for a performance in aid of the funds of the project of establishing a National Theatre as a memorial to Shakespear,* I have identified the Dark Lady with Mistress Mary Fitton.* First, let me say that I do not contend that the Dark Lady was Mary Fitton, because when the case in Mary's favor (or against her, if you please to consider that the Dark Lady was no better than she ought to have been) was complete, a portrait of Mary came to light and turned out to be that of a fair lady, not of a dark one. That settles the question, if the portrait is authentic, which I see no reason to doubt, and the lady's hair undyed, which is perhaps less certain. Shakespear rubbed in the lady's complexion in his sonnets mercilessly; for in his day black hair was as unpopular as red hair was in the early days of Queen Victoria. Any tinge lighter than raven black must be held fatal to the strongest claim to be the Dark Lady. And so, unless it can be shewn that Shakespear's sonnets exasperated Mary Fitton into dyeing her hair and getting painted in false colors, I must give up all pretence that my play is historical. The later suggestion of Mr Acheson* that the Dark Lady, far from being a maid of honor, kept a tavern in Oxford, and was the mother of Davenant* the poet, is the one I should have adopted had I wished to be up to date. Why, then, did I introduce the Dark Lady as Mistress Fitton?

Well, I had two reasons. The play was not to have been written by me at all, but by Dame Edith Lyttelton;* and it was she who suggested a scene of jealousy between Queen Elizabeth and the Dark Lady at the expense of the unfortunate Bard. Now this, if the Dark Lady was a maid of honor, was quite easy. If she were a tavern landlady, it would have strained all probability. So I stuck to Mary Fitton. But I had another and more personal reason. I was, in a manner, present at the birth of the Fitton theory. Its parent and I had become acquainted; and he used to consult me on obscure passages in the sonnets, on which, as far as I can remember, I never succeeded in throwing the faintest light, at a time when nobody else thought my opinion, on that or any other subject, of the slightest importance. I thought it would be friendly to immortalize him, as the silly literary saying is, much as Shakespear immortalized Mr W.H.,* as he said he would, simply by writing about him.

Let me tell the story formally.

Thomas Tyler*

Throughout the eighties at least, and probably for some years before, the British Museum reading room was used daily by a gentleman of such astonishing and crushing ugliness that no one who had once seen him could ever thereafter forget him. He was of fair complexion, rather golden red than sandy; aged between forty-five and sixty; and dressed in frock coat and tall hat of presentable but never new appearance. His figure was rectangular, waistless, neckless, ankleless, of middle height, looking shortish because, though he was not particularly stout, there was nothing slender about him. His ugliness was not unamiable: it was accidental, external, excrescential.* Attached to his face from the left ear to the point of his chin was a monstrous goitre, which hung down to his collar bone, and was very inadequately balanced by a smaller one on his right eyelid. Nature's malice was so overdone in his case that it somehow failed to produce the effect of repulsion it seemed to have aimed at. When you first met Thomas Tyler you could think of nothing else but whether surgery could really do nothing for him. But after a very brief acquaintance you never thought of his disfigurements at all, and talked to him as you might to Romeo or Lovelace;* only, so many people, especially women, would not risk the preliminary ordeal, that he remained a man apart and a bachelor all his days. I am not to be frightened or prejudiced by a tumor; and I struck up a cordial acquaintance with him, in the course of which he kept me pretty closely on the track of his work at the Museum,* in which I was then, like himself, a daily reader.

He was by profession a man of letters of an uncommercial kind. He was a specialist in pessimism; had made a translation of Ecclesiastes* of which eight copies a year were sold; and followed up the pessimism of Shakespear and Swift* with keen interest. He delighted in a hideous conception which he called the theory of the cycles, according to which the history of mankind and the universe keeps eternally repeating itself without the slightest variation throughout all eternity; so that he had lived and died and had his goitre before and would live and die and have it again and again and again. He liked to believe that nothing that happened to him was completely novel: he was persuaded that he often had some recollection of its previous occurrence in the last cycle. He hunted out allusions to this favorite theory in his three favorite pessimists. He tried his hand occasionally at deciphering ancient inscriptions, reading them as people seem to read the stars, by discovering bears and bulls and swords and goats where, as it seems to me, no sane human being can see anything but stars higgledy-piggledy. Next to the translation of Ecclesiastes, his *magnum opus* was his work on Shakespear's Sonnets, in which he accepted a previous identification of Mr W. H., the 'onlie begetter' of the sonnets, with the Earl of Pembroke (William Herbert), and promulgated his own identification of Mistress Mary Fitton with the Dark Lady. Whether he was right or wrong about the Dark Lady did not matter urgently to me: she might have been Maria Tompkins* for all I cared. But Tyler would have it that she was Mary Fitton; and he tracked Mary down from the first of her marriages in her teens to her tomb in Cheshire, whither he made a pilgrimage and whence returned in triumph with a picture of her statue, and the news that he was convinced she was a dark lady by traces of paint still discernible.

In due course he published his edition of the Sonnets,* with the evidence he had collected. He lent me a copy of the book, which I never returned. But I reviewed it in the Pall Mall Gazette* on the 7th of January 1886, and thereby let loose the Fitton theory in a wider circle of readers than the book could reach. Then Tyler died, sinking unnoted like a stone in the sea. I observe that Mr Acheson, Mrs Davenant's champion, calls him Reverend. It may very well be that he got his knowledge of Hebrew in reading for the Church; and there was always something of the clergyman or the schoolmaster in his dress and air. Possibly he may actually have been ordained. But he never told me that or anything else about his affairs; and his black pessimism would have shot him violently out of any church at present established in the West. We never talked about affairs: we talked about Shakespear, and the Dark Lady, and Swift, and Koheleth,* and the cycles, and the mysterious moments when a feeling came over us that this had happened to us before, and about the forgeries of the Pentateuch* which were offered for sale to the British Museum, and about literature and things of the spirit generally. He always came to my desk at the Museum and spoke to me about something or other, no doubt finding that people who were keen on this sort of conversation were rather scarce. He remains a vivid spot of memory in the void of my forgetfulness, a quite considerable and dignified soul in a grotesquely disfigured body.

Frank Harris*

To the review in the Pall Mall Gazette I attribute, rightly or wrongly, the introduction of Mary Fitton to Mr Frank Harris. My reason for this is that Mr Harris wrote a play* about Shakespear and Mary Fitton; and when I, as a pious duty to Tyler's ghost, reminded the world that it was to Tyler we owed the Fitton theory, Frank Harris, who clearly had not a notion of what had first put Mary into his head, believed, I think, that I had invented Tyler expressly for his discomfiture; for the stress I laid on Tyler's claims must have seemed unaccountable and perhaps malicious on the assumption that he was to me a mere name among the thousands of names in the British Museum catalogue. Therefore I make it clear that I had and have personal reasons for remembering Tyler, and for regarding myself as in some sort charged with the duty of reminding the world of his work. I am sorry for his sake that Mary's portrait is fair, and that Mr W. H. has veered round again from Pembroke to Southampton;* but even so his work was not wasted: it is by exhausting all the hypotheses that we reach the verifiable one; and after all, the wrong road always leads somewhere.

Frank Harris's play was written long before mine. I read it in manuscript before the Shakespear Memorial National Theatre was mooted; and if there is anything except the Fitton theory (which is Tyler's property) in my play which is also in Mr Harris's it was I who annexed it from him and not he from me. It does not matter anyhow, because this play of mine is a brief trifle, and full of manifest impossibilities at that; whilst Mr Harris's play is serious both in size, intention, and quality. But there could not in the nature of things be much resemblance, because Frank conceives Shakespear to have been a broken-hearted, melancholy, enormously sentimental person, whereas I am convinced that he was very like myself: in fact, if I had been born in 1556 instead of in 1856, I should have taken to blank verse and given Shakespear a harder run for his money than all the other Elizabethans put together. Yet the success of Frank Harris's book on Shakespear gave me great delight.

To those who know the literary world of London there was a sharp stroke of ironic comedy in the irresistible verdict in its favor. In critical literature there is one prize that is always open to competition, one blue ribbon that always carries the highest critical rank with it. To win, you must write the best book of your generation on Shakespear. It is felt on all sides that to do this a certain fastidious refinement, a delicacy of taste, a correctness of manner and tone, and high academic distinction in addition to the indispensable scholarship and literary reputation, are needed; and men who pretend to these qualifications are constantly looked to with a gentle expectation that presently they will achieve the great feat. Now if there is a man on earth who is the utter contrary of everything that this description implies; whose very existence is an insult to the ideal it realizes; whose eye disparages, whose resonant voice denounces, whose cold shoulder jostles every decency, every delicacy, every amenity, every dignity, every sweet usage of that quiet life of mutual admiration in which perfect Shakespearean appreciation is expected to arise, that man is Frank Harris. Here is one who is extraordinarily qualified, by a range of sympathy and understanding that extends from the ribaldry of a buccaneer to the shyest tendernesses of the most sensitive poetry, to be all things to all men, yet whose proud humor it is to be to every man, provided the man is eminent and pretentious, the champion of his enemies. To the Archbishop he is an atheist, to the atheist a Catholic mystic, to the Bismarckian Imperialist* an Anacharsis Klootz,* to Anacharsis Klootz a Washington,* to Mrs Proudie* a Don Juan, to Aspasia* a John Knox:* in short, to everyone his complement rather than his counterpart, his antagonist rather than his fellow-creature. Always provided, however, that the persons thus affronted are respectable persons.* Sophie Perovskaia, who perished on the scaffold for blowing Alexander II* to fragments, may perhaps have echoed Hamlet's

> Oh God, Horatio, what a wounded name—
> Things standing thus unknown—I leave behind!*

but Frank Harris, in his Sonia,* has rescued her from that injustice, and enshrined her among the saints. He has lifted the Chicago anarchists* out of their infamy, and shewn that, compared with the Capitalism that killed them, they were heroes and martyrs. He has done this with the most unusual power of conviction. The story, as he tells it, inevitably and irresistibly displaces all the vulgar, mean, purblind, spiteful versions. There is a precise realism and an unsmiling, measured, determined sincerity which gives a strange dignity to the work of one whose fixed practice and ungovernable impulse it is to kick conventional dignity whenever he sees it.

Harris 'durche Mitleid wissend'*

Frank Harris is everything except a humorist, not, apparently, from stupidity, but because scorn overcomes humor in him. Nobody ever dreamt of reproaching Milton's Lucifer* for not seeing the comic side of his fall; and nobody who has read Mr Harris's stories desires to have them lightened by chapters from the hand of Artemus Ward.* Yet he knows the taste and the value of humor. He was one of the few men of letters who really appreciated Oscar Wilde,* though he did not rally fiercely to Wilde's side until the world deserted Oscar in his ruin. I myself was present at a curious meeting between the two, when Harris, on the eve of the Queensberry trial,* prophesied to Wilde with miraculous precision exactly what immediately afterwards happened to him, and warned him to leave the country. It was the first time within my knowledge that such a forecast proved true. Wilde, though under no illusion as to the folly of the quite unselfish suit-at-law he had been persuaded to begin, nevertheless so miscalculated the force of the social vengeance he was unloosing on himself that he fancied it could be stayed by putting up the editor of The Saturday Review* (as Mr Harris then was) to declare that he considered Dorian Grey* a highly moral book, which it certainly is. When Harris foretold him the truth, Wilde denounced him as a fainthearted friend who was failing him in his hour of need, and left the room in anger. Harris's idiosyncratic power of pity saved him from feeling or shewing the smallest resentment; and events presently proved to Wilde how insanely he had been advised in taking the action, and how accurately Harris had gauged the situation.

The same capacity for pity governs Harris's study of Shakespear,* whom, as I have said, he pities too much; but that he is not insensible to humor is shewn not only by his appreciation of Wilde, but by the fact that the group of contributors* who made his editorship of The Saturday Review so remarkable, and of whom I speak none the less highly because I happened to be one of them myself, were all, in their various ways, humorists.

'Sidney's Sister: Pembroke's Mother'*

And now to return to Shakespear. Though Mr Harris followed Tyler in identifying Mary Fitton as the Dark Lady, and the Earl of Pembroke as the addressee of the other sonnets and the man who made love successfully to Shakespear's mistress, he very characteristically refuses to follow Tyler on one point, though for the life of me I cannot remember whether it was one of the surmises which Tyler published, or only one which he submitted to me to see what I would say about it, just as he used to submit difficult lines from the sonnets.

This surmise was that 'Sidney's sister: Pembroke's mother' set Shakespear on to persuade Pembroke* to marry, and that this was the explanation of those earlier sonnets which so persistently and unnaturally urged matrimony on Mr W. H. I take this to be one of the brightest of Tyler's ideas, because the persuasions in the sonnets are unaccountable and out of character unless they were offered to please somebody whom Shakespear desired to please, and who took a motherly interest in Pembroke. There is a further temptation in the theory for me. The most charming of all Shakespear's old women, indeed the most charming of all his women, young or old, is the Countess of Rousillon in All's Well That Ends Well.* It has a certain individuality among them which suggests a portrait. Mr Harris will have it that all Shakespear's nice old women are drawn from his beloved mother;* but I see no evidence whatever that Shakespear's mother was a particularly nice woman or that he was particularly fond of her. That she was a simple incarnation of extravagant maternal pride like the mother of Coriolanus in Plutarch,* as Mr Harris asserts, I cannot believe: she is quite as likely to have borne her son a grudge for becoming 'one of these harlotry players'* and disgracing the Ardens. Anyhow, as a conjectural model for the Countess of Rousillon, I prefer that one* of whom Jonson wrote

> Sidney's sister: Pembroke's mother:
> Death ere thou has slain another,
> Learned and fair and good as she,
> Time shall throw a dart at thee.

But Frank will not have her at any price, because his ideal Shakespear is rather like a sailor in a melodrama; and a sailor in a melodrama must adore his mother. I do not at all belittle such sailors. They are the emblems of human generosity; but Shakespear was not an emblem; he was a man and the author of Hamlet, who had no illusions about his mother. In weak moments one almost wishes he had.

Shakespear's Social Standing

On the vexed question of Shakespear's social standing Mr Harris says that Shakespear 'had not had the advantage of a middle-class training.' I suggest that Shakespear missed this questionable advantage, not because he was socially too low to have attained to it, but because he conceived himself as belonging to the upper class from which our public school boys are now drawn. Let Mr Harris survey for a moment the field of contemporary journalism. He will see there some men who have the very characteristics from which he infers that Shakespear was at a social disadvantage through his lack of middle-class training. They are rowdy, ill-mannered, abusive, mischievous, fond of quoting obscene schoolboy anecdotes, adepts in that sort of blackmail which consists in mercilessly libelling and insulting every writer whose opinions are sufficiently heterodox to make it almost impossible for him to risk perhaps five years of a slender income by an appeal to a prejudiced orthodox jury; and they see nothing in all this cruel blackguardism but an uproariously jolly rag, although they are by no means without genuine literary ability, a love of letters, and even some artistic conscience. But he will find not one of the models of this type (I say nothing of mere imitators of it) below the rank that looks at the middle class, not humbly and enviously from below, but insolently from above. Mr Harris himself notes Shakespear's contempt for the tradesman and mechanic, and his incorrigible addiction to smutty jokes. He does us the public service of sweeping away the familiar plea of the Bardolatrous* ignoramus, that Shakespear's coarseness was part of the manners of his time, putting his pen with precision on the one name, Spenser,* that is necessary to expose such a libel on Elizabethan decency. There was nothing whatever to prevent Shakespear from being as decent as More* was before him, or Bunyan* after him, and as self-respecting as Raleigh* or Sidney, except the tradition of his class, in which education or statesmanship may no doubt be acquired by those who have a turn for them, but in which insolence, derision, profligacy, obscene jesting, debt contracting, and rowdy mischievousness, give continual scandal to the pious, serious, industrious, solvent bourgeois. No other class is infatuated enough to believe that gentlemen are born and not made by a very elaborate process of culture. Even kings are taught and coached and drilled from their earliest boyhood to play their part. But the man of family (I am convinced that Shakespear took that view of himself) will plunge into society without a lesson in table manners, into politics without a lesson in history, into the city without a lesson in business, and into the army without a lesson in honor.

It has been said, with the object of proving Shakespear a laborer, that he could hardly write his name. Why? Because he 'had not the advantage of a middle-class training.' Shakespear himself tells us, through Hamlet, that gentlemen purposely wrote badly lest they should be mistaken for scriveners;* but most of them, then as now, wrote badly because they could not write any better. In short, the whole range of Shakespear's foibles: the snobbishness, the naughtiness, the contempt for tradesmen and mechanics, the assumption that witty conversation can only mean smutty conversation, the flunkeyism towards social superiors and insolence towards social inferiors, the easy ways with servants which is seen not only between The Two Gentlemen of Verona and their valets,* but in the affection and respect inspired by a great servant like Adam:* all these are the characteristics of Eton and Harrow,* not of the public elementary* or private adventure school.* They prove, as everything we know about Shakespear suggests, that he thought of the Shakespears and Ardens as families of consequence, and regarded himself as a gentleman under a cloud through his father's ill luck in business, and never for a moment as a man of the people. This is at once the explanation of and excuse for his snobbery. He was not a parvenu trying to cover his humble origin with a purchased coat of arms:* he was a gentleman resuming what he conceived to be his natural position as soon as he gained the means to keep it up.

*This Side Idolatry**

There is another matter which I think Mr Harris should ponder. He says that Shakespear was but 'little esteemed by his own generation.' He even describes Jonson's description of his 'little Latin and less Greek'* as a sneer, whereas it occurs in an unmistakeably sincere eulogy of Shakespear, written after his death, and is clearly meant to heighten the impression of Shakespear's prodigious natural endowments by pointing out that they were not due to scholastic acquirements. Now there is a sense in which it is true enough that Shakespear was too little esteemed by his own generation, or, for the matter of that, by any subsequent generation. The bargees on the Regent's Canal* do not chant Shakespear's verses as the gondoliers in Venice are said to chant the verses of Tasso* (a practice which was suspended for some reason during my stay in Venice: at least no gondolier ever did it in my hearing). Shakespear is no more a popular author than Rodin is a popular sculptor or Richard Strauss a popular composer. But Shakespear was certainly not such a fool as to expect the Toms, Dicks, and Harrys of his time to be any more interested in dramatic poetry than Newton,* later on, expected them to be interested in fluxions.* And when we come to the question whether Shakespear missed that assurance which all great men have had from the more capable and susceptible members of their generation that they were great men, Ben Jonson's evidence disposes of so improbable a notion at once and for ever. 'I loved the man,' says Ben, 'this side idolatry, as well as any.' Now why in the name of common sense should he have made that qualification unless there had been, not only idolatry, but idolatry fulsome enough to irritate Jonson into an express disavowal of it? Jonson, the bricklayer, must have felt sore sometimes when Shakespear spoke and wrote of bricklayers as his inferiors. He must have felt it a little hard that being a better scholar, and perhaps a braver and tougher man physically than Shakespear, he was not so successful or so well liked. But in spite of this he praised Shakespear to the utmost stretch of his powers of eulogy: in fact, notwithstanding his disclaimer, he did not stop 'this side idolatry.' If, therefore, even Jonson felt himself forced to clear himself of extravagance and absurdity in his appreciation of Shakespear, there must have been many people about who idolized Shakespear as American ladies idolize Paderewski,* and who carried Bardolatry, even in the Bard's own time, to an extent that threatened to make his reasonable admirers ridiculous.

Shakespear's Pessimism

I submit to Mr Harris that by ruling out this idolatry, and its possible effect in making Shakespear think that his public would stand anything from him, he has ruled out a far more plausible explanation of the faults of such a play as Timon of Athens* than his theory that Shakespear's passion for the Dark Lady 'cankered and took on proud flesh in him, and tortured him to nervous breakdown and madness.'* In Timon the intellectual bankruptcy is obvious enough: Shakespear tried once too often to make a play out of the cheap pessimism which is thrown into despair by a comparison of actual human nature with theoretical morality, actual law and administration with abstract justice, and so forth. But Shakespear's perception of the fact that all men, judged by the moral standard which they apply to others and by which they justify their punishment of others, are fools and scoundrels, does not date from the Dark Lady complication: he seems to have been born with it. If in The Comedy of Errors and A Midsummer Night's Dream* the persons of the drama are not quite so ready for treachery and murder as Laertes* and even Hamlet himself (not to mention the procession of ruffians who pass through the latest plays) it is certainly not because they have any more regard for law or religion. There is only one place in Shakespear's plays where the sense of shame is used as a human attribute; and that is where Hamlet is ashamed, not of anything he himself has done, but of his mother's relations with his uncle. This scene* is an unnatural one: the son's reproaches to his mother, even the fact of his being able to discuss the subject with her, is more repulsive than her relations with her deceased husband's brother.

Here, too, Shakespear betrays for once his religious sense by making Hamlet, in his agony of shame, declare that his mother's conduct makes 'sweet religion a rhapsody of words.'* But for that passage we might almost suppose that the feeling of Sunday morning in the country which Orlando describes so perfectly in As You Like It* was the beginning and end of Shakespear's notion of religion. I say almost, because Isabella in Measure for Measure* has religious charm, in spite of the conventional theatrical assumption that female religion means an inhumanly ferocious chastity. But for the most part Shakespear differentiates his heroes from his villains much more by what they do than by what they are. Don Juan in Much Ado* is a true villain: a man with a malicious will; but he is too dull a duffer to be of any use in a leading part; and when we come to the great villains like Macbeth, we find, as Mr Harris points out, that they are precisely identical with the heroes: Macbeth is only Hamlet incongruously committing murders and engaging in hand-to-hand combats. And Hamlet, who does not dream of apologizing for the three murders he commits, is always apologizing because he has not yet committed a fourth, and finds, to his great bewilderment, that he does not want to commit it. 'It cannot be,' he says, 'but I am pigeon-livered, and lack gall to make oppression bitter; else, ere this, I should have fatted all the region kites with this slave's offal.'* Really one is tempted to suspect that when Shylock asks 'Hates any man the thing he would not kill?'* he is expressing the natural and proper sentiments of the human race as Shakespear understood them, and not the vindictiveness of a stage Jew.*

Gaiety of Genius

In view of these facts, it is dangerous to cite Shakespear's pessimism as evidence of the despair of a heart broken by the Dark Lady. There is an irrepressible gaiety of genius which enables it to bear the whole weight of the world's misery without blenching.* There is a laugh always ready to avenge its tears of discouragement. In the lines which Mr Harris quotes only to declare that he can make nothing of them, and to condemn them as out of character, Richard III, immediately after pitying himself because

> There is no creature loves me
> And if I die no soul will pity me,

adds, with a grin,

> Nay, wherefore should they, since that I myself
> Find in myself no pity for myself?*

Let me again remind Mr Harris of Oscar Wilde. We all dreaded to read De Profundis:* our instinct was to stop our ears, or run away from the wail of a broken, though by no means contrite, heart. But we were throwing away our pity. De Profundis was de profundis indeed: Wilde was too good a dramatist to throw away so powerful an effect; but none the less it was de profundis in excelsis.* There was more laughter between the lines of that book than in a thousand farces by men of no genius. Wilde, like Richard and Shakespear, found in himself no pity for himself. There is nothing that marks the born dramatist more unmistakeably than this discovery of comedy in his own misfortunes almost in proportion to the pathos with which the ordinary man announces their tragedy. I cannot for the life of me see the broken heart in Shakespear's latest works. 'Hark, hark! the lark at heaven's gate sings'* is not the lyric of a broken man; nor is Cloten's comment that if Imogen* does not appreciate it, 'it is a vice in her ears which horse hairs, and cats' guts, and the voice of unpaved eunuch to boot, can never amend,'* the sally of a saddened one. Is it not clear that to the last there was in Shakespear an incorrigible divine levity, an inexhaustible joy that derided sorrow? Think of the poor Dark Lady having to stand up to this unbearable power of extracting a grim fun from everything. Mr Harris writes as if Shakespear did all the suffering and the Dark Lady all the cruelty. But why does he not put himself in the Dark Lady's place for a moment as he has put himself so successfully in Shakespear's? Imagine her reading the hundred and thirtieth sonnet!

> My mistress' eyes are nothing like the sun;
> Coral is far more red than her lips' red;
> If snow be white, why then her breasts are dun;*
> If hairs be wire, black wires grow on her head;
> I have seen roses damasked,* red and white,
> But no such roses see I in her cheeks;
> And in some perfumes is there more delight
> Than in the breath that from my mistress reeks.*
> I love to hear her speak; yet well I know
> That music hath a far more pleasing sound.
> I grant I never saw a goddess go:
> My mistress, when she walks, treads on the ground.
>   And yet, by heaven, I think my love as rare
>   As any she belied with false compare.*

Take this as a sample of the sort of compliment from which she was
never for a moment safe with Shakespear. Bear in mind that she was not
a comedian; that the Elizabethan fashion of treating brunettes as ugly
women must have made her rather sore on the subject of her complexion; that no human being, male or female, can conceivably enjoy being
chaffed* on that point in the fourth couplet about the perfumes; that
Shakespear's revulsions, as the sonnet immediately preceding shews,
were as violent as his ardors, and were expressed with the realistic
power and horror that makes Hamlet say that the heavens got sick when
they saw the queen's conduct; and then ask Mr Harris whether any
woman could have stood it for long, or have thought the 'sugred'* compliment worth the cruel wounds, the cleaving of the heart in twain,*
that seemed to Shakespear as natural and amusing a reaction as the bur-
lesquing of his heroics by Pistol,* his sermons by Falstaff,* and his
poems by Cloten* and Touchstone.*

Jupiter and Semele

This does not mean that Shakespear was cruel: evidently he was not;
but it was not cruelty that made Jupiter reduce Semele to ashes:* it was
the fact that he could not help being a god nor she help being a mortal.
The one thing Shakespear's passion for the Dark Lady was not, was
what Mr Harris in one passage calls it: idolatrous.* If it had been, she
might have been able to stand it. The man who dotes 'yet doubts; suspects, yet strongly loves,'* is tolerable even by a spoilt and tyrannical
mistress; but what woman could possibly endure a man who dotes without doubting; who *knows* and who is hugely amused at the absurdity of
his infatuation for a woman of whose mortal imperfections not one
escapes him: a man always exchanging grins with Yorick's skull,* and
inviting 'my lady' to laugh at the sepulchral humor of the fact that
though she paint an inch thick* (which the Dark Lady may have done),
to Yorick's favor she must come at last. To the Dark Lady he must
sometimes have seemed cruel beyond description: an intellectual
Caliban.* True, a Caliban who could say

> Be not afeard: the isle is full of noises,
> Sounds and sweet airs that give delight and hurt not.
> Sometimes a thousand twangling instruments
> Will hum about mine ears; and sometimes voices,
> That, if I then had waked after long sleep,
> Will make me sleep again; and then, in dreaming,
> The clouds, methought, would open and shew riches

> Ready to drop on me: that when I wak'd
> I cried to dream again.*

which is very lovely; but the Dark Lady may have had that vice in her ears which Cloten dreaded:* she may not have seen the beauty of it, whereas there can be no doubt at all that of 'My mistress' eyes are nothing like the sun,' &c.,* not a word was lost on her.

And is it to be supposed that Shakespear was too stupid or too modest not to see at last that it was a case of Jupiter and Semele? Shakespear was most certainly not modest in that sense. The timid cough of the minor poet was never heard from him.

> Not marble, nor the gilded monuments
> Of princes, shall outlive this powerful rhyme*

is only one out of a dozen passages in which he (possibly with a keen sense of the fun of scandalizing the modest coughers) proclaimed his place and his power in 'the wide world dreaming of things to come.'* The Dark Lady most likely thought this side of him insufferably conceited; for there is no reason to suppose that she liked his plays any better than Minna Wagner* liked Richard's music dramas: as likely as not, she thought The Spanish Tragedy* worth six Hamlets. He was not stupid either: if his class limitations and a profession that cut him off from actual participation in great affairs of State had not confined his opportunities of intellectual and political training to private conversation and to the Mermaid Tavern,* he would probably have become one of the ablest men of his time instead of being merely its ablest playwright. One might surmise that Shakespear found out that the Dark Lady's brains could no more keep pace with his than Anne Hathaway's,* if there were any evidence that their friendship ceased when he stopped writing sonnets to her. As a matter of fact the consolidation of a passion into an enduring intimacy generally puts an end to sonnets.

That the Dark Lady broke Shakespear's heart, as Mr Harris will have it she did, is an extremely unShakespearian hypothesis. 'Men have died from time to time, and worms have eaten them; but not for love,'* says Rosalind. Richard of Gloster, into whom Shakespear put all his own impish superiority to vulgar sentiment, exclaims

> And this word 'love,' which greybeards call divine,
> Be resident in men like one another
> And not in me: I am myself alone.*

Hamlet has not a tear for Ophelia:* her death moves him to fierce disgust for the sentimentality of Laertes by her grave;* and when he discusses the scene with Horatio immediately after, he utterly forgets her, though he is sorry he forgot himself, and jumps at the proposal of a fencing match to finish the day with. As against this view Mr Harris pleads Romeo,* Orsino,* and even Antonio;* and he does it so penetratingly that he convinces you that Shakespear did betray himself again and again in these characters; but self-betrayal is one thing; and self-portrayal, as in Hamlet and Mercutio,* is another. Shakespear never 'saw himself,' as actors say, in Romeo or Orsino or Antonio. In Mr Harris's own play Shakespear is presented with the most pathetic tenderness. He is tragic, bitter, pitiable, wretched and broken among a robust crowd of Jonsons and Elizabeths; but to me he is not Shakespear because I miss the Shakespearian irony and the Shakespearian gaiety. Take these away and Shakespear is no longer Shakespear: all the bite, the impetus, the strength, the grim delight in his own power of looking terrible facts in the face with a chuckle, is gone; and you have nothing left but that most depressing of all things: a victim. Now who can think of Shakespear as a man with a grievance? Even in that most thoroughgoing and inspired of all Shakespear's loves: his love of music (which Mr Harris has been the first to appreciate* at anything like its value), there is a dash of mockery. 'Spit in the hole, man; and tune again.'* 'Divine air! Now is his soul ravished. Is it not strange that sheep's guts should hale the souls out of men's bodies?'* 'An he had been a dog that should have howled thus, they would have hanged him.'* There is just as much Shakespear here as in the inevitable quotation about the sweet south and the bank of violets.*

I lay stress on this irony of Shakespear's, this impish rejoicing in pessimism, this exultation in what breaks the hearts of common men, not only because it is diagnostic of that immense energy of life which we call genius, but because its omission is the one glaring defect in Mr Harris's otherwise extraordinarily penetrating book. Fortunately, it is an omission that does not disable the book as (in my judgment) it disabled the hero of the play, because Mr Harris left himself out of his play, whereas he pervades his book, mordant, deep-voiced, and with an unconquerable style which is the man.

The Idol of the Bardolaters

There is even an advantage in having a book on Shakespear with the Shakespearian irony left out of account. I do not say that the missing chapter should not be added in the next edition: the hiatus is too great: it leaves the reader too uneasy before this touching picture of a writhing worm substituted for the invulnerable giant. But it is none the less probable that in no other way could Mr Harris have got at his man as he has. For, after all, what is the secret of the hopeless failure of the academic Bardolaters to give us a credible or even interesting Shakespear, and the easy triumph of Mr Harris in giving us both? Simply that Mr Harris has assumed that he was dealing with a man, whilst the others have assumed that they were writing about a god, and have therefore rejected every consideration of fact, tradition, or inter-pretation, that pointed to any human imperfection in their hero. They thus leave themselves with so little material that they are forced to begin by saying that we know very little about Shakespear. As a matter of fact, with the plays and sonnets in our hands, we know much more about Shakespear than we know about Dickens or Thackeray: the only difficulty is that we deliberately suppress it because it proves that Shakespear was not only very unlike the conception of a god current in Clapham, but was not, according to the same reckoning, even a respect-able man. The academic view starts with a Shakespear who was not scurrilous; therefore the verses about 'lousy Lucy'* cannot have been written by him, and the cognate passages in the plays are either strokes of character-drawing or gags interpolated by the actors. This ideal Shakespear was too well behaved to get drunk; therefore the tradition that his death was hastened by a drinking bout with Jonson and Drayton* must be rejected, and the remorse of Cassio* treated as a thing observed, not experienced: nay, the disgust of Hamlet at the drinking customs of Denmark* is taken to establish Shakespear as the superior of Alexander* in self-control, and the greatest of teetotalers.

Now this system of inventing your great man to start with, and then rejecting all the materials that do not fit him, with the ridiculous result that you have to declare that there are no materials at all (with your waste-paper basket full of them), ends in leaving Shakespear with a much worse character than he deserves. For though it does not greatly matter whether he wrote the lousy Lucy lines or not, and does not really matter at all whether he got drunk when he made a night of it with Jonson and Drayton, the sonnets raise an unpleasant question which does matter a good deal; and the refusal of the academic Bardolaters to discuss or even mention this question has had the effect of producing a silent verdict against Shakespear. Mr Harris tackles the question openly, and has no difficulty whatever in convincing us that Shakespear was a man of normal constitution sexually, and was not the victim of that most cruel and pitiable of all the freaks of nature: the freak which transposes the normal aim of the affections.* Silence on this point means condemnation; and the condemnation has been general throughout the present generation, though it only needed Mr Harris's fearless handling of the matter to sweep away what is nothing but a morbid and very disagreeable modern fashion. There is always some stock accusation brought against eminent persons. When I was a boy every well-known man was accused of beating his wife. Later on, for some unexplained reason, he was accused of psychopathic derangement. And this fashion is retrospective. The cases of Shakespear and Michel Angelo* are cited as proving that every genius of the first magnitude was a sufferer; and both here and in Germany there are circles in which such derangement is grotesquely reverenced as part of the stigmata of heroic powers. All of which is gross nonsense. Unfortunately, in Shakespear's case, prudery, which cannot prevent the accusation from being whispered, does prevent the refutation from being shouted. Mr Harris, the deep-voiced, refuses to be silenced. He dismisses with proper contempt the stupidity which places an outrageous construction on Shakespear's apologies in the sonnets for neglecting that 'perfect ceremony'* of love which consists in returning calls and making protestations and giving presents and paying the trumpery attentions which men of genius always refuse to bother about, and to which touchy people who have no genius attach so much importance. No reader who had not been tampered with by the psychopathic monomaniacs could ever put any construction but the obvious and innocent one on these passages. But the general vocabulary of the sonnets to Pembroke (or whoever 'Mr W. H.' really was) is so overcharged according to modern ideas that a reply on the general case is necessary.

Shakespear's alleged Sycophancy and Perversion

That reply, which Mr Harris does not hesitate to give, is two-fold: first, that Shakespear was, in his attitude towards earls, a sycophant; and, second, that the normality of Shakespear's sexual constitution is only too well attested by the excessive susceptibility to the normal impulse shewn in the whole mass of his writings. This latter is the really conclusive reply. In the case of Michel Angelo, for instance, one must admit that if his works are set beside those of Titian or Paul Veronese,* it is impossible not to be struck by the absence in the Florentine of that susceptibility to feminine charm which pervades the pictures of the Venetians. But, as Mr Harris points out (though he does not use this particular illustration) Paul Veronese is an anchorite* compared to Shakespear. The language of the sonnets addressed to Pembroke, extravagant as it now seems, is the language of compliment and fashion, transfigured no doubt by Shakespear's verbal magic, and hyperbolical, as Shakespear always seems to people who cannot conceive so vividly as he, but still unmistakeable for anything else than the expression of a friendship delicate enough to be wounded, and a manly loyalty deep enough to be outraged. But the language of the sonnets to the Dark Lady is the language of passion: their cruelty shews it. There is no evidence that Shakespear was capable of being unkind in cold blood. But in his revulsions from love, he was bitter, wounding, even ferocious; sparing neither himself nor the unfortunate woman whose only offence was that she had reduced the great man to the common human denominator.

In seizing on these two points Mr Harris has made so sure a stroke, and places his evidence so featly that there is nothing left for me to do but to plead that the second is sounder than the first, which is, I think, marked by the prevalent mistake as to Shakespear's social position, or, if you prefer it, the confusion between his actual social position as a penniless tradesman's son taking to the theatre for a livelihood, and his own conception of himself as a gentleman of good family. I am prepared to contend that though Shakespear was undoubtedly sentimental in his expressions of devotion to Mr W. H. even to a point which nowadays makes both ridiculous, he was not sycophantic if Mr W. H. was really attractive and promising, and Shakespear deeply attached to him. A sycophant does not tell his patron that his fame will survive, not in the renown of his own actions, but in the sonnets of his sycophant. A sycophant, when his patron cuts him out in a love affair, does not tell his patron exactly what he thinks of him. Above all, a sycophant does not write to his patron precisely as he feels on all occasions; and this rare kind of sincerity is all over the sonnets. Shakespear, we are told, was 'a very civil gentleman.'* This must mean that his desire to please people and be liked by them, and his reluctance to hurt their feelings, led him into amiable flattery even when his feelings were not strongly stirred. If this be taken into account along with the fact that Shakespear conceived and expressed all his emotions with a vehemence that sometimes carried him into ludicrous extravagance, making Richard offer his kingdom for a horse* and Othello declare of Cassio that

> Had all his hairs been lives, my great revenge
> Had stomach for them all,*

we shall see more civility and hyperbole than sycophancy even in the earlier and more coldblooded sonnets.

Shakespear and Democracy

Now take the general case pled against Shakespear as an enemy of democracy by Tolstoy,* the late Ernest Crosbie* and others, and endorsed by Mr Harris. Will it really stand fire? Mr Harris emphasizes* the passages in which Shakespear spoke of mechanics and even of small master tradesmen as base persons whose clothes were greasy, whose breath was rank, and whose political imbecility and caprice moved Coriolanus to say to the Roman Radical who demanded at least 'good words' from him

> He that will give good words to thee will flatter
> Beneath abhorring.*

But let us be honest. As political sentiments these lines are an abomination to every democrat. But suppose they are not political sentiments! Suppose they are merely a record of observed fact. John Stuart Mill* told our British workmen that they were mostly liars. Carlyle* told us all that we are mostly fools. Matthew Arnold and Ruskin* were more circumstantial and more abusive. Everybody, including the workers themselves, know that they are dirty, drunken, foul-mouthed, ignorant, gluttonous, prejudiced: in short, heirs to the peculiar ills of poverty and slavery, as well as co-heirs with the plutocracy to all the failings of human nature. Even Shelley* admitted, 200 years after Shakespear wrote Coriolanus, that universal suffrage was out of the question. Surely the real test, not of Democracy, which was not a live political issue in Shakespear's time, but of impartiality in judging classes, which is what one demands from a great human poet, is not that he should flatter the poor and denounce the rich, but that he should weigh them both in the same balance. Now whoever will read Lear and Measure for Measure will find stamped on his mind such an appalled sense of the danger of dressing man in a little brief authority,* such a merciless stripping of the purple from the 'poor, bare, forked animal'* that calls itself a king and fancies itself a god, that one wonders what was the real nature of the mysterious restraint that kept 'Eliza and our James'* from teaching Shakespear to be civil to crowned heads, just as one wonders why Tolstoy was allowed to go free when so many less terrible levellers* went to the galleys or Siberia. From the mature Shakespear we get no such scenes of village snobbery as that between the stage country gentleman Alexander Iden and the stage Radical Jack Cade.* We get the shepherd in As You Like It,* and many honest, brave, human, and loyal servants, beside the inevitable comic ones. Even in the Jingo play,

Henry V, we get Bates and Williams* drawn with all respect and honor as normal rank and file men. In Julius Caesar, Shakespear went to work with a will when he took his cue from Plutarch* in glorifying regicide and transfiguring the republicans. Indeed hero-worshippers have never forgiven him for belittling Caesar and failing to see that side of his assassination which made Goethe denounce it* as the most senseless of crimes. Put the play beside the Charles I of Wills, in which Cromwell* is written down to a point at which the Jack Cade of Henry VI becomes a hero in comparison; and then believe, if you can, that Shakespear was one of them that 'crook the pregnant hinges of the knee where thrift may follow fawning.'* Think of Rosencrantz, Guildenstern,* Osric,* the fop who annoyed Hotspur,* and a dozen passages concerning such people! If such evidence can prove anything (and Mr Harris relies throughout on such evidence) Shakespear loathed courtiers.

If, on the other hand, Shakespear's characters are mostly members of the leisured classes, the same thing is true of Mr Harris's own plays and mine. Industrial slavery is not compatible with that freedom of adventure, that personal refinement and intellectual culture, that scope of action, which the higher and subtler drama demands. Even Cervantes had finally to drop Don Quixote's* troubles with innkeepers demanding to be paid for his food and lodging, and make him as free of economic difficulties as Amadis de Gaul.* Hamlet's experiences simply could not have happened to a plumber. A poor man is useful on the stage only as a blind man is: to excite sympathy. The poverty of the apothecary* in Romeo and Juliet produces a great effect, and even points the sound moral that a poor man cannot afford to have a conscience; but if all the characters of the play had been as poor as he, it would have been nothing but a melodrama of the sort that the Sicilian players* gave us here; and that was not the best that lay in Shakespear's power. When poverty is abolished, and leisure and grace of life become general, the only plays surviving from our epoch which will have any relation to life as it will be lived then will be those in which none of the persons represented are troubled with want of money or wretched drudgery. Our plays of poverty and squalor, now the only ones that are true to the life of the majority of living men, will then be classed with the records of misers and monsters, and read only by historical students of social pathology.

Then consider Shakespear's kings and lords and gentlemen! Would even John Ball* or Jeremiah* complain that they are flattered? Surely a more mercilessly exposed string of scoundrels never crossed the stage. The very monarch who paralyses a rebel by appealing to the divinity that hedges a king, is a drunken and sensual assassin, and is presently killed contemptuously before our eyes in spite of his hedge of divinity. I could write as convincing a chapter on Shakespear's Dickensian prejudice against the throne and the nobility and gentry in general as Mr Harris or Ernest Crosbie on the other side. I could even go so far as to contend that one of Shakespear's defects is his lack of an intelligent comprehension of feudalism.* He had of course no prevision of democratic Collectivism.* He was, except in the commonplaces of war and patriotism, a privateer through and through. Nobody in his plays, whether king or citizen, has any civil public business or conception of such a thing, except in the method of appointing constables, to the abuses in which he called attention quite in the vein of the Fabian Society.* He was concerned about drunkenness and about the idolatry and hypocrisy of our judicial system; but his implied remedy was personal sobriety and freedom from idolatrous illusion in so far as he had any remedy at all, and did not merely despair of human nature. His first and last word on parliament was 'Get thee glass eyes, and, like a scurvy politician, seem to see the thing thou dost not.'* He had no notion of the feeling with which the land nationalizers of today regard the fact that he was a party to the enclosure of common lands at Wellcome.* The explanation is, not a general deficiency in his mind, but the simple fact that in his day what English land needed was individual appropriation and cultivation, and what the English Constitution needed was the incorporation of Whig principles of individual liberty.

Shakespear and the British Public

I have rejected Mr Harris's view that Shakespear died broken-hearted of 'the pangs of love despised.'* I have given my reasons for believing that Shakespear died game, and indeed in a state of levity which would have been considered unbecoming in a bishop. But Mr Harris's evidence does prove that Shakespear had a grievance and a very serious one. He might have been jilted by ten dark ladies and been none the worse for it; but his treatment by the British Public was another matter. The idolatry which exasperated Ben Jonson was by no means a popular movement; and, like all such idolatries, it was excited by the magic of Shakespear's art rather than by his views. He was launched on his career as a successful playwright by the Henry VI trilogy,* a work of no originality, depth, or subtlety except the originality, depth, and subtlety of the feelings and fancies of the common people. But Shakespear was not satisfied with this. What is the use of being Shakespear if you are not allowed to express any notions but those of Autolycus?* Shakespear did not see the world as Autolycus did: he saw it, if not exactly as Ibsen did (for it was not quite the same world), at least with much of Ibsen's power of penetrating its illusions and idolatries, and with all Swift's horror* of its cruelty and uncleanliness.

Now it happens to some men with these powers that they are forced to impose their fullest exercise on the world because they cannot produce popular work. Take Wagner and Ibsen for instance! Their earlier works are no doubt much cheaper than their later ones; still, they were not popular when they were written. The alternative of doing popular work was never really open to them: had they stooped they would have picked up less than they snatched from above the people's heads. But Handel* and Shakespear were not held to their best in this way. They could turn out anything they were asked for, and even heap up the measure. They reviled the British Public, and never forgave it for ignoring their best work and admiring their splendid commonplaces; but they produced the commonplaces all the same, and made them sound magnificent by mere brute faculty for their art. When Shakespear was forced to write popular plays to save his theatre from ruin, he did it mutinously, calling the plays As *You* Like It, and Much Ado About Nothing. All the same, he did it so well that to this day these two genial vulgarities are the main Shakespearean stock-in-trade of our theatres. Later on Burbage's power and popularity as an actor enabled Shakespear to free himself from the tyranny of the box office, and to express himself more freely in plays consisting largely of monologue to be spoken by a great actor from whom the public would stand a good deal. The history of Shakespear's tragedies has thus been the history of a long line of famous actors, from Burbage and Betterton* to Forbes Robertson; and the man of whom* we are told that 'when he would have said that Richard died, and cried A horse! A horse! he Burbage cried'* was the father of nine generations of Shakspearean playgoers, all speaking of Garrick's Richard,* and Kean's Othello,* and Irving's Shylock,* and Forbes Robertson's Hamlet* without knowing or caring how much these had to do with Shakespear's Richard and Othello and so forth. And the plays which were written without great and predominant parts, such as Troilus and Cressida,* All's Well That Ends Well, and Measure for Measure, have dropped on our stage as dead as the second part of Goethe's Faust* or Ibsen's Emperor or Galilean.*

Here, then, Shakespear had a real grievance; and though it is a sentimental exaggeration to describe him as a broken-hearted man in the
face of the passages of reckless jollity and serenely happy poetry in his
latest plays, yet the discovery that his most serious work could reach
success only when carried on the back of a very fascinating actor
who was enormously overcharging his part, and that the serious
plays which did not contain parts big enough to hold the overcharge
were left on the shelf, amply accounts for the evident fact that
Shakespear did not end his life in a glow of enthusiastic satisfaction
with mankind and with the theatre, which is all that Mr Harris can
allege in support of his broken-heart theory.* But even if Shakespear
had had no failures, it was not possible for a man of his powers to
observe the political and moral conduct of his contemporaries without
perceiving that they were incapable of dealing with the problems
raised by their own civilization, and that their attempts to carry out the
codes of law and to practise the religions offered to them by great
prophets and law-givers were and still are so foolish that we now call
for The Superman,* virtually a new species, to rescue the world from
mismanagement. This is the real sorrow of great men; and in the face
of it the notion that when a great man speaks bitterly or looks melancholy he must be troubled by a disappointment in love seems to me
sentimental trifling.

If I have carried the reader with me thus far, he will find that trivial
as this little play of mine is, its sketch of Shakespear is more complete
than its levity suggests. Alas! its appeal for a National Theatre as
a monument to Shakespear failed to touch the very stupid people who
cannot see that a National Theatre is worth having for the sake of the
National Soul. I had unfortunately represented Shakespear as treasur-
ing and using (as I do myself) the jewels of unconsciously musical
speech which common people utter and throw away every day; and this
was taken as a disparagement of Shakespear's 'originality.' Why was
I born with such contemporaries? Why is Shakespear made ridiculous
by such a posterity?

Postscript 1933

The recent death of Frank Harris has refreshed the interest of the
sketch of him in this preface, especially as he died in the act of finishing
a curious biography* of me which has attracted a good deal of notice,
and which is truthful as to its record of bare facts, though its critical
side is badly lamed through Frank's having lost touch with me before

the end of the nineteenth century, and never reconsidered his estimates in the light of my later exploits.

The appeal for a national theatre with which the play concludes, and for the sake of which it was written, elicited applause but no subscriptions. Two years ago a great Shakespear Memorial Theatre was completed at Stratford-upon-Avon through the efforts of Sir Archibald Flower,* replacing the old Shakespear theatre which owed its existence to his family; but Sir Archibald had wasted no time in appealing to Shakespear's countrymen: he had turned to America and received a noble response. The attempt to establish a National Theatre in London to commemorate Shakespear's exploits in that old city, now expanded into a concentration camp much too big for any civic consciousness, was and still is a complete failure, though there is enough money (not English money, of course) available to carry out the project if the Government would provide a site, and the municipality forgo its rates, as foreign Governments and municipalities do.

THE DARK LADY OF THE SONNETS

*Fin de siècle** 15–1600. Midsummer night on the terrace of the Palace at Whitehall,* overlooking the Thames. The Palace clock chimes* four quarters and strikes eleven.*

*A Beefeater** on guard. A Cloaked Man approaches.*

THE BEEFEATER. Stand. Who goes there? Give the word.

THE MAN. Marry! I cannot. I have clean forgotten it.

THE BEEFEATER. Then cannot you pass here. What is your business? Who are you? Are you a true man?

THE MAN. Far from it, Master Warder. I am not the same man two days together: sometimes Adam,* sometimes Benvolio,* and anon the Ghost.*

THE BEEFEATER [*recoiling*] A ghost! Angels and ministers of grace defend us!*

THE MAN. Well said, Master Warder. With your leave I will set that down in writing; for I have a very poor and unhappy brain for remembrance. [*He takes out his tablets and writes*]. Methinks this is a good scene, with you on your lonely watch, and I approaching like a ghost in the moonlight. Stare not so amazedly at me; but mark what I say. I keep tryst* here tonight with a dark lady. She promised to bribe the warder. I gave her the where-withal: four tickets for the Globe Theatre.*

THE BEEFEATER. Plague on her!* She gave me two only.

THE MAN [*detaching a tablet*] My friend: present this tablet, and you will be welcomed at any time when the plays of Will Shakespear are in hand. Bring your wife. Bring your friends. Bring the whole garrison. There is ever plenty of room.

THE BEEFEATER. I care not for these new-fangled plays.* No man can understand a word of them. They are all talk.* Will you not give me a pass for The Spanish Tragedy?*

THE MAN. To see The Spanish Tragedy one pays, my friend. Here are the means. [*He gives him a piece of gold*].

THE BEEFEATER [*overwhelmed*] Gold! Oh, sir, you are a better paymaster than your dark lady.

THE MAN. Women are thrifty, my friend.

THE BEEFEATER. Tis so, sir. And you have to consider that the most open handed of us must een cheapen that which we buy every day. This lady has to make a present to a warder nigh every night of her life.

THE MAN [*turning pale*] I'll not believe it.

THE BEEFEATER. Now you, sir, I dare be sworn, do not have an adventure like this twice in the year.

THE MAN. Villain: wouldst tell me that my dark lady hath ever done thus before? that she maketh occasions to meet other men?

THE BEEFEATER. Now the Lord bless your innocence, sir, do you think you are the only pretty man in the world? A merry lady, sir: a warm bit of stuff. Go to: I'll not see her pass a deceit on a gentleman that hath given me the first piece of gold I ever handled.

THE MAN. Master Warder: is it not a strange thing that we, knowing that all women are false, should be amazed to find our own particular drab* no better than the rest?

THE BEEFEATER. Not all, sir. Decent bodies, many of them.

THE MAN [*intolerantly*] No. All false. All. If thou deny it, thou liest.

THE BEEFEATER. You judge too much by the Court,* sir. There, indeed, you may say of frailty that its name is woman.*

THE MAN [*pulling out his tablets again*] Prithee say that again: that about frailty: the strain of music.*

THE BEEFEATER. What strain of music, sir? I'm no musician, God knows.

THE MAN. There is music in your soul: many of your degree have it very notably. [*Writing*] 'Frailty: thy name is woman!' [*Repeating it affectionately*] 'Thy name is woman.'

THE BEEFEATER. Well, sir, it is but four words. Are you a snapper-up of such unconsidered trifles?*

THE MAN [*eagerly*] Snapper-up of—[*he gasps*] Oh! Immortal phrase! [*He writes it down*]. This man is a greater than I.

THE BEEFEATER. You have my lord Pembroke's* trick, sir.

THE MAN. Like enough: he is my near friend. But what call you his trick?

THE BEEFEATER. Making sonnets by moonlight. And to the same lady too.

THE MAN. No!

THE BEEFEATER. Last night he stood here on your errand, and in your shoes.

THE MAN. Thou, too, Brutus!* And I called him friend!

THE BEEFEATER. Tis ever so, sir.

THE MAN. Tis ever so. Twas ever so. [*He turns away, overcome*]. Two Gentlemen of Verona! Judas! Judas!!

THE BEEFEATER. Is he so bad as that, sir?

THE MAN [*recovering his charity and self-possession*] Bad? O no. Human, Master Warder, human. We call one another names when we are offended, as children do. That is all.

THE BEEFEATER. Ay, sir: words, words, words.* Mere wind, sir. We fill our bellies with the east wind,* sir, as the Scripture hath it. You cannot feed capons so.*

THE MAN. A good cadence. By your leave [*He makes a note of it*].

THE BEEFEATER. What manner of thing is a cadence, sir? I have not heard of it.

THE MAN. A thing to rule the world with, friend.

THE BEEFEATER. You speak strangely, sir: no offence. But, an't like you, you are a very civil gentleman; and a poor man feels drawn to you, you being, as twere, willing to share your thought with him.

THE MAN. Tis my trade. But alas! the world for the most part will none of my thoughts.

Lamplight streams from the palace door as it opens from within.

THE BEEFEATER. Here comes your lady, sir. I'll to t'other end of my ward. You may een take your time about your business: I shall not return too suddenly unless my sergeant comes prowling round. Tis a fell sergeant, sir: strict in his arrest.* Good een, sir; and good luck! [*He goes*].

THE MAN. 'Strict in his arrest'! 'Fell sergeant'! [*As if tasting a ripe plum*] O-o-o-h! [*He makes a note of them*].

*A Cloaked Lady gropes her way from the palace and wanders along the terrace, walking in her sleep.**

THE LADY [*rubbing her hands as if washing them*]* Out, damned spot. You will mar all* with these cosmetics. God made you one face; and you make yourself another.* Think of your grave, woman, not ever of being beautified.* All the perfumes of Arabia* will not whiten this Tudor* hand.

THE MAN. 'All the perfumes of Arabia'! 'Beautified'! 'Beautified'! a poem in a single word. Can this be my Mary? [*To the Lady*] Why do you speak in a strange voice, and utter poetry for the first time? Are you ailing? You walk like the dead. Mary! Mary!*

THE LADY [*echoing him*] Mary! Mary!* Who would have thought that woman to have had so much blood in her!* Is it my fault that my counsellors put deeds of blood on me? Fie! If you were women you would have more wit than to stain the floor so foully. Hold not up her head so: the hair is false. I tell you yet again, Mary's buried: she cannot come out of her grave.* I fear her not: these cats that dare jump into thrones though they be fit only for men's laps must be put away. Whats done cannot be undone.* Out, I say.* Fie! a queen, and freckled!*

THE MAN [*shaking her arm*] Mary, I say: art asleep?

The Lady wakes; starts; and nearly faints. He catches her on his arm.

THE LADY. Where am I? What art thou?*

THE MAN. I cry your mercy.* I have mistook your person all this while. Methought you were my Mary:* my mistress.

THE LADY [*outraged*] Profane fellow:* how do you dare?

THE MAN. Be not wroth with me, lady. My mistress is a marvellous proper woman.* But she does not speak so well as you. 'All the perfumes of Arabia'! That was well said: spoken with good accent and excellent discretion.*

THE LADY. Have I been in speech with you here?

THE MAN. Why, yes, fair lady. Have you forgot it?

THE LADY. I have walked in my sleep.

THE MAN. Walk ever in your sleep, fair one; for then your words drop like honey.*

THE LADY [*with cold majesty*] Know you to whom you speak, sir, that you dare express yourself so saucily?*

THE MAN [*unabashed*] Not I, not care neither. You are some lady of the Court, belike. To me there are but two sorts of women: those with excellent voices, sweet and low, and cackling hens that cannot make me dream. Your voice has all manner of loveliness in it. Grudge me not a short hour of its music.

THE LADY. Sir: you are overbold.* Season your admiration for a while with—*

THE MAN [*holding up his hand to stop her*] 'Season your admiration for a while—'

THE LADY. Fellow: do you dare mimic me to my face?*

THE MAN. Tis music. Can you not hear? When a good musician sings a song, do you not sing it and sing it again till you have caught and fixed its perfect melody? 'Season your admiration for a while': God! the history of man's heart is in that one word admiration. Admiration! [*Taking up his tablets*] What was it? 'Suspend your admiration for a space—'

THE LADY. A very vile jingle of esses. I said 'Season your—'

THE MAN [*hastily*] Season: ay, season, season, season. Plague on my memory, my wretched memory! I must een write it down. [*He begins to write, but stops, his memory failing him*]. Yet tell me which was the vile jingle? You said very justly: mine own ear caught it even as my false tongue said it.

THE LADY. You said 'for a space.' I said 'for a while.'*

THE MAN. 'For a while' [*he corrects it*]. Good! [*Ardently*] And now be mine neither for a space nor a while, but for ever.

THE LADY. Odds my life! Are you by chance making love* to me, knave?

THE MAN. Nay: tis you who have made the love: I but pour it out at your feet. I cannot but love a lass that sets such store by an apt word.

Therefore vouchsafe, divine perfection of a woman—no: I have said that before somewhere;* and the wordy garment of my love for you must be fire-new—*

THE LADY. You talk too much, sir. Let me warn you: I am more accustomed to be listened to than preached at.

THE MAN. The most are like that that do talk well. But though you spake with the tongues of angels,* as indeed you do, yet know that I am the king of words—

THE LADY. A king, ha!

THE MAN. No less. We are poor things, we men and women—

THE LADY. Dare you call me woman?

THE MAN. What nobler name can I tender you? How else can I love you? Yet you may well shrink from the name: have I not said we are but poor things? Yet there is a power that can redeem us.

THE LADY. Gramercy for your sermon, sir. I hope I know my duty.

THE MAN. This is no sermon, but the living truth. The power I speak of is the power of immortal poesy. For know that vile as this world is, and worms as we are, you have but to invest all this vileness with a magical garment of words to transfigure us and uplift our souls til earth flowers into a million heavens.

THE LADY. You spoil your heaven with your million. You are extravagant. Observe some measure in your speech.

THE MAN. You speak now as Ben* does.

THE LADY. And who, pray, is Ben?

THE MAN. A learned bricklayer who thinks that the sky is at the top of his ladder, and so takes it on him to rebuke me for flying. I tell you there is no word yet coined and no melody yet sung that is extravagant and majestical enough for the glory that lovely words can reveal. It is heresy to deny it: have you not been taught that in the beginning was the Word? that the Word was with God? nay, that the Word *was* God?*

THE LADY. Beware, fellow, how you presume to speak of holy things. The Queen is the head of the Church.*

THE MAN. You are the head of my Church when you speak as you did at first. 'All the perfumes of Arabia'! Can the Queen speak thus? They say she playeth well upon the virginals.* Let her play so to me; and I'll kiss her hands. But until then, *you* are my Queen; and I'll kiss those lips that have dropt music on my heart.* [*He puts his arms about her*].

THE LADY. Unmeasured impudence! On your life, take your hands from me.

The Dark Lady comes stooping along the terrace behind them like *a running thrush. When she sees how they are employed, she rises angrily to her full height, and listens jealously.*

THE MAN [*unaware of the Dark Lady*] Then cease to make my hands tremble with the streams of life you pour through them. You hold me as the lodestar holds the iron:* I cannot but cling to you. We are lost, you and I: nothing can separate us now.

THE DARK LADY. We shall see that, false lying hound, you and your filthy trull.* [*With two vigorous cuffs, she knocks the pair asunder, sending the man, who is unlucky enough to receive a right-handed blow, sprawling on the flags*]. Take that, both of you!

THE CLOAKED LADY [*in towering wrath, throwing off her cloak and turning in outraged majesty on her assailant*] High treason!

THE DARK LADY [*recognizing her and falling on her knees in abject terror*] Will: I am lost: I have struck the Queen.

THE MAN [*sitting up as majestically as his ignominious posture allows*] Woman: you have struck WILLIAM SHAKESPEAR!!!!!!

QUEEN ELIZABETH [*stupent*] Marry, come up!!! Struck William Shakespear quotha!* And who in the name of all the sluts and jades and light-o'-loves and fly-by-nights* that infest this palace of mine, may William Shakespear be?

THE DARK LADY. Madam: he is but a player. Oh, I could have my hand cut off—

QUEEN ELIZABETH. Belike you will, mistress. Have you bethought you that I am like to have your head cut off as well?

THE DARK LADY. Will: save me. Oh, save me.

ELIZABETH. Save you! A likely savior, on my royal word! I had thought this fellow at least an esquire;* for I had hoped that even the vilest of my ladies would not have dishonored my Court by wantoning* with a baseborn servant.

SHAKESPEAR [*indignantly scrambling to his feet*] Baseborn! I, a Shakespear of Stratford! I, whose mother was an Arden!* baseborn! You forget yourself,* madam.

ELIZABETH [*furious*] S'blood!* do I so? I will teach you—

THE DARK LADY [*rising from her knees and throwing herself between them*] Will: in God's name anger her no further. It is death. Madam: do not listen to him.

SHAKESPEAR. Not were it een to save your life, Mary, not to mention mine own, will I flatter a monarch who forgets what is due to my family. I deny not that my father was brought down to be a poor bankrupt;* but twas his gentle blood* that was ever too generous for trade. Never did he disown his debts. Tis true he paid them not; but it is an attested truth that he gave bills for them; and twas those bills, in the hands of base hucksters, that were his undoing.

ELIZABETH [*grimly*] The son of your father shall learn his place in the presence of the daughter of Harry the Eighth.*

SHAKESPEAR [*swelling with intolerant importance*] Name not that inordinate man in the same breath with Stratford's worthiest alderman.* John Shakespear wedded but once: Harry Tudor was married six times. You should blush to utter his name.

THE DARK LADY ⎱ [*crying out together*] ⎰ Will: for pity's sake—

ELIZABETH ⎰ ⎱ Insolent dog—

SHAKESPEAR [*cutting them short*] How know you that King Harry was indeed your father?

ELIZABETH ⎱ Zounds!* Now by—[*she stops to grind her teeth with rage*].

THE DARK LADY ⎰ She will have me whipped through the streets. Oh God! Oh God!

SHAKESPEAR. Learn to know yourself better, madam. I am an honest gentleman of unquestioned parentage, and have already sent in my demand for the coat-of-arms that is lawfully mine. Can you say as much for yourself?

ELIZABETH [*almost beside herself*] Another word; and I begin with mine own hands the work the hangman shall finish.

SHAKESPEAR. You are no true Tudor: this baggage* here has as good a right to your royal seat as you. What maintains you on the throne of England? Is it your renownèd wit? your wisdom that sets at nought the craftiest statesmen of the Christian world? No. Tis the mere chance that might have happened to any milkmaid, the caprice of Nature that made you the most wondrous piece of beauty* the age hath seen. [*Elizabeth's raised fists, on the point of striking him, fall to her side*]. That is what hath brought all men to your feet, and founded your throne on the impregnable rock of your proud heart,* a stony island in a sea of desire. There, madam, is some wholesome blunt honest speaking for you. Now do your worst.*

ELIZABETH [*with dignity*] Master Shakespear: it is well for you that I am a merciful prince. I make allowance for your rustic ignorance. But remember that there are things which be true, and are yet not seemly to be said (I will not say to a queen; for you will have it that I am none) but to a virgin.

SHAKESPEAR [*bluntly*] It is no fault of mine that you are a virgin, madam, albeit tis my misfortune.

THE DARK LADY [*terrified again*] In mercy, madam, hold no further discourse with him. He hath ever some lewd jest on his tongue. You hear how he useth me! calling me baggage and the like to your Majesty's face.

ELIZABETH. As for you, mistress, I have yet to demand what your business is at this hour in this place, and how you come to be so concerned with a player that you strike blindly* at your sovereign in your jealousy of him.

THE DARK LADY. Madam: as I live and hope for salvation—

SHAKESPEAR [*sardonically*] Ha!

THE DARK LADY [*angrily*]—ay, I'm as like to be saved as thou that believest naught save some black magic of words and verses—I say, madam, as I am a living woman I came here to break with him for ever. Oh, madam, if you would know what misery is, listen to this man that is more than man and less at the same time. He will tie you down to anatomize your very soul:* he will wring tears of blood from your humiliation; and then he will heal the wound with flatteries that no woman can resist.

SHAKESPEAR. Flatteries! [*Kneeling*] Oh, madam, I put my case at your royal feet. I confess to much. I have a rude tongue:* I am unmannerly: I blaspheme against the holiness of anointed royalty; but oh, my royal mistress, AM I a flatterer?

ELIZABETH. I absolve you as to that. You are far too plain a dealer to please me. [*He rises gratefully*].

THE DARK LADY. Madam: he is flattering you even as he speaks.

ELIZABETH [*a terrible flash in her eye*] Ha! Is it so?

SHAKESPEAR. Madam: she is jealous; and, heaven help me! not without reason. Oh, you say you are a merciful prince; but that was cruel of you, that hiding of your royal dignity* when you found me here. For how can I ever be content with this black-haired, black-eyed, black-avised* devil again now that I have looked upon real beauty and real majesty?

THE DARK LADY [*wounded and desperate*] He hath swore to me ten times over that the day shall come in England when black women, for all their foulness, shall be more thought on than fair ones. [*To Shakespear, scolding at him*] Deny it if thou canst. Oh, he is compact of lies and scorns. I am tired of being tossed up to heaven and dragged down to hell at every whim that takes him. I am ashamed to my very soul that I have abased myself to love one that my father would not have deemed fit to hold my stirrup—one that will talk to all the world about me—that will put my love and my shame into his plays and make me blush for myself there—that will write sonnets about me that no man of gentle strain would put his hand to. I am all disordered: I know not what I am saying to your Majesty: I am of all ladies most deject and wretched—*

SHAKESPEAR. Ha! At last sorrow hath struck a note of music out of thee. 'Of all ladies most deject and wretched.' [*He makes a note of it*].

THE DARK LADY. Madam: I implore you give me leave to go. I am distracted with grief and shame. I—

ELIZABETH. Go [*The Dark Lady tries to kiss her hand*]. No more. Go. [*The Dark Lady goes, convulsed*].* You have been cruel to that poor fond wretch, Master Shakespear.

SHAKESPEAR. I am not cruel, madam; but you know the fable of Jupiter and Semele. I could not help my lightnings scorching her.

ELIZABETH. You have an overweening conceit of yourself, sir, that displeases your Queen.

SHAKESPEAR. Oh, madam, can I go about with the modest cough of a minor poet, belittling my inspiration and making the mightiest wonder of your reign a thing of nought? I have said that 'not marble nor the gilded monuments of princes shall out-live'* the words with which I make the world glorious or foolish at my will. Besides, I would have you think me great enough to grant me a boon.*

ELIZABETH. I hope it is a boon that may be asked of a virgin Queen without offence, sir. I mistrust your forwardness; and I bid you remember that I do not suffer persons of your degree (if I may say so without offence to your father the alderman) to presume too far.

SHAKESPEAR. Oh, madam, I shall not forget myself again; though by my life, could I make you a serving wench, neither a queen nor a virgin should you be for so much longer as a flash of lightning might take to cross the river to the Bankside.* But since you are a queen and will none of me, nor of Philip of Spain,* nor of any other mortal man, I must een contain myself as best I may, and ask you only for a boon of State.

ELIZABETH. A boon of State already! You are becoming a courtier like the rest of them. You lack advancement.*

SHAKESPEAR. 'Lack advancement.' By your Majesty's leave: a queenly phrase. [*He is about to write it down*].

ELIZABETH. [*striking the tablets from his hand*] Your tables begin to anger me, sir. I am not here to write your plays for you.

SHAKESPEAR. You are here to inspire them, madam. For this, among the rest, were you ordained. But the boon I crave is that you do endow a great playhouse, or, if I may make bold to coin a scholarly name for it, a National Theatre,* for the better instruction and gracing of your Majesty's subjects.

ELIZABETH. Why, sir, are there not theatres enow on the Bankside and in Blackfriars?*

SHAKESPEAR. Madam: these are the adventures of needy and desperate men that must, to save themselves from perishing of want, give the sillier sort of people what they best like; and what they best like, God knows, is not their own betterment and instruction, as we well see by the example of the churches, which must needs compel men to frequent them, though they be open to all without charge. Only when there is a matter of a murder, or a plot, or a pretty youth in petticoats, or some naughty tale of wantonness, will your subjects pay the great cost of good players and their finery, with a little profit to boot. To prove this I will tell you that I have written two noble and excellent plays setting forth the advancement of women of high nature and fruitful industry even as your Majesty is: the one a skilful physician,* the other a sister devoted to good works.* I have also stole from a book of idle wanton tales two of the most damnable foolishnesses in the world,* in the one of which a woman goeth in man's attire* and maketh impudent love to her swain,* who pleaseth the groundlings* by overthrowing a wrestler;* whilst, in the other, one of the same kidney* sheweth her wit by saying endless naughtinesses to a gentleman as lewd as herself.* I have writ these to save my friends from penury, yet shewing my scorn for such follies and for them that praise them by calling the one As You Like It, meaning that it is not as *I* like it, and the other Much Ado About Nothing, as it truly is. And now these two filthy pieces drive their nobler fellows from the stage,* where indeed I cannot have my lady physician presented at all, she being too honest a woman for the taste of the town. Wherefore I humbly beg your Majesty to give order that a theatre be endowed out of the public revenue for the playing of those pieces of mine which no merchant will touch, seeing that his gain is so much greater with the worse than with the better. Thereby you shall also encourage other men to undertake the writing of plays who do now despise it and leave it wholly to those whose counsels will work little good to your realm. For this writing of plays is a great matter, forming as it does the minds and affections of men in such sort that whatsoever they see done in show on the stage, they will presently be doing in earnest in the world, which is but a larger stage. Of late, as you know, the Church taught the people by means of plays; but the people flocked only to such as were full of superstitious miracles and bloody martyrdoms;* and so the Church, which also was just then brought into straits by the policy of your royal father, did abandon and discountenance the art of playing; and thus it fell into the hands of poor players and greedy merchants that had their pockets to look to and not the greatness of this your kingdom. Therefore now must your Majesty take up that good work that your Church hath abandoned, and restore the art of playing to its former use and dignity.

ELIZABETH. Master Shakespear: I will speak of this matter to the Lord Treasurer.*

SHAKESPEAR. Then am I undone,* madam; for there was never yet a Lord Treasurer that could find a penny for anything over and above the necessary expenses of your government, save for a war or a salary for his own nephew.*

ELIZABETH. Master Shakespear: you speak sooth;* yet cannot I in any wise mend it. I dare not offend my unruly Puritans* by making so lewd a place as the playhouse a public charge; and there be a thousand things to be done in this London of mine before your poetry can have its penny from the general purse. I tell thee, Master Will, it will be three hundred years and more before my subjects learn that man cannot live by bread alone,* but by every word that cometh from the mouth of those whom God inspires. By that time you and I will be dust beneath the feet* of the horses, if indeed there be any horses then, and men be still riding instead of flying. Now it may be that by then your works will be dust also.

SHAKESPEAR. They will stand, madam: fear not for that.

ELIZABETH. It may prove so. But of this I am certain (for I know my countrymen) that until every other country in the Christian world, even to barbarian Muscovy and the hamlets of the boorish Germans, have its playhouse at the public charge, England will never adventure. And she will adventure then only because it is her desire to be ever in the fashion, and to do humbly and dutifully whatso she seeth everybody else doing. In the meantime you must content yourself as best you can by the playing of those two pieces which you give out as the most damnable ever writ, but which your countrymen, I warn you, will swear are the best you have ever done. But this I will say, that if I could speak across the ages to our descendants, I should heartily recommend them to fulfil your wish; for the Scottish minstrel hath well said that he that maketh the songs of a nation is mightier than he that maketh its laws;* and the same may well be true of plays and interludes.* [*The clock chimes* the first quarter. The warder returns on his round*]. And now, sir, we are upon the hour when it better beseems a virgin queen to be abed than to converse alone with the naughtiest of her subjects. Ho there! Who keeps ward on the queen's lodgings tonight?

THE WARDER. I do, an't please your majesty.*

ELIZABETH. See that you keep it better in future. You have let pass a most dangerous gallant even to the very door of our royal chamber. Lead him forth; and bring me word when he is safely locked out; for I shall scarce dare disrobe until the palace gates are between us.

SHAKESPEAR [*kissing her hand*] My body goes through the gate into the darkness, madam; but my thoughts follow you.

ELIZABETH. How! to my bed!

SHAKESPEAR. No, madam, to your prayers, in which I beg you to remember my theatre.

ELIZABETH. That is my prayer to posterity. Forget not your own to God; and so goodnight, Master Will.

SHAKESPEAR. Goodnight, great Elizabeth. God save the Queen!

ELIZABETH. Amen.

Exeunt severally: she to her chamber: he, in custody of the warder, to the gate nearest Blackfriars.

AYOT ST LAWRENCE,
20th June 1910.

MACBETH SKIT

MACBETH SKIT

SCENE V

Inverness. Macbeth's castle.*
Enter Lady Macbeth,* reading a letter.

LADY M. 'They met me in the day of success; and I have learned by the perfectest* report, they have more in them than mortal knowledge. When I burned in desire to question them further, they made themselves air, into which they vanished. Whiles I stood rapt in the wonder of it, came missives* from the king,* who all-hailed me 'Thane of Cawdor;'* by which title, before, these weird sisters* saluted me, and referred me to the coming on of time, with 'Hail, king that shalt be!' This have I thought good to deliver* thee, my dearest partner of greatness, that thou mightst not lose the dues of rejoicing, by being ignorant of what greatness is promised thee. Lay it to thy heart, and farewell.'
Glamis* thou art, and Cawdor, and shalt be
What thou art promised: yet do I fear thy nature;
It is too full o' the milk of human kindness
To catch the nearest* way: thou wouldst be great;
Art not without ambition, but without
The illness* should attend it: what thou wouldst highly,
That wouldst thou holily; wouldst not play false,
And yet wouldst wrongly win: thou'ldst have, great Glamis,
That which cries 'Thus thou must do, if thou have it;
And that which rather thou dost fear to do
Than wishest should be undone.' Hie* thee hither,
That I may pour my spirits in thine ear.
And chastise with the valor of my tongue
All that impedes thee from the golden round,*
Which fate and metaphysical* aid doth seem
To have thee crown'd withal.

Enter a Messenger.

What is your tidings?

MESS. The king comes here to-night.

LADY M. Thou'rt mad to say it:
Is not thy master with him? who, were't so,
Would have inform'd for preparation.

MESS. So please you, it is true: our thane is coming:
   One of my fellows had the speed of* him.
   Who, almost dead for breath, had scarcely more
   Than would make up his message.

LADY M.   Give him tending;
   He brings great news. [*Exit Messenger*].
                                   The raven* himself is hoarse
That croaks the fatal entrance of Duncan
Under my battlements. Come, you spirits
That tend on mortal thoughts,* unsex me here,
And fill me, from the crown to the toe, top-full
Of direst cruelty! make thick my blood,
Stop up the access and passage to remorse,
That no compunctious* visitings of nature
Shake my fell* purpose, nor keep peace between
The effect and it!* Come to my woman's breasts,
And take my milk for gall, you murdering ministers,*
Wherever in your sightless* substances
You wait on nature's mischief! Come thick night,
And pall thee in the dunnest* smoke of hell,
That my keen knife see not the wound it makes,
Nor heaven peep through the blanket of the dark
To cry 'Hold, hold!'

Enter Macbeth.
                                   Great Glamis! worthy Cawdor!
Greater than both, by the all-hail hereafter!
Thy letters have transported me beyond
This ignorant present, and I feel now
The future in the instant.

MACBETH. My dearest girl;
   I am never tired of hearing you
   Express yourself in that magnificent way.
   Duncan comes here tonight.*

LADY M. And when goes hence?

MACBETH. Tomorrow: so the old man says.*

LADY M.   O, never
   Shall sun that morrow see!
   Your face, my thane, is as a book where men

May read strange matters. To beguile the time,*
Look like the time; bear welcome in your eye,
Your hand, your tongue: look like the innocent flower,
But be the serpent under 't. He that's coming
Must be provided for: and you shall put
This night's great business into my dispatch;*
Which shall to all our nights and days to come
Give solely sovereign sway and masterdom.

(*During this speech Macbeth tries to play up to it. When she says 'Look like the time' he takes out a turnip watch;* bears welcome in his eye and hand and tongue; looks like the innocent flower and then like the serpent under it.*)

MACBETH. We will proceed no further in this business*—you see, deary, I am trying to put it in your style, though its rather out of my line. We will, as I was saying, proceed no further in this business—in short, chuck it.* The old man has been fearfully good to me; and ever since I cut that man in two in the war,* everybody has been uncommonly kind to me. I enjoy being popular. You dont, I know; but I do. It may be a weakness; but if I were to murder the old man the very first night he is staying with us, I should lose sympathy. I really dont think people would like it.

LADY M.   Was the hope drunk
Wherein you dress'd yourself? hath it slept since?
And wakes it now, to look so green and pale*
At what it did so freely? From this time
Such I account thy love. Art thou afeard
To be the same in thine own act and valour
As thou art in desire? Wouldst thou have that
Which thou esteem'st the ornament of life,*
And live a coward in thine own esteem,
Letting 'I dare not' wait upon 'I would,'
Like the poor cat i' the adage?*

MACBETH. Like what?*

LADY M. (*Louder*) Like the cat.*

MACBETH. Oh, the cat. In the *what*, did you say?

LADY M. In the adage.

MACBETH. Never heard of it. Your language is beyond me, my dear girl. However, if you want to know what I am afraid of, I'm afraid of

the police. I dare do all that may become a man*—a law abiding
man, you understand—without getting him into trouble. Who dares
do more is—well, he isnt *me*.

LADY M.   What beast was't then
That made you break* this enterprise to me?
When you durst do it, then you were a man;
And, to be more than what you were, you would
Be so much more the man.*

MACBETH. Look here: I don't follow this.

LADY M.   Nor time nor place
Did then adhere,* and yet you would make both, and
They have made themselves, and that their fitness now
Does unmake you. I have given suck, and know
How tender 'tis to love the babe that milks me:
I would, while it was smiling in my face,
Have pluck'd my nipple from his boneless gums,
And dash'd the brains out, had I so sworn as you
Have done to this.

MACBETH. No you wouldn't, darling. It sounds all right; but one
doesn't do these things,* believe me. Besides, Duncan wont behave
in that way: he was weaned about 75 years ago. Suppose we fail?

LADY M.   We *fail*!!

MACBETH. [*Prosaically*] Yes, fail.

LADY M. But screw your courage to the sticking-place,*
And we'll not fail. When Duncan is asleep—
Whereto the rather shall his day's hard journey
Soundly invite him—his two chamberlains*
Will I with wine and wassail* so convince,*
That memory, the warder of the brain,
Shall be a fume, and the receipt* of reason
A limbec* only:

MACBETH. What the devil is a limbec?*

LADY M. [*Putting her hand over his mouth to shut him up, and proceeding*].
                                          when in swinish sleep
Their drenched natures lie as in a death,

What cannot you and I perform upon
The unguarded Duncan? What not put upon
His spongy* officers, who shall bear the guilt
Of our great quell?*

MACBETH. [*Reflecting*] A limbec must be an alembic; and an alembic
is the sort of thing you see in an apothecary's shop—a sort of illicit
still. But hang me if I know what you mean by this great quell. I never
met a woman who could talk over my head as you do. What do you
expect me to say, darling?

LADY M. Bring forth men-children only:
For thy undaunted mettle should compose
Nothing but males.*

MACBETH. Capital!* Just how I wanted to turn *it*. As I understand you,
the two Johnnies* who sleep in the room with Duncan will be drunk.
By the way, you neednt trouble to make them drunk: you can depend
on them for that: they havnt been sober after nine o'clock since they
were children. The old man cant keep awake for ten minutes at any
hour, even when *you* are talking to him. All I have to do is to stick
their dirks* into him. It's great. By George,* its immense! How do
you think of such things. Everybody'll say they did it. Eh? What?

LADY M. Who dares receive it other,
As we shall make our griefs and clamor roar
Upon his death?*

MACBETH. [*Tragically*] I am settled (I mean Duncan is)
And buck up each—each—each—

LADY M. Each corporal agent to this terrible feat—*

MACBETH. Yes—give us a chance, old girl—[*again tragically*] Each
corporal agent to these terrible feet*—Look here: what's wrong with
my feet?

MISS MCCARTHY.* Gerald:* come off it. I shall never make
a Shakepearian actor of you. [*She leads him ignominiously from the
stage*].

Curtain.
Jan 1916

CYMBELINE REFINISHED

A VARIATION ON SHAKESPEAR'S ENDING

FOREWORD

THE practice of improving Shakespear's plays, more especially in the matter of supplying them with what are called happy endings, is an old established one which has always been accepted without protest by British audiences. When Mr Harley Granville-Barker, following up some desperate experiments by the late William Poel,* introduced the startling innovation of performing the plays in the West End of London exactly as Shakespear wrote them, there was indeed some demur; but it was expressed outside the theatre and led to no rioting. And it set on foot a new theory of Shakespearean representation. Up to that time it had been assumed as a matter of course that everyone behind the scenes in a theatre must know much better than Shakespear how plays should be written, exactly as it is believed in the Hollywood studios today that everyone in a film studio knows better than any professional playwright how a play should be filmed. But the pleasure given by Mr Granville-Barker's productions shook that conviction in the theatre; and the superstition that Shakespear's plays as written by him are impossible on the stage, which had produced a happy ending to King Lear,* Cibber's Richard III,* a love scene* in the tomb of the Capulets between Romeo and Juliet before the poison takes effect, and had culminated in the crude literary butcheries successfully imposed on the public and the critics as Shakespear's plays by Henry Irving* and Augustin Daly* at the end of the last century, is for the moment heavily discredited. It may be asked then why I, who always fought fiercely against that superstition in the days when I was a journalist-critic, should perpetrate a spurious fifth act to Cymbeline,* and do it too, not wholly as a literary *jeu d'esprit*,* but in response to an actual emergency in the theatre when it was proposed to revive Cymbeline at no less sacred a place than the Shakespear Memorial Theatre at Stratford-upon-Avon.*

Cymbeline, though one of the finest of Shakespear's later plays now on the stage, goes to pieces in the last act. In fact I mooted the point myself by thoughtlessly saying that the revival would be all right if I wrote a last act for it. To my surprise this blasphemy was received with acclamation; and as the applause, like the proposal, was not wholly jocular, the fancy began to haunt me, and persisted until I exorcised it by writing the pages which ensue.

I had a second surprise when I began by reading the authentic last act carefully through. I had not done so for many years, and had the common impression about it that it was a cobbled-up affair by several hands, including a vision in prison accompanied by scraps of quite ridiculous doggerel.

For this estimate I found absolutely no justification nor excuse. I must have got it from the last revival of the play at the old Lyceum theatre,* when Irving, as Iachimo,* a statue of romantic melancholy, stood dumb on the stage for hours (as it seemed) whilst the others toiled through a series of *dénouements* of crushing tedium, in which the characters lost all their vitality and individuality, and had nothing to do but identify themselves by moles on their necks,* or explain why they were not dead.* The vision and the verses were cut out as a matter of course; and I ignorantly thanked Heaven for it.

When I read the act as aforesaid I found that my notion that it is a cobbled-up *pasticcio* by other hands was an unpardonable stupidity. The act is genuine Shakespear to the last full stop, and late phase Shakespear in point of verbal workmanship.*

The doggerel* is not doggerel: it is a versified masque,* in Shakespear's careless woodnotes wild,* complete with Jupiter as *deus ex machina*,* eagle and all, introduced, like the Ceres scene in The Tempest,* to please King Jamie,* or else because an irresistible fashion had set in, just as at all the great continental opera houses a ballet used to be *de rigueur*. Gounod had to introduce one into his Faust, and Wagner into his Tannhäuser, before they could be staged at the Grand Opera in Paris.* So, I take it, had Shakespear to stick a masque into Cymbeline. Performed as such, with suitable music and enough pictorial splendor, it is not only entertaining on the stage, but, with the very Shakespearean feature of a comic jailor which precedes it, just the thing to save the last act.

Without it the act is a tedious string of unsurprising *dénouements* sugared with insincere sentimentality after a ludicrous stage battle. With one exception the characters have vanished and left nothing but dolls being moved about like the glass balls in the game of solitaire until they are all got rid of but one. The exception is the hero, or rather the husband of the heroine, Leonatus Posthumus.* The late Charles Charrington,* who with his wife Janet Achurch broke the ice for Ibsen in England,* used to cite Posthumus as Shakespear's anticipation of his Norwegian rival. Certainly, after being theatrically conventional to the extent of ordering his wife to be murdered, he begins to criticize, quite on the lines of Mrs Alving in Ghosts,* the slavery to an inhuman ideal of marital fidelity which led him to this villainous extremity. One may say that he is the only character left really alive in the last act; and as

I cannot change him for the better I have left most of his part untouched. I make no apology for my attempt to bring the others back to dramatic activity and individuality.

I should like to have retained Cornelius* as the exponent of Shakespear's sensible and scientific detestation of vivisection. But as he has nothing to say except that the Queen is dead, and nobody can possibly care a rap whether she is alive or dead, I have left him with her in the box of puppets that are done with.

I have ruthlessly cut out the surprises that no longer surprise anybody. I really could not keep my countenance over the identification of Guiderius* by the mole on his neck. That device was killed by Maddison Morton,* once a famous farce writer, now forgotten by everyone save Mr Gordon Craig* and myself. In Morton's masterpiece, Box and Cox,* Box asks Cox whether he has a strawberry mark on his left arm. 'No' says Cox. 'Then you are my long lost brother' says Box as they fall into one another's arms and end the farce happily. One could wish that Guiderius had anticipated Cox.

Plot has always been the curse of serious drama, and indeed of serious literature of any kind. It is so out-of-place there that Shakespear never could invent one. Unfortunately, instead of taking Nature's hint and discarding plots, he borrowed them all over the place and got into trouble through having to unravel them in the last act, especially in The Two Gentlemen of Verona and Cymbeline. The more childish spectators may find some delight in the revelation that Polydore and Cadwal* are Imogen's long lost brothers and Cymbeline's* long lost sons; that Iachimo* is now an occupant of the penitent form and very unlike his old self; and that Imogen is so dutiful that she accepts her husband's attempt to have her murdered with affectionate docility. I cannot share these infantile joys. Having become interested in Iachimo, in Imogen, and even in the two long lost princes, I wanted to know how their characters would react to the *éclaircissement** which follows the battle. The only way to satisfy this curiosity was to rewrite the act as Shakespear might have written it if he had been post-Ibsen and post-Shaw instead of post-Marlowe.*

In doing so I had to follow the Shakespearean verse pattern to match the 89 lines of Shakespear's text which I retained. This came very easily to me. It happened when I was a child that one of the books I delighted in was an illustrated Shakespear, with a picture and two or three lines of text underneath it on every third or fourth page. Ever since, Shakespearean blank verse has been to me as natural a form of literary expression as the Augustan English* to which I was brought up in

Dublin, or the latest London fashion in dialogue. It is so easy that if
it were possible to kill it it would have been burlesqued to death by
Tom Thumb,* Chrononhotonthologos,* and Bombastes Furioso.* But
Shakespear will survive any possible extremity of caricature.

I shall not deprecate the most violent discussion as to the propriety
of meddling with masterpieces. All I can say is that the temptation to do
it, and sometimes the circumstances which demand it, are irresistible.
The results are very various. When a mediocre artist tries to improve on
a great artist's work the effect is ridiculous or merely contemptible.
When the alteration damages the original, as when a bad painter
repaints a Velasquez* or a Rembrandt,* he commits a crime. When the
changed work is sold or exhibited as the original, the fraud is indictable.
But when it comes to complete forgery, as in the case of Ireland's
Vortigern,* which was much admired and at last actually performed as
a play by Shakespear, the affair passes beyond the sphere of crime and
becomes an instructive joke.

But what of the many successful and avowed variations? What about
the additions made by Mozart to the score of Handel's Messiah?*
Elgar,* who adored Handel, and had an unbounded contempt for all
the lesser meddlers, loved Mozart's variations, and dismissed all purist
criticism of them by maintaining that Handel must have extemporized
equivalents to them on the organ at his concerts. When Spontini*
found on his visit to Dresden that Wagner had added trombone parts*
to his choruses, he appropriated them very gratefully. Volumes of variations on the tunes of other composers were published as such by
Mozart and Beethoven, to say nothing of Bach* and Handel, who
played Old Harry* with any air that amused them. Would anyone now
remember Diabelli's vulgar waltz* but for Beethoven's amazing variations, one of which is also a variation on an air from Don Giovanni?*

And now consider the practice of Shakespear himself. Tolstoy*
declared that the original Lear is superior to Shakespear's rehandling,
which he abhorred as immoral. Nobody has ever agreed with him. Will
it be contended that Shakespear had no right to refashion Hamlet? If he
had spoiled both plays, that would be a reason for reviving them without Shakespear's transfigurations, but not for challenging Shakespear's
right to remake them.

Accordingly, I feel no qualm of conscience and have no apology to
make for indulging in a variation on the last act of Cymbeline. I stand
in the same time relation to Shakespear as Mozart to Handel, or Wagner
to Beethoven. Like Mozart, I have not confined myself to the journey-
man's job of writing 'additional accompaniments': I have luxuriated in

variations. Like Wagner dealing with Gluck's overture to *Iphigenia in Aulis** I have made a new ending for its own sake.* Beethoven's Ninth Symphony* towers among the classic masterpieces; but if Wagner had been old enough in his Dresden days not only to rescore the first and greatest movement as he did, but to supply the whole work with a more singable ending I should not have discouraged him; for I must agree with Verdi* that the present ending, from the change to six-four onward, though intensely Beethovenish, is in performance usually a screaming voice destroying orgy.*

I may be asked why all my instances are musical instead of literary. Is it a plot to take the literary critics out of their depth? Well, it may have that good effect; but I am not aiming at it. It is, I suppose, because music has succeeded to the heroic rank taken by literature in the sixteenth century. I cannot pretend to care much about what Nat Lee did in his attempts to impart Restoration gentility to Shakespear,* or about Thomas Corneille's bowdlerization of Molière's *Festin de Pierre*,* or any of the other literary precedents, though I am a little ashamed of being found in the company of their perpetrators. But I do care a good deal about what Mozart did to Handel, and Wagner to Gluck; and it seems to me that to discuss the artistic morality of my alternative ending without reference to them would be waste of time. Anyhow, what I have done I have done;* and at that I must leave it.

I shall not press my version on managers producing Cymbeline if they have the courage and good sense to present the original word-forword as Shakespear left it, and the means to do justice to the masque. But if they are halfhearted about it, and inclined to compromise by leaving out the masque and the comic jailor and mutilating the rest, as their manner is, I unhesitatingly recommend my version. The audience will not know the difference; and the few critics who have read Cymbeline will be too grateful for my shortening of the last act to complain.

Ayot Saint Lawrence
December 1945

CYMBELINE REFINISHED

ACT V*

A rocky defile.* A wild evening. Philario,* in armor, stands on a tall rock, straining his eyes to see into the distance. In the foreground a Roman captain, sword in hand, his helmet badly battered, rushes in panting. Looking round before he sits down on a rock to recover his breath, he catches sight of Philario.

CAPTAIN. Ho there, signor! You are in danger there.
    You can be seen a mile off.

PHILARIO [*hastening down*] Whats your news?
    I am sent by Lucius* to find out how fares
    Our right wing led by General Iachimo.*

CAPTAIN. He is outgeneralled.* There's no right wing now.
    Broken and routed, utterly defeated,
    Our eagles* taken and the few survivors
    In full flight like myself. And you?

PHILARIO.   My news
    Is even worse. Lucius, I fear, is taken.
    Our centre could not stand the rain of arrows.

CAPTAIN. Someone has disciplined these savage archers.
    They shoot together and advance in step:
    Their horsemen trot in order to the charge
    And then let loose th' entire mass full speed.
    No single cavaliers but thirty score*
    As from a catapult four hundred tons
    Of horse and man in one enormous shock
    Hurled on our shaken legions. Then their chariots
    With every axle furnished with a scythe
    Do bloody work. They made us skip, I promise you. Their slingers!
    [*He points to his helmet*]
    —Well: see their work! Two inches further down
    I had been blind or dead. The crackbrained Welshmen
    Raged like incarnate devils.

PHILARIO.   Yes: they thought
  We were the Britons. So our prisoners tell us.

CAPTAIN. Where did these bumpkins get their discipline?

PHILARIO. Ay: thats the marvel. Where?

CAPTAIN.   Our victors say
  Cassivelaunus* is alive again.
  But thats impossible.

PHILARIO.   Not so impossible
  As that this witless savage Cymbeline,*
  Whose brains were ever in his consort's head,
  Could thus defeat Roman-trained infantry.

CAPTAIN. 'Tis my belief that old Belarius,*
  Banned as a traitor, must have been recalled.
  That fellow knew his job. These fat civilians
  When we're at peace, rob us of our rewards
  By falsely charging us with this or that;
  But when the trumpet sounds theyre on their knees to us.

PHILARIO. Well, Captain, I must hasten back to Lucius
  To blast his hopes of any help from you.
  Where, think you, is Iachimo?

CAPTAIN.   I know not.
  And yet I think he cannot be far off.

PHILARIO. He lives then?

CAPTAIN.   Perhaps. When all was lost he fought
  Like any legionary, sword in hand.
  His last reported word was 'Save yourselves:
  Bid all make for the rocks; for there
  Their horsemen cannot come'. I took his counsel;
  And here I am.

PHILARIO.   You were best come with me.
  Failing Iachimo, Lucius will require
  Your tale at first hand.

CAPTAIN.   Good. But we shall get
  No laurel crowns* for what we've done today.

Exeunt together. Enter Posthumus* dressed like a peasant, but wearing a Roman sword and a soldier's iron cap. He has in his hand a bloodstained handkerchief.

POSTHUMUS. Yea, bloody cloth,* I'll keep thee; for I wish'd
    Thou shouldst be colour'd thus. You married ones,
    If each of you should take this course, how many
    Must murder wives much better than themselves
    For wrying* but a little? O Pisanio!*
    Every good servant does not all commands:
    No bond,* but to do just ones. Gods, if you
    Should have ta'en vengeance on my faults, I ne'er
    Had liv'd to put on this:* so had you sav'd
    The noble Imogen to repent, and struck
    Me (wretch) more worth your vengeance. But, alack,
    You snatch some hence for little faults: that's love,
    To have them fall no more. You some permit
    To second ills with ills, each elder worse,
    And make them dread it, to the doers' thrift;*
    But Imogen is your own: do your best wills,
    And make me blest to obey! I am brought hither
    Among the Italian gentry, and to fight
    Against my lady's kingdom: 'tis enough
    That, Britain, I have kill'd thy mistress. Peace!
    I'll give no wound to thee. I have disrobed me
    Of my Italian weeds,* and drest myself
    As does a Briton peasant; so I've fought
    Against the part* I came with; so I'll die
    For thee, O Imogen, even for whom my life
    Is every breath a death; and thus unknown,
    Pitied nor hated, to the face of peril
    Myself I'll dedicate. Let me make men know
    More valour in me than my habits shew.
    Gods, put the strength o' the Leonati* in me!
    To shame the guise o' the world, I'll begin
    The fashion, less without and more within.

He is hurrying off when he is confronted with Iachimo, battle stained, hurrying in the opposite direction. Seeing a British enemy he draws his sword.

POSTHUMUS. Iachimo! Peace, man: 'tis I, Posthumus.

IACHIMO. Peace if you will. The battle's lost and won.
Pass on.

POSTHUMUS. Do you not know me?

IACHIMO.   No.

POSTHUMUS.   Look closer.
You have some reason to remember me
And I to hate you. Yet we're sworn friends.

IACHIMO. By all the gods, Leonatus!

POSTHUMUS.   At your service,
Seducer of my wife.*

IACHIMO.   No more of that.
Your wife, Posthumus, is a noble creature.
I'll set your mind at rest upon that score.

POSTHUMUS. At rest! Can you then raise her from the grave?
Where she lies dead to expiate* our crime?

IACHIMO. Dead! How? Why? When? And expiate! What mean you?

POSTHUMUS. This only: I have had her murdered, I.
And at my best am worser than her worst.

IACHIMO. We are damned for this. [*On guard*] Let's cut each other's
throats.

POSTHUMUS [*drawing*] Ay, let us.

*They fight furiously. Enter Cymbeline, Belarius, Guiderius, Arviragus,**
Pisanio, with Lucius and Imogen as Fidele: both of them prisoners*
guarded by British soldiers.

BELARIUS [*taking command instinctively*] Part them there. Make fast*
the Roman.

Guiderius pounces on Iachimo and disarms him. Arviragus pulls
Posthumus back.

ARVIRAGUS. In the King's presence sheath your sword, you lout.

IACHIMO. In the King's presence I must yield perforce;*
But as a person of some quality
By rank a gentleman, I claim to be

Your royal highness's prisoner, not this lad's.

LUCIUS. His claim is valid, sir. His blood is princely.

POSTHUMUS. 'Tis so: he's noble.

CYMBELINE. What art thou?

POSTHUMUS. A murderer.

IMOGEN. His voice! His voice! Oh, let me see his face. [*She rushes to Posthumus and puts her hand on his face*].

POSTHUMUS. Shall's have a play with this? There lies thy part [*he knocks her down with a blow of his fist*].

GUIDERIUS. Accursed churl: take that. [*He strikes Posthumus* and brings him down on one knee*].

ARVIRAGUS. You dog, how dare you [*threatening him*].

POSTHUMUS. Soft, soft, young sirs. One at a time, an 't please you. [*He springs up and stands on the defensive*].

PISANIO [*interposing*] Hands off my master! He is kin to the king.

POSTHUMUS [*to Cymbeline*] Call off your bulldogs, sir. Why all this coil* About a serving boy?

CYMBELINE. My son-in-law!

PISANIO. Oh, gentlemen, your help. My Lord Posthumus: You ne'er killed Imogen till now. Help! help!

IMOGEN. Oh, let me die. I heard my husband's voice
Whom I thought dead; and in my ecstasy,
The wildest I shall ever feel again,
He met me with a blow.*

POSTHUMUS. Her voice. 'Tis Imogen.
Oh, dearest heart, thou livest. Oh, you gods,
What sacrifice can pay you for this joy?

IMOGEN. You dare pretend you love me.

POSTHUMUS. Sweet, I dare
Anything, everything. Mountains of mortal guilt
That crushed me are now lifted from my breast.
I am in heaven that was but now in hell.

You may betray me twenty times again.

IMOGEN. Again! And pray, when have I e'er betrayed you?

POSTHUMUS. I had the proofs. There stands your paramour.*
Shall's have him home? I care not, since thou liv'st.

IMOGEN. My paramour! [*To Iachimo*] Oh, as you are a gentleman,
Give him the lie.

IACHIMO.   He knows no better, madam.
We made a wager, he and I, in Italy
That I should spend a night in your bedchamber.

IMOGEN [*to Posthumus*] You made this wager! And I'm married to you!

POSTHUMUS. I did. He won it.

IMOGEN.   How? He never came
Within my bedchamber.

IACHIMO.   I spent a night there.
It was the most uncomfortable night
I ever passed.

IMOGEN.   You must be mad, signor.
Or else the most audacious of all liars
That ever swore away a woman's honor.

IACHIMO. I think, madam, you do forget that chest.

IMOGEN. I forget nothing. At your earnest suit
Your chest was safely housèd in my chamber;
But where were you?

IACHIMO.   I? I was in the chest [*Hilarious sensation*].
And on one point I do confess a fault.
I stole your bracelet while you were asleep.

POSTHUMUS. And cheated me out of my diamond ring!

IACHIMO. Both ring and bracelet had some magic in them
That would not let me rest until I laid them
On Mercury's* altar. He's the god of thieves.
But I can make amends. I'll pay for both
At your own price, and add one bracelet more
For the other arm.

POSTHUMUS.   With ten thousand ducats*
  Due to me for the wager you have lost.

IMOGEN. And this, you think, signors, makes good to me
  All you have done, you and my husband there!

IACHIMO. It remedies what can be remedied.
  As for the rest, it cannot be undone.
  We are a pitiable pair. For all that
  You may go further and fare worse; for men
  Will do such things to women.

IMOGEN.   You at least
  Have grace to know yourself for what you are.
  My husband thinks that all is settled now
  And this a happy ending!

POSTHUMUS.   Well, my dearest,
  What could I think? The fellow did describe
  The mole upon your breast.*

IMOGEN.   And thereupon
  You bade your servant kill me.

POSTHUMUS.   It seemed natural.

IMOGEN. Strike me again; but do not say such things.

GUIDERIUS. An if you do, by Thor's great hammer stroke*
  I'll kill you, were you fifty sons-in-law.

BELARIUS. Peace, boy: we're in the presence of the king.

IMOGEN. Oh, Cadwal, Cadwal, you and Polydore,*
  My newfound brothers, are my truest friends.
  Would either of you, were I ten times faithless,
  Have sent a slave to kill me?

GUIDERIUS [shuddering]   All the world
  Should die first.

ARVIRAGUS.   Whiles we live, Fidele,
  Nothing shall harm you.

POSTHUMUS.   Child: hear me out.
  Have I not told you that my guilty conscience
  Had almost driven me mad when heaven opened

And you appeared? But prithee,* dearest wife,
How did you come to think that I was dead?

IMOGEN. I cannot speak of it: it is too dreadful.
I saw a headless man drest in your clothes.

GUIDERIUS. Pshaw! That was Cloten:* son, he said, to the king.
I cut his head off.

CYMBELINE.   Marry, the gods forefend!*
I would not thy good deeds should from my lips
Pluck a hard sentence: prithee, valiant youth,
Deny 't again.

GUIDERIUS.   I have spoke it, and I did it.

CYMBELINE. He was a prince.

GUIDERIUS. A most incivil* one: the wrongs he did me
Were nothing prince-like; for he did provoke me
With language that would make me spurn the sea
If it could so roar to me. I cut off 's head;
And am right glad he is not standing here
To tell this tale of mine.

CYMBELINE.   I am sorry for thee:
By thine own tongue thou art condemn'd, and must
Endure our law: thou 'rt dead.* Bind the offender,
And take him from our presence.

BELARIUS.   Stay, sir king:
This man is better than the man he slew,
As well descended as thyself, and hath
More of thee merited than a band of Clotens
Had ever scar for.* [*To the Guard*] Let his arms alone,
They were not born for bondage.

CYMBELINE.   Why, old soldier,
Wilt thou undo the worth thou art unpaid for,
By tasting of our wrath? How of descent
As good as we?

GUIDERIUS.   In that he spake too far.

CYMBELINE. And thou shalt die for 't.

BELARIUS.   We will die all three:

But I will prove that two on 's* are as good
As I have given out him.

CYMBELINE. Take him away.
The whole world shall not save him.

BELARIUS. Not so hot.*
First pay me for the nursing of thy sons;
And let it be confiscate all so soon
As I've received it.

CYMBELINE. Nursing of my sons!

BELARIUS. I am too blunt and saucy: here's my knee.
Ere I arise I will prefer* my sons.
Then spare not the old father. Mighty sir:
These two young gentlemen that call me father,
And think they are my sons, are none of mine.
They are the issue of your loins, my liege,
And blood of your begetting.

CYMBELINE. How? my issue?

BELARIUS. So sure as you your father's. These your princes
(For such and so they are) these twenty years
Have I train'd up: those arts they have as I
Could put into them; my breeding was, sir, as
Your highness knows.* Come hither, boys, and pay
Your loves and duties to your royal sire.

GUIDERIUS. We three are fullgrown men and perfect strangers.
Can I change fathers as I'd change my shirt?*

CYMBELINE. Unnatural whelp! What doth thy brother say?

ARVIRAGUS. I, royal sir? Well, we have reached an age
When fathers' helps are felt as hindrances.
I am tired of being preached at.

CYMBELINE [*to Belarius*] So, sir, this
Is how you have bred my puppies.

GUIDERIUS. He has bred us
To tell the truth and face it.

BELARIUS. Royal sir:
I know not what to say: not you nor I

Can tell our children's minds. But pardon him.
If he be overbold the fault is mine.

GUIDERIUS. The fault, if fault there be, is in my Maker.
I am of no man's making. I am I:
Take me or leave me.

IACHIMO [*to Lucius*] Mark well, Lucius, mark.
There spake the future king* of this rude island.

GUIDERIUS. With you, Sir Thief, to tutor me? No, no:
This kingly business has no charm for me.
When I lived in a cave methought a palace
Must be a glorious place, peopled with men
Renowned as councillors, mighty as soldiers,
As saints a pattern of holy living,
And all at my command were I a prince.
This was my dream. I am awake today.
I am to be, forsooth,* another Cloten,
Plagued by the chatter of his train of flatterers,
Compelled to worship priest invented gods,*
Not free to wed the woman of my choice,*
Being stopped at every turn by some old fool
Crying 'You must not', or, still worse, 'You must'.
Oh no, sir: give me back the dear old cave
And my unflattering four footed friends.
I abdicate, and pass the throne to Polydore.*

ARVIRAGUS. Do you, by heavens? Thank you for nothing, brother.

CYMBELINE. I'm glad you're not ambitious. Seated monarchs
Do rarely love their heirs. Wisely, it seems.

ARVIRAGUS. Fear not, great sir: we two have never learnt
To wait for dead men's shoes, much less their crowns.

GUIDERIUS. Enough of this. Fidele: is it true
Thou art a woman, and this man thy husband?

IMOGEN. I am a woman, and this man my husband.
He would have slain me.

POSTHUMUS.   Do not harp on that.*

CYMBELINE. God's patience, man, take your wife home to bed.

You're man and wife: nothing can alter that.
Are there more plots to unravel? Each one here,
It seems, is someone else. [*To Imogen*] Go change your dress
For one becoming to your sex and rank.
Have you no shame?

IMOGEN.   None.

CYMBELINE.   How? None!

IMOGEN.   All is lost.
Shame, husband, happiness, and faith in Man.
He is not even sorry.

POSTHUMUS.   I'm too happy.

IACHIMO. Lady: a word. When you arrived just now
I, as you saw, was hot on* killing him.
Let him bear witness that I drew on him
To avenge your death.

IMOGEN.   Oh, do not make me laugh.
Laughter dissolves too many just resentments,
Pardons too many sins.

IACHIMO.   And saves the world
A many thousand murders. Let me plead for him.
He has his faults; but he must suffer yours.
You are, I swear, a very worthy lady;
But still, not quite an angel.

IMOGEN.   No, not quite,
Nor yet a worm. Subtle Italian villain!
I would that chest had smothered you.

IACHIMO.   Dear lady
It very nearly did.

IMOGEN.   I will not laugh.
I must go home and make the best of it
As other women must.

POSTHUMUS.   Thats all I ask. [*He clasps her*].

BELARIUS. The fingers of the powers above do tune
The harmony of this peace.

LUCIUS.   Peace be it then.
For by this gentleman's report and mine
I hope imperial Cæsar* will reknit
His favour with the radiant Cymbeline,
Which shines here in the west.

CYMBELINE.   Laud we the gods,
And let our crooked smokes climb to their nostrils
From our blest altars. Publish we this peace
To all our subjects. Set we forward: let
A Roman and a British ensign* wave
Friendly together: so through Lud's town* march,
And in the temple of great Jupiter
Our peace we'll ratify; seal it with feasts.
Set on there!* Never was a war did cease,
Ere bloody hands were wash'd, with such a peace.*

[*Curtain*]

SHAKES VERSUS SHAV

A PUPPET PLAY

PREFACE

THIS in all actuarial probability is my last play* and the climax of my eminence, such as it is. I thought my career as a playwright was finished when Waldo Lanchester* of the Malvern Marionette Theatre,* our chief living puppet master, sent me figures of two puppets, Shakespear and myself, with a request that I should supply one of my famous dramas for them, not to last longer than ten minutes or thereabouts. I accomplished this feat,* and was gratified by Mr Lanchester's immediate approval.

I have learnt part of my craft as conductor of rehearsals (producer,* they call it) from puppets. Their unvarying intensity of facial expression, impossible for living actors, keeps the imagination of the spectators continuously stimulated. When one of them is speaking or tumbling and the rest left aside, these, though in full view, are invisible, as they should be. Living actors have to learn that they too must be invisible while the protagonists are conversing, and therefore must not move a muscle nor change their expression, instead of, as beginners mostly do, playing to them and robbing them of the audience's undivided attention.

Puppets have also a fascination of their own, because there is nothing wonderful in a living actor moving and speaking, but that wooden headed dolls should do so is a marvel that never palls.

And they can survive treatment that would kill live actors. When I first saw them in my boyhood nothing delighted me more than when all the puppets went up in a balloon and presently dropped from the skies with an appalling crash on the floor.

Nowadays the development of stagecraft into filmcraft may destroy the idiosyncratic puppet charm. Televised puppets could enjoy the scenic backgrounds of the cinema. Sound recording could enable the puppet master to give all his attention to the strings he is manipulating, the dialogue being spoken by a company of first-rate speakers as in the theatre. The old puppet master spoke all the parts himself in accents which he differentiated by Punch-and-Judy* squeaks and the like. I can imagine the puppets simulating living performers so perfectly that the spectators will be completely illuded.* The result would be the death of puppetry; for it would lose its charm with its magic. So let reformers beware.

Nothing can extinguish my interest in Shakespear. It began when I was a small boy, and extends to Stratford-upon-Avon, where I have attended so many bardic festivals that I have come to regard it almost as a supplementary birthplace of my own.

No year passes without the arrival of a batch of books contending that Shakespear was somebody else. The argument is always the same. Such early works as Venus and Adonis, Lucrece, and Love's Labour's Lost,* could not possibly have been written by an illiterate clown and poacher who could hardly write his own name. This is unquestionably true. But the inference that Shakespear did not write them does not follow. What does follow is that Shakespear was not an illiterate clown but a well read grammar-schooled son in a family of good middle-class standing, cultured enough to be habitual playgoers and private entertainers of the players.

This, on investigation, proves to be exactly what Shakespear was. His father, John Shakespear, Gent, was an alderman who demanded a coat of arms which was finally granted. His mother was of equal rank and social pretension. John finally failed commercially, having no doubt let his artistic turn get the better of his mercantile occupation, and leave him unable to afford a university education for William, had he ever wanted to make a professional scholar of him.

These circumstances interest me because they are just like my own.* They were a considerable cut above those of Bunyan and Cobbett,* both great masters of language, who nevertheless could not have written Venus and Adonis nor Love's Labour's Lost. One does not forget Bunyan's 'The Latin I borrow.'* Shakespear's standing was nearer to Ruskin's, whose splendid style owes much more to his mother's insistence on his learning the Bible by heart than to his Oxford degree.

So much for Bacon-Shakespear* and all the other fables founded on that entirely fictitious figure Shaxper or Shagsper the illiterate bumpkin.

Enough too for my feeling that the real Shakespear might have been myself, and for the shallow mistaking of it for mere professional jealousy.

Ayot Saint Lawrence,
1949

SHAKES VERSUS SHAV

Shakes enters and salutes the audience with a flourish of his hat.

SHAKES. Now is the winter of our discontent
   Made glorious summer by the Malvern sun.*
   I, William Shakes, was born in Stratford* town,
   Where every year a festival* is held
   To honour my renown not for an age
   But for all time.* Hither I raging come
   An infamous impostor to chastize,
   Who in an ecstasy of self-conceit
   Shortens my name to Shav, and dares pretend
   Here to reincarnate my very self,
   And in your stately playhouse to set up
   A festival, and plant a mulberry*
   In most presumptuous mockery of mine.
   Tell me, ye citizens of Malvern,
   Where I may find this caitiff.* Face to face
   Set but this fiend of Ireland and myself;
   And leave the rest to me.* [*Shav enters*]. Who art thou?
   That rearst a forehead almost rivalling mine?

SHAV. Nay, who art thou, that knowest not these features
   Pictured throughout the globe? Who should I be
   But G.B.S.?

SHAKES. What! Stand, thou shameless fraud.
   For one or both of us the hour is come.
   Put up your hands.

SHAV. Come on.*

They spar. Shakes knocks Shav down with a straight left and begins counting him out, stooping over him and beating the seconds with his finger.*

SHAKES. Hackerty-backerty* one, Hackerty-backerty two,
   Hackerty-backerty three...Hackerty-backerty nine—

At the count of nine Shav springs up and knocks Shakes down with a right to the chin.

SHAV [*counting*] Hackerty-backerty one,...Hackerty-backerty ten. Out.

SHAKES. Out! And by thee! Never. [*He rises*]. Younger you are
By full three hundred years, and therefore carry
A heavier punch than mine; but what of that?
Death will soon finish you; but as for me,
Not marble nor the gilded monuments
Of princes—

SHAV. —shall outlive your powerful rhymes.
So you have told us: I have read your sonnets.*

SHAKES. Couldst write Macbeth?*

SHAV. No need. He has been bettered
By Walter Scott's Rob Roy.* Behold, and blush.

Rob Roy and Macbeth appear, Rob in Highland tartan and kilt with claymore, Macbeth in kingly costume.*

MACBETH. Thus far into the bowels of the land
Have we marched on without impediment.*
Shall I still call you Campbell?

ROB [*in a strong Scotch accent*] Caumill me no Caumills.*
Ma fet is on ma native heath: ma name's Macgregor.

MACBETH. I have no words. My voice is in my sword. Lay on, Rob Roy;
And damned be he that proves the smaller boy.*

He draws and stands on guard. Rob draws; spins round several times like a man throwing a hammer; and finally cuts off Macbeth's head at one stroke.

ROB. Whaur's your Wullie Shaxper the noo?*

Bagpipe and drum music, to which Rob dances off.

MACBETH [*headless*] I will return to Stratford: the hotels
Are cheaper there. [*He picks up his head, and goes off with it under his arm to the tune of British Grenadiers*].*

SHAKES. Call you this cateran*
Better than my Macbeth, one line from whom
Is worth a thousand of your piffling plays.

SHAV. Quote one. Just one. I challenge thee. One line.

SHAKES. 'The shardborne beetle with his drowsy hum.'*

SHAV. Hast never heard of Adam Lindsay Gordon?*

SHAKES. A name that sings. What of him?

SHAV.   He eclipsed
   Thy shardborne beetle. Hear his mighty lines. [*Reciting*]
   'The beetle booms adown the glooms
   And bumps among the clumps.'*

SHAKES [*roaring with laughter*] Ha ha! Ho ho! My lungs like chanticleer
   Must crow their fill.* This fellow hath an ear.
   How does it run? 'The beetle booms—

SHAV. Adown the glooms—

SHAKES. And bumps—

SHAV. Among the clumps.' Well done, Australia!

   Shav laughs.

SHAKES. Laughest thou at thyself? Pullst thou my leg?

SHAV. There is more fun in heaven and earth, sweet William,
   Than is dreamt of in your philosophy.*

SHAKES. Where is thy Hamlet? Couldst thou write King Lear?

SHAV. Aye, with his daughters all complete. Couldst thou
   Have written Heartbreak House?* Behold my Lear.

   A transparency is suddenly lit up, shewing Captain Shotover seated, as
   in Millais' picture called North-West Passage,* with a young woman of
   virginal beauty.*

SHOTOVER [*raising his hand and intoning*]* I built a house for my
   daughters and opened the doors thereof
   That men might come for their choosing, and their betters spring
   from their love;
   But one of them married a numskull: the other a liar wed;
   And now she must lie beside him even as she made her bed.

THE VIRGIN.* 'Yes: this silly house, this strangely happy house, this
   agonizing house, this house without foundations. I shall call it
   Heartbreak House.'

SHOTOVER. Enough. Enough. Let the heart break in silence.*

*The picture vanishes.**

SHAKES. You stole that word from me: did I not write
    'The heartache and the thousand natural woes
    That flesh is heir to'?*

SHAV.   You were not the first
    To sing of broken hearts. I was the first
    That taught your faithless Timons* how to mend them.

SHAKES. Taught what you could not know. Sing if you can
    My cloud capped towers, my gorgeous palaces,
    My solemn temples. The great globe itself,
    Yea, all which it inherit, shall dissolve—*

SHAV. —and like this foolish little show of ours
    Leave not a wrack behind.* So you have said.
    I say the world will long outlast our day.
    Tomorrow and tomorrow and tomorrow*
    We puppets shall replay our scene. Meanwhile,
    Immortal William dead and turned to clay
    May stop a hole to keep the wind away.
    Oh that that earth which kept the world in awe
    Should patch a wall t' expel the winter's flaw!*

SHAKES. These words are mine, not thine.

SHAV.   Peace, jealous Bard:
    We both are mortal. For a moment suffer
    My glimmering light to shine.

*A light appears between them.**

SHAKES. Out, out, brief candle!* [*He puffs it out*].

Darkness. The play ends.

APPENDIX A

MATERIAL CUT FROM THE PLAY
HOW HE LIED TO HER HUSBAND

SHE (taking the flowers without look at them and obviously temporizing) Teddy isn't in yet.

HE Well let us take that calmly: let us go to the theatre as if nothing had happened, and tell him when we come back. Now or three hours hence; to-day or to-morrow; what does that matter, provided all is done in honor, without shame or fear.

SHE What did you get tickets for?—~~Parsifal~~ (Lohengrin)?*

HE I tried; but ~~Parsifal~~ (Lohengrin) was sold out for to-night. (He takes out two ~~Vaudeville~~ (Court)* Theatre tickets)

SHE Then what did you get?

HE Can you ask me? What is there besides ~~Parsifal~~ (Lohengrin) that we two could endure, except Candida?

SHE (springing up) Candida! No, I won't go to it again, Henry (she tosses the flowers on to the piano) It is that play that has done all the mischief. I'm very sorry I ever saw it: it ought to be stopped.

HE (amazed) Aurora!

SHE Yes, I mean it.

HE That divinest love poem—the poem that gave us courage to speak to one another—that revealed to us what we really felt for one another—that—

SHE Just so. It put a lot of stuff into my head that I should never have dreamt of for myself. I imagined myself just like Candida.

HE (catching her hands and looking earnestly at her) You were right. You are like Candida.

SHE (snatching her hands away) Oh, stuff! And I thought you were just like Eugene. (looking critically at him) Now that I come to look at you, you are rather like him, too.

(Applause and laughter, Mr ~~Arnold Daly~~ (Granville Barker)* grins feebly at the audience)

Play resumed*

(She throws herself discontentedly into the nearest seat, which happens to be the bench at the piano. He goes to her, standing over her with one knee on the bench)

HE   (very earnestly) Aurora: if Candida had loved Eugene she would have gone out into the night with him without a moment's hesitation.

SHE   (with equal earnestness) Henry: do you know what's wanting in that play?

HE   There is nothing wanting in it.

SHE   Yes there is. There's a Georgina wanting in it. If Georgina had been there to make trouble, that play would have been a true-to-life tragedy. Now I'll tell you something about it that I have never told you before.

HE   What is that?

SHE   I took Teddy to it. I thought it would do him good; and so it would if I could only have kept him awake. Georgina came too; and you should have heard the way she went on about it. She said it was downright immoral, and that she knew the sort of woman that encourages boys to sit on the hearthrug and make love to her. She was just preparing Teddy's mind to poison it about me.

HE   Let us be just to Georgina, dearest—

SHE   Let her deserve it first. Just to Georgina, indeed!

HE   She really sees the world in that way. That is her punishment.

SHE   How can it be her punishment when she likes it. It'll be my punishment when she brings her budget of poems to Teddy. I wish you'd have some sense and sympathize with my position a little.

HE   (going away from the piano and beginning to walk about rather testily) My dear: I really dont care about Georgina or about Teddy. All these squabbles belong to a plane on which I am, as you say, no use. I have counted the cost; and I do not fear the consquences. After all what is there to fear? Where is the difficulty? What can Georgina do? What can your husband do? What can anybody do?

APPENDIX B

MATERIAL CUT FROM THE PLAY
PRESS CUTTINGS

MITCHENER (<u>rising majestically</u>) I search the pages of history in vain for a parallel to such a speech made by a Private to a general. I shall get Mrs Farrell to deal with you. (<u>He goes to the door and calls</u>) Mrs Farrell. But for the coherence of your remarks I should conclude that you were drunk. As it is you must be mad.

(<u>Mrs Farrell looks in</u>)

MRS FARRELL what is the matter with this man. His language and ideas have reached a pitch of insubordination, never, I firmly believe, previously attained in the records of the human race.

MRS FARRELL Never mind the lad. He got a touch of the sun on sentry last week.

MITCHENER Nonsense! Sunstroke is allowed only in the Indian army. If this man wants to have sunstroke he must enlist for foreign service and for twenty years. Compulsory home service does not include sunstroke.

MRS FARRELL Have it your own way. Send him to the guard-room; and I'll talk to him when Ive got the uniform for you. (<u>She goes out</u>)

THE ORDERLY I call it cowardly, that. Just cowardly.

MITCHENER How dare you accuse me of cowardice.

THE ORDERLY To set Mrs Farrell on me. I can stand up to you: you know I cant stand up to her. And me with a sunstroke too.

MITCHENER Dont flatter yourself that you have some fancy variety of madness. This is common English lunacy. You shall be placed under restraint at once. Call the guard.

THE ORDERLY Thats all very well as long as a man does it. But when he doesnt, where are you?

MITCHENER This is a thing absolutely beyond belief. A soldier is ordered to right about face and march; and he doesnt stir.

THE ORDERLY Why should he?

MITCHENER May I ask, do you intend to remain in this room for ever?

THE ORDERLY Ask me to go politely and I'll go. Speak as you ought to speak to a respectable Shoreditch tradesman; and youll get civility from me. Dont order me: request me.

MITCHENER You don't know what youre talking about. I dont request you to leave the room: I command you. The essence of command is incivility. You can choose whether you can comply with a request. You have no choice but to obey a command.

THE ORDERLY Well, youve given your order; and I havent obeyed it; and I dont intend to. I'm fed up with orders.

MITCHENER When I describe your conduct and language to the Court Martial, I shall simply not be believed.

THE ORDERLY So much the better for me.

MITCHENER Not at all: youll be punished all the same: they must pretend to believe me. Let me solemnly warn you that this can have only one end. You'll be dismissed from the army in disgrace, without a character.

THE ORDERLY You dont suppose I want to stay in the army, do you?

MITCHENER No, sir; you want to leave your country undefended, I suppose.

THE ORDERLY Rot. I want to leave that corner in Pall Mall* where I got sunstroke undefended: the police'll look after it all right. Let me get back to Shoreditch, and I'll look after the country all right. If the Germans come, just send me down a gun; and I'll turn out all right. Same as the Boers* did, you know. It's men youll want then, and not right-about-facers.

MITCHENER Dont talk halfpenny paper rubbish to me, sir. You think yourself a brave Briton; but let me tell you, sir, that when men are left to their own initiative, they run away when bullets begin to fly.

THE ORDERLY Jolly good job too. Let both sides run for it, I say; and save the taxpayer's pocket. Whats the good of a battle except to give the like of you a job? I tell you straight I dont want to be shot; and neither does any German that ever I met.

MITCHENER You'll change your note, my man, when you wake up some morning and find Shoreditch full of Germans.

THE ORDERLY It's full of them already. Theyre almost the same as Englishmen. I dont hold with war: whats the good of people killin one another? If we was all killed there'd be nobody left to shave.

MITCHENER Miserable, soulless, ignorant barber that you are, it is war that creates the necessity for military service; and military service is the greatest school of character in the world.

THE ORDERLY Tell that to the marines. Why, if a poor chap lets out that he's been a soldier, he cant get a job. When you wanted short service, all you generals said that the old soldier was an old fraud. Now you make him out an angel. Look at me, Ive had six months of service. I was a decent barber. Am I a decent soldier?

MITCHENER No. You are a disgrace to humanity. You have slandered an honorable body of men who give their lives for the defence of the country. And you actually demand that the crime of striking your office—a crime worse than parricide—be put on the same footing as a black eye given to any vulgar civilian. Is it possible that you have ever felt an impulse to commit so horrible—so unnatural an offence?

THE ORDERLY Yes I have. Every time you says 'Right-about-face' to me, I feel that I want to give you one in the eye.

EXPLANATORY NOTES

HOW HE LIED TO HER HUSBAND

The preface was first published in 1907, in *John Bull's Other Island, How He Lied to Her Husband, Major Barbara* (London: Constable, 1907). However, the original preface was considerably longer than the version presented here: Shaw published this truncated version in the standard edition of *John Bull's Other Island, How He Lied to Her Husband, Major Barbara* (London: Constable, 1931). The material he cut from the 1907 edition was used in the preface to *Mrs Warren's Profession*.

The play-text exists in a number of substantially different versions. The first public performance of the original play-text took place at the Berkeley Lyceum Theatre in New York on 26 September 1904, then Shaw revised it for public performance in London at the Royal Court Theatre on 28 February 1905 (an earlier copyright reading in London had been given at the Victoria Hall on 27 August 1904). Shaw slightly altered the text again for the first English publication in 1907, in *John Bull's Other Island, How He Lied to Her Husband, Major Barbara* (London: Constable, 1907). Then he made changes for this revised version published here, which first appeared as *John Bull's Other Island, with, How He Lied to Her Husband, and Major Barbara* (London: Constable, 1931). In addition, a German translation by Siegfried Trebitsch (1868–1956) appeared as 'Wie er ihren Mann belog' in the *Berliner Tageblatt*, 28 November 1904, pp. 17–19.

5 *pièce d'occasion*: (Fr.) artistic work written for a special event.

Arnold Daly: née Peter Christopher Arnold Daly (1875–1927), American actor and producer, he secured the rights to Shaw's *Candida* in 1903, and his production then played for 150 performances. Shaw added the phrase 'the late' to describe Daly when revising the preface in 1930 (*HHL* Hol, fo. 1).

The Man of Destiny: a short play by Shaw about Napoleon's early career. Shaw originally intended the drama in 1895 for Henry Irving (1838–1905), although Irving never played the part. Instead, Arnold Daly added to his success with *Candida* by putting *The Man of Destiny* onstage in New York at the Carnegie Lyceum in February 1904, and then at the Garrick in September 1905.

Othello: Shakespeare's play, written probably in early 1604. Ironically, as the final part of this book shows, Shaw did often take his theatrical cue from the work of Shakespeare.

point of honor: the preface now ends quite abruptly here after Shaw's decision, in 1930, to cut away the original conclusion that he had included in the 1907 Constable edition of the play, and use those deleted words instead for the preface to *Mrs Warren's Profession*.

6 *Cromwell Road*: a street in the traditionally fashionable and wealthy area of South Kensington, London. Today the road has become a major artery

between London and the West, but when Shaw wrote his play Cromwell Road was a far quieter residential area, and the houses built here from 1855 to 1885 provided a model for the houses in other nearby estates. In 1886, Shaw had written a book review in which he wondered 'whether Michel Angelo could have afforded to live in the Cromwell-road, even if he had made up his mind to endure the architecture there' ('Ouida's Latest Novel', review originally published in the *Pall Mall Gazette*, 25 January 1886; repr. in *Bernard Shaw's Book Reviews*, ed. Brian Tyson, 2 vols (University Park: Pennsylvania State University Press, 1991), i. 105–8, at 106). However, this setting was not the original production setting for the play, but one that Shaw included for the 1905 version at the Court Theatre in London. Before that, for Arnold Daly's US premiere of the work in 1904, the setting was not 'her flat in Cromwell Road' but 'her house in New York' (*HHL* Carb, fo. 1).

6 *South Kensington fashion*: Shaw knew the pretensions of this area very well. In 1876, as a 19-year-old, he had moved to London for the first time, staying with his mother for about four years at 13 Victoria Grove, a mile away from the Cromwell Road setting of this play. In 1909 Shaw reflected that, during a performance of *How He Lied to Her Husband* at St James's Theatre in London, 'the stalls received it with dull resentment because the vulgar South Kensington woman in it was one of themselves' (*CL* ii. 886, letter of 29 November 1909). The earliest publicly performed version of the play, the 1904 script set in New York, does not include the reference to 'South Kensington fashion', but simply asks for 'as much luxury as the management can afford', before Shaw adjusted the script for the 1905 production in London (*HHL* Carb, fo. 1).

hearth: the area around the fireplace, usually the focal point of the room.

dressed for the theatre: in 1900, one French writer observed that, in the British theatre, 'people go in evening dress and feel as if they were at a party' (*Manchester Guardian*, 20 February 1900, p. 6).

South Kensington female: in the first publicly performed version of the script, Aurora is a New Yorker rather than a Londoner. The version of the script used in 1904 entirely lacks the rather damning novelistic direction, which Shaw added for the first printing of the play in 1907: '*she has an air of being a young and beautiful woman; but as a matter of hard fact, she is, dress and pretensions apart, a very ordinary South Kensington female of about 37, hopelessly inferior in physical and spiritual distinction to the beautiful youth*' (*HHL* Carb, fo. 1).

7 *I'm the only Aurora in London*: Shaw changed this line for London production in 1905; during the 1904 production in the United States it had read, 'I'm the only Aurora in New York' (*HHL* Carb, fo. 2).

8 *workbox*: a box for keeping materials such as those used for sewing.

9 *all London*: Shaw changed this line in 1905 for the production at London's Court Theatre. For the earlier US premiere the line had read 'all New York' (*HHL* Carb, fo. 5).

10 *Come!*: in the versions of the play that existed before 1930 there was a great deal more text here, which involved discussion of the contemporary stage and Shaw's play *Candida*. Shaw wrote this additional material originally in 1904, edited it in 1905, and published it in 1907, but then cut the material in 1930 for fear that the references had become too dated. The deleted text is included in Appendix A.

stand it: before the 1931 standard edition, the text read here 'stand it, like that half baked clergyman in the play? He'd just kill you'. But in 1930, Shaw worried that the allusion to his earlier play *Candida* was too dated and cut the line.

Greek ideal: here Shaw refers to the athletic ideas of ancient Greece, where the presentation of a well-formed male physique was connected to the political and moral ideal of the good male citizen.

pugilism: Shaw himself became fascinated by boxing in the 1880s. He even entered his name in the Queensberry Amateur Boxing Championships in 1883. Shaw also wrote a novel about a boxer, *Cashel Byron's Profession* (first published 1886), adapted the story into a stage play in *The Admirable Bashville* (produced 1902), and enjoyed a close friendship with the world heavyweight boxing champion Gene Tunney (1897–1978).

11 *fender*: the metal frame before the fire, which stops hot coals toppling onto the floor.

Perfect love casteth out fear: cf. 1 John 4:18.

12 *flapdoodle*: nonsense.

fiveshillingsworth: in the first publicly performed 1904 version of the play, set in New York, this had read 'a dollar's worth', but Shaw changed it for the British production in 1905 (*HHL* Carb, fo. 12).

15 *I hear him tapping . . . said anything*: Shaw altered these lines for the 1905 London production. In the New York production in 1904 Aurora had said instead, 'I hear him kicking his gums [shoes] off (she comes down to the hearth) Oh, I wish I were a thousand miles away', to which Henry replied 'The sooner it's over the better' (*HHL* Carb, fo. 15).

city man: a denizen of the City of London, with the implication of involvement in business or financial work. The earliest publicly performed version of the play was set in New York, so in this 1904 version, the line read instead 'Her husband comes in. He has a momentous air, but shows no sign of displeasure: rather the contrary' (*HHL* Carb, fo. 15).

snuggery: a cosy room, especially one of small size, where a person might retire for some peace and quiet.

16 *Swinburne's Songs Before Sunrise*: an 1871 collection of poems by Algernon Charles Swinburne (1837–1909), which he viewed as 'lyrics for the crusade' of Italian and global republicanism (see Catherine Maxwell, *Swinburne* (Tavistock: Northcote House, 2006), 59).

rosy fingered Aurora: Aurora is the Roman goddess of the dawn, depicted here with the Homeric epithet 'rosy-fingered' (rhododactylos).

16 *Apjohn: thats really very ready of you . . . I will be proud to have you about
    the house*: Shaw changed this line for the 1905 London performance: for
    the earlier 1904 New York production it had read 'Henry Apjohn: you are
    a young man of resource', allowing Bompas to assert his maturity over
    Apjohn (*HHL* Carb, fo. 15).

17 *Dont overdo it, old chap*: this rather British-sounding line was adjusted for
    the 1905 London performance at the Court Theatre. Before that, in New
    York, it had been delivered as 'Well, there I think you are overdoing it: I do
    indeed' (*HHL* Carb, fo. 17).

    Apjohn . . . Fool of myself: Shaw changed this line for the 1905 London
    performance. For the earlier 1904 New York production it had read 'Young
    man: youre almost too clever too live. Or else I am making a fool of myself',
    but Shaw adjusted the line for the London production in a way that reduces
    the emphasis on the age gap between the two men (*HHL* Carb, fo. 15).

18 *slipping*: a defensive strategy performed by quickly moving the head right,
    left, or backwards in order to evade another fighter's punches. To do this
    successfully, the boxer must rotate the upper body slightly by pivoting the
    hips and shoulders.

    penny-a-lining puppies: writers paid at only a penny a line, and hence
    producing work of little literary value.

    actor-managers: actors who also run theatres or theatre companies.

    repertory theatre: a theatre that performs works from a repertoire of plays,
    with the staged works being rotated regularly.

    Bedford Park: a suburb of London then known for the bohemian and artis-
    tic tendencies of its residents. Denizens included Shaw's lover Florence
    Farr (1860–1917), and his literary rivals W. B. Yeats (1865–1935) and
    Arthur Wing Pinero (1855–1934).

    Ascot: a fashionable race meeting held at Ascot in Berkshire each June.

19 *What is Mrs Bompas to you . . . d'ye hear*: this set of lines delivered by
    Teddy Bompas is full of references to Aurora's British identity, and was
    incorporated into the 1905 London performance at the Court Theatre.
    When the play was previously performed in New York during 1904, Teddy
    Bompas had delivered a quite different speech at this point, emphasizing
    Aurora's American identity. In the US performance version of the play,
    the speech had been as follows:

>   What is Mrs Bompas to you, I'd like to know? I'll tell you what Mrs
>   Bompas is. She's the handsomest woman in New York, and the clever-
>   est, and the most attractive to men who know a good thing when they
>   see it, whatever she may be to conceited puppies that think nothing's
>   good enough for them. Three Presidents of the United States of
>   America have danced with my wife, and been glad and proud to do it.
>   In this very room a man of the highest position in Europe confessed to
>   me that his feelings for Mrs Bompas were not consistent with his duty
>   to me as his host. One of the first professional poets in Boston wrote

a sonnet to her worth all your amateur trash. (<u>with gathering fury</u>) But she isn't good enough for <u>you</u>! You regard her with coldness—with indifference; and you have the cheek to tell me so to my face. For two pins I'd bash your face in to teach you manners. Introducing a handsome woman to you is casting pearls before swine—(<u>shouting at him</u>) <u>swine</u> d'ye hear? (*HHL* carb, fo. 20)

20 *You dont mean it!*: this line was changed for the 1905 London performance at the Court Theatre to get rid of an Americanism. In 1904 the New York production of the play had seen the line delivered as 'Is that so?', with Henry replying 'Yes, it is so, and a lot more so' (instead of 'Yes, I do mean it, and a lot more too') (*HHL* Carb, fo. 21).

My dear chap, why didnt you say so before?: this British-sounding line was added for the 1905 London performance at the Court Theatre. Before that, in New York, it had been delivered as 'Oh, well, I suppose I must apologise' (*HHL* Carb, fo. 21).

Take his hand: this line was adjusted for the 1905 London performance at the Court Theatre to get rid of an Americanism. In 1904 the New York production had seen the line delivered as 'Shake' (*HHL* Carb, fo. 22).

vinegar and brown paper: a British folk-medicine remedy for headaches, famously described in the nursery rhyme 'Jack and Jill'.

a real kindness to us both: this line was adjusted for the 1905 London performance at the Court Theatre to get rid of an Americanism. In 1904 the New York production had seen the line delivered as 'real kind of you' (*HHL* Carb, fo. 22).

21 *Oh, I don't mind. I am past minding anything*: at this point until Shaw's 1930 revision of the play there was more text, which involved references to Shaw's play *Candida*. Shaw later cut this material in 1930 for fear that the references had become too dated. The deleted text from first printed text in 1907 is below:

HE. Oh, *I* dont mind. I am past minding anything. I have grown too fast this evening.

SHE. How old are you, Henry?

HE. This morning I was eighteen. Now I am—confound it! I'm quoting that beast of a play [*he takes the Candida tickets out of his pocket and tears them up viciously*].

(Shaw, *How He Lied to Her Husband*, in Shaw, *John Bull's Other Island* (1907 edn), 125–44, at 144).

How He Lied to Her Husband: in 1904 and 1905, Shaw had suggested the following stage direction to close the play, although he deleted it before the first published version in 1907:

<u>CURTAIN</u>
(<u>Hisses. Manager takes a call and is pelted off</u>

Threatening cries of 'Author, Author' lights turned out—EXEUNT
    OMNES [all go out]
(*HHL* carb, fo. 23).

PASSION, POISON, AND PETRIFACTION

The preface was first written as 'Notes' and included in the typescript of
Shaw's production copy (see *PPP* Type). It was published, also as 'Notes', following (rather than preceding) the play-text and without the final sentence, in
Harry Furniss's Christmas Annual (London: n.pub., 1905), then (with the final
sentence added) in *Translations and Tomfooleries* (London: Constable, 1926),
and republished under the same title by Constable in 1932.

The play was first performed in Regent's Park on 14 July 1905. The text was
published in *Harry Furniss's Christmas Annual*, with illustrations (London:
n.pub., 1905), and privately published for copyright in the United States in
1905. It was then published as *Translations and Tomfooleries* (London: Constable,
1926) and republished under the same title by Constable in 1932.

23 *PETRIFACTION*: conversion into stone.

    Gazogene: a portable device for making fizzy drinks.

    Barns and Booths: the play was first performed in a booth in Regent's Park,
and the script takes its cue from melodrama, a theatrical form often performed during the early twentieth century by travelling players in barns,
tents, or other makeshift venues. However, when Shaw first wrote his
manuscript he may have been less certain about the setting: he did not
originally describe the text as being for 'Barns and Booths' but as 'A new
and original Tragedy in One Act' (*PPP* Hol, fo. 1).

25 *Cyril Maude*: actor and theatre manager (1862–1951). Early in Shaw's
playwriting career, Maud accepted *You Never Can Tell* for an 1897 production at the Haymarket Theatre, a leading London venue, which led to
rehearsals but no performance.

    The Actors' Orphanage: a charity established in 1896, which in 1906
opened a home for the orphans and illegitimate children of actors on
Morland Road, Croydon.

    Vanbrugh . . . Pawle: Irene Vanbrugh (1872–1949), actor and wife of Dion
Boucicault the younger (1859–1929); Nancy Price (1880–1970), actor
and author, who had played the shop-girl Hilda Gunning in *Letty* (1904)
by Pinero—a part which foreshadowed Shaw's Eliza Doolittle in
Pygmalion; George Patrick Huntley (1868–1927), Irish actor known for
his comic roles; Fred Eric Lewis Tuffley (1855–1935), English actor, who
mainly specialized in comedy; Arthur Williams (1844–1915), English
popular comedian, who by 1905 had become a star of the musical theatre;
John Lennox Pawle (1872–1936), a thickset, London-born actor, who
would go on to perform in Hollywood films during the late 1910s and
early 1920s.

Bill Bailey: a popular song originally titled 'Bill Bailey, Won't You Please Come Home?' (1902), written by the song-and-dance man Hughie Cannon (1877–1912). The lyrics contain indications of adultery.

26 *bed-sitting room*: a room or apartment that acts as both a bedroom and a sitting-room.

a fashionable quarter of London: Shaw's unpublished manuscript is slightly more specific about the location, and includes a nod to William Shakespeare (1564–1616), beginning:

> Place. The West End of London
> Period. Not for an age but for all time. (*PPP* Hol, fo. 2)

'Not for an age but for all time' is taken from the eulogy to Shakespeare written by the poet and playwright Benjamin ('Ben') Jonson (1572–1637), which opens the 1623 folio of Shakespeare's work (Jonson's line is, 'He was not of an age, but for all time!') (Jonson, *The Oxford Authors: Ben Jonson*, ed. Ian Donaldson (Oxford: Oxford University Press, 1985), 454).

bootjack: a device for pulling off boots.

27 *Magnesia*: a mineral thought by some alchemists to be one of the ingredients of the philosopher's stone (the mythical substance that could potentially turn cheap metals into gold or silver, and prolong life indefinitely). In the 1870s an English pharmacist, Charles Henry Phillips (1820–82), invented 'Milk of Magnesia', an alkaline water suspension and suspended form of magnesium hydroxide. This was used as a heartburn treatment and a laxative, had been sold and advertised under that name in the United States since at least 1880, and looks something like the lime-and-water remedy that Magnesia creates during the play.

embracing her: it is clear here that Phyllis initiates this contact, although Shaw had first envisaged this as more mutual, the manuscript reading 'They embrace' (*PPP* Hol, fo. 8).

saturnine: gloomy.

I'll do't: recalls Hamlet's line as he plans to stab the praying Claudius, 'And now I'll do't' (*Hamlet*, III. iii. 74).

reached Heaven: in the manuscript Shaw included a more specific reference to Shakespeare at this point, with George Fitztollemache delivering l. 106 from *Macbeth* III. iv. After the music ceases George was originally going to raise his dagger and deliver the line, ' "Why so, being going, I am a man again" Shakespear! She dies' (*PPP* Hol, fo. 9).

29 *powders*: in order to make carbon dioxide when water is added, the gazogene needs to be loaded with a dry mixture of tartaric acid and sodium bicarbonate.

Oh, yes, of course: in the manuscript Shaw had given Adolphus a more apologetic line instead of this one, writing, 'I beg your pardon' (*PPP* Hol, fo. 14).

a loving cup: a drink shared to demonstrate unity or friendship.

466 *Explanatory Notes*

29 *Pledge me*: drink with me as a gesture of goodwill.

Adolphus: Shaw had originally intended Adolphus to start singing at this point, in the manuscript wanting the character to deliver the first two lines of 'Drink to me only with thine eyes', a song based on a 1616 poem by Ben Jonson (1572–1637), 'Song: To Celia'. The song was to be interrupted by George Fitztollemache declaring 'Oh, in heaven's name' and Magnesia's complaint 'I cannot bear it, Adolphus' (*PPP* Hol, fo. 15).

30 *Sensation*: the nature of this sensation was made clear by Shaw in his manuscript version of the play, where he wrote '<u>Thunder. Clash of cymbals. Red limes</u> [lights]. <u>Magnesia screams and lets down her hair</u>' (*PPP* Hol, fo. 16).

31 *a peppermint lozenge*: a sweet tablet flavoured with peppermint.

32 *the plaster ceiling*: before the widespread use of plasterboard in the 1930s, ceilings in London would usually be constructed using strips of wood (laths) that were then covered with a lime-based mortar, often incorporating horsehair.

Flakes of plaster: Shaw suggested that, in performance, '<u>Ice wafers and tops of old wedding cakes will come in useful here</u>' (*PPP* Hol, fo. 25).

33 *chevaux de fries*: (Fr.) protective lines of spines (a figurative use taken from the defensive instrument of war used to prevent cavalry charges). Shaw misspells it: the last word should be *frise*.

curl papers: pieces of soft paper, in which Phyllis's hair is twisted so that it will retain its curl when the paper is removed.

34 *washstand ewer*: a jug ordinarily used for hand-washing.

Fitztollemache: Shaw wrote 'they' in his manuscript, indicating that Magnesia and possibly Phyllis should also have been involved in making Adolphus drink (*PPP* Hol, fo. 31).

35 *potman . . . flagon*: like a drunk shaking the final drops from a bottle of liquor.

chords cease: in his manuscript, Shaw demanded here 'Clash of cymbals' (*PPP* Hol, fo. 32).

naw tore moy ahse dahn: Shaw obviously worried about the comprehensibility of this line, adding to his manuscript the explanatory note 'Nigh tore my house down' (*PPP* Hol, fo. 33).

36 *eze gorn ez awd ez niles*: he's gone as hard as nails.

Whew!: Shaw's manuscript included here the policeman delivering the explanatory line, 'He's a ton weight' (*PPP* Hol, fo. 35).

Trafalgar Square: public square in central London, featuring statues including the central figure of Horatio Nelson (1758–1805).

Aushd pat im in the cestern an worsh it aht of im: I should put him in the cistern and wash it out of him.

37 *chack it*: chuck it, i.e. stop it.

Horficer: Officer (addressed to the policeman).

lancet: a surgical instrument with a point like a lance, used for making incisions.

quadrille: a square dance.

38 *copper*: Shaw includes a joke here in the form of a pun. 'Copper' is a slang term for a policeman, but also refers to the conductive metal that is often used as a lightning rod.

After life's fitful fever they sleep well: a comic adaptation of Lady Macbeth's comment on King Duncan, 'After life's fitful fever he sleeps well' (*Macbeth*, III. ii. 25). Her husband's earlier attempt at stabbing her while she was sleeping also offers an echo of Shakespeare's play.

ashpan: small bowl for collecting tobacco ash.

The rest is silence: cf. *Hamlet*, III. ii. 316.

National Anthem: 'God Save the King', the British national anthem, for which the spectators would have been expected to rise to their feet.

PRESS CUTTINGS

The preface was published in *Translations and Tomfooleries* (London: Constable, 1926) and republished under the same title by Constable in 1932.

The play was first performed at the Court Theatre on 9 July 1909. The play-text was published as *Press Cuttings: A Topical Sketch Compiled from the Editorial and Correspondence Columns of the Daily Papers, etc* (London: Constable, 1909). It was subsequently collected in *Translations and Tomfooleries* (London: Constable, 1926), and republished under the same title by Constable in 1932.

The title *Press Cuttings* is a reference to items snipped from newspapers, and *Women's War* in the subtitle refers to the campaign for women to have the right to vote in public elections.

41 *Lord Chamberlain*: an officer of the royal household under whom the Master of the Revels was appointed in 1494 (see note to p. 272), and whose powers over the stage were bolstered by Acts in 1737 and 1843. By the time Shaw was writing, the Lord Chamberlain exercised censorship of stage plays by requiring theatre managers to submit scripts for approval before production. When the Court Theatre sent the script of *Press Cuttings* to the censor before the planned production of the work in July 1909, the reader of plays responded on 24 June: 'I beg to call your attention to the endorsement on every "Licence for Representation" "No offensive personalities, or representations of living persons to be permitted on the stage". / I am returning the copy in order to give you the opportunity of eliminating all personalities expressed or understood' (HRC Lic).

General Bones and Mr Johnson: Shaw had to comply with the requirements of the British censor, and so for performance changed the name of Mitchener to 'Bones' and Balsquith to 'Johnson': 'Bones' and 'Johnson' were characters who performed in the Christy Minstrels group of blackface performers.

41 *General Mitchener . . . is not the late Lord Kitchener*: Mitchener's name appears to be an amalgam of Viscount Alfred Milner (1854–1925) the politician and colonial administrator, and Horatio Herbert Kitchener (1850–1916), the army officer and colonial administrator who led a campaign to reconquer the Sudan, worked as chief of staff during the South African War (1899–1902), and became commander-in-chief of the British army between 1902 and 1909. Privately, however, Shaw described the fictional character as 'a caricature' of Frederick Sleigh Roberts (1832–1914), the field marshal who led in the Second Anglo-Afghan War, the South African War, and was the last commander-in-chief of the British army in 1901–4. Shaw also claimed the part alluded to the army officer Prince George, Duke of Cambridge (1819–1904). For a production in Vienna in 1915, Shaw suggested the actor playing the role 'makes up as Admiral von Tirpitz' (1849–1930), the military leader who was prominent in Germany during the reign of Kaiser Wilhelm II (*CL* iii. 304, letter of 28 July 1915).

Balfour-Asquith: an amalgam of Arthur James Balfour (1848–1930), Conservative politician and prime minister from 1902 to 1905, and Herbert Henry Asquith (1852–1928), Liberal politician and prime minister from 1908 to 1916.

42 *first of April*: the choice of April Fools' Day points to the subversive nature of Shaw's script.

three years hence: 1912 (the script was written and published in 1909).

War Office: department of the British government taking responsibility for the administration of the British army which existed until 1964 and was led by the secretary of state for war. Mitchener is here in the building in which the work of this department was conducted, located in London at the junction of Horse Guards Avenue and Whitehall.

Votes for Women: adopted as the slogan of the women's suffrage movement (see note to p. 43) from 13 October 1905. The slogan apparently came into use after Emmeline Pankhurst (1858–1928), Christabel Pankhurst (1880–1958), and Annie Kenney (1879–1953) found it impossible to use a banner with the longer slogan, 'Will the Liberal Party Give Votes for Women?' The play *Votes for Women!* by Elizabeth Robins (1862–1952) was staged at the Royal Court Theatre in April–May 1907, and portrayed a suffragette rally in Trafalgar Square.

Orderly: soldier who attends to the minor tasks and orders demanded by a superior officer.

door-scraper: a small, horizontal metal bar fixed at just above ground level near a door, allowing those entering a building to scrape dirt from their footwear.

flags: flagstones.

downfaces: browbeats and outsmarts.

afraid of these women: in October 1906, the feminist-socialist Anne Cobden-Sanderson (1823–1926) had protested with the Women's Social and Political Union at Westminster, and she—as well as nine other women—had been arrested and imprisoned. Shaw responded in *The Times* with a satirical letter, from which *Press Cuttings* ultimately developed, stating: 'This is a terrible moment in our national life. We are not often so thoroughly frightened . . . Ten women—ten petticoated, long-stockinged, corseted females have hurled themselves on the British Houses of Parliament . . . the measures which have always been deemed sufficient to protect the House of Commons against men are not to be trusted against women' (Shaw, 'Woman Suffrage', *The Times*, 31 October 1906, p. 8).

dashed: a euphemism for 'damned'.

43 *dursent*: dare not.

pepperily: in an irritable manner.

Right about face: turn 180 degrees right (so you are facing back on yourself).

Votes for monkeys!: in his unpublished typescript, Shaw originally added here an even more absurd demand, 'Votes for cockroaches' (*PC* Type, fo. 3).

Suffraget: a female supporter of the cause of women's political enfranchisement (the right to vote in public elections). The term (more generally feminized with the '-ette' ending) is particularly associated with the British activists of the Women's Social and Political Union, established by Emmeline Pankhurst in 1903, whose members adopted militant tactics including law breaking and hunger striking.

Balsquith: this compound name was frequently used in the satirical magazine *Punch*, and recalls both Arthur Balfour and Herbert Asquith (see note to p. 157).

44 *Bellachristina*: the suffragette Christabel Pankhurst, eldest daughter of Emmeline Pankhurst.

Holloway: the female-only prison where Christabel Pankhurst was imprisoned in late 1908, along with other suffragettes.

French chalk: a kind of talc, used as a dry lubricant for gloves.

Camberwell: the scarcely exalted status of Camberwell, in south London, is discussed in Shaw's later play *Geneva* (1938), where one character from the area declares that 'the west end may turn up its nose at Camberwell', and another character describes the area as 'totally indistinguishable from any other part of London' (Shaw, *Geneva, Cymbeline Refinished, Good King Charles* (London: Constable, 1946), 32, 97).

Tariff Reformer: a political figure supporting the idea of an extended tariff on goods from overseas.

Sandstone: if Shaw felt General Mitchener was 'a caricature' of Frederick Sleigh Roberts, it is likely that General Sandstone, with his nickname of 'Old Red', alludes to the real-life figure of General Redvers Henry Buller

(1839–1908) who had the nickname of 'Old Buller'. Just as Mitchener and Sandstone are rivals in the play, so in real life Roberts and Buller were rival generals during the South African War of 1899–1902. During that conflict, Roberts's 'severe criticisms' of Buller appeared in the press (see *Manchester Guardian*, 18 April 1900, p.5), and Roberts eventually replaced Buller as commander-in-chief in South Africa (with Kitchener acting as chief of staff). In *Press Cuttings*, Shaw imagines the fictional Sandstone having an 'unworkable' military plan to use against the suffragettes of the future, and the playwright may have been thinking of Buller's tactics in South Africa, which were widely considered a failure following the influential criticism of *The Times's* correspondent Leo Amery (1873–1955).

44 *Westminster*: the British parliament at the Palace of Westminster. At the end of March 1909, while Shaw was writing this play, the National Women's Social and Political Union convened a mock parliament, chaired by Emmeline Pankhurst, which met at Caxton Hall and then moved to Westminster. *The Times* reported that 'a number of members of the Women's Social and Political Union attempted to force an entrance to the House of Commons at New Palace-yard gates, and considerable disorder took place. The police were very tolerant, but as the disorder continued it became absolutely necessary to make several arrests . . . they had been deputed to convey a resolution to Mr. Asquith' ('Woman Suffrage', *The Times*, 31 March 1909, p. 12). The protests continued on 1 April, the date on which Shaw's play is set.

45 *Parliament Square*: the square at the north-west end of the Palace of Westminster.

Wellington: Arthur Wellesley, 1st Duke of Wellington (1769–1852), who defeated Napoleon (1769–1821) at the Battle of Waterloo (18 June 1815).

Helen and Georgina: this is a likely allusion to Marie Brackenbury (1866–1945) and Georgina Brackenbury (1865–1949), the two suffragette daughters of General Charles Brackenbury (1831–90). The two women were arrested in February 1908 at a protest outside the House of Commons, and given a six-week prison sentence.

46 *Bill*: the draft of an Act of Parliament submitted to the legislature for discussion and adoption as an Act.

Reform Acts: those Acts of Parliament that reformed the franchise and greatly increased the proportion of the population eligible to vote during the nineteenth and early twentieth centuries.

magistracy responsible only to a Council of War: a group of law officers answering only to a group of military officers (indicating a special emergency situation).

India: the Indian system of government was far from a representative democracy. The Governor-General (representing the British monarch) ruled the country, and since 1773 had been aided and advised by an executive council, which from 1861 was run as a cabinet where councillors took particular portfolios.

Irish parliament voted for its own extinction: an Irish parliament met in Dublin from 1297, but with the Act of Union in 1800 the parliament was abolished and its powers transferred to Westminster. In the Irish parliament itself, a motion pledging to retain the body's independence was defeated by 138 votes to 96 on 16 January 1800, and on 6 February the proposals for a legislative union were approved by 158 votes to 115.

47 *To dare, to dare, and again to dare*: the words of George-Jacques Danton (1759–94), minister of justice following the deposition of the monarchy in France in August 1792 during the French Revolution. When hostile armies from Prussia and Austria were invading France, Danton made a speech of revolutionary encouragement on 2 September 1792 ('Il nous faut de l'audace, encore de l'audace, toujours de l'audace') (*Danton: Documents authentiques*, ed. Alfred Bougeart (Brussels: A. Lacroix, 1861), 119).

Maxim's Silencer: a suppressor which attaches to a gun in order to limit the noise and flash of the firing weapon.

human life: in his unpublished typescript, Shaw originally added here a comment by Mitchener, 'Seriously, Balsquith, this atrocious murder must convince you of the absolute necessity for the sternest measures' (*PC* Type, fo. 8).

what a soldier is for: in his unpublished typescript, Shaw originally added here a retort by Mitchener, 'Certainly not. He is paid to shoot other people' (*PC* Type, fo. 8).

48 *universal compulsory military service*: Shaw's play (written in 1909 but set in 1912) predicts that compulsory military service will be introduced in 1911. In fact, conscription came slightly later for England, Scotland, and Wales (but not Ireland), being imposed from 1916 to 1919.

Times Book Club: founded in 1905, this club advertised reduced prices for selected books, publicized via *The Times* newspaper. Shaw had entered into a public spat over the club in 1907, after other authors and publishers boycotted it over fears of the effect on other booksellers. Shaw supported it and even published a special edition of some of his plays under the imprint of *The Times* Book Club. As part of this 'book war', the club began selling the biography *Lord Randolph Churchill* (1906) by Lord Rosebery (1847–1929) as an enormous loss leader, and the popularity of that volume provides a model for the fictional reminiscences of Mitchener here.

curate: a deputy or assistant to a parish priest.

49 *Chubbs-Jenkinson*: several elements in the story of Chubbs-Jenkinson and the curate are reminiscent of the 'guards scandal' that was widely reported in the British and international press during 1903. In 1902, three young officers in the 1st Battalion Grenadier Guards had been subject to 'ragging', or severe beating, for minor infringements of the rules, such as leaving the barracks in uniform to get a haircut. However, these victims were extremely well connected: they consisted of the eldest son of the 4th Duke of Wellington (1849–1934), the son of Lord Belhaven (1840–1920), and a nephew of Lord De Saumarez (1843–1937). By December 1902, the

three peers had complained to Lord Roberts, commander-in-chief of the British army, about the way that their young relatives were treated. The matter came to broader public attention when a rear admiral, who was also an uncle of one of the punished young men, wrote an explosive letter (Basil E. Cochrane, 'The Recent Incidents in the Grenadier Guards', *The Times*, 10 February 1903, p. 5) that was widely reprinted, pointing out that his nephew had been educated at Oxford but had suffered in the Grenadier Guards under a system of 'inhumanity' where young officers deemed to have broken the rules would be handed over to a kangaroo court of other young officers, and almost invariably sentenced to a brutal flogging. Following these revelations, Lord Roberts sought to punish the commanding officer, and so breathed fresh life into the press controversy.

49 *leader of the Labor Party*: a number of socialist groups and trade unions cooperated together, and joined under the official name 'The Labour Party' from February 1906. In 1904 the Royal Commission on Army Reform recommended introducing compulsory military service, but the socialist newspaper the *Labour Leader* said this was 'as hateful to British tradition as slavery', and in 1909 the Labour Party conference passed a resolution declaring that 'the immunity from compulsory military service which our nation enjoys, is one of the greatest heritages of freedom' (*Labour Leader*, 3 June 1904, and *Independent Labour Party Conference Report* (1909), 84; both quoted by Paul Ward, *Red Flag and Union Jack* (Woodbridge: Boydell, 1998), 116).

the House: i.e. House of Commons, the lower house of the UK Parliament.

soda king: manufacturer of soda water, popular in Europe after the Paris Exposition of 1867.

50 *subalterns*: junior officers, below the rank of captain.

peerage: a class or rank of nobility.

51 *Bobby Bessborough*: possibly a reference to Vere Brabazon Ponsonby, 9th Earl of Bessborough (1880–1956). He had attended Cambridge rather than Oxford University, and stood, unsuccessfully, as a unionist parliamentary candidate in 1906. After Shaw had written *Press Cuttings*, Ponsonby would be elected an MP in 1910 and 1913.

A pasteboard one: a flimsy or unsubstantial one.

Alliance Office: possibly refers to the office (located from 1882 at No. 1 St James's Street SW1) of the Alliance British and Foreign Life and Fire Assurance Company.

goes out: in his unpublished typescript, Shaw originally added here the following lines:

> BALSQUITH. Mitchener: do you fully take in the situation? Do you grasp that public opinion holds Old Red responsible for this flogging.
>
> MITCHENER. I tell you again I care nothing for public opinion.
>
> BALSQUITH. But Lady Richmond also holds him responsible.

MITCHENER. Then he is lost. Poor old Sandstone!

BALSQUITH. Yes; but you are found.

(*PC* Type, fo. 13).

52 *adjutant or your aide-de-camp*: an officer appointed to act as an aide to a senior officer.

Hegel: the German philosopher Georg Wilhelm Friedrich Hegel (1770–1831) famously wrote in his lectures: 'what experience and history teach us is this, that peoples and governments have never learned anything from history, or acted on principles deduced from it' (Hegel, *Lectures on the Philosophy of History*, trans. by J. Sibree (London: Bohn, 1861), 6).

four more Dreadnoughts: in 1898, the First Fleet Act in Germany sought to develop a high-seas battle fleet. In the ensuing years, this triggered an Anglo-German arms race, with the prospect of German dominance of the oceans causing panic in Britain. In 1905, Britain commissioned its first dreadnought, a battleship that was bigger, faster, and better armed than any earlier vessel. In response, Germany began constructing its own dreadnoughts. By 1909, the British public had taken up the slogan of 'We want eight, and we won't wait' to pressurize the Liberal government into building more of these ships (Henry W. Lucy, 'From the Cross Benches', *The Observer*, 4 April 1909, p. 9).

54 *Jingo civilian*: someone who boasts of his country's readiness for a fight.

Monaco enjoys no security: Monaco is a tiny principality in western Europe, surrounded on three sides by France and on one side by the Mediterranean, and situated 5 miles from the Italian border. It had been buffeted by a number of European events in its recent history: after the French Revolution, Monaco was annexed to the French between 1793 and 1814; following Napoleon's defeat, it was placed under Anglo-Sardinian protection in 1815; then, in the Revolutionary year of 1848, Monaco lost its neighbouring towns of Roquebrune and Menton; finally, its independence was restored by treaty in 1861.

Zeppelin airships: the large, long, and cylindrical German flying machines of the early twentieth century. A Zeppelin bombing raid provides the climax to Shaw's 1919 play *Heartbreak House*.

coaling-station: a port designed for loading coal, especially as fuel for steam vessels.

Lambeth: area of south London. Between 1909 and 1913 the Fabian Women's Group spent time researching the everyday circumstances and economic circumstances of working-class families there. The report appeared as *Round About a Pound a Week* (London: G. Bell and Sons, 1913).

55 *The president is Lady Corinthia Fanshawe; and the secretary is Mrs. Banger*: in real life, the Women's National Anti-Suffrage League was inaugurated on 21 July 1908, with Lady Jersey (1849–1945), the political hostess and philanthropist, presiding as 'chairman' of the organization. The athletic,

intelligent, and unmarried Gertrude Bell (1868–1926) took the role of honorary secretary, and was soon writing to *The Times* to declare that the new league could only be hindered by 'A territorial army of Amazons' (Bell, 'The National Anti-Suffrage League', *The Times*, 20 August 1908, p. 6).

56 *Daughter of Lord Broadstairs*: the real-life chair of the Women's National Anti-Suffrage League, Lady Jersey, was the eldest daughter of Baron Leigh (1824–1905), who had been a supporter of technical education. He was a Liberal who voted for Irish Home Rule in 1893 and hosted Gladstone in 1895.

automatic turbine man: Shaw may be alluding here to the real-life figure of Lord John Fisher (1841–1920), the influential naval admiral who helped introduce the turbine engine to HMS *Dreadnought* and the British fleet, which allowed faster speeds of travel.

charwoman: a woman hired by the day to do domestic chores. Shaw declared that, with this play, 'The only really sympathetic woman in it is a charwoman' (*CL* ii. 843, letter of 14 May 1909).

Chamber o Military Glory: in the early years of the twentieth century the 'Hall of Tableaux' at the Madame Tussaud's waxworks exhibition displayed scenes of a military, naval, and historical nature.

Music Halls: venues used for a style of popular entertainment typically consisting of singing, dancing, comedy, and novelty acts. There might be as many as twenty or twenty-five 'turns' in one evening's entertainment, and the format enjoyed great popularity in the second half of the 1800s and the early 1900s.

Variety Theatres: in the late 1800s, the popular music halls tended to be remodelled so that patrons, rather than sitting at individual supper tables, would sit in an auditorium in something resembling theatre seating. The halls became known as 'Palaces of Variety' and the older traditions of audiences eating, drinking, and behaving boisterously disappeared. The Variety Theatres also developed more complex, twice nightly, programmes of fare, including ballets and short plays. To a considerable extent, the term 'music hall' continued to be used interchangeably with the term 'variety'.

jook: duke.

57 *pleased as Punch*: very satisfied.

the supertax is put up to twenty shillings in the pound: on 29 April 1909, Asquith's government had introduced to the House of Commons a 'People's Budget', with proposed high taxes on the well-off, including a 'supertax' of 6*d*. in the pound on incomes over £5,000.

Poet Laureate: the poet formally selected as an officer of the Royal Household, expected to compose verse for significant royal and national occasions. The Poet Laureate at the time of the play's composition and setting was the—now largely forgotten—writer Alfred Austin (1835–1913).

Mansion House: official residence of the Lord Mayor of London, and a centre of government, entertaining, and other functions of the City of London.

seamy: the roughest, most degraded side. Shaw here uses term figuratively, and in the following line uses the term literally in reference to the underside (the side with seams) of General Sandstone's uniform.

58 *divilmint*: devilment, or evil.

59 *Fair caution*: quite an extraordinary or alarming person.

I sor im op it: I saw him hop it, or run away.

Shoreditch: an East End area of London. From the mid-nineteenth century, Shoreditch had been a major centre of the furniture trade, but by the start of the twentieth century was increasingly marked by overcrowding and poverty. In a *Saturday Review* piece of 9 April 1898, Shaw describes Shoreditch as 'a neighbourhood in which the Saturday Review is comparatively little read' (*Our Theatres in the Nineties*, 3 vols (London: Constable, 1932), iii. 351).

when I drew the number . . . it gev me the ump: when I had to be inducted into the army through participating in a compulsory draft lottery it upset and annoyed my mother, and it made me feel ill-humoured.

the drill: military exercise/training.

sergeant: a senior role of responsibility within the soldier rather than the officer ranks of the British army.

'*Fours*': arrange yourself into lines of four.

Lieutenant: a rank held by a British army officer below the rank of captain. Usually those from these ranks—the officers—would take on more leadership responsibilities, and would often come from a more exclusive social group. But Shaw's orderly emphasizes that the officers may have less common sense than the other ranks and even than the horses.

State visit to the Coal Trust: formal ceremonial visit to a body working in the united interests of a group of collieries. In 1909 the term 'Coal Trust' was commonly used about the coal industry in the United States: Shaw was likely using the American example to imagine the near future of Britain, where there were coal amalgamations in South Wales (such as the group of companies that formed the Cambrian Combine in 1906) and where there had been serious discussion about railway amalgamation and pooling agreements on traffic in 1909.

Threes: i.e. you should have arranged yourself into lines of three.

bally: euphemism for 'bloody'.

60 *Stepney*: part of London's East End that developed rapidly in the nineteenth century, filling with immigrants and the urban poor to a density of 158 people per acre by 1911, and becoming known for violence, poverty, and poor living conditions.

60 *discharge bought for him by his relations*: in real life, when Shaw wrote the play there had been no recent alteration in the regulations for the purchase of discharge. A soldier and/or his family had the automatic right to purchase discharge within the first three months of service, and after that period it was an 'indulgence' that had to be agreed by his commanding officer and the relevant brigade commander. After twenty-one years' service a soldier could apply for discharge without purchase. The 1908 and 1912 King's Regulations say the same thing about this, although in the play Shaw obviously imagined that this situation may have changed by 1912. His thinking may have been prompted by a case raised in the Commons during February 1908 in which a mother claimed she had been refused the right to purchase a son's discharge under the 'Widows' Act' (it was pointed out that there was no such Act and the discharge had been turned down under existing regulations). Shaw may also have been thinking about the bill for national military service brought forward in the Lords in May 1909 by the National Service League: the bill failed, but it proposed the abolition of discharge by purchase.

City o London alderman: the chief officer of a ward in the City of London, a rank below that of Lord Mayor.

Poltroon: coward, wretch.

sentry-box: small wooden construction in which a sentry can stand during bad weather without abandoning his post.

two years ard: two years of doing hard labour, heavy manual work.

61 *Call the guard . . . March*: in his unpublished typescript, Shaw originally added (1) a moment when Mitchener calls in Mrs Farrell before calling in the guard, (2) an extensive set of lines after 'March' . The missing lines are each included in this volume in Appendix B.

62 *compulsory service*: in real life, the National Service League did introduce a bill to the House of Lords in May 1909, providing compulsory military service for all men aged between 18 and 30. The bill failed, but Shaw imagines this measure having been passed in 1911, with the support of the popular press.

halfpenny papers: a series of halfpenny morning papers was launched from 1896, aimed at the lower middle class, with titles including the *Daily Mail*, *The Sun*, and *The Star*. They focused on melodramatic tales, stories of accidents, and crime news; they described politics with the apparently common-sense approach of the ordinary man in the street, and were less expensive than *The Times* or the *Daily Telegraph*, which focused primarily upon public affairs and politics.

Richmond Park nightingale: in 1904, King Edward VII (1841–1910) encouraged greater public access to this park, which had originally been established as a royal hunting park, and which was situated in an attractive part of what is now south-west London. In 1906 the *Daily Mail* was reporting that nightingales did occasionally appear here ('Haunts of the Nightingale', *Daily Mail*, 14 May 1906, p. 5).

63 *pusillanimity*: cowardice.

an XVIII century horse pistol: a large pistol carried on the saddle when riding a horse.

64 *Waterloo*: the Battle of Waterloo (18 June 1815), which saw the final defeat of Napoleon by the armies of Wellington and Blücher.

Kassassin: a battle at the Egyptian village of Kassassin/Qassasin took place in August 1882, during the Anglo-Egyptian War of that year. An English force led by General Graham (1789–1867) occupied the lock, and then fought with a number of Egyptian battalions. A further battle then took place in September 1882, when one English colonel found himself under attack by three squadrons of his Egyptian enemy, and, according to *The Times*, 'charged the nearest body with such fury that he killed 10 of the enemy and took four horses' ('Egypt', *The Times*, 12 September 1882, p. 5).

police courts: courts that have jurisdiction over a number of minor charges.

blood and iron, as was well said by Bismarck: Otto von Bismarck (1815–98), the minister-president of Prussia, gave a famous 1862 speech entitled 'Blood and Iron' (*Blut und Eisen*) which encouraged military readiness.

65 *Napoleon*: Napoleon sponsored what became known as the Napoleonic Code, which left women in a subordinate position to men, with divorce proceedings favouring fathers and husbands, and men maintaining control of children and family property. In 1897, Shaw had premiered his own short satirical play about Napoleon's career, *The Man of Destiny*.

Queen Elizabeth: Elizabeth I (1533–1603), queen of England and Ireland.

'made in Germany': one of the great worries of Britain's newspapers in the late nineteenth and early twentieth centuries was that the country was losing its industrial advantage and that many products used in Britain—including even military medals—were being 'made in Germany'. In addition, Alfred Milner (1854–1925), on whom the character of Mitchener was partly based, had himself been born in Hesse-Darmstadt, and spent much of his youth in Germany, including three years of education at a *Gymnasium* (a particularly academic school). Consequently, his enemies sometimes saw 'Germanic' or 'Teutonic' tendencies in his behaviour.

66 *raising her revolver*: perhaps recalls the incident in 1893, when the actress Elizabeth Robins (1862–1952) rejected Shaw's advances. As Shaw put it, 'I have interviewed beautiful women before; but none of them were ever so noble as to threaten to shoot me' (*CL* i. 380, letter of 5 February 1893).

F in alt: high F, in the octave directly above the topmost line of the treble stave.

Patti: Adelina Patti (1843–1919), an Italian soprano who, during the nineteenth century, performed operatic music to great acclaim.

E flat: a tone below the high F that Corinthia is claiming to reach.

67 *sarrusophones*: brass instruments of the oboe class, played with a double reed.

Tosti's Goodbye for Ever: the song 'Addio' by the Italian composer Paolo Tosti (1846–1916) had enjoyed great popular success during the Victorian era, with its chorus of 'Goodbye Forever! Goodbye Forever!' (quoted by David Ewen, *Great Composers, 1300–1900* (New York: Wilson, 1966), 385).

67 *Knightsbridge*: the Knightsbridge Barracks in central London. Mitchener appears to be referring to an event like the grand ball held there on 1 July 1880.

Tush!: an exclamation expressing contempt.

tenor: the adult male singing voice situated between the bass and counter-tenor or alto: the range of notes usually goes from the octave below middle C to the A above middle C.

68 *combinations*: combination garments, close-fitting underwear usually worn by women or children, and made up of a combined undershirt/chemise and drawers.

69 *Salic Law*: the law of the French monarchy whereby females were excluded from the line of succession.

New Zealand women have the vote: women gained the vote in 1893 in New Zealand, becoming the first women in a self-governing country to do so.

70 *Antony and Cleopatra*: the lovers of Shakespeare's play. At the start of that script, Mark Antony—who is one of the three men (triumvirs) ruling Rome, and already married—is enjoying an affair with Cleopatra, the beautiful queen of Egypt. When Antony later fights one of the other triumvirs, his brother-in-law Octavius Caesar, at sea, Cleopatra commands a fleet, and Antony's ships lose once Cleopatra's force flees and Antony follows her. Mitchener implies that in the 'game of Antony and Cleopatra' there is a danger of such a woman—uncontrolled and immoral, as he sees things—taking charge of society. Shaw gave his own theatrical response to Shakespeare's script in the 1898 play *Caesar and Cleopatra*.

Wagner's music: the music of Richard Wagner (1813–83), the German composer and theatrical artist, includes *Tristan und Isolde* and *Der Ring des Nibelungen*. Shaw published his own commentary on Wagner's *Ring* in the 1898 work *The Perfect Wagnerite*.

71 *take care of the pence, the pounds will take care of themselves*: take care of small sums of money and you will always have plenty. In Shaw's *Pygmalion*, Higgins observes 'Take care of the pence and the pounds will take care of themselves is as true of personal habits as of money' (Shaw, *Androcles and the Lion, Overruled, Pygmalion* (London: Constable, 1931), 230).

Liberal and Unionist Free Traders: the Liberal and Unionist Party was formed in 1886 when a group of those from the Liberal Party, led by Joseph Chamberlain (1836–1914) and the Marquess of Hartington (1833–1908), split away because of disagreements over Irish Home Rule. When Joseph Chamberlain launched tariff reform in 1903 he clashed with Hartington (now Duke of Devonshire) over the principle of free trade (that is, having no tariff barriers) and a number of Devonshire-supporting Liberal Unionists (who supported free trade) migrated back to the Liberal Party.

Factory Acts: the statutes 42 Geo. III. c. 73 (1802), 3 & 4 Will. IV. c. 103 (1833), and certain subsequent Acts, designed to regulate the conditions of employment for factory workers, especially for women and children.

72 *No: it's no use . . . has been tried*: in his unpublished typescript, Shaw originally added here a different set of lines:

> BALSQUITH. (Earnestly) Mitchener: Bellachristina has been invited to the Powerscourt garden party; and everybody is saying they had no idea she was such a nice girl.
>
> MITCHENER. You don't say so.
>
> BALSQUITH. I do.
>
> MITCHENER. Then all is indeed lost.
>
> ASQUITH. After all, you know, I dont suppose votes for women will make much difference. It hasnt in the other countries in which it has been tried.
>
> (*PC* Type, fo. 42)

that Pankhurst lot: those associated with Emmeline and Christabel Pankhurst (see notes to pp. 42, 44).

put them in quad: put them in prison.

73 *Sergeant-at-Arms*: an officer of each of the two Houses of Parliament, whose duties involve enforcing the commands of the House and arresting offenders.

leader of the House: in the House of Commons, the member of the government who officially leads the proceedings of the House.

comes: Shaw envisaged the following stage positioning here:

Mitchener——Mrs Farrell——Balsquith
(*PC* Type, fo. 44).

74 *Elephant*: Eliza lives in Elephant and Castle, an area of south London that Shaw described in his deleted act of *Back to Methuselah* (*A Glimpse of the Domesticity of Franklyn Barnabas*) as 'not a place at which tram cars stay: it is a point of continual departure and continual return. It is an ark which sends out doves every minute, and to which the doves return when the waters have abated' (Shaw, *The Black Girl in Search of God and Some Lesser Tales* (London: Constable, 1934), 230).

sthreel: streel (elsewhere rendered by Shaw as 'sthreal'), untidy/disreputable woman or slut.

I'm no chicken: I'm no longer young.

75 *Who's Who*: an annual publication giving biographical information on influential figures in British life.

Arra: an expression of excitement.

G'lang: go along with you.

scald: scurvy fellow.

collapsing: Shaw envisaged the following stage positioning here:

                              Mrs Farrell
Orderley——Mitchener——Lady Corinthia——Balsquith
(*PC* Type, fo. 46).

76 *Egeria*: a female counsellor, Egeria being the nymph who advised the
legendary second king of Rome, Numa Pompilius, and taught him how to
govern.

   lieutenant: Shaw is again emphasizing that the officers (among whom the
   lieutenants are numbered) may need to be less competent than those men
   from the other, supposedly less exclusive, ranks.

                              OVERRULED

The preface was published in *Androcles and the Lion, Overruled, Pygmalion*
(London: Constable, 1916), and republished under the same title by Constable
for the standard edition in 1931.

   Shaw first considered *Trespassers will be Prosecuted* as a title for the play but
changed it after discovering that a play of the same title by Michael Arabian
(1876–1957) had been produced at Manchester's Gaiety Theatre in 1909 and
1910. *Overruled* was first performed at London's Duke of York's Theatre on 14
October 1912. The play-text was first published in German, in a translation by
Siegfried Trebitsch, as 'Es hat nicht sollen sein' in the *Neue Freie Presse*
(Vienna), 23 March 1913, pp. 38–45. The original text was first published in
English as 'Overruled: A Dramatic Study' in the *English Review* (May 1913),
179–97, and in *Hearst's Magazine* (New York) (May 1913), 681–96. The script
was first published in book form as *Androcles and the Lion, Overruled, Pygmalion*
(London: Constable, 1916), and republished under the same title by Constable
for the standard edition in 1931.

81 *condign*: fitting or appropriate.

82 *Women may, Napoleon said . . . idle woman*: Napoleon noted 'Love is the
   occupation of the idle man, the distraction of the warrior, the stumbling
   block of the sovereign' (quoted by H. A. L. Fisher, *Napoleon* (London:
   Oxford University Press, 1956), 209).

   Joseph: a significant figure in Genesis, one of the sons of Jacob/Israel who
   is sold into slavery by jealous brothers, but rises to become the second
   most important man in Egypt, bringing Jacob/Israel to settle on good
   land in Egypt.

   Potiphar's wife: in Genesis (39:7–10), Joseph, having been sold into slavery, is bought by the Egyptian captain Potiphar, who promotes Joseph to
   run the household. Potiphar's wife repeatedly, and unsuccessfully, tries to
   bed Joseph. He flees, but she denounces him as her seducer and he is
   imprisoned.

83 *Brieux's Bourgeois aux Champs*: Eugène Brieux (1858–1932), a realist
   dramatist praised by Shaw for putting taboo issues on the stage. As Shaw
   put it, 'Europe has today a Sophocles in the person of Eugène Brieux'

(Shaw's lecture, 'On the Nature of Drama', 28 February 1914, quoted in Charlotte Shaw, 'Foreword', Eugène Brieux, *Damaged Goods* (London: Fifield, 1917), pp. v–xvi, at p. xiii). In the 1910 volume *Three Plays by Brieux*, one of the plays (*Maternité* or *Maternity*) was translated by Charlotte Shaw, whilst Bernard Shaw contributed a preface. A realistic depiction of countryside life is found in Brieux's three-act comedy of 1914, *Le Bourgeois aux champs* (The City Man in the Country).

Malvolio and Sir Toby: two characters from *Twelfth Night* by William Shakespeare. Malvolio is the austere steward (who is asked by Sir Toby, 'Dost thou think because thou art virtuous there shall be no more cakes and ale?'). Sir Toby, by contrast, remains a licentious figure (who, with his friends, is condemned by Malvolio because they 'gabble like tinkers' and 'make an alehouse of my lady's house'). See *Twelfth Night*, II. iii. 98 and 76–7.

voluptuary: someone addicted to sensual pleasures.

84 *Lucrezia Borgia . . . Messalina . . . Cenci*: Lucrezia Borgia (1480–1519) was an Italian noblewoman, daughter of Pope Alexander VI, a figure often linked with the criminality and excess of the Borgia family; as Shaw indicates, she was perhaps not the instigator of Borgia crimes, but was exploited by her father and brother. Messalina Valeria (died 48 CE) was the third wife of the Roman emperor Claudius, famous for her alleged promiscuity and ruthlessness. Beatrice Cenci (1577–99) was an Italian noblewoman famous for reputedly participating in the murder of her abusive father.

La Rochefoucauld: François VI, duc de La Rochefoucauld (1613–80), who stated, 'Abundance of Men would never have been in *Love*, if they had never been entertained with any discourse of *Love*' (*The Moral Maxims and Reflections of the Duke de la Rochefoucauld*, ed. George H. Powell (London: Methuen, 1912), 56).

Rousseau: Jean-Jacques Rousseau (1712–78), philosopher and essayist, who detailed the fate of his five illegitimate children in his posthumously published *Confessions* (1782, 1789). Rousseau wrote, 'My third child was therefore carried to the foundling hospital as well as the two former, and the next two were disposed of in the same manner; for I have had five children in all' (Rousseau, *Confessions, Complete in One Volume* (London: Reeves and Turner, 1861), 269).

85 *The favorite subject of farcical comedy*: when Shaw had drafted his preface, he originally began at this point (*Over* Type, fo. 1).

Restoration Comedy: a mode of comedy that came to the fore after the Restoration of the Stuart monarchy (1660), often focusing on the manners of elite society, sexual infidelity, and the complexities of arranging a marriage. For the first time in London, these plays featured women appearing in acting roles.

Palais Royal farce: the Théâtre du Palais-Royal in Paris, which opened in 1831 and specialized in farce and vaudeville. In England the term 'Palais-Royal farce' became associated with translations of suggestive plays by

French writers such as Georges Feydeau (1862–1921), whose preferred comic theme was the way that a husband or wife might strive to conceal adulterous liaisons.

85 *Parisian school*: adultery was a recurring theme for Alexandre Dumas *fils* (1824–95), who produced three plays on the subject between 1871 and 1873 alone. Writers including Émile Augier (1820–89) and Victorien Sardou (1831–1908) followed his cue, leading Henry James (1843–1916) to conclude of French dramatists that 'adultery is their only theme' (James, 'The Parisian Stage', *The Nation*, 9 January 1873, pp. 23–4).

Ibsen: Henrik Ibsen (1828–1906), influential Norwegian playwright, who from the 1870s set about writing a series of plays—which became internationally famous—about contemporary social issues. In Britain, Shaw became one of Ibsen's major exponents, writing one of the first English-language studies of Ibsen's work, *The Quintessence of Ibsenism* (1891).

put them out of countenance: in an earlier draft of the preface, Shaw uses the more strongly worded phrase, 'swept it into the dustbin' (*Over* Type, fo. 9).

86 *heresiarch*: a founder or leader of heresy.

Francesca and Paolo: the adulterous lovers Francesca Da Rimini and Paolo Malatesta described in the second circle of hell in canto 5 of the *Inferno* by Italian poet Dante Alighieri (1265–1321).

popular plays: in his earlier draft of the preface, Shaw planned to make a slightly different point in this sentence, writing that 'they were quite wrong in assuming that the so-called sex dramas which they declared to be the only real dramas really deal with sex' (*Over* Type, fo. 9).

Molière: (1622–73) French dramatist and author of acclaimed plays including *Tartuffe* and *Le Misanthrope*.

Don Quixote: novel by Miguel de Cervantes (1547–1616) published in two volumes in 1605 and 1615.

Othello: the protagonist of Shakespeare's play, who strangles his wife in bed after becoming possessed by the false belief that she has been unfaithful to him.

Romeo and Juliet: Shakespeare's play, probably written in 1595, in which the apothecary speaks a grand total of seven lines.

87 *Thackeray*: William Makepeace Thackeray (1811–63), novelist.

Dickens: Charles Dickens (1812–70), novelist.

Macbeth . . . Macduff: Macbeth is the titular character of Shakespeare's well-known play, probably written about 1606. During Act II, Macbeth murders Duncan, the king of Scotland. Subsequently, in the climactic fifth act of the play, Macduff, the thane of Fife, kills Macbeth.

Tristan and Isolde: three-act opera of 1865 by Wagner. The second act is set in a castle at night, where Isolde waits for Tristan while her husband is away hunting. There Tristan and Isolde consummate their love and are then discovered. The lovers tend to ignore external circumstances and instead focus upon their inner feelings.

88 *Alsatia*: a lawless place, where criminals would be immune from arrest.

89 *Disillusive*: tending to disillusion.

Sophocles: (496–409 BCE), tragedian of the ancient Greek theatre.

Granville Barker . . . Reinhardt . . . Moscow Art Theatre: Harley Granville Barker (1877–1946) was a dramatist and theatre director. The real name of Max Reinhardt (1873–1943), theatre manager and director, was Max Goldmann. Moscow Art Theatre was a Russian theatre of naturalism founded in 1898 by Konstantin Stanislavsky (1863–1938) and Vladimir Nemirovich-Danchenko (1858–1943).

Cibber . . . Garrick . . . Richard III: Cibber (1671–1757) was a theatre manager, actor, and writer. David Garrick (1717–79) was an actor and dramatist. He gave his first London performance as Shakespeare's Richard III in October 1741 in Goodman's Fields Theatre. The performance was revelatory, and the actor's costuming in this part was well remembered, thanks to a famed 1745 painting by William Hogarth (1697–1764).

trunk hose and plumes: full, bag-like breeches, covering the upper thighs and hips, and feathers.

Plantagenets: the royal dynasty that ruled in England from Henry II in 1154 to Richard III in 1485.

George III: (1738–1820), king of Great Britain and Ireland from 1760, and then king of the United Kingdom from the Act of Union of 1801 until 1820.

Sheridan's Critic . . . Buckingham's Rehearsal: a play by Richard Brinsley Sheridan (1751–1816), *The Critic: or, a Tragedy Rehearsed* (1779) gives a comic take on the world of playwrights and theatre critics. *The Rehearsal* (1671) is a play written by George Villiers, 2nd Duke of Buckingham (1592–1628) and his collaborators, which satirized contemporary heroic drama.

Fielding: in *Tom Jones* (1749) by Henry Fielding (1707–54), the character of Partridge attends a performance of *Hamlet*, with Garrick in the lead role. Partridge praises the actor playing the king, but is told that Hamlet is played by the best actor. '"He the best player!" cries Partridge, with a contemptuous sneer, "why, I could act as well as he myself. I am sure, if I had seen a ghost, I should have looked in the very same manner, and done just as he did"' (Fielding, *Tom Jones*, ed. John Bender and Simon Stern (Oxford: Oxford University Press, 1996), 752).

Garrick's Hamlet: David Garrick performed as *Hamlet* in 1742, and then reprised the role for almost three and a half decades until 1776. His performances came at a time when audiences were beginning to respond to the inner emotions and feelings of *Hamlet*, with Garrick revealing the overriding grief that governed much of the character's behaviour.

Calvé's intensely real Carmen: Emma Calvé (1858–1942), French soprano whose acclaimed version in the title role of *Carmen* by Georges Bizet (1838–75) was given verisimilitude by the fact that, in preparation for the part, she had gone to Spain and modelled her behaviour on the flirtatious cigarette girls she observed in Seville. Shaw declared that she 'wrecked an innocently pretty opera' by introducing the 'rapscallionly Carmen of real life' (Shaw, review of 2 November 1895, in *Our Theatres in the Nineties*, i. 235).

90 *Don Giovanni . . . Zerlina*: the version of the libertine Don Juan as presented in the 1787 opera by Wolfgang Amadeus Mozart (1756–91) and librettist Lorenzo da Ponte (1749–1838). Zerlina is the newly married peasant woman whom Don Giovanni attempts to seduce in the opera.

92 *Sibthorpe Juno*: key character in Shaw's play *Overruled*.

an earnest and distinguished British moralist: possibly Frederick Jackson of Hindhead (born 15 August 1832), who wrote to Shaw on 3 May 1913: 'I have just read "Over-ruled", and quite understand why you never show me your M.S.S. Your last play is only Congreve and water. You need above all things a change of air and scene. Try the out-of-the-way parts of Provence, or better still take a look at the Temple of Neptune at Paestum, then have a good purge, and you will return home as sound as a roach' (British Library, Add. MS 50539, ALS 3 May 1913, fos. 21–2).

doctrine of original sin: influential concept established by St Augustine of Hippo (354–430), describing the tendency towards evil that is innate in all human beings and was inherited from Adam after the Fall.

Black Death: epidemic that killed perhaps a quarter of Europe's population in 1347–50.

salvarsan: an arsenic compound used to treat syphilis.

93 *chesterfield*: a stuffed-over sofa with a back and two ends, one of which is sometimes adjustable.

seaside hotel: Shaw had originally intended more geographical specificity here, writing 'a pretty room in a hotel in Harwich' (*Over* Type, fo. 1). Harwich is a port in Essex, and if the characters met there it would imply that their trips around the world had already completed. Shaw's revised location of a non-specific seaport hotel (perhaps somewhere in the Pacific) might indicate instead that the characters were meeting midway through the journey.

dandyism: the style of a person who strives, above all, to be fashionable.

Juno: the name of the chief goddess in Roman mythology, wife of Jupiter, and the goddess of marriage.

I don't want to be tired and sorry . . . I don't want you to be tired and sorry: these lines carry a sexual implication that worried the British censor. Although the play was allowed a licence for public performance, one official at the Lord Chamberlain's office noted, 'I am not sure if the allusion to being "tired" when "horrid" is quite innocent' (British Library, Add. MS 65987F, *Overruled*, D.D. note of 30 September 1912).

94 *making love to me*: this is meant in the (now archaic) sense of courting or paying amorous attention to someone.

96 *matter with them*: in his draft, Shaw added an additional line of exposition here, 'My sisters were always pulling me up for it; but I keep on doing it all the same' (*Over* Type, fo. 6).

97 *a libertine*: an individual, usually a man, who remains unhindered by moral opinion, particularly with regard to sexual relations: a promiscuous or dissolute person.

Don Juan: the fictional character who symbolizes libertinism. He was the subject of a drama by Spanish playwright Tirso de Molina (1584–1648), and features in many subsequent literary works, including the third act of Shaw's 1903 play *Man and Superman*.

sit: actors may wish to consider that at one point when writing the play Shaw envisaged a different onstage positioning here, writing 'stand' instead of 'sit' (*Over* Type, fo. 8).

99 *drink*: Gregory may be nodding towards the beer produced by the Pockthorpe Brewery in Norwich. There is also potentially an echo of 'sip'/'sup forth' in Sibthorpe's name.

Gregory, which sounds like a powder: medical powders tended to be sold under the names of particular individuals, such as Dover's powder for colds, and James's powder for fevers. 'Gregory's powder' was a laxative, named after its inventor James Gregory (1753–1821).

101 *like Tannhäuser in the hill of Venus*: in the opera *Tannhäuser* (premiered 1845) by Wagner, Act I begins with the young Tannhäuser in the underground realm of Venus, where he has spent the year with the goddess of love, whose erotic powers and sensuality he praises. Nonetheless, Tannhäuser expresses his desire to be back in the outside world.

102 *Suez*: city, port, and ancient trading site, on the coast of northern Egypt. Sibthorpe Juno has therefore headed south-east at the same time as his wife has headed west.

103 *'Farewell and adieu to you dear Spanish ladies'*: the song 'Spanish Ladies', an old British sailing song, possibly derives from the period in the mid-1790s when British ships would dock in Spanish harbours (with Britain and Spain then allies against France).

Gibraltar: although Gibraltar shares a short land border of less than a mile with Andalusian province of Cádiz, Gibraltar itself is not part of Spain, having been formally held by Britain since the Treaty of Utrecht in 1713.

What eloquence!: in his draft, Shaw had written instead, 'This is a perfectly silly way to talk' (*Over* Type, fo. 16).

world for him: in his draft, Shaw added the following extra lines at this point, 'He is frightfully sentimental: one of those men that ought to have a dozen wives; only hes so conscientious and so affectionate, I darent suggest such a thing to him' (*Over* Type, fo. 17).

104 *spinal tonic*: a medicinal substance that restores or increases the healthy condition of the spine.

104 *Seraphita*: the name of an 1835 novel by Honoré de Balzac (1799–1850), about a mysterious figure in Norway. This figure is ambisexual: appearing as male to some (such as the character Minna, who is drawn to the man Séraphitus), and as female to others (such as the character Wilfred, who is attracted to the woman Séraphita).

Sally . . . Lunn . . . joke: Sally Lunn is a type of teacake, its name perhaps deriving from the French *soleil et lune* (sun and moon) or from the name of the cake-seller Solange Luyon/Sally Lunn.

107 *Mr Lunn*: in his draft, Shaw planned to include the following extra lines at this point:

> MRS LUNN. Is this your wife, Mr June. Wont you introduce me.
>
> MRS JUNO. How do you do? (they shake hands)
>
> MRS LUNN. Nice pair of husbands we've got, havnt we?
>
> (*Over* Type, fo. 25)

111 *polyandry*: a form of polygamy in which one woman has two or more husbands or male sexual partners at the same time.

112 *uxorious*: devotedly or dotingly attached to a wife.

115 *footling*: talking foolishly.

THE INCA OF PERUSALEM

The preface was published in *Heartbreak House, Great Catherine, and Playlets of the War* (London: Constable, 1919), and republished under the same title by Constable for the standard edition in 1931.

The play was first performed at the Birmingham Repertory Theatre, 7 October 1916. The play-text was first published in *Heartbreak House, Great Catherine, and Playlets of the War* (London: Constable, 1919), and republished under the same title by Constable for the standard edition in 1931.

The title *The Inca of Perusalem* references the name of the emperor/king in Peru before the Spanish conquest; in this play, the Inca bears a close similarity to the German Kaiser Wilhelm II (1859–1941). The invented country Perusalem is a pun on 'Peru', where the Incas once lived, and 'Preussen' (Prussia), the state that was the cradle of Imperial Germany. We may also hear an echo of 'Jerusalem', the ancient holy city which Shaw would visit in 1931.

121 *Caesar*: autocrat/emperor.

knowing better himself: in Shaw's 1898 play *Caesar and Cleopatra*, Julius Caesar (100–44 BCE) reflects on Roman battles in Egypt, 'this has been a mad expedition. We shall be beaten . . . I am an old man—worn out now' (Shaw, *Three Plays for Puritans* (London: Constable, 1934), 149).

deleted everything . . . a foul blow: most notably, when Shaw reviewed the rough proof of his 1915 rehearsal copy of the play, he made a revision to delete one of the stage directions (see note to p. 133). He did this in part because of the Lord Chamberlain's directions to ensure that the Inca did not look too much like the German Kaiser. One of the official readers noted that the Inca was 'obviously the German Emperor', and the company presenting Shaw's work were instructed to 'see that the make up of the Inca does not too closely resemble the German Emperor' (British Library, LCP Corr 1915-3885 *The Inca of Perusalem*, letter by G. S. Street of 11 November 1915 and letter by Trundell of 15 November 1915).

122 *archdeacon*: the chief deacon, originally the main attendant to a bishop.

emoluments: the amount of money he earns from his office.

Roosenhonkers-Pipstein: this fictional multimillionaire was originally called simply 'Pipstein' until Shaw revised his rehearsal copy before sending it to the printers in 1915. Shaw presumably felt that the double-barrelled name, with potentially antisemitic connotation, sounded more comical (see *Inc* Type).

123 *fifteen million dollars*: in his typescript, Shaw suggested a figure of three millions as the figure here, with Rosenhonkers-Pipstein possessing 'four millions' rather than sixteen million dollars at the time of his death (see *Inc* Type, fo. 2). This may not have been that he was envisaging a poorer multimillionaire, but was likely thinking in British pounds rather than US dollars (one pound on the outbreak of the First World War falling to be worth just under four dollars).

Mammon: worldly goods and money, regarded as a false god, or evil influence.

securities: tradable financial assets. Shaw suggested in his typescript the figure of 'ten thousand' rather than fifty thousand dollars a year as a settlement. As he revised the piece he likely made the change as he began to think of the wealth of his millionaires in US dollars rather than British pounds (see *Inc* Type, fo. 2).

The speculative ones . . . whole show burst up: Ermyntrude's financial investments have either been risky and unrewarding, or have involved more certain ventures that have nonetheless had to pay out to various creditors until reaching a final point of failure.

a hundred thousand dollars: Shaw wrote this amount as '£20,000' in his typescript, shifting from UK to US currency as the best measure of great wealth (*Inc* Type, fo. 3).

What!: in his draft of the play, Shaw ended the prologue with this exclamation (*Inc* Type, fo. 3).

124 *workhouse*: an establishment where the destitute could access board and lodging, with inmates ordinarily required to work for those benefits.

126 *the war*: the First World War (1914–18).

128 *pothouse*: an alehouse or pub.

Alas, madam . . . an eminent medical man: Shaw considered creating a more pugnacious version of this waiter. The typescript shows that Shaw did not at first consider the waiter to have been a former medic at all, but when Shaw revised his rehearsal copy in 1915 he decided that the waiter had a medical background and wanted the character to speak with the words, 'I will not bear this. I have never been taken for so before. How dare you? Do you know that I am an eminent medical man?' (*Inc* Type, fo. 8).

130 *armaments contractor*: in his typescript, Shaw wrote a line here with a very different implication. The printed line appears to share the same focus on arms dealing as his play *Major Barbara* (1905), but Shaw's typescript for *The Inca of Perusalem* refers not to 'some fat armaments contractor' but to 'some beef baron or oilshop king millionaire or sausage millionaire' (*Inc* Type, fo. 10).

decayed professional person disguised as a waiter: Shaw did not at first see the waiter as having once been a medic, but having a far lower social status, and so in an earlier draft this line read 'lout of a stable boy dressed like a waiter' (*Inc* Type, fo. 10).

I shake its dust off my feet: cf. Matthew 10:14.

133 *The Inca . . . cloak*: this stage direction had, in Shaw's typescript, made explicit the connection between the Inca and the real-life German leader. Shaw had written: '*The Inca, in a German military uniform, very stiff, very solemn, advances with a marked and imposing stage walk; stops; clicks his heels and bows. He strongly resembles the Kaiser, and copies his moustache.*' However, Shaw's rough proof of the 1915 rehearsal copy of the play, which he labelled 'to comply with Licence', indicated that he wanted the direction changed to '*The Inca, a handsome gentleman on the elderly side of middle age, in a military uniform and military moustaches, very stiff, very solemn, advances with a marked and imposing stage walk; stops; clicks his heels; bows.*' When he created a revised rough proof of the play in 1918, Shaw approved the version of the direction that appears in this volume (*Inc* Proof, fo. 12).

Allerhöchst: (Ger.) most high/highest of all.

Providence: when revising his typescript Shaw changed this from 'God', perhaps in order to avoid provoking the censor with a reference to the deity (*Inc* Type, fo. 15).

134 *Arminius*: also known as Hermann (18? BCE–19 CE), the German tribal leader who led a major victory over the Romans in the Teutoburg Forest in 9 CE.

Shipskeel canal: a fictional waterway named after the ship's keel, part of the bottom of a boat.

Henry the Birdcatcher: this was the nickname given to Henry I (876–936 CE), who, according to legend, was laying snares for birds when he learned of his election as king of Germany.

half a million Perusalem dollars: in his typescript Shaw wrote 'four million Perusalem dollars' here, but changed the figure when he prepared his rehearsal copy in 1915. He kept the ensuing reference to ten million dollars unchanged, however, perhaps wanting to exaggerate how much the value of the brooch had increased (*Inc* Type, fo. 17).

135 *I ask you!*: in Shaw's typescript he envisaged this line continuing, 'I dare-
     say it would look nice on the chest of a brewer's horse at the annual show
     in Regent's Park; but I am not a brewer's horse' (*Inc* Type, fo. 17).

     daughter-in-law: in his typescript Shaw wrote 'consort' here, giving the
     relationship a different implication (*Inc* Type, fo. 17).

     *The Inca would not allow his son to marry you . . . only other human being on
     it*: originally Shaw's typescript described a rather different set of relation-
     ships, reading, 'The Inca would not marry you if you were on a desert
     island and you were the only other human being on it' (*Inc* Type, fo. 18).

     morganatic: a marriage in which a man of high rank marries a wife of lower
     rank, but neither the wife nor any potential children have a claim to the
     husband's possessions or title.

     dragoon: a cavalry soldier.

     When I marry the Inca's son . . . that moustache: in the typescript this line
     had read, 'When I marry the Inca, Captain, I shall make him order you to
     cut off your moustache' (*Inc* Type, fo. 18).

     By all the thunders of Thor: Thor (Thunder) was a god shared by the early
     Germanic peoples, characterized by his great strength.

136 *I say No*: Shaw's typescript included another line here, possibly removed
     because of the author's justifiable fear that the censor would find the refer-
     ence too insulting about the monarchy: 'These wretched throned insects
     might be commercial travellers for anything anyone cares for their miser-
     able moustaches' (*Inc* Type, fo. 19).

     Kultur: civilization and culture as expressed in the German language, and
     a term used in a discomforting sense during the world wars as connoting
     a racial superiority connected to imperialism and militarism.

137 *Well, he started it, you know*: at one stage Shaw intended Ermyntrude to
     say quite the reverse here. The typescript corrects the line from 'How
     wicked of them to rebel against him'. The Inca was to respond, 'Do you
     know why they rebel against him? They hate him because he is a lever of
     peace: a sincere Christian. He has kept the peace for years' (*Inc* Type,
     fos. 20–1).

     trinitrotoluene: used as a high explosive that is insensitive to shock and can
     be melted; better known by its abbreviation, TNT.

     grief: at this point, Shaw's typescript contains the following extra lines that
     Shaw erased as he revised the work:

     Ermyntrude. Is it possible that the Inca is one of the great
        misunderstood?

     The Inca. Misunderstood. O Heavens, madam, how much
        misunderstood! You little know. But enough. The heart knoweth its
        own bitterness. And it is, after all, the penalty of greatness (he sits
        down again exhausted by his emotions).

     (*Inc* Type, fo. 22).

137 *His Imperial Highness Prince Eitel . . . Wilson*: a fictional compound of various national leaders. The first two names recall the eldest two sons of Kaiser Wilhelm II: Crown Prince Wilhelm (1882–1951) and Prince Eitel Friedrich (1883–1942). The names then recall, in turn, George V of Britain (1865–1936), Franz Joseph I of Austria (1830–1916), Alexander I of Yugoslavia (1888–1934), Nicholas II of Russia (1868–1918), Victor Emmanuel III of Italy (1869–1947), Albert I of Belgium (1875–1934), Theodore Roosevelt of the United States (1858–1919), and Woodrow Wilson of the United States (1856–1924).

138 *Chips and Spots and Lulu and Pongo and the Corsair and the Piffler and Jack Johnson the Second*: these seven figures may call to mind the seven children of the real-life Kaiser Wilhelm II, namely Crown Prince Wilhelm, Prince Eitel Friedrich, Prince Adalbert (1884–1948), Prince August Wilhelm (1887–1949), Prince Oskar (1888–1958), Prince Joachim (1890–1920), and Princess Viktoria Luise (1892–1980).

Strauss's Sinfonia Domestica: Richard Strauss (1864–1949) was the German composer of *Symphonia Domestica* (Domestic Symphony, premiered in 1904), a tone poem written for a large orchestra.

mouth organ: harmonica.

any of these young degenerates: in Shaw's typescript this judgemental line originally read simply 'they' (*Inc* Type, fo. 24).

139 *Admiral von Cockpits*: intended to recall the real-life Admiral von Tirpitz (1849–1930), who expanded the German navy in the build-up to the First World War and was a dominant figure during the reign of Kaiser Wilhelm II.

Angel Gabriel: the angel who functions as God's messenger and tells the Virgin Mary that she will be the mother of Jesus in Luke 1:28.

General Von Schinkenburg: intended to recall the real-life General von Hindenburg (1847–1934), the military leader known for his resilience and strategic brilliance.

Schinkenburg!: at this point in his typescript Shaw included the lines: 'Have you ever heard of the doctor who could cure fits and nothing else, and gave all his patients fits so that he might cure them? They died of what was really the matter with them' (*Inc* Type, fo. 25).

Bedrock the Great: the name of this fictional monarch recalls that of Frederick the Great (1712–86), long-reigning king of Prussia who greatly enlarged his kingdom and proved a brilliant military leader. However, the British censor felt that the fictional 'Bedrock' also alluded to Queen Victoria (1819–1901), and so requested in 1915 that the reference was cut before performance (HRC Lic).

140 *the Inca's uncle*: intended to recall Edward VII, one of the real-life uncles of Kaiser Wilhelm II. Edward, with his many mistresses and his lengthy period as heir apparent, had been the 'playboy prince'. In 1915 the British censor felt troubled by this line, wanting it cut from performance and writing, 'As this obviously means King Edward it may be thought

disrespectful to his memory' (British Library, LCP Corr 1915-3885 *The Inca of Perusalem*, Letter by G. S. Street of 11 November 1915). Accordingly, Shaw edited the reference for his 1915 rehearsal copy of the play, which he described as being 'Cut to comply with Licence'. Shaw's proofs reveal him revising the line as follows, 'Why, hang it all, madam, if it were a mere family matter, the Inca's <relatives would be> ~~uncle would have been~~ as great ~~a man~~ as the Inca. ~~And well, everyone knows what the Inca's uncle was~~' (*Inc* Proof, fo. 20).

duffers: people who are ill-suited to their role, being incompetent or useless.

France after 1871: the Third French Republic of 1871–1940.

St Helena: an extremely remote tropical island in the Atlantic, to which the British exiled Napoleon Bonaparte in 1815, and where he died six years later.

Acropolis: the ancient citadel of Athens.

Velasquez: the Spanish artist Diego Velázquez (1599–1660); a famous collection of his paintings was held at the Prado Museum in Madrid.

Bayreuth: the city in east-central Germany where the composer Richard Wagner settled in 1872, and where he founded his famous music festival in 1876 in order to showcase his own compositions.

shot . . . as indeed he very nearly was: when Wagner was nearly 36 years old, he played a role in the 1849 May Uprising in Dresden. Afterwards, he narrowly escaped arrest and fled to Switzerland. Meanwhile, twelve thousand people suspected of supporting the revolution were rounded up, and twenty-six fleeing students hidden in a single room were taken out and shot.

from the Carpathians to the Rocky Mountains: from the mountains of eastern Europe to those of North America.

141 *india-rubber stamp*: a person or institution whose power is formal but not real.

American President: Woodrow Wilson.

American fashion: in his typescript Shaw added the explanatory line here, 'American voting papers are the longest in the world' (*Inc* Type, fo. 29).

statue of Liberty . . . on its tomb: raised in 1876, with the statue being placed upon a granite pedestal inside the courtyard of the star-shaped walls of Fort Wood (which had once been used to repel the British during the War of 1812). The Inca here indicates that, despite such symbolism, the United States is the 'tomb' of liberty because its president is all-powerful and the government does what it likes.

142 *Mahometan faith*: an archaic way of describing a follower of Islam (now considered inaccurate terminology because it implies the worship of the prophet Muhammad (*c.*570–632 CE)). In 1915, the British censor wanted this part of the script changed in performance, writing of his discomfort over the 'marriage idea with the allusion to the Empress: this seems

beyond fair' (British Library, LCP Corr 1915-3885 *The Inca of Perusalem*, Letter by G. S. Street of 11 November 1915). However, Shaw does not appear to have ever changed the reference.

142 *war bread*: the nutritionally substandard 'Kriegsbrot' or 'K' bread eaten in Germany during the war, with the ingredients often including a large amount of potato.

does not even allow himself wine at dinner: this alludes to the public example of King George V, who, in response to a prime ministerial campaign for teetotalism for the duration of the war, issued a famous statement on 6 April 1915 declaring: 'By the King's command, no wines, spirits, or beer will be consumed in any of his Majesty's houses' ('The King's Pledge', *Manchester Guardian*, 9 August 1915, p. 6). The British censor complained about this part of Shaw's play, pointing to 'The allusion to King George's abstinence from wine. I think that should be cut out' (British Library, LCP Corr 1915-3885 *The Inca of Perusalem*, Letter by G. S. Street of 11 November 1915). Accordingly, Shaw deleted the reference for his 1915 rehearsal copy of the play, which he described as being 'Cut to comply with Licence' (*Inc* Proof, front cover).

style: at this point Shaw had added the following extra lines, which he deleted when he prepared his 1915 rehearsal copy of the play:

> The Inca. (With towering scorn) Indeed, madam? Are you so important? Of course not. We are only kings, rulers of the people and servants of ~~God~~ Providence and hard fare and hard work is good enough for us. But you are a lady's maid: you must have luxuries, spendors, extravagances, infinitesimal insect that you are.

> Ermyntrude. Well, sir, you cant have it both ways, you know. If you are great you must put up with plain living and high thinking. If you are a petty ~~creature~~ little insect like me, you need petty comforts. Besides, Sir, you should not call me an insect.

(*Inc* Type, fo. 32)

143 *hyphenated millionaire*: i.e. a multi-millionaire.

implacable enemy: Britain.

Many fine young men are dying while you wait: at this point, Shaw had planned to include some harsh words about the folly of men dying in the war. The lines were deleted entirely by the time he came to produce a revised rough proof of the play in 1918, at a time when the scale of the wartime slaughter had become clear. But in the version he prepared as a rehearsal copy in 1915 he included the following lines (although he crossed through some words as he corrected those 1915 proofs):

> ERMYNTRUDE. .... Many fine young men are dying while you wait.

> THE INCA. ~~There are plenty more where they came from, madam.~~ ~~My own life is at stake; and I think I have shown that I value it very~~ ~~highly.~~ Well, can you expect me to value the lives of people who

actually boast of their readiness to sacrifice their lives in a quarrel that not one in a thousand of them understands? For every man killed or hurt, I have rescued ~~four men~~ <hundreds> from unworthy drudgeries, shrewish wives, squalling children, and all the horrors of home. Yet not one of them says as much as Thank you, sire. Besides, madam—this is strictly between ourselves—why the devil do they fight if they dont want to?

ERMYNTRUDE. Because you make them.

THE INCA. Stuff! How can I? I am only one man; and they are millions. Do you suppose they would really kill each other if they didnt want to, merely for the sake of my beautiful eyes.

(*Inc* Proof, fo. 24).

O'FLAHERTY V.C.

The preface was published in *Heartbreak House, Great Catherine, and Playlets of the War* (London: Constable, 1919), and republished by Constable for the standard edition in 1931.

The play was first performed by 40th Squadron, Royal Flying Corps, on the Western Front in Belgium, 17 February 1917, and first performed profession-ally at New York's 39th Street Theatre, 21 June 1920. The play-text was first published in *Hearst's Magazine* (New York) (August 1917), 88–91. It was then published in England as part of the collected edition *Heartbreak House, Great Catherine, and Playlets of the War* (London: Constable, 1919), and republished under the same title by Constable for the standard edition in 1931.

In the title, *V.C.* is a reference to Victoria Cross: a British military and naval decoration awarded for demonstrative bravery in battle. The play had a different subtitle, 'An Interlude in the Great War of 1914', when originally published in 1917 in *Hearst's Magazine*, but that was changed on publication by Constable in 1919, when the play appeared without any subtitle (in *Heartbreak House, Great Catherine, and Playlets of the War* (London: Constable, 1919)). When the standard edition was published in 1931, the title appeared as *O'Flaherty V.C.: A Recruiting Pamphlet*.

147 *Dublin Castle*: the seat of British rule in Ireland until 1922.

REMEMBER BELGIUM: this recruitment poster called to mind German wartime atrocities in Belgium—a country, like Ireland, of relatively small size and predominantly Roman Catholic population.

FORGET AND FORGIVE: Irish nationalists tended to remember 800 years of 'English' tyranny, going back to the Anglo-Norman invasions of the twelfth century. Such tyranny included the plantations of the sixteenth and seventeenth centuries, as well as the execution of those who had led notable rebellions against the Crown in 1798 and 1803.

Belgium and its broken treaty: the Treaty of London in 1839 had seen Germany and the other major powers agree to maintain Belgium's neu-trality, yet Germany invaded in August 1914.

147 *Limerick and its broken treaty*: in 1691 the Treaty of Limerick concluded the war in Ireland between defeated Jacobites and victorious supporters of William of Orange. The treaty guaranteed generous terms for Catholics in Ireland, yet the articles were not honoured and, soon afterwards, a set of restrictive penal laws were imposed, discriminating against Catholics.

rebellion: the Easter Rising of 24–9 April 1916, an insurrection that took place almost entirely in Dublin and saw the proclamation of an Irish Republic.

long drawn out ferocity: after the Easter Rising, fifteen high-profile insurgents were executed over nine days (3–12 May 1916), something that helped change the popular mood in Ireland from hostility towards the rebels to broad support for them.

John Bull: England. Shaw famously used this name in the title of his 1904 comedy about Ireland, *John Bull's Other Island*.

ruins of Dublin: after the Easter Rising, Shaw had argued elsewhere that 'It is greatly to be regretted that so very little of Dublin has been demolished. The General Post Office was a monument, fortunately not imperishable, of how extremely dull eighteen-century pseudo-classic architecture can be. Its demolition does not matter. What does matter is that all the Liffey slums have not been abolished' (Shaw, 'Some Neglected Morals of the Irish Rising', *New Statesman*, 6 May 1916, pp. 105–6).

Louvain: small Belgium university town, 16 miles east of Brussels, famed for its university and Gothic architecture (nicknamed 'the Oxford of Belgium'). Towards the start of the First World War, between 25 and 30 August 1914, it was the scene of an infamous set of German war crimes, including the burning of the seventeenth-century library and the killing of civilians, events that were widely reported in the British press.

148 *secession in America*: during the American Civil War of 1861–5, Irish soldiers fought for the Confederate side in units such as the 6th Louisiana Infantry (the 'Irish Tigers'). Irish soldiers also fought in large numbers for the Union side during the war, with most Irish-Americans having settled in the northern states which remained loyal to the United States government.

termagants: quarrelsome and violent women.

colleen: girl.

Volumnia: mother of Coriolanus in Shakespeare's *Coriolanus* (a play probably written in 1608). She boasts of having raised her son for war, declaring, 'Thou art my warrior; | I holp to frame [helped to make] thee' (V. iii. 63–4).

rout of the Fifth Army: on 21 March 1918, the British Fifth Army faced the major German offensive, Operation Michael, across a 42-mile stretch of the Western Front. The Fifth Army failed to withstand this spring offensive, lost 150,000 men, and was disbanded.

Irish Conscription: on 25 March 1918, the British cabinet made plans for conscription in Ireland to recruit 150,000 men from the country. In April, there followed widespread protests, and the government, fearing another Irish uprising, backed away from the proposal.

British blockade: between 1914 and 1919, Britain and the Allied Powers conducted a naval operation to prevent Germany and the Central Powers from importing food and raw materials by sea.

149 *God Save the King*: see note to p. 38.

It's a Long Way to Tipperary: a British music-hall song written in 1912 by Jack Judge (1872–1938), which enjoyed great popularity amongst the British soldiers during the First World War. Tipperary is a town and county in the province of Munster, Ireland.

O'Flaherty: when Shaw first wrote the play he consistently spelt the name 'O'Flaharty', but corrected it to O'Flaherty in his typescript copy. The first mention of 'O'Flaharty' in the typescript also included an additional description of his weariness, describing the soldier as 'desperately tired', but Shaw also deleted this reference before publication (*OVC* Type, fo. 1).

baronet: a titled order, the lowest hereditary one, ranking just below a baron.

recruiting: the British government formed a parliamentary Recruiting Committee in August 1914, and during the committee's sixteen-month existence it organized 12,000 meetings and arranged 20,000 speeches. Shaw heard an enthusiastic recruitment speech by Horatio Bottomley (1860–1933), and commented, 'It's exactly what I expected: the man gets his popularity by telling people with sufficient bombast just what they think themselves and therefore want to hear'. Shaw's comment reported by Cyril Scott, *My Years of Indiscretion* (London: Mills & Boon, 1924), 231.

the quality: those of good social position.

150 *king . . . queen*: George V (1865–1936) and his consort Mary of Teck (1867–1953).

Bedad: by God.

bet: beaten.

Flanders: the Flemish-speaking northern half of Belgium, where the flat agricultural areas became wartime battlefields.

he is our king; and it's our own country, isnt it?: this assertion was a major point of contention during the First World War in Ireland, with many nationalists expressing their dissent. For example, in October 1914, at Liberty Hall in Dublin a banner was famously hung up that declared 'We Serve Neither King Nor Kaiser, But Ireland'. By Easter 1916, a group of rebels had launched an uprising and issued the Proclamation of the Irish Republic, which asserted the 'right of the people of Ireland to the ownership of Ireland and to the unfettered control of Irish destinies' and highlighted the 'long usurpation of that right by a foreign people and government' (reproduced in Charles Townshend, *1916: The Irish Rebellion* (London: Allen Lane, 2005), p. xx).

the divil a perch of it ever I owned: nothing at all, not even 1/160 of an acre, did I ever own.

Parnell: Charles Stewart Parnell (1846–91) led the struggle for Irish Home Rule in the late 1900s, and was known as the 'uncrowned king of Ireland'.

151 *kanatt*: sly, tricky rogue.

the cross of Monasterboice: the imposing St Mulredach's Cross (17 feet 8 inches tall), located at Monasterboice, a ruined monastic settlement in Co. Louth, Ireland.

Fenian: member of a revolutionary organization formed in 1858 by Irishmen determined to rid Ireland of government from Westminster.

St Patrick: the patron saint of Ireland, where the absence of snakes gave rise to the legendary story that this fifth-century figure had driven them out of the country.

French was on the sea . . . Shan Van Vocht: O'Flaherty's mother has been singing a well-known ballad from 1842 about the 1798 rebellion in Ireland, where the 'Shan Van Vocht' ('the poor old woman') of the song's title is the female personification of Ireland and 'the Orange' refers to the Protestant ascendancy in Ireland.

152 *funking*: backing out of, because of fear.

Kaiser: Wilhelm II of Germany, the king of England's first cousin.

the Prussian guard: an elite German army force, whose members earned a solid reputation as shock troops. Shaw's typescript specified that they were 'twelve six-foot four guardsmen' (*OVC* Type, fo. 6).

153 *have a mass said*: the common Roman Catholic practice of requesting a priest to offer Mass (a Eucharistic service) for the repose of the soul of someone who has died.

Bavarians: those from Bavaria, in south-east Germany, where the majority of the population was Catholic, just as on the island of Ireland. Shaw's typescript played down O'Flaherty's kill-rate here, and read, '"have a mass said for the souls of them twelve Germans you killed" says he, "for they were Bavarians and good Catholics"' (*OVC* Type, fo. 7).

Boshes: derogatory term for German soldiers.

we shall never beat the Boshes: in his typescript, Shaw included the less derisory 'Germans' here (*OVC* Type, fo. 8).

Horatio Bottomley: (1860–1933), a journalist and MP who edited *John Bull*, a popular weekly magazine. During the war, he addressed large audiences as part of the recruiting campaign, giving music-hall-style turns that encouraged men to volunteer for the fighting. However, he had long been associated with swindling, get-rich schemes, and dubious journalism. By 1922 he would be imprisoned for fraud.

Lord Lieutenant: the representative of the British Crown in Ireland until 1922.

154 *Boshes . . . Boshes*: again, in his typescript, Shaw included the less derisory 'Germans' at the two points in O'Flaherty's speech here (*OVC* Type, fo. 8).

Englishmen that was as poor as ourselves and maybe as good as ourselves: in Shaw's typescript this line was less ambiguous: 'men that was as poor as ourselves and as good as ourselves' (*OVC* Type, fo. 9).

little pension: a regular payment of sixpence three farthings a day.

155 *holy water*: water blessed by a Catholic priest and used to purify the faithful.

156 *Pathans*: the Pashto-speaking people living in India and Afghanistan.

weeshy: very small.

conversion: i.e. to Roman Catholicism.

on the bottle: nourishing her when young by means of a feeding bottle. That is, O'Flaherty's mother has breastfed the wealthy child at the expense of her own daughter Annie.

collar of gold that Malachi won from the proud invader: O'Flaherty is quoting from the verse 'Let Erin Remember the Days of Old' (1808) by Thomas Moore (1779–1852), in which the Irish poet describes how 'Malachi wore the collar of gold, | Which he won from her proud invader' (*The Poetical Works of Thomas Moore* (Philadelphia: J. Crissy, 1845), 321). The verse describes how the tenth-century Irish monarch Malachy Mor fought against the Danes and managed to take a collar of gold from one as a trophy of victory.

157 *Gladstone*: William Ewart Gladstone (1809–98), Liberal prime minister who, in the late nineteenth century, strove unsuccessfully to bring Home Rule to Ireland.

Asquith: Liberal prime minister who introduced the third Home Rule Bill to Parliament on 11 April 1912 (after Gladstone's two unsuccessful attempts in 1886 and 1893). Although Asquith's bill passed, it never took effect due to being postponed by the First World War.

Home Rule: self-government rather than Westminster rule in Ireland, through the establishment of an Irish national parliament.

Redmond: John Redmond (1856–1918), Irish nationalist politician and leader of the Irish Parliamentary Party from 1900 until 1918.

158 *lost tribes of the house of Israel*: ten of the twelve Hebrew tribes that, after the death of Moses, took possession of Canaan, but which disappeared after the Assyrian conquest of 721 BCE.

goddess Venus: Roman goddess of love.

Killiney Bay off Bray Head: particularly attractive part of the Co. Dublin coastline, to the south of the city. Shaw had a glimpse of it, and considered it his happiest time, when the family moved to a cottage here in his youth.

Moses built the seven churches: the picturesque valley of Glendalough, 22 miles from Dublin, contains seven churches, constructed between the tenth and the twelfth centuries. Moses is the Hebrew prophet who led his people out of Egyptian slavery in the Book of Exodus.

Lazarus was buried in Glasnevin: Glasnevin is a large cemetery in Dublin which opened in 1832. Lazarus is the biblical character who (in John 11) has been dead for four days before being brought back to life by Christ.

158 *Cork*: town in the south of Ireland, a distance of 289 miles, as the crow flies, from Shakespeare's English birthplace of Stratford-upon-Avon.

Whisht: hush.

hold your whisht: be quiet.

159 *Dinny darlint*: Dennis darling.

the old red coat: the last time that British soldiers fought in scarlet tunics was at Ginnis in the Sudan during December 1885, although the 'redcoats' were long remembered in melodramatic plays on the Irish stage. Khaki became the colour of service dress in the British army from 1902.

bosthoon: awkward, senseless person.

160 *spalpeen*: rascal.

Boshes: in his typescript, Shaw included the less derisory 'Germans' here (*OVC* Type, fo. 21).

161 *the heathen Mahomet that put a corn in his ear . . . the pigeon come to pick it out and eat it*: O'Flaherty recycles a disparaging and once-common story that the prophet Muhammad had trained a bird in this way to trick disciples.

a Pharisee: a legalistic and self-righteous person, sharing those traits associated with the Pharisees of the New Testament.

162 *old age pension . . . only sixty-two*: British state pensions had been introduced in 1908, when the age for qualifying for a pension had been fixed at 70. The payment of a pension was subject to strict tests of means and character.

acushla: darling.

Tessie: Shaw originally intended O'Flaherty to use the more formal name 'Teresa' here (*OVC* Type, fo. 23).

German gold . . . German silver: German gold is imitation gold leaf; German silver is a silver-white alloy of copper, zinc, and nickel, usually used for utensils.

Bosh: this line and the surrounding discussion of German gold and silver was included as Shaw made handwritten changes to his typescript, when he added in other insulting references to the Germans in order to echo the real-life way that British troops described their enemy (*OVC* Type, fo. 24).

163 *alanna*: my child.

plakeen: small panel or piece.

her waist where it used to be . . . other ladies had it: the queen's critics thought that she was a dreary figure, and her clothes were somewhat anachronistic. The queen was certainly not part of the fashionable set, and so her clothing here is described as being cut in a less stylish way than that of those around her. The queen's gowns tended to look back to the Edwardian period and to the pomp of Empire.

the popshop in Drumpogue: the pawnshop in Drumpogue, a fictional locale. In Irish, 'Drum' = the ridge, 'Pogue' = kiss.

she didnt know what to say to me: Shaw's friend Beatrice Webb (1858–1943) would later describe meeting the queen, saying, 'she was painfully at a loss of what to say to me. To avoid silence I told her about our visit to Ireland' (Webb, *The Diary of Beatrice Webb*, iv, ed. Norman and Jeanne MacKenzie (Cambridge, MA: Harvard University Press, 1985), 228).

Sixpence three farthings a day: in his typescript Shaw left the monetary figure blank, as he needed to do some research to check what the pension actually was (*OVC* Type, fo. 25).

164 *the divil a penny*: not a penny.

gets her into trouble: there is a double meaning here, being 'in trouble' signifies being caught in some mischief, but the term was also used to describe the condition of a pregnant woman who was not yet married.

bad scran: colloquialism, literally meaning 'bad scraps of food'.

165 *Tessie*: Shaw originally intended O'Flaherty to use the more formal name 'Teresa' here (*OVC* Type, fo. 23).

Ochone: Alas!

heart scalded: bitterly upset.

bad cess: bad luck.

166 *Sir Horace Plunkett*: Horace Plunkett (1854–1932), a politician and agricultural reformer who believed that the small farmer in Ireland needed to have greater autonomy, and drew inspiration from the agricultural modernization of Denmark and the co-operative movement in Britain. Shaw first met Plunkett in 1908, and became a good friend.

separation allowance: a portion of a soldier's pay, usually matched by the government, that was sent home to make sure that his dependants avoided impoverishment.

167 *sheeps' eyes*: amorous glances.

a flea in your ear: a harsh rebuke.

sloothering: wheedling/cajoling.

AUGUSTUS DOES HIS BIT

The play was first performed at the Court Theatre on 21 January 1917. The play-text was first published, together with the preface, in *Heartbreak House, Great Catherine, and Playlets of the War* (London: Constable, 1919), and republished under the same title (again with the preface) by Constable for the standard edition in 1931.

173 *Commander-in-Chief*: Field-Marshal Sir Douglas Haig (1861–1928), commander-in-chief of the British armed forces on the Western Front from December 1915 until the end of the First World War. He invited

Shaw to visit the front in January 1917, with Shaw accepting the offer and arriving in early February. Shaw subsequently judged Haig to be 'a first rate specimen of the British gentleman and conscientiously studious soldier' who was 'steadied by a well-closed mind' (Shaw, *What I Really Wrote about the War* (London: Constable, 1931), 244). As a result of his visit, Shaw produced the piece 'Joy Riding at the Front' (*What I Really Wrote about the War*, 240–70).

173 *the Stage Society*: a London play-producing organization, founded to showcase drama of artistic merit that might not be produced on the commercial stage, and which commenced operations with a production of Shaw's *You Never Can Tell* in 1899. Actors performed for little or no money; plays were characteristically staged for one or two nights in between runs of other performances at commercial playhouses; and some of the productions—such as Shaw's *Mrs Warren's Profession* (1902)—had been refused a licence by the censor. The society performed *Augustus Does His Bit* on 21 January 1917, at the Court Theatre in London.

persona grata: (Lat.) a person, especially a diplomat, acceptable to certain others.

Eddystone: the lighthouse, erected in 1882, which marks the dangerous Eddystone Rocks, south-west of Plymouth.

174 *The Morning Post*: a daily London newspaper founded in 1772 and absorbed into the *Daily Telegraph* in 1937. The *Post* was conservative and tended to adopt an attitude of deference towards the powerful and wealthy.

the G.R.'s: the elderly home-defence corps of volunteers named Georgius Rex after the king (George V). Their age profile meant that, at times, they gained derisory nicknames including 'Gorgeous Wrecks'.

175 *Defence of the Realm Act*: an Act passed in August 1914, four days after Britain entered the First World War, handing extensive powers to the government, with the Act's scope extending into many areas of civilian life by 1917–18.

176 *Huns*: derogatory term for Germans. The Huns were originally a nomadic people, whose warriors terrified Europe and the Roman Empire during the fourth and fifth centuries. The name was applied to Germany after Kaiser Wilhelm II (1859–1941) gave his 'Hun address' in 1900, urging German soldiers departing to suppress the Boxer Rising in China to be ruthless like the Huns. The name stuck after Rudyard Kipling (1865–1936) published the 1914 poem 'For All We Have and Are', warning that 'The Hun is at the gate!' (*The Times*, 2 September 1914, p. 9).

war saving: emphasizing the importance of individual thrift in order to help the war effort. A parliamentary War Saving Committee was highlighting the need for British people to economize in May 1916, shortly before Shaw wrote the play.

178 *pennorth*: as much as could be bought for a penny.

quart: a quarter of a gallon (two pints).

179 *Board of Trade*: an arm of government with some responsibilities for trading and employment. Part of this board, in 1916, formed the Ministry of Labour.

Minister of Munitions: a new government post created in 1915 to coordinate the manufacture and supply of weaponry and ammunition for the war effort.

Yours not to reason why: yours is but to do and die: cf. 'The Charge of the Light Brigade' (1854) by Alfred Tennyson (1809–92): 'Their's not to reason why, | Their's but to do and die' (Alfred Lord Tennyson, *Selected Poems*, ed. Christopher Ricks (London: Penguin, 2007), 215).

180 *the Tower*: the Tower of London, on the north bank of the Thames, well known as a traditional place of imprisonment.

181 *marchioness*: a woman with the rank of marquess (a hereditary nobleman ranked below a duke and above an earl).

mirror . . . comb . . . moustache pomade . . . his toilet: the equipment needed when dressing, arranging the hair, and preparing to face the world. A moustache pomade was a scented oil or ointment for dressing male facial hair.

182 *Royal Commissions*: commissions of inquiry/committees appointed by the monarch on government recommendation.

Radical papers: press which emerged to countrywide prominence in the first half of the nineteenth century, appealing to a predominantly working-class audience, and unifying different groups of workers by showing their shared concerns. In May 1913 Shaw helped to establish the left-wing weekly review, the *New Statesman*.

beau sabreur: (Fr.) 'handsome swordsman', at one time the nickname of Joachim Murat (1767–1815), Napoleon's cavalry commander and later king of Naples.

quarry in Hulluch: in April 1916, four months before Shaw wrote this play, the Battle of Hulluch in northern France saw the British soldiers of the 16th (Irish) Division suffering because of the chlorine and phosgene gas deployed by the German army.

183 *Nelson in the Baltic*: Sir Horatio Nelson (1758–1805), who was second-in-command under Vice-Admiral Sir Hyde Parker (1739–1807), led a British victory over the Danes at the Battle of Copenhagen in April 1801. Nelson famously helped win the battle by ignoring the signals being sent by his superior, putting his telescope to his blind eye and commenting, 'I really do not see the signal' (quoted by Terry Coleman, *The Nelson Touch* (Oxford: Oxford University Press, 2002), 259).

Ruhleben: a First World War internment camp near Berlin.

Pomeranian: region on the south coast of the Baltic Sea.

184 *Foreign Office*: the governmental department handling relations with other countries. Shaw had originally wanted this piece of dialogue by the lady to begin with the affirmation, 'It is indeed most urgent, I must explain', but he cut this from the proofs before publication (*Aug* Play, fo. 16).

184 *Ritz Hotel*: luxury hotel in Piccadilly, London, opened in 1906 by the Swiss-born César Ritz (1850–1918).

War Office: department of the British government which existed until 1964 and was led by the secretary of state for war. The office took responsibility for the administration of the British army.

185 *Knightsbridge barracks*: barracks based on the southern edge of Hyde Park, just three-quarters of a mile from Buckingham Palace. Members of the Household Calvary based at the barracks perform ceremonial duties at the palace.

188 *humorously makes a paralytic attempt to stand at attention*: Shaw changed this line on the proof copy before the piece was printed, originally intending the clerk to have a quite different reaction: '*is compelled to retreat towards the door*' (*Aug* Play, fo. 21).

191 *Colonel Bogey*: a golfing term taken from the mythical 'Colonel Bogey'. The term was used in the 1800s, and later became the name of a popular march, composed in 1914 by Frederick Joseph Ricketts (1891–1945).

ANNAJANSKA, THE BOLSHEVIK EMPRESS

In his original proofs, Shaw had suggested instead the title 'Annajanska, the Wild Grand Duchess: From the Russian of Gregory Biessipoff'. He may here have decided to present the work as a translation from a Russian original in order to overcome his wartime unpopularity, although the fictional Russian name chosen (with its prominent 'GBS') gave an indication of the true author's identity (*Anna* Proof, title page).

The play was first performed at the London Coliseum on 21 January 1918. The play-text was first published, along with the preface, in *Heartbreak House, Great Catherine, and Playlets of the War* (London: Constable, 1919), and republished under the same title (again with preface) by Constable for the standard edition in 1931.

197 *bravura*: piece requiring great skill in performance, written to test the ability of the actors.

Lillah McCarthy . . . Man and Superman . . . Androcles: Lillah McCarthy (1875–1960), actress and theatre manager, took the role of Ann Whitefield in the first production of Shaw's *Man and Superman*, in 1905 at the Court Theatre, and would go on to play many other theatrical roles created by Shaw. McCarthy also took the role of Lavinia in the first production of his *Androcles and the Lion* (given at the St James's Theatre in 1913).

Charles Ricketts: (1866–1931), artist and art collector, probably best-known in his lifetime for his theatre designs, which included the first production of Shaw's *Saint Joan* in 1924.

Mrs Siddons, Sir Joshua Reynolds, and Dr Johnson: Sarah Siddons (1755–1831), actress, was an acquaintance of Samuel Johnson (1709–84), author and lexicographer, who suggested to her that she play Queen Katherine in the 1613 play by Shakespeare and John Fletcher (1579–1625), *Henry*

VIII, which proved one of her great theatrical successes. One of the best-known images of Siddons is the painting of her as *The Tragic Muse* (1784) by Joshua Reynolds (1723–92), painter and art theorist. He met Samuel Johnson in about 1756, and Johnson later described him as 'almost the only man whom I call a friend' (quoted in James Boswell, *The Life of Samuel Johnson* (London: Charles Tilt, 1840), 148). Reynolds also painted one of the most recognizable images of Johnson in 1756/7.

Coliseum variety theatre: a large entertainment venue in London, seating 2,359 spectators. Designed by Frank Matcham (1854–1920), it opened in 1904.

Tchaikovsky's 1812: the overture written by Peter Ilich Tchaikovsky (1840–93) in 1880 to commemorate Russia's victory over Napoleonic France in 1812.

198 *Beotia*: a fictional post-revolutionary republic, which echoes the name of the ancient Greek district of Boeotia (location of significant theatrical stories including that of Oedipus). The fictional 'Beotia' is also evidently designed to sound like 'Russia', which in real life had experienced a revolution beginning in March 1917 (NS), shortly before Shaw wrote his play that December. Beotia is later mentioned in Shaw's 1932 play, *Too True to be Good*, where one character declares that everyone is asking for a visa for Beotia, also known as 'The Union of Federated Sensible Societies, sir. The U.F.S.S. Everybody wants to go there now' (London: Constable, 1934), 103.

provisional government: in real-life Russia, a provisional government had been established following the toppling of Tsar Nicholas II (1868–1918) in March 1917 (NS). However, that provisional government only survived until November, when it was in turn overthrown by the Bolsheviks.

the prime minister has shot himself: in real life, the first leader of the Russian Provisional Government in 1917 was Prince Lvov (1861–1925), a social reformer who came to power in March but resigned in July after he found himself unable to satisfy the demands of an increasingly radical population. He was followed by the moderate socialist leader Aleksandr Kerensky (1881–1970), who lasted from August to November. Neither man shot himself, but both fled the country following the Bolshevik takeover.

extreme left fellow: a fictional version of Lenin (1870–1924), leader of the Bolshevik Revolution.

Maximilianists: fictional version of the Bolsheviks, whose name literally means 'one of the majority'. In real life, under the leadership of Lenin, they seized control of the Russian government in November 1917.

Oppidoshavians: the invented name combines 'Opposition' and 'Shavian'. In real-life Russia, the Mensheviks, the group that had split in opposition from the Bolsheviks between 1903 and 1912, were closer to Shaw's Fabians than the Bolsheviks; the Mensheviks favoured a more gradual development towards socialism rather than immediate violent change.

198 *Moderate Red Revolutionaries*: another fictional faction, whose name chimes with that of the real-life Socialist Revolutionary Party. The Socialist Revolutionary Party had been the largest socialist group in Russia during 1917, but divided over the Revolution in November.

carbon sheets: thin sheets of paper coated with carbon on one side, used to make copies of a document as it is being typed.

199 *the revolution*: a fictional version of the Russian Revolution of 1917; in the first part (in March) the imperial government of the Tsar was overthrown, in the second part (in November), the Bolsheviks toppled the Provisional Government of Aleksandr Kerensky.

the Panjandrums of Beotia: a fictional version of the Romanov dynasty, which ruled Russia from 1613 until 1917. Panjandrum is usually a mock title for a mysterious figure of significant authority.

My Panjandrum is deposed: based on the events of March 1917, when, following riots in St Petersburg (then Petrograd), Tsar Nicholas was urged to abdicate by the army and the legislature. He accordingly gave up the Crown and was placed under house arrest in Petrograd, before being sent to Siberia in August. After the Bolshevik takeover he was moved south to Ekaterinburg, where he and his family were murdered in 1918.

Jew: it is likely that Shaw is thinking here of the real-life Aleksandr Kerensky, whose background as a lawyer was well known, and who was, for example, described in the *People* as 'that semi-Jew' ('Why Kerensky Fell', *People*, 23 December 1917, p. 6). Strammfest's description of being appointed commander-in-chief sounds like Shaw may have been reimagining Kerensky's appointment of Lavr Kornilov (1870–1918) as commander-in-chief on 1 August 1917. The *New Statesman* had been rooting for Kerensky just before Shaw wrote his play, writing (17 November 1917) that 'Kerensky may yet disappear in the maelstrom, but his name will not die. He will be remembered for his passionate self-immolation, for the suffering through which he did his work, and for his deep human feeling' (Sir Lewis Namier, 'Russian and the Bolsheviks', reproduced in Stephen Howe (ed.), *Lines of Dissent: Writing from the New Statesman 1913–1988* (London: Verso, 1988), 37–42, at 42).

gutter press: newspapers whose journalists pay most attention to sensational stories of sex and crime.

200 *the vote*: in July 1917, the Russian Provisional Government gave women aged over 20 the right to vote, and they were able to use this right during the elections to the Constituency Assembly in November that year. Russia therefore became the first major European power to grant the vote to women.

I would have given it to her with both hands: presumably meaning that he would have beaten her with his two fists.

201 *G.H.Q.*: General Headquarters.

Panderobajensky Hussars: a fictional light cavalry regiment, with a name echoing that of the real-life Preobrazhensky Regiment, one of the most famous and most elite units of the Imperial Russian Army. The fictional regiment in the play has a named affiliation to the Panjandrum (Russian cavalry regiments tended to have the name of a significant Russian general or the name of a Russian or European royal family that provided the unit's honorary colonel). In real life, during 1907–8, Tsar Nicholas II restored the Hussar regiments that Alexander III (1845–94) had dissolved, and provided them with elaborate and distinctive uniforms. The Hussar units generally disintegrated during the First World War, although some of the officers subsequently joined the Red Army.

203 *give the man a cross*: an award, presumably based on the real-life Cross of St George, a Russian military decoration given for extreme bravery.

comrade: title adopted by Socialists and Communists as a prefix to a surname. The title was intended to do away with sexual and social distinctions.

204 *Peter Piper*: character in an English alliterative nursery rhyme ('Peter Piper picked a peck of pickled pepper . . .').

Clergyman's sore throat: an inflamed pharynx, as afflicting clergymen and others who overstrain their voices.

205 *Proletarians of all lands, unite*: cf. *The Communist Manifesto* (1848) by Karl Marx (1818–83) and Friedrich Engels: 'Working men of all countries, unite!' (ed. Jeffrey C. Isaac (New Haven: Yale University Press, 2012), 103).

the Marseillaise: French national anthem, composed in 1792 by Claude-Joseph Rouget de Lisle (1760–1836); a revolutionary song urging 'Aux armes, citoyens' ('To arms, citizens').

Hakonsburg . . . Potterdam . . . Premsylople: all fictional locations.

206 *knouted*: flogged with a whip or scourge.

dowager: woman who has been widowed, and enjoys the title and status that derives from her late husband.

207 *single tax*: a tax, originally upon land values, which was proposed as a way of simplifying the tax system by replacing all other taxes. The proposal originated in the publication by Henry George (1839–97), *Progress and Poverty* (1879).

no annexations and no indemnities: Strammfest here reflects the confusion about Russian official attitudes towards the war during 1917. The Bolsheviks eventually won power with the popular slogan 'Peace, Land, Bread' and would sign a peace treaty with Germany in March 1918. Before that, the Provisional Government had tried to continue the war and to launch a new offensive on the Eastern Front in June 1917. Meanwhile, the Socialist leaders of the Soviet of Workers' and Soldiers' Deputies (elected by popular mandate and so providing a powerful rival to the unelected leaders of the Provisional Government) approved only a defensive war, but actually wanted the unrealistic prospect of simply halting the conflict, through a general peace without annexations or indemnities.

208 *destruction*: when Shaw prepared the play for performance in 1918 there
were some additional lines included here that he erased by the time it was
being printed in 1919, but which make more explicit the nursery-rhyme
reference. The lines are:

> [*With an impatient jerk of her ankle, she kicks the dynasty out; then
> suddenly brightens up; dances to Strammfest; and bends caressingly
> over him*]. Peterkin: you know what Grandmama taught you:
>
> Humpty Dumpty sat on a wall
>
> Humpty Dumpty had a great fall.
>
> Well, we are Humpty Dumpty. I think we always were Humpty Dumpty.
>
> (*Anna* Proof, p. 16)

All the king's horses and all the king's men: cf. the English nursery rhyme
'Humpty Dumpty'.

God knows I would!: In the first performed version of the play, given by
Lillah McCarthy in 1918, the ensuing section—right up until the Grand
Duchess's line 'I will tell you. The war can save it'—was not delivered.
Instead the Grand Duchess was simply to say 'You see: it is impossible.
Well, I have not come here to save our wretched family and our bloodstained crown. [*Resolutely*] I am come to save the revolution', and
Strammfest was to reply, 'Stupid as I am, I have come to think that I had
better save that than save nothing. But what can save the revolution against
such revolutionists?' This made the first performance considerably shorter
than the current text, with Shaw adding the additional lines printed here
before publication in 1919 (*Anna* Proof, pp. 16–17).

new order: honour for merit.

209 *golden calf to worship*: cf. Exodus 32:4–6. The Israelites made and worshipped the icon of the golden calf while Moses was fetching the Ten
Commandments from Mount Sinai.

changeling: a child secretly swapped for another during infancy.

210 *Karl Marx*: Shaw himself had spent time reading Marx's writings. William
Archer (1856–1924) famously recalled visiting the British Museum in the
1880s and seeing the young and unknown Irishman studying *Das Kapital*
in French (W.A., *The World*, 14 December 1892, p. 14).

211 *Bolshevism*: the Communistic form of government seen in Russia following the Bolshevik Revolution in November 1917.

THE SHEWING-UP OF BLANCO POSNET

The preface (including the postscript) was first published in *The Doctor's
Dilemma, Getting Married, The Shewing-up of Blanco Posnet* (London:
Constable, 1911), and republished under the same title by Constable for the
standard edition in 1932. Part of the preface, labelled here 'The Rejected

Statement', was privately printed in 1909 as *Statement of the Evidence in Chief of George Bernard Shaw before the Joint-Committee on Stage Plays (Censorship and Theatre Licensing)* (Edinburgh: R & R Clark, 1909).

The play was first performed in public by the Abbey Theatre company, which gave a run of the play in Dublin from 25 August 1909 (the company may have tried out the piece in Liverpool on 10 April 1909). The play-text was privately printed for copyright in London and New York in 1909, first published in English in 1911 as *The Doctor's Dilemma, Getting Married, & The Shewing-up of Blanco Posnet* (London: Constable, 1911), and republished under the same title by Constable for the standard edition in 1932. A German translation by Siegfried Trebitsch appeared as 'Blanco Posnets Erweckung' during the autumn of 1909 in *Der Merker* (Vienna) in three parts: 25 October, pp. 79–81; 10 November, pp. 112–16; 25 November, pp. 159–65.

Shaw explained the title to Leo Tolstoy (1828–1910), the Russian writer of fiction, plays, and essays, as follows: ' "Shewing up" is American slang for unmasking a hypocrite' (*CL* ii. 900, letter of 14 February 1910).

217 *Select Committee of both Houses of Parliament*: during the early twentieth century, writers including Shaw protested against theatrical censorship. In 1909, the Westminster Parliament responded by setting up a joint select committee, consisting of members of the House of Lords and the House of Commons, under the chairmanship of Herbert Samuel (see note to p. 223). Shaw and others gave evidence to the committee, which ended up concluding, in a 500,000-word report, that the Lord Chamberlain's role should be retained, but that submitting plays to him for licensing should be optional. It would be legal to stage an unlicensed play, but managers would risk being prosecuted by the Director of Public Prosecutions (see note to p. 265) or by the Attorney General. Shaw felt this basically left the situation unchanged.

Bluebook: an official British government publication.

Barrie . . . Carr: James Matthew Barrie (1860–1937), novelist and playwright, was the creator of Peter Pan. Johnston Forbes Robertson (1853–1937) was described by Shaw as being capable of performing with 'continuous charm, interest, and variety which are the result not only of his well-known grace and accomplishment as an actor, but of a genuine delight—the rarest thing on our stage—in Shakespear's art' (review of 2 October 1897, reproduced in *Our Theatres in the Nineties*, iii. 206). Shaw read *The Devil's Disciple* to Forbes Robertson in 1897 and later wrote the part of Caesar in *Caesar and Cleopatra* for the actor to play. Cecil Raleigh (1856–1914) was an actor and dramatist; John Galsworthy (1867–1933), a novelist and dramatist; Laurence Housman (1865–1959), a writer and artist. Herbert Beerbohm Tree (1852–1917), an actor and theatre manager; William Leonard Courtney (1850–1928), a journalist and philosopher; William Schwenck Gilbert (1836–1911), dramatist best known for his collaborations with the composer Arthur Sullivan. Arthur Bingham Walkley (1855–1926) was a theatre critic; Lena Ashwell (original name Lena Margaret Pocock, married name Lena Margaret Simpson) (1872–1957), an actress and theatre manager. Gilbert Murray (1866–1957) was a classical scholar and acclaimed translator who gave an influential re-evaluation of Euripidean drama; George Alexander (1858–1918), an actor and theatre manager; George Edwardes (1855–1915), a musical theatre producer. Joseph William Comyns Carr (1849–1916), was an author, gallery owner, and theatre manager.

217 *Speaker of the House of Commons*: James William Lowther, 1st Viscount Ullswater (1855–1949).

Bishop of Southwark: Edward Stuart Talbot (1844–1934).

Caine . . . Chesterton: Thomas Henry Hall Caine (1853–1931), novelist and dramatist, wrote the bestselling novel *The Eternal City*; Israel Zangwill (1864–1926) was a writer whose best-known work includes the novel *Children of the Ghetto* and the play *The Melting Pot*; Squire Bancroft (1841–1926) was an actor-manager; G(ilbert). K. Chesterton (1874–1934) was a novelist and essayist, known for books such as *The Man Who Was Thursday*.

218 *His Majesty's Stationery Office*: HMSO, the official publisher for both UK Houses of Parliament.

Charles Dickens in Little Dorrit: novel published by Dickens in serial form between 1855 and 1857, attacking the English legal system.

the best of all possible worlds: the words of Gottfried Leibniz (1646–1716) in his *Essays on the Goodness of God, the Freedom of Man and the Origin of Evil* (1710).

French Revolution: the effort in France, between 1789 and 1799, to end the *ancien régime* and establish a new order, as a consequence of which it became involved in a series of wars with other countries in Europe.

219 *Lord Chamberlain*: see note to p. 41.

Privy Council: formal group of advisers to the monarch.

in camera: (Lat.) 'in chamber', i.e. in private.

Office of Examiner of Plays: the Lord Chamberlain was formally the censor of the stage, but from the 1720s onwards, the task was actually performed by his Examiner of Plays, and in later years the examiner was aided by several other official readers. By Shaw's time, the Lord Chamberlain's role was mainly to sign off the report that had been issued by the readers and examiners.

220 *the king*: Edward VII. When a command performance of Shaw's play *John Bull's Other Island* was arranged for the king in 1905, Shaw had joked, 'Short of organizing a revolution I have no remedy' (*CL* ii. 522, letter of 14 March 1905).

Mrs Warren's Profession: play written by Shaw in 1893, and banned by the Lord Chamberlain because of its discussion of prostitution (the 'profession' of the title).

Nonconformist conscience: Dissenting Protestant preachers had long been warning about the dangers of the theatre, that, for instance, 'the Theatre must remain a power for mischief, and, therefore, must have the unqualified condemnation of the holy and good' (Revd A. Hervey, *Nottingham Theatre: The Warning!*, quoted by Jo Robinson, 'The Performance of Anti-Theatrical Prejudice', *Nineteenth Century Theatre and Film*, 35/2 (2008), 10–28, at 14).

Liberal Government: the government being led by Herbert Asquith since April 1908.

the City: also known as 'the Square Mile', run by the City of London Corporation, Britain's oldest local government, and including most of the financial sector of London.

221 *west end of London*: the major theatre and entertainment centre of the English capital since the nineteenth century.

222 *two guineas*: a guinea signifies the amount of 21 shillings. It was the reading fee required to be paid for all plays submitted to the Lord Chamberlain before they could be approved for the public stage.

is so much Greek: is unintelligible.

223 *Vigilance Societies and Municipalities*: Vigilance Societies were groups that developed in the nineteenth century and aimed to pursue 'social purity' by campaigning against the promotion of 'vices' such as prostitution, masturbation, and homosexuality. For example, the American reformer Anthony Comstock (1844–1915) led a long campaign against obscenity in literature, founded the New York Society for the Suppression of Vice, and locked horns with Shaw, who criticized 'Comstockery' (*CL* ii. 559, letter of *c*.22–3 September 1905). Municipalities are towns with self-government.

plays by Ibsen ... Brieux ... Barker ... me: Ibsen's play *Ghosts* (premiered 1882) gives indications of incest and depicts the effects of syphilis being passed on to a son from his adulterous father. *Ghosts* was banned from the public stage in Britain between 1891 and 1914. Brieux's play *Damaged Goods* (first rehearsed 1901), which warned against the dangers of promiscuity and showed the dangers of passing on syphilis, was banned in 1902 until belatedly thought to teach an admirable lesson during the First World War and finally brought to the public London stage in 1917. Shaw appears to have seen a private production, given by the 'Authors' Producing Society' on 1 March 1914 at the Little Theatre in John Street (programme in HRC, Shaw Collection, Vertical Files, box 706, folder G237). Barker's play *Waste* tells of a politician having an affair with a woman and thereby causing her to undergo a lethal illegal abortion. The script was refused a licence in 1907, and only approved in 1920. Shaw's play *Mrs Warren's Profession* deals with the subject of prostitution. It was first submitted to the Lord Chamberlain, and rejected, in 1898. The play was regularly resubmitted, but not licensed until 1924.

Unionist: the 1895 UK general election saw a coalition of Liberal and Conservative Unionists gain power (i.e. those opposed to Gladstonian

Home Rule for Ireland). The opposing Liberals regained power in 1905 as a minority administration and then won the general election of 1906, remaining in power until 1915.

223 *Robert Vernon Harcourt . . . Gladstone era*: Robert Vernon Harcourt (1878–1962) sat in parliament as Liberal MP between 1908 and 1918. He was the son of Sir William Harcourt (1827–1904), the leader of the Liberal Party in 1896–8.

a couple of plays: Harcourt's comic play *An Angel Unawares* appeared onstage in 1905, and another comedy, *A Question of Age*, was produced (for two underwhelming performances only) at the Royal Court in 1906. The *Sketch* described how 'It is "G.B.S" who has incited and spurred him to write plays, and from the older dramatist the younger has received valuable hints and much good advice' ('Heard in the Green Room', *The Sketch*, 26 July 1905, p. 27).

Chancellor of the Duchy of Lancaster: a ministerial role in the British government, effectively minister without portfolio. Officially, the figure administers the estates and rents of the Duchy (ducal territory) of Lancaster.

Herbert Samuel (now Postmaster-General): Samuel (1870–1963), Liberal politician who from 1909 held the position of Chancellor of Duchy of Lancaster, and in 1910–14 was Postmaster General, in charge of the postal service.

Alfred Mason: (1865–1948) a novelist who between 1906 and 1910 acted as Liberal MP for Coventry.

Arms and the Man: Mason appeared in the first production of Shaw's play *Arms and the Man* in 1894, but failed to find other acting work in the West End.

Hugh Law . . . son of an Irish Chancellor: Hugh Law (1872–1943) sat in the House of Commons as Irish Parliamentary Party MP for West Donegal between 1902 and 1918. His father, Hugh Law (senior) (1818–83), was Lord Chancellor for Ireland between 1881 and 1883.

224 *Colonel Lockwood*: Amelius Mark Richard Lockwood (1847–1928), Conservative MP between 1892 and 1917. His education at Eton was scarcely that of the 'average' man, but he did enjoy popularity across party lines in the House of Commons, where he was referred to as 'Uncle Mark'.

made a Bunthorne blench: Reginald Bunthorne, the poet in the comic opera *Patience* (1881) by Gilbert and Sullivan, who walked 'down Piccadilly with a poppy or a lily in your mediaeval hand' (W. S. Gilbert, *Patience; or, Bunthorpe's Bride* (New York: Doubleday, 1902), 26). Bunthorne calls to mind the taboo-busting Pre-Raphaelite poet and painter Algernon Swinburne (1837–1909). To blench is to shy away.

Lord Gorell: John Gorell Barnes (1848–1913), judge.

Lord Plymouth: Robert George Windsor-Clive (1857–1923), Conservative politician and philanthropist.

Shakespear Memorial project: a fund to create a memorial to Shakespeare began in 1903 when a wealthy retired wine merchant Richard Badger (1819–1907), who had grown up in Stratford, wrote to *The Times* promising to contribute £1,000 towards raising commemorative statues in Stratford and in London (Badger, 'National Statues to Shakespeare', *The Times*, 28 May 1903, p. 10). By 1905 this pledge had spawned a Shakespeare Memorial Committee, of which Lord Plymouth (1857–1923) became chairman. In 1908 the group endorsed 'an architectural Monument including a statue' in London's Portland Place ('The Shakespeare Memorial', *The Times*, 24 April 1908, p. 10).

Shakespear Memorial National Theatre: after Lord Plymouth's committee announced their 1908 plan to raise a statue of Shakespeare in London, the issue gained wider public attention. In *The Times* Sir John Hare (1844–1921; real name John Joseph Fairs), the stage actor and theatre manager, wrote that Shakespeare 'raised the most indestructible monument to his genius by the works he has left us, and it requires no blocks of stone or marble to keep his memory green' ('The Shakespeare Memorial', *The Times*, 10 March 1908, p. 8). Shortly afterwards, a group supporting Hare's viewpoint held a meeting at the Lyceum Theatre, with Shaw prominently positioned on the platform, calling for 'the establishment of a national theatre as a memorial to Shakespeare' ('Shakespeare Memorial', *The Times*, 10 April 1908, p. 8). Lord Plymouth had written a tactful note to this assembly, pointing out that his committee too wanted to see 'the furtherance of serious drama'. Representatives of his original Shakespeare Memorial Committee and the rival National Theatre group met on 23 July 1908, and agreed to join together as the 'Shakespeare Memorial National Theatre General Committee', forming a joint twenty-three-member executive that included Shaw ('The Shakespeare Memorial', *The Times*, 23 June 1908, p. 12).

Lords Lytton and Esher: Victor Alexander George Robert Bulwer-Lytton (1876–1947) acted as president of the meeting at the Lyceum Theatre in May 1908 (see previous note). Reginald Baliol Brett (1852–1930), 2nd Viscount Esher, was part of the Shakespeare Memorial Committee (see previous note) and was then one of those who suggested a meeting with the representatives of the rival National Theatre group.

Lord Willoughby de Broke . . . amateur actor: Richard Greville Verney (1869–1923), Conservative politician, had formed an acting company in 1896 with his wife, the 'Kineton Amateurs', whose members performed in Warwickshire and Oxfordshire. They tended to perform at theatres and halls in aid of charitable causes, and favoured comedies including *Home* by T. W. Robertson (1829–71), *White Bait at Greenwich* by John Maddison Moreton (1811–91), and *Lady Huntworth's Experiment* by R. C. Carton (1853–1928). Lord Willoughby de Broke took on both directing and acting duties for the group.

Lord Newton: Thomas Wodehouse Legh (1857–1942), Conservative politician.

224 *Lord Ribblesdale, the argute*: Thomas Lister (1854–1925), Liberal politician. Argute means subtle and shrewd.

225 *Hamlet*: the theme of incest is a notable feature of Shakespeare's play, in
which Gertrude marries her brother-in-law Claudius (the 'incestuous,
murd'rous, damnèd Dane', V. ii. 283).

Oedipus . . . The Cenci . . . Maternité . . . Les Avariés . . . Monna Vanna: in
Oedipus Tyrannos, the play by Sophocles first performed c.430–426 BCE,
the main character discovers that he has unwittingly killed his own father,
married his own mother, and that therefore he has produced daughters
who are also his own half-sisters. *The Cenci*, a five-act tragedy published in
1819 by Percy Bysshe Shelley (1792–1822), revolves around the villainous
Count Francesco Cenci, who rapes his own daughter. She, in turn, then
helps organize the Count's murder. *Brieux's Maternité* (1903) is a play
dealing with the issues of abortion and birth control. Charlotte Shaw
(1857–1943) was responsible for introducing her husband to this work,
having read it in 1906 and feeling 'an event had occurred and a new possession come into my life' (Mrs Bernard Shaw, 'Foreword', in Brieux,
Damaged Goods, trans. John Pollock (London: A. C. Fifield, 1914), p. v).
She subsequently made her own translation of the play. The Shaws are
also likely to have seen the play being performed by the Incorporated
Stage Society in April 1906 (programme in HRC, Shaw Collection,
Vertical Files, box 706, folder G237). *Les Avariés* ('Damaged Goods') is
a 1901 play by Brieux that describes a protagonist who has contracted
syphilis. *Monna Vanna* is a 1902 play by Belgian dramatist Maurice
Maeterlinck (1862–1949), banned because it features, at one point, the
title character being commanded to go to the tent of a general wearing
nothing except her cloak. *The Athenaeum* noted that the decision to censor
this work 'makes us the laughing stock of Europe' ('Dramatic Gossip',
The Athenaeum, 21 June 1902, p. 796).

226 *Committee of 1892*: an earlier parliamentary select committee had also
been appointed to look at the licensing and regulation of theatres and
places of entertainment. This committee reported on 2 June 1892, and
Shaw took great interest in its proceedings, during which Shaw's friend
William Archer (along with a relatively small number of other dramatists)
argued against censorship. Nonetheless, the 1892 committee endorsed the
status quo, and approved the work of an earlier select committee in 1866,
which had concluded 'That the censorship of plays has worked satisfactorily, and that it is not desirable that it should be discontinued' (*Report
from the Select Committee on Theatrical Licenses and Regulations* (Shannon:
Irish University Press, 1970 [facsimile of 1866 edn]), p. x).

Sir Henry Irving: real name John Henry Brodribb (1838–1905), actor-
manager described by Shaw as 'for thirty years the foremost actor in
London' (Shaw, *The Drama Observed*, ed. Bernard F. Dukore (University
Park, Pennsylvania: Pennsylvania State University Press, 1993), iii. 1115).

227 *hoisting of them with their own petard*: blowing of them up in the air by their
own bomb; see *Hamlet*, III. iv. 204.

viva voce: (Lat.) 'with the living voice', by oral examination.

228 *everyone else can get it for the same price too*: Shaw printed his evidence privately as the pamphlet *Statement of the Evidence in Chief of George Bernard Shaw before the Joint-Committee on Stage Plays (Censorship and Theatre Licensing)* (Edinburgh: R & R Clark, 1909).

yeoman's service: a useful job, like that of a faithful servant.

Free Churches: Shaw means the Nonconformists who tended to be suspicious of theatre.

The Times published: see Shaw, 'The Select Committee on the Censorship', *The Times*, 2 August 1909, p. 6, and 'Mr. Shaw and the Committee', *The Times*, 6 August 1909, p. 7.

231 *Bluebook, pp. 46–53*: here Shaw is again referring to the *Report from the Joint Select Committee on the Stage Plays (Censorship)*.

232 *since 1892*: Shaw's play *Widowers' Houses* was his first play to reach the stage, appearing on 9 and 13 December 1892 at London's Royalty Theatre.

Society of Authors: group founded in 1884 to lobby for the interests of writers.

Three of them have been refused licences: *Mrs Warren's Profession* (banned in 1893), *The Shewing-up of Blanco Posnet* (banned in May 1909), and *Press Cuttings* (banned in June 1909).

a licence has since been granted: *Press Cuttings* was resubmitted later in 1909, with the names of the main characters changed, and was granted a licence in August.

a comedy of mine: in 1903, Shaw's play *Arms and the Man* (first performed 1894), which had been translated into German as *Helden* (Heroes), was suggested for production at the Burgtheater, a prominent theatre in Vienna. The theatre's director sent the script to the *Hoftheaterzensor*, the official with special jurisdiction over the court theatres, asking for an unofficial view of the work. A reply came back from the Literary Bureau under the Ministry of Foreign Affairs to say that, although from the censorship point of view there were no objections, the timing was 'inopportune'. After all, the play is set during the Serbo-Bulgarian War of 1885, and in 1902–3 there were again tensions in that region. The Burgtheater quietly dropped the play, but Shaw circulated the story of the play's suppression widely, believing 'It is very desirable that the action of the Censor . . . should get into the newspapers' (letter of 23 February 1903, in Shaw, *Bernard Shaw's Letters to Siegfried Trebitsch*, ed. Samuel A. Weiss (Stanford, CA: Stanford University Press, 1986), 44). Eventually the play appeared in Vienna on 27 December 1904.

One of the plays so suppressed: on 20 October 1905, the moral crusader Anthony Comstock warned that the upcoming US premiere of *Mrs Warren's Profession* was 'one of Bernard Shaw's filthy products' ('Comstock at it Again', *New York Times*, 25 October 1905, p. 1). On 27 October the premiere occurred at New Haven's Hyperion Theatre, produced by

Arnold Daly, but the following day the show was banned by the mayor and police chief (neither having seen the show), with the police declaring the play 'grossly indecent and not fit for public presentation' ('Daly's New Shaw Play Barred in New Haven', *New York Times*, 29 October 1905, p. 1). Daly took the play to New York's Garrick Theatre two days later, and between 2,000 and 3,000 people had to be turned away at the door. The city's police commissioner made cuts to the play in advance of the New York premiere, but after he attended the performance he consulted with the city's mayor and informed the Garrick's manager that the play was banned and everyone associated with the performance would be arrested for offending public decency. In fact, only Daly and the Garrick's manager ended up facing charges, and were acquitted. The play subsequently appeared at the Manhattan Theatre in March 1907.

233 *leading-strings*: straps designed to guide a child when learning to walk.

Linnaeus: Carolus Linnaeus (1707–78), naturalist who devised the modern system for classifying organisms.

234 *Darwin . . . Samuel Butler*: Charles Darwin (1809–82), the famous naturalist and originator of the theory of natural selection; Alfred Russel Wallace (1823–1913), a naturalist and evolutionary theorist; Thomas Henry Huxley (1825–95), a biologist and 'Darwin's bulldog'. Hermann von Helmholtz (1821–94), a scientist and philosopher; John Tyndall (1820–93), an experimental physicist and exponent of a scientific naturalism that challenged the established religious world-view. Herbert Spencer (1820–1903), sociologist and philosopher, was an advocate of the evolutionary model of the natural world. Thomas Carlyle (1795–1881), an essayist and historian who rejected Christianity; John Ruskin (1819–1900), an art critic and social thinker; Samuel Butler (1835–1902), a writer and artist, whose thinking about evolution particularly affected Shaw.

Greek and Roman Catholic censorships: the *Index Librorum Prohibitorum* was a list (until 1966) of publications forbidden by the Catholic Church: the list included the treatise *Zoonomia* (1794–6) by Erasmus Darwin (1731–1802), which describes a theory of evolution, although his grandson Charles Darwin's *On the Origin of Species* (1859) was never included.

Hampden . . . Galileo: John Hampden (1595–1643) was an MP who opposed Charles I (1600–49) over ship money, thus challenging the monarch's authority in the build-up to the English Civil Wars; George Washington (1732–99), commander-in-chief of the colonial armies during the American Revolution and then first president of the United States in 1789–97; Martin Luther (1483–1546), theologian and religious reformer who helped trigger the Protestant Reformation; Galileo Galilei (1564–1642), philosopher and scientist whose astronomic observations helped establish the heliocentric (sun rather than earth-centred) view of the solar system, and resulted in the Inquisition moving against him.

Mahometanism: see note to p. 142.

as Anarchism is thought of and dealt with today: anarchism attracted a number of artists and thinkers, but a series of Anarchist terrorist attacks took place from the 1890s, including the high-profile murders of King Umberto I of Italy (1844–1900), President William McKinley of the United States (1843–1901), and President Sadi Carnot of France (1837–94). Accordingly, newspapers, police, and judges often acted harshly when faced with Anarchists. The *New York Times*, for example, urged, 'whenever there is reason to suppose that the Anarchist element is to be met, it should be met with rifles and Gatling guns' ('The Chicago Murders', *New York Times*, 6 May 1884, p. 4).

Clapham: an area of south London.

Constantinople: city, now known as Istanbul, situated on the Bosphorus.

235 *Whigs*: the British 'Act of Toleration', passed in 1689, had become totemic for nineteenth-century Whigs, the party formed to represent the views of religious dissenters, industrialists, and reformers. That Act had granted toleration for religious dissenters, although in a rather limited way (only applying to those Protestant Nonconformists who believed in the Holy Trinity).

Catholic Emancipation . . . admission of Jews to parliament: Catholic emancipation relates to the granting of political and civil liberties to Roman Catholics in Britain and Ireland, effected by an Act of 1829. Until 1858, Jews technically could not take seats in Parliament because an oath of allegiance needed to be made on a copy of the New Testament. This was amended by the Jews Relief Act in 1858, with Lionel de Rothschild (1808–79) becoming Westminster's first serving Jewish MP.

236 *Tom Paine's centenary*: hundredth anniversary of the death of Thomas Paine (1737–1809), the author and revolutionary who influentially advocated American independence. *The Times* published a laudatory article to mark the centenary of Paine's death, 'The Greatest of Pamphleteers', 8 June 1909, p.10.

Proudhon: Pierre-Joseph Proudhon (1809–65), journalist and libertarian socialist who, in 1840, declared 'Property is theft!' (Proudhon, *What is Property?*, trans. Donald R. Kelley and Bonnie G. Smith (Cambridge: Cambridge University Press, 1993), 14).

Lord Liverpool or Lord Brougham: Robert Banks Jenkinson (1770–1828), 2nd Earl Liverpool, was prime minister, 1812–27. His Tory administration was responsible for prosecuting editors and publishers and, in 1819, introducing a repressive Newspaper Stamp Duties Act that imposed a fourpence stamp duty on all periodicals costing less than sixpence. Henry Peter Brougham (1778–1868), Lord Chancellor, 1830–4, was a popular Whig politician who argued against the stamp duty on newspapers, declaring the tax 'by far the most hurtful of these bad taxes in one essential particular. The instruction of the working classes in the country districts, where it is most wanted, has been almost entirely prevented by it . . . Our only chance of making those poor people read was, by wrapping up good information of a lasting value in news' (*Hansard's Parliamentary Debates, 11 March–18 April 1853* (London: Cornelius Buck, 1853), col. 1135).

236 *Inquisition . . . Star Chamber*: the Inquisition was an ecclesiastical tribunal of the Roman Catholic Church for suppressing heresy and punishing heretics. Star Chamber was a court which grew out of the medieval king's council and was used by Charles I to enforce unpopular policies and so became associated with oppression of the king's opponents.

get rid of the Star Chamber . . . did not get rid of the Inquisition: Star Chamber was abolished by the Long Parliament in 1641, a year before the outbreak of civil war; the Spanish Inquisition was in fact permanently abolished in 1834.

Laisser-Faire: (Fr.) 'let do', the principle that government ought to steer clear of the action of individuals, particularly in trade and industrial matters.

237 *Bakounine*: Mikhail Bakunin (1814–76), political writer and revolutionary anarchist.

Julius Cæsar: Shakespeare's play, probably written in 1599, in which the title character only speaks 6 per cent of the words and is stabbed to death in the third act.

Tsar of Russia: Nicholas II, who had faced a serious revolutionary movement in 1905 and was indeed executed by the Bolsheviks in 1918.

Governor-General of India: Gilbert Kynynmoud, 4th Earl of Minto (1845–1914), who faced growing Indian nationalism and became the target of assassination attempts.

Goethe: Johann Wolfgang von Goethe (1749–1832), German writer.

regicides of 1649: those responsible for the execution of King Charles I.

Plutarchian republicanism: the Greek author and biographer Plutarch (46–after 119 CE), who helped establish the 'great man' notion of history, in which the course of events was mainly altered by notable individuals.

Brutus . . . Ravaillac . . . Charlotte Corday: Marcus Junius Brutus (*c.*85–42 BCE) was the leading murderer of Julius Caesar (100–44 BCE); François Ravaillac of Angoulême (1578–1610) assassinated King Henri IV of France (1553–1610); Charlotte Corday (1768–93) murdered French Revolutionary Jean-Paul Marat (1743–93) in his bath.

scouted: mocked and rejected.

His Majesty's Theatre in London: Herbert Beerbohm Tree performed in an acclaimed *Julius Caesar* at His Majesty's Theatre in June 1909. Tree himself took the role of Anthony before the packed house, prompting *The Observer* to comment that never before had anyone 'conveyed so fully the Shakespearean spirit of passionate oratory in its mob-swaying effect. Repeated calls brought the actor-manager again and again before the curtain' ('Julius Cæsar', *The Observer*, 27 June 1909, p. 6).

suppress the play completely in Calcutta and Dublin: for fear of encouraging Indian and Irish nationalists who might take violent action against British rule.

Lord Frederick Cavendish, Presidents Lincoln and McKinley . . . Sir Curzon Wyllie: Frederick Cavendish (1836–82), chief secretary for Ireland, was murdered in the 1882 Phoenix Park murders by the Invincibles, an extremist group of Fenians. Abraham Lincoln (1809–65), 16th president of the United States, was murdered by John Wilkes Booth (1838–65); William McKinley (1843–1901), 25th president of the United States, was murdered by Leon Czolgosz (1873–1901). Sir Curzon Wyllie (1848–1909), a British army officer, was murdered by the Indian nationalist Madan Lal Dhingra (1883–1909), while attending an event given by the National Indian Association in South Kensington, London.

officered by two European Powers of the first magnitude: Bulgaria was supported by Russia, whose officers had been training and commanding Bulgaria's army since the 1870s. On the other side, Serbia's king Milan I (1854–1901) had so many Austrian advisers and patrons that the *Manchester Guardian* reported that Bulgarian 'victories were Austrian defeats' ('Foreign Telegrams', *Manchester Guardian*, 26 November 1885, p. 8).

238 *it gave offence in Rome*: *Arms and the Man* was staged at Rome's Teatro Argentina at the end of March 1909, and according to the *Morning Post* 'proved to be one of the greatest failures ever seen on the Italian stage', with audiences regarding the play as 'a studied insult to the profession of arms' ('Italian Versions of Mr Shaw's Plays', *Morning Post*, 1 April 1909, p. 8).

Coercion Act . . . Habeas Corpus Act . . . martial law: a Coercion Act refers to those measures beginning with the Suppression of Disturbances Act (1833), which allowed the Lord Lieutenant to designate a particular district as being disturbed and therefore to suspend ordinary constitutional liberties. The Habeas Corpus Act of 1679 safeguarded individual liberty and prevented unlawful imprisonment. Martial law refers to government by military authority, with ordinary civil law suspended, usually for the purpose of maintaining order in times of unrest.

Act of 1843: Theatre Regulation Act of 1843, which bolstered the powers of the Lord Chamberlain. All plays had to be submitted to him one week before the planned first night, and he could ban any show 'whenever he shall be of opinion that it is fitting for the Preservation of Good Manners, Decorum or of the Public Peace' (6 & 7 Vict., c 68, section 14).

fine art: Henry Irving became the first actor to be knighted, in 1895, and thus in this respect putting dramatic art on a par with other art forms such as music and painting.

239 *Lord Rosebery . . . eulogize Cromwell*: Archibald Philip Primrose (1847–1929), prime minister, 1894–5, and writer, delivered a speech in 1899 to celebrate the erection of a statue of Oliver Cromwell (1599–1658), Lord

Protector of England, Ireland, and Scotland (1653–80), outside the Houses of Parliament, praising Cromwell as someone who 'used his gifts in statesmanship and in war to raise and to maintain the power and the empire of England' ('The Statue Erected', *The Times*, 15 November 1899, p. 9).

239 *the American law against obscenity . . . makes the magistrate virtually a censor*: in 1873, Anthony Comstock managed to promote a Congressional Act for the Suppression of Trade in, and Circulation of, Obscene Literature and Articles of Immoral Use. However, the notion of 'obscenity' itself was left vague and open to contrasting legal interpretation.

240 *Eschylus and Europides*: Aeschylus (545/4–456/55 BCE) and Euripides (*c.*484–406 BCE), tragedians of the ancient Greek theatre.

241 *Milton . . . Chesterfield . . . Bentham*: John Milton (1608–74) was an English poet and polemicist. Philip Dormer Stanhope, 4th Earl of Chesterfield (1694–1773), was a politician who opposed the 1737 stage-licensing bill, and made an eloquent speech against it in the House of Lords, arguing that the Lord Chamberlain was being given 'a more absolute power than we trust even to the king himself' (Chesterfield, *The Works of Lord Chesterfield* (New York: Harper, 1855), 67). Jeremy Bentham (1748–1832) was a philosopher who developed utilitarianism.

whipper-in: during a hunt, an assistant who keeps hounds from straying by using a whip.

242 *An Englishman's Home*: patriotic play first staged at the Wyndham's Theatre. The drama appeared anonymously but was written by Guy du Maurier (1865–1915), and depicted a suburban English family suffering as England is invaded by the 'Nearlander' forces (*An Englishman's Home* (New York: Harper, 1909), 2).

refused to license a parody of it: in February 1909, the Lord Chamberlain refused to license a five-minute burlesque of *An Englishman's Home*, which Harry Gabriel Pélissier (1874–1913) had planned to produce at the Apollo Theatre. On 1 March Pélissier mocked the censor's decision by staging another sketch (as part of 'The Follies' show at the Apollo) that recalled elements from *An Englishman's Home*.

another play: Shaw is presumably referring to his own play *Press Cuttings*, which was refused a licence on 24 June 1909.

St James's Palace: official residence of the monarch.

Mikado: emperor.

entente cordiale: (Fr.) friendly understanding.

243 *Carlyle's essay on the prophet*: Carlyle wrote a lecture, 'The Hero as Prophet', in 1840, praising the prophet Muhammad for his 'candid ferocity' but describing Islam as 'a confused form of Christianity' (Carlyle, *On Heroes, Hero-worship, & the Heroic in History* (New York: Wiley and Putnam, 1846), 51).

criticized as an impostor: British Christians had produced translations of the Quran that were critical of the prophet Muhammad. For example,

George Sale (1697?–1736) made a version of *The Koran: or, Alcoran of Mohammed*, which includes a note 'To the Reader' that accuses the prophet of 'imposing a false religion on mankind' (London: William Tegg, 1877, p. vi). John Medows Rodwell (1808–1900) published *The Koran* (London: Dent, 1909), in a version that includes an introduction accusing the prophet of having 'frequently descended to deliberate invention and artful rhetoric' (p. viii).

reviled as Mahound: in medieval Europe, Muhammad had his name corrupted in this way in order to denigrate the prophet. For example, in the fourteenth-century York Mystery Plays, the character of Satan yells out 'Help, Mahound' (Richard Beadle and Pamela M. King (eds), *York Mystery Plays* (Oxford: Oxford University Press, 1984), 248).

Dean and Chapter of St Paul's: the clerics running the Anglican cathedral in London built by Christopher Wren (1632–1723).

ex officio: (Lat.) in virtue of his office.

Primate: chief bishop.

244 *Gaiety Theatre*: a West End theatre that became synonymous with musical comedy, by contrast with His Majesty's Theatre, where Beerbohm Tree established a Shakespeare festival in 1905. Edwardes ran the Gaiety for thirty years from 1885.

Northampton: town in the East Midlands, over 67 miles from London.

Divorçons of the late Victorien Sardou: Sardou was famed for his development of the bourgeois well-made play, and disparaged by Shaw. However, with Sardou's 1880 play *Divorçons* (Let's Get a Divorce!)—a play of sexual innuendo inspired by French plans to legalize divorce—Shaw did confess to being 'unable to maintain this unfavorable attitude' as the piece manifested such 'witty liveliness' ('The New Magda and the New Cyprian', a review of 6 June 1896, in Shaw, *Our Theatres in the Nineties*, ii. 150–1).

a very amusing comedy: *A Modern Aspasia* by Hamilton Fyfe (1869–1951), performed at the Aldwych Theatre by the Stage Society in June 1909, and featuring a man being shared between his wife and mistress.

(Report, page 330): *Report from the Select Committee on Theatres and Places of Entertainment: with proceedings; minutes of evidence; appendix; and index* (Shannon: Irish University Press, 1970 [facsimile of 1892 edn])

245 *illegal operation*: an abortion, illegal in Great Britain until 1967.

Imperial Theatre: playhouse in Westminster which opened in 1876 (as the Royal Aquarium Theatre). It was closed to make way for the Methodist Central Hall, which was erected at that location, at the corner of Tothill Street and Storey's Gate, from 1907. But the Stage Society was nonetheless able to stage the banned play *Waste* by Granville Barker at the site in November 1907.

a West End manager: it remains unclear which particular West End manager Shaw was referring to here. The Haymarket Theatre hosted the banned play *The Breaking Point* by Edward Garnett (1868–1937) in

April 1908, and the Imperial Theatre hosted Granville Barker's forbidden play *Waste* in November 1907, both under the auspices of the Stage Society. But the censor was evaded in other ways in the West End as well. For example, Janet Achurch (1863–1916) and her husband, Charles Charrington (1854–1926), translated a play by Octave Feuillet (1821–90) called *Julie* and proposed to produce it at the Criterion. The licence was refused, but the censor then agreed to allow a production if one sentence was cut from the script. In performance, Achurch uttered the line anyway, but in a quiet voice.

246 *prompt copy*: copy of the play script prepared for the prompter's use in performance.

A Doll's House: Ibsen's play appeared on the London stage, at the Novelty Theatre, in 1889.

247 *one play by Sophocles*: *Oedipus Tyrannos*, banned in England in the early twentieth century: in 1904 Beerbohm Tree had been refused permission to stage the piece at His Majesty's Theatre in response to an informal request to the censor, although in November 1910 a licence was granted to perform the translation of the play by Gilbert Murray. The playwright Henry Arthur Jones (1851–1929) commented wryly that 'if any considerable body of Englishmen are arranging to marry their mothers, whether by accident or design, it must be stopped at once. But it is not a frequent occurrence in any class of English society. Throughout the course of my life I have not met more than six men who were anxious to do it' (quoted by Frank Fowell and Frank Palmer, *Censorship in England* (London: Frank Palmer, 1913), 275).

248 *Freethinker*: someone who thinks independently of authority and doubts religious dogma. The notion that Euripides had such doubts comes from his dramas and from the interpretation of them that is found in the comic work of Aristophanes (*c*.450–*c*.388 BCE). In Aristophanes' *Thesmophoriazusae*, for example, one character claims that Euripides' work on tragedies 'has got all the men believing that there aren't any gods' (trans. Alan H. Sommerstein (Warminster: Aris & Phillips, 1994), 61), and in the *Frogs* Euripides is described as 'god-detested scum' (trans. Alan H. Sommerstein (Warminster: Aris & Phillips, 1996), 111).

mise-en-scène: (Fr.), 'placing on stage', staging.

one of the plays: *The Chorus Lady*, by James Forbes (1871–1938), which when staged at the Vaudeville in April 1909 featured a scene in which chorus girls appear in their New-York dressing room. *The Times* declared that these 'pretty girls' managed 'to reveal many secrets of feminine attire' ('Vaudeville Theatre', *The Times*, 20 April 1909, p. 10), although *The Observer* commented that the play, overall, provided 'the idea of stage life that you might expect from the "Church Monthly"' ('Prince's Theatre', *The Observer*, 17 May 1910, p. 6).

London County Council: governmental body established in 1888 by the Local Government Act. The County Council's Theatres and Music Halls

Committee (established 1889) regulated London's music halls and theatres (apart from the actual stage plays, which remained regulated by the Lord Chamberlain).

249 *police des mœurs*: (Fr.) morality police.

Secretary of State: minister presiding over a government department.

ecclesiastical referee: although English-language theatre originated with the performance of Christian religious stories, churchmen often attacked the theatre for its immorality. For example, *The Era* reported that one cleric 'was in particular extremely anxious to prevent any collision between the lambs of the elect and the children of Satan, as he conscientiously believed his followers and the Corps Dramatique to be' ('Theatrical Recollections', *The Era*, 23 November 1856, p. 10).

Public Health Acts: a number of Acts that reduced mortality in UK towns during the final part of the nineteenth century by reforming sanitation and ensuring the enforcement of basic standards of cleanliness and hygiene.

recent deputation: leading theatre writers, including John Galsworthy, Gilbert Murray, and J. M. Barrie, felt riled by the censorship of *The Breaking Point*, a second-rate play by Edward Garnett. They made elaborate plans for taking a protest to the prime minister, Henry Campbell-Bannerman (1836–1908). According to William Archer in November 1907: 'The Dramatic authors of England are to assemble in Trafalgar Square. Barrie will address them from the base of Nelson's column, and the Savoy Orchestra will play "Britons never will be slaves"' (quoted by George Jefferson, *Edward Garnett: A Life in Literature* (London: Jonathan Cape, 1982), 120). A procession was then planned, with a number of unlikely features, including W. B. Yeats (1865–1939) carrying an effigy of the censor George Alexander Redford (1840–1916). Unfortunately the prime minister was ill, and the event never took place. Instead a small deputation, led by Barrie and Arthur Wing Pinero (but not Shaw), met with the Home Secretary, Herbert Gladstone (1854–1930), in February 1908.

250 *Finance Bill*: in November 1909, Conservative leader Arthur Balfour brought Conservatives in the House of Lords to reject the redistributive Finance Bill, which had been brought forth by the Liberal government of Herbert Asquith. Usually the Lords would not reject a money bill, and, after a period of constitutional crisis and a general election, the Finance Act was given Royal Assent in April 1910.

251 *factory code*: the code of Factory Acts that imposed health-and-safety rules, regulated working hours, and protected children, passed mainly by Liberal governments in the nineteenth century.

Public Health and Building Acts: nineteenth-century Acts that developed boards of health in England and Wales, and allowed building structures to be regulated.

252 *From the Restoration to the days of Macready*: from the Restoration of the English monarchy in 1660 to the days of William Charles Macready (1793–1873), actor and theatre manager.

252 *drive the prostitutes from his theatre*: Macready, when manager of Drury Lane between 1841 and 1843, proposed that prostitutes should only be allowed into the gallery, through a separate pay-office, and by passing through a dismantled lobby.

253 *long-run managers*: those producing long-running plays, often delivered by acting companies that toured cities across the UK. By the time Shaw wrote this, the work of the long-run managers had seen off the earlier stock companies of the nineteenth century (those earlier companies had been engaged for a season at a theatre, and rotated a series of plays during the engagement).

Prohibitionist Teetotaller: an abstainer who advocates restricting the making and selling of alcohol.

254 *mandamus*: (Lat.), 'we command', writ.

255 *County Council or City Corporation*: a county council is a governing body of a county; a city corporation is the civic authority of a city.

Sabbath-breaking: failing to observe Sunday, the Sabbath in Christianity.

Attorney-General: first ministerial law officer of the British government.

laws against blasphemy: these laws included elements of 1 Edw. 6 c. 1 (An Act against such persons as shall irreverently speak against the Sacrament of the Altar). The laws also included the 1819 Criminal Libel Act (60 Geo 3 & 1 Geo. 4 c. 8), which included the word 'blasphemous'; the Metropolitan Police Act of 1839 (2 & 3 Vict. c. 47); and the Town Police Clauses Act of 1847 (51 & 52 Vict. c. 64).

Archbishop of Canterbury: the primate of all England in the Anglican Church, a role taken at that time by Randall Thomas Davidson (1848–1930).

256 *Hermes of Praxiteles*: Greek sculpture of the naked Hermes (messenger God) and the infant Dionysus (god of wine), supposedly created by the sculptor Praxiteles in the fourth century BCE, and discovered in 1877.

Measure for Measure: Shakespeare's play written in 1603 or 1604, which revolves around the question of whether Isabella will sacrifice her virginity in order to save her brother, who has been found guilty of fornication, and involves characters including the brothel-running 'Mistress Overdone'.

259 *first-nighter*: person who attends the first night that a play is given for the public.

successful march: Alexander had been manager of St James's Theatre in London from 1891 until his death in 1918.

purlieus: outskirts.

Isle of Dogs: area in east London on the banks of the Thames; that is to say that the king has not gone very far.

261 *Rhine maidens*: the three water nymphs (named Woglinde, Wellgunde, and Flosshilde) who open and close the opera cycle *Der Ring des Nibelungen* by Richard Wagner. They frolic in the river with their treasure at the start of *Das Rheingold* (1869), and at the end of *Götterdämmerung* (1876) they drag the character of Hagen down into the depths of the water.

Les Huguenots: five-act opera premiered in 1836 by Giacomo Meyerbeer (1791–1864), about the love between Catholic Valentine and Protestant Raoul. The second act features a chorus of bathing beauties, who chase 'Gloom from every heart' (New York: Charles D. Koppel, [1836?]), 20.

King's Proctor: an official with the right to intervene on behalf of the Crown in divorce and certain other cases in which suppression of the facts or other impropriety is alleged.

Sterne's Sentimental Journey: *A Sentimental Journey Through France and Italy* (1768), a novel by Laurence Sterne (1713–68) based on his own travels, which parodies novel-writing and the penning of travel journals. Sterne's work contains an obscene subtext, such as when the novel ends with one of the characters grabbing the chambermaid: 'So that when I stretch'd out my hand, I caught hold of the Fille de Chambre's END OF VOL. II' (Sterne, *A Sentimental Journey*, ed. Melvyn New and W. G. Day (Indianapolis: Hackett, 2006), 165).

King Lear: Shakespeare's play published in a first quarto of 1608 (with a different text of the play appearing in the folio of 1623). In both versions the dead Cordelia appears immediately after Albany declares 'The gods defend her!' (V. iii. 252).

the most appalling blasphemy: Shaw was likely thinking of Gloucester's lines, 'As flies to wanton boys are we to th' gods: | They kill us for their sport' (IV. i. 35–6).

262 *Ibsen's Brand*: Ibsen's five-act verse tragedy was first published in 1866. The title character is an uncompromising Lutheran priest whose mother, wife, and son die, and whose people turn on him. At the end of the play Brand dies, calling out, 'God, I plunge into death's night,— | Shall they wholly miss thy Light | Who unto man's utmost might | Will'd—?' (an unnamed voice replies, 'He is the God of love') (Ibsen, *Brand*, trans. C. H. Herford (London: William Heinemann, 1912), 262).

Clyde Fitch's The Woman in the Case: a drawing-room melodrama by the leading American dramatist Clyde Fitch (1865–1909), which features one character being suspected of murder after having an affair with a villainous woman who 'had an itch for a vice that nothing could cure!' (*The Woman in the Case* (New York: Little, Brown, 1915), 43).

Magna Charta: (Lat.) 'Great Charter', alternative spelling for the Magna Carta, which granted the English personal and political liberties in 1215 and made the king subject to the rule of law.

Blake, Zola, and Swinburne: William Blake (1757–1827), poet and artist, sought to denounce the cruelties enacted by the Christian Churches. He expressed radical religious beliefs, such as 'The Bible or <Peculiar> Word of God, Exclusive of Conscience or the Word of God Universal, is that Abomination which like the Jewish ceremonies is for ever removed & henceforth every man may converse with God & be a King & Priest in his own house' (Blake, *The Complete Poetry & Prose of William Blake*, ed.

David V. Erdman (rev. edn, Berkeley and Los Angeles: University of California Press, 1982), 615). Émile Zola (1840–1902), novelist and political activist, sought to describe some of the truths of the human condition in his naturalistic writing, and his English publisher, Henry Vizetelly (1820–94), was twice prosecuted under the Obscene Publications Act. In the House of Commons in 1888, Zola's work was described as 'only fit for swine' (quoted by Phillip Walker, *Zola* (Oxford: Routledge, 1985), 211). Algernon Charles Swinburne (1837–1909) was a poet and literary reviewer whose poetry contains references to subjects that his contemporaries considered taboo, including incest, lesbianism, hermaphroditism, and necrophilia.

262 *mulcted*: punished (by a fine).

263 *victualler*: person licensed to sell alcohol.

King John . . . Henry VII: John (1167–1216), king of England, who on 16 June 1215 confirmed the final draft of the Magna Carta at Runnymede, and by mid-July had written to Pope Innocent, asking him to annul the charter. Henry VII (1457–1509), king of England and lord of Ireland, first of the Tudor monarchs.

cutting off the ears of eminent Nonconformist divines: in the 1630s, the Star Chamber punished a number of individual Puritans who had criticized the Anglican bishops, ordering that they spend some time in the pillory, and further ordering the removal of ears from John Bastwick (1595?–1654), William Prynne (1600–69), Alexander Leighton (*c*.1570–1649), and Henry Burton (bapt. 1578–d. 1647/8).

264 *[it does not, by the way, except in the crudest police cases]*: this is Shaw's insertion.

Archbishop Laud: William Laud (1573–1645), archbishop of Canterbury who faced trumped-up charges of treason and advancing popery, and was executed in 1645.

Act of the Long Parliament in 1641: the English Parliament summoned in November 1640, which, in its early months, brought down the king's advisers and took other measures that raised tensions between parliament and the king, one early act being the abolition of Star Chamber.

265 *Transubstantiation*: the Roman Catholic doctrine that, during the Eucharist, the substance of the bread and wine is changed into the body and blood of Christ.

Quarter Sessions: a court of limited criminal and civil jurisdiction and of appeal.

Director of Public Prosecutions: the office, established in 1879, had power to institute and conduct criminal proceedings where the usual course of proceedings was likely to be ineffective. The Director of Public Prosecutions could also assist chief police officers and others wishing to begin proceedings.

266 *municipal aldermen*: local councillors.

Jenny Geddes: (dates unknown), supposed religious activist (who may never have existed at all) who is usually said to have begun the demonstrations against Charles I's new Scottish prayer book when it was used in Edinburgh for the first time in 1637. Allegedly, as the dean of St Giles's Cathedral read from the book, Geddes threw a folding stool at him.

Passion Play at Oberammergau: this event, which is still performed to this day, was first staged following a 1633 vow that, if the village was spared from plague, the residents would perform a play about Christ's suffering and death in each decade, in perpetuity.

267 *Wagner's Parsifal*: opera first premiered in 1882, Wagner's retelling of the myth of the Holy Grail (the cup used by Christ at the Last Supper).

miracle of the Mass: the Eucharistic service, a dramatic performance of which occurs in Act I of Wagner's *Parsifal*. The Duchess Carolyne von Wittgenstein (1819–87) protested against what she saw as Wagner's mockery of the Holy Sacrament.

Covent Garden: site of a London theatre since 1732. The theatre in place since 1858 has been mainly given over to operatic performances.

Holy Ghost: one of the three consubstantial persons, known as the Holy Trinity, that makes up the Christian God (along with God the Father and God the Son). A dove hovers over Parsifal's head at the end of Wagner's opera.

Primrose League: a popular organization of local branches established in 1883 to support Conservative ideas of Crown, Church, and Empire.

269 *Press Laws (especially in Egypt, India, and Ireland)*: laws concerning what publishers could print, particularly in troublesome colonies of the British Empire.

270 *Sweet Lavender, Peter Pan, The Silver King*: *Sweet Lavender* was a sentimental comedy by Arthur Wing Pinero which premiered in 1888 and then ran for 684 performances. *Peter Pan; or, The Boy Who Wouldn't Grow Up* was a popular play first produced for 150 performances in 1904 by J. M. Barrie. *The Silver King* was a melodramatic play written by Henry Arthur Jones and Henry Herman (1832–94), opening in 1882 for 289 performances.

desuetude: disuse.

272 *Master of the Revels*: official of the English royal household in the 1500s and 1600s, responsible for organizing the court's masques and dramatic entertainments. By the later 1500s he had become responsible for licensing and censoring plays.

Henry VIII: (1491–1547), king of England and later also of Ireland.

Synge's The Playboy of the Western World: 1907 comedy by John Millington Synge (1871–1909) in which the lead character wins popularity in the West of Ireland by boasting of parricide. The first week of performances at the Abbey Theatre in Dublin saw riotous objections to the work.

Irish National Theatre: the Abbey Theatre in Dublin, where Synge's *Playboy of the Western World* was first played.

Lady Gregory . . . Yeats: Isabella Augusta Gregory (1852–1932), playwright and literary patron, and William Butler Yeats (1865–1939), poet and playwright, were co-founders and co-directors of the Abbey Theatre.

brought the play to London: the Abbey brought *Blanco Posnet* to London's Aldwych Theatre on 5 December 1909.

273 *two eminent actors (one retired)*: Sir Squire Bancroft (1841–1926), actor-manager, who had found himself wealthy enough to retire as manager in 1885, and only very occasionally acted on the stage after that; and Sir John Hare, who had finished his career as manager in 1895 but still performed regularly as an actor until 1917.

an Oxford professor of literature: Professor Walter Alexander Raleigh (1861–1922), literary scholar.

two eminent barristers: Sir Edward Carson (1854–1935), politician and lawyer; and Stanley Owen Buckmaster (1861–1934), politician and lawyer.

Estate of the Realm: a collective group of the body politic, the three estates usually consisting of lords spiritual (bishops who are peers), lords temporal (peers), and the commons.

274 *old English tithe barn*: a barn for holding tithe-corn, the tenth of a farm's produce given to a Church. Shaw explained to Tolstoy that the play 'is a very crude melodrama, which might be played in a mining camp to the roughest audience' (*CL* ii. 900, letter of 14 February 1910).

Sheriff: the figure who—sometimes with deputies—executes civil and criminal process throughout a county, takes responsibility for prisons and their inmates, attends courts, and keeps the peace. Shaw told the producer of a 1926 revival of the play that the Sheriff 'must not dress and make-up as one of the boys: he should be clean, respectably dressed, wellspoken, and obviously a substantial man and the boss' (*CL* iv. 31, letter of 11 November 1926).

pioneers of civilization: those who migrated west to settle and develop American territory (which was already well known to Native Americans) between the mid-1700s and mid-1800s.

shucking nuts: removing the shells from nuts. The copy that Shaw prepared in 1909 for theatre rehearsals specified that the women should sit in the following arrangement:

HANNAH

LOTTIE   EMMA

JESSIE   BABSY

(*SUBP* Type, fo. 1).

slattern: a woman who is untidy in her habits or appearance.

somebody: in an earlier draft of the play, Shaw gave this character a rather different ending to her speech, adding at this point, 'Well, I say, let them

use it on a horse thief that is a curse to everybody and not on one another'
(*SUBP* Rev, fo. 1).

275   *a spree*: merrymaking, rough amusement, or sport.

Vigilance Committee: group of vigilantes, self-appointed for the purposes
of maintaining justice.

stolen: in an early draft of the play, Shaw included some additional lines
here to explain more about the relationship between the genders in this
society:

> HANNAH. Why didnt her husband do it for her?
>
> BRIDGET. He had his own work to do.
>
> HANNAH. She could have spared him easier than the horse.
>
> JANE. That is why we think so much of horse-thieving and so little of
> killing a man, I suppose.
>
> (*SUBP* Rev, fo. 3)

277   *blackguard*: villain.

delirium tremens: (Lat.), 'trembling delirium', a type of delirium induced
by excessive drinking of alcohol, and characterized by quaking and various
delusions of the senses.

varmint: troublesome person.

Angels ever bright and fair . . . Take, oh take me to your care: lyrics from the
libretto *Theodora* (1750) by Thomas Morrell (1703–84) for an oratorio by
Handel (1685–1759), about a Christian saint martyred under Roman persecution (Handel, *Theodora: An Oratorio* (London: Walsh, [n.d.]), 35).

278   *Oh woman, in our hours of ease, / Uncertain, coy, and hard to please*: from
the epic poem *Marmion* (1808) by Walter Scott (1771–1832). The poem
concerns the 1513 Battle of Flodden (*The Poetical Works of Sir Walter Scott*
(Boston: Phillips, Sampson, 1852), 300).

When pain and anguish wring the brow, / A ministering angel thou: lines also
taken from Scott's *Marmion* (p. 301). Shaw then planned, in an early
prepublication version of his script, to include the following lines:

> STRAPPER. It wont make much difference to you, anyhow, whether
> they tore your eyes out or not, as long as we can see to hang you.
>
> BLANCO. Let cats delight / To bark and bite.
>
> (*SUBP* Rev, fos. 8–9)

279   *blinded soul*: in an early prepublication version of his script, Shaw then
planned to include the following rather grisly lines:

> BLANCO. And round up the horse as well.
>
> STRAPPER. If I had my way I'd make you tell where that horse is, if
> I had to roast every inch of skin off your carcass first.
>
> BLANCO. Perhaps I ate him, Strapper.
>
> (*SUBP* Rev, fo. 11)

280 *I distrained on it for what you owed me*: I confiscated it from Elder Daniels in order to obtain satisfaction for the debt.

281 *God fulfils Himself in many ways*: cf. 'The Passing of Arthur' (1869) by Alfred Tennyson (line 409), in *Tennyson: Selected Poems*, ed. by Michael Millgate (Oxford: Oxford University Press, 1963), 175–90, at 188.

Went on the spree: went for a spell of drunken carousing.

Cheese it: leave off.

'Shake not the dying sinner's sand': cf. the epic poem *Marmion* by Walter Scott (p. 303).

282 *temperance reformers*: the American Temperance Society was formed in 1826, advocating total abstinence from alcohol.

the tempter: in a prepublication version of his script, Shaw then planned to include some words to clarify Elder Daniels's thoughts about sobriety and work. The character was supposed to continue: 'There's not a man in this town as would employ a teetotaller. When one comes here he has to git. And why? Because we know from the Bible that | Satan will find mischief still | For idle hands to do' (*SUBP* Rev, fo. 16).

off it: in a prepublication version of his script, Shaw then planned to include a line indicating the moral thinking of Boozy Daniels. In deleting this line, Shaw foregrounded Boozy's self interest, as the deleted line was to read:

ELDER DANIELS. (fervently) You think doing right doesnt pay. Youre wrong it always pays better than doing wrong, though fools throw a good man's profits in his teeth to keep their own rags and poverty in countenance.

(*SUBP* Rev, fo. 16)

He cometh like a thief in the night: cf. 1 Thessalonians 5:2, 'the Lord so cometh as a thief in the night'.

He always has a trick up His sleeve . . . as far as hanging me goes: all of Blanco's lines in this dialogue were repeatedly highlighted by the Lord Chamberlain's office in 1909, marking them as being unacceptable for public performance because of their blasphemous implication. The censor first pointed this out to the management of His Majesty's Theatre in London. Then, when the management of Manchester's Gaiety Theatre resubmitted the script later in the year, the censor sent a somewhat exasperated note to say, 'I observe that this print copy contains the passages originally objected to . . . in fact I should say that the copy now before me is practically identical. Under these circumstances it would clearly be impossible for the Examiner of Plays to recommend the issue of the Lord Chamberlain's Licence for Representation, in its present form' (British Library, Add. MS 65866E, *The Shewing Up of Blanco Posnet*, and HRC Lic). In 1916, the play was resubmitted to the Lord Chamberlain's office, where a different reader confirmed that 'The passages in which Posnet rails at God as "a sly one", "a mean one" etc. . . . must offend many by their outrageous blasphemy; and I can only follow my predecessors by holding that unless these speeches are deleted, the Play is not recommended for License' (HRC Lic).

284 *surplices*: vestments of white linen with wide sleeves and often reaching the floor, characteristically worn by those—such as priests and choristers—leading church services.

285 *comes back*: in a prepublication version of his script, Shaw then planned to include the following lines which show how profoundly Blanco had been affected by his encounter with the woman and child:

> BLANCO. How did you come in so pat what I spoke of you? I'll find out whether you're real, now. (He comes towards him)
>
> STRAPPER. (Drawing his pistol) You want me to cheat the Sheriff, do you? Don't you think it. Stand back, or I'll break your leg with a bullet. You won't hang any easier for that.
>
> BLANCO. Feel him, Boozy. Is he real? That's all I want to find out.
>
> ELDER DANIELS. (Making a pretence of feeling Strapper's arm) He's real, Blanco: solid as hickory.
>
> (*SUBP* Rev, fo. 22)

Foxing: lying.

rottenest: in a prepublication version of his script, Shaw intended to emphasize Blanco's contempt for Strapper even more strongly here. Shaw planned to include Blanco delivering the following insult: 'The game boils in me at every word that comes from your rotten heart and dirty mouth' (*SUBP* Rev, fo. 33).

hanged for a sheep as a lamb: you may as well be hanged for a great deal as for a little. This proverb alludes to a traditional penalty for sheep-stealing.

A woman! Oh Lord!: Blanco's response here is slightly ambiguous, but in an early prepublication version of his script, Shaw spelled out more specifically what Blanco is thinking. Instead of the exclamation 'A woman! Oh Lord!', Blanco was going to say, 'There's not a woman in this rotten town that wouldn't swear a man's life away just for the lark of seeing him lynched' (*SUBP* Rev, fo. 24).

spree: in an early prepublication version of his script, Shaw then planned for Feemy to add a clarifying detail about the chronology of the evening, 'You was the last thing I saw out of my window before I turned in' (*SUBP* Rev, fo. 25).

286 *die game*: Feemy responds violently to this line, and the reason for the strength of her reaction is partly explained by a line that Shaw cut from the published version of the text. In a prepublication version of his script, Shaw planned for Blanco to add a reference to Feemy being eternally doomed, 'You and I are born blackguards, Feemy: we'll keep one another up to the mark until we're both safe in hell' (*SUBP* Rev, fo. 26).

289 *'a Daniel come to judgment'*: Blanco refers here to the line spoken by Shylock in Shakespeare's *The Merchant of Venice* (IV. i. 217). It refers to an episode

related in Daniel 13 (a chapter not included within the Protestant Bible since it is regarded as Apocryphal), in which a beautiful married woman called Susannah is falsely accused of promiscuity, but is correctly judged innocent by the youthful Daniel.

290 *than you*: in an early prepublication version of his script, Shaw gave a greater emphasis at this point to Elder Daniels's discomfort with Blanco's line of questioning. Shaw had planned to include the following lines that do not appear in the published text:

> ELDER DANIELS. Why do you want to bring that up, you foolish lost sinner, after my doing all I could to keep it back? That was why you stole the horse.
>
> BLANCO. Never you mind that. Just you answer this.
>
> (*SUBP* Rev, fo. 35).

291 *I did*: the horse never appears in the play, but at this point Shaw did plan for Feemy to describe the animal: 'You know—the one with the white place and the stockings'. Shaw deleted that reference before publication (*SUBP* Rev, fo. 36).

Oh you liar!: the violence of Feemy's interjection here was emphasized in an early prepublication version of his script, where Shaw added: 'STRAPPER (Restraining her) Be quiet. Let him talk' (*SUBP* Rev, fo. 37).

I accuse the fair Euphemia . . . with a pair of tongs: this is the second part of the script that drew repeated objection from the British censor. He objected to the sexual promiscuity implied in Blanco's lines here (British Library, Add. MS 65866E, *The Shewing Up of Blanco Posnet*, and HRC Lic).

292 *Book of Books*: the Bible. Potentially here alluding to Proverbs 5:5, 'the lips of a strange woman drop as an honeycomb, and her mouth is smoother than oil . . . Her feet go down to death; her steps take hold on hell'.

taking the primrose path: pursuing pleasure in a way that will probably bring ruin (the phrasing potentially alludes to Shakespeare's *Hamlet*, I. iii. 49 and *Macbeth* II. iii. 15).

293 *What would he look at a rainbow for?*: Blanco's interest in the rainbow was explained more clearly in lines that Shaw deleted from the text prior to publication. In a prepublication version of his script, Shaw planned to include the following:

> BLANCO. Did you notice where the end of that rainbow touched the prairie? That is where I should look for the horse if it was mine.
>
> ELDER DANIELS. I told you he was not right in his head, Sheriff. What would he look at a rainbow like that for if he was in his senses?
>
> (*SUBP* Rev, fo. 41)

cinch: firm or secure hold.

shammin mad: pretending to be crazy.

Cut it short: when he published the play, Shaw deleted a line here that showed Blanco retaliating to the foreman's insult. Shaw had intended for Blanco to

give the feisty response to the foreman, 'When your turn comes, there wont
be any delay, because they'll find the horse, and you on it' (*SUBP* Rev, fo. 42).

294 *By Gum!*: By God!

And theyve got the thief too: when Shaw prepared the play for publication,
he cut a line here that would have emphasized both Blanco's hostility to
the other characters and the way that Blanco shares their curiosity. In an
early prepublication version of his script, Shaw planned for Blanco to ask,
'Got who, you fool? What are you talking about?' (*SUBP* rev, fo. 45).

295 *jade*: hussy.

croup: childhood inflammatory disease affecting the larynx and trachea,
characterized by a sharp distinctive cough, and often proving fatal in
a short time.

little Judas: traitor, a reference to the biblical character of Judas Iscariot
(d. *c.*30 CE), the Apostle who betrayed Christ.

296 *dabbled red crest*: his stained/soiled hair arranged in an upright tuft.

betraying him with a kiss: cf. Luke 22:48, 'Jesus said unto him, Judas,
betrayest thou the Son of man with a kiss?'

297 *holt*: hold, grip.

299 *jiggered*: this term is used as a substitute for a profane oath.

maypole: tall thin woman.

sleep: although Nestor may appear to be unconscious in this published
version of the script, Shaw had intended the character to speak the lines
that would stir Blanco into preaching. Before publication, Shaw deleted
the following lines that he had drafted:

> NESTOR Don't make ~~me~~ <him> cry again, Robert. Have
> compassion. Where's your wit. Why don't you ask him does his
> mother know he's out?

> BLANCO. Because they're afraid they might grow to be as ghastly
> a thing as you that never was either a young man or an old one
> because you never were a man at all (suddenly raising his head)
> Boys: hand him out; and I'm going to preach . . .

(*SUBP* rev, fos. 54–5)

300 *Skiddoo*: go away.

failure: in an early prepublication version of his script, Shaw then planned for
Blanco to deliver some additional lines about the nature of morality in the USA:

> BLANCO . . . I tell you this glorious Republic has started on a wrong
> notion—a notion of two paths—the broad one leading to destruc-
> tion and the straight and narrow one going the other way.

> THE OTHER BOY A few there be that find it.

> BLANCO. A rotten sight fewer find the other way, my lad. I tell you
> that every man that pretends to be on one of these paths has one
> foot in the other all the time. Here is brother Daniels, your Elder,

set out to be a good man. Well, he's a rotten failure at it—a whiskey-selling, money-lending fraud.

ELDER DANIELS. I never said I hadnt my faults, Blanco. But I humbly hope for mercy in the end.

BLANCO. Aye: sneak out of it. Beg your way into heaven instead of kicking down the door and going in by right as a real good man would. But I dont reproach you brother. Am I any better?

ELDER DANIELS. No, Blanco. (Great laughter)

BLANCO. Who said I was? I'm a worse sort of fraud, because I'm a commoner sort.

(*SUBP* Rev, fos. 57–8)

300 *turning-the-other-cheek*: cf. Christ's words in Matthew 5:39, 'whosoever shall smite thee on thy right cheek, turn to him the other also'.

vale of tears: used in some translations of Psalm 84 (the 'valle lacrimarum' of the Vulgate translation), the phrase used by Christians to refer to the sorrows of earthly life.

the golden rule: 'Therefore all things whatsoever ye would that men should do to you, do ye even so to them' (Matthew 7:12) / 'And as ye would that men should do to you, do ye also to them likewise' (Luke 6:31).

301 *rips*: coarse, immoral, disreputable women.

302 *bully*: capital, first rate.

What do you know about Him . . . get it off me again: Blanco's two lengthy dialogues about God here were substantially revised in order to make them less blasphemous than Shaw originally intended. In an early prepublication version of his script, Shaw intended to highlight the incompetence and powerlessness of God by having Blanco saying (instead of the lines published in 1911):

Not even Him. He was beat by the croup. Why did the child die? First He made the croup when He was thinking of one thing; and then He made the child when he was thinking of something else; and the croup got past Him and killed the child. Some of us will have to find out how to kill the croup, I guess. That's a man's work if you like: I think I'll turn doctor, just on the chance of getting back on Him by doing something He couldn't do. But dont lets have any more rot about good men and bad men and the two paths. In future I shall do what Ive blooming got to do: thats how I size it up.

(*SUBP* Rev, fo. 60)

would there: in an early prepublication version of his script, Shaw planned here for Blanco to make the declaration, 'A blessed consolation!' The fact that Shaw deleted this reference prior to publication indicates that, although the censor found the perceived blasphemy in the published text unacceptable, Shaw had planned a script that was somewhat more irreligious in places (*SUBP* Rev, fo. 62).

Seek the path . . . good and bad: this passage has a strongly biblical emphasis. The Book of Psalms repeatedly makes reference to the 'paths of the
Lord', most famously Psalm 23:3 ('he leadeth me in the paths of right-
eousness for his name's sake'). Matthew 7:13–14 declares how 'wide is the
gate, and broad is the way, that leadeth to destruction . . . strait is the gate,
and narrow is the way, which leadeth unto life'. Elsewhere, Galatians 3:28
announces that 'There is neither Jew nor Greek, there is neither bond nor
free, there is neither male nor female: for ye are all one in Christ Jesus'.

303 *same as when you swore a lie to save my neck*: Shaw emphasized the importance
of this line. In a letter to the producer of a revival of the play in 1926, Shaw
wrote, 'Without that line the audience thinks that Feemy did not see Blanco on
the horse and was perjuring herself at the beginning, whereas the whole point
of the thing is that she was telling the truth, but at the last moment "went soft"
and called on God to strike her dead (at the risk of being taken at her word) if
she ever saw him or the horse' (*CL* iv. 31, letter of 11 November 1926).

GREAT CATHERINE (WHOM GLORY STILL ADORES)

The Author's Apology for Great Catherine was first published in abbreviated
form in *Everybody's Magazine* (New York) (February 1915), 193–212, then in
Heartbreak House, Great Catherine, and Playlets of the War (London: Constable,
1919), and republished under the same title by Constable for the standard edition in 1931.

The play was first performed at London's Vaudeville Theatre on 18
November 1913. The play-text was first published in German translation as *Die
Grosse Katharina* in the *Neue Rundschau* (Berlin) (April 1914); Shaw's English
script was first published in *Everybody's Magazine* (New York) (February
1915), 193–212, with illustrations by Henry Raleigh (1880–1944). It was first
published in England in the anthology *Heartbreak House, Great Catherine, and
Playlets of the War* (London: Constable, 1919), and republished under the same
title by Constable for the standard edition in 1931.

307 *Great Catherine*: German-born Empress Catherine II, known as 'Catherine
the Great', is remembered as one of Russia's greatest monarchs (r. 1762–96).
During her time in power, Russia expanded rapidly, extending into Crimea
and into much of Poland. Her rule also saw widespread legal and administrative reforms.

Grimm . . . Voltaire: Friedrich Melchior Grimm (1723–1807) was an
author and critic. Voltaire was the pen name of François-Marie Arouet
(1694–1778), the humanistic, sceptical, and empirical philosopher with
whom Catherine the Great corresponded. His prolific output in a variety
of forms rivalled that of Shaw, and, like Shaw, Voltaire was known for
a ready wit as well as a willingness to demolish conventional religious and
cultural beliefs. Shaw's contemporaries sometimes made comparisons
between him and Voltaire, and thus, in *Great Catherine*, Voltaire resembles
a kind of proto-Shaw, another argumentative writer who suffers from
headaches and will make 'you laugh whilst he is convincing you'. (339)

307 *Patiomkin*: Grigory Aleksandrovich Potemkin (1739–91), the military strategist, statesman, and lover of Catherine the Great, was the subject of many unverifiable stories, including the rumour that he and Catherine were secretly married. For almost two decades he was the most powerful man in Russia, and remained close to Catherine even when she took other lovers. Jeremy Bentham admired Potemkin as 'Prince of Princes', but others looked upon the statesman's political scheming and sexual appetites with less affection. An early German publication about Potemkin labelled him 'Prince of Darkness': J. F. E. Albrecht, *Pansalvin, Fürst der Finsternis, und seine Geliebte* (Germanien [Gera]: Heinsius, 1794). Shaw deliberately chose to render the character's name as 'Patiomkin' in the play after coming to believe that 'Potemkin is wrong and out of date' (British Library, Add. MS 50572, 'La Grande Catherine', fo. 3).

humbug: trick.

Peters, Elizabeths, and Catherines: Peter I ('the Great', 1672–1725), Peter II (1715–30), Peter III (1728–62); Elizabeth Petrovna (1709–62); Catherine I, originally called Marta Skowronska (1684–1727).

308 *harlequinade*: a sort of pantomime.

Guignol Theatre: dramatic entertainment characterized by short pieces of a sensational, violent, and macabre nature; chiefly performed at the Théâtre du Grand Guignol in Paris.

Byron: George Gordon Noel Byron (1788–1824), poet who, in *Don Juan*, ignored most of Catherine's work and characterized her as a woman of large sexual appetite.

English country gentleman: i.e. the character Edstaston.

bushels of plays: Catherine authored numerous comedies, historical plays, and opera libretti. Her best-known play is her comedy *Oh, These Times!* (1772).

'the onlie begetter': cf. the dedication of Shakespeare's sonnets to 'Mr. W.H.'.

Gertrude Kingston: real name Gertrude Angela Kohnstamm (1862–1937), actress.

309 *Pinero's Trelawny of the Wells*: comic play by Arthur Wing Pinero, in which the middle-aged character of Mrs Telfer declares of queens that 'I have played thirteen of 'em. And, as parts, they are not worth a tinker's oath' (London: Heinemann, 1899), 45.

a tinker's oath: something neither scarce nor valuable.

as Wagner and Thomas Hardy have done: between 1904 and 1908 Thomas Hardy (1840–1928) published the experimental verse drama *The Dynasts* that was subtitled 'a drama of the Napoleon wars, in three parts, nineteen acts, & one hundred and thirty scenes' (London: Macmillan, 1910). The major innovation of Richard Wagner was the *Gesamtkunstwerk* (total theatre), an aesthetic combination of poetry, music, dance, and theatre architecture.

310 *Horatios*: a reference to the emotionally uncomplicated and relatively undeveloped character who is a loyal friend to Hamlet in Shakespeare's play.

Shakespear's Orlandos and Bassanios and Bertrams: Orlando is the brave male character who marries Rosalind in *As You Like It* (probably written early 1600); Bassanio wins Portia in *The Merchant of Venice* (probably written in 1596) by famously picking a lead casket over a gold or silver one; and Bertram features in *All's Well that Ends Well* (probably written in 1605), where he is married to Helena. Not one of these figures has the depth or complexity of Hamlet or Macbeth.

Burbage: Richard Burbage (1568–1619), actor who collaborated with Shakespeare. He first brought some of Shakespeare's best-known characters to the stage, and was named in Shakespeare's will.

twenty arms like an Indian god: Shaw is likely thinking of figures such as Ganesha, who is often depicted with four arms; the goddess of destruction Kali, with up to eighteen arms; and the guardian deity Yamantaka, with thirty-two arms.

Kean . . . Sullivan: the actors Edmund Kean (1787–1833) and Barry Sullivan (1821–91). Sullivan's performances at Dublin's Theatre Royal between 1870 and 1873 had a profound and lasting effect on Shaw.

Knowles . . . Tennyson: Sheridan Knowles (1784–1862), playwright who created a number of plays for William Macready at Covent Garden in the 1820s and 1830s; Edward Bulwer-Lytton (1803–73), politician and writer, who wrote five plays for William Macready between 1836 and 1840; William Gorman Wills (1828–91), dramatist and portrait painter, whose *Charles I* was performed for 180 nights in 1872–3 with the part of the king played by Henry Irving; Alfred, Lord Tennyson: the poet whose first successful stage piece was *The Cup*, starring Irving and Ellen Terry (see note to p. 310), in 1881, with Irving later producing Tennyson's *Thomas à Becket* in 1893.

Robertson . . . Pinero . . . Barrie: Thomas William Robertson (1829–71), playwright credited with writing sixty-one plays in his short life, whose 'cup-and-saucer' dramas reacted against melodramatic excess. Shaw watched a revival of Roberton's best-known work *Caste* in 1879, and declared, 'After years of sham heroics and superhuman balderdash, *Caste* delighted everyone by its freshness, its nature, its humanity' (Shaw, *The Drama Observed*, ed. Dukore, iii. 877). Arthur Wing Pinero, playwright whose work sought to deal with social problems of day-to-day existence, such as *The Second Mrs Tanqueray* (1893) in which a 'woman with a past' commits suicide. Nonetheless, in the *Saturday Review* in the late 1890s, Shaw had declared 'my school is in violent reaction against that of Mr Pinero' (G.B.S., 'Mr. Pinero's New Play', review of 16 March 1895, repr. in Shaw, *Our Theatres in the Nineties*, i. 59–66, at 65). Barrie created Peter Pan, but also authored the 1902 historical play *Quality Street*, which discusses the restrictions of gender, and *The Admirable Crichton*, a satirical take on contemporary attitudes towards class. At one point Shaw declared, 'He gave you the impression that for all his playfulness he had hell in his soul' (Shaw, *The Drama Observed*, Dukore, iv. 1479).

310 *Caesar*: in Shaw's 1898 play *Caesar and Cleopatra* the author set out a fictional version of the relationship between Julius Caesar and Cleopatra, but sought to replace Shakespeare's version of Caesar with a character who would be 'a simple return to nature and history' (Shaw, quoted by Archibald Henderson, *George Bernard Shaw: Man of the Century* (New York: Appleton-Century-Crofts, 1956), 556). Shaw therefore looked to Forbes-Robertson, the best-known Shakespearean actor of the day, to help make the point that Shakespeare had been transcended or replaced. Forbes-Robertson played Shaw's Caesar in 1906–7.

Ellen Terry: (1847–1928), actress who exchanged numerous letters with Shaw at the turn of the century. Shaw invited her to play Lady Cecily Waynflete in his play *Captain Brassbound's Conversion*, having based the character on her. Terry later reflected, 'we developed a perfect fury for writing to each other! Sometimes the letters were on business, sometimes they were not, but always his were entertaining, and mine were, I suppose, "good copy" as he drew the character of Lady Cecily Waynflete in *Brassbound* entirely from my letters' (Terry, 'Mr Shaw', in *Shaw: Interviews and Recollections*, ed. A. M. Gibbs (Houndmills: Macmillan, 1990), 162–3, at 163).

Captain Brassbound's Conversion: play that revolves around its sole female character, Lady Cecily Waynflete. Shaw told Terry, 'never was there a part so deeply written for a woman as this for you' (quoted by Hesketh Pearson, *Bernard Shaw: His Life and Personality* (New York: Atheneum, 1963), 213). Janet Achurch originally played the part when the piece premiered in 1900, but Terry consequently took the role at the Royal Court in 1906.

The Devil's Disciple: Shaw's play of 1897 about the character of Dick Dudgeon, who in the American War of Independence appears to be a dangerous freethinker ('the devil's disciple'), but is actually altruistic and self sacrificing.

cordon bleu: (Fr.) 'blue ribbon', usually worn as part of the insignia of a knightly order.

potboiler: a dramatist who creates works to make a living by pandering to popular taste and ignoring artistic quality.

311 *Richard Mansfield*: (1857–1907), an actor and producer who actually disliked Shaw, but enjoyed a long New York run when he produced and starred in *The Devil's Disciple*, which provided Shaw's first financial success in the theatre.

William Terriss . . . assassinated: (1847–97), actor known for playing heroic roles, who told Shaw in February 1896 that he planned to do an international tour, and would like to include in his repertoire a play containing 'every "surefire" melodramatic situation' (quoted by Michael Holroyd, *Bernard Shaw*, 4 vols (London: Chatto & Windus, 1988–92), i. 393). Terriss was fatally stabbed in December 1897 as he arrived at the stage door of the Adelphi Theatre. The murderer was a fellow actor, Richard Arthur / Archer Prince (1865–1936) who had become delusional.

Frankenstein's monster: an ugly and hotchpotch creation which might end up punishing its creator, as in Mary Shelley's *Frankenstein; or, the Modern Prometheus* (1818).

Louis Calvert: (1859–1923), actor, who in the mid-1890s was playing parts in an assortment of Shakespeare plays (including *Julius Caesar*, *Richard II*, and *Antony and Cleopatra*), but who in 1904 took the role of Broadbent in Shaw's *John Bull's Other Island* at the Court Theatre.

Mrs Patrick Campbell: Beatrice Stella Campbell, née Tanner (1865–1940), who had played significant roles in plays such as Pinero's *The Second Mrs Tanquery* before, in 1914, she starred as Eliza Doolittle in Shaw's *Pygmalion* at His Majesty's Theatre.

Helen of Euripides: many felt that the best performance of the actress Gertrude Kingston was her portrayal of Helen in Granville Barker's 1905 version of *The Trojan Women* by Euripides. Shaw had suggested this casting to Granville Barker, 'comparing her, not with the ideal Helen of your imagination, but with the next best Helen you are likely to get' (quoted in Bernard F. Dukore, *Bernard Shaw, Director* (London: George Allen & Unwin, 1971), 40).

'How oft the sight of means to do ill deeds makes deeds ill done!': lines spoken by the titular character in Shakespeare's *King John*, IV. ii. 218–19.

312 *Winter Palace, St Petersburg*: residence of the Russian tsars. The fourth and final Winter Palace, a building of considerable pomp and luxury, was built in 1754–62 by the Italian architect Bartolomeo Francesco Rastrelli (1700–71). In 1762, Catherine assumed the throne and dismissed Rastrelli, replacing much of the Baroque interior with Neoclassical decor.

Versailles du Roi Soleil: in France between 1661 and 1710, the 'Sun King' (Louis XIV, 1638–1715) transformed the Palace of Versailles into an enormous and opulent complex to glorify the monarchy.

roubles: the main monetary unit of Russia, with a rouble being worth 100 kopeks.

313 *Varinka*: Varvara Engelhardt (1757–1815), who was, in real life, both the niece and the lover of Potemkin.

Cossack: name of a warlike Turkish people occupying land to the north of the Black Sea. From their number came the body of horsemen that formed an important element of the Russian army.

old Fritz of Prussia: Frederick the Great, king of Prussia, 1740–86.

kvass: a Russian fermented drink with a low alcohol content.

General Volkonsky: Prince Mikhail Volkonskii (1713–89), a well-known aristocrat who supported Catherine when she seized the throne.

314 *Sot!*: a person who stupefies himself by drinking alcohol.

315 *Light Dragoon*: originally the British Army's mounted infantry, whose members often won a reputation for bravery. Notoriously, during the

Crimean War (1853–6), the 13th Light Dragoons were at the forefront of the doomed Charge of the Light Brigade.

315 *Edstaston*: a fictional caricature of Englishness. Charlotte Shaw's family on her mother's side (the Kirbys) owned the estate of Edstaston, near the county town of Wem in Shropshire, and in 1905 Bernard Shaw spent an enjoyable visit there with his sister-in-law and her husband. Shaw later wrote that, in the play, the character's name should be 'pronounced Ette-stass-tun', and described the character as demonstrating 'English stiffness' (British Library, Add. MS 50572, 'La Grande Catherine', fos. 5–6).

316 *rebellion in America*: the American Revolutionary War of 1775–83. During 1776, the year in which this play is set, Congress adopted its Declaration of Independence (on 4 July), announcing the separation of thirteen North American British colonies from Great Britain.

317 *Cambridge*: the university based in East Anglia since the thirteenth century.

Bunker's Hill: the Battle of Bunker Hill, fought in Charlestown on 17 June 1775, during the Siege of Boston. This first major battle of the American Revolutionary War saw the British suffer heavy casualties of more than 1,000 soldiers, and showed that—although the British Army won a tactical victory—those Crown forces could be matched by the colonists. Shaw had originally thought about naming the 'battle of Nimeguen' here, referring to a force of 4,000 English soldiers who fought a bloody battle with the French after signing a treaty in 1677 (*GC* Type, fo. 10).

vinegar borle: vinegar bottle (delivered in intoxicated voice, in the same way that 'letter' has just been rendered 'lerrer').

319 *paladin*: a famous, knightly hero.

321 *what happened to Peter . . . Orlov murdered him*: Peter III, emperor of Russia, married Catherine in 1745 but alienated her and became deeply unpopular. Catherine believed he was planning to divorce her, and so overthrew him to become empress in his place. He formally abdicated, and was put into the custody of one of her supporters who had plotted to overthrow him, Aleksey Grigoryevich Orlov (1737–1808), whose brother was also Catherine's lover. Orlov murdered Peter on 18 July 1762. Catherine may not have ordered the killing, although public opinion held her responsible.

petit lever: (Fr.) the ceremonial event where a select group from the court served the monarch as she rose, dressed, and prepared for the day.

322 *toilette*: (Fr.) the process of washing/dressing/arranging the hair.

Fi donc!: (Fr.) For shame!

Popof: Vasily Stephanovich Popov (1745–1822), Potemkin's secretary chancellor.

324 *Princess Dashkoff*: Ekaterina Romanovna Dashkova (1743–1810), a Russian princess and author who founded the Russian Academy and aided the coup that brought Catherine to power.

Naryshkin, the Chamberlain: Lev Naryshkin (1733–99), a witty and aristocratic chamberlain, considered by the real Catherine at one point to be 'the most trustworthy person I have among this nation' (quoted by Simon Dixon, *Catherine the Great* (London: Profile, 2009), 143).

Potztausend!: (Ger.) 'Upon my soul!', strong expression of astonishment.

325 *Elizabeth*: Tsar Elizabeth Petrovna, who on her death passed the throne to Catherine's husband Peter III.

kopek: a Russian copper coin.

326 *March him baby, / Baby, baby, / Lit-tle ba-by bumpkins*: to be sung to the following tune:

(*GC* Type, fo. 26).

in canon, a third above: Varinka starts the same piece after a delay, and harmonizes (as in the notation above, singing in an interval of a major third above the notes sung by Patiomkin).

327 *sober in Siberia*: i.e. exiled to Siberia. For example, Catherine sent Aleksandr Nikolayevich Radishchev (1749–1802) to Siberia after he wrote *A Journey from St Petersburg to Moscow* (1790), which had been designed to inform the monarch about poor living conditions.

328 *fishfag*: a woman who sells fish, a fishwife.

Schweig, du Hund: (Ger.) Silence, you dog.

329 *Mr Pitt's business*: William Pitt the Elder (1708–78), prime minister 1756–61 and 1766–8. At the time in which this play is set, Pitt was ill, but he would speak out in 1777 in an abortive attempt to prevent the American colonies from breaking away.

332 *Neva*: major river in St Petersburg.

coxcomb: a foolish, conceited, vain person.

334 *epigastrium*: the upper central abdomen.

Holy Nicholas: St Nicholas (fourth century CE), patron saint of Russia.

the Gazette: the *London Gazette*, an official British government journal.

335 *He has broken my sweetbread*: a sweetbread is a pancreas. Originally Shaw intended this line not to be 'broken my sweetbread' but to read 'break my sword in two' (*GC* Type, fo. 39).

336 *polonaise*: a stately and slow dance, originating in Poland, revolving mainly around a complicated march of dancers in couples.

a brass band: Shaw specified that he needed 'to have one of the new gramophones to play the ballroom music with the effect of a first rate military band whenever the curtains are opened in the last scene' (*CL* iv. 40, letter of 2 February 1927).

337 *Also [the German word]*: so.

 exsufflicate: puffed up, inflated.

338 *Donnerwetter!*: (Ger.) Oh my goodness!

 Peter the Great: Peter I believed his son, Alexis (1690–1719), guilty of treasonously trying to overthrow him. Alexis was condemned to death, and died from the after-effects of torture.

339 *L'Homme aux Quarante Écus*: *The Man of Forty Crowns*, a piece written by Voltaire in 1768, consisting of dialogues, letters, and commentaries. Voltaire (a landowner himself) reacts here against a proposal by the economist Le Mercier de la Rivière (1719–1801) to replace all taxes with a single tax on land income.

 Ausgezeichnet!: (Ger.) Admirable/fantastic!

 Wie komisch!: (Ger.) How strange!

 Church of England: the Christian Established Church in England. Voltaire, whilst believing in the reality of a benign deity, felt repelled by institutional Christianity.

340 *Geliebter!*: (Ger.) Beloved!

343 *Redowa*: the music for a ballroom dance in 3/4 or 3/8 time, based on Bohemian folk music.

345 *[ironically, in German] So!*: I see!

 Alle Wetter!!!: (Ger.) My goodness!!!

346 *Spire View . . . Devon*: an imaginary address in the county of Devon, in the south-west of England.

THE SIX OF CALAIS

The Prefatory was published in *The Simpleton, The Six, and the Millionairess: Being Three More Plays by Bernard Shaw* (London: Constable, 1936).

 Shaw gave this piece the early working title of *The Bourgeois de Calais* (*Six* MS, fo. 1). It was first performed at Regent's Park Open Air Theatre on 17 July 1934. The play-text was privately printed in English in 1934, and a German translation by Siegfried Trebitsch was published as 'Die Sechs von Calais' in the *Neue Freie Press* (Vienna), 25 December 1934, pp. 25–8. In 1936 Shaw's script was published as part of the anthology *The Simpleton of the Unexpected Isles; Six of Calais; The Millionairess* (London: Constable, 1936).

351 *coiffure*: style of wearing her hair and attiring her head.

 Great Edward's grandson and his queen Philippa: Edward III (1312–77), who was grandson of Edward I (1239–1307), and Philippa of Hainault (c.1310/15–69).

 thrasonic: boastful.

 Edward Plantagenet the Third: Edward III. By traditional accounts, his father, Edward II (1284–1327), struggled to reign in the powerful barons.

Edward II was then executed after his queen Isabella (1292–1358) moved to depose him by uniting with the baronial figure of Roger Mortimer (*c*.1287–1339). Although the queen and Mortimer then installed Edward III on the throne, and started to govern in his name, by the time of his eighteenth birthday the young king ordered Mortimer seized and executed, and began the period of his own personal rule.

rent their garments: in the Bible, the rending or tearing of clothes is often a sign of rage or distress.

352 *Richelieu*: historical verse drama of 1839 by Bulwer-Lytton.

The School For Scandal: comic play first performed in 1777, written by Richard Brinsley Sheridan.

As You Like It: in Shakespeare's play, Rosalind is the quick-witted heroine and Jaques a somewhat detached observer who delivers the famous speech beginning 'All the world's a stage' (II. vii. 138–65).

Millamant: witty character in *The Way of the World*, a play by William Congreve (1670–1729) first performed in 1700.

concupiscent: lustful.

Siddons: see note to p. 197. In reality, for the first performance of Shaw's play the part of Philippa was taken by Phyllis Neilson-Terry (1892–1977).

Froissart: Jean Froissart (*c*.1333–*c*.1400), poet and historian of the Hundred Years War, whose account of the Siege of Calais (in his *Chronicles*) helped Shaw to write his play. The quotation here appears adapted from either Barry St Leger's *Stories from Froissart* (London: Henry Colburn, 1832), 258; or *The Chronicles of Froissart*, trans. by Lord Berners (New York: Collier Press, 1910), 75.

ON THE HIGH SEAS: four days before Shaw wrote this, he began sailing from Cape Town on board RMS *Windsor Castle*, for a seventeen-day return cruise to Southampton.

353 *last day of the siege*: in 1346, the English troops of Edward III won the Battle of Crécy against the French troops of Philip VI. Afterwards, the port of Calais withstood an English siege for nearly a year until being starved out. Calais finally surrendered on 4 August 1347.

Edward III: king of England and lord of Ireland, and duke of Aquitaine. When Shaw wrote a description of the Siege of Calais in 1920, prior to writing the play itself in 1934, he was already denigrating Edward's actions by writing: 'Instead of admiring the men of Calais for holding out against him so long, and yielding only to famine, he, in mere doglike vengeance, demanded that they should send him six of their leading citizens that he might murder them in cold blood . . . He wanted the animal satisfaction of hurting the thing that had hurt him; and he clamored for the heads of his six enemies to be cut off' (*Six* Pref).

Philippa of Hainault: originally from Hainault (Hainaut) in what is now Belgium, she became Edward's wife and queen of England. The marriage required a papal dispensation because the two were second cousins, and the wedding was confirmed at York Minster in 1328. When Shaw wrote a description of the Siege of Calais in 1920, prior to writing the play itself in 1934, he was already praising Philippa by declaring: 'she must have been extraordinarily skilful in managing her husband. She then said that she wanted the six burgesses to do what she liked with. Edwafd [*sic*], furious as he was, knew better than to refuse. He only permitted himself to say that he wished she were somewhere else, not specifying the place, as a modern husband might have done, And [*sic*] he handed over the six burgesses. They were awaiting death in their shirts, and they had had little to eat for a year. With the practicality of her sex, she dressed them and fed them before setting them free' (*Six* Pref).

353 *flying*: Shaw's 1934 proof of the play adds an additional direction here, '*The engines of the besiegers, mostly movable wooden towers, rear themselves behind the tents*', but Shaw came to realize the impracticality of this direction and revised it after the first performance in Regent's Park on 17 July 1934 (*Six* Proof 1, p. 1).

Black Prince: Edward of Woodstock (1330–76), eldest son of Edward III and Philippa of Hainault. He was 17 at the end of the siege of Calais, but would never ascend to the throne, suffering from what were probably repeated attacks of dysentery, and dying at the age of 45. Shaw had not included this character in the script until a very late stage: he had originally given the prince's lines to the nobleman Sir Walter Manny, and only changed this when correcting the proofs, introducing the character of the Black Prince, and relegating Manny to a minor, unspeaking role in the play (*Six* Proof 1). The Black Prince's name may refer to the colour of his armour or his 'black' reputation in France.

John of Gaunt: (1340–99), fourth son of Edward III and Philippa of Hainault. He was 7 years old, and the earl of Richmond, at the end of the siege of Calais.

wax: a fit of anger. Shaw's 1934 proof of the play originally indicated a more formal relationship between John of Gaunt and Edward III here, with John referring to 'The King' rather than 'father' (*Six* Proof 1, p. 1).

Gogswoons: by God. Corruption of 'God's wounds', an expression used, for example, in *The Taming of the Shrew*, viii. 33.

aged 35: Shaw added this detail to the script before publication but after the play's first performance. In reality the king was 34 at the time of the events described in the drama (*Six* Proof 2, p. 1).

354 *herald*: an officer who bears messages between princes or sovereign powers.

unborn child: in his *Chronicles*, Jean Froissart describes the queen as being 'great with child' at the end of the siege of Calais. Froissart refers to the unborn child as Princess Margaret (1346–61), although in reality Margaret had been born in Windsor more than a year before, and it is more likely that Froissart was thinking of the queen being pregnant with her largely forgotten and short-lived son Thomas (summer 1347–8?), who was born at Windsor Castle.

355 *burgesses*: citizens of the town.

aged 33: Shaw added this detail at a late stage to his play, after the first performance but before the play was first published. In reality, the queen's date of birth is uncertain: she may have been born on 24 June 1310 but may not have been born until 1315, so she could have been between 31 and 37 at the time of the events depicted (*Six* Proof 2, title page).

posset: a drink, often given for medicinal reasons, usually made from hot milk mixed with alcohol and flavoured with sugar, spices or herbs.

St Anne: mother of the Virgin Mary, and patron saint of new mothers.

356 *malingreuse*: (Fr.) female person with a sickly appearance.

Sir Walter Manny: Sir Walter Mauny (*c.*1310–72), soldier and son of the Lord of Masny in Hainault, settled in England in 1327 after arriving in the country as a page to Philippa of Hainault. In 1920, Shaw saw him as one of the two heroes of the Siege of Calais, writing that 'The honors are to Queen Philippa and to Sir Walter Marny, to pity, chivalry and generosity'. When Shaw wrote the play in 1934 he originally gave the character of Manny a far larger part as the king's uncle. But before the script was first acted, Shaw decided to give all of Manny's lines to the Black Prince instead, and cut the words 'uncle', 'niece', and 'nephew' from the text (as well as apologizing to the producer at the Regent's Park theatre, where the play was being premiered, for sending a copy where 'you will find considerable confusion as to the way he [the Black Prince] is addressed'). (*Six* Syd, title page; and *Six* Pref).

Lords Derby, Northampton, and Arundel: Henry of Lancaster (*c.*1310–61) who was made earl of Derby in 1337 and who took part in the siege of Calais until the surrender; William de Bohun (*c.*1312–60), 1st Earl of Northampton, a close associate of Edward III; De Bohun participated in the early part of the siege of Calais; Richard Fitzalan (*c.*1313–76), 3rd Earl of Arundel and 8th Earl of Surrey, who was with the king at the siege of Calais.

Eustache de St Pierre: (*c.*1287–1371), one of the chief defenders of Calais, who led the delegation begging for mercy at the cost of their own lives. Shaw originally described this figure as 'the eldest burgess, the venerable Eustache de St Pierre', although he cut that description from the play before publication (*Six* Proof 2, p. 5).

de Wissant . . . d'Oudebolle: in the *Chronicles*—which guided Shaw when writing the play—Jean Froissart describes Piers de Wissant as one of the six who volunteered to suffer on behalf of the rest of Calais, and as the brother of Jacques de Wissant, who also volunteered. Jacques de Wissant is named in Froissart's *Chronicles* as one of the six who offered himself on behalf of the rest of Calais. He was apparently the owner of a rich family estate. Jean d'Aire is named in Froissart's *Chronicles* as the second man, after Eustache de St Pierre, who opted to sacrifice himself in exchange for the rest of Calais. According to Froissart, he was a well-respected and rich burgher with two beautiful daughters. Gilles d'Oudebolle is not named in the *Chronicles* by Froissart, as the historian names only four of the six burghers.

356 *Piers de Rosty (nicknamed Hardmouth)*: the most insolent of the burghers of Calais and a figure not named by Froissart. In 1934, when the play was premiered, Shaw wrote a programme note arguing that Auguste Rodin (1840–1917), who created the sculpture *The Bourgeois de Calais* in 1884–6, 'contributed the character of Peter Hardmouth; but his manner of creation was that of a sculptor and not that of a playwright. Nothing remained for me to do but correct Froissart's follies and translate Rodin into words.' Peter Hardmouth remained unnamed in Shaw's actual script, however, until the version that the author revised for publication after the play had been premiered: until then the character had simply been included in the text as 'the sixth' (*Six* Proof 2, p. 4).

357 *Peter*: i.e. Piers de Rosty, *not* Piers de Wissant.

his grandfather: Edward I, king of England and lord of Ireland, and duke of Aquitaine. Edward was known for his impressive achievements: he showed himself a peacemaker in Europe, mobilized massive military resources, and developed parliament.

Fie: an exclamation expressing reproach or disgust.

by Holy Paul: by St Paul; an expression used in, for example, *Richard III*, I. iii. 45.

360 *baulked of*: made to miss or omit intentionally.

shriven: having made confession of their sins (and therefore ready to face death and judgement).

what to expect: at the Battle of Crécy (1346) the English used cannon, the first recorded example of firearms being used during pitched battle in the Western world. Then at Calais, Edward besieged the town and at first refused any terms to the starving people.

trulls: prostitutes. See note to p. 409.

362 *scullion*: the lowest kind of domestic servant.

Holy Rood: the cross upon which Jesus died.

363 *Henpecked!*: ruled over or domineered by a wife.

mercer: person who deals in textiles, and especially fine fabrics.

countenance: moral support.

haberdasher: someone who deals in articles relating to dress, such as thread or ribbon.

Champagne: province in the north-east of France.

364 *cur*: dog.

stone: Shaw had intended Peter to respond to this put-down with the defiant line 'I can bite still with the teeth I have left', but cut that line after the first performance and before the play was published (*Six* Proof 2, p. 12).

distaff: the staff on which wool or flax would be wound in traditional spinning, and hence associated with women's work.

spunk: spirit (but also, from the 1890s, a slang term for seminal fluid).

donkey's bray: Shaw asked the first producer of the play, at the Open Air Theatre in Regent's Park, 'Can you find an actor who can bray like a donkey?' (card included to Sydney Carroll with *Six* Proof 1).

365 *distance*: in his 1934 proof Shaw had originally intended the written script to conclude with details of where and when the play had been composed, 'THE END / IN THE ATLANTIC / APPROACHING THE CHANNEL / 16th *May* 1934' (*Six* Proof 1, p. 12).

THE BRITISH PARTY SYSTEM

The play-text was printed as part of the third chapter of Shaw's *Everybody's Political What's What?* (London: Constable, 1944). I have found no record of a public performance being given. The title of the play refers to the system of politics based on competition between different organized groups.

369 *municipalities*: town, city, or district with local self-government.

Conservative . . . Progressive parties: the Conservatives are a major political party in the UK which grew out of the former Tory Party, and have tended to be supportive of traditional institutions. The Progressives are the political grouping that has generally opposed the Conservatives, and worked towards reform and change in society.

municipal councils and corporations: local rather than national governing bodies.

Althorp: the estate in Northamptonshire owned by the Spencer family since 1508.

William the Third: William of Orange (1650–1702), born in The Hague in the Netherlands and involved in a number of wars against the Catholic king of France. In 1689 he and his wife Mary were crowned joint rulers of England, Scotland (where he is known as William II), and Ireland in what became known as the 'Glorious Revolution'. He ousted the Catholic James II and VII (1633–1701), who was his maternal uncle and father-in-law, and thus ensured that Protestantism retained its position of primacy in Britain.

Robert Spencer: (1641–1702), 2nd Earl of Sunderland (from infancy), and a prominent British statesman. After serving as ambassador, he became secretary of state in 1679 for Charles II. He acted as adviser to both of the Catholic-leaning monarchs, Charles II and his successor James II, and announced his own conversion to Catholicism in 1688. With the invasion of the staunchly Protestant William of Orange, Spencer fled to the Netherlands. But in 1690 he returned to England, converted back to Anglicanism, and began to advise William. Spencer's keen political instincts proved valuable to the post-1689 monarchy, and the king repeatedly sought Spencer's advice from 1692. In particular, as Shaw notes, Spencer advised William to select all of his ministers from one political party, telling William to drop his policy of achieving a balanced ministry of both Tory and Whig figures, and instead favour the Whigs.

369 *Charles II*: (1630–85), king of England, Scotland, and Ireland.

Scarlet Woman of Rome: the Roman Catholic Church, perceived by some Protestants to be prefigured by the 'scarlet' woman of Revelation 17:4.

your country: Robert Spencer was born in Paris in 1641. The nobles and Paris Parlement had risen against the Crown in 1648.

Bourbons: the House of Bourbon, which produced the kings of France from 1589 to 1792 (including the epitome of absolute monarchy, Louis XIV, who occupied the throne from 1643 to 1714). England fought Louis's France in the War of the Grand Alliance from 1689 to 1697.

France's best general: January 1695 had seen the death of the duc de Luxembourg (1628–95), France's undefeated general.

Amsterdam: William III came from the Netherlands, the capital city of which has been widely recognized as Amsterdam since the early 1800s. After becoming British king, he had a fraught relationship with Amsterdam, where regents suspected him of subordinating Dutch interests to those of England.

Stadtholder: governor of a province or provinces. As stadtholder of Dutch provinces from 1672 to 1688, William enjoyed influence over municipal appointments, and gained the right to purge town administrations. However, Amsterdam was unusual in that the stadtholder there did not have the power to appoint the chief magistrate (equivalent to an English mayor).

370 *Pope*: head of the Roman Catholic Church, a position occupied from 1691 to 1700 by Innocent XII (1615–1700).

fat Bourbon bigot: Louis XIV (1638–1715), who revoked the Edict of Nantes—which had guaranteed some religious liberty to French Protestants—and who oversaw the persecution of that religious minority.

in Louis' pocket: in December 1688, James II and VII had been allowed to flee to France, where he died in 1701.

Whig . . . Tory: in about 1679 the term Whig was originally applied to the political faction opposed to James II and VII becoming king on the grounds of his Catholicism, the term Tory applied to the political faction supporting James's hereditary right.

371 *elector of Hanover*: when the British monarch Queen Anne (1665–1714) died without leaving any surviving children, the man who had been elector of Hanover from 1698 (and who had been in charge of day-to-day government of that electorate since 1694), Georg Ludwig (1660–1727), became George I, king of Britain and Ireland.

your sister-in-law's children continue to die: Queen Anne produced eighteen children, only five of whom were born alive, and only one of whom survived infancy (although that surviving boy also died in 1700).

enclosure of commons: converting areas of commonly held land into private property by use of boundaries or fences.

billeting: across early modern Europe, it had been common to quarter troops among local populations, with those civilians expected to bear the burden of providing food and shelter to the soldiers. When William of Orange arrived in England, the delicacy of the political situation meant that from 1688 billeting in private houses was forbidden except with pre-payment and permission of the owner. Soldiers were quartered in public houses and inns instead, except in Ireland, where billeting soldiers with local civilians continued.

window tax: a tax calculated on the basis of the number of windows in a house, imposed on England and Wales between 1696 and 1851.

372 *his seat*: the right to sit as Member of Parliament.

No Popery: anti-Catholicism.

Lilburne the Leveller: John Lilburne (1615?–57), member of the English Levellers who tried to level differences of position and rank among men.

died in the same year: 1702.

373 *Sunderland's son Charles*: Charles Spencer, 3rd Earl of Sunderland (1675–1722), was the son and heir of Robert Spencer. In 1695, Charles Spencer became a member of the House of Commons, and although his father had joined the Tories in 1694, Charles became a loyal Whig. Charles acted as Lord Lieutenant of Ireland, Lord Privy Seal, and Lord President of the Council. At the time that he appears in Shaw's play (1720) he was First Lord of the Treasury (a post he held between 1718 and 1721). In effect, he was now what we might recognize as prime minister, but, as Shaw's play anticipates, Charles Spencer's career would be ruined by the South Sea Bubble (a speculation mania that centred on the South Sea Company that traded largely in slaves with Spanish America, see note to p. 374). Spencer had helped to launch the scheme, seeing a chance to consolidate the national debt and reduce the interest payable, and so when the stock crashed he was held responsible by an angry public. Nonetheless, he found himself acquitted of the accusation of corruption thanks to a strong defence by Walpole. Spencer resigned as First Lord of the Treasury in April 1721, and was succeeded by Walpole.

Robert Walpole: Walpole (1676–1745) is generally regarded as the first prime minister of Britain, having acted as both First Lord of the Treasury and Chancellor of the Exchequer in 1715–17 and in 1721–42. The king, George I, struggled to speak English and felt uninterested in parliamentary business, so left Walpole to chair a grouping of ministers, which would be the forerunner of the later British cabinet. Walpole also occupied 10 Downing Street, which has been the home of British prime ministers ever since. But Shaw had little affection for this historic figure, describing him (in the preface to *Plays Unpleasant*) as corrupt.

373 *leads the Opposition to the Peerage Bill*: Walpole played a key part in defeating the Peerage Bill of 1719, which would have limited the monarch's ability to create new peers. On 7 December Walpole made one of his finest speeches, in opposition to the bill, which was duly defeated by 269 votes to 177.

St James's Park: large park in central London, surrounded by the Palace of Westminster, St James's Palace, and Buckingham Palace.

plain as a pikestaff: a proverbial phrase meaning extremely clear or obvious (a pikestaff is a kind of walking stick).

kill kingship with a single chop of the axe in Whitehall: the beheading of Charles I on 30 January 1649, against the wall of the Banqueting House in Whitehall.

Restoration: the return of the monarchy in England, Scotland, and Ireland in 1660, following the period of the Commonwealth.

374 *You are a peer: I am a commoner*: Sunderland became heir to the earldom of Sunderland in 1688 on the death of his elder brother.

House of Lords is the springboard from which you plunged into politics at 21: in real life, Spencer entered the House of Commons in 1695, and took a seat in the Lords on the death of his father in 1702. In the Lords, the young Sunderland played an active role, helping to defeat the Occasional Conformity Bill of 1703.

the shelf on which I shall be laid by at three score and ten: where I shall be put at the end of my life (three score and ten being the nominal length of a human life, i.e. $3 \times 20 + 10 = 70$ years).

South Sea madness: the South Sea company was a British joint-stock venture designed to reduce the national debt. The company had a monopoly to trade with South America, and stock in the company soared in value as part of a wider market boom. The price reached its peak on 24 June but the bubble burst in August, leaving the public finances in a parlous stage and generating calls for vengeance from those who had been ruined. Walpole led the official response to the crisis, gaining him an image—which is somewhat untrue—of a statesman who remained apart from the fever of speculation and who engaged with the business simply in order to assist his nation.

it will be the end of you politically: following the South Sea Bubble, Spencer resigned and was replaced by Walpole as First Lord of the Treasury in April 1721. Spencer died in April 1722.

THE DARK LADY OF THE SONNETS

Sonnets are short lyric poems of fourteen lines often expressing the travails of a lover. In 1609 a volume of 154 sonnets by William Shakespeare was published in a quarto version—the only printed edition in his lifetime—although some sonnets had circulated as early as 1598. More than four-fifths of this sonnet sequence celebrates a fair, male youth in strikingly homoerotic terms. The last twenty-eight sonnets, however, are addressed to a woman, the 'dark lady' (so called because of her black hair and eyes, and dull grey-brown skin). These poems describe the narrator's desire for sex with her. The critical view of Shakespeare that predominated in the nineteenth century tended to see the sequence as a biographical conundrum to be solved, and the 'dark lady' as a real historical person to be identified.

Shaw's preface was published in *Misalliance, The Dark Lady of the Sonnets, and Fanny's First Play* (London: Constable, 1914), and republished under the same title by Constable for the standard edition in 1932. The postscript of 1933 is reproduced from Shaw, *The Complete Prefaces of Bernard Shaw* (London: Paul Hamlyn, 1965), 770.

The play was first performed on 24 November 1910 at London's Haymarket Theatre. The play-text was first published in a German translation by Siegfried Trebitsch as 'Die schwarze Dame der Sonette', in the *Neue Freie Presse* (Vienna), 25 December 1910, pp. 31–6. Shaw's English version was published in the *English Review* (January 1911), 258–69, and *Redbook Magazine* (New York) (January 1911), 417–32. The script was then published in *Misalliance, The Dark Lady of the Sonnets, and Fanny's First Play* (London: Constable, 1914), and later republished under the same title by Constable for the standard edition in 1932.

379 *pièce d'occasion*: (Fr.) play written for a particular occasion.

a National Theatre as a memorial to Shakespear: this project enjoyed eventual but not immediate success. Two sites were abortively purchased for the National Theatre of the UK: the first in Gower Street in 1913, the second in Cromwell Gardens in 1937. But the National Theatre only began giving performances in 1963, when it was temporarily based at the Old Vic Theatre in London until a permanent home on the South Bank opened in 1976. The impetus to remember Shakespeare was taken up by the Royal Shakespeare Company (RSC), which the artistic director Peter Hall conceived as a state-supported, national company with actors on long contracts. The RSC was established in 1961, and developed the old Shakespeare festival at Stratford into a permanent company that performed throughout the whole year.

Mary Fitton: Fitton (bapt. 1578, d. 1641) had been at Elizabeth's court as maid of honour since roughly 1597, and in 1600 began a love affair with William Herbert (1580–1630). At a meeting of the New Shakspere Society in 1884, the scholar Thomas Tyler (1826–1902) argued that she must have been the 'dark lady' of Shakespeare's sonnets, and he continued arguing that case in subsequent publications. The theory gained widespread acceptance, particularly as her lover, William Herbert, had the same initials as the 'Mr W.H.' to whom the sonnet sequence is dedicated. However, as Shaw acknowledges, the identification was challenged by those who pointed to evidence that Fitton had a fair complexion.

379 *Mr Acheson*: Arthur Acheson (1864–1930), Shakespeare scholar and author of *Mistress Davenant: The Dark Lady of Shakespeare's Sonnets* (London: Bernard Quaritch, 1913).

Davenant: William Davenant (1606–68), dramatist, theatre manager, and poet, who according to John Aubrey (1626–97), jokingly commented that he 'writ with the very spirit that did Shakespeare, and seemed contented enough to be thought his son' (Aubrey, *Brief Lives*, ed. John Buchanan-Brown (London: Penguin, 2000), 101).

Edith Lyttelton: (1865–1948), author, close friend of Shaw, and member of the Shakespeare Memorial National Theatre Committee.

380 *Mr W.H.*: the figure to whom Shakespeare's Sonnets are dedicated.

Thomas Tyler: theological and literary scholar who suffered from birth with a goitrous disfigurement. He edited an 1886 edition of the Sonnets, and in his introduction argued that Mary Fitton was the 'dark lady'. He furthered his case in his 1890 edition of *Shakespeare's Sonnets* and his 1898 publication *The Herbert-Fitton Theory: A Reply*.

excrescential: redundant.

Romeo or Lovelace: Romeo Montague is one of the title characters of Shakespeare's *Romeo and Juliet*, described by Juliet as having 'a flow'ring face' (III. ii. 73). Richard Lovelace is the attractive-looking aristocrat who rapes the virtuous title character of the lengthy novel *Clarissa* by Samuel Richardson (1689–1761).

the Museum: in 1857, the British Museum Library opened a round reading room, with an impressive domed roof, where numerous writers would work. Shaw studied here after moving to London in 1876.

Ecclesiastes: Old Testament book of wisdom literature which Thomas Tyler translated to produce his study *Ecclesiastes, a Contribution to its Interpretation* (London: Williams & Norgate, 1874).

Swift: Jonathan Swift (1667–1745), writer and clergyman.

381 *Maria Tompkins*: i.e. anyone.

his edition of the Sonnets: William Shakespeare, *Shakspere's Sonnets, the First Quarto, 1609. A Facsimile in Photo-Lithography . . . with an Introduction by T. Tyler* (London: C. Praetorius, 1886).

I reviewed it in the Pall Mall Gazette: unsigned review, 'The Truth About Shakespeare', *Pall Mall Gazette*, 7 January 1886, pp. 4–5. Here Shaw praises Tyler for producing 'a masterpiece of critical sagacity'.

Koheleth: or Qoheleth, the writer of the book of Ecclesiastes.

the forgeries of the Pentateuch: in 1883 the Polish antiquities dealer Moses W. Shapira (*c*.1830–84) offered to the British Museum an apparently ancient manuscript, which followed the order of the Book of Deuteronomy but included some noteworthy variations not seen elsewhere. The manuscript had already been denounced as a forgery by experts in Germany, and in 1884 their British colleagues agreed. A disgraced Shapira committed suicide, although some researchers have since claimed that he may have been offering a genuine fragment of a Dead Sea Scroll.

382 *Frank Harris*: (1856–1931), writer who created the play *Shakespeare and His Love*, which recycled the idea that Mary Fitton was the 'dark lady' of Shakespeare's sonnets. Harris and Shaw were two Irish-born journalists and thinkers who emerged onto London's intellectual scene at roughly the same time. In the 1890s, Harris edited the *Saturday Review*, a publication for which Shaw wrote theatre reviews. At this stage, Harris looked the more successful figure: Harris had married a rich widow, was well connected in London, and was even considering a career as an MP. Shaw, by contrast, found himself struggling as an unsuccessful novelist and badly paid critic. But their respective statuses reversed at the start of the twentieth century. Shaw married his own millionairess in 1898 and went on to become one of London's leading personalities and cultural figures. Harris meanwhile edited a series of disastrously loss-making publications, showed himself to be an insatiable womanizer, and became a pariah in London society. Harris later wrote about his sexual adventures in the scandalous autobiography *My Life and Loves*, 4 vols (Paris: [privately printed], 1922–7).

wrote a play: Harris's *Shakespeare and His Love* was written by 1904 and apparently submitted to Granville Barker and J. E. Vedrenne (1867–1930) at the Court Theatre, who did not put it on stage but did pass it to Shaw. When Harris published the play in 1910 he attached an angry introduction saying that he had heard about Shaw's *The Dark Lady of the Sonnets*, and although he had not yet read that drama, 'it looks as if he had annexed my theory bodily so far as he can understand it, and the characters to boot' (Harris, *Shakespeare and His Love: A Play in Four Acts and an Epilogue* (London: Frank Palmer, 1910), p. viii). In an early version of the preface, Shaw wrote more about encountering Harris's play (although these lines did not appear in the published version of the preface): 'Mr. Harris alludes in his book to a play of his which has not yet been published or performed, and of which Shakespeare is the hero. Now it happens, by an accident for which Mr. Harris is not responsible, that I found or rather made (for I never lose an opportunity of reading anything of Mr. Harris's) an opportunity of reading this play' (*DLS* Carb, fo. 25).

Southampton: Henry Wriothesley, 3rd Earl of Southampton (1573–1624), courtier and literary patron.

383 *the Bismarckian Imperialist*: Bismarck's Prussian imperial state bolstered an authoritarian leadership and ensured the prominence of privileged social groups.

Anacharsis Klootz: pseudonym of Jean-Baptiste du Val-de-Grâce, baron de Cloots (1755–94), Prussian-born radical participant in the French Revolution, who declared that the whole world shared the democratic ideals of the Revolution.

Washington: first president of the United States in 1789–97, during which time his government maintained a neutral position with regard to the French Revolutionary Wars (1792–1802).

383 *Mrs Proudie*: the wife of the Bishop of Barchester, and a figure much concerned with maintaining appearances in *Barchester Towers* (1857) by Anthony Trollope (1815–82).

Aspasia: Aspasia of Miletus (fifth century BCE), mistress of Pericles, the Athenian statesman. In one account, she is said to have run a brothel.

John Knox: (*c*.1514–72), religious reformer, who from the Elizabethan period was taken up with enthusiasm by the Puritan segment of the Church of England.

To the Archbishop he is an atheist . . . respectable persons: Stanley Weintraub has observed, these 'lines explain much about the Shaw/Harris relationship. Shaw was cool, scrupulous, precise, generous, humane. Beneath the post of self-advertising egoist he was a shy man; beneath the clown's motley he masked a philosophic mood; beneath the Bunyanesque preacher he was a sentimental Irish romantic. While Shaw's sexual temperature was low, the Irish-born Harris, who fancied himself as a sentimental romantic, possessed a compulsion for lechery' ('Introduction', in Weintraub (ed.), *The Playwright and the Pirate: Bernard Shaw and Frank Harris: A Correspondence* (Gerrards Cross: Colin Smythe, 1982), pp. vii–xx, at pp. xii–xiii).

Sophie Perovskaia . . . Alexander II: Perovskaia (1853–81) was a Russian revolutionary who was hanged for her involvement in coordinating the bomb attack that killed Tsar Alexander II (1818–81).

Oh God, Horatio, . . . leave behind: cf. *Hamlet*, V. ii. 351–2.

his Sonia: refers to the short story 'Sonia', published in Frank Harris's *Montes the Matador and Other Stories* (London: Grant Richards, 1900). Here, the female revolutionary is described by one character as 'the one divine thing in the world, with her smiling pale face and God-illumined eyes'. When the fictional version of Sophie Perovskaia is about to hang, 'her courage lifted the soul and made the place sacred' (p. 253).

Chicago anarchists: refers to Harris's novel *The Bomb* (London: Long, 1908), about the Chicago bombing of 1886.

'Durch Mitleid Wissend': (Ger.) 'Made wise through pity', words taken from Wagner's opera *Parsifal* (Act I, Scene 2 ('Grail scene'), line 54, in Wagner, *Parsifal* (London: John Calder, 1986), 98).

384 *Milton's Lucifer*: central character in *Paradise Lost*, Milton's epic poem published in 1667.

Artemus Ward: pseudonym of Charles Farrar Browne (1834–67), American humorist who delivered comic lectures and influenced the work of Mark Twain (1835–1910).

Oscar Wilde: (1854–1900), writer. Shaw knew of Wilde's family in Dublin; then in the 1870s–80s Shaw was invited to the London at-homes of Wilde's mother, where he met Oscar, and the two men developed a rivalrous friendship.

the Queensberry trial: the 9th Marquess of Queensberry (1844–1900) felt enraged by the homosexual relationship that had developed between his son and Wilde. Queensberry left a misspelled card at Wilde's club accusing the author of 'posing as a somdomite', and Wilde then unwisely opted to pursue a libel action against the marquess (quoted by Merlin Holland, *Irish Peacock & Scarlet Marquess* (London: Fourth Estate, 2003), 300). However, the accusation of homosexuality was true, and Wilde thus endured public disgrace and imprisonment.

The Saturday Review: the *Saturday Review of Politics, Literature, Science, and Art*, a weekly Conservative London publication that appeared between 1855 and 1938. Frank Harris acted as proprietor-editor from 1894 to 1898.

Dorian Grey: Oscar Wilde's only novel, *The Picture of Dorian Gray*, the first version of which was published by *Lippincott's Magazine* in 1890. The novel tells of a man who retains an attractive appearance whilst debauchery affects his hidden portrait. Shaw idiosyncratically renders 'Gray' as 'Grey'.

study of Shakespear: Shaw refers here to Harris's book, *The Man Shakespeare and His Tragic Life Story* (London: Frank Palmer, 1909), in which Harris explains that Shakespeare 'was passion's slave, and had himself experienced with his dark mistress, Mary Fitton, the ultimate degradation of lust' (p. 301).

group of contributors: as editor of the *Saturday Review*, Harris solicited contributions from figures including Shaw; the art critic Dugald Sutherland MacColl (1859–1948); poet critic Arthur Symons (1865–1945); and drama critic Max Beerbohm (1872–1956).

'Sidney's Sister: Pembroke's Mother': lines from a poem about Mary Herbert, countess of Pembroke (1561–1621), 'Epitaph on the Countess of Pembroke' (in *The Works of Ben Jonson* (Boston: Phillips, Sampson, 1853), 815). Although the lines have often been ascribed to Ben Jonson, they were perhaps more likely written by William Browne (1590/1–c.1645). Mary Herbert herself was a writer and literary patron; the sister of courtier and poet Sir Philip Sidney (1554–86), who dedicated his *Arcadia* to her; and also the mother of William Herbert (1580–1630).

385 *Pembroke*: William Herbert, son of Mary Herbert.

Countess of Rousillon in All's Well That Ends Well: countess in Shakespeare's play who assists in arranging the marriage of her son to her ward.

his beloved mother: Mary Arden (c.1537–1608).

mother of Coriolanus in Plutarch: Greek biographer Plutarch (46–119 CE). The translation of Plutarch's work by Thomas North (c.1535–c.1603), entitled *Lives of the Noble Grecians and Romans*, provided source material for Shakespeare's play.

'one of these harlotry players': cf. Shakespeare's *Henry IV, part 1*, II. iv. 325.

that one: Mary Herbert, the subject of Ben Jonson's ensuing lines.

386 *Bardolatrous*: term coined by Shaw to describe those who blindly worshipped Shakespeare and whose efforts led to misguided interpretations of Shakespeare's work.

386 *Spenser*: Edmund Spenser (*c.*1552–99), poet, and administrator in Ireland, best known for his allegorical poem *The Faerie Queene* (1590, 1596).

More: Thomas More (1478–1535), Lord Chancellor, humanist, martyr, and author of *Utopia* (1516). Since Shaw wrote these lines, More's 'decent' nature has been questioned by revisionist writers, most notably by the English novelist Hilary Mantel (1952–).

Bunyan: John Bunyan (bapt. 1628, d. 1688), author, best known for *The Pilgrim's Progress* (1678/9).

Raleigh: Sir Walter Raleigh (1554–1618), explorer, courtier, and poet.

scriveners: professional penmen or scribes. Hamlet declares: 'I once did hold it [think] (as our statists [statemen] do) | A baseness [beneath me] to write fair, and laboured much | How to forget that learning' [scribes being lower-class workers] (V. ii. 34–6).

387 *The Two Gentlemen of Verona and their valets*: in Shakespeare's play written in about 1587, Valentine has a comic servant named Speed, and Proteus has a comic servant named Launce.

Adam: the kindly servant in *As You Like It*.

Eton and Harrow: boarding schools which were originally founded or endowed for public use (Eton in 1440 by Henry VI (1421–72), Harrow in 1572 by John Lyon (*c.*1514–92)), and later, chiefly from the nineteenth century, developed into fee-paying private secondary schools.

public elementary: the 1891 Elementary Education Act effectively introduced free rudimentary schooling. From this date, public elementary schools received 10 shillings a year from the state for each child taught, and schools in receipt of such grants could not ask for additional fees from pupils.

private adventure school: school established by an educational entrepreneur, which survived on the basis of charging fees to pupils.

coat of arms: in 1596, John Shakespeare was granted a coat of arms, about twenty-five years after he had first applied for them, in an application probably reactivated by William, who may himself have been keen to highlight his own status as a gentleman. The yellow colour of this design and its motto *Non sancz droict* (Not without right) were mocked in Jonson's *Every Man Out of His Humour*, where the clown Sogliardo proposes the motto 'Not without mustard' (ed. Helen Ostovich (Manchester: Manchester University Press, 2001), 232).

This Side Idolatry: cf. Jonson's eulogy for Shakespeare (1640), 'I lov'd the man, and doe honour his memory (on this side Idolatry) as much as any' (Jonson, *Timber, or Discoveries Made upon Men and Matter*, in *Oxford Authors: Ben Jonson*, 539).

'little Latin and less Greek': Jonson's eulogy to Shakespeare, which opens the 1623 folio of Shakespeare's work, described the bard as having 'small Latin, and less Greek' (*The Oxford Authors: Ben Jonson*, 454).

Regent's Canal: 9-mile-long waterway in central London.

Tasso: Torquato Tasso (1544–95), Italian poet, author of *Gerusalemme liberata*.

Newton: Isaac Newton (1642–1727), mathematician and natural philosopher.

fluxions: Newtonian mathematical term, referring to the rate at which a flowing or varying quantity increases its magnitude.

388 *Paderewski*: Ignacy Jan Paderewski (1860–1941), pianist who became prime minister of Poland in 1919.

Timon of Athens: Shakespeare and Thomas Middleton (bapt. 1580, d. 1627) wrote *Timon of Athens* in about 1606.

'cankered . . . nervous breakdown and madness': quotation from Frank Harris's study *The Man Shakespeare and His Tragic Life-Story*, 247.

The Comedy of Errors and A Midsummer Night's Dream: Shakespeare's plays, probably written about 1594 and 1596 respectively.

Laertes: the character who, in revenge for the deaths of his sister Ophelia and father Polonius, fatally fights Hamlet with an envenomed sword.

This scene: *Hamlet*, III. v.

389 *'sweet religion a rhapsody of words'*: cf. *Hamlet*, III. v. 45–6, 'sweet religion makes | A rhapsody of words'.

the feeling . . . which Orlando describes so perfectly in As You Like It: refers to Orlando's lines, 'If ever you have looked on better days, | If ever been where bells have knolled to church' (*As You Like It*, II. vii. 111–13).

Isabella in Measure for Measure: in Shakespeare's play, Isabella is a novice in a convent.

Don Juan in Much Ado: in Shakespeare's play *Much Ado about Nothing*, probably written in 1598, Don John is a bastard who confesses 'I am a plain-dealing villain' (I. iii. 23). Shaw spells the name idiosyncratically.

'It cannot be . . . offal': cf. *Hamlet*, II. ii. 473–6.

'Hates any man the thing he would not kill?': cf. *The Merchant of Venice*, IV. i. 66.

a stage Jew: an anti-Semitic comic bogeyman of the early modern theatre.

blenching: shying away.

390 *There is no creature loves me . . . pity myself*: cf. *Richard III*, V. iv. 180–3.

De Profundis: letter written by Wilde to his lover about his time in Reading Gaol, describing his fall from grace and his attempts to turn from despair. The letter was posthumously named *De Profundis* ('out of the depths'), the first two words of the Latin version of Psalm 130.

de profundis in excelsis: (Lat.) 'out of the depths' + 'in the highest', the latter occurring in the religious phrase 'Gloria in excelsis Deo' (Glory to God in the highest) as found in the Christian hymn known as the Greater Doxology. The former is found in Psalm 130, 'Out of the depths I cry to you, O Lord'.

'Hark, hark! the lark at heaven's gate sings': cf. *Cymbeline*, II. iii. 16.

390 *Cloten . . . Imogen*: in *Cymbeline* Cloten is the malevolent son of the evil queen in *Cymbeline*. He is eventually beheaded after opting to disguise himself in order to rape Imogen, the king's daughter and virtuous wife of Posthumus.

'it is a vice . . . amend': cf. *Cymbeline*, II. iii. 24–5. Cloten is attempting to use the music to woo Imogen: it does not work.

dun: dull grey-brown.

damasked: having the hue of the damask rose/ornamented with variegated colours.

reeks: exhales.

As any she belied with false compare: any woman described with misleading similies.

391 *chaffed*: vexed or irritated.

'sugred': in 1598 the writer and translator Francis Meres (1565/6–1647) described Shakespeare's 'sugred Sonnets among his private friends' (*Palladis Tamia. Wits Treasury. Being the Second Part of Wits Commonwealth*, fos. 281ᵛ–2ʳ, quoted by Jane Kingsley-Smith, *The Afterlife of Shakespeare's Sonnets* (Cambridge: Cambridge University Press, 2019), 14).

cleaving of the heart in twain: see Gertrude's line in *Hamlet*, 'O Hamlet, thou hast cleft my heart in twain' (III. iv. 153).

Pistol: soldier who appears in *Henry IV, part 2* (probably written in 1598), *Henry V* (probably written in 1599), and *The Merry Wives of Windsor* (probably written in 1600). In the latter play, Pistol's boasting serves as a parody of the king's epic language.

Falstaff: fat and boastful (but cowardly) drinker who appears in *Henry IV, part 1* (probably written 1596/7), *Henry IV, part 2*, and *The Merry Wives of Windsor*. He often speaks like a clergyman, but does so playfully.

Cloten: in *Cymbeline*, he considers impressing Imogen with music and poetic utterance, suggestively telling his musicians, 'If you can penetrate her with your fingering, so; we'll try with tongue too' (II. iii. 12–13).

Touchstone: in *As You Like It*, the jester at the court of Duke Frederick (who has usurped his own brother's dukedom). In III. ii he offers a parodic love poem that concludes, 'He that sweetest rose will find | Must find love's prick, and Rosalind' (93–4).

made Jupiter reduce Semele to ashes: the god Jupiter sired a child (Bacchus) by Semele, who was a human woman. However, when she asked to see her lover in his full splendour, his lightning set her on fire. In order to save the child, Jupiter created a surrogate womb from a gash in his thigh, and sewed the foetus inside.

idolatrous: in *The Man Shakespeare*, Frank Harris wrote of Shakespeare that 'The story of his idolatrous passion for Mary Fitton is the story of his life' (p. 212).

dotes 'yet doubts; suspects, yet strongly loves': cf. *Othello*, III. iii. 166.

Yorick's skull: in *Hamlet* the title character handles the skull of the dead court-jester, Yorick.

paint an inch thick: wear a thick layer of cosmetics or make-up, cf. *Hamlet*, V. i. 158.

Caliban: misshapen, feral character in Shakespeare's *The Tempest* (probably written in 1611). He is the son of the sorceress Sycorax and has apparently tried to rape Miranda.

392 *Be not afeard . . . I cried to dream again*: Caliban's lines in *The Tempest*, III. ii. 126–34.

Cloten dreaded: refers again to Cloten's line in *Cymbeline*, where he worries that Imogen may fail to appreciate the music that he has arranged for her ('it is a vice in her ears'), *Cymbeline*, II. iii. 23–5.

&c.: i.e. the insulting message of Sonnet 130 and its ilk.

Not marble . . . rhyme: cf. Sonnet 55.

'the wide world dreaming of things to come': cf. Sonnet 107.

Minna Wagner: Minna Planer (1809–66), German actor and first wife of the composer Richard Wagner. The marriage lasted until her death but was characterized by prolonged periods of separation.

The Spanish Tragedy: a popular tragedy written in about 1587 by Thomas Kyd (bapt. 1558, d. 1594) and staged by 1592.

Mermaid Tavern: well-known tavern in lower Bread Street associated with leading figures of the seventeenth century. Shaw is referring to the legend that Shakespeare may have drunk here and had witty clashes with Ben Jonson, a story which disappointingly lacks any supporting evidence. The teetotal Shaw originally added a debunking line at this point in his preface to say that, if Shakespeare was looking for intellectual and political training, the Mermaid Tavern was 'quite the most hopeless place in England from that point of view' (*DLS* Carb, fo. 24).

Anne Hathaway: (*c*.1556–1623), wife of William Shakespeare.

'Men have died from time to time . . . but not for love': cf. *As You Like It*, IV. i. 80–1.

And this word 'love' . . . alone: cf. *Henry VI, part 3*, V. vi. 82–4.

Ophelia: rejected lover of Hamlet and daughter of Polonius (Polonius being the character that Hamlet accidentally kills). After her father's death and Hamlet's rejection, Ophelia goes mad and is subsequently found drowned.

Laertes by her grave: refers to *Hamlet*, V. i. 238–9, where Hamlet confronts the grieving Laertes: 'Woot weep? Woot fight? Woot fast? Woot tear thyself? | Woot drink up eisel, eat a crocodile?'

393 *Romeo*: according to Frank Harris's book, *The Man Shakespeare*, Shakespeare 'painted his own portrait in all the critical periods of life: as a sensuous youth given over to love and poetry in Romeo' (p. 54).

Orsino: duke of Illyria in Shakespeare's *Twelfth Night* (probably written late 1601). Like Romeo, Orsino begins the play in love with a different woman to the one that he loves by the end (Orsino's affections moving from Olivia to Viola). In *The Man Shakespeare*, Harris wrote that 'inconstancy was a characteristic of sensuality and belonged to Shakespeare himself', and expressed the view that, with Orsino, 'Shakespeare as we know him in Romeo is depicted again with insistence on a few salient traits: here, too, we have the poet of the Sonnets masquerading as a Duke and the protagonist of yet another play' (p. 131).

393 *Antonio*: eponymous merchant in Shakespeare's *The Merchant of Venice*. He is a somewhat one-dimensionally honourable and generous character, and Frank Harris claimed 'Antonio is Shakespeare himself' (*The Man Shakespeare*, 185).

Mercutio: witty and acerbic friend of Romeo in *Romeo and Juliet*, who is killed by Juliet's cousin Tybalt while Romeo attempts to intervene.

Mr Harris has been the first to appreciate: Harris argued that 'Shakespeare praises music so frequently and so enthusiastically that we must regard the trait as characteristic of his deepest nature' (*The Man Shakespeare*, 136).

'Spit in the hole, man; and tune again': cf. *The Taming of the Shrew*, vi. 38. This means to wet the hole that contains the tuning peg (to improve the peg's grip).

'Divine air! . . . bodies?': cf. *Much Ado about Nothing*, II. iii. 49–50.

'An he had been a dog . . . hanged him': cf. *Much Ado about Nothing*, II. iii. 71–2.

the sweet south and the bank of violets: refers to Duke Orsino's opening speech in *Twelfth Night*, where Orsino describes music that 'came o'er my ear like the sweet sound | That breathes upon a bank of violets' (I. i. 5–6). For Frank Harris, this speech 'contains the completest, the most characteristic, confession of Shakespeare's feelings ever given in a few lines' (*The Man Shakespeare*, 130).

394 *'lousy Lucy'*: a poem that has been suggested as being written by the young Shakespeare about Sir Thomas Lucy (*c*.1532–1600), mocking Lucy who supposedly punished Shakespeare for poaching on Lucy's lands. The poem includes the lines, 'If Lousy is Lucy, as some folk miscall it, | Then Lucy is Lousy whatever befall it' (printed in Sabrina Feldman (ed.), *The Apocryphal William Shakespeare* (Indianapolis: Dog Ear, 2011), 5). The authenticity of the poem is questionable, and it was unprinted before the eighteenth century.

Drayton: Michael Drayton (1563–1631), poet.

Cassio: character in *Othello* who at one stage gets drunk.

the disgust of Hamlet . . . Denmark: Hamlet condemns Claudius 'as he drains his draughts of Rhenish down' (I. iv. 9), and then Hamlet observes that 'This heavy-headed revel east and west | Makes us traduced and taxed of other nations. | They clepe us drunkards' (I. iv. 17–19). Hamlet is also disgusted at the revelry he sees when he thinks the Court should still be mourning the death of his father. Shaw reacted to his own father's alcoholic excesses by embracing teetotalism.

Alexander: Alexander the Great (356–323 BCE) famously exercised self-control over the 'pleasures of the body', although famed for his excessive drinking.

the freak which transposes the normal aim of the affections: i.e. homosexuality. The evident homophobia of these remarks sits awkwardly with Shaw's earlier sympathetic description of Oscar Wilde's downfall.

395 *Michel Angelo*: Michelangelo (1475–1564), painter, architect, sculptor, and poet. His letters express strong feelings of attachment to young men, and his artworks show a preoccupation with the male nude.

'perfect ceremony': cf. Sonnet 23. Frank Harris's book, *The Man Shakespeare*, observed that this 'is the sonnet upon which all those chiefly rely who wish to condemn Shakespeare' for being homosexual, but claims that phrases such as 'the perfect ceremony of love's rite' actually 'form an astonishingly small base on which to raise so huge and hideous a superstructure' (pp. 234–5).

Titian . . . Veronese: the painters Tiziano Vecelli (1488/90–1576) and Paolo Veronese (1528–88).

anchorite: a hermit.

396 *'a very civil gentleman'*: Shaw appears to be quoting the words of his own play here. 'A very civil gentleman' is a phrase used by the Beefeater to describe Shakespeare at the start of *The Dark Lady of the Sonnets*.

kingdom for a horse: cf. *Richard III*, V. vi. 13.

Had all his hairs . . . all: cf. *Othello*, V. ii. 76–7.

397 *Tolstoy*: Tolstoy's 'Shakespeare and the Drama' (1906) castigates Shakespeare. Tolstoy argues that Shakespeare's 'elevation of the lords' reveals how the English dramatist 'despises the crowd' (Tolstoy, *Tolstoy on Shakespeare*, trans. V. Tchertkoff and I.F.M. (New York: Funk & Wagnalls, 1906), 94).

Ernest Crosbie: Ernest Crosby (1856–1907), author of the essay 'Shakespeare's Attitude Towards the Working Classes', which attacked Shakespeare because the playwright 'was unable to conceive of any situation rising to the dignity of tragedy in other than royal and ducal circles'. The essay was printed together with Tolstoy's essay and a letter from Shaw in *Tolstoy on Shakespeare*, 127–8.

Harris emphasizes: in *The Man Shakespeare*, Frank Harris argued that Shakespeare imbued Coriolanus with 'his [Shakespeare's] own delicate senses and neuropathic loathing for mechanic slaves with "greasy aprons" and "thick breaths rank of gross diet"' (p. 316).

He that will give good words to thee . . . abhorring: cf. *Coriolanus* I. i. 149–50.

John Stuart Mill: (1806–73), philosopher and economist. In his *Thoughts on Parliamentary Reform*, he wrote that the lower classes are 'mostly habitual liars' (Mill, *Essays on Politics and Society*, ed. J. M. Robson (Toronto: University of Toronto Press; London: Routledge and Kegan Paul, 1977), 312–40, at 338).

397 *Carlyle*: the historian and essayist commented of the population of the
     British Isles that they were 'twenty-seven millions mostly fools' (Stump-
     Orator, 1 May 1850, repr. in *The Works of Thomas Carlyle*, xx. *Latter-Day
     Pamphlets*, ed. Henry Duff Traill (Cambridge: Cambridge University
     Press, 1898), 208.

     Matthew Arnold and Ruskin: Matthew Arnold (1822–88), poet and critic,
     observed in England and France a 'constitutional preference for the ani-
     mal over the intellectual life' (Arnold, *The Popular Education of France*
     (London: Longman, Green: 1861), 170). Ruskin described his work at the
     London Working Men's College as being 'directed not to making a car-
     penter an artist, but to making him happier as a carpenter' (Ruskin's
     words before a Royal Commission on art education in 1857, reproduced in
     Ruskin, *On the Old Road: A Collection of Miscellaneous Essays, Pamphlets,
     &c.* (Orpington: G. Allen, 1885), 572).

     Shelley: the poet wrote in his pseudonymous 1817 essay 'A Proposal for
     Putting Reform to the Vote': 'With respect to Universal Suffrage, I confess
     I consider its adoption, in the present unprepared state of public knowledge
     and feeling, a measure fraught with peril' (*The Prose Works of Percy Bysshe
     Shelley*, ed. R. H. Shepherd (London: Chatto & Windus, 1888), 365).

     a little brief authority: cf. *Measure for Measure*, II. ii. 122.

     'poor, bare, forked animal': cf. *King Lear*, III. iv. 85.

     'Eliza and our James': the line is taken from Ben Jonson's elegy 'To the
     Memory of my Beloved', which praises Shakespeare as the 'Soul of the
     age' whose dramas 'did so take Eliza, and our James' (*Oxford Authors: Ben
     Jonson*, 454–5).

     levellers: those who sought to erase social distinctions of position or rank.
     Tolstoy, a communitarian Christian, drew upon the Bible to develop his
     ideas of equality.

     Alexander Iden and the stage Radical Jack Cade: towards the end of *Henry
     VI, part 2* Jack Cade is wanted for inciting a negative kind of populist
     revolt against the reigning monarch, and is hiding in the woods. Because
     he is hungry, he climbs into the garden of Alexander Iden, a self-described
     'esquire of Kent', in order to find food. Cade describes Iden as the 'Lord
     of the soil', and Iden kills him (IV. x. 37, 21).

     shepherd in As You Like It: the character of Silvius, who suffers unrequited
     love for Phebe but eventually wins her.

398 *in . . . Henry V, we get Bates and Williams*: in Shakespeare's play of 1599
     Bates and Williams are ordinary soldiers who encounter the (disguised)
     king on the eve of the Battle of Agincourt.

     cue from Plutarch: the translation by Thomas North (*c.*1535–*c.*1603) of
     a work by Plutarch entitled *Lives of the Noble Grecians and Romans* (1579)
     furnished Shakespeare with source material for his play.

     Goethe denounce it: Goethe labelled Caesar's murder 'the most repulsive
     deed' ('der abgeschmacktesten Tat') in *Materialien zur Geschichte der*

Farbenlehre ('Materials towards a History of Colour Theory', in *Goethes Werke*, xiv, ed. Dorothea Kuhn (Munich: C. H. Beck, 1994), 45).

Charles I of Wills . . . Cromwell: William Gorman Wills (1828–91), playwright and painter, whose play *Charles I* appeared at the Lyceum in 1872, with Henry Irving in the role of the king. Oliver Cromwell's depiction in the play *Charles I* by William Gorman Wills (1828–91) caused some in the press to complain about the derogatory nature of the portrayal.

'crook the pregnant hinges of the knee . . . fawning': cf. *Hamlet*, III. ii. 48–9.

Rosencrantz, Guildenstern: one-time friends of Hamlet in Shakespeare's play who have agreed to spy on the prince for the usurping king Claudius. They are reported dead by the end of the play.

Osric: a courtier who is mocked and rebuked by Hamlet for a lack of wit.

the fop who annoyed Hotspur: in Shakespeare's play *Henry IV, part 1*, the nobleman Hotspur is riled by 'a certain lord, neat and trimly dress'd' who appears after Hotspur has been fighting a battle at Homildon and 'made me mad | To see him shine so brisk, and smell so sweet, | And talk so like a waiting gentlewoman' (I. iii. 28–68).

Don Quixote: in his novel *Don Quixote* Cervantes introduces a sense of economic realism, which is not present in other chivalric tales, when the title character meets an innkeeper who asks about his financial status. 'Don Quixote replied that he had not a penny, since he had never read in histories concerning knights-errant of any knight that had' (*The Adventures of Don Quixote*, trans. J. M. Cohen (Harmondsworth: Penguin, 1954), 42).

Amadis de Gaul: Amadís de Gaula, the protagonist of a popular chivalric romance bearing his name, the earliest surviving version of which comes from a Spanish edition of 1515.

apothecary: character in *Romeo and Juliet* who fatefully sells poison to Romeo, commenting that 'My poverty but not my will consents' (V. i. 75).

Sicilian players: the Sicilian Players of actor-manager Giovanni Grasso (1873–1930). They performed at London's Lyric Theatre and Manchester's Gaiety Theatre in March and April 1910, delivering the play *Omerta*, about an innocent man who is imprisoned for murder and on release finds that the woman he loves has married the real killer.

John Ball: (d. 1381), priest, radical preacher, and leader of the Peasants' Revolt, during which he preached that God created all men equal.

Jeremiah: Hebrew prophet (d. *c.*570 BCE), who was willing to condemn the king as one who 'buildeth his house by unrighteousness, and his chambers by wrong' (Jeremiah 22:13).

399 *feudalism*: system that prevailed in Europe during the Middle Ages in which a vassal received land from someone of higher rank, in return for service.

democratic Collectivism: ownership of the land by the whole community, managed for the benefit of the people as a whole, with everyone having equal rights and a say in making significant decisions.

399 *Fabian Society*: British organization operating from January 1884, critiquing laissez-faire capitalism, and aiming to establish a democratic socialist state. Shaw first attended a Fabian meeting in May 1884, became a member four months later, and wrote many important Fabian tracts.

'Get thee glass eyes, and . . . dost not': cf. *King Lear*, IV. vi. 150–2.

Wellcome: Welcombe, near Stratford. Here Shakespeare earned tithe income from his freeholds, and when the fields were enclosed he risked a reduction in this income. Hence in 1614 he managed to gain an agreement that would compensate him 'for all such loss, detriment and hindrance' (quoted in S. Schoenbaum, *William Shakespeare: A Compact Documentary Life* (rev. edn, Oxford: Oxford University Press, 1987), 283). Evidently, he had worked to protect his own financial interests rather than putting his efforts into helping those in Stratford who sought to protect the common land from enclosures.

'the pangs of love despised': cf. *Hamlet*, III. i. 73, 'The pangs of despisèd love'.

Henry VI trilogy: trilogy probably written by Shakespeare and others including perhaps Christopher Marlowe (bapt. 1564, d. 1593) and Thomas Nashe (bapt. 1567, d. *c*.1601). The trilogy was most likely set down in 1590 (*part 2*), in 1590–1 (*part 3*), and early 1592 (*part 1*).

400 *Autolycus*: roguish character in Shakespeare's *The Winter's Tale* (written 1609–11) who disguises himself to trick people, and entertains with sometimes bawdy songs.

Swift's horror: Swift's *A Modest Proposal* (1729) points to the world's cruelty by satirically suggesting cannibalism as a solution to Irish poverty, and his 'The Lady's Dressing Room' (1732) indicates a misogynistic horror at uncleanliness.

Handel: George Frideric Handel (1685–1759), English composer of German birth.

Betterton: Thomas Betterton (bapt. 1635, d. 1710), actor and theatre manager, often considered the best English actor between Burbage (1568–1619) and David Garrick (1717–79).

the man of whom: Richard Burbage.

he Burbage cried: the words from 'Iter Boreale', the most widely circulated poem by Richard Corbet (1582–1635). The poem describes a man who 'mistooke a player for a King' by confusing Richard Burbage with Richard III (quoted by Pauline Kiernan, *Staging Shakespeare at the New Globe* (Houndmills: Macmillan, 1999), 51–2).

Garrick's Richard: David Garrick performed his impressively dynamic Richard III in London on 19 October 1741 at Goodman's Fields Theatre.

Kean's Othello: the final stage performance of Edmund Kean came on 25 March 1833, when he played Othello opposite his son's Iago.

Irving's Shylock: Henry Irving became closely associated with the part of Shylock, a character he tended to play in a sympathetic way and which he first brought to the Lyceum Theatre in November 1879. His production ran for 250 performances and afterwards remained in Irving's repertoire for twenty-four years. Shaw wrote in the *Saturday Review* that Irving's portrayal 'was simply not Shylock at all; and when his own creation came into conflict with Shakespear's, as it did quite openly in the Trial scene, he simply played in flat contradiction of the lines, and it positively acted Shakespear off the stage' (review of 26 September 1896; repr. in Shaw, *Our Theatres in the Nineties*, ii. 198).

Forbes Robertson's Hamlet: Johnston Forbes Robertson played the part of Hamlet at the London Lyceum in September 1897. His physically grace-ful interpretation of the character proved the actor's most successful role, and his final professional appearance came in the same part in April 1916, when he was 63. Shaw reviewed Forbes Robertson as Hamlet on 2 October 1897 for the *Saturday Review*, and praised the actor as 'just the sort of actor that Hamlet requires' (reprinted in Shaw, *Our Theatres in the Nineties*, iii. 201).

Troilus and Cressida: Shakespeare's play, probably written in 1602.

second part of Goethe's Faust: the first part of Goethe's two-part play was first performed in 1819, and the second in 1854. In this second part, Faust summons Helen of Troy and has a son with her (only for the son to die and take Helen with him), and Faust is ultimately saved and raised to heaven.

Ibsen's Emperor or Galilean: Ibsen's longest play, constructed in two parts (of five acts each), and published in 1873. It revolves around the Roman Empire of the fourth century CE, and the final twelve years of the emperor Julian the Apostate (331/2–363 CE). Ibsen regarded the drama as his masterpiece.

401 *his broken-heart theory*: in *The Man Shakespeare*, Frank Harris declared that he had 'purposely drawn special attention to Shakespeare's weakness and despair', which the Bard supposedly felt at the end of his career (p. 349).

The Superman: in the thought of Friedrich Nietzsche (1844–1900), the Superman (Übermensch) is the perfect and superior man of the future who transcends conventional Christian morality. Shaw helped popularize the term with his 1903 play *Man and Superman*, but he subsequently wrote a careful qualification: 'It is assumed that Nietzsche gained his European reputation by a senseless glorification of selfish bullying as the rule of life, just as it is assumed, on the strength of the single word Superman (Ubermensch) borrowed by me from Nietzsche, that I look for the salva-tion of society to the despotism of a single Napoleonic Superman, in spite of my careful demonstration of the folly of that outworn infatuation' ('Preface to Major Babara' [1906], in Shaw, *John Bull's Other Island, How He Lied to Her Husband, Major Barbara* (London: Constable, 1930), 211. As the twentieth century wore on, however, Shaw's endorsement of vari-ous dictators showed that he had not necessarily heeded that qualification.

curious biography: Shaw does not really tell the truth here in referring to the biography. Harris did know Shaw in the late 1890s, when Harris acted as editor of the *Saturday Review* and Shaw was the journal's drama critic.

Although the two drifted apart, they enjoyed a burgeoning correspondence between 1915 and Harris's death in 1931, and Shaw remained closely involved in the preparation of the biography. Shaw provided Harris with letters that were used in the volume, with that correspondence sometimes having been judiciously edited by Shaw. As Stanley Weintraub puts it, 'Harris completed only sixty-five faltering pages before his health cracked altogether and ghostwriter Frank Scully took over, completing the job by the use of paid researchers and Shaw's letters.' Furthermore, Weintraub observes that, before publication, 'When Harris died in the south of France, in self-exile both from England and America, Shaw felt that he not only had to complete the book but rewrite it—in the pompous Harrisian style—to pay for Harris's obsequies [and to help Harris's widow financially]', 'Then he wrote a characteristically paradoxical postscript in his own name to give the book a further push' (Weintraub, *The Unexpected Shaw* (New York: Ungar, 1982), 209–10). The volume was published as Frank Harris, *Frank Harris on Bernard Shaw: an Unauthorised Biography Based on Firsthand Information, with a Postscript by Mr Shaw* (London: Gollancz, 1931). On the day of publication, it sold 27,000 copies in London alone (see Weintraub, 'Introduction', in *The Playwright and the Pirate*, p. xviii).

402 *Sir Archibald Flower*: (1865–1950), a brewing magnate and part of the family that had founded the Shakespeare Memorial Theatre in Stratford. From 1900 he acted as chairman of the trustees of Shakespeare's birthplace and of the Shakespeare Memorial Theatre, and after the playhouse burnt down in 1926, Flower worked to ensure that a replacement was built. He solicited donations from the United States, including taking the actors on a fundraising tour of America in 1928, with the replacement building opening in 1932.

403 *Fin de siècle*: (Fr.) end of the century.

Palace at Whitehall: London home of the English monarch from 1530 until 1698, and once the largest royal palace in Europe, complete with four tennis courts, bowling alley, and cockpit (a ring for cockfighting).

chimes: Shaw wrote to the producer Charles Ricketts about the music that should sound as soon as the curtain is raised: 'My notion is simply a long sustained mysterious note on the bassoon and the Westminster chimes presently played in single notes by the harp, which will finally strike the hour on its lowest E (I think Big Ben is in E). The music stops when the Warder challenges Shakespear' (*CL* ii. 952, letter of 21 November 1910).

Beefeater: member of the Yeomen of the Guard, the monarch's bodyguard.

Adam: according to legend and tradition, Shakespeare himself played Adam, the character of the faithful old servant, in *As You Like It*.

Benvolio: Romeo's cousin in *Romeo and Juliet*.

anon the Ghost: the character of Shakespeare ('the man') claims that every now and then he would play the ghost of Old Hamlet.

Angels and ministers of grace defend us!: the title character's line in *Hamlet*, I. iv. 40.

tryst: mutual appointment.

Globe Theatre: the London theatre that (in its first incarnation) produced work from 1599 to 1613, and provided a venue for some of Shakespeare's best-known plays.

Plague on her!: the curse 'plague upon' repeatedly occurs in Shakespeare's plays, the plague being a mortal threat to those living at the time.

I care not for these new-fangled plays: the construction 'I care not for' is repeatedly used in Shakespeare, but perhaps is most famously associated with Sir Andrew Aguecheek in *Twelfth Night*, who asserts, 'I care not for good life' (II. iii. 33).

They are all talk: the same criticism was repeatedly levelled at Shaw.

The Spanish Tragedy: there were eleven published editions of Kyd's work between 1592 and 1633, a total unmatched by any of Shakespeare's plays.

404 *drab*: untidy and dirty woman.

the Court: the place where Queen Elizabeth lived and held state, attended by her retinue.

frailty . . . its name is woman: cf. line spoken by Hamlet in *Hamlet*, I. ii. 146, 'Frailty, thy name is woman'.

strain of music: recalls Orsino's words at the start of *Twelfth Night*, 'That strain again, it had a dying fall' (I. i. 4).

snapper-up of such unconsidered trifles: line spoken by Autolycus in *The Winter's Tale*, IV. iii. 25.

405 *lord Pembroke*: William Herbert. Here Shaw is playing on the idea that both Shakespeare and Herbert might have been infatuated by the gentlewoman Mary Fitton. Herbert's real-life affair with Fitton was supposedly characterized by Fitton disguising herself as a man to visit his lodgings. The affair ended in pregnancy, death of her young baby, and public disgrace.

Brutus: Shakespeare gave a sympathetic version of this historical figure in *Julius Caesar*, and the line here echoes the famous '*Et tu, Brute?*' of III. i. 77.

words, words, words: see *Hamlet*, II. ii. 189.

fill our bellies with the east wind: see Job 15:2, 'Should a wise man utter vain knowledge, and fill his belly with the east wind?'

You cannot feed capons so: see *Hamlet*, III. ii. 82. A capon is a castrated cock.

406 *Tis a fell sergeant, sir: strict in his arrest*: see 'this fell sergeant, Death, | Is strict in his arrest' (*Hamlet*, V. ii. 294–5), which refers to a cruel officer who is rigorous and unceasing in his arrest (in *Hamlet*, the arrest is the stopping of Hamlet's speech as he dies).

walking in her sleep: Shaw suggested that there should be 'A shimmering from the fiddles when the light heralds Elizabeth, continuing more or less until she wakes, when it stops abruptly' (*CL* ii. 952, letter of 21 November 1910).

406 *rubbing her hands as if washing them*: at the start of this section (where the Lady quotes famous lines from a number of well-known Shakespeare plays) she calls to mind the figure of Lady Macbeth from *Macbeth*, V. i, where Lady Macbeth, wracked with guilt, walks in her sleep, 'rubs her hands' as if 'washing her hands', and declares 'Out, damned spot!'

mar all: recalls 'You mar all with this starting' in *Macbeth*, V. i. 38.

you make yourself another: see *Hamlet*, III. i. 138–9. 'God hath given you one face and you make yourself another'.

beautified: made beautiful or more beautiful. In *Hamlet*, II. ii. 109–10, Hamlet has described Ophelia as 'most beautified' in a letter, and Ophelia's father Polonius comments, 'That's an ill phrase, a vile phrase: "beautified" is a vile phrase'.

All the perfumes of Arabia: see *Macbeth*, V. i. 42. Arabia was known in early modern England for its spices.

Tudor: of the line of English sovereigns descended from Owen Tudor (*c*.1400–61), the second husband of Catherine of Valois (1401–37), widow of Henry V (1386–1422). The Tudor line lasted from Henry VII to Elizabeth I.

You walk like the dead. Mary! Mary!: Mary Fitton, courtier and gentlewoman.

Mary! Mary!: Mary Stewart (1542–87), also known as Mary Queen of Scots. She was the only surviving child of James V, king of Scots (1512–42), and Elizabeth I's cousin. Mary reigned in Scotland from 1542, but an uprising forced her to abdicate in 1567, and afterwards she fled to England to seek Elizabeth's protection. Mary was Elizabeth's closest relative, but in 1558 Mary had also claimed the English throne as her own, and her claim was supported by potentially rebellious English Catholics. From 1568 Mary thus began a lengthy period of almost two decades in English captivity. Finally, on 1 February 1587, Elizabeth signed the warrant that authorized Mary's death, and an executioner cut off Mary's head with three blows. Elizabeth remained troubled by her cousin's fate, signified by Shaw here with an adaptation of Lady Macbeth's line from *Macbeth*, V. i. 33–4.

Who would have thought that woman to have had so much blood in her: see *Macbeth*, V. i. 33–4, 'who would have thought the old man to have had so much blood in him?'

she cannot come out of her grave: adaptation of *Macbeth*, V. i. 52: 'Banquo's buried. He cannot come out on's grave'.

Whats done cannot be undone: see *Macbeth*, V. i. 55.

Out, I say: see *Macbeth*, V. i. 30.

freckled: perhaps recalling Prospero's insult to Caliban in *The Tempest*, I. ii. 283: 'freckled whelp, hag-born'.

What art thou?: potentially recalls *Hamlet*, I. i. 44, 'What art thou that usurp'st this time of night'.

cry your mercy: see *King Lear*, III. iv. 139.

Methought you were my Mary: recalls *King Lear*, IV. vii. 61, 'Methinks I should know you, and know this man'.

Profane fellow: see *Cymbeline*, II. iii. 115.

marvellous proper woman: see *Richard III*, I. ii. 250: 'a marv'lous proper man'.

spoken with good accent and excellent discretion: see *Hamlet*, II. ii. 371: 'Fore God, my lord, well spoken, with good accent and good discretion'.

407 *drop like honey*: this recalls the 1598 description given by Francis Meres (1565/6–1647) of 'honey-tonged Shakespeare' (Meres, *Palladis Tamia* (1598), quoted in Feldman, *The Apocryphal William Shakespeare*, 183).

you dare express yourself so saucily: this may recall the opening of *King Lear*, I. i. 17, 'this knave came something saucily'.

overbold: see *Macbeth*, III. v. 3, 'saucy and over-bold'.

Season your admiration for a while with: see *Hamlet*, I. ii. 192.

mimic me to my face: may recall *Othello*, V. ii. 79, 'Weep'st thou for him to my face?'

You said 'for a space'. I said 'for a while': the Lady's version of the line, without so many 'esses', is the one that appears in *Hamlet*, 'Season your admiration for a while'.

making love: meaning to woo, as in Macbeth, III. i. 125.

408 *divine perfection of a woman—no: I have said that before somewhere*: Shakespeare used the phrase in *Richard III* (I. ii. 75), which was written in perhaps 1592 or 1594, and so already scripted by the time that *The Dark Lady of the Sonnets* is set (at the end of the 1500s). By contrast, *Macbeth* would not be written until about 1606 and *Hamlet* in about 1600, with Shaw's play suggesting that Elizabeth I played a part in the creation of those later works.

fire-new: newly coined. May recall *Love's Labour's Lost*, I. i. 176: 'A man of fire-new words'.

spake with the tongues of angels: see 1 Corinthians 1:13, 'Though I speak with the tongues of men and of angels, and have not charity, I am become as sounding brass, or a tinkling cymbal'.

Ben: Benjamin ('Ben') Jonson, the poet and playwright, whose stepfather was a bricklayer and who was himself also attached to the trade for a long period of his life (he made payments to the Tylers' and Bricklayers' Company as early as 1595 and as late as 1611). At the start of the 1623 Folio, Jonson's poem described his 'beloved' Shakespeare, as 'Soul of the age! | The applause, delight, the wonder of our stage!' But from the eighteenth century, critics tended to feel shocked by Jonson's apparent opinions that 'Shakespear wanted Arte' and that Shakespeare had 'small Latin and less Greek', and Shaw here develops the idea of the two playwrights rebuking one another (see *Ben Jonson's Conversations with William*

Drummond of Hawthornden, ed. R. F. Patterson (London: Blackie, 1923), 5; and *Oxford Authors: Ben Jonson*, 454–5).

408 *in the beginning was the Word . . . the Word was God*: see John 1:1, 'In the beginning was the Word, and the Word was with God, and the Word was God'.

head of the Church: the Act of Supremacy of 1559 described the queen as supreme governor of the Church of England (the earlier 1534 Act of Supremacy recognized Henry VIII as 'Supreme Head of the Church of England'). Both Acts sought to emphasize the authority of the English monarch rather than the Pope in Rome.

409 *virginals*: a small keyboard musical instrument common in sixteenth- and seventeenth-century England. Also, in this instance, 'virginals' provides a pun on Elizabeth I's persona as the 'Virgin Queen'.

music on my heart: see 'The Rime of the Ancient Mariner' by Samuel Taylor Coleridge (1772–1834), 'the silence sank | Like music on my heart' (*The Oxford Authors: Samuel Taylor Coleridge*, ed. H. J. Jackson (Oxford: Oxford University Press, 1985), 62).

The Dark Lady: i.e. Mary Fitton, arriving for her assignation with Shakespeare. Shaw wrote, 'I am not quite sure about this; but there might be some music when the Dark Lady enters, rising rapidly to a climax and breaking off when she boxes their ears' (*CL* ii. 952, letter of 21 November 1910).

the lodestar holds the iron: as the needle of a magnet points to the guiding pole star. There is potentially an allusion here to *A Midsummer Night's Dream*, I. i. 183, 'Your eyes are lodestars'.

trull: female prostitute. An insult found in, for example, *Henry VI, part 3*, I. iv. 114; and *Antony and Cleopatra*, III. vi. 95.

quotha: indeed! (as found, for example, in *Pericles*, II. i. 71).

jades . . . light-o'-loves . . . fly-by-nights: jades are hussies; light-o'-loves inconstant women or harlots; and fly-by-nights are addicted to nocturnal excursions.

esquire: a man of the higher order of English gentry, ranking just below a knight.

wantoning: engaging in lascivious behaviour.

410 *an Arden*: Shakespeare's mother Mary came from the Ardens, a distinguished Warwickshire family which could trace its pedigree back to the 1086 Domesday Book, where the clan's extensive landholdings were recorded.

You forget yourself: this may offer a reminder of the same phrase in *Julius Caesar*, IV. ii. 79.

S'blood!: an oath that euphemistically shortens 'God's blood'. Characteristically used by Falstaff in *Henry IV, part 1*.

a poor bankrupt: Shakespeare's father, John (*c*.1530–1601), was an ambitious man who worked as a glover and whittawer (dresser of light-coloured leather). John prospered until the 1570s, marrying into a high-status family, buying property in Stratford, and taking a prominent civic role in the town. However, in the 1570s, he was dealing illegally in wool (something restricted to authorized merchants) and was also prosecuted for usury. By the end of that decade he was in debt, he mortgaged some of his wife's inheritance in 1578, and lost that inheritance shortly afterwards when unable to repay the amount.

gentle blood: see *Richard III*, IV. iv. 50.

Harry the Eighth: Henry VIII.

worthiest alderman: Shakespeare's father, John, was a social climber. John achieved the civic post of alderman (a senior town councillor) in 1565, and in 1568 he won election as bailiff for a year, the highest office in Stratford. In 1571 he became chief alderman and deputy bailiff. However, by 1572, he saw a collapse in both his finances and his social prestige. John Shakespeare stopped attending council meetings after 1576, and was replaced as an alderman in 1586.

Zounds!: an oath that euphemistically shortens 'by God's wounds'. Used by Shakespearean characters including Othello, Richard III, and Aaron.

411 *baggage*: good-for-nothing woman, as used at the opening of *The Taming of the Shrew*, i. 3.

piece of beauty: a phrase used in *The Winter's Tale*, IV. iv. 32.

proud heart: a term repeated in Shakespeare's sonnets 140 and 141.

do your worst: may recall 'do thy worst', which is repeated in Shakespeare's sonnets 19 and 92.

strike blindly: potentially recalls Hamlet's attack on the figure he believes to be the king, behind the arras in *Hamlet*, III. iv.

anatomize your very soul: in *King Lear*, III. vi. 65, we find 'let them anatomize Regan': a suggestion later gruesomely literalized in the 1971 play *Lear* by Edward Bond (1934–).

412 *rude tongue*: the phrasing here may recall *Richard II*, III. iv. 75.

royal dignity: the phrasing here may recall *Henry VI, part 2*, III. iii. 195.

black-avised: dark-complexioned.

of all ladies most deject and wretched: see *Hamlet*, III. i. 149.

The Dark Lady goes, convulsed: Shaw revised this section in his rough proofs of the play. He originally included the following lines at this point:

> ELIZABETH. Go [*the Dark Lady tries to kiss her hand*]. Go. No more. The rest is silence. [*The Dark Lady goes*].
>
> SHAKESPEAR. Good. Good.
>
> ELIZABETH. What mean you by good?
>
> SHAKESPEARE. 'The rest is silence'. I shall kill somebody with that—in a play.
>
> (British Library, Add. MS 50626, *The Dark Lady of the Sonnets*, p. 11).

413 *not marble nor the gilded monuments of princes shall out-live*: see Shakespeare's
     Sonnet 55, ll. 1–2. At this point in the sonnet sequence, the speaker is
     boasting that his verse will outlast palaces and other buildings, keeping the
     fair youth's virtues alive until doomsday.

     a boon: an entreaty, or petition.

     Bankside: area of land, now in the Borough of Southwark in London,
     which took its name from the medieval embankment along the River
     Thames. In Shakespeare's time Bankside was close to the City, but
     remained outside the jurisdiction of the City authorities, and so became
     known for various ill-regarded activities, including theatre-going, animal
     baiting, and brothel visiting (the area became known as 'the stews' in part
     because of these 'stewhouses').

     Philip of Spain: (1527–98), king of Spain and Portugal, and husband of
     Elizabeth's half-sister, Mary I, from 1554 until her death.

     lack advancement: see *Hamlet*, III. ii. 302.

     a National Theatre: an anachronism in the world of the play, but designed
     to speak to Britain in 1910, when the play was first performed. Three years
     afterwards, in 1913, the National Theatre Executive Committee pur-
     chased the freehold of a London site on which it was planned to build the
     theatre (although it eventually took until 1976, on an entirely different
     site, for the UK's National Theatre to open in a building of its own).

     Blackfriars: the playhouse known as the 'first Blackfriars' was run by John
     Lyly in the 1580s. James Burbage subsequently built another indoor play-
     house in the area, where Shakespeare's company performed from 1609 to
     1642. The Blackfriars precinct, as part of an area once occupied by a mon-
     astery, was free from the Lord Mayor's jurisdiction.

414 *the one a skilful physician*: Shakespeare's *All's Well that Ends Well* tells of
     Helena, a physician's daughter who herself manages to cure the king of
     France who is suffering with a fistula (the king's courtiers believe that the cure
     is connected to witchcraft or to sex rather than to the skills of a physician).
     Unlike characters such as Viola in *Twelfth Night* or Rosalind in *As You Like
     It*, Helena does not dress as a man, and Shaw felt that the play was strik-
     ingly modern, writing in 1921 that *All's Well that Ends Well* 'anticipates
     Ibsen' (Shaw, *The Drama Observed*, iv. 1377).

     the other a sister devoted to good works: in *Measure for Measure*, Isabella is
     a novice in a convent who seeks to defend her brother. He has been con-
     demned to death for fornication. Like Elizabeth I, Isabella realizes the
     value of her virginity, which becomes central to the plot after Angelo
     agrees to spare her brother's life in exchange for sex with her.

     book of idle wanton tales . . . foolishnesses in the world: Shaw's play here criti-
     cizes *As You Like It* and *Much Ado About Nothing*, although Shakespeare's
     inspiration did not come from just one source. The former draws upon the
     prose romance *Rosalynde* (1590) by Thomas Lodge (*c.*1558–1625), and
     Lodge recycles an old romance story that had already been reworked by

Ludovico Ariosto (1474–1533), Matteo Bandello (1485–1561), and Edmund Spenser (*c.*1552–99). Shaw actually changed this line in his play at a late stage to sound more condemnatory of Shakespeare. Up until Shaw corrected the 1910 proofs of *The Dark Lady of the Sonnets*, the line made no mention of him having 'stole' anything but instead read 'I have also writ two of the most damnable foolishnesses in the world' (British Library, Add. MS 50626, *The Dark Lady of the Sonnets*, p. 9).

a woman goeth in man's attire: i.e. Rosalind in *As You Like It*, who disguises herself as the shepherd Ganymede.

swain: i.e. the young man, Orlando de Boys, who ends up marrying Rosalind at the conclusion of *As You Like It*.

groundlings: people who stand in the 'ground' or pit of the theatre, the least expensive area, and hence figures of relatively unrefined taste.

overthrowing a wrestler: in *As You Like It* (I. ii) Orlando fights Charles, the personal wrestler of the usurping Duke Ferdinand. The audience learns that Charles has broken the ribs of his earlier opponents, but Orlando manages to defeat him and demonstrate bravery in a scene that is dismissed here as a crowd-pleaser. Shaw had written about this aspect of the play as early as 1885, when he had seen a disappointing production at the St James's Theatre, and observed, 'Charles the Wrestler would have made a good start for the play in spite of Orlando, whose stupidity I never before fully realised' (*CL* i. 126, letter of 16 March 1885).

of the same kidney: of the same sort.

a gentleman as lewd as herself: i.e. Beatrice and Benedick in *Much Ado About Nothing*, who spend time wittily insulting each other before finally agreeing to marry.

drive their nobler fellows from the stage: there is an anachronism here. *All's Well that Ends Well* was written in early 1605, probably adapted by Thomas Middleton (bapt. 1580, d. 1627) in 1621, and had its first recorded performance in 1741. *Measure for Measure* was written in 1603 or 1604, performed at court in December 1604, and had adaptations made by Middleton in 1621 or 1622. Yet Shaw's play was supposed to be set at the end of the 1500s. In describing these later plays being driven from the stage, Shaw is primarily criticizing the taste not of Shakespeare's time but of the early twentieth century, reprising an argument he made in 1905, where he expressed his preference for 'real studies of life and character in—for instance—*Measure for Measure* and *All's Well that Ends Well*', and his disappointment that 'the public would not have them, and remains of the same mind still, preferring a fantastic sugar doll, like Rosalind, to such serious and dignified studies of women as Isabella and Helena' (Shaw, *The Drama Observed*, ed. Dukore, iii. 1105). As the end of *The Dark Lady of the Sonnets* makes clear, Shaw hoped that a National Theatre might be able to withstand such commercial pressures.

full of superstitious miracles and bloody martyrdoms: during the medieval period, drama was used to convey Christian stories and teaching to a largely illiterate population. Miracle plays presented the life, miracles, and martyrdom of the saints, whilst mystery plays told stories from the Bible, including the crucifixion of Christ.

415 *Lord Treasurer*: William Cecil (1520/1–98), who served as Lord Treasurer 1572–98; or Thomas Sackville (*c*.1536–1608), who served as Lord Treasurer 1599–1608. As the historical discussion moves into present-day concerns about establishing the National Theatre, Shaw wanted the figure of the Lord Treasurer to bring to mind the image of the prime minister of the day, Herbert Henry Asquith.

am I undone: may recall the repetition of *The Taming of the Shrew*, V. i. 53: 'O, I am undone I am undone!'

a salary for his own nephew: recalls Robert Cecil (1830–1903) (the namesake of Elizabeth I's secretary of state) the man who, when prime minister (1895–1902), opted to appoint his own nephew Arthur Balfour as chief secretary for Ireland in 1887, which, it has been suggested, gave rise to the expression 'Bob's your uncle' (to mean 'everything will turn out fine' / 'there you have it').

sooth: truth.

Puritans: the English Protestants who wished to purge the English Church of Roman Catholic influence, and who often felt hostile towards the playhouses. The theatre, after all, was an idle amusement; could potentially spread Catholic ideas; and contradicted the commandment against making graven images. In 1642, under Puritan influence, the Long Parliament ordered the closure of the playhouses.

cannot live by bread alone: see Matthew 4:4, 'Man shall not live by bread alone, but by every word that proceedeth out of the mouth of God'.

dust beneath the feet: may recall *King Lear*, V. iii. 134, 'dust below thy foot'.

the Scottish minstrel hath well said . . . he that maketh its laws: Andrew Fletcher of Saltoun (1653?–1716), the Scottish patriot who was fighting for the Scottish parliament in 1704 (shortly before that parliament ceased to function in 1707), wrote that he knew of a wise man who 'believed if a man were permitted to make all the ballads, he need not care who should make the laws of a nation' (*Political Works of Andrew Fletcher* (London: Bettesworth, 1732), 372).

interludes: the ending that follows in the script was written on 22 November 1910, and was a last-minute addition for the production at the Haymarket that opened on 24 November. Up until that point, Shaw had scripted a different ending for the play after the word 'Interludes'. The original ending is as follows:

> ELIZABETH . . . And now, sir, I see my Court approach; and to shew them that I am no ignorant city madam that makes her husband bedeck her with jewels instead of encouraging the arts and honoring their professors, I will dance a measure with you before them all if you have the skill to step it.

SHAKESPEARE I am but an indifferent dancer, madam, and for that
am most commonly set to play old men. The air is my element, not
the earth. But with your Majesty for my partner I will think I am
treading the plains of heaven; and that shall satisfy even my spirit.
So vouchsafe me your royal hand; and to't.

They lead a dance, in which the Court joins.

(CURTAIN)

(*DLS* Type, fos. 21–2).

chimes: Shaw envisaged these as being provided as 'single notes by the
harp' (*CL* ii. 952, letter of 21 November 1910).

an't please your majesty: see *Henry V*, IV. vii. 105.

MACBETH SKIT

Shaw's script includes printed sections from Shakespeare's original play that
he literally cut and pasted onto the page. For this edition the printed sections
that Shaw cut and pasted wholesale from Shakespeare will be printed in a
smaller point size to distinguish them from the text that Shaw wrote in his own
hand. The actors for whom Shaw wrote the text decided not to perform this
drama and there is no record of a public performance being given. The play-text
was first published by Bernard F. Dukore, as 'Macbeth Skit', in *Educational
Theatre Journal*, 19/3 (1967), 343–8.

419 *Scene V: Inverness. Macbeth's castle*: this skit begins at the moment in
Shakespeare's play when Macbeth's wife first enters (I. v). At this point
the audience has already seen the three witches, and has seen Macbeth
(based on the historical figure of MacBheatha mac Fhionnlaigh, king of
Scotland 1040–57) arrive as a war hero. He has been bravely and bloodily
battling the rebels of the Thane of Cawdor. The audience has also seen the
current king, Duncan, feeling impressed by Macbeth, and deciding to
hand over the Thane's land and title to Macbeth. Macbeth, meanwhile,
has met the three weird sisters (the witches), who predict that he will
become thane of Cawdor, and then king of Scotland. They also riddlingly
indicate that future kings of Scotland will come from the line of Banquo,
Macbeth's companion. The news then arrives that Macbeth *has* been
made thane of Cawdor, and Macbeth realizes that this first part of the
prophecy is correct. Macbeth's thoughts turn towards the kingship, and
he meets Duncan, who declares his plan to visit Macbeth's castle at
Inverness. The scene with which Shaw opens his skit begins with an unat-
tended Lady Macbeth reading a letter that Macbeth has sent to her,
informing her of these developments and the witches' prophecy. She is
excited by the prospect of her husband becoming king.

Lady Macbeth: this title is actually never spoken in Shakespeare's play
(where she is variously termed 'Macbeth's Wife', 'Macbeth's Lady',
'Wife', and 'Lady'). Yet her name has popular recognition, with ambitious

wives (particularly political wives) often being labelled a 'Lady Macbeth'. Shakespeare's character is based on the eleventh-century figure of Gruoch ingen Boite, and in 2010, the playwright David Greig (1969–) premiered his play *Dunsinane* which reimagined Macbeth's wife as the figure 'Gruach'.

419 *perfectest*: most accurate.

missives: messages.

king: the historical Duncan I (*c*.1001–40), king of Scotland 1034–40.

'Thane of Cawdor': clan chief or overlord of Cawdor, a location 12 miles from Inverness.

weird sisters: the three witches.

deliver: tell.

Glamis: location in Angus, in the north-east of Scotland. Macbeth is the thane, or clan chief, of this location at the start of the play.

nearest: most convenient.

illness: evilness, badness.

Hie: hasten.

golden round: crown.

metaphysical: supernatural.

420 *had the speed of*: outdistanced.

raven: ominous bird.

mortal thoughts: murderous thoughts.

compunctious: remorseful.

fell: cruel.

The effect and it: my plan and its achievement.

ministers: helpers.

sightless: invisible.

dunnest: darkest.

My dearest girl . . . Duncan comes here tonight: this is the first jarringly twentieth-century phrasing in the skit. Shakespeare's text reads simply: 'My dearest love, | Duncan comes here tonight' (I. v. 54–5).

so the old man says: Shakespeare's text has 'as he purposes' (I. v. 56).

421 *beguile the time*: deceive everyone.

my dispatch: her management/oversight.

a turnip watch: a wind-up pocket watch. Shaw is perhaps mocking the famously anachronistic striking clock in Shakespeare's *Julius Caesar* (II. i. 192).

We will proceed no further in this business: at this point in the text, Shaw cuts an entire scene from Shakespeare's original play (I. vi, the scene in which King Duncan arrives at Inverness and greets Lady Macbeth). Shaw also cuts Macbeth's famous soliloquy which begins, 'If it were done when 'tis done'. Instead, Shaw moves straight to Macbeth's line at I. vii. 32 of Shakespeare's text. That line itself, 'We will proceed no further in this business' is directly lifted from Shakespeare's play, but the rest of Macbeth's speech in that paragraph is Shaw's invention.

chuck it: get rid of it.

I cut that man in two in the war: Shaw originally wrote more informally here, 'I chopped that Johnny in two in the battle' (*MacS* Draft, fo. 1).

green and pale: ill.

ornament of life: crown.

Like the poor cat i' the adage: Lady Macbeth refers to the saying, 'The cat wanted fish but would not wet her feet'.

Like what?: in Shakespeare's original text, Macbeth responds to his wife's line about the 'poor cat i' th' adage' by declaring, 'Prithee, peace. | I dare do all that may become a man' (I. vii. 45–6). But Shaw's play takes a far more comic turn at this point, as Macbeth fails to understand the early modern English being spoken by his wife, and employs words that are not used by Shakespeare (such as 'police').

Like the cat: this is the first time that Shaw wishes Lady Macbeth to speak a line that is supplemental to Shakespeare's text. All of her earlier lines were transplanted directly from Shakespeare's *Macbeth* I. v and vii. This added line is not, however, a twentieth-century invention (as the lines spoken by the character of Shaw's Macbeth tend to be), but is simply a repetition of part of Shakespeare's I. vii. 45.

422 *I dare do all that may become a man*: a rare moment when Shaw's Macbeth speaks a line from Shakespeare's original play (I. vii. 47).

break: broach.

man: Shaw slightly reordered this section. He originally intended Lady Macbeth to speak her next line ('Nor time nor place | Did then adhere, and yet you would make both') at this point before Macbeth's interjection 'Look here: I dont follow this' (*MacS* Type, fo. 4).

adhere: agree.

one doesn't do these things: in Henrik Ibsen's celebrated 1879 play *A Doll's House*, Krogstad says of Nora's ideas about suicide 'People don't do that sort of thing' (Ibsen, *The League of Youth: The Pillars of Society: A Doll's House*, ed. William Archer (London: Walter Scott, 1904), 285–389, at 351). Similarly, in *Hedda Gabler* (1891), after the title character does actually kill herself, Judge Brack concludes the play by declaring, 'people don't *do* such things' (*Rosmersholm: The Lady from the Sea: Hedda Gabler*, ed. William Archer (London: Walter Scott, [1907?]), 241–364, at 364). The apostrophe on 'doesn't', unusual for Shaw, appears in the original.

sticking-place: notch holding a string on a crossbow. Although the meaning may be somewhat obscure, this line was nonetheless included in the popular musical *Hamilton* (2015).

422 *chamberlains*: gentlemen of the bedchamber.

wassail: drink.

convince: overpower.

receipt: receptacle.

limbec: Shaw highlights the obscurity of some of Shakespeare's language, which has often proved indecipherable to later audiences. 'Limbec' is a corrupted version of 'alembic', and refers to an early apparatus used for distilling, consisting of two connected vessels with fumes rising into the upper section. Shaw had in fact originally included here a slightly more clarifying line to say that an alembic is used to 'distil illicit whiskey with' (*MacS* Draft, fo. 2).

What the devil is a limbec?: in his draft, Shaw had preferred here, 'What the dickens is a limbec?' (*MacS* Draft, fo. 1).

423 *spongy*: drunken.

quell: refers to the action or an act of quelling something or someone, i.e. murdering them.

Bring forth men-children . . . Nothing but males: for the first time, Lady Macbeth speaks a line that Shakespeare originally gave to her husband, Macbeth (I. vii. 72–4).

Capital!: excellent, first-rate. Delivered here as an exclamation of approval.

Johnnies: a term applied humorously or contemptuously to various classes of men. Macbeth refers here to the two grooms who will be framed during his murdering of the king.

dirks: daggers.

By George: at one point Shaw wrote here, 'By St George', before correcting his typescript (*MacS* Type, fo. 6).

Who dares receive it . . . death?: Shaw's Lady Macbeth is now once more speaking lines that Shakespeare wrote for his Lady Macbeth.

Each corporal agent to this terrible feat: here Lady Macbeth delivers a line that Macbeth speaks in the Shakespearean original (I. vii. 79–80). This time, however, there is a metatheatrical dimension to this swapping: the text implies that the actor playing Shaw's Macbeth is forgetting his lines and that the actor playing Lady Macbeth needs to prompt him. Corporal here means corporeal or bodily.

to these terrible feet: the original Shakespearean line is 'to this terrible feat', i.e. the murder of Duncan. Changing the line allows Shaw to make a punning joke, and although he included in his typescript the idea that Macbeth would speak the original Shakespearean line, Shaw then changed the text in order to make the pun clearer, making 'this terrible feat' into 'these terrible feet' (*MacS* Type, fo. 7).

Miss McCarthy: Shaw intended Lady Macbeth to be played by Lilla McCarthy.

Gerald: Shaw intended the part of Macbeth to be played by the West End actor Gerald du Maurier.

CYMBELINE REFINISHED

The foreword was first privately published in 1937, for distribution at performances of the play at the Embassy Theatre London. It was subsequently published in *Geneva, Cymbeline Refinished, & Good King Charles* (London: Constable, 1946).

The play was first performed at London's Embassy Theatre on 16 November 1937. The play-text was privately printed by R. & R. Clarke in 1937. It was published in the *London Mercury*, 37 (February 1938), 373–89, and then in the collection *Geneva, Cymbeline Refinished, & Good King Charles* (London: Constable, 1946).

427 *Granville-Barker . . . William Poel*: Granville Barker (see note to p. 454) played Richard II for the actor, director and writer William Poel (1852–1934) in 1899, and was profoundly influenced by Poel's approach to Shakespeare. Poel founded the Elizabethan Stage Society, which gave thirty productions of Shakespeare plays between 1894 and 1905, and attempted to recreate the theatrical conditions of the Elizabethan stage. Granville Barker himself produced notable versions of *The Winter's Tale* and *Twelfth Night* in 1912, and *A Midsummer Night's Dream* in 1914.

happy ending to King Lear: the poet and playwright Nahum Tate (*c*.1652–1715) produced a version of *King Lear* in which Lear, Cordelia, and Gloucester all survive; and this version held the stage well into the nineteenth century.

Cibber's Richard III: Cibber created a revised version of *Richard III*, consisting of 2,053 lines: only 795 are from Shakespeare's play, 1,069 are by Cibber, and the rest are lifted from other Shakespeare plays.

love scene: figures including David Garrick included a love scene between Romeo and Juliet in the tomb.

Henry Irving: the stage actor appeared in numerous Shakespeare plays and did cut them. Indeed, Shaw declared 'He does not merely cut plays; he disembowels them' (Shaw, *The Drama Observed*, ed. Bernard F. Dukore (University Park: Pennsylvania State University Press, 1993), vol. i, p. xxi). However, Shaw's criticism is rather unfair as Irving cut the texts less severely than many of his contemporaries, and restored Shakespeare's rather than Cibber's version of *Richard III* to the stage.

Augustin Daly: (1838–99), dramatist and theatre manager, who brought to London his edited versions of Shakespeare's texts, which Shaw declared 'his fricassees of Shakespeare' (Shaw, *Dramatic Opinions and Essays* (New York: Brentano's, 1928), 46).

Cymbeline: Shakespeare's play *Cymbeline* (produced by 1611) has a rather complicated plot, and appears to leap in time between Renaissance Italy and first-century Britain. Cymbeline, the king of Britain, has a beautiful daughter Imogen, who has secretly married the poor but noble character of Posthumus Leonatus. Cymbeline banishes Posthumus, and Imogen is instead lined up to marry the son of Cymbeline's evil queen (the king's stepson Cloten). In Italy, Posthumus then meets Iachimo, who bets that he can seduce Imogen. Iachimo makes the attempt, is rejected, but tricks Posthumus into believing that the seduction has been successful. Posthumus is so infuriated that he decides to have Imogen murdered: but she learns of the plot, disguises herself as a boy, and travels to Wales. Here, she encounters two men who are her brothers but were kidnapped years before. Imogen's potential husband, the villainous Cloten, now arrives and one of the brothers kills him. Imogen then drinks a potion which makes her appear dead, and the grieving brothers leave her body next to that of Cloten. Nonetheless, she revives, and, is traumatized by thinking that Cloten's headless body is that of her real husband Posthumus. Imogen then joins the Roman army—which has meanwhile invaded Britain—acting as a page. Her husband Posthumus and the treacherous Iachimo are also travelling with the Romans, with the former feeling distraught about having apparently had Imogen killed. Posthumus thus allows himself to be captured by the British, but the god Jupiter now promises to intervene. Finally, then, Cymbeline summons the prisoners, and Posthumus and Imogen are reunited. A remorseful Iachimo is forgiven, the identity of the kidnapped British sons is revealed, and the evil queen dies.

427 *jeu d'esprit*: (Fr.) playful display of wit.

Shakespear Memorial Theatre at Stratford-upon-Avon: the new art-deco theatre, by Elisabeth Scott (1898–1972), opened in Stratford in 1932.

428 *old Lyceum theatre*: London theatre where Irving had been manager for twenty-three years from 1878. The theatre had, in 1903, been demolished apart from the walls and portico, and then rebuilt to house music-hall shows.

Iachimo: the villain in *Cymbeline*, played by Irving at the Lyceum in September 1896.

moles on their necks: Guiderius' 'sanguine star' on his neck confirms his identity.

not dead: Imogen had been thought dead, but had only taken a potion that made her appear so.

and late phase Shakespear in point of verbal workmanship: Shaw included this sentence in the 1946 printing of the foreword, but when the text had first been printed in 1937 Shaw included a more fulsome description of Shakespeare's *Cymbeline*, by writing instead 'and first quality Shakespear at that as far as the verbal workmanship is concerned' (*CR* Pamp, fo. 4).

doggerel: badly composed writing.

masque: courtly dramatic entertainment, in which dancing and music often played a key role.

woodnotes wild: cf. the line by John Milton about Shakespeare warbling 'his native woodnotes wild' in the poem 'L'Allegro' (Milton, *The Major Works*, ed. Stephen Orgel and Jonathan Goldberg (Oxford: Oxford University Press, 1991), 22–5, at 25).

Jupiter as deus ex machina: Jupiter, the Roman king of the gods, descends onto the stage in *Cymbeline*, V. iv, hurling a thunderbolt and sitting on an eagle. Shaw is using the literal meaning of the Latin phrase *deus ex machina*, 'the god from a machine'.

Ceres scene in The Tempest: *The Tempest*, IV. i, which features a masque in which the Roman goddess of agriculture, Ceres, appears.

King Jamie: James VI and I, king of England, Scotland, and Ireland.

Gounod . . . Wagner . . . Grand Opera in Paris: the requirement by the Paris Opéra, the leading French opera company (founded 1669), for a ballet to be included within each opera often necessitated revisions from the composer. When *Faust* (premiered 1859) was revived in 1869 by the Opéra, its composer Charles Gounod (1818–93) added music for a long ballet scene, while Wagner added the Venusberg ballet to Act I of *Tannhäuser* (premiered 1845) for the 1861 revival there.

Leonatus Posthumus: secretly married to Imogen but comes to believe that she is unfaithful and commands her murder. In the final scene he expresses his remorse, yet also strikes Imogen to the ground when she tries to reveal her identity, as she is dressed as a boy and he does not recognize her.

Charles Charrington: stage name of Charles Martin, actor.

broke the ice for Ibsen in England: in 1889, the 23-year-old Achurch, manager of the Novelty Theatre in London, appeared as Nora in the first English production of *A Doll's House*. Charrington played the part of Dr Rank. In 1894 Achurch played Rita in Ibsen's *Little Eyolf*, and Shaw praised her for performing with 'all her old originality and success' (Shaw, *Shaw's Dramatic Criticism (1895–1898)* (Westport, CT: Greenwood, 1971), 197).

Mrs Alving in Ghosts: Mrs Alving realizes, as she tells Pastor Manders, that her dead husband remained 'After nineteen years of marriage, as dissolute—in his desires at any rate—as he was before you married us' (Ibsen, *Ghosts: An Enemy of the People*: *The Wild Duck*, ed. William Archer (London: Walter Scott, 1908), 7–102, at 14).

429 *Cornelius*: a physician who, in *Cymbeline*, I. vi, presents the villainous queen with poisonous compounds that she has requested. When he asks why, she declares that she wants to try them 'on such creatures as | We count not worth the hanging (but none human)'. He replies, 'Your highness | Shall from this practice but make hard your heart'.

Guiderius: Cymbeline's oldest son, who was kidnapped as a small child and raised in a cave.

Maddison Morton: (1811–91), playwright who wrote more than 125 plays.

Gordon Craig: (1872–1966), theatre director and designer, who labelled Maddison Morton 'the funniest playwright that England ever had' (Craig's view remembered by Kenneth Tynan in a letter of 14 July 1967, in

Tynan, *Kenneth Tynan Letters*, ed. Kathleen Tynan (London: Random House, 1998), 408).

429 *Box and Cox*: this first appeared at the Lyceum Theatre in November 1847, and is Maddison Morton's best-known farce.

Polydore and Cadwal: the names under which Guiderius and Arvirargus respectively, Cymbeline's sons, have been raised since being kidnapped as children.

Cymbeline: see note to pp. 577-8.

Iachimo: the man who tricked Leonatus Posthumus into believing that Imogen (Posthumus' wife) was unfaithful, but who subsequently expresses remorse.

éclaircissement: (Fr.) clearing up of what had been unknown.

post-Marlowe: Christopher Marlowe died in 1593.

Augustan English: seventeeth- and eighteenth-century English literature, which saw writers trying to emulate writers such as Virgil (70-19 BCE) and Horace (65 BCE-8 CE), who wrote during the reign of Caesar Augustus (27 BCE-14 CE).

430 *Tom Thumb*: satirical play, performed and published in 1730 (and published in a revised version in 1731), by Henry Fielding (1707-54). The script mocks the bombast of grandiose stage tragedies.

Chrononhotonthologos: satirical play of 1734 by Henry Carey (1687-1743). The script, which appeared under the pseudonym 'Benjamin Bounce', mocks heroic tragedy.

Bombastes Furioso: farcical play of 1810 by William Barnes Rhodes (1772-1826). The script mocks the style of contemporary tragedy.

Velasquez: Diego Velázquez (bapt. 1599, d. 1660), painter.

Rembrandt: Rembrandt van Rijn (1606-69), painter.

Ireland's Vortigern: William Henry Ireland (1775-1835), who forged a variety of documents supposedly written by and to Shakespeare, and who also 'discovered' a new play supposedly by Shakespeare, *Vortigern*, which was accepted for performance at Drury Lane, where it was produced on 2 April 1796, and howled from the stage.

additions made by Mozart to . . . Handel's Messiah: Handel premiered his oratorio *Messiah* in 1742. Wolfgang Amadeus Mozart subsequently rescored the piece for performance in 1789.

Elgar: Edward William Elgar (1857-1934), composer and conductor, who died shortly before Shaw wrote this play and had been a good friend of the playwright.

Spontini: Gaspare Spontini (1774-1851), composer and conductor.

Wagner had added trombone parts: in November 1844, Wagner attended rehearsals of Spontini's opera *La Vestale* (1807). Spontini was leading the rehearsals, and according to Wagner himself, 'I asked Spontini why he had omitted using trombones during the splendid triumphal march in the first act'. An astonished Spontini 'requested me to add trombones to the march so that they could be included at the next rehearsal' (Wagner, *My Life*, trans. Andrew Gray, ed. Mary Whittall (Cambridge: Cambridge University Press, 1983), 282).

Beethoven . . . Bach: Ludwig van Beethoven (1770–1827) and Johann Sebastian Bach (1685–1759), both German composers.

played Old Harry: play the devil with, work mischief upon.

Diabelli's vulgar waltz: Beethoven wrote his thirty-three Diabelli Variations (1823) for piano, at the invitation of composer Anton Diabelli (1781–1858), who had composed the original waltz.

Don Giovanni: in variation 22 of the Diabelli Variations, Beethoven quotes from the start of Mozart's 1787 opera *Don Giovanni*.

Tolstoy: in his essay 'Shakespeare and the Drama' (1906), Tolstoy denounces the 'immoral works of Shakespeare', and devotes considerable attention to *King Lear*, arguing that compared to the anonymous Elizabethan play *King Leir* (which had been performed by 1594), Shakespeare's characters 'have been strikingly weakened and deprived of force by him, as compared with their appearance in the older drama' (*Tolstoy on Shakespeare*, 124, 56).

431 *Gluck's overture to Iphigenia in Aulis*: Christoph Willbald Gluck (1714–87) created the opera that first appeared onstage in 1774, and in 1847 Wagner produced a revised version. Wagner commented that 'only my treatment of the overture, the sole piece from this work with which the critics were previously familiar from the traditional feeble renditions, aroused any great objection' (Wagner, *My Life*, 338).

own sake: for the 1937 version of the foreword, Shaw originally added here, 'though Mozart's attempt was quite presentable', pointing to the 1781 opera *Idomeneo* by Mozart, which echoed some of Gluck's *Iphigenia in Aulis*. For the revised 1946 version of the foreword Shaw considered writing the reverse, that 'Mozart's conventional num-tum finish is not good enough', before deleting the reference to Mozart altogether (*CR* Var, p. 135).

Beethoven's Ninth Symphony: Wagner repeatedly conducted and commented upon Beethoven's Ninth, and had made a piano reduction of the piece as early as 1830. Shaw refers to Wagner's preparation of the symphony in Dresden, where, in 1846, Wagner had adjusted the orchestration. As Wagner put it in his autobiography, where previously passages marked 'forte' had simply included a doubling of wind instruments, he sought instead to 'give as expressive a rendering as possible' (Wagner, *My Life*, 330).

Verdi: Giuseppe Verdi (1813–1901), operatic composer who complained of Beethoven's Ninth Symphony that 'No one will ever approach the sublimity of the first movement, but it will be an easy task to write as badly for voices as is done in the last movement' (quoted in Jean-Pierre Barricelli, *Melopoiesis* (New York: New York University Press, 1988), 143).

431 *orgy*: when Shaw's preface was first printed in 1937, he included an additional sentence here to conclude the paragraph, adding 'A sacredly noble work should not end in the madhouse'. He removed that sentence for the 1946 printing of the foreword (*CR* Pamp, fo. 4).

Nat Lee . . . impart Restoration gentility to Shakespear: Nathaniel Lee (d. 1692), actor and playwright, included many linguistic echoes of Shakespeare when writing the Roman tragedy *Lucius Junius Brutus* (1680). The dedication Lee added to this work observes that 'Shakespeare's Brutus with much ado beat himself into the heads of a blockish age' (ed. by John Loftis (Lincoln: University of Nebraska Press, 1967), 5).

Thomas Corneille's bowdlerization of Molière's Festin de Pierre: Molière staged his play *Dom Juan; ou, Le Festin de pierre* ('Don Juan; or, The Feast of Stone') in 1665, and triggered some objection because of its perceived impiety. In 1673, at the request of Molière's widow, the drama was rescripted by Thomas Corneille (1625–1709) as *Le Festin de Pierre*.

what I have done I have done: Shaw echoes the words of Pontius Pilate in John 19:22 ('What I have written, I have written'), who is questioned about having labelled Christ 'the King of the Jews'.

432 *Act V*: in Shakespeare's play this act ties up a number of the plot details. It begins with Cymbeline summoning his two sons (Guiderius and Arviragus, although he does not recognize who they are) to thank them. Although the brothers have arrived with the Roman army, they have actually been fighting for Britain. The news arrives that the queen has died, after having confessed that she did not love Cymbeline and that she planned to poison him. Iachimo and Posthumus are brought in, together with Imogen who is disguised as the boy Fidele. Iachimo confesses his own trickery in trying to win his bet about Imogen's seduction. Posthumus tries to attack him, but Imogen reveals who she is, and so the married couple are reunited. The courtier Belarius then unveils the identity of Cymbeline's two sons. Posthumus forgives Iachimo, and Cymbeline forgives the Romans, allowing them all to return home. Shaw decided to rewrite this final act, finding it largely, as he put it in his foreword, 'a tedious string of unsurprising *dénouements* sugared with insincere sentimentality' (p. 428). Although Shaw found that the masque elements could potentially save a performance, he nonetheless deleted the appearance of the god Jupiter, with all of the accompanying music and spectacle. Shaw focused instead upon articulating the previously unspoken reactions of Shakespeare's human characters, most notably adding in the feelings of Imogen to her husband's attempted murder, and the feelings of the king's sons to the discovery of their biological father.

defile: a narrow pass or gorge between mountains. The setting is first-century Britain, during a Roman invasion which has been launched because king Cymbeline has refused to pay a British tribute to Rome.

Philario: an Italian friend of Posthumus.

Lucius: the Roman ambassador to Britain, Caius Lucius.

General Iachimo: the character who has pretended to seduce Imogen earlier in the play, now a commander of the invading Roman army.

outgeneralled: outmanoeuvred, beaten in military skill.

eagles: symbol known as the standard of a Roman legion.

score: a group of twenty. So thirty score is 600.

433 *Cassivelaunus*: the real-life chief of the Cassi people in Buckingham, Bedfordshire, and Hants. He was reputedly a brave and skilful leader who, in 54 BCE, resisted Caesar's second expedition to Britain.

Cymbeline: character based loosely upon the historical figure of Cunobellus, who is described in the account of ancient Britain by Raphael Holinshed (?–*c*.1580), as a ruler in pre-Roman Britain at the time of the birth of Christ.

Belarius: this character is the British lord who was exiled as a traitor and who then kidnapped Cymbeline's two sons and raised them as his own. At this point in the play, however, Belarius has returned to help Cymbeline repel the Roman invaders.

laurel crowns: emblems of victory, using leaves of the bay laurel.

434 *Posthumus*: (Lat.) 'born after his father died'. He is the secret husband of Imogen, who nonetheless was tricked into believing that she was unfaithful to him, and so commanded her murder, something he now regrets. Full of guilt, he enlisted in the Roman army, but in this speech he vows, for the sake of Imogen, to fight for Britain instead. Shaw felt that Posthumus had to be played by a large actor, and was reportedly disappointed with the casting of Geoffrey Toone (1910–2005) in the role for the 1937 premiere: at rehearsals, Shaw told Toone, 'Ah, you're all wrong for the part—you're all wrong. No, you mustn't jump about the stage like that—you should walk around exactly as if you had big diver's boots on you' (Shaw quoted by Earl Grey, HRC, Sound recording, Interview with Basil Langton and Earl Grey, 3 July 1962).

Yea, bloody cloth: this soliloquy is the first part of the Shaw text that is imported with little alteration from the Shakespearean original (V. i. 1–33).

wrying: straying.

Pisanio: Posthumus' servant, who we know is indeed 'good' because earlier in the original play Posthumus charged him with murdering Imogen, but Pisanio refused and instead told Imogen of this plan, sending her into hiding.

bond: obligation.

put on this: instigate Imogen's murder.

You some permit . . . to the doers' thrift: you let some people reinforce one sin with another—each sin worse than the last—and make them avoid sins that might be advantageous.

weeds: clothes.

part: side, i.e. against the Romans.

434 *Leonati*: (Lat.) 'born of a lion'. Posthumus' father also fought bravely against the Romans, and so gained this title for the family.

435 *Seducer of my wife*: although Iachimo and Posthumus are friends, earlier in Shakespeare's play Iachimo used trickery to pretend that he had seduced Imogen.

　　expiate: extinguish the guilt of.

　　Guiderius, Arviragus: Cymbeline's sons, kidnapped in childhood by Belarius and so unknown to Cymbeline at this point.

　　Imogen as Fidele: since her husband attempted to murder her, Imogen has been disguised as a boy (Lat. *fides* = 'faith').

　　Make fast: bind.

　　perforce: of necessity.

436 *strikes Posthumus*: in Shakespeare's original, Posthumus strikes Fidele at V. vi. 229 (not knowing Fidele to be Imogen), but no one else physically responds to this. In the violent response of Guiderius and Arviragus that we see here, Shaw was attempting to construct a more realistic version of Shakespeare's scene.

　　coil: tumult and trouble.

　　met me with a blow: in Shakespeare's play, after Imogen/Fidele is struck down by Posthumus, she revives only to berate an entirely different character, Pisanio (for, she believes, trying to poison her earlier in the play). Only after that digression (V. vii. 236–61) does she return to her husband and ask him 'Why did you throw your wedded lady from you?' (V. vii. 262). Shaw felt that this was an unrealistic response, and instead keeps Imogen's focus upon her husband's behaviour. She reflects that her wild 'ecstasy' has now gone for ever, and goes on to treat his words with scepticism.

437 *paramour*: lover.

　　Mercury: the Roman messenger god, known for his cunning (equivalent of Greek Hermes).

438 *ducats*: gold coins.

　　The mole upon your breast: earlier in the play, Iachimo convinced Posthumus that Imogen had been unfaithful by describing this particular detail of her naked body.

　　Thor's great hammer stroke: Thor, see note to p. 135, is not a character mentioned by Shakespeare. Thor's thunderbolt is represented by his hammer.

　　Cadwal . . . Polydore: see note to p. 429.

439 *prithee*: I pray thee, please.

　　Cloten: the evil queen's son, and so Cymbeline's stepson. He was beheaded by Cymbeline's son Guiderius after he had decided to dress as Posthumus in order to rape Imogen.

　　Marry, the gods forefend: an expression of surprise, 'the gods forbid'.

　　incivil: barbarous.

dead: going to be put to death.

Had ever scar for: ever earned by battle scars.

440 *on 's*: of us.

hot: rapidly.

prefer: advance.

Marry, the gods forfend . . . As your highness knows: this is the second point in the text (and the longest) where Shaw imports a large amount of the original Shakespearean text with little alteration (V. vi. 287–341).

as I'd change my shirt: in Shakespeare's text, Cymbeline's two sons remain conspicuously silent while their father discovers their identity, only speaking afterwards to declare that they loved Imogen as soon as they met her. Shaw is determined to introduce greater realism into the reaction of the sons.

441 *future king*: Iachimo assumes Guiderius will inherit the crown and rule Britain after the death of Cymbeline.

forsooth: in truth.

priest invented gods: here Shaw bluntly contradicts the conclusion of Shakespeare's play, which has Cymbeline, in the final lines of the script, declaring 'Laud we the gods' (V. vi. 475).

Not free to wed the woman of my choice: when first performed in 1937 this line strongly called to mind the abdication of King Edward VIII (1894–1972), who had given up the throne in December 1936 in order to marry the divorced American socialite Wallis Simpson (1896–1986). The *Daily Express* reported that when the play was first performed, 'Gasps came from the opening-night audience at the Embassy Theatre last night when they heard lines on abdication' (17 November 1937, p. 1). When the play was approved by the British censor, the reader commented that Shaw 'gets in his views on the disadvantages of being a King'. The official reader had underlined both 'free to wed the woman of my choice' and, a few lines later, 'I abdicate' (British Library, Lord Chamberlain's Papers, Add. MSS 67084 L. *Cymbaline* [*sic*] *Unfinished* [*sic*]).

I abdicate, and pass the throne to Polydore: Guiderius appears to move here from ancient Britain to England at the time when Shaw wrote the play. This line (and those immediately before it about the advice of counsellors) recall the recent abdication of Edward VIII. On performance in 1937, the *New Statesman* noted that Shaw's drama contained 'a few wise-cracks about the Abdication' (quoted by E. J. West, 'Shaw, Shakespeare, and *Cymbeline*', *Theatre Annual* (September 1950), 7–24, at 18).

harp on that: dwell on the subject. This line is Shaw's invention, but does carry an echo of Polonius' declaration in *Hamlet*, 'Still harping on my daughter' (*Hamlet*, II. ii. 185).

442 *hot on*: eager to set about.

443 *Cæsar*: Roman emperor, who has just sent his armies into Britain because of Cymbeline's refusal to pay a tribute.

443 *ensign*: banner.

Lud's town: London.

Set on there!: go forward.

let / A Roman . . . such a peace: the final six lines of Shaw's text are the same as the final six lines of Shakespeare's play (V. vi. 478–84).

SHAKES VERSUS SHAV

Parts of the preface first appeared in 'Mr Shaw on Puppets and Actors', *The Times*, 5 August 1949, p. 4. It was then published in full as a programme note for the Lanchester Marionette Theatre's Malvern performances of the play, 9 August–3 September 1949, and in 'Shakes vs. Shav—the Bout of the Centuries', *New York Times*, 4 September, magazine section, pp. 14–15, 33. The preface was also printed, along with the play, in the *Arts Council Bulletin*, 113 (September 1949), 5–9. However, Shaw felt that he had not authorized this latter printing in the monthly thruppence magazine of the Arts Council (in a mix-up, he had seemingly given permission to the puppeteer Waldo Lanchester for the text to be printed by the 'British Council'). Shaw wrote a letter to Eric White of the Arts Council: 'Gracious heavens what have you done? Infringed my British copyright and all but thrown it into the public domain in the USA. Damages, thousands of pounds, and millions of dollars hard cash. On Lanchester's authorisation! He has no authority. I am the sole owner' (Shaw's letter of 2 September 1949, in the possession of Waldo Lanchester and read aloud on HRC, Sound recordings, Waldo Lanchester interview with Basil Langton, interview of 7 July 1962 at 39 Henley Street, Stratford-on-Avon, R2566). The preface was subsequently printed, with Shaw's authorization, in *Buoyant Billions, Farfetched Fables, & Shakes Versus Shav* (London: Constable, 1950).

The title of the play is an abbreviation of 'William Shakespeare versus George Bernard Shaw'. It was first performed at the Lyceum Hall, Malvern, on 9 August 1949. The play-text was first publicly printed in the *Arts Council Bulletin*, 113 (September 1949), 5–9, in what Shaw felt was an unauthorized edition. The first authorized public printing came in *Buoyant Billions, Farfetched Fables, & Shakes Versus Shav* (London: Constable and Company, 1950).

447 *my last play*: Shaw actually wrote one more play, *Why She Would Not*, before his death in 1950.

Waldo Lanchester: (1897–1978), puppeteer.

Malvern Marionette Theatre: theatre run from 1936 to 1949 by Waldo Lanchester and his wife Muriel.

feat: prior to publication, Shaw originally added at this point in his preface 'in two days' (*SvS* Type, fo. 1).

producer: the equivalent of today's 'director'.

Punch-and-Judy: traditional English puppet show usually presented in a collapsible booth.

illuded: tricked.

448   *Venus and Adonis, Lucrece, and Love's Labour's Lost*: *Venus and Adonis* and *Lucrece* are Shakespeare poems, the first probably written between 1592 and 1593 (when the theatres closed due to an outbreak of plague), the second written by 9 May 1594. *Love's Labour's Lost* is a play written by Shakespeare most probably in late 1594.

just like my own: Shaw was born into a downwardly mobile family with some artistic ability. The Shaws were members of the Protestant ascendancy in Ireland, a position of relative social prestige, but Shaw's father, George Carr Shaw (1815–85), was a failing corn merchant and alcoholic. Shaw's mother, Bessie Shaw (1830–1913), had skill as a pianist and singer. In the preface to *Immaturity*, Shaw wrote, 'I sing my own class: the Shabby Genteel, the Poor Relations, the Gentlemen who are No Gentlemen' (*Immaturity* (London: Constable, 1931), p. viii).

Cobbett: William Cobbett (1763–1835), journalist, farmer, and politician.

'The Latin I borrow': in *The Pilgrim's Progress* (1678/9), Bunyan's character appears to be acknowledging the limitations of his education.

Bacon-Shakespear: the theory that Shakespeare's plays were really written by Sir Francis Bacon (1561–1626), the philosopher, essayist, and statesman. This theory was promoted by the author and teacher Delia Bacon (1811–59, no relation to Francis) and became widespread in the late Victorian period.

449   *Now is the winter of our discontent . . . sun*: Shakespeare first appears delivering an adapted version of the two lines with which Richard III opens Shakespeare's play. When *Shakes Versus Shav* premiered in Malvern, this line was pre-recorded by Lewis Casson (1875–1969) playing the part of Shakespeare. The show was advertised as featuring a celebrated cast directed by Sir Lewis Casson, and the other lines were pre-recorded by Ernest Thesiger (1879–1961) as Shaw, Russell Thorndike (1885–1972) as Macbeth, Archie Duncan (1914–79) as Rob Roy, Cecil Trouncer (1898–1953) as Captain Shotover, and Isabel Dean (1918–97) as Ellie Dunn. Malvern is the Worcestershire spa town where the play was first performed, in the Waldo Lanchester Marionette Theatre at the Lyttelton Hall. When Waldo Lanchester toured the play to other locations he changed the onstage scenery slightly in order to make the setting clear. Shaw specified that for the production given in Malvern 'there will be no scenery: only a background, floorground, and ceiling (if any) of rich dark green stuff or even black velvet', but when Lanchester performed in different locations he added a backcloth showing a tapestry representation of Great Malvern priory church, with a scroll showing the word 'Malvern' (*CL* iv. 839, letter of 20 January 1949).

Stratford: the market town where Shakespeare was baptized and buried lies about 30 miles from Malvern.

a festival: Stratford-upon-Avon had seen sporadic Shakespeare festivals ever since the actor-manager David Garrick had organized a jubilee festival there in 1769. When the town erected a permanent Shakespeare theatre in 1879, an eight-day drama festival was organized, which became an annual festival featuring visiting actors every April until 1919, after which the theatre always had a resident company. Shaw himself gave a well-reported toast to Shakespeare at the annual birthday luncheon in 1925, in which he made a plea for a new theatre at Stratford 'which should not only be a permanent home for the acting of Shakespeare but a training school' ('Shakespeare's Birthday', *Manchester Guardian*, 24 April 1925, p. 8). The following year the old building burned down and in 1932 a new Memorial Theatre opened, where the Shakespeare festivals continued. Meanwhile, 30 miles away, Malvern established a drama festival in 1929 to showcase the work of Shaw, based on what took place in Stratford. Barry Jackson (1879–1961) had seen the Three Choirs Festival (a music festival given by the choirs of Hereford, Gloucester, and Worcester cathedrals) as well as the Shakespeare festivals in Stratford, and, as he put it, 'it struck me that a festival of that kind, with perhaps some modern plays, ought to be acceptable elsewhere; there ought to be people who were fond of the drama apart from those going to Stratford for Shakespeare; and I thought Malvern would be a very good place. And I was walking with him [Shaw] on the [Malvern] hills one day and he said yes it would be very nice' (HRC, Barry Jackson interview with Basil Langton, Longton—Transcripts of Recorded Interviews, I-J, box 1, folder 5. Interview of 13 January 1960).

449 *not for an age / But for all time*: cf. Ben Jonson's poem in the 1623 first folio of Shakespeare's plays, 'He was not of an age, but for all time!' (*Oxford Authors: Ben Jonson*, 454).

And in your stately playhouse to set up / A festival, and plant a mulberry: in an early unpublished typescript, Shaw specified here Shakespeare should be more scathing about the Malvern festival, with these lines rendered as 'And on these hills a playhouse is set up | Wherein to host a fraudulent festival' (*SvS* Type, fo. 1).

caitiff: wretch.

And leave the rest to me: in an early unpublished typescript, Shaw specified here that Shakespeare should display an even more pugnacious attitude towards Shaw. Instead of the published line, Shakespeare was to declare: 'Within my fists' length bring him; if he scape me | Heaven forgive me too' (*SvS* Type, fo. 1).

Put up your hands / Come on: in an early unpublished typescript, Shaw specified here greater animosity between Shakespeare and Shaw. Instead of the published lines, Shaw originally wrote:

> SHAKES. The devil take thy soul.
>
> SHAW. Thou prayest not well. Put up your hands. Come on.
>
> (*SvS* Type, fo. 2)

counting him out: in boxing the competitors are given a count of ten seconds after being knocked down. If a boxer does not rise before the count ends, he is out.

Hackerty-backerty: nonsense words used here to make sure the seconds of the count are extended to an appropriately full length.

450 *your sonnets*: Shav is referring in particular here to Sonnet 55, which includes the declaration, 'Not marble nor the gilded monuments | Of princes shall outlive this powerful rhyme' (ll. 1–2).

Macbeth: see headnote to *Macbeth Skit*, p. 419.

Walter Scott's Rob Roy: a historical novel by Walter Scott, published in 1817, with the titular character being Rob Roy MacGregor, a Scottish drover-turned-outlaw who, after the Jacobite rising of 1715, kills a traitor who betrays the Stuart cause.

claymore: a Scottish sword. In an early unpublished typescript, Shaw originally specified here that the puppets of Rob Roy and Macbeth should be 'smaller than those of Shakespeare and Shaw' and should 'enter together upstage' (*SvS* Type, fo. 6).

Have we marched on without impediment: cf. *Richard III*, V. ii. 4.

Caumill me no Caumills: do not call me Campbell. Shaw is here giving a version of some of Rob Roy's lines in Walter Scott's novel: 'do not Maister or Campbell me—my foot is on my native heath, and my name is MacGregor!' (Scott, *Waverley Novels: Centenary Edition*, iv. *Rob Roy* (Edinburgh: Adam & Charles Black, 1871), 385).

Lay on, Rob Roy . . . boy: see *Macbeth*, V. i. 34–5, 'Lay on Macduff, | And damned be him that first cries, "Hold, enough!"' Shaw believed, as he put it, that 'My remotest known ancestor was Macduff' (*Leader Magazine*, 23 March 1946, p. 9).

cuts off Macbeth's head at one stroke: for the puppeteers, this is the most technically difficult part of the piece to perform. When Waldo Lanchester premiered the piece, the head on the Macbeth figure was more or less rigid up to the moment of throwing it off, and then it was lifted by strings that went underneath the neck and lifted the whole head from the centre pin, tilting the head forward and onto the floor. Lanchester also ran a loose string from the top of the head of the Macbeth puppet down through the puppet's hand and up to the puppeteer's control, allowing the head to be picked up again by the puppet.

Whaur's your Wullie Shaxper the noo?: Where's your Willie Shakespeare now? In an early unpublished typescript, Shaw rendered this line of Rob Roy's as, 'Thus perish all the Sassenachs in Scotland' (*SvS* Type, fo. 7).

British Grenadiers: a tune dating from at least the early eighteenth century, and almost certainly performed by British soldiers during conflicts including the American Revolutionary War and the Crimean War. The sung lyrics begin: 'Some talk of Alexander, and some of Hercules, | Of Hector and Lysander, and such great names as these; | But of all the world's brave heroes, there's none that can compare, | With a tow row, row row row, to the British grenadier' (*The Book of English Songs*, ed. Charles Mackay (London: Houlston & Wright [1857?]), 213–14).

cateran: Highland marauder.

451 *'The shardborne beetle with his drowsy hum'*: see *Macbeth*, III. ii. 43. Shardborne signifies a beetle that carries itself on scaly wings, and perhaps means 'born in the dung'.

451 *Adam Lindsay Gordon*: (1833–70) a nineteenth-century poet and horse-man, who was educated in England and moved to Australia at the age of 20. He wrote popular ballads and enjoyed sufficient public acclaim that, in 1917, four thousand people took part in an annual pilgrimage to his grave. In 1934, the Duke of York unveiled the poet's bust in Westminster Abbey. However, Gordon's reputation declined during the twentieth century and he is now largely forgotten. Shaw apparently added 'Well done, Australia!' to his script at a late stage in order to avoid offending any Australian visit-ors who came to see his play (HRC, Sound recordings, Waldo Lanchester interview with Basil Langton, interview of 7 July 1962 at 39 Henley Street, Stratford-on-Avon, R2566).

'The beetle booms adown the glooms / And bumps among the clumps': not actually a line by Adam Lindsay Gordon but a version of a line from the poem 'Dusk Song—The Beetle' by the American writer James Whitcomb Riley (1849–1916): 'The beetle booms adown the glooms | And bumps along the dusk' (*The Complete Poetical Works of James Whitcomb Riley* (Bloomington: Indiana University Press, 1993), 148).

My lungs like chanticleer / Must crow their fill: taken from *As You Like It*, II. vii. 30. 'My lungs begin to crow like chanticleer' (chanticleer being a traditional name for a rooster). Shaw originally added at this point in an early unpublished typescript another criticism of Shaw's opinion by Shakespeare, who was to comment, instead of 'This fellow hath an ear | How does it run?', the lines: 'Call you this balderdash | Immortal verse? Ha! ha!' (*SvS* Type, fo. 7).

There is more fun in heaven and earth, sweet William, / Than is dreamt of in your philosophy: see *Hamlet*, I. v. 165–6, 'There are more things in heaven and earth, Horatio, | Than are dreamt of in our philosophy'.

Heartbreak House: Shaw's three-act play first published in 1919, in which an octogenarian inventor and his daughter, who live in a house shaped like a ship, are visited by a number of people. The drama features various arguments about morality, and concludes with an air raid that kills a rich businessman as well as a burglar, but spares the rest of the household who refuse to shelter from the bombs and appear excited by the attack. Ultimately the play functions as a kind of national fable, predicting an apocalyptic future and showing England to be a ship of fools.

Captain Shotover: an eccentric 88-year-old inventor who runs a rather bohemian household, partly an autobiographical portrayal of Shaw him-self, and partly based on the seafaring father of actress Lena Ashwell. Ashwell's father had retired to a sailing vessel on the River Tyne, where he had fitted out the stern as his own quarters.

Millais' picture called North-West Passage: the 1874 painting by John Everett Millais (1829–96) depicts a grim old seaman sitting in a chair, gripping the hand of a young woman who kneels at his feet. Millais painted the piece when an English expedition was setting off for the North-West Passage, an unnavigable sea route around North America that had become associated with death and failure.

raising his hand and intoning: the lines that Shotover speaks here are taken from the end of Act I of *Heartbreak House*, where the elderly captain describes the two daughters who have caused his heart to break like that of Lear. In that moment in *Heartbreak House*, Shotover describes his daughters Lady Utterword (who has married Sir Hastings Utterword, 'governor of all the crown colonies in succession') and Hesione Hushabye (who has married the fantasist Hector Hushabye and reduced him to a 'household pet') (*Heartbreak House* (London: Constable, 1931), 46, 96). Shaw found a clear link between these characters and those of Shakespeare, commenting of Shotover's daughters in 1917, 'I don't find them much more popular than Goneril and Regan' and later labelling Shotover 'a modernized King Lear' (*CL* iii. 498, letter of 10 August 1917; Hesketh Pearson, *George Bernard Shaw: His Life and Personality* (New York: Atheneum, 1963), 363). When the words spoken here by Shotover appear in Shaw's original text of *Heartbreak House*, only the first three lines of the poem are actually delivered by the captain (originally, Shotover delivers the words up to 'numskull', then the character of Hector declares 'The other a liar wed', and then Hesione Hushabye completes the stanza; see *Heartbreak House*, 78–9).

'Yes . . . Heartbreak House': the words spoken here by the Virgin do not follow the previous lines in Shaw's original play *Heartbreak House*. Rather, they are spoken in Act III of that play by Ellie Dunn, a young woman who ends up in a kind of mystical union with the 88-year-old captain. In *Heartbreak House*, by the time that she speaks these words, Ellie has been holding Shotover as he sleeps and describing him as her 'natural captain, my spiritual husband and second father' (p. 132). Ellie has been taught by her actual father to confuse Shakespearean stories for reality, and she delivers the line above shortly after she has observed, 'There seems to be nothing real in the world except my father and Shakespear' (p. 129). If the two daughters of Shotover are versions of Goneril and Regan, then Ellie can be viewed as a reimagining of *King Lear*'s Cordelia.

Let the heart break in silence: a line spoken by Captain Shotover in Act III of *Heartbreak House*.

452 *vanishes*: Shaw originally added at this point in an early unpublished typescript another criticism of Shaw's writing by the fictional version of Shakespeare, who was to comment 'This nothing means to me. Tis not blank verse' (*SvS* Type, fo. 8).

'The heartaches and the thousand natural woes / That flesh is heir to': see *Hamlet*, III. i. 63–4, 'The heartache and the thousand natural shocks | That flesh is heir to'.

Timons: Shakespeare and Middleton's play *Timon of Athens* revolves around a rich Athenian who is ruined by his own generosity, is abandoned by those who once flattered him, and curses the city, taking off to dwell in a cave where he lives alone and full of misanthropic thoughts.

My cloud capped towers . . . shall dissolve: see *The Tempest*, IV. i. 152–4, 'The cloud-capped towers, the gorgeous palaces, | The solemn temples, the great globe itself, | Yea, all which it inherit, shall dissolve'.

452 *and like this foolish little show of ours / Leave not a wrack behind*: Shaw completes the quotation with a variant on the line from *The Tempest*, IV. i. 155–6, 'And, like this insubstantial pageant faded, | Leave not a rack behind' (a 'rack' is a wind-blown cloud).

Tomorrow and tomorrow and tomorrow: see *Macbeth*, V. v. 18.

Immortal William dead . . . winter's flaw: see *Hamlet*, V. i. 174–7, 'Imperious Caesar, dead and turned to clay, | Might stop a hole to keep the wind away. | O, that that earth which kept the world in awe | Should patch a wall t'expel the winter's flaw!' Here, 'flaw' signifies a violent gust of wind.

A light appears between them: in an early unpublished typescript, Shaw originally specified here 'A glowing light bulb descends', and planned to show the bulb being apparently puffed out onstage by the Shaw puppet (*SvS* Type, fo. 5). The revised idea of a light suddenly appearing, however, posed problems for the puppeteers, so Waldo Lanchester explained that when he staged the play he felt 'the only thing to do is to bring down an electric bulb, which we had a nice little miniature candle flame, electric candle flame, which wasn't very bright, it was one of a very ancient carbon filament. We just let it down on a thin flex, let it down and had a switch on the top, lit it up, and just pulled the cable and it came down between them, and then when Shakespeare steps and says "out, out brief candle" we just switched it off and at the same time my wife dimmed the stage out into blackness' (HRC, Sound recordings, Waldo Lanchester interview with Basil Langton, interview of 7 July 1962 at 39 Henley Street, Stratford-on-Avon, R2566).

Out, out, brief candle: see *Macbeth*, V. v. 22.

APPENDIX A

A large piece of text featured in the printed version of *How He Lied to Her Husband* in 1907, and was cut by Shaw before the publication of the standard edition of his work in 1931 for fear that the references to his earlier play *Candida* had become too dated. The deleted text appears in Appendix A, showing the earlier adjustments that Shaw made to change his 1904 New York text for 1905 production in London. In performance these lines would have been delivered after Henry Apjohn's line 'there is no malice, no grudge, between us. Come!' on p. 10]. The text is taken from *HHL* Carb, fos. 6–9.

453 ~~Parsifal~~ ⟨*Lohengrin*⟩: when Shaw prepared his play for performance in New York, he felt that Wagner's *Parsifal* should be the opera for which Apjohn should have attempted to purchase tickets. *Parsifal* had received its first ever performance outside Germany in New York's Metropolitan Opera House during December 1903. This acclaimed production of Wagner's opera cost thousands of dollars to stage, and attracted a first-night audience of 7,000, mostly well-known society types. However, the opera did not appear in England until February 1914, when it played at the Royal Opera House, Covent Garden. So when Shaw adjusted his script for London

performance in 1905, following the earlier New York production, he changed the opera to *Lohengrin*, which had been seen on London stages since 1875.

~~*Vaudeville*~~ ⟨*Court*⟩: from January 1904, Shaw's *Candida* had appeared at the Vaudeville Theatre on Forty-fourth Street, near Fifty Avenue, in New York, under the management of Winchell Smith (1871–1933). The building was later known as the Berkeley Lyceum. When Shaw prepared *How He Lied to Her Husband* for London, he changed the name of the theatre to the Court Theatre, where *Candida* had played from April 1904.

454 *Mr* ~~*Arnold Daly*~~ ⟨*Granville Barker*⟩: Daly played the part of Marchbanks in *Candida* during its successful New York run, and then took the part of Apjohn in *How He Lied to Her Husband*. In London, however, Granville Barker played Marchbanks in *Candida* and then played Apjohn in *How He Lied to Her Husband*. Shaw therefore adjusts the names of the actors here.

Applause and laughter . . . Play resumed: these stage directions were deleted for the 1907 printing of the play.

APPENDIX B

Appendix B consists of two sets of material that Shaw cut from *Press Cuttings* prior to publication in 1909. The lines in the first set were supposed to appear in the text after Mitchener says, 'You shall be placed under restraint at once. Call the guard' on p. 61]. The lines in the second set were originally planned to appear in *Press Cuttings* on p. 48 after Mitchener says, 'Thats nothing to you. You have your orders: obey them. Do you hear? Right about face. March.' The texts are taken from *PC* Type, fos. 25–9.

456 *Pall Mall*: a short but fashionable street in Westminster, connecting St James's Street to Trafalgar Square. The War Office was based here, in Cumberland House, from the mid-1800s until 1906.

Boers: the 'Boer War', or South African War, saw Britain fight two Afrikaner republics between October 1899 and May 1902. Britain won, but the conflict was the costliest that the nation fought in the period between the Napoleonic Wars and the First World War.

American Literature

British and Irish Literature

Children's Literature

Classics and Ancient Literature

Colonial Literature

Eastern Literature

European Literature

Gothic Literature

History

Medieval Literature

Oxford English Drama

Philosophy

Poetry

Politics

Religion

The Oxford Shakespeare

A complete list of Oxford World's Classics, including Authors in Context, Oxford English Drama, and the Oxford Shakespeare, is available in the UK from the Marketing Services Department, Oxford University Press, Great Clarendon Street, Oxford OX2 6DP, or visit the website at www.oup.com/uk/worldsclassics.

In the USA, visit www.oup.com/us/owc for a complete title list.

Oxford World's Classics are available from all good bookshops. In case of difficulty, customers in the UK should contact Oxford University Press Bookshop, 116 High Street, Oxford OX1 4BR.

RUDYARD KIPLING	**Plain Tales from the Hills**
	War Stories and Poems
D. H. LAWRENCE	**The Rainbow**
	Sons and Lovers
	Women in Love
WYNDHAM LEWIS	**Tarr**
KATHERINE MANSFIELD	**Selected Stories**
ROBERT FALCON SCOTT	**Journals**
ROBERT TRESSELL	**The Ragged Trousered Philanthropists**
VIRGINIA WOOLF	**Between the Acts**
	Flush
	Jacob's Room
	Mrs Dalloway
	The Mark on the Wall and Other Short Fiction
	Night and Day
	Orlando: A Biography
	A Room of One's Own and Three Guineas
	To the Lighthouse
	The Voyage Out
	The Waves
	The Years
W. B. YEATS	**The Major Works**

Late Victorian Gothic Tales
Literature and Science in the
  Nineteenth Century

JANE AUSTEN   Emma
                               Mansfield Park
                               Persuasion
                               Pride and Prejudice
                               Selected Letters
                               Sense and Sensibility

MRS BEETON   Book of Household Management

MARY ELIZABETH BRADDON   Lady Audley's Secret

ANNE BRONTË   The Tenant of Wildfell Hall

CHARLOTTE BRONTË   Jane Eyre
                               Shirley
                               Villette

EMILY BRONTË   Wuthering Heights

ROBERT BROWNING   The Major Works

JOHN CLARE   The Major Works

SAMUEL TAYLOR COLERIDGE   The Major Works

WILKIE COLLINS   The Moonstone
                               No Name
                               The Woman in White

CHARLES DARWIN   The Origin of Species

THOMAS DE QUINCEY   The Confessions of an English
                                 Opium-Eater
                               On Murder

CHARLES DICKENS   The Adventures of Oliver Twist
                               Barnaby Rudge
                               Bleak House
                               David Copperfield
                               Great Expectations
                               Nicholas Nickleby